California Civil Procedure Handbook

California Civil Procedure Handbook

Rules, Selected Statutes and Cases,
and Comparative Analysis

2021–2022 Edition

Walter W. Heiser
PROFESSOR OF LAW
UNIVERSITY OF SAN DIEGO SCHOOL OF LAW

Supplemental Course Materials for Use with All
First-Year Civil Procedure Casebooks

CAROLINA ACADEMIC PRESS
Durham, North Carolina

ISBN 978-1-5310-2356-0
eISBN 978-1-5310-2357-7
ISSN 1949-6116

Carolina Academic Press
700 Kent Street
Durham, North Carolina 27701
(919) 489-7486
www.cap-press.com

Printed in the United States of America

Contents

Part One

California Civil Procedure

Chapter I

Introduction to California Civil Procedure

A. Sources of California Procedural Laws

1. "Written Law"

According to section 1895 of the California Code of Civil Procedure, all laws in California are either "written" or "unwritten." The written law is contained in the California Constitution and statutes, and in the United States Constitution and statutes. CCP § 1897. Unwritten law is law "not promulgated and recorded . . . but which is, nevertheless, observed and administered in the courts. . . . It has no certain repository, but is collected from the reports of the decisions of the courts, and the treatises of learned men." CCP § 1899.

The United States Constitution and Laws. Although the origins of specific California procedural laws lie elsewhere, the United States Constitution is in one sense the ultimate source. Both as a conceptual proposition and an actual check when challenged, all state procedural laws must be consistent with the requirements of the Fourteenth Amendment. The federal Due Process Clause provides the ultimate "fairness" standard by which state procedural statutes, rules, and court actions are measured. *See, e.g., Kulko v. Superior Court,* 436 U.S. 84, 98 S. Ct. 1690, 56 L. Ed. 2d 132 (1978) (California state court's exercise of personal jurisdiction over a nonresident parent in child support action violated federal Due Process Clause); *Randone v. Appellate Department,* 5 Cal. 3d 536, 96 Cal. Rptr. 709, 488 P.2d 13 (1971), *cert. denied,* 407 U.S. 924 (1972) (Then-existing California attachment statute, which authorized prejudgment attachment without notice and an opportunity for a hearing, violated Due Process Clause).

The California Constitution. In addition to a general Due Process provision which mirrors that of the United States Constitution, the California Constitution contains a number of more specific sections which help define our civil litigation process. For example, Section 16 of Article I provides with respect to civil jury trials:

> Trial by jury is an inviolate right and shall be secured to all, but in a civil cause three-fourths of the jury may render a verdict. * * * In a civil cause a jury may be waived by the consent of the parties expressed as prescribed by statute.

The California Code of Civil Procedure. The California Code of Civil Procedure (hereinafter, "CCP"), consisting of hundreds of statutes, is the primary source of procedural law for California state courts. This Code covers such topics as subject matter jurisdiction, statutes of limitations, joinder of parties and claims, service of process, pleadings and motions, attachment, trial and pretrial motions, extraordinary writs, appeals, judgments, and enforcement of judgments.

Unlike the relatively succinct Federal Rules of Civil Procedure that apply in federal trial courts, the California Code is lengthy, comprehensive, and quite detailed. For example, Federal Rule 56 delineates the standards and procedures for summary judgment motions in less than one page, but CCP § 437c takes 2-1/2 pages of similar size type; Federal Rule 30 specifies the procedures for oral depositions in 2-1/4 pages, CCP §§ 2025.010–2025.620 require more than 10 pages to cover the same topic. The code approach employed by California usually means that most specific procedural questions can be answered by simply locating the relevant Code sections.

Other statutory codes also contain important procedural provisions, often limited to particular types of cases. *See, e.g.,* Government Code § 900 *et seq.* (procedures for presentation of claims against public entities and officials under the California Tort Claims Act); Family Code §§ 200–291 (procedures relating to dissolution of marriage and related proceedings); Civil Code §§ 1780–1784 (remedies and procedures for actions under the Consumers Legal Remedies Act); Evidence Code §§ 450–460 (judicial notice); Business & Professions Code §§ 6146–6149 (limitations on contingent fee agreements).

California Rules of Court. Pursuant to the authority contained in the California Constitution and in various code sections, the Judicial Council of California has adopted numerous state-wide rules of practice and procedure. These Rules of Court supplement statutory and constitutional provisions, and have the force of law. The Rules of Court were reorganized and renumbered effective January 1, 2007.

The scope of the numerous and detailed California Rules of Court is difficult to characterize. Some rules govern procedures in the appellate courts, Rules 8.1–8.1125, Cal. Rules of Ct.; others fine-tune civil pretrial and trial procedures in the superior court, Rules 3.1–3.2120. Some specifically relate to family law proceedings, some to coordination of civil actions, and others to court-annexed arbitration and mediation. Rules 5.475–5.5, 3.500–3.550, 3.800–3.878, Cal. Rules of Ct. Some cover seemingly mundane topics, such as the form and size requirements of papers presented for filing specified in Rules 2.100–2.119; others provide essential information on important matters not covered elsewhere, such as the time deadlines for filing a notice of appeal in Rules 8.104 & 8.108. The criteria for publication of appellate opinions, for example, are found in Rules 8.1100–8.1125 and no place else.

You might think a detailed Code of Civil Procedure plus hundreds of state-wide Rules of Court would provide sufficient bases for the regulation of civil procedure. Unfortunately, the California courts do not. Pursuant to the authority provided by CCP § 575.1 and Government Code § 68070(a), each county has promulgated numerous local rules applicable to civil actions in its superior courts. Typically they govern such areas of local variation as the format and filing requirements for papers, the procedures for scheduling hearings, telephonic rulings, and special rules for specific departments. With the advent of the Trial Court Delay Reduction Act, local rules have taken on increased importance.

2. "Unwritten" Law

Judicial Decisions. Judicial decisions are a prevalent source of procedural law. The courts not only interpret the written law, but possess the inherent power to make procedural law. *See, e.g., La Sala v. American Savings & Loan Assn.*, 5 Cal. 3d 864, 872, 97 Cal. Rptr. 849, 489 P.2d 1113 (1971) (Adopting procedures for class actions); *Green v. Obledo*, 29 Cal. 3d 126, 145–46, 172 Cal. Rptr. 206, 624 P.2d 256 (1981) (Same).

The general rule is that judicial decisions in civil actions are given retroactive effect. This means that a decision of the California Supreme Court overruling a former decision or announcing a new rule of law should normally apply to all actions that already have been filed or litigated but are not yet final. *See, e.g., Newman v. Emerson Radio Corp.*, 48 Cal. 3d 973, 978, 258 Cal. Rptr. 592, 772 P.2d 1059 (1989) (Observing that the California courts have consistently applied tort decisions retroactively even when those decisions declared new causes of action); *Peterson v. Superior Court*, 31 Cal. 3d 147, 151–52, 181 Cal. Rptr. 784, 642 P.2d 1305 (1982) (Concluding new rule announced by Supreme Court that punitive damages are recoverable from intoxicated driver who causes personal injury should be applied retroactively).

However, the courts have recognized exceptions to the general rule when considerations of fairness and public policy precluded retrospective operation of judicial decisions. *See, e.g., Newman v. Emerson Radio Corp., supra* (Collecting cases); *Moradi-Shalal v. Fireman's Fund Ins. Companies*, 46 Cal. 3d 287, 250 Cal. Rptr. 116, 758 P.2d 58 (1988) (Judicial reinterpretation of a statute to preclude private third-party causes of action for unfair insurer practices not given retroactive effect; considerations of fairness and public policy required prospective application to permit those who had already embarked on litigation to receive the benefit of the court's express prior ruling on which they had relied).

Publication of Appellate Court Opinions. Decisions on the merits by the California Supreme Court and Courts of Appeal must be in writing with the court's reasons stated. Art. VI, § 14, Cal. Const. All such written opinions of the Supreme Court are published in the Official Reports (*i.e.*, the multi-volume *California Reports*). Rule 8.1105(a), Cal. Rules of Ct.

An opinion of the Court of Appeal, however, is published in the Official Reports (*i.e.*, the multi-volume *California Appellate Reports*) only if it satisfies one of the criteria for publication set forth in Rule 8.1105(c) (*e.g.*, the opinion establishes a new rule of law, addresses or creates an apparent conflict in the law, involves a legal issue of continuing public interest, invokes a previously overlooked rule of law, etc.). Because these criteria discourage publication, only approximately 17% of the judicial opinions rendered by the various Courts of Appeal in civil appeals are published. *See* Judicial Council of California, *2014 Court Statistics Report*, Courts of Appeal, Figure 30: Civil Appeals for 2012–13. Partial publication is also authorized and is frequently utilized.

If the Court of Appeal determines that only portions of its opinion meet the standards for publication, it can order publication of only those portions. Rule 8.1110(a). The unpublished parts are treated as an unpublished opinion. Rule 8.1110(c).

The California Supreme Court has the power to change the publication status of a Court of Appeal opinion by ordering that an opinion certified for publication is not to be published or, more rarely, that an opinion not certified for publication is to be published. Rule 8.1105(e)(2). A grant of review by the California Supreme Court does not automatically affect the Court of Appeal's certification for publication. Rule 8.1105(e)(1)(B). However, the California Supreme Court may order depublication of part of an opinion anytime after granting review. Rule 8.1105(e)(2).

Citation of Unpublished Opinions Prohibited. What difference does it make whether or not an opinion is published? Plenty. Generally, subject to certain limited exceptions, an unpublished opinion cannot be cited or relied on by a court or a party in any other action or proceeding. Rule 8.1115, Cal. Rules of Ct. Because an unpublished or depublished opinion can not be cited, it has no precedential value. *See, e.g., Nelson v. Justice Court*, 86 Cal. App. 3d 64, 66, 150 Cal. Rptr. 39 (1978); *Heaton v. Marin County Employees Retirement Bd.*, 63 Cal. App. 3d 421, 431, 133 Cal. Rptr. 809 (1976). Improper citation to an unpublished opinion in an appellate brief may result in the imposition of sanctions. *See Alicia T. v. County of Los Angeles*, 222 Cal. App. 3d 869, 885–86, 271 Cal. Rptr. 513 (1990) (Monetary sanctions imposed against appellant's counsel for repeatedly citing depublished cases).

Learned Treatises. The California courts often rely on legal treatises and secondary authorities to illuminate gray areas of the law. The most authoritative treatise by far is the ten-volume *California Procedure* authored by Bernard E. Witkin, now in its fifth edition (2008) and supplemented annually. First published in 1954, Witkin's treatise has been cited thousands of times over the years in judicial opinions. Another influential treatise is Weil and Brown, *Civil Procedure Before Trial*, a loose-leaf service published by The Rutter Group and updated annually.

Secondary authorities, such as learned treatises, are not themselves law and do not have the binding force of statutes, court rules, or judicial precedents. Nevertheless, they can be quite persuasive. For example, when construing unclear procedural statutes, the California courts frequently rely on legislative histories contained in Judicial Council, California Law Revision Commission Official Comments, or legislative committee reports to ascertain legislative intent. *See Bonanno v. Central Contra Costa Transit Authority*, 30 Cal. 4th 139, 148, 132 Cal. Rptr. 2d 341, 65 P.3d 807 (2003) (Official Comments are "persuasive, albeit not conclusive, evidence" of legislative intent).

B. California Judicial System

The following profile of the California judicial system is reproduced, in part, from *California Judicial Branch* and *California Courts*, with additions and modifications taken from *2017 Court Statistics Report, Statewide Caseload Trends 2006–2007 Through 2015–2016*, published by the Judicial Council of California.

California Judicial Branch

The California court system—the largest in the nation, with more than 2,000 judicial officers, 19,000 court employees, and more than 6.2 million cases—serves over 39 million people. The state Constitution vests the judicial power of California in the Supreme Court, Courts of Appeal, and superior courts. The Constitution also provides for the formation and functions of the Judicial Council, the policymaking body for the state courts and other agencies.

California Supreme Court

The Supreme Court of California is the state's highest court. Its decisions are binding on all other California courts. The court conducts regular sessions in San Francisco, Los Angeles, and Sacramento; it may also hold special sessions elsewhere.

Membership. One Chief Justice and six associate justices are appointed by the Governor and confirmed by the Commission on Judicial Appointments. The appointments are confirmed by the public at the next general election; justices also come before voters at the end of their 12-year terms. To be considered for appointment, a person must be an attorney admitted to practice in California or have served as a judge of a court of record in this state for 10 years immediately preceding appointment (Cal. Const., art. VI, § 10).

Jurisdiction. The Supreme Court has original jurisdiction in proceedings for extraordinary relief in the nature of mandamus, certiorari, and prohibition. The court also has original jurisdiction in habeas corpus proceedings (Cal. Const., art. VI, § 10).

The state Constitution gives the Supreme Court the authority to review decisions of the state Courts of Appeal (Cal. Const., art. VI, §12). This reviewing power enables the Supreme Court to decide important legal questions and to maintain uniformity in the law. The court selects specific issues for review, or it may decide all the issues in a case (Cal. Const., art. VI, § 12). The Constitution also directs the high court to review all cases in which a judgment of death has been pronounced by the trial court (Cal. Const., art. VI, § 11). Under state law, these cases are automatically appealed directly from the trial court to the Supreme Court (Pen. Code §1239(b)).

Business Transacted. Total filings increased slightly from the previous year, with 8,079 (civil=1,121) filings in 2015–2016 compared with 7,868 filings in 2014–15. Dispositions increased from 7,560 in 2014–15 to 7,946 in 2015–16. Twenty-three automatic appeals (death penalty cases) were disposed of in 2015–16, compared to nineteen in 2014–15. Filings of original proceedings in 2015–16 numbered 2,804, up from 2,727 in 2014–15. Filings in State Bar disciplinary proceedings in 2015–16 reached a total of 1,031.

The number of written opinions remained the same, with 76 in 2015–16 and in 2014–15. The Supreme Court ordered seventeen (17) Court of Appeal opinions depublished in 2015–16, down from twenty-one (21) in 2014–15. The Supreme Court continued to meet its commitment to issue decisions within 90 days of oral argument or submission of the last brief.

Petitions for Review. The total number of petitions for review of Court of Appeal decisions increased slightly from 4,041 in 2014–15 to 4,193 in 2015–16. Petitions for review in civil appeals totaled 1,083 in 2015–16, down slightly from 1,158 in 2014–15. An additional 234 civil writ petitions were filed in 2015–16, compared to 237 in 2014–15. Petitions for review in criminal appeals were at 3,110 in 2015–16, compared to 2,883 in 2014–15.

The Supreme Court granted only 55 (civil=31, criminal=24) petitions for review for expected decision in 2015–16, down from 61 the previous year. It also granted and held 34 petitions pending an expected decision in a lead case. An additional 46 petitions were granted and immediately transferred back to a Court of Appeal for further proceedings. Grants for all three reasons totaled 135, or 3 percent of petitions acted upon. As in prior years, there was a higher percentage of grants in civil matters (6%) than in criminal matters (3%).

Original Proceedings. Civil original proceedings totaled 288, and criminal totaled 2,516 in 2015–16. Habeas corpus petitions constitute the bulk of criminal writ petitions. With the exception of habeas corpus petitions, most such writ petitions seek review of interlocutory decisions of lower courts.

Courts Of Appeal

Established by a constitutional amendment in 1904, the Courts of Appeal are California's intermediate courts of review. California has six appellate districts, each with at least one division. The six appellate districts are composed of 19 divisions and 105 justices. District headquarters are: First District, San Francisco; Second District, Los Angeles; Third District, Sacramento; Fourth District Division One, San Diego; Fifth District, Fresno; and Sixth District, San Jose. The Legislature has constitutional authority to create new Court of Appeal districts and divisions (Cal. Const., art. VI, §3).

Membership. Each district (or division, in the case of the Second and Fourth Districts) has a presiding justice and two or more associate justices. The total number of justices was 105 in 2015–16. Appellate justices are appointed by the Governor and confirmed by the Commission on Judicial Appointments. The same rules that govern the selection of Supreme Court justices apply to those serving on the Courts of Appeal.

Jurisdiction. Courts of Appeal have appellate jurisdiction when superior courts have original jurisdiction, and in certain other cases prescribed by statute. Like the Supreme Court, they have original jurisdiction in habeas corpus, mandamus, certiorari, and prohibition proceedings (Cal. Const., art. VI, §10). There were 20,217 contested matters in the Courts of Appeal during the 2015–16 fiscal year.

Business Transacted. A total of 20,217 notices of appeal and original proceedings were filed in the Courts of Appeal in 2015–16, down slightly from 20,661 in 2014–15. Filings of records of appeal decreased slightly from 13,607 in 2014–15 to 13,296 in 2015–16. A total of 5,935 notices of appeal were filed in civil cases (3,840 records of appeal).

Total filings of original writ proceedings dropped slightly to 6.921 cases in 2015–16. Likewise, civil original writ proceedings dropped slightly to 1,781, and criminal filings of original proceedings to 4,791. During the same year, 1,690 civil writ petitions were summarily denied, another 98 were disposed of by written opinion.

Total dispositions increased slightly from the previous year to 22,931 in 2015–16. Written opinions also increased slightly to 9,967 cases (total civil=2,917) in 2015–16.

Trial Court Affirmative Rate. Among cases disposed by written opinion, there was little change from the previous year in the proportions of cases affirmed, reversed, and dismissed. As in previous fiscal years, approximately 79% of civil appeals decided by opinion, and 91 % of criminal appeals, were affirmed during 2015–16.

Opinions Certified for Publication. Cases are decided by three-judge panels. Decisions of the panels, known as opinions, are published in the California Appellate Reports if those opinions meet certain criteria for publication. In general, the opinion is published if it establishes a new rule of law, involves a legal issue of continuing public interest, criticizes existing law, or makes a significant contribution to legal literature (Cal. Const., art. VI, §14; Rules of Court, rule 8.1105(c)). During fiscal year 2015–16, eight (8%) percent of Court of Appeal opinions were certified as meeting the criteria for publication, the same as in the previous year. The highest publication rates were for original proceedings (15%) and civil appeals (15%), followed by juvenile (5%) and criminal appeals (4%).

Case-Processing Time. Statewide, half of the civil appeals disposed of by opinion in 2015–16 took more than 506 days from notice of appeal to decision. The outlook was somewhat better for criminal appeals, for which the statewide median time from filing of notice of appeal to decision was 427 days.

In both civil and criminal appeals, studies indicate that most case delay is beyond an appellate court's control. For example, appellate courts typically must wait a significant amount of time for the trial court record to be completed. The period from the filing of the record to the filing of the appellant's and respondent's briefs consti¬tutes another large block of time. After the record and briefs are filed, most Courts of Appeal decide cases quite promptly.

Superior Courts

Membership, qualifications. The superior courts have 1,726 authorized judges and 287 commissioners and referees. The California Legislature determines the number of judges in each court. Superior court judges serve six year terms and are elected by county voters on a nonpartisan ballot at a general election. Vacancies are filled through appointment by the Governor. A superior court judge (with the exception of former municipal court judges in unified courts) must have been an attorney admitted to practice law in California or have served as a judge of a court of record in this state for at least 10 years immediately preceding election or appointment.

Jurisdiction. Superior courts now have trial jurisdiction over all criminal cases including felonies, misdemeanors, and traffic matters. They also have jurisdiction over all civil cases including family law, probate, juvenile, and general civil matters. More than 6.2 million cases were filed in the trial courts at over 500 court locations throughout the state during 2015 –2016 (a 9% decline over the past year). Appeals in limited civil cases (where $25,000 or less is at issue) and misdemeanors are heard by the appellate division of the superior court. When a small claims case is appealed, a superior court judge decides the case.

Business Transacted. Superior court filings fell from 6,850,075 in 2014–15 to 6,217,800 in 2015–16. There were 5,488,900 dispositions in 2015–16, down from the number in 2014–15.

Civil case filings (excluding marital and family law petitions) decreased from 721,520 in 2014–15 to 712,299 in 2015–16. However, personal injury, property damaged, and wrongful death filings increased somewhat from 54,004 in 2014–15 to 56,615 in 2015–16. Domestic–related filings (marital and family law petitions) increased from 380,994 in 2014–15 to 387,849 in 2015–16. Criminal case filings decreased to 4,946,881 in 2015–16.

Only three (3) percent of all unlimited civil cases were disposed of by jury trials, and one (1) percent of limited civil cases, in 2015–16. Likewise, only three (3) percent of felony dispositions were by jury trial. The total number of all civil and criminal jury trials in 2015–16 was 9,279.

Civil Cases. Total civil filings in all case categories equaled 712,299 during 2015–16. Of these, only 201,390 were unlimited civil cases, 352,562 were limited civil cases, 138,520 were family law (marital) cases, and 158,347 were small claims court cases. Civil dispositions in all case categories totaled 676,074, including 182,679 unlimited civil cases. Only 1,142 unlimited civil cases were decided by jury trials, or 3 percent. Over 80% of all civil cases were dismissed before trial during 2015–16, including 4.5% for delay in prosecution.

Case–Processing Time. Civil case processing time increased somewhat compared to previous years. In 2015–16, 64% of all unlimited civil cases were disposed of within 12 months, 76% within 18 months, and 83% within 24 months. Likewise, 82% of limited civil cases were disposed of within 12 months, 90% within 18 months, and 93% within 24 months. Criminal case processing time did not change significantly, with 85% of all felonies being disposed of in less than 12 months.

Court System Agencies

The Constitution also provides for agencies concerned with judicial administration: Judicial Council Commission on Judicial Appointments, Commission on Judicial Performance, and Habeas Corpus Resource Center. Their duties are described below.

Judicial Council. Chaired by the Chief Justice, the Judicial Council is the governing body of the California courts. The California Constitution directs the Judicial Council to provide policy guidelines to the courts, make recommendations annually to the Governor and Legislature, and adopt and revise California Rules of Court in the areas of court administration, practice and procedure. The council performs its constitutional and other functions with the support of its staff agency, the Administrative Office of the Courts.

The 21 voting members of the Judicial Council consist of the Chief Justice, one Associate Justice of the Supreme Court, 3 justices of the Courts of Appeal, 10 judges of the superior courts, 4 attorney members appointed by the State Bar Board of Governors, and 1 member from each house of the Legislature. The Council also has approximately 11 advisory members, who include court executives or administrators. The council performs most of its work through internal committees and advisory committees and task forces.

Commission on Judicial Appointments. The Governor's appointees to the Supreme Court and the Courts of Appeal must be confirmed by the Commission on Judicial Appointments. No appellate appointment is final until the commission has filed its approval with the Secretary of State.

Commission on Judicial Performance. The California Constitution provides for a Commission on Judicial Performance, which deals with the censure, removal, retirement, or private admonishment of judges and commissioners for either misconduct or inability to perform their duties on account of permanent disability.

Chapter II

Statutes of Limitations, Attorney Fees, Court Costs, and Related Matters

A. Statutes of Limitations

The first step in resolving a statute of limitations problem is to ascertain the length of the statutorily prescribed period for a cause of action. Section 312 of the Code of Civil Procedure then requires that the action be commenced within that period after the cause of action has "accrued." The next question is to determine when a cause of action has "accrued" such that the statutory limitation period begins to run. The answer to this question can be quite complex in California. The Code of Civil Procedure does not provide a general definition of "accrual" applicable to all statutes of limitations. Instead, the California courts have traditionally provided the general rules regarding accrual, as our principal case below illustrates. However, the Legislature has defined the accrual point for certain specific causes of action, such as medical malpractice, CCP § 340.5; legal malpractice, CCP § 340.6; childhood sexual abuse, CCP § 340.1(a); injury due to exposure to asbestos, CCP § 340.2; and breach of contract for sale of goods, Commercial Code § 2725(2).

Jolly v. Eli Lilly & Company

Supreme Court of California

44 Cal. 3d 1103, 245 Cal. Rptr. 658, 751 P.2d 923 (1988)

PANELLI, JUSTICE.

This case presents the following questions: whether a plaintiff, in a suit for personal injury caused by a defective drug, who is unaware of any specific facts establishing wrongful conduct on the part of any drug manufacturer, may delay bringing an action until she discovers such facts; whether a claim, otherwise barred by the statute of limitations, can be revived due to our decision in *Sindell v. Abbott Laboratories* (1980) 26 Cal. 3d 588 [163 Cal. Rptr. 132, 607 P.2d 924, 2 A.L.R.4th 1061], in which we held that a plaintiff who is unable to identify the particular manufacturer of a fungible drug that caused injury to her can state a claim by joining defendants who manufactured a substantial percentage of the market share of the allegedly defective drug; and whether the filing of the class action in *Sindell, supra*, tolled the statute of limitations for members of the putative class until the class was denied certification. We answer these questions in the negative and so conclude that the suit is time-barred.

I. *Facts*

Plaintiff Jolly was born in 1951. In 1972, she first learned that while she was *in utero* her mother had ingested the synthetic drug estrogen diethylstilbestrol (DES) for the prevention of miscarriage. Plaintiff was told in 1972 that DES daughters could suffer injuries. Therefore, she went to a DES clinic at the UCLA Medical Center for a checkup. She was diagnosed as having adenosis, a precancerous condition that required careful monitoring. In 1976, she had an abnormal pap smear and underwent a dilation and curettage, a surgical procedure to remove abnormal tissue. In 1978, plaintiff underwent a complete hysterectomy and a partial vaginectomy in order to remove malignancy. As of 1972, plaintiff was aware, or at least suspected, that her condition was a result of her mother's ingestion of DES during pregnancy.

Starting in 1972, plaintiff attempted to discover the manufacturer of the DES ingested by her mother. Efforts were increased in 1976 and 1978 when plaintiff's condition became acute. Unfortunately, the doctor who prescribed the drug had died, and plaintiff was unable to locate his records. Although the dispensing pharmacist did remember filling the DES prescription, he did not recall or have records pertaining to the specific brand used. This was not unusual since DES was a fungible drug, that is, hundreds of pharmaceutical companies made DES from a single agreed formula. The hospital where plaintiff was born was of no assistance because plaintiff's mother did not use DES while there.

At least as of 1978, plaintiff was aware of the pendency of one or more DES suits alleging that DES manufacturers were liable to those injured due to their failure to test or failure to warn. Although she believed that DES had caused her injuries and that those who marketed DES had wrongfully marketed a defective product, there is no conclusive evidence in the record to show that a reasonable investigation by plaintiff in 1978 would have disclosed specific proven facts that would establish any wrongful conduct on the part of a DES drug manufacturer. In fact, even today defendants allege that DES is not defective, but for purposes of summary judgment have admitted the allegation of some defectiveness.

Further, plaintiff believed that she had no cause of action if she could not identify the particular manufacturer of the drug her mother took during pregnancy. Because her efforts to identify that manufacturer were unsuccessful, plaintiff did not file suit.

In March 1980, we decided *Sindell v. Abbott Laboratories, supra,* 26 Cal. 3d 588, and held that if a plaintiff could not identify the precise drug manufacturer of the ingested DES, she could state a cause of action against the DES manufacturers of a substantial percentage of the market share of the drug. Defendants would be liable, assuming the remaining material allegations in the complaint were proven, unless they could disprove their involvement. Almost one year after *Sindell,* plaintiff Jolly brought this action.

Defendants moved for summary judgment, asserting that the action was barred by Code of Civil Procedure section 340, subdivision (3),[2] setting forth a one-year statute of limitations period for an action "for injury . . . caused by the wrongful act or neglect of another." Although conceding the applicability of the one-year statutory period, plaintiff denied that the suit was time-barred. She asserted that the statute did not commence until she learned of the *Sindell* decision, because only then did she realize that she would be able to successfully bring her claim.

Plaintiff maintained that *Sindell* created a new cause of action by redefining "causation." Prior to *Sindell*, she claimed, only the specific manufacturer of the pills that were ingested was deemed to have "caused" the injury. After *Sindell*, according to plaintiff, it was the generic drug DES that "caused" the harm, and therefore all DES manufacturers were tortfeasors.

The trial court granted defendants' motion and entered judgment in their favor. The Court of Appeal reversed, relying on its earlier decision in *Kensinger v. Abbott Laboratories* (1985) 171 Cal. App. 3d 376 [217 Cal. Rptr. 313]. The Court of Appeal did not address Jolly's main argument, that the statute could not begin to run until after our decision in *Sindell, supra,* 26 Cal. 3d 588, except by way of a footnote declining to adopt her position. We granted defendants Eli Lilly and Company, Rexall Drug Company, and E.R. Squibb and Sons, Inc.'s subsequent petition for review.

II. *The Kensinger Decision*

As previously noted, both sides agree that the one-year limitations period of section 340, subdivision (3) applies to this case. Both sides also agree that the common law rule, that an action accrues on the date of injury (*Lambert v. McKenzie* (1901) 135 Cal. 100, 103 [67 P. 6]), applies only as modified by the "discovery rule." The discovery rule provides that the accrual date of a cause of action is delayed until the plaintiff is aware of her injury and its negligent cause.[4] (*Sanchez v. South Hoover Hospital, supra,* 18 Cal. 3d 93, 99.) A plaintiff is held to her actual knowledge as well as knowledge that could reasonably be discovered through investigation of sources open to her. (*Id.* at p. 101.) The parties differ as to what constitutes sufficient knowledge to start the statute running.

The Court of Appeal applied *Kensinger, supra,* 171 Cal. App. 3d 376, a factually similar case, and found that it was a question of fact as to whether the statute of limitations

---

2. All further statutory references are to the Code of Civil Procedure [CCP] unless otherwise indicated. [Effective January 1, 2003, the one-year statute of limitations for personal injury actions in former CCP § 340(3) was increased to two years by new CCP § 335.1.]

4. Defendants argue that the statute should commence when the plaintiff knows of her injury and its *factual* cause. Although that position has been adopted in some jurisdictions (*see e.g., United States v. Kubrick* (1979) 444 U.S. 111 [100 S. Ct. 352, 62 L. Ed. 2d 259] [concerning the Federal Tort Claims Act]; *Anthony v. Koppers Co., Inc.* (1980) 284 Pa. Super. 81 [425 A.2d 428, 436], *revd. on other grounds,* (1981) 496 Pa. 119 [436 A.2d 181]), it is not the rule in California. (*See, e.g., Sanchez v. South Hoover Hospital* (1976) 18 Cal. 3d 93, 99 [132 Cal. Rptr. 657, 553 P.2d 1129]; *Gutierrez v. Mofid* (1985) 39 Cal. 3d 892, 896 [218 Cal. Rptr. 313, 705 P.2d 886].)

began to run more than one year before plaintiff Jolly filed her complaint. The *Kensinger* court acknowledged the well established rule that ignorance of the legal significance of known facts or the identity of the defendant would not delay the running of the statute — only ignorance of one or more "critical facts" could have that effect.

However, the key point in *Kensinger* was its determination that one "critical fact" was knowledge of some wrongful conduct. Specifically, the court held that a plaintiff may have "no knowledge of facts indicating wrongdoing by a particular defendant. In such a situation, litigation might be premature for lack of knowledge of any *factual basis* for imputing fault to a manufacturer rather than ignorance of supportive legal theories. . . . Knowledge of the occurrence and origin of harm cannot necessarily be equated with knowledge of the factual basis for a legal remedy. . . ." (171 Cal. App. 3d at pp. 383–384; italics added.) Accordingly, the *Kensinger* court held that the statutory clock did not begin to tick until the plaintiff knew or reasonably should have known of the facts constituting wrongful conduct, as well as the fact of her injury and its relation to DES.[5] The Court of Appeal, applying *Kensinger*, held that it could not be said that "as a matter of law" Jolly was or should have been aware of *facts* establishing wrongdoing, e.g., "either failure to test or failure to warn," until within one year of the date she filed suit.

The rule proposed in *Kensinger* goes too far.[6] Under the discovery rule, the statute of limitations begins to run when the plaintiff suspects or should suspect that her injury was caused by wrongdoing, that someone has done something wrong to her.[7] As we said in *Sanchez* and reiterated in *Gutierrez*, the limitations period begins once the plaintiff " 'has notice or information of circumstances to put a reasonable person *on inquiry. . . .*' " * * * A plaintiff need not be aware of the specific "facts" necessary to establish the claim; that is a process contemplated by pretrial discovery. Once the plaintiff has a suspicion of wrongdoing, and therefore an incentive to sue, she must decide whether to file suit or sit on her rights. So long as a suspicion exists, it is clear that the plaintiff must go find the facts; she cannot wait for the facts to find her.

For example, in *Miller v. Bechtel Corp.* (1983) 33 Cal. 3d 868 [191 Cal. Rptr. 619, 663 P.2d 177], we held that plaintiff was barred by the statute of limitations from

---

5. Plaintiff maintains that the *Kensinger* rule was foreshadowed by prior California authority. However, the cases that she cites do no more than set out the discovery rule as previously described. They do not directly address the question of whether a suspicion of wrongdoing without knowledge of particular facts establishing misconduct will begin the statutory period. (*See Young v. Haines* (1986) 41 Cal. 3d 883 [226 Cal. Rptr. 547, 718 P.2d 909] [effect of fraudulent concealment by a physician]; *Brown v. Bleiberg* (1982) 32 Cal. 3d 426 [186 Cal. Rptr. 228, 651 P.2d 815] [same]; *Gutierrez, supra*, 39 Cal. 3d 892 [same]; * * * *Martinez-Ferrer v. Richardson-Merrell, Inc.* (1980) 105 Cal. App. 3d 316 [164 Cal. Rptr. 591] [effect on statute of limitations when plaintiff might have had no cause of action at earlier point in time, but believed that he did].)

6. We recognize that some jurisdictions have adopted rules similar to that set out in *Kensinger*. (*See, e.g., Anthony v. Abbott Laboratories* (R.I. 1985) 490 A.2d 43 (relied on in *Kensinger*); *Dawson v. Eli Lilly & Co.* (D.D.C. 1982) 543 F. Supp. 1330; *Lopez v. Swyer* (1973) 62 N.J. 267 [300 A.2d 563].) However, as will be shown, the rule in California is otherwise.

7. In this context, "wrong," "wrongdoing," and "wrongful" are used in their lay understanding.

pursuing her suit for fraud, even though she filed suit soon after she discovered facts confirming her long-held suspicion that her former husband had concealed the true worth of his assets during dissolution negotiations. We noted that the plaintiff had doubts at the time she signed the dissolution agreement as to the actual value of her husband's Bechtel stock. However, neither she nor her attorney took adequate steps then to investigate the matter. Years later, when the stock was sold for an amount well beyond that stated during the dissolution discussions, plaintiff brought suit. We held that her early suspicion put her on inquiry notice of the potential wrongdoing, which an investigation would have confirmed. Her failure timely to investigate barred the action. This conclusion was reached over a strong dissent, in which it was argued that the statute of limitations should not begin to run until plaintiff discovered the *facts* constituting the misconduct — her mere suspicion was not enough.

Another case in point is *Gray v. Reeves* (1977) 76 Cal. App. 3d 567. In *Gray*, a plaintiff suffered an allergic reaction to a drug in 1971, but delayed filing suit against the prescribing doctor and manufacturer until 1973. The Court of Appeal affirmed the trial court's award of summary judgment for defendants based on the statute of limitations. The court noted plaintiff's admission that in 1971 he knew that defendants "did something wrong." Even without specific facts as to why the drug was defective, plaintiff was on notice at that time that he had a potential cause of action. (*See also Graham v. Hansen* (1982) 128 Cal. App. 3d 965, 972–973 [180 Cal. Rptr. 604] ["If plaintiff believes because of injuries she has suffered that someone has done something wrong" the statutory period begins].)

The foregoing is fully consistent with the policy of deciding cases on the merits as well as the policies underlying the statute of limitations. In *Davies v. Krasna* (1975) 14 Cal. 3d 502, 512 [121 Cal. Rptr. 705, 535 P.2d 1161, 79 A.L.R.3d 807], we held that the fundamental purpose of the statute is to give defendants reasonable repose, that is, to protect parties from defending stale claims. A second policy underlying the statute is to require plaintiffs to diligently pursue their claims. Because a plaintiff is under a duty to reasonably investigate and because a *suspicion* of wrongdoing, coupled with a knowledge of the harm and its cause, will commence the limitations period, suits are not likely to be unreasonably delayed, and those failing to act with reasonable dispatch will be barred. At the same time, plaintiffs who file suit as soon as they have reason to believe that they are entitled to recourse will not be precluded.[8]

While resolution of the statute of limitations issue is normally a question of fact, where the uncontradicted facts established through discovery are susceptible of only one legitimate inference, summary judgment is proper. In this case it is clear that application of the discovery rule supports the trial court's judgment. Plaintiff stated that as early as 1978 she was interested in "obtaining more information" about DES because she wanted to "make a claim"; she felt that someone had done something wrong to

---

8. To the extent that *Kensinger, supra*, 171 Cal. App. 3d 376, conflicts with the foregoing, it is disapproved. Of course, nothing stated herein affects the well-established rule that the ignorance of the legal significance of known facts or the identity of the wrongdoer will not delay the running of the statute.

her concerning DES, that it was a defective drug and that she should be compensated.[9] She points to no evidence contradicting her candid statements. Thus, plaintiff is held to her admission; she suspected that defendants' conduct was wrongful during 1978— well over a year before she filed suit. This suspicion would not have been allayed by any investigation. To the contrary, a timely investigation would have disclosed numerous articles concerning DES and many DES suits filed throughout the country alleging wrongdoing.

Plaintiff's contention that our decision in *Sindell* redefined "causation" and "wrongful," providing the crucial "fact" necessary for her to suspect wrongdoing, is without merit. * * * At this point it is necessary only to point out the oft-stated rule that it is the discovery of facts, not their legal significance, that starts the statute. All of the facts set out in *Sindell* that are relevant to plaintiff's case were either already known by her in 1978 or could have been discovered through a reasonable investigation.[11] Indeed, plaintiff admits that she learned of no new facts between 1978 and 1980.

In sum, the limitations period begins when the plaintiff suspects, or should suspect, that she has been wronged. Here, plaintiff suspected as much no later than 1978. Because she did not file suit until 1981, her suit, unless otherwise saved, is time-barred.[13]

[The Supreme Court then determined that the plaintiff's claim, otherwise barred by the statute of limitations, was not revived by the court's decision in *Sindell v. Abbott Laboratories, supra*. Next, the court rejected the plaintiff's argument that the filing of the class action in *Sindell, supra*, tolled the statute of limitations with respect to individual members of the putative class, such as the plaintiff, until the class was denied certification in 1982.]

---

9. Specifically, the following dialogue was contained in plaintiff's deposition and was part of the motion for summary judgment:

"Q:Why at that time were you interested in obtaining more information [about the DES ingested by plaintiff's mother]?
"A:To see if I had any type of recourse.
"Q:You mean in terms of making a claim or recovering from someone for your injury?
"A:Sure, yes.
"Q:In 1978 did you feel that you should have some kind of recourse?
"A:Yes.
"Q:You felt that someone had done something wrong to you?
"A:Yes.
"Q:And that you should be compensated for it?
"A:Yes.
"Q:You believed at that time, in 1978, that DES was a defective drug, is that right?
"A:Yes."

11. This case does not present us with a situation where the plaintiff conducted a prompt investigation and brought suit as soon as the results of the investigation were known, but even so filed her claim after the limitations period had expired. In such a situation, the cause of action might still be timely. (*See Whitfield v. Roth* (1974) 10 Cal. 3d 874, 887–889 [112 Cal. Rptr. 540, 519 P.2d 588] [concerning the 100-day period set forth in the Government Tort Claims Act].)

13. Plaintiff's failure to file suit despite her suspicion of wrongdoing is not surprising in the context of this case. By her own admission, her real reason for delaying action was that she did not know *whom* to sue, not that she did not know *whether* to sue.

III. *Conclusion*

The judgment of the Court of Appeal is reversed. The cause is remanded with instructions to affirm the judgment of the trial court in favor of defendants.

Notes and Questions Regarding Statutes of Limitations

(1) Effective January 1, 2003, the statute of limitations for assault, battery, wrongful death, and personal injury actions "caused by the wrongful act or neglect of another," has been increased to two years. CCP § 335.1. The statute of limitations for other intentional torts, such as libel, slander, and false imprisonment, remains one year. CCP § 340.

(2) The California discovery rule sets forth two alternative tests for triggering the limitations period: (1) a subjective test requiring actual suspicion by the plaintiff that the injury was caused by wrongdoing and (2) an objective test requiring a showing that a reasonable person would have suspected the injury was caused by wrongdoing. *Jolly, supra*, 44 Cal. 3d at 1110. The first to occur under these two tests begins the limitations period. *Id.* What constitutes "reasonable suspicion"? Does it depend on the nature of the injury? What constitutes "actual suspicion"? Does obtaining a second opinion from another doctor about the propriety of your ongoing medical treatment by your doctor constitute "actual suspicion" that your doctor has committed malpractice, thereby starting the statute of limitations? *See Kitzig v. Nordquist*, 81 Cal. App. 4th 1384, 97 Cal. Rptr. 2d 762 (2000).

(3) Note that the California Supreme Court in *Jolly* did not modify the traditional common law rule that ignorance of the legal significance of known facts will not delay the running of the statute of limitations. What does this rule mean?

(4) Another important limitation on the discovery rule adopted in *Jolly* is the well-established California rule that the ignorance of the identity of the wrongdoer will not delay the running of the statute of limitations. In other words, the statute of limitations begins to run when the plaintiff knows of her injury, its cause, and suspects wrongdoing, even though the plaintiff does not know *who* caused her injury. This was particularly a problem for the plaintiff in *Jolly*.

(5) Related to the issue of delayed discovery of injury is the question of how substantial must an injury be to trigger the commencement of the relevant statute of limitations. The modern California rule is: Although a right to recover nominal damages will not trigger the running of the period of limitation, "the infliction of appreciable and actual harm, however uncertain in amount, will commence the statutory period." *Davies v. Krasna*, 14 Cal. 3d 502, 514, 121 Cal. Rptr. 705, 535 P.2d 1161 (1975).

(6) *Legislative Modification of the Discovery Rule.* In a number of specific areas the Legislature has statutorily defined when certain causes of action accrue. Some of these statutory provisions simply codify the common law doctrine, but others modify, and in some instances eliminate, the discovery rule. The most notable is contained in section 2725 of the Commercial Code, which sets forth a four-year statute of limitations for actions for breach of any contract for sale of goods. Section 2725(2) states that

"a cause of action accrues when the breach occurs, regardless of the aggrieved party's lack of knowledge of the breach." Another is CCP § 337.15, which contains a ten-year limitation for actions against real estate developers, contractors, and architects for property damages arising our of a latent deficiency, which accrues upon "the substantial completion of the development or improvement." CCP § 337.15(a).

Some special statutes adopt the discovery rule but include a superceding limitation period which accrues on the date of injury. The two most notable examples are CCP § 340.5, which governs actions for injury or death against health care providers based on professional negligence; and CCP § 340.6, which governs actions against attorneys for wrongful acts. Section 340.5 generally requires that a medical negligence action be commenced within three years of the date of injury or one year after discovery of the injury, "whichever occurs first." Likewise, § 340.6 generally requires that an attorney malpractice action be commenced within four years from the date of the wrongful act or one year after discovery of the wrongful act, "whichever occurs first." Both statutes contain some exceptions and special tolling provisions, and must be examined closely.

(7) *Tolling.* After a cause of action has accrued, there are a number of situations in California that will toll (*i.e.*, suspend) the running of a statutory limitation period. Many of these general tolling provisions are set forth in sections 351–358 of the Code of Civil Procedure. For example, if a person has a "disability" within the meaning of CCP § 352 at the time a cause of action accrues, the applicable statute of limitations is suspended during the time of such "disability." Section 352(a) defines "disability" to mean that the person is "under the age of majority" or "insane."

(a) One of the most controversial tolling provisions is contained in CCP § 351, which tolls the statute of limitations during the time that the defendant is absent from California. In *Abramson v. Brownstein*, 897 F.2d 389 (9th Cir. 1990), the U.S. Court of Appeals held that CCP § 351, when applied to nonresident defendants, violates the Commerce Clause of the U.S. Constitution. The *Abramson* court ruled the § 351 forced a nonresident defendant to choose between being present in California for several years or forfeiture of the limitations defense and, as such, was an impermissible burden on interstate commerce.

A subsequent decision concluded that § 351 violates the Commerce Clause not only as applied to nonresident defendants, but also as applied to resident defendants who travel in the course of interstate commerce. *Filet Menu, Inc. v. Cheng*, 71 Cal. App. 4th 1276, 84 Cal. Rptr. 2d 384 (1999). However, the court emphasized that its conclusion was limited to travel for facilitation of interstate commerce — tolling statutory periods for the duration of out-of-state travel unrelated to interstate commerce, such as for vacation trips or to attend college, does not violate the Commerce Clause. *Id.*, at 1283–84. For a discussion of the constitutionality of absence-based tolling provisions, see Walter W. Heiser, *Can the Tolling of Statutes of Limitations Based on the Defendant's Absence from the State Ever Be Consistent with the Commerce Clause?*, 76 Mo. L. Rev. 385 (2011) (arguing that CCP § 351 violates the Commerce

Clause when applied to a resident defendant who is temporarily absent from California regardless of the reason for the interstate travel).

(b) Other specific tolling provisions are included in special statutes of limitations. *See, e.g.,* CCP § 340.5 (medical malpractice statute of limitations tolled upon proof of fraud, intentional concealment, or presence of foreign body in the person of the injured person); CCP § 340.6 (Legal malpractice statute of limitations tolled during the time plaintiff has not sustained actual injury, the attorney continues to represent the plaintiff, the attorney willfully conceals facts, or the plaintiff is under a legal or physical disability). Specific tolling provisions in special statutes may constitute the exclusive bases for tolling. *See, e.g., Belton v. Bowers Ambulance Service,* 20 Cal. 4th 928, 86 Cal. Rptr. 2d 107, 978 P.2d 591 (1999) (Holding no tolling provision outside of CCP § 340.5 can extend the three-year maximum time period for commencement of a medical malpractice action, § 340.5 does not provide the exclusive basis for tolling the one-year limitation period); CCP § 352(b) (Special tolling provisions of the California Tort Claims Act, and not the traditional "disability" tolling provisions of CCP § 352(a), apply to tort claims against a public entity or employee).

(8) *Equitable Tolling.* In addition to statutory tolling provisions, the California courts have created judicial tolling doctrines based on concepts of fairness, typically when the plaintiff has filed a timely action against the defendant but in the wrong court or tribunal. The three elements necessary to establish the doctrine of equitable tolling are: (1) timely notice to the defendant, (2) lack of prejudice to the defendant, and (3) reasonable and good faith conduct on the part of the plaintiff. *Addison v. State of California,* 21 Cal. 3d 313, 146 Cal. Rptr. 224, 578 P.2d 941 (1978) (Holding that the statute of limitations was tolled during the period that plaintiff's state law claims were pending before a federal court and until that court declined to exercise jurisdiction, where the plaintiff had timely filed these claims against the defendants in the federal court); *Elkins v. Derby,* 12 Cal. 3d 410, 115 Cal. Rptr. 641, 525 P.2d 81 (1974) (Holding the "several remedies" rule tolls the running of the limitations period when an injured person has several fora or procedures available to remedy the injury and, reasonably and in good faith, pursues one against the defendant).

(9) *Equitable Estoppel.* Under certain circumstances, a defendant may be estopped from asserting an applicable statute of limitations where the defendant's fraudulent conduct has induced the plaintiff to delay filing an action until after the expiration of the limitations period. *See, e.g, Muraoka v. Budget Rent-A-Car,* 160 Cal. App. 3d 107, 206 Cal. Rptr. 476 (1984) (Holding defendant, whose promise of settlement fraudulently induce plaintiff to delay filing civil action, was equitably estopped from asserting the statute of limitations defense); *Bernson v. Browning-Ferris Industries of California, Inc.,* 7 Cal. 4th 926, 30 Cal. Rptr. 2d 440, 873 P.2d 613 (1994) (Holding defendant equitably estopped from raising the statute of limitations defense where defendant fraudulently concealed the cause of action against defendant and the plaintiff exercised reasonable diligence, but could not discover the relevant information within the limitations period).

(10) *Commencement.* Section 350 of the Code of Civil Procedure states that an action is commenced, with respect to statutes of limitations in the Code of Civil Procedure, "when the complaint is filed." Note, however, that special statutory schemes modify the general rule of "commencement" by inserting a prerequisite to the filing of the complaint. *E.g.,* CCP § 340.5 (Requiring a medical malpractice plaintiff to give a defendant at least 90 days' prior notice of intention to file a complaint); California Tort Claims Act, Gov. Code § 900 *et. seq.* (Requiring as a precondition to tort litigation against most public entities and employees that the plaintiff file a written claim with the appropriate state or local agency); Fair Employment and Housing Act, Gov. Code § 12900 *et. seq.* (Requiring a plaintiff to file a claim with the Department of Fair Employment and Housing as a condition precedent to a lawsuit for discrimination under the Act).

(11) *Laches.* Statutes of limitations apply to all civil causes of action, whether in law or in equity. CCP § 312. In addition, California recognizes the doctrine of laches, which applies specifically to actions seeking equitable remedies (*e.g.,* injunctions). If the defense of laches is established, the court will refuse equitable relief even though the relevant statutory period of limitations has not yet expired. *See Conti v. Board of Civil Service Commissioners,* 1 Cal. 3d 351, 82 Cal. Rptr. 337, 461 P.2d 617 (1969) (Citing numerous other cases). The basic elements of this judge-made doctrine are "(1) The failure to assert a right, (2) for some appreciable delay, (3) which results in prejudice to the adverse party." *In re Marriage of Powers,* 218 Cal. App. 3d 626, 642, 267 Cal. Rptr. 350 (1990).

B. Attorney Fees

California follows the so-called "American Rule" with respect to the recovery of attorney fees which, in the absence of an established exception, requires each party to bear its own attorney fees. *See, e.g., Serrano v. Unruh,* 32 Cal. 3d 621, 627, 186 Cal. Rptr. 754, 652 P.2d 985 (1982); *Alyeska Pipeline Co. v. Wilderness Society,* 421 U.S. 240, 247–57, 95 S. Ct. 1612, 44 L. Ed. 2d 141 (1975). California does recognize many exceptions based on fee-shifting statutes, judge-made equitable doctrines, and contractual provisions. Not only does the Legislature authorize parties to allocate attorney fees by agreement, CCP § 1021; it also makes an otherwise unilateral contractual right to recover attorney fees reciprocally binding upon all parties in an action to enforce the contract, Civil Code § 1717.

The Legislature has enacted numerous fee-shifting statutes which authorize courts to award reasonable attorney fees to the prevailing party. *E.g.,* CCP § 1021.5 (Private Attorney General Statute), CCP § 1028.5 (actions between small business and state regulatory agency), Government Code § 6259(d) (Public Records Act), Government Code § 12965(b) (Fair Employment and Housing Act), and Civil Code § 1811.1 (Retail Installment Sales Act).

The U.S. Congress has also enacted numerous fee-shifting statutes which may apply when a party seeks enforcement of the federal statute in state court. *See, e.g., Sokolow v.*

County of San Mateo, 213 Cal. App. 3d 231, 261 Cal. Rptr. 520 (1989) (Superior Court directed to award attorney fees under both 42 U.S.C. § 1988 and CCP § 1021.5 in civil rights action); *Green v. Obledo*, 161 Cal. App. 3d 678, 207 Cal. Rptr. 830 (1984) (Superior Court must apply federal fee-shifting statute when federal claim brought in state court).

These statutory and contractual bases for recovery of attorney fees constitute very significant departures from the American Rule. In addition, although perhaps less significant in overall impact, the California courts have created several exceptions to the American Rule based on equitable theories. These include the "common fund," "substantial benefit," "private attorney general," and "third-party tort" doctrines. *See, e.g., Serrano v. Priest*, 20 Cal. 3d 25, 141 Cal. Rptr. 315, 569 P.2d 1303 (1977); *Prentice v. North American Title Guaranty Corp.*, 59 Cal. 2d 618, 30 Cal. Rptr. 821, 381 P.2d 645 (1963).

Consideration of these judge-made exceptions still does not provide a complete picture of attorney fee recovery in California. In appropriate situations, a court may award attorney fees as a sanction for bad faith litigation, CCP § 128.7; for misuse of the discovery process, CCP §§ 2023.010–2023.030; and for frivolous appeals, CCP § 907, Rule 8.276, Cal. Rules of Ct.

Graham v. DaimlerChrysler Corp.
Supreme Court of California
34 Cal. 4th 553, 21 Cal. Rptr. 3d 331, 101 P.3d 140 (2004)

MORENO, JUSTICE.

In this case defendant offered to repurchase a truck that had been marketed with false statements about its towing capacity. This offer came after a lawsuit plaintiffs filed against defendant seeking this repurchase remedy, but before any kind of court judgment was rendered. Plaintiffs were awarded substantial attorney fees under Code of Civil Procedure section 1021.5. Defendant raises several issues regarding those fees. The first is whether we should reconsider the catalyst theory, recognized by this court in *Westside Community for Independent Living, Inc. v. Obledo* (1983) 33 Cal. 3d 348 [188 Cal. Rptr. 873, 657 P.2d 365] (*Westside Community*). Under the catalyst theory, attorney fees may be awarded even when litigation does not result in a judicial resolution if the defendant changes its behavior substantially because of, and in the manner sought by, the litigation. We conclude the catalyst theory should not be abolished but clarified. In order to be eligible for attorney fees under section 1021.5, a plaintiff must not only be a catalyst to defendant's changed behavior, but the lawsuit must have some merit, as discussed below, and the plaintiff must have engaged in a reasonable attempt to settle its dispute with the defendant prior to litigation. Because these limitations on the catalyst theory are to some degree new and were not addressed by the parties or the trial court, we remand for reconsideration of the trial court's award of attorney fees in this case.

Defendant also contends the trial court erred in concluding that the present lawsuit substantially benefited a large group of people or the general public, as required by section 1021.5. We conclude the trial court did not abuse its discretion in making that conclusion. Finally, defendant, while conceding that a plaintiff could be awarded attorney fees for attorney fee litigation, contends that these fees should not be enhanced beyond the "lodestar" amount. We do not endorse such a categorical rule, but we explain below that fees for fee litigation usually should be enhanced at a significantly lower rate than fees for the underlying litigation, if they are enhanced at all. We therefore will remand the cause to the trial court to recalculate the amount of the fee in light of the principles discussed below, assuming it finds on remand that plaintiffs are eligible for some attorney fees.

I. STATEMENT OF FACTS

The facts, taken largely from the Court of Appeal's opinion, are as follows:

DaimlerChrysler incorrectly marketed its 1998 and 1999 Dakota R/T trucks as having a 6,400-pound towing capacity when they could actually tow only 2,000 pounds. The error occurred because the Dakota R/T was a sporty version of an existing truck model, which could tow 6,400 pounds. However, to obtain a sporty design, DaimlerChrysler lowered the suspension on the Dakota R/T, thus reducing its towing capacity.

The reduced towing capacity was a potential risk factor. The lowered suspension meant that towing more than 2,000 pounds would cause the suspension to bottom out, stressing the frame and increasing fatigue and wear. The DaimlerChrysler response team considered this a potential safety issue.

Buyers who wanted to tow more than 2,000 pounds were told they could do so only if their Dakota R/T was modified with a trailer hitch costing $300. The factory installed some of these hitches, while other buyers who wanted to tow had dealer-installed or after-market hitches attached.

Nationwide, DaimlerChrysler sold or leased fewer than 7,000 of the Dakota R/T's in the two relevant years. Fewer than 1000 affected R/T's were sold in California during the two years.

By February 1999, DaimlerChrysler set up a response team to address the problem. By June 1999, DaimlerChrysler had taken steps to replace the incorrect marketing materials, owners manuals, and engine and door labels for not-yet-sold Dakota R/T's, although public agency investigation revealed that brochures misrepresenting the trucks' towing capacity were still being distributed as of August 1999. DaimlerChrysler also had notified existing buyers of the error, told them not to attempt to tow more than 2,000 pounds, and provided them with the same modified materials. Simultaneously, DaimlerChrysler began to address remedial measures for customers who had bought or leased their Dakota R/T's under the incorrect marketing program.

Many Dakota R/T buyers never intended to tow more than 2,000 pounds. When informed by DaimlerChrysler of the error, most of those customers were satisfied with DaimlerChrysler's offers of cash and merchandise.

Initially, DaimlerChrysler offered $300 refunds to buyers who had purchased hitches of that amount. By the summer, DaimlerChrysler authorized dealers to repurchase or replace Dakota R/T's on a case-by-case basis, but only for customers who demanded such a remedy.

On July 29, 1999, the Santa Cruz County District Attorney contacted DaimlerChrysler about the problem, threatened legal action, and requested DaimlerChrysler's input before acting. On August 10, 1999, the California Attorney General notified DaimlerChrysler it had joined the Santa Cruz County District Attorney. The public agencies requested a response by the end of August 1999.

Plaintiffs filed their case on August 23, 1999, in Los Angeles County Superior Court. Plaintiffs alleged they all bought 1999 Dakota R/T's from various DaimlerChrysler dealers. Only Graham lived and bought his truck in California. Plaintiffs alleged DaimlerChrysler marketed, sold, and warranted their 1998 and 1999 Dakota R/T's as capable of towing 6400 pounds when the trucks actually could tow only 2000 pounds. Plaintiffs alleged DaimlerChrysler acknowledged the error by letter to all purchasers dated June 16, 1999. Plaintiffs alleged they notified DaimlerChrysler of their (1) trucks' failure to comply with the warranted towing capacity, and (2) revocation of their acceptance of their trucks on July 19, 1999. Plaintiffs sought (but never obtained) class certification for all those who bought Dakota R/T's nationwide. Plaintiffs alleged a single breach of express warranty cause of action. Plaintiffs sought return of their purchase or lease payments, compensatory damages, and attorney fees. Also on August 23, 1999, the Detroit News contacted DaimlerChrysler's legal counsel about plaintiffs' case. DaimlerChrysler's counsel claimed DaimlerChrysler had responded appropriately to the marketing error, including offering buybacks to customers who requested it. Plaintiffs faxed their complaint to DaimlerChrysler the same day. The next day, August 24, 1999, DaimlerChrysler's employee newsletter ran an article on plaintiffs' case.

DaimlerChrysler's response team met throughout August 1999. The team knew about both public agency inquiries and the response deadline. Indeed, DaimlerChrysler wrote the public agencies that its internal approval process prohibited a response by August 31, but promised a response by September 8, 1999. On September 10, 1999, DaimlerChrysler issued its offer to all previous Dakota R/T buyers of repurchase or replacement. In response to later inquiries, response team members conceded they were aware of the class action lawsuit filed in California before DaimlerChrysler's September 10, 1999, letter offering repurchase or replacement to all Dakota R/T buyers.

DaimlerChrysler demurred to the complaint. Plaintiffs filed an amended complaint, acknowledging DaimlerChrysler's offer of, among other remedies, repurchase or replacement of the trucks for all previous buyers. The trial court sustained the demurrer without leave to amend and dismissed the case, finding it was moot because DaimlerChrysler already had offered all purchasers the relief plaintiffs sought. Meanwhile, the public agencies continued to pursue legal action against DaimlerChrysler, pointing to the fact that the erroneous marketing of the Dakota R/T continued as late as September 1999. In late 2000, DaimlerChrysler settled the public agency investigations by paying a $75,000 fine and agreeing to ensure that the marketing error did not reoccur. Nationwide, 2549 Dakota R/T buyers opted for repurchase or replacement. Another 3,101 buyers opted for service contracts and parts coupons. The total value of these offers exceeded $15 million. Fewer than 1,000 of the R/T buyers were Californians.

Although plaintiffs' case was dismissed, the parties continued to litigate plaintiffs' entitlement to attorney fees. DaimlerChrysler insisted throughout that plaintiffs were not entitled to attorney fees, contending plaintiffs had no effect on DaimlerChrysler's recognition of the problem and decision to offer all buyers repurchase or replacement. For over a year, there were hotly contested discovery and other motions to clarify the facts described above. The court held a lengthy evidentiary hearing on October 18, 2000. DaimlerChrysler contended that the Dakota R/T response team was not even aware of the litigation until after September 10, 1999, when its repurchase offer was made, a position that the trial court found to lack credibility.

The trial court filed its final order awarding attorney fees on July 6, 2001. The court concluded after its review of the declarations and documentary evidence presented that DaimlerChrysler's "position that the lawsuit was not a catalyst was largely a transparent fabrication. . . ." It rejected DaimlerChrysler's argument that plaintiffs' action was unnecessary because of the enforcement action of the Santa Cruz County District Attorney and the California Attorney General. The trial court found that these agencies "had only made an inquiry and had not commenced any proceeding when plaintiffs filed this action. Further [those agencies] were only concerned with DaimlerChrysler's false advertising materials and never sought any remedies on behalf of the consumers who acquired these vehicles while they were being misrepresented."

In addition to finding that plaintiffs were the successful party, the trial court found the other requirements of section 1021.5 had been met. It found that the lawsuit "resulted in the enforcement of an important right affecting the public interest, . . . the protection and enforcement of consumer rights, including highway safety," and that "as a result of the lawsuit, thousands of consumers received pecuniary benefits and enhanced safety. Thousands more are likely to benefit from it if DaimlerChrysler and/or other manufacturers are deterred from similar conduct in the future."

The court also concluded that "DaimlerChrysler should pay plaintiffs attorneys fees in the interest of justice. Plaintiffs' attorney fees will otherwise go unpaid. Fees cannot be paid out of the benefits conferred upon the consumers because DaimlerChrysler . . . distributed the benefits of [its] offer to the consumers without any discussion with plaintiffs or their attorneys. Justice is served by encouraging lawyers to bring meritorious consumer cases, of which this action is an example."

The trial court found the lodestar fee amount was $329,620 through the October 18, 2000, hearing, with a multiplier of 2.25 for the fees incurred until the October 18, 2000, hearing, including fees for litigating attorney fees, and applied no multiplier for time thereafter. The court awarded no fees for work after April 23, 2001. The total award was $762,830.

The Court of Appeal affirmed. It observed that the United States Supreme Court had recently rejected the catalyst theory as a basis for attorney fee awards under various federal statutes in *Buckhannon Board & Care Home, Inc. v. West Virginia Dept. of*

Health & Human Resources (2001) 532 U.S. 598 [121 S. Ct. 1835, 149 L. Ed. 2d 855] (*Buckhannon*). But the court declined to follow the United States Supreme Court's lead, noting that the catalyst theory has been long recognized in California. The court also rejected arguments that the litigation was not in the public interest and that it did not benefit a substantial number of people. Further, the court concluded that the trial court did not abuse its discretion in awarding fees for seeking fees, and in permitting those fees to be enhanced over the basic lodestar amount. We granted review.

II. DISCUSSION

A. *Whether the Catalyst Theory Should Be Abolished*

An important exception to the American rule that litigants are to bear their own attorney fees is found in section 1021.5.[2] As we have stated: "The Legislature adopted section 1021.5 as a codification of the private attorney general doctrine of attorney fees developed in prior judicial decisions. [Citation.] Under this section, the court may award attorney fees to a 'successful party' in any action that 'has resulted in the enforcement of an important right affecting the public interest if: (a) a significant benefit, whether pecuniary or nonpecuniary, has been conferred on the general public or a large class of persons, (b) the necessity and financial burden of private enforcement are such as to make the award appropriate, and (c) such fees should not in the interest of justice be paid out of the recovery, if any.' . . . [T]he private attorney general doctrine 'rests upon the recognition that privately initiated lawsuits are often essential to the effectuation of the fundamental public policies embodied in constitutional or statutory provisions, and that, without some mechanism authorizing the award of attorney fees, private actions to enforce such important public policies will as a practical matter frequently be infeasible.' Thus, the fundamental objective of the doctrine is to encourage suits enforcing important public policies by providing substantial attorney fees to successful litigants in such cases." (*Maria P. v. Riles* (1987) 43 Cal. 3d 1281, 1288–1289 [240 Cal. Rptr. 872, 743 P.2d 932] (*Maria P.*).)

In order to effectuate that policy, we have taken a broad, pragmatic view of what constitutes a "successful party." "Our prior cases uniformly explain that an attorney fee award may be justified even when plaintiff's legal action does not result in a favorable final judgment. (*Westside Community*, [*supra*,] 33 Cal. 3d 348, 352 [188 Cal. Rptr. 873, 657 P.2d 365]; *see also Press v. Lucky Stores, Inc.* (1983) 34 Cal. 3d 311 [193 Cal. Rptr. 900, 667 P.2d 704] [although their action had become moot, plaintiffs were awarded fees under § 1021.5 because they had achieved the relief they sought through preliminary injunction].) * * * The trial court in its discretion 'must realistically assess the litigation

---

2. In its entirety, section 1021.5 provides: "Upon motion, a court may award attorneys' fees to a successful party against one or more opposing parties in any action which has resulted in the enforcement of an important right affecting the public interest if: (a) a significant benefit, whether pecuniary or nonpecuniary, has been conferred on the general public or a large class of persons, (b) the necessity and financial burden of private enforcement, or of enforcement by one public entity against another public entity, are such as to make the award appropriate, and (c) such fees should not in the interest of justice be paid out of the recovery, if any. * * *"

and determine, from a practical perspective, whether or not the action served to vindicate an important right so as to justify an attorney fee award' under section 1021.5.

The catalyst theory is an application of the above stated principle that courts look to the practical impact of the public interest litigation in order to determine whether the party was successful, and therefore potentially eligible for attorney fees. We specifically endorsed that theory in *Westside Community, supra*, 33 Cal. 3d 348. * * * The *Westside Community* court, although endorsing the catalyst theory . . . , nonetheless went on to conclude that no attorney fees were owed in that case because there was no demonstrable causal connection between the lawsuit and the government's action. (*Westside Community, supra*, 33 Cal. 3d at pp. 353–354.)

We continue to conclude that the catalyst theory, in concept, is sound. The principle upon which the theory is based—that we look to the "impact of the action, not its manner of resolution" (*Folsom, supra*, 32 Cal. 3d at p. 685)—is fully consistent with the purpose of section 1021.5: to financially reward attorneys who successfully prosecute cases in the public interest, and thereby "'prevent worthy claimants from being silenced or stifled because of a lack of legal resources.'" (*Folsom, supra*, 32 Cal. 3d at p. 683.) We therefore reaffirm our endorsement of the catalyst theory.

DaimlerChrysler argues that we should reevaluate that endorsement in light of the rejection of the catalyst theory by the United States Supreme Court in *Buckhannon, supra*, 532 U.S. 598. At the outset we state what hardly needs stating: that United States Supreme Court interpretation of federal statutes does not bind us to similarly interpret similar state statutes. Indeed, in the realm of attorney fees for private attorneys general, this court has markedly diverged from United States Supreme Court precedent. In *Serrano v. Priest* (1977) 20 Cal. 3d 25 [141 Cal. Rptr. 315, 569 P.2d 1303] (*Serrano III*), an opinion that predated the effective date of section 1021.5 (*see Serrano v. Unruh* (1982) 32 Cal. 3d 621, 624, fn. 1 [186 Cal. Rptr. 754, 652 P.2d 985] (*Serrano IV*)), this court rejected the holding of *Alyeska Pipeline Co. v. Wilderness Society* (1975) 421 U.S. 240 [95 S. Ct. 1612, 44 L. Ed. 2d 141] that attorney fees cannot be awarded on a private attorney general theory absent express statutory authorization. (*Serrano III, supra*, 20 Cal. 3d at pp. 46–47.) More recently, we unanimously declined to follow the United States Supreme Court's rejection of the use of a contingency fee multiplier in calculating private attorney general fees. (*Ketchum v. Moses* (2001) 24 Cal. 4th 1122, 1137–1139 [104 Cal. Rptr. 2d 377, 17 P.3d 735] (*Ketchum*).) We reaffirmed that the "'fashioning of equitable exceptions' to the California rule that parties must bear their own costs 'is a matter within the sole competence of this court.'" (*Id.* at p. 1137.) As explained below, we do not find the reasoning of the five-to-four majority in *Buckhannon* persuasive, and decline to apply its holding to section 1021.5.

A good deal of the *Buckhannon* court's reason for rejecting the catalyst theory turns on the definition of "prevailing party." The *Buckhannon* majority found the term "prevailing party" to be "a legal term of art," defined according to Black's Law Dictionary (7th ed. 1999) at page 1145 as "'[a] party in whose favor a judgment is rendered, regardless of the amount of damages awarded—in certain cases, the court will award attorney's fees to the prevailing party—Also termed *successful party.*'" (*Buckhannon, supra*, 532 U.S. at p. 603.) This definition, together with prior court decisions, led the *Buckhannon* majority to conclude that a "prevailing party" must be a party that has brought about a "'material alteration of the legal relationship of the parties,'" which could include both a "judgment [] on the merits," and a settlement agreement "enforced through a consent decree."

The *Buckhannon* majority concluded that "the 'catalyst theory' falls on the other side of the line from these examples. It allows an award where there is no judicially sanctioned change in the legal relationship of the parties. Even under a limited form of the 'catalyst theory,' a plaintiff could recover attorney's fees if it established that the 'complaint had sufficient merit to withstand a motion to dismiss for lack of jurisdiction or failure to state a claim on which relief may be granted.' [Citation.] This is not the type of legal merit that our prior decisions, based upon plain language and congressional intent, have found necessary. . . . A defendant's voluntary change in conduct, although perhaps accomplishing what the plaintiff sought to achieve by the lawsuit, lacks the necessary judicial *imprimatur* on the change. Our precedents thus counsel against holding that the term 'prevailing party' authorizes an award of attorney's fees *without* a corresponding alteration in the legal relationship of the parties." (*Buckhannon, supra*, 532 U.S. at p. 605.)

We agree with DaimlerChrysler that the terms "prevailing party" and "successful party," as used in section 1021.5, are synonymous. We also agree that in the context of section 1021.5, the term "party" refers to a party to litigation, and therefore precludes an award of attorney fees when no lawsuit has been filed. (*See* Black's Law Dict. (4th rev. ed. 1968) p. 1278 ["Party" is a technical term having a precise meaning in legal parlance; it refers to "those by or against whom a suit is brought . . . , the party plaintiff or defendant. . . ."]; . . . But we are aware of no judicial construction or legislative usage in California that limits the terms "prevailing party" or "successful party" to the meaning found in the most recent edition of Black's Law Dictionary to the exclusion of other meanings, as DaimlerChrysler, following the *Buckhannon* majority, argues.

We therefore turn to the "usual and ordinary meaning" of the statutory language in order to discern legislative intent. The term "successful party," as ordinarily understood, means the party to litigation that achieves its objectives. We agree with the dissenting opinion in *Buckhannon*: "In everyday use, 'prevail' means 'gain victory by virtue of strength or superiority: win mastery: triumph.' Webster's Third New International Dictionary 1797 (1976). There are undoubtedly situations in which an individual's goal is to obtain approval of a judge, and in those situations, one cannot 'prevail' short of a judge's formal declaration. In a piano competition or a figure skating contest, for example, the person who prevails is the person declared winner by the judges. However, where the ultimate goal is not an arbiter's approval, but a favorable alteration of actual circumstances, a formal declaration is not essential. . . . [¶] A lawsuit's ultimate purpose is to achieve actual relief from an opponent. Favorable judgment may be instrumental in gaining that relief. Generally, however, 'the judicial decree is not the end but the means. At the end of the rainbow lies not a judgment, but some action (or cessation of action) by the defendant. . . .' [Citation.] On this common understanding, if a party reaches the 'sought-after destination,' then the party 'prevails' regardless of the 'route taken.' [Citation.]" (*Buckhannon, supra,* 532 U.S. at pp. 633–634 (dis. opn. of Ginsburg, J.).)

DaimlerChrysler also makes a number of policy arguments. Like the *Buckhannon* majority, it argues that "[a] request for attorney's fees should not result in a second major litigation" (*Buckhannon, supra,* 532 U.S. at p. 609), and that the catalyst theory would require a complex causal determination. "Among other things, a 'catalyst theory' hearing would require analysis of the defendant's subjective motivations in changing its conduct, an analysis that 'will likely depend on a highly factbound inquiry and may turn on reasonable inferences from the nature and timing of the defendant's change in conduct.'" (*Ibid.*) We find persuasive the argument of the *Buckhannon* dissent that although some time may be expended in fact finding under the catalyst theory, it is at least as likely as not that the catalyst rule "'saves judicial resources,' [citation] by encouraging 'plaintiffs to discontinue litigation after receiving through the defendant's acquiescence the remedy initially sought.'" (*Buckhannon, supra,* 532 U.S. at p. 640 (dis. opn. of Ginsburg, J.).)

Nor are we persuaded that cases decided under a catalyst theory will inevitably give rise to complex and time-consuming litigation over the issue of causality. Case law, as well as our own judicial experience, suggests that catalyst theory cases may be resolved by relatively economical, straightforward inquiries by trial court judges close to and familiar with the litigation. Moreover, the defendant in such cases knows better than anyone why it made the decision that granted the plaintiff the relief sought, and the defendant is in the best position to either concede that the plaintiff was a catalyst or to document why the plaintiff was not. We are unpersuaded that DaimlerChrysler's inability or unwillingness to do either in the present case, thereby prolonging the litigation, is necessarily attributable to the inherent difficulty of catalyst theory cases.

DaimlerChrysler further argues that overall, the benefits that the catalyst rule is supposed to possess are dwarfed by the harms the rule will engender. It contends the evil to which the catalyst rule is addressed — that meritorious plaintiffs and plaintiffs' attorneys will be deprived of attorney fees by a favorable settlement — will be a relatively rare occurrence. * * * On the other hand, DaimlerChrylser argues the catalyst rule could encourage nuisance suits by unscrupulous attorneys hoping to obtain fees without having the merits of their suit adjudicated. * * *

We, of course, have no way of quantifying the magnitude of the potential and actual abuses by plaintiffs under a catalyst rule or by defendants under its absence. DaimlerChrysler and the *Buckhannon* majority's prediction — that defendants' change of behavior depriving worthy plaintiffs of attorney fees will be relatively rare — is one we cannot verify. But as plaintiffs argue, what is objectionable about elimination of the catalyst theory is not only that in a given case an attorney will be unjustly deprived of fees, but that attorneys will be deterred from accepting public interest litigation if there is the prospect they will be deprived of such fees after successful litigation. (*See*

Chemerinsky, *Closing the Courthouse Doors to Civil Rights Litigants* (2003) 5 U.Pa. J .Const.L. 537, 547.) As matters stand now, public interest attorneys often take a considerable risk that they will not be paid at all because they will not prevail in the litigation or because they will be deemed ineligible for fees under section 1021.5, as when the suit is adjudged not to be sufficiently in the public interest. Abolition of the catalyst theory will increase an already considerable risk. As plaintiffs' attorney succinctly states: "[I]t defies common sense to think attorneys who take meritorious public interest cases with the expectation that they will be compensated if they obtained favorable results for their clients will not be deterred from doing so if the defendant can litigate tenaciously, then avoid paying their fees by voluntarily providing relief before a court order is entered."

Nor do we believe that avoiding this increased risk of public interest litigation must inevitably come at the expense of rewarding a significant number of extortionate lawsuits. We can adopt sensible limitations on the catalyst theory that discourage the latter without putting a damper on lawsuits that genuinely provide a public benefit. Our starting point in this endeavor is the observation that the Legislature has assigned responsibility for awarding fees under section 1021.5 "not to automatons unable to recognize extortionists, but to judges expected and instructed to exercise 'discretion.'" (*Buckhannon, supra*, 532 U.S. at p. 640 (dis. opn. of Ginsburg, J.).) * * * A number of circuits of the United States Court of Appeals, prior to *Buckhannon*, adopted a version of the catalyst theory that required not only a causal connection between the lawsuit and the relief obtained but also a determination that defendant's conduct was required by law. Generally speaking, the "required by law" prong was tantamount to a finding that the lawsuit was "not frivolous, unreasonable, or groundless."

This court has not explicitly adopted the above two-pronged test. We now do so. The trial court must determine that the lawsuit is not "frivolous, unreasonable or groundless", in other words that its result was achieved "by threat of victory, not by dint of nuisance and threat of expense." The determination the trial court must make is not unlike the determination it makes when asked to issue a preliminary injunction, i.e., not a final decision on the merits but a determination at a minimum that "'the questions of law or fact are grave and difficult.'" (*Wilms v. Hand* (1951) 101 Cal. App. 2d 811, 815 [226 P.2d 728]; . . .)

In addition to some scrutiny of the merits, we conclude that another limitation on the catalyst rule proposed by the Attorney General, appearing as amicus curiae, should be adopted by this court. The Attorney General proposes that a plaintiff seeking attorney fees under a catalyst theory must first reasonably attempt to settle the matter short of litigation. We believe this requirement is fully consistent with the basic objectives behind section 1021.5 and with one of its explicit requirements—the "necessity . . . of private enforcement" of the public interest. Awarding attorney fees for litigation when those rights could have been vindicated by reasonable efforts short of litigation does not advance that objective and encourages lawsuits that are more opportunistic than authentically for the public good. Lengthy prelitigation negotiations are not required, nor is it necessary that the settlement demand be made by counsel, but a plaintiff must at least notify the defendant of its grievances and proposed remedies and give the defendant the opportunity to meet its demands within a reasonable time. What constitutes a "reasonable" time will depend on the context.

Applying the catalyst rule, as discussed above, to the present case, the trial court applied the first prong of the rule to conclude that the lawsuit was in fact a substantial causal factor in DaimlerChrysler's change in policy with respect to its willingness to repurchase or replace the Dakota R/T or to offer consumers substantial discounts. DaimlerChrysler does not contend that the trial court's ruling on that point is unsupported by substantial evidence. But it is unclear whether the trial court considered the merits of the suit, and the trial court did not consider whether plaintiffs attempted to reasonably settle the matter short of litigation. We therefore remand the matter for a determination of whether plaintiffs are eligible for attorney fees under the catalyst rule as articulated above.

B. *Trial Court Did Not Abuse Its Discretion in Finding the Substantial Benefit and Public Interest Prongs of Section 1021.5 Were Met*

DaimlerChrysler also contends that the attorney fee award must be overturned in its entirety because it failed to confer "a significant benefit . . . on the general public or large class of persons" as required by section 1021.5. This contention need not detain us long. We will uphold the trial court's decision to award attorney fees under section 1021.5, unless the court has abused its discretion. (*Hewlett v. Squaw Valley Ski Corp.* (1997) 54 Cal. App. 4th 499, 544 [63 Cal. Rptr. 2d 118].) It is well settled that attorney fees under section 1021.5 may be awarded for consumer class action suits benefiting a large number of people. (*Beasley v. Wells Fargo Bank* (1991) 235 Cal. App. 3d 1407, 1417–1418 [1 Cal. Rptr. 2d 459] [upholding an award of section 1021.5 attorney fees for class action against bank charging excess credit card fees].) As *Beasley* recognizes, section 1021.5 requires both a finding of a significant benefit conferred on a substantial number of people and a determination that the "subject matter of the action implicated the public interest." (*Beasley, supra*, at p. 1418.)

In the present case, the trial court found that the problem addressed by the lawsuit implicated an issue of public safety, and that the lawsuit benefited thousands of consumers and potentially thousands more by acting as a deterrent to discourage lax responses to known safety hazards. In light of the facts reviewed in the first part of this opinion, we conclude the trial court did not abuse its discretion in finding that the lawsuit met the substantial benefit and public interest requirements of section 1021.5.[9]

---

9. The dissent appears to question the rule stated in *Beasley* that a consumer class action suit conferring significant benefits on a large number of people vindicating a right of substantial societal importance can be the basis of an award of section 1021.5 attorney fees. It cites in support of its position *Flannery v. California Highway Patrol* (1998) 61 Cal. App. 4th 629, 635–636 [71 Cal. Rptr. 2d 632], a case involving a single plaintiff's lawsuit under the Fair Employment and Housing Act. But *Flannery* merely held that a plaintiff who enforces a statutory right is not necessarily entitled to section 1021.5 fees when the primary effect of the suit is to vindicate an individual economic interest. *Flannery* does not contravene the rule in *Beasley*. Nor does the dissent's reweighing and recharacterization of the evidence persuade us that the trial court's conclusion — that the lawsuit itself furthered

C. *Whether There Should Be a Multiplier for Attorney Fees for Litigating Attorney Fees*

In the present case, a large percentage of the attorney fees were awarded for litigation to obtain fees under section 1021.5. As noted, the lodestar amount calculated by the trial court was $329,620, and that amount was multiplied by an enhancement of 2.25, for a total $762,830. The trial court based the enhancement on "the contingency nature [of the litigation], the delay in payment and the quality of the result." DaimlerChrysler argues that there should be no enhancement for fees for fee-related litigation, or "fees on fees." Assuming the trial court concludes on remand that plaintiffs are entitled to some attorney fees, we address for its benefit whether it appropriately awarded enhancements for fees on fees. We conclude that, while fees for attorney fee litigation under section 1021.5 may be enhanced under some circumstances, that enhancement should generally be lower than fees awarded in the underlying litigation.

We first review some general principles regarding the calculation of attorney fees in public interest litigation. As we recently explained, under our decision in *Serrano III*, a court assessing attorney fees begins with a touchstone or lodestar figure, based on the 'careful compilation of the time spent and reasonable hourly compensation of each attorney . . . involved in the presentation of the case.' [Citation omitted.] We expressly approved the use of prevailing hourly rates as a basis for the lodestar, noting that anchoring the calculation of attorney fees to the lodestar adjustment method '"is the only way of approaching the problem that can claim objectivity, a claim which is obviously vital to the prestige of the bar and the courts."' [Citation omitted.] In referring to 'reasonable' compensation, we indicated that trial courts must carefully review attorney documentation of hours expended; 'padding' in the form of inefficient or duplicative efforts is not subject to compensation. [Citation omitted.]

"Under *Serrano III*, the lodestar is the basic fee for comparable legal services in the community; it may be adjusted by the court based on factors including . . . (1) the novelty and difficulty of the questions involved, (2) the skill displayed in presenting them, (3) the extent to which the nature of the litigation precluded other employment by the attorneys, (4) the contingent nature of the fee award. [Citation omitted.] The purpose of such adjustment is to fix a fee at the fair market value for the particular action. In effect, the court determines, retrospectively, whether the litigation involved a contingent risk or required extraordinary legal skill justifying augmentation of the unadorned lodestar in order to approximate the fair market rate for such services. The '"experienced trial judge is the best judge of the value of professional services rendered in his court, and while his judgment is of course subject to review, it will not be disturbed unless the appellate court is convinced that it is clearly wrong."'"(*Ketchum, supra,* 24 Cal. 4th at pp. 1131–1132.)

---

the public interest by resulting in extensive consumer remedies, which served as a deterrent to future conduct jeopardizing public safety—was unsupported by substantial evidence.

One of the most common fee enhancers, and one used by the trial court in the present case, is for contingency risk. We reaffirmed the propriety of a contingency risk enhancement in *Ketchum*: "The economic rationale for fee enhancement in contingency cases has been explained as follows: 'A contingent fee must be higher than a fee for the same legal services paid as they are performed. The contingent fee compensates the lawyer not only for the legal services he renders but for the loan of those services. The implicit interest rate on such a loan is higher because the risk of default (the loss of the case, which cancels the debt of the client to the lawyer) is much higher than that of conventional loans.' (Posner, Economic Analysis of Law (4th ed. 1992) pp. 534, 567.) 'A lawyer who both bears the risk of not being paid and provides legal services is not receiving the fair market value of his work if he is paid only for the second of these functions. If he is paid no more, competent counsel will be reluctant to accept fee award cases.'" (*Ketchum, supra*, 24 Cal. 4th at pp. 1132–1133.)

Turning to the question of compensation for fee-related litigation, we first note it is well established that plaintiffs and their attorneys may recover attorney fees for fee-related matters. As we stated: "the [private attorney general] doctrine will often be frustrated, sometimes nullified, if awards are diluted or dissipated by lengthy, uncompensated proceedings to fix or defend a rightful fee claim." (*Serrano IV, supra*, 32 Cal. 3d at p. 632; *see also Ketchum, supra*, 24 Cal. 4th at p. 1141.)

While DaimlerChrysler does not dispute that fees for fee-related litigation may be awarded, it asks this court to hold that there should be no multiplier for fees on fees. It cites to several out-of-state cases that have disallowed such multipliers, principally because fee litigation is tangential to the primary litigation and of less social value. * * *

Courts awarding attorney fees under section 1021.5 also may generally differentiate between the contingency risk undertaken during the litigation on the merits and the risk undertaken for litigation on fees. The risk that an attorney takes in the underlying public interest litigation has two components: the risk of not being a "successful party," i.e., of not prevailing on the merits, and the risk of not establishing eligibility for an attorney fee award. (*Serrano III, supra*, 20 Cal. 3d at p. 49.) * * * Generally speaking, by the time of the commencement of fee litigation in section 1021.5 cases, the first and perhaps most substantial component of risk, that of not being a successful party, has been eliminated. What remains is the second component, that plaintiffs may not be able to establish eligibility for fees, i.e., to establish that the litigation confers "a 'significant benefit' . . . 'on the general public or a large class of persons'" (*Beasley v. Wells Fargo Bank, supra*, 235 Cal. App. 3d at pp. 1417–1418) or that there was the "'necessity and financial burden of private enforcement,'" making the award appropriate (*Hammond v. Agran* (2002) 99 Cal. App. 4th 115, 121 [120 Cal. Rptr. 2d 646]).

Although in the present case, as in other catalyst theory cases, plaintiffs had not established themselves as the successful party at the beginning of the fee litigation, and some enhancement for that risk may be justified, the achievement of their litigation objective before fee litigation would reduce somewhat the uncertainty over their "successful party" status. The fact that the risk of fee litigation is generally less than the risk of litigation on the merits of the suit justifies a lower attorney-fee multiplier for the former, if one is given at all. We do not believe a lower multiplier on fees for less risky fee litigation will deter attorneys from accepting worthwhile public interest cases.

III. DISPOSITION

The judgment of the Court of Appeal affirming the award of attorney fees in the present case is reversed, and the cause is remanded for proceedings consistent with the views expressed in this opinion.

GEORGE, C.J., KENNARD, J., and WERDEGAR, J., concurred.

DISSENT: CHIN, JUSTICE. — I dissent.

Plaintiffs filed a simple seven-page complaint alleging a single cause of action for breach of warranty after the defendant had already acknowledged its marketing mistake and was taking steps to correct it, and while the Santa Cruz County District Attorney and the California Attorney General were investigating the matter and preparing to take appropriate action. The complaint constituted plaintiffs' entire legal effort regarding the underlying lawsuit. They obtained no judicial ruling of any kind in their favor. Nevertheless, to date, plaintiffs have parlayed this complaint into an award of attorney fees of $762,830, most of it for work unrelated to the underlying lawsuit. Now the majority remands the matter for yet more litigation. I disagree for several reasons.

This court has never awarded attorney fees to a party with no judicial ruling in its favor. We should not start now. Relying solely on federal cases that have been overruled and California cases that either *denied* attorney fees or involved a plaintiff with a judicial ruling in its favor, the majority permits an award of attorney fees to the plaintiffs as the "prevailing" or "successful" party. To do so, it adopts the so-called catalyst theory, a theory that was once prevalent in federal courts, but that the United States Supreme Court has now repudiated. We should not resurrect it.

Moreover, plaintiffs do not qualify for attorney fees even under the majority's catalyst theory. Their lawsuit was unnecessary when filed, it was moot within days of its filing, and it conferred no substantial public benefit. Plaintiffs have also failed to show their suit had any merit in light of the corrective steps defendant had already taken. The majority implicitly recognizes that plaintiffs failed to justify their award of attorney fees, but it inexplicably remands the matter for yet more litigation, which will undoubtedly increase plaintiffs' attorney fee demand to a truly astronomic amount. I disagree here also. No reason appears to give plaintiffs a second chance to try to prove what they failed to prove the first time. Courts should seek to resolve litigation, not perpetuate it.

Finally, the majority permits qualifying plaintiffs to receive not only (1) attorney fees for litigating the underlying lawsuit, but *also* (2) a multiplier on those fees, and *also* (3) attorney fees for litigating their entitlement to attorney fees, and *also* (4) a multiplier on the fees for litigating entitlement to fees. I disagree on the final point. Surely, awarding fees for the underlying litigation, with a potential multiplier, *plus* fees for litigating entitlement to fees, is sufficient. A multiplier for litigating fees on fees is excessive and can only lead to outrageously inflated awards like the one here, where a simple complaint is transformed into an award of over three-quarters of a million dollars.

The majority today goes further than this court has ever gone before—indeed, so far as I can tell, further than any other court has ever gone—in permitting plaintiffs to win large attorney fee awards. I cannot agree. Lest California truly become a mecca for plaintiffs and plaintiffs' attorneys throughout the country, we need to be at least somewhat in step with the rest of the country.

II. DISCUSSION

A. *California should not adopt the catalyst theory*

"California follows what is commonly referred to as the American rule, which provides that each party to a lawsuit must ordinarily pay his own attorney fees. [Citations omitted.] The Legislature codified the American rule in 1872 when it enacted Code of Civil Procedure section 1021, which states in pertinent part that 'Except as attorney's fees are specifically provided for by statute, the measure and mode of compensation of attorneys and counselors at law is left to the agreement, express or implied, of the parties. . . .'" (*Trope v. Katz* (1995) 11 Cal. 4th 274, 278–279 [45 Cal. Rptr. 2d 241, 902 P.2d 259].) Code of Civil Procedure section 1021.5, enacted in 1977, provides an exception to this American rule. * * *

In *Buckhannon, supra*, 532 U.S. 598, the high court relied on the plain meaning of the word "prevailing" to reject the catalyst theory. Here, the language of Code of Civil Procedure section 1021.5 militates much more strongly against the catalyst theory. The federal statutes simply give trial courts discretion to allow the "prevailing party" attorney fees. Code of Civil Procedure section 1021.5, however, permits an award only to a "successful" (which is synonymous with "prevailing") party in an action "which has resulted in the *enforcement* of an important *right* affecting the public interest. . . ." (Italics added.) The italicized words mean that the plaintiffs must have *compelled* the defendant's conduct to protect some "right." (*See* Black's Law Dict., *supra*, at p. 549 [defining "enforcement" as "[t]he act or process of compelling compliance with a law, mandate, or command"].)

But voluntary action is not compelled action. Without some judicially enforceable order, there is no way to know whether the action was voluntary or compelled. Persons and entities act voluntarily in response to a lawsuit for many reasons, some unrelated to the lawsuit's merits: to avoid the expense of litigation or bad publicity, to foster good public relations, to make an improvement or take other useful action not required by law, perhaps simply to put the litigation behind and move on. The pressure to yield voluntarily to a lawsuit's demands, even if not legally required, is exacerbated by the circumstance that historically attorney fee awards have not gone in both directions. Although the statutes do not prohibit awards to prevailing defendants, the private attorney general doctrine has generally resulted only in attorney fee awards to the prevailing plaintiffs and not also to the prevailing defendants. Thus, unlike the plaintiffs who can hope to be reimbursed for their attorney fees, the defendants generally cannot expect to receive compensation from the plaintiffs for *their* attorney fees.

Those defendants who choose to fight a lawsuit lose even when they win; they must pay their attorneys themselves, which can be very expensive even for the victor. This circumstance places the defendants under great pressure to settle a lawsuit, even if unmeritorious, as soon as possible.

A "judicial *imprimatur*" on a defendant's change in conduct is thus necessary to show that the plaintiff actually enforced a legal right. Merely eliciting a voluntary action is not enforcing a legal right. But the catalyst theory simply *assumes* the defendant's action was required to right a legal wrong; it *assumes* the defendant had acted unlawfully. This assumption is contrary to the requirements of Code of Civil Procedure section 1021.5.

The majority argues the catalyst theory is needed to eliminate risk in public interest litigation. But there will always be risk. * * * The private at torney general doctrine inherently contains both a risk and a cost. A line must be drawn somewhere to balance this risk and this cost. I would hold that the statute here draws the necessary line by requiring some kind of a judicial imprimatur before a plaintiff can be considered to be a successful or prevailing party that enforced an important public right.

The potential for awards of this kind can also greatly increase the possibility of undue pressure to settle meritless claims.* * * Indeed, the private attorney general doctrine, even without the catalyst theory and multipliers on fees on fees, gives the plaintiffs a great advantage in settlement negotiations. The defendants generally have to pay their own attorney fees. Thus, those defendants who litigate rather than sell out as cheaply as possible as soon as possible face not the *risk*, but the near *certainty*, that they will incur attorney fees they will not recover. They also risk incurring a potentially substantial award for the *opponents'* attorney fees. The plaintiffs, by contrast, merely face the *possibility* they will not be compensated for their own attorney fees; they run little risk of having to pay their opponents' attorney fees. And to compensate for even this possibility, the private attorney general doctrine permits courts to add a multiplier to the plaintiffs' attorney fees, which can be very rewarding, as this case illustrates. The plaintiffs thus have relatively little incentive to settle, defendants a very strong need to settle. I see no need for the catalyst theory to provide yet more incentive to plaintiffs.

For all of these reasons, I would not adopt the catalyst theory as a basis for awarding attorney fees. I would conclude that before a party can be considered to be a successful or prevailing party under Code of Civil Procedure section 1021.5 or Government Code section 12965, subdivision (b), there must be some court-ordered change in the legal relationship between the plaintiff and the defendant in the plaintiff's favor.

B. *Plaintiffs have not established entitlement to attorney fees even under the majority's catalyst theory*

Even accepting the majority's catalyst theory, plaintiffs have failed to establish entitlement to attorney fees for several reasons. * * * For *any* plaintiff (including those who actually win their lawsuit) to receive attorney fees, the action must have "resulted in the enforcement of an important right affecting the public interest. . . ." (Code Civ. Proc., § 1021.5.) "A decision which has as its primary effect the vindication of the litigant's personal rights is not one which brings into play the attorney fees provisions of [Code of Civil Procedure] section 1021.5." (*In re Head* (1986) 42 Cal. 3d 223, 228 [228 Cal. Rptr. 184, 721 P.2d 65].) Plaintiffs' complaint was solely for breach of warranty. It sought only class certification (which plaintiffs never obtained), an award of "compensatory damages for breach of warranty," and attorney fees. This action was, at most, a vindication of personal rights, not an important right affecting the general public.

C. *Plaintiffs should not receive a multiplier for litigating fees on fees*

The majority also holds that a plaintiff may recover, as attorney fees, not only its fees incurred prosecuting the underlying litigation, with a multiplier, and its fees incurred litigating its entitlement to attorney fees (i.e., fees on fees), but also a *multiplier* on fees on fees. I appreciate the majority's attempt to limit the size of such multipliers. The majority's efforts might help reduce the instances of the tail wagging the dog like here, where the fee for litigating fees on fees is nine times greater than the fee for litigating the underlying lawsuit. But I would hold that a multiplier is never appropriate for litigating fees on fees. The majority disagrees with courts from other states that have considered this question and, tellingly, cites no out-of-state cases supporting its conclusion. If, as the majority claims, the private attorney general doctrine is intended to encourage societally useful lawsuits (like the majority finds this one to be), and not merely to swell attorneys' coffers, permitting fees for work expended on the actual lawsuit plus a multiplier, and permitting attorneys to be paid for their efforts in obtaining those fees plus that multiplier, is a sufficient incentive. A multiplier on fees generated litigating fees, which, as here, can make the overall reward truly absurd compared to the effort regarding the underlying litigation, is not necessary.

III. CONCLUSION

At a time when Californians are increasingly concerned about extortionate lawsuits against businesses, large and small, and worried that the legal climate in California is so unfriendly to businesses that many are leaving the state and others are deterred from coming here in the first place, today's ruling goes in exactly the wrong direction. And it goes further in that direction than this court has ever gone before. We should interpret and apply California's private attorney general statutes sensibly to encourage responsible litigation while also keeping attorney fee judgments within reasonable bounds and maintaining some semblance of balance between the litigation positions of the plaintiffs and the defendants.

Because the majority does not do so, I dissent. I would reverse the judgment of the Court of Appeal.

BAXTER, J., and BROWN, J., concurred.

Notes and Questions Regarding Recovery of Attorney Fees

(1) *Code of Civil Procedure § 1021.* Section 1021 authorizes the parties to a contract to include an agreement as to who will recover attorney fees in the event of subsequent litigation. Section 1021 is not limited to contract actions; the parties may also agree to

recovery of attorney fees in any tort actions which may arise from their underlying transactional relationship. *See, e.g., Palmer v. Shawback*, 17 Cal. App. 4th 296, 21 Cal. Rptr. 2d 575 (1993); *Lerner v. Ward*, 13 Cal. App. 4th 155, 16 Cal. Rptr. 2d 486 (1993); *Xuereb v. Marcus & Millichap, Inc.*, 3 Cal. App. 4th 1338, 5 Cal. Rptr. 2d 154 (1992).

(2) *Civil Code § 1717.* Where a contractual provision makes recovery of attorney's fees available for only one party, Civil Code § 1717 makes this right to recover reciprocally binding and awards attorney fees to "the party prevailing on the contract, whether he or she is the party specified in the contract or not." Civil Code § 1717 expressly limits this reciprocal remedy only to an action "on a contract" or "to enforce that contract." The courts have construed this language to preclude application of § 1717 to a tort cause of action unless intertwined with a contract cause of action. *See, e.g., Reynolds Metals Co. v. Alperson*, 25 Cal. 3d 124, 129, 158 Cal. Rptr. 1, 599 P.2d 83 (1979) ("Where a cause of action based on the contract providing for attorney's fees is joined with other causes of action beyond the contract, the prevailing party may recover attorney's fees under section 1717 only as they relate to the contract action"); *Lerner v. Ward, supra* (Section 1717 not applicable because plaintiffs dismissed contract cause of action at inception of trial and proceeded only on tort theory that defendant fraudulently induced them to enter real property purchase agreement); *Xuereb v. Marcus & Millichap, Inc., supra* (Section 1717 not applicable to action arising out of real estate transaction because plaintiffs submitted their case to jury on negligence and other tort theories but not on the pleaded breach of contract cause of action).

(3) *Code of Civil Procedure § 1021.5.* The Legislature adopted CCP § 1021.5 in 1977 as a codification of the private attorney general doctrine developed in prior judicial decisions such as *Serrano v. Priest*, 20 Cal. 3d 25, 141 Cal. Rptr. 315, 569 P.2d 1303 (1977). *See Maria P. v. Riles*, 43 Cal. 3d 1281, 1294, 240 Cal. Rptr. 872, 743 P.2d 932 (1987); *Conservatorship of Whitley v. Maldonado*, 50 Cal. 4th 1206, 117 Cal. Rptr. 3d 342, 241 P.3d 840 (2010) (Discussing the statutory requirements and concluding that a litigant's personal nonpecuniary motives for bringing an action may not be used to disqualify that litigant from obtaining attorney fees under CCP § 1021.5). The right to attorney fees under CCP § 1021.5 is similar to, but independent from, the right under the federal Civil Rights Attorneys' Fees Awards Act, 42 U.S.C. § 1988. *See, e.g., Sokolow v. County of San Mateo*, 213 Cal. App. 3d 231, 243–50, 261 Cal. Rptr. 520 (1989) (Comparing "prevailing party" requirements under the state and federal statutes); *Olson v. Automobile Club of Southern California*, 42 Cal. 4th 1142, 74 Cal. Rptr. 3d 81, 179 P.3d 882 (2008) (Like the federal statute, a prevailing party is not entitled to an award of expert witness fees in addition to attorney fees under § 1021.5).

(4) *Lodestar Method of Calculating Attorney Fees Award.* California courts usually follow the "lodestar" method when calculating the amount of an award of attorney fees. *See, e.g., Press v. Lucky Stores, Inc.*, 34 Cal. 3d 311, 193 Cal. Rptr. 900, 667 P.2d 704 (1983); *Serrano v. Priest*, 20 Cal. 3d 25, 141 Cal. Rptr. 315, 569 P.2d 1303 (1977). This method requires the trial court to first determine the lodestar figure by multiplying the time spent on the case by a reasonable hourly rate for each attorney. Once the lodestar figure is determined, the court must consider a variety of other factors which

may justify either the augmentation or the diminution of the lodestar amount. Most importantly, for example, the lodestar amount may be reduced (*i.e.*, a "negative multiplier") to reflect the relative degree of success achieved by the prevailing party. *See, e.g., Californians for Responsible Toxics Management v. Kizer*, 211 Cal. App. 3d 961, 259 Cal. Rptr. 599 (1989) (Upholding trial court's 35% fractional multiplier where plaintiff achieved limited success through lawsuit). However, as *Graham v. DaimlerChrysler* indicates, the lodestar amount may also be enhanced (*i.e.*, a "positive multiplier") based on several factors, including the novelty and difficulty of the questions involved and the contingent nature of the fee award. *See, e.g., Beasley v. Wells Fargo Bank*, 235 Cal. App. 3d 1407, 1 Cal. Rptr. 2d 459 (1991) (Upholding increase of attorney fees awarded pursuant to CCP § 1021.5 based on 1.5 multiplier applied to lodestar amount); *City of Oakland v. Oakland Raiders*, 203 Cal. App. 3d 78, 249 Cal. Rptr. 606 (1988) (Lodestar amount of $853,756 increased to $2 million).

(5) *Other State Statutory Authority for an Award of Attorney Fees.* Although CCP § 1021.5 is the most utilized fee-shifting statute, the California Legislature has enacted over 300 other statutes which authorize an award of attorney fees to the prevailing party. *See* CEB, *California Attorney Fee Awards, Selected California Fee-Shifting Statutes*, §§ 3.80–3.128 (3d ed. 2015), for a survey of these various statutes by subject. Some of the more important of these fee-shifting statutes include Government Code § 12965(b) (Fair Employment and Housing Act authorizes an award of attorney fees to prevailing party in actions brought under the Act); Government Code § 800 (Prevailing party entitled to award of fees in civil action to review administrative proceeding determination where determination the result of arbitrary or capricious action by government entity or official); Labor Code § 218.5 (Prevailing party shall be awarded attorney fees in action for nonpayment of wages or fringe benefits); CCP § 1036 (Inverse condemnation actions); Civil Code §§ 1794, 1811.1 & 2983.4 (Actions under consumer protection statutes); Civil Code § 1942.4(b), § 1942.5(g) (Tenant actions for breach of habitability or retaliatory eviction); and Family Code §§ 2030–2034 (Attorney fee award in family law cases based on relative circumstances of parties).

C. Recovery of Costs by the Prevailing Party

The right of a party to recover costs is purely statutory. *Perko's Enterprises, Inc. v. RRNS Enterprises*, 4 Cal. App. 4th 238, 241, 5 Cal. Rptr. 2d 470 (1992); *McIntosh v. Crandall*, 47 Cal. App. 2d 126, 127–128, 117 P.2d 380 (1941). Set forth below are the relevant statutory provisions governing recovery of costs in general civil actions:

CALIFORNIA CODE OF CIVIL PROCEDURE (2021)

Section 1032. Recovery of costs by prevailing party as matter of right.

(a) As used in this section, unless the context clearly requires otherwise:

(1) "Complaint" includes a cross-complaint.

(2) "Defendant" includes a cross-defendant, a person against whom a complaint is filed, or a party who files an answer in intervention.

(3) "Plaintiff" includes a cross-complainant or a party who files a complaint in intervention.

(4) "Prevailing party" includes the party with a net monetary recovery, a defendant in whose favor a dismissal is entered, a defendant where neither plaintiff nor defendant obtains any relief, and a defendant as against those plaintiffs who do not recover any relief against that defendant. If any party recovers other than monetary relief and in situations other than as specified, the "prevailing party" shall be as determined by the court, and under those circumstances, the court, in its discretion, may allow costs or not and, if allowed may apportion costs between the parties on the same or adverse sides pursuant to rules adopted under Section 1034.

(b) Except as otherwise expressly provided by statute, a prevailing party is entitled as a matter of right to recover costs in any action or proceeding.

(c) Nothing in this section shall prohibit parties from stipulating to alternative procedures for awarding costs in the litigation pursuant to rules adopted under Section 1034.

Section 1033.5. Items allowable as costs.

(a) The following items are allowable as costs under Section 1032:

(1) Filing, motion, and Jury fees.

(2) Juror food and lodging while they are kept together during trial and after the jury retires for deliberation.

(3)

(A) Taking, video recording, and transcribing necessary depositions, including an original and one copy of those taken by the claimant and one copy of depositions taken by the party against whom costs are allowed.

(B) Fees of a certified or registered interpreter for the deposition of a party or witness who does not proficiently speak or understand the English language.

(C) Travel expenses to attend depositions.

(4) Service of process by a public officer, registered process server, or other means, . . .

(5) Expenses of attachment including keeper's fees.

(6) Premiums on necessary surety bonds.

(7) Ordinary witness fees pursuant to Section 68093 of the Government Code.

(8) Fees of expert witnesses ordered by the court.

(9) Transcripts of court proceedings ordered by the court.

(10) Attorney's fees, when authorized by any of the following:

    (A) Contract.

    (B) Statute.

    (C) Law.

(11) Court reporter fees as established by statute.

(12) Court interpreter fees for a qualified court interpreter authorized by the court for an indigent person represented by a qualified legal services project, as defined in Section 6213 of the Business and Professions Code or a pro bono attorney, as defined in Section 8030.4 of the Business and Professions Code.

(13) Models, the enlargements of exhibits and photocopies of exhibits, and the electronic presentation of exhibits, including costs of rental equipment and electronic formatting, may be allowed if they were reasonably helpful to aid the trier of fact.

(14) Fees for the electronic filing or service of documents through an electronic filing service provider if a court requires or orders electronic filing or service of documents.

(15) Fees for the hosting of electronic documents if a court requires or orders a party to have documents hosted by an electronic filing service provider. This paragraph shall become inoperative on January 1, 2022.

(16) Any other item that is required to be awarded to the prevailing party pursuant to statute as an incident to prevailing in the action at trial or on appeal.

(b) The following items are not allowable as costs, except when expressly authorized by law:

    (1) Fees of experts not ordered by the court.

    (2) Investigation expenses in preparing the case for trial.

    (3) Postage, telephone, and photocopying charges, except for exhibits.

    (4) Costs in investigation of jurors or in preparation for voir dire.

    (5) Transcripts of court proceedings not ordered by the court.

(c) An award of costs shall be subject to the following:

    (1) Costs are allowable if incurred, whether or not paid.

    (2) Allowable costs shall be reasonably necessary to the conduct of the litigation rather than merely convenient or beneficial to its preparation.

    (3) Allowable costs shall be reasonable in amount.

    (4) Items not mentioned in this section and items assessed upon application may be allowed or denied in the court's discretion.

(5)(A) If a statute of this state refers to the award of "costs and attorney's fees," attorney's fees are an item and component of the costs to be awarded and are allowable as costs pursuant to subparagraph (B) of paragraph (10) of subdivision (a). A claim not based upon the court's established schedule of attorney's fees for actions on a contract shall bear the burden of proof. Attorney's fees allowable as costs pursuant to subparagraph (B) of paragraph (10) of subdivision (a) may be fixed as follows: (i) upon a noticed motion, (ii) at the time a statement of decision is rendered, (iii) upon application supported by affidavit made concurrently with a claim for other costs, or (iv) upon entry of default judgment. Attorney's fees allowable as costs pursuant to subparagraph (A) or (C) of paragraph (10) of subdivision (a) shall be fixed either upon a noticed motion or upon entry of a default judgment, unless otherwise provided by stipulation of the parties.

(B) Attorney's fees awarded pursuant to Section 1717 of the Civil Code are allowable costs under Section 1032 as authorized by subparagraph (A) of paragraph (10) of subdivision (a).

Notes and Questions Regarding Recovery of Costs

(1) *Allowable Costs.* A prevailing party is entitled to recover costs as a matter of right. CCP §§ 1021, 1032(b). Section 1033.5(a) specifies those items generally recoverable as costs of right; section 1033.5(b) specifies those costs not recoverable, "unless expressly authorized by law." An item not specifically allowable under § 1033.5(a) nor prohibited under § 1033.5(b) may nevertheless be recoverable in the discretion of the court. CCP § 1033.5(c)(4).

(2) *Prevailing Party Under CCP § 1032.* Section 1032(a) clearly defines who is the "prevailing party" in a variety of typical situations. The proper interpretation of these statutory definitions is not so clear, however, in less typical applications. In *McLarand, Vasquez & Partners, Inc. v. Downey Savings & Loan Ass'n*, 231 Cal. App. 3d 1450, 282 Cal. Rptr. 828 (1991), for example, the plaintiff filed a complaint seeking damages against the defendant for breach of contract and tortious denial of contract. The defendant cross-complained against the plaintiff, seeking damages for breach of contract, negligence, and related claims. Following a jury trial, general verdicts denying relief to both parties were entered. Is the defendant the only "prevailing party" pursuant to § 1032(a) (4)? Or are both parties "prevailing parties" under §§ 1032(a)(1)–(4), and both entitled to an award of costs, because the defendant filed a cross-complaint against the plaintiff and neither party was successful on its action? Is § 1032(a)(2), which defines a "defendant" to include a cross-defendant, of any relevance to this issue?

The court in *McLarand* held that where both parties are denied relief on their respective claims, the defendant is entitled to an award of costs but the plaintiff is not. The court rejected an interpretation of § 1032 which would make both parties "prevailing parties" and therefore both entitled to an award of costs, commenting that the "practical effect of such a result would be to conclude the prevailing party is the one who spends the most." *Id.* at 1453. What did the court mean by this comment? Do you agree with the *McLarand* court's interpretation of § 1032? Why?

(3) *Procedures.* The procedures for claiming and for contesting costs are set forth in Rule 3.1700 of the California Rules of Court. A prevailing party who claims costs must serve and file a memorandum of costs within the time specified in the Rule, usually 15 days after entry of judgment; any motion to strike or to tax costs must be served and filed within an equally short period of time.

(4) *Costs Must Be Reasonably Necessary.* Costs that are allowable as a matter of right or as a matter of discretion must be reasonable in amount and must be "reasonably necessary to the conduct of the litigation rather than merely convenient or beneficial to its preparation." CCP § 1033.5(c)(2) & (3). Technological advances in the conduct of litigation have complicated the "reasonably necessary" determination. *See Science Applications Int'l Corp. v. Superior Court*, 39 Cal. App. 4th 1095, 46 Cal. Rptr. 2d 332 (1995) (Finding expenses incurred for a graphics communication system and for editing of videotape depositions for effective presentation of the testimony to the jury were not "reasonably necessary"); *but see Bender v. County of Los Angeles*, 217 Cal. App. 4th 968, 159 Cal. Rptr. 3d 204 (2013) (Affirming trial court's finding that the synchronizing of videotaped depositions, including the cost of employing a projectionist to recover and retrieve excerpts selected by counsel, both enhanced counsel's advocacy during trial and was reasonably necessary to the conduct of the litigation).

(5) *Effect of Statutory Offers to Compromise on Recovery of Costs.* The costs allowed under CCP § 1032 may be withheld or augmented pursuant to CCP § 998. Section 998 authorizes a party to serve upon any other party a written offer to allow judgment to be taken in accordance with the terms and conditions stated in the offer. If the offer made by a defendant is not accepted and the plaintiff fails to obtain a more favorable judgment, the plaintiff shall not recover his or her post-offer costs and shall pay the defendant's costs from the time of the offer. § 998(c). If an offer made by a plaintiff is not accepted and the defendant fails to obtain a more favorable judgment the court, in its discretion, may require the defendant to pay a reasonable sum to cover the costs of the services of expert witnesses, in addition to plaintiff's costs. § 998(d).

Chapter III

Pleadings

A. The Complaint

1. Code Pleading

California's pleading system derives from the Field Code reforms of the mid-19th century. New York's adoption of a Code of Civil Procedure followed closely upon the 1848 Report of the Commissioners on Practice and Pleadings of New York and its head, David Dudley Field. California, which joined the Union in 1850, chose the "modern" system of the time for its pleading model. The Field Code abolished the common law forms of action, merged law and equity, limited the types of pleadings, limited the effects of technical errors, and required pleading only the "facts constituting the cause of action." *See* CCP §§ 307, 422.10, 425.10, and 475.

California remains nominally a "code pleading" state. It has declined to follow the notice pleading model of the federal rules. Section 425.10(a) still requires the complaint to contain "a statement of the facts constituting the cause of action, in ordinary and concise language." However, California has liberalized the code pleading requirements. Case law reflects a reduced concern with pleading ultimate facts in precisely the correct format. Although the elements of a cause of action must be present in a pleading, if the allegations give sufficient notice of plaintiff's factual theory, this is usually sufficient. Alternative and inconsistent theories may be asserted. *Shepard & Morgan v. Lee & Daniel, Inc.*, 31 Cal. 3d 256, 182 Cal. Rptr. 351, 643 P.2d 968 (1982). Joinder of claims and parties has been liberalized by adopting rules similar to (and in many cases identical to) the federal rules. Amendment is liberally allowed through trial. The Judicial Council has also adopted Official Form Pleadings—complaints, cross-complaints and answers—for several basic types of claims and causes of action. *See* CCP § 425.12. Identifying California as a code pleading state is thus both misleading and an oversimplification.

Section 422.10 lists the pleadings in California courts: "The pleadings allowed in civil actions are complaints, demurrers, answers and cross-complaints."

Semole v. Sansoucie

Court of Appeal of California, Second Appellate District

28 Cal. App. 3d 714, 104 Cal. Rptr. 897 (1972)

HERNDON, ACTING PRESIDING JUSTICE.

Plaintiffs (appellants) appeal from the order dismissing this action brought against respondent to recover damages for wrongful death. The dismissal was entered after respondent's demurrer to appellants' second amended complaint had been sustained without leave to amend on the ground that no cause of action had been stated.

The original complaint, filed on July 11, 1966, alleges that on May 9, 1966, appellants' son, John Semole, was fatally injured while loading piggyback trailers onto railroad flatcars. It named as defendants the decedent's employer, Pacific Motor Trucking Company, and a fellow employee, Robert J. Sansoucie, respondent herein, and 10 Does.

On December 11, 1970, the court below granted the motion of the defendant corporation for summary judgment and dismissed the action as to that defendant on the ground that the action against decedent's employer was barred by Labor Code section 3601 which, with inapplicable exceptions, limits the remedy to the recovery of workmen's compensation. Appellants took no appeal from that judgment but have sought to maintain the action against respondent, decedent's fellow employee, by invoking Labor Code section 3601, subdivision (a)(3) which read at that time as follows: "(a) Where the conditions of compensation exist, the right to recover such compensation, pursuant to the provisions of this division is, except as provided in Section 3706, the exclusive remedy for injury or death of an employee against the employer or against any other employee of the employer acting within the scope of his employment, except that an employee, or his dependents in the event of his death, shall, in addition to the right to compensation against the employer, have a right to bring an action at law for damages against such other employee, as if this division did not apply, in the following cases: . . .

"(3) When the injury or death is proximately caused by an act of such other employee which evinces a reckless disregard for the safety of the employee injured, and a calculated and conscious willingness to permit injury or death to such employee."

* * * Respondent filed a general demurrer to the complaint and sought a dismissal of the action on the grounds: (1) that summons was not served upon him within the three-year period as provided in Code of Civil Procedure section 581a; and (2) that the action was barred by Labor Code section 3601.

[The trial court refused to dismiss the action on the first ground but sustained the demurrer, with leave to amend, on the ground that the complaint did not allege facts sufficient to state a cause of action under Labor Code section 3601, subdivision (a) (3). Plaintiffs filed a first and a second amended complaint. In each case, defendant demurred on the ground that a cause of action under Labor Code section 3601, subdivision (a)(3), had still not been stated. The last demurrer was sustained] without leave to amend, "pursuant to points and authorities filed." Thus, the first issue presented is whether or not the second amended complaint alleges facts sufficient to state a cause of action.

The Complaint Does Set Forth Facts Sufficient to State a Cause of Action

The earlier versions of the complaint charged respondent with negligence and reckless disregard for the safety of others. Since this action is subject to the provisions of Labor Code section 3601, above quoted, they were manifestly insufficient to state a claim, for they failed to allege the "calculated and conscious willingness to permit injury or death" required by the statute.

In an effort to remedy the indicated deficiency, the second amended complaint, the charging allegations of which are set forth in full in the margin,[1] included an allegation cast in the words of the statute. Citing the rule that allegations of "wilful misconduct" require that the facts must be stated more fully than in ordinary negligence cases (*Snider v. Whitson*, 184 Cal. App. 2d 211 [7 Cal. Rptr. 353]), respondent contends that the complaint must be held inadequate.

No cases dealing precisely with the question before the court have been cited, nor has our independent investigation uncovered any, and so our inquiry must necessarily be rooted in general principles.

It is well settled that "[in] considering the sufficiency of a pleading, we are bound by the rule that on appeal from a judgment entered on demurrer, the allegations of the complaint must be liberally construed with a view to attaining substantial justice among the parties. (Code Civ. Proc., § 452.)" (*Youngman v. Nevada Irrigation Dist.*, 70 Cal. 2d 240, 244–245 [74 Cal. Rptr. 398, 449 P.2d 462].) Obviously, the complaint must be read as a whole (*Smith v. Kern County Land Co.*, 51 Cal. 2d 205, 207 [331 P.2d 645]), and each part must be given the meaning it derives from the total context wherein it appears.

The Supreme Court has consistently stated the guideline that "a plaintiff is required only to set forth the essential facts of his case with reasonable precision and with particularity sufficient to acquaint a defendant with the nature, source and extent of his cause of action." (*Youngman v. Nevada Irrigation Dist.*, *supra*, 70 Cal. 2d at p. 245; *Smith v. Kern County Land Co.*, *supra*, 51 Cal. 2d at p. 209.) It has also been stated that "[the] particularity required in pleading facts depends on the extent to which the defendant in fairness needs detailed information that can be conveniently provided by the plaintiff; less particularity is required where the defendant may be assumed to have knowledge of the facts equal to that possessed by the plaintiff." (*Jackson v. Pasadena City School Dist.*, 59 Cal. 2d 876, [31 Cal. Rptr. 606, 382 P.2d 878]; *Burks v. Poppy Construction Co.*, 57 Cal. 2d 463, 474 [20 Cal. Rptr. 609, 370 P.2d 313].) This seems particularly applicable to a wrongful death action where none of the plaintiff-heirs was present at the site of the fatal injury.

---

1. "VII. That this action is brought pursuant to Section 3601(a)(3) of the Labor Code of the State of California.

"VIII. That on or about the 9th day of May, 1966, at about 4:00 P.M. the defendant Robert J. Sansoucie among other things backed the aforementioned tractor and trailer into an area without first inspecting whether the area was safe and without looking into the area he was backing into.

"IX. That said conduct is prohibited by the Vehicle Code of the State of California and the Rules and Regulations governing the operation of motor vehicles by Pacific Motor Trucking Company.

"X. That the defendants further operated the vehicle in a reckless disregard for the safety and calculated and conscious willingness to permit injury or death to such fellow employees."

Finally, it must be noted that the modern discovery procedures necessarily affect the amount of detail that should be required in a pleading. (*See Dahlquist v. State of California*, 243 Cal. App. 2d 208, 212–213 [52 Cal. Rptr. 324].)

Applying these principles to the case at bar, we hold that the complaint, though hardly a model of pleading, stated a cause of action. The statutory requirement is that the death be caused by a fellow-employee's act "which evinces a reckless disregard for the safety of the employee injured, and a calculated and conscious willingness to permit injury or death to such employee." (Lab. Code, § 3601, subd. (a)(3).) In substance, the complaint alleges that respondent failed to inspect the area into which he was backing and that he acted with the state of mind required by the statute.

* * * Respondent contends that paragraph X of the complaint is only a characterization—a conclusion of law—with no additional factual support. "The distinction between conclusions of law and ultimate facts is not at all clear and involves at most a matter of degree. [Citations omitted.] For example, the courts have permitted allegations which obviously included conclusions of law and have termed them 'ultimate facts' or 'conclusions of fact.'" (*Burks v. Poppy Construction Co., supra*, 57 Cal. 2d at p. 473.)

In *Smith v. Kern County Land Co., supra*, 51 Cal. 2d 205, the issue was whether an allegation that defendant "desired and wished" that plaintiff come onto his land to remove tree stumps and roots was a sufficient averment of plaintiff's status as an invitee, not a licensee. The Supreme Court ruled, at page 208: "This allegation is not, as defendant contends, a mere conclusion of law. The cases it relies on are readily distinguishable. *Wheeler v. Oppenheimer*, 140 Cal. App. 2d 497 [295 P.2d 128], held only that the technical term 'bad faith' was a conclusion of law. *Faulkner v. California Toll Bridge Authority*, 40 Cal. 2d 317 [253 P.2d 659], held to be legal conclusions the allegations that an investigation was 'insufficient' and that acts were 'arbitrary capricious, fraudulent, wrongful and unlawful.' The applicability of each of these words depends on more than, as in the case at bar, the mere presence of a state of mind."

The pleading in the case at bar is not as clearly susceptible to that distinction as the pleading in *Smith*. But we do feel that the allegation here possesses enough of a factual thrust that we cannot agree with respondent's contention that it is only a characterization that adds no additional factual support.

In *Jones v. Oxnard School Dist.*, 270 Cal. App. 2d 587, 593 [75 Cal. Rptr. 836], the court stated: "The applicable principle is that the 'conclusion of law—ultimate fact' dichotomy is not an absolute but that the fair import of language used in the pleading must be received to determine whether the adversary has been fairly apprised of the factual basis of the claim against him." That, we think, places the dichotomy in its proper perspective. * * *

Notes and Questions on the Sufficiency of the Complaint

(1) *Semole* illustrates the two issues present in evaluating the sufficiency of a complaint, and by analogy any pleading in the code pleading system. Since the complaint must contain "a statement of the *facts* constituting the *cause of action*," it must be both

formally sufficient—the "facts" must be in the appropriate style of "ultimate facts"—and these facts must present each of the elements of one or more "cause[s] of action." In *Semole*, there was no question that the elements necessary to recover under the statute were clearly present—plaintiff used the very words of the statute, "calculated and conscious willingness to permit injury or death," in the complaint. Defendant objected that the allegation required more factual content and that it should be disregarded as merely a "conclusion of law."

(2) *Federal Court Pleading Standard Compared.* For several decades, pleading a fact-based cause of action was not necessary in federal court as long as the pleading gives the defendant "fair notice of what the plaintiff's claim is and the grounds upon which it rests." *Conley v. Gibson*, 355 U.S. 41, 47, 78 S. Ct. 99, 2 L. Ed. 2d 80 (1957). However, two recent U.S. Supreme Court decisions construing federal Rule 8(a)(2), *Bell Atlantic Corp. v. Twombly*, 550 U.S. 544, 127 S. Ct. 1955, 167 L. Ed. 2d 929 (2007), and *Ashcroft v. Iqbal*, 556 U.S. 662, 129 S. Ct. 1937, 173 L. Ed. 2d 868 (2009), disapproved of this traditional "notice" pleading approach. Instead, the Supreme Court adopted the following new standard for federal courts:

> To survive a motion to dismiss, a complaint must contain sufficient factual matter, accepted as true, to "state a claim to relief that is plausible on its face." [*Bell AtlanticCorp. v. Twombly*, 550 U.S. 544, 570 (2007).] A claim has facial plausibility when the plaintiff pleads factual content that allows the court to draw the reasonable inference that the defendant is liable for the misconduct alleged. *Id.*, at 556. . . .
>
> Two working principles underlie our decision in *Twombly*. First, the tenet that a court must accept as true all of the allegations contained in a complaint is inapplicable to legal conclusions. Threadbare recitals of the elements of a cause of action, supported by mere conclusory statements, do not suffice. *Id.*, at 555. (Although for the purposes of a motion to dismiss we must take all of the factual allegations in the complaint as true, we "are not bound to accept as true a legal conclusion couched as a factual allegation"). Rule 8 marks a notable and generous departure from the hyper-technical, code-pleading regime of a prior era, but it does not unlock the doors of discovery for a plaintiff armed with nothing more than conclusions. Second, only a complaint that states a plausible claim for relief survives a motion to dismiss. *Id.*, at 556. Determining whether a complaint states a plausible claim for relief will . . . be a context-specific task that requires the reviewing court to draw on its judicial experience and common sense. But where the well-pleaded facts do not permit the court to infer more than the mere possibility of misconduct, the complaint has alleged—but it has not "show[n]"—"that the pleader is entitled to relief." Fed. Rule Civ. Proc. 8(a)(2).
>
> In keeping with these principles a court considering a motion to dismiss can choose to begin by identifying pleadings that, because they are no more than conclusions, are not entitled to the assumption of truth. While legal conclusions can provide the framework of a complaint, they must be supported

by factual allegations. When there are well-pleaded factual allegations, a court should assume their veracity and then determine whether they plausibly give rise to an entitlement to relief.

Ashcroft v. Iqbal, supra, 129 S. Ct. at 1949–1950

How does the new federal pleading standard compare with the standard endorsed in *Semole*? Does the new federal standard require more or less fact-based pleading than the *Semole* standard? Would the complaint in *Semole* have survived a demurrer (i.e., a motion to dismiss for failure to state a claim) if the California court had applied the new federal standard? In your opinion, which of these two standards represents the better approach to pleading? Why?

(3) Under traditional code pleading, the pleader can err by being either too general—using conclusions of law—or too specific—pleading evidence. *See Careau & Co. v. Security Pacific Business Credit, Inc.,* 222 Cal. App. 3d 1371, 272 Cal. Rptr. 387 (1990) (A complaint must allege the ultimate facts necessary to the statement of an actionable claim).

(4) *Heightened Pleading Requirements.* Causes of action based on fraud must be specifically pleaded; a general pleading of the legal conclusion of fraud is insufficient. *Stansfield v. Starkey,* 220 Cal. App. 3d 59, 269 Cal. Rptr. 337 (1990). Each of the elements of fraud—false representation of a material fact, knowledge of its falsity, intent to defraud, justifiable reliance, and resulting damage—must be alleged in full, factually and specifically. *See Id.; Nagy v. Nagy,* 210 Cal. App. 3d 1262, 1268–69, 258 Cal. Rptr. 787 (1989) (Complaint which lacked an allegation of a definite amount of damage held not to state a cause of action for fraud); *Wilhelm v. Pray, Price, Williams & Russell,* 186 Cal. App. 3d 1324, 231 Cal. Rptr. 355 (1986) (Complaint which failed to specifically plead factual basis for knowledge of falsity and justifiable reliance held not to state fraud cause of action).

(5) *Official Form Pleadings.* The Judicial Council of California has developed and approved Official Form pleadings—complaints, cross-complaints, and answers—for optional use for several basic of causes of action. CCP § 425.12. The Official Form of the "Complaint for Personal Injury, Property Damage, Wrongful Death—Motor Vehicle Cause of Action." is reproduced below:

2. Statement of Damages

Code of Civil Procedure § 425.10(b) provides that in superior court actions to recover actual or punitive damages for personal injury or wrongful death, the amount sought is *not* to be stated. Apparently passed to avoid publicizing inflated claims against individuals and particularly health care providers, section 425.10(b) must be read with section 425.11 that gives a defending party the right at any time to request "a statement setting forth the nature and amount of damages being sought." *See also* CCP § 425.115 (statement preserving right to seek punitive damages). Even if not demanded, the statement must be served before a default may be taken. *See Schwab v. Rondel*

PLD-PI-001

ATTORNEY OR PARTY WITHOUT ATTORNEY (Name, State Bar number, and address):	FOR COURT USE ONLY
TELEPHONE NO: FAX NO. (Optional): E-MAIL ADDRESS (Optional): ATTORNEY FOR (Name):	

SUPERIOR COURT OF CALIFORNIA, COUNTY OF
STREET ADDRESS:
MAILING ADDRESS:
CITY AND ZIP CODE:
BRANCH NAME:

PLAINTIFF:

DEFENDANT:

☐ DOES 1 TO _____

COMPLAINT—Personal Injury, Property Damage, Wrongful Death
☐ **AMENDED** (Number):
Type (check all that apply):
☐ **MOTOR VEHICLE**   ☐ **OTHER** (specify):
     ☐ **Property Damage**   ☐ **Wrongful Death**
     ☐ **Personal Injury**   ☐ **Other Damages** (specify):

Jurisdiction (check all that apply):   CASE NUMBER:
☐ **ACTION IS A LIMITED CIVIL CASE**
   Amount demanded   ☐ does not exceed $10,000
                 ☐ exceeds $10,000, but does not exceed $25,000
☐ **ACTION IS AN UNLIMITED CIVIL CASE** (exceeds $25,000)
☐ **ACTION IS RECLASSIFIED** by this amended complaint
     ☐ from limited to unlimited
     ☐ from unlimited to limited

1. **Plaintiff** (name or names):
   alleges causes of action against **defendant** (name or names):

2. This pleading, including attachments and exhibits, consists of the following number of pages:

3. Each plaintiff named above is a competent adult
   a. ☐ **except plaintiff** (name):
      (1) ☐ a corporation qualified to do business in California
      (2) ☐ an unincorporated entity (describe):
      (3) ☐ a public entity (describe):
      (4) ☐ a minor   ☐ an adult
         (a) ☐ for whom a guardian or conservator of the estate or a guardian ad litem has been appointed
         (b) ☐ other (specify):
      (5) ☐ other (specify):
   b. ☐ **except plaintiff** (name):
      (1) ☐ a corporation qualified to do business in California
      (2) ☐ an unincorporated entity (describe):
      (3) ☐ a public entity (describe):
      (4) ☐ a minor   ☐ an adult
         (a) ☐ for whom a guardian or conservator of the estate or a guardian ad litem has been appointed
         (b) ☐ other (specify):
      (5) ☐ other (specify):

☐ Information about additional plaintiffs who are not competent adults is shown in Attachment 3.

Page 1 of 3

Form Approved for Optional Use
Judicial Council of California
PLD-PI-001 [Rev. January 1, 2007]

COMPLAINT—Personal Injury, Property Damage, Wrongful Death

Code of Civil Procedure, § 425.12
www.courtinfo.ca.gov

American LegalNet, Inc.
www.FormsWorkflow.com

PLD-PI-001

SHORT TITLE:	CASE NUMBER:

4. ☐ Plaintiff *(name):*

  is doing business under the fictitious name *(specify):*

  and has complied with the fictitious business name laws.

5. Each defendant named above is a natural person

 a. ☐ **except** defendant *(name):*
   (1) ☐ a business organization, form unknown
   (2) ☐ a corporation
   (3) ☐ an unincorporated entity *(describe):*

   (4) ☐ a public entity *(describe):*

   (5) ☐ other *(specify):*

 c. ☐ **except** defendant *(name):*
   (1) ☐ a business organization, form unknown
   (2) ☐ a corporation
   (3) ☐ an unincorporated entity *(describe):*

   (4) ☐ a public entity *(describe):*

   (5) ☐ other *(specify):*

 b. ☐ **except** defendant *(name):*
   (1) ☐ a business organization, form unknown
   (2) ☐ a corporation
   (3) ☐ an unincorporated entity *(describe):*

   (4) ☐ a public entity *(describe):*

   (5) ☐ other *(specify):*

 d. ☐ **except** defendant *(name):*
   (1) ☐ a business organization, form unknown
   (2) ☐ a corporation
   (3) ☐ an unincorporated entity *(describe):*

   (4) ☐ a public entity *(describe):*

   (5) ☐ other *(specify):*

 ☐ Information about additional defendants who are not natural persons is contained in Attachment 5.

6. The true names of defendants sued as Does are unknown to plaintiff.

 a. ☐ Doe defendants *(specify Doe numbers):* _____ were the agents or employees of other named defendants and acted within the scope of that agency or employment.

 b. ☐ Doe defendants *(specify Doe numbers):* _____ are persons whose capacities are unknown to plaintiff.

7. ☐ Defendants who are joined under Code of Civil Procedure section 382 are *(names):*

8. This court is the proper court because

 a. ☐ at least one defendant now resides in its jurisdictional area.

 b. ☐ the principal place of business of a defendant corporation or unincorporated association is in its jurisdictional area.

 c. ☐ injury to person or damage to personal property occurred in its jurisdictional area.

 d. ☐ other *(specify):*

9. ☐ Plaintiff is required to comply with a claims statute, **and**

 a. ☐ has complied with applicable claims statutes, **or**

 b. ☐ is excused from complying because *(specify):*

COMPLAINT—Personal Injury, Property
Damage, Wrongful Death

PLD-PI-001

SHORT TITLE:	CASE NUMBER:

10. The following causes of action are attached and the statements above apply to each *(each complaint must have one or more causes of action attached):*
   a. ☐ Motor Vehicle
   b. ☐ General Negligence
   c. ☐ Intentional Tort
   d. ☐ Products Liability
   e. ☐ Premises Liability
   f. ☐ Other *(specify):*

11. Plaintiff has suffered
   a. ☐ wage loss
   b. ☐ loss of use of property
   c. ☐ hospital and medical expenses
   d. ☐ general damage
   e. ☐ property damage
   f. ☐ loss of earning capacity
   g. ☐ other damage *(specify):*

12. ☐ The damages claimed for wrongful death and the relationships of plaintiff to the deceased are
   a. ☐ listed in Attachment 12.
   b. ☐ as follows:

13. The relief sought in this complaint is within the jurisdiction of this court.

14. **Plaintiff prays** for judgment for costs of suit; for such relief as is fair, just, and equitable; and for
   a. (1) ☐ compensatory damages
      (2) ☐ punitive damages
      The amount of damages is *(in cases for personal injury or wrongful death, you must check (1)):*
      (1) ☐ according to proof
      (2) ☐ in the amount of: $

15. ☐ The paragraphs of this complaint alleged on information and belief are as follows *(specify paragraph numbers):*

Date:

▶

_____   _____
(TYPE OR PRINT NAME)   (SIGNATURE OF PLAINTIFF OR ATTORNEY)

PLD-PI-001 [Rev. January 1, 2007]   **COMPLAINT—Personal Injury, Property**   Page 3 of 3
                                       Damage, Wrongful Death

SHORT TITLE:	CASE NUMBER:

CAUSE OF ACTION—Motor Vehicle

_____
(number)

ATTACHMENT TO ☐ Complaint ☐ Cross - Complaint

(Use a separate cause of action form for each cause of action.)

Plaintiff *(name):*

MV- 1. Plaintiff alleges the acts of defendants were negligent; the acts were the legal (proximate) cause of injuries and damages to plaintiff; the acts occurred

on *(date):*

at *(place):*

MV- 2. DEFENDANTS

  a. ☐ The defendants who operated a motor vehicle are *(names):*

    ☐ Does _____ to _____

  b. ☐ The defendants who employed the persons who operated a motor vehicle in the course of their employment are *(names):*

    ☐ Does _____ to _____

  c. ☐ The defendants who owned the motor vehicle which was operated with their permission are *(names):*

    ☐ Does _____ to _____

  d. ☐ The defendants who entrusted the motor vehicle are *(names):*

    ☐ Does _____ to _____

  e. ☐ The defendants who were the agents and employees of the other defendants and acted within the scope of the agency were *(names):*

    ☐ Does _____ to _____

  f. ☐ The defendants who are liable to plaintiffs for other reasons and the reasons for the liability are ☐ listed in Attachment MV-2f ☐ as follows:

    ☐ Does _____ to _____   **Page** _____

Page 1 of 1

Form Approved for Optional Use
Judicial Council of California
PLD-PI-001(1) [Rev. January 1, 2007]

CAUSE OF ACTION—Motor Vehicle

Code of Civil Procedure 425.12
www.courtinfo.ca.gov

American LegalNet, Inc.
www.FormsWorkflow.com

Homes, Inc., 53 Cal. 3d 428, 280 Cal. Rptr. 83, 808 P.2d 226 (1991) (Default judgment invalid because plaintiff did not serve defendant a statement of damages).

In some instances, the Legislature imposes additional restrictions on the pleading of punitive damages claims. For example, CCP § 425.13 bars inclusion of a punitive damages claim in a complaint seeking damages against a health care provider arising out of professional negligence unless the plaintiff first demonstrates to the court a "substantial probability" that the plaintiff "will prevail" on the claim. A plaintiff may not amend the complaint to include a punitive damages claim unless the plaintiff first demonstrates, by affidavits or declarations, that she possesses a legally sufficient claim that is supported by competent, admissible evidence. *College Hospital, Inc. v. Superior Court*, 8 Cal. 4th 704, 34 Cal. Rptr. 898, 882 P.2d 894 (1994).

3. Truth in Pleadings

Section 128.5 sanctions and new section 128.7. In 1981 the Legislature passed Code of Civil Procedure § 128.5. This section authorizes trial courts to "order a party, the party's attorney, or both to pay any reasonable expenses, including attorney's fees, incurred by another party as a result of *bad faith actions or tactics* that are frivolous or solely intended to cause unnecessary delay." CCP § 128.5(a) [emphasis added]. The section has had much less impact than the 1983–93 version of federal Rule 11. To be considered frivolous, a bad faith action or tactic had to be "totally and completely without merit or for the sole purpose of harassing an opposing party." § 128.5(b)(2). In addition, the California appellate courts have divided on the question of whether subjective bad faith is required in order to impose sanctions. CCP § 128.5 was amended in 2017 to authorize a trial court to order a party to pay reasonable expenses, including attorney's fees, "incurred by another party as a result of actions or tactics, made in bad faith, that are frivolous or solely intended to cause unnecessary delay."

As a result of these limitations, in 1994 the Legislature added a new § 128.7 to the Code of Civil Procedure. Section 128.7 is patterned directly on Rule 11 of the Federal Rule of Civil Procedure. The section requires "[e]very pleading, petition, written notice of motion, or other similar paper shall be signed by at least one attorney of record in the attorney's individual name" or by a party not represented by an attorney. CCP § 128.7(a). The heart of the section, § 128.7(b), imposes on the attorney or party a series of "certifications" any time the attorney or party makes a "presentation" to the court:

> (b) By presenting to the court, whether by signing, filing, submitting, or later advocating, a pleading, petition, written notice of motion, or other similar paper, an attorney or unrepresented party is certifying that to the best of the person's knowledge, information, and belief, formed after an inquiry reasonable under the circumstances, all of the following conditions are met:
>
> > (1) It is not being presented primarily for an improper purpose, such as to harass or to cause unnecessary delay or needless increase in the cost of litigation.

(2) The claims, defenses, and other legal contentions therein are warranted by existing law or by a nonfrivolous argument for the extension, modification, or reversal of existing law or the establishment of new law.

(3) The allegations and other factual contentions have evidentiary support or, if specifically so identified, are likely to have evidentiary support after a reasonable opportunity for further investigation or discovery.

(4) The denials of factual contentions are warranted on the evidence or, if specifically so identified, are reasonably based on a lack of information or belief.

Like the current version of federal Rule 11, sanctions are discretionary with the court, not mandatory, upon finding a violation of one of the certifications. Also like Rule 11, there is a "safe harbor" provision. A party served with a motion for CCP § 128.7 sanctions ordinarily has 21 days in which to withdraw or correct the challenged paper before the motion is filed. § 128.7(c)(1). Sanctions are "limited to what is sufficient to deter" repetition of the conduct. Paying the injured party's attorneys fees as a sanction is limited to specified circumstances and when "warranted for effective deterrence." § 128.7(d). Under § 128.7(d) sanctions may be made payable to the court. *See Kane v. Hurley*, 30 Cal. App. 4th 859, 35 Cal. Rptr. 2d 809 (1994) and *Levy v. Blum, supra*, 92 Cal. App. 4th at 635–38, for thorough discussion of this issue and CCP § 128.5 and § 128.7 generally; and *Marriage of Schnabel*, 30 Cal. App. 4th 747, 36 Cal. Rptr. 2d 682 (1994), for a discussion of the imposition of sanctions, pursuant to CCP § 907, for a frivolous appeal.

Voluntary Dismissal to Avoid Section 128.7 Sanctions. The "safe harbor" provision of CCP § 128.7(c)(1) requires that the party seeking sanctions follow a two step procedure. First, the party must serve a notice of motion for sanctions on the offending party at least 21 days before filing the motion with the court, which specifically describes the sanctionable conduct. Service of the motion on the offending party begins a 21-day safe harbor period during which the sanctions motion may not be filed with the court. If the pleading is withdrawn, the motion for sanctions may not be filed with the court. If the pleading is not withdrawn, the motion for sanctions may then be filed. *See Levy v. Blum, supra*, 92 Cal. App. 4th at 637.

If a plaintiff's complaint is dismissed during the 21-day safe harbor period, either voluntarily or involuntarily, the trial court no longer has the authority to award sanctions under § 128.7(c)(1). *See, e.g., Hart v. Avetoom*, 95 Cal. App. 4th 410, 115 Cal. Rptr. 2d 511 (2002); *Malovec v. Hamrell*, 70 Cal. App. 4th 434, 82 Cal. Rptr. 2d 712 (1999). The *Hart* court observed that allowing a party to serve and file a sanctions motion after the conclusion of the case would completely defeat the purpose of the safe harbor provision. How so? What is the purpose of the safe harbor provision? Does the trial court still have the authority to award sanctions under § 128.7(c)(1) where the plaintiff has not withdrawn the offending complaint, but the trial court has sustained a demurrer to the complaint without leave to amend, before the 21-day safe harbor period has passed? *See Banks v. Hathaway, Perrett, Webster, Powers & Chrisman*, 97 Cal. App. 4th 949, 118 Cal. Rptr. 2d 803 (2002) (An order sustaining a demurrer without leave to amend does not bar a motion for § 128.7 sanctions unless the order is reduced to a judgment before the sanctions motion is served and filed).

Does a plaintiff's voluntary dismissal of his action with prejudice, after defendant's motion for § 128.7 sanctions has been filed and taken under submission, deprive the trial court of authority to grant the motion and impose sanctions on plaintiff for filing an improper complaint? *See Eichenbaum v. Alon*, 106 Cal. App. 4th 967, 131 Cal. Rptr. 2d 296 (2003) (The availability of § 128.7 sanctions against an offending plaintiff who has voluntarily dismissed his action depends upon whether the sanctions motion was filed before or after dismissal).

B. Amendments

1. California's Relation Back Doctrine

Barrington v. A.H. Robins Co.

Supreme Court of California

39 Cal. 3d 146, 216 Cal. Rptr. 405, 702 P.2d 563 (1985)

BROUSSARD, JUSTICE.

[Plaintiff filed suit against her doctor, the manufacturer of Darvon, and Doe's 1 through 40, alleging medical malpractice and negligent failure to warn of the dangers involved in taking the drug. Plaintiff subsequently substituted A.H. Robins Co. for one of the fictitious Doe defendants, and filed an amended complaint alleging a new cause of action against Robins. This new cause alleged that the instrument causing her injury was a defective Dalkan Shield intrauterine device manufactured by Robins. The California Supreme Court concluded that the amended complaint did not relate back, and discussed the relation back doctrine at length].

We . . . traced the evolution of the relation back doctrine in *Smeltzley v. Nicholson Mfg. Co.* (1977) 18 Cal. 3d 932 [136 Cal. Rptr. 269, 559 P.2d 624, 85 A.L.R.3d 121], and formulated a general rule: An amended complaint relates back to the original complaint, and thus avoids the statute of limitations as a bar against named parties substituted for fictitious defendants, if it: (1) rests on the same general set of facts as the original complaint; and (2) refers to the same accident and same injuries as the original complaint. (*Id.*, at pp. 936–937.)

[The] contention that the Dalkon Shield cause of action does not relate back is supported by *Coronet Manufacturing Co. v. Superior Court* (1979) 90 Cal. App. 3d 342 [153 Cal. Rptr. 366]. In *Coronet*, the original complaint in an action for wrongful death alleged that plaintiffs' daughter was electrocuted while using a dangerous instrumentality—a defective hair dryer. The defendants were the corporation that manufactured the hair dryer and a number of Doe component suppliers. The amended complaint, which identified Coronet for the first time as one of the Doe component suppliers, was filed after the statute of limitation had run as to the original complaint. The amended complaint, however, alleged that the dangerous instrumentality was a lamp socket and switch manufactured by Coronet rather than a hair dryer.

The court held that the amended complaint did *not* relate back to the original complaint, and was thus barred by the statute of limitations. The court announced that an amended complaint relates back only if it is based on the same operative facts, and refers to the same "offending instrumentality" and "accident." The amended complaint before the court did not relate back because "[the] difference between being electrocuted by a hair dryer and being electrocuted by a table lamp is as great as being electrocuted by the hair dryer and being poisoned by some improperly processed food found on the kitchen shelf. Although they relate to a single death at a single location, they are different 'accidents' and involve different instrumentalities." (*Id.*, at p. 347).

Similarly, . . . the new cause of action in the present case does not relate back because it, too, involves separate and distinct "offending instrumentalities" and "accidents." The original complaint alleged that the offending instrumentality was Doctor Taras' negligent medical treatment and the failure of Dr. Taras and Darvon Manufacturer to warn of the dangers involved in taking the prescription drug Darvon. The alleged accident was her ingestion of that drug. By contrast, the amended complaint alleged that the offending instrumentality was a defective and unsafe Dalkon Shield designed, manufactured, and sold by Robins. The alleged accident was tubal-ovarian abscesses and an infection resulting from her use of the Dalkon Shield. * * *

Notes and Questions Regarding Relation Back Doctrine

(1) As *Barrington* illustrates, the California courts typically state the current relation back doctrine as requiring that the amended complaint not only must rest on the "same general set of facts," but also must involve the "same accident and same injuries" and refer to the "same offending instrumentality" as the original complaint. *See, e.g., Smetlzley v. Nicholson Mfg. Co.*, 18 Cal. 3d 932, 934, 136 Cal. Rptr. 269, 559 P.2d 624 (1977); *Branick v. Downey Savings & Loan Ass'n*, 39 Cal. 4th 235, 243–44, 46 Cal. Rptr. 3d 66, 138 P.3d 214 (2006). For criticisms of these additional restrictions on the basic "same general set of facts" standard, *see* Walter W. Heiser, *Relation Back of Amended Complaints: The California Courts Should Adopt a More Pragmatic Approach*, 44 Santa Clara L. Rev. 643 (2004).

Professor Heiser explains why the use of the "same accident," "same injury," and "same instrumentality" tests as prerequisites to relation back is inconsistent with the modern view of civil litigation where discovery and pretrial orders, not pleadings, define the issues for trial. Heiser, *Relation Back, supra*, at 660–72, 695–97. He argues that the "same general set of facts" standard should be applied in a pragmatic manner, which would focus on whether the defendant will be unfairly surprised and therefore unduly prejudiced by the amended complaint. *Id.* at 687–95. The key inquiry is whether, during the course of pretrial discovery, the defendant was already made aware of, and already has gathered facts responding to, the new allegations in the amendment. *Id.* Do you agree with these arguments? What problems do you see with such a pragmatic approach?

(2) *Federal Rule 15(c)(2) compared.* By requiring an amended complaint to refer to the "same injury" in addition to the "same general set of facts," the California relation back rule is more restrictive than its federal counterpart under Rule 15(c)(2), F.R.C.P., which authorizes relation back in federal court when the amended complaint refers to the "same conduct, transaction, or occurrence" set forth in the original pleading. For example, assume in a car crash case that the plaintiff files a timely complaint against the defendant other driver seeking damages for property damage to her vehicle. After the statute of limitations has expired, the plaintiff files an amended complaint seeking personal injury damages caused by the same accident. The amended complaint would relate back to the original complaint under Federal Rule 15(c)(2) because they both refer to the same occurrence — the car crash. But the amended complaint would not relate back under the California doctrine because it alleges a different injury than the original complaint. *See Sidney v. Superior Court,* 198 Cal. App. 3d 710, 717, n.4, 244 Cal. Rptr. 31 (1988).

2. California's Fictitious ("Doe") Defendant Practice

California's unique "Doe defendant practice" is significantly more liberal than that recognized in other jurisdictions and in federal practice. *See* James E. Hogan, *California's Unique Doe Defendant Practice: A Fiction Stranger Than Truth,* 30 Stan. L. Rev. 51, 88–101 (1977). California allows plaintiffs to name as Doe defendants parties whom the plaintiff has no reason to believe even exist solely as insurance against the statute of limitations bar. Designed to mitigate the harsh effects of California's short statutes of limitations, particularly in personal injury actions, California's "Doe defendant practice" permits relation back to the date of the original pleading in a broad variety of circumstances unknown to the federal courts under Rule 15(c)(3), F.R.C.P. Ordinarily relation back is allowed by the simple expedient of substituting the new defendant for one of the "Does."

California's "Doe defendant practice" has evolved through case law interpreting three rather innocent-looking statutes: Sections 474, 350, and 583.210 of the California Code of Civil Procedure. These statutes have existed in some form or other since the original Practice Act of 1851. Section 474 is the legislative centerpiece of the fictitious defendant practice, providing in pertinent part:

> When the plaintiff is ignorant of the name of a defendant, he must state that fact in the complaint, . . . and such defendant may be designated in any pleading or proceeding by any name, and when his true name is discovered, the pleading or proceeding must be amended accordingly; . . .

As will be discussed in *Streicher v. Tommy's Electric Company,* reproduced *infra,* the California courts have construed CCP § 474 to include a relation back concept.

Streicher v. Tommy's Electric Company

Court of Appeal of California, Sixth Appellate District

164 Cal. App. 3d 876, 211 Cal. Rptr. 22 (1985)

Panelli, Justice.

Plaintiff appeals from a judgment of dismissal entered after defendants' demurrer to an amended complaint was sustained without leave to amend on the ground the statute of limitations barred the action. We reverse.

FACTS

On October 4, 1979, plaintiff Frank Streicher filed a complaint for personal injuries sustained on July 16, 1979, at a construction site when certain radio-controlled overhead garage doors opened causing him to fall from the scaffolding upon which he was working. The complaint named as defendants Shippers Development Company (general contractor), Salinas Steel Builders, Inc. (subcontractor), Jack's Overhead Door Company, Inc. and John Hendrix (independent contractors and installers of the electronic doors), as well as four fictitious business entities (Black, White, Blue, and Grey Companies), three fictitious individuals comprising Grey Company as a partnership (Does One, Two, and Three), and ninety-seven additional fictitious defendants (Does Four through One Hundred).

The first paragraph of the complaint alleged that the true names and capacities of the fictitious defendants were unknown to plaintiff, but stated that when these were ascertained plaintiff would move to amend the complaint accordingly. Paragraph six alleged a cause of action for negligence, charging that defendants owned, possessed and controlled the construction site, that they had provided an unsafe workplace through their failure, among other things, to "supervise and control the installation and operation of radio-controlled overhead garage doors" on the worksite, and that such negligence resulted in plaintiff's injuries.

On May 18, 1982, two years and ten months after the accident, and after settlement was obtained with the named defendants, Streicher filed a first amended complaint against respondents Tommy's Electric Company and Shima American Corporation and Does Four through One Hundred. It alleged respondents designed, manufactured, marketed and sold the radio-controlled overhead door openers involved in the accident and that these openers had been defectively designed and would malfunction without human intervention. The amended complaint stated causes of action for negligence, breach of express and implied warranty, and strict products liability.[1]

---

1. On April 29, 1982, prior to the filing of his amended complaint, Streicher served upon Shima American Corporation (Shima) a summons and a copy of the original complaint. The proof of service indicated Shima had been served as fictitious defendant "Doe Five," but the summons accompanying the complaint did not so indicate. On May 17, 1982 plaintiff and respondents stipulated to plaintiff's filing of the amended complaint, but the stipulation also indicated it did not constitute a waiver by respondents "to answer or otherwise plead" to the amended complaint.

On June 17, 1982, respondents demurred to the first amended complaint on the ground that the claim was barred by the one year statute of limitations (Code Civ. Proc., § 340, subd. (3)). Respondents also moved the court to judicially notice, pursuant to Evidence Code sections 452 and 453, all the pleadings and records in its file on this case including a cross-complaint filed by Jack's Overhead Doors (one of the named defendants) and a complaint in intervention filed by Industrial Indemnity Co. (plaintiff's employer's workers' compensation carrier), both filed in February of 1980, which included respondents among the named defendants and alleged causes of action for indemnity based on a products liability theory.

Respondents argued in their moving papers that since plaintiff's amended complaint did not substitute respondents for any of the fictitiously named defendants in his original complaint, the amended complaint was in fact adding new defendants to the action and that this was not permissible after the running of the one-year statute of limitations. Respondents further argued that even if plaintiff's defective substitution of fictitious defendants was cured, the provisions of Code of Civil Procedure section 474,[2] allowing the amendment to relate back to the filing of the original complaint, did not apply because in February of 1980 plaintiff had notice of respondents' identity through the filing of the cross-complaint and intervention pleadings, yet he had nevertheless failed to exercise due diligence in amending his complaint before the expiration of the statute of limitations in July 1980.

Streicher opposed respondents' demurrer and moved for leave to amend his complaint in order to properly substitute respondents for specifically named fictitious defendants, arguing his failure to do so constituted a procedural error which could be easily cured. Streicher also argued the benefits afforded by section 474 should apply because he was not aware of any facts constituting the basis for a products liability cause of action against respondents until March 30, 1982, when an electronics expert indicated that the electronic door controllers involved in the accident were defective.

The court sustained respondents' demurrer without leave to amend on the ground the statute of limitations barred the action. The court's minute order also noted that plaintiff's early pleadings were consistent with his belief that "before March 30, 1982 . . . [he] had no basis for an action against the two defendants." This appeal followed.

DISCUSSION

On appeal, Streicher contends the trial court erroneously sustained the demurrer and abused its discretion in denying him leave to amend the complaint to cure his failure to specifically substitute respondents for fictitious defendants named in the original complaint. We find these contentions meritorious.

---

2. Unless otherwise indicated, further statutory references are to the Code of Civil Procedure. Section 474 provides in pertinent part: "When the plaintiff is ignorant of the name of a defendant, he must state that fact in the complaint, . . . and such defendant may be designated in any pleading or proceeding by any name, and when his true name is discovered, the pleading or proceeding must be amended accordingly. . . ."

Preliminarily we must determine whether Streicher's first amended complaint, absent his defective substitution of respondents for the fictitiously named defendants, relates back to the filing date of the original complaint under section 474, thus defeating the bar of the statute of limitations.

"The purpose of . . . section 474 is to enable a plaintiff who is ignorant of the identity of the defendant to file his complaint before his claim is barred by the statute of limitations. There is a strong policy in favor of litigating cases on their merits, and the California courts have been very liberal in permitting the amendment of pleadings to bring in a defendant previously sued by fictitious name." (*Barrows v. American Motors Corp.* (1983) 144 Cal. App. 3d 1, 7 [192 Cal. Rptr. 380], citing *Austin v. Massachusetts Bonding & Insurance Co.* (1961) 56 Cal. 2d 596, 600, 602, 603 [15 Cal. Rptr. 817, 364 P.2d 681]; *see also Motor City Sales v. Superior Court* (1973) 31 Cal. App. 3d 342, 345 [107 Cal. Rptr. 280].) It is also well settled that the amended pleading will relate back to the date of filing of the original complaint provided it seeks recovery on the same general set of facts as alleged in the original complaint. (*Austin v. Massachusetts Bonding & Insurance Co., supra,* 56 Cal. 2d at p. 600; *Barnes v. Wilson* (1974) 40 Cal. App. 3d 199, 203 [114 Cal. Rptr. 839]; *Smeltzley v. Nicholson Mfg. Co.* (1977) 18 Cal. 3d 932, 937 [136 Cal. Rptr. 269, 559 P.2d 624, 85 A.L.R.3d 121]; *Barrows v. American Motors Corp., supra,* 144 Cal. App. 3d at p. 7.) Moreover, it is clear that where the original complaint contains standard Doe allegations alleging negligence theories, it is proper to amend the complaint to bring in other defendants on warranty and products liability; since the amendment involves the same accident and injury, the amendment relates back to satisfy the statute of limitations. (*Barrows v. American Motors Corp., supra,* 144 Cal. App. 3d at p. 7; *Garrett v. Crown Coach Corp.* (1968) 259 Cal. App. 2d 647 [66 Cal. Rptr. 590].)

However, in order to claim the benefits of section 474, plaintiff's ignorance of defendant's true name must be genuine and not feigned. (*Stephens v. Berry* (1967) 249 Cal. App. 2d 474, 477 [57 Cal. Rptr. 505]; *Schroeter v. Lowers* (1968) [260 Cal. App. 2d 695, 67 Cal. Rptr. 270].) We must therefore look to see whether plaintiff knew defendant's true name at the time he filed his original complaint. Plaintiff's requisite ignorance of defendant's name under section 474 has been expansively interpreted by the courts to encompass situations where "he knew the identity of the person but was ignorant of the facts giving him a cause of action against the person [Citations omitted], or knew the name and all the facts but was unaware that the law gave him a cause of action against the fictitiously named defendant and discovered that right by reason of decisions rendered after the commencement of the action. [Citations omitted.]" (*Marasco v. Wadsworth* (1978) 21 Cal. 3d 82, 88 [145 Cal. Rptr. 843, 578 P.2d 90], quoting with approval *Barnes v. Wilson, supra,* 40 Cal. App. 3d at p. 205.) Moreover, section 474's ignorance requirement "is restricted to the knowledge of the plaintiff *at the time of filing of the complaint*" (*Munoz v. Purdy* (1979) 91 Cal. App. 3d 942, 947 [154 Cal. Rptr. 472], italics added; *Mishalow v. Horwald* (1964) 231 Cal. App. 2d 517, 522–523 [41 Cal. Rptr. 895]), "and does not relate to steps that should be taken *after* the filing of the action." (91 Cal. App. 3d at p. 947.)

Guided by the foregoing principles we turn to the case at bar. Streicher's original complaint contained standard "Doe" allegations against fictitious defendants then unknown, as required by section 474. Although the original complaint alleged a cause of action for negligence against all defendants for failing to provide a safe place to work, it was proper to amend the complaint to bring in the defectively substituted defendants on the additional warranty and products liability theories of recovery since the amendment involved the same accident and injury alleged in the original complaint. (*See Smeltzley v. Nicholson Mfg. Co., supra,* 18 Cal. 3d at p. 937.) It is undisputed that at the time Streicher's original complaint was filed he was ignorant of respondents' identity or of their participation in designing, manufacturing or selling the electronic door openers involved in the accident. Likewise Streicher did not know at this time any facts which would indicate the possibility the door openers were defectively designed as such flaw in design was not externally visible.

Respondents contend, nevertheless, that Streicher did not "in good faith" avail himself of the provisions of section 474 because four months after his original complaint was filed he was alerted, through the filing of cross-complaint and intervention pleadings, of respondents' role in manufacturing and distributing the electronic door devices and of the possibility they could be sued under a products liability theory of recovery. As pointed out above, plaintiff's *actual knowledge at the time* the suit is filed is dispositive in triggering the application of section 474's fictitious defendant provisions (*Mishalow v. Horwald, supra,* 231 Cal. App. 2d at p. 522; *Munoz v. Purdy, supra,* 91 Cal. App. 3d at p. 947). Further, it remains undisputed that at the time of the filing of the original complaint Streicher was ignorant of respondents' identity or of their status as manufacturers and distributors of the defective door openers. Moreover, there is *no* requirement under section 474 that plaintiff exercise reasonable diligence in discovering either the true identity of fictitious defendants or the facts giving him a cause of action against such persons after the filing of a complaint and up to the expiration of the applicable limitation period. (*Munoz v. Purdy, supra,* 91 Cal. App. 3d at pp. 947–948; *Barrows v. American Motors Corp., supra,* 144 Cal. App. 3d at p. 10, fn.4.) As aptly stated by the court in *Munoz, supra,* "the interjection of a discovery standard into section 474 would lead to the harmful practice in all litigation of requiring that all persons who might conceivably have some connection with the lawsuit be specifically named in order to avoid the sanctions of the failure to comply with the inquiry requirements of section 474." (91 Cal. App. 3d at pp. 947–948.)

Respondent also argues that, irrespective of appellant's lack of knowledge of the true identity of the fictitiously named defendants at the time he filed the original complaint, he was nonetheless "dilatory" in filing the amended complaint once he acquired knowledge of the true identity of those defendants fictitiously named. Respondent contends that unreasonable delay in filing the *amendment* after actual discovery of the true identity of a fictitiously named defendant can bar a plaintiff's resort to the fictitious name procedure. Some authority for this proposition can be found in *Barrows v. American Motors Corp., supra,* 144 Cal. App. 3d at pages 8–9, and in *Barnes v. Wilson, supra,* 40 Cal. App. 3d 199 at page 206. Here, however the trial court was only dealing with a demurrer to the amended complaint. "Defendant's demurrer, however, tests only the sufficiency of the pleadings. Nothing in the pleadings suggests that plaintiff, after learning of his cause of action against defendant, was dilatory in amending his complaint, or that defendant suffered prejudice from such delay. [citation]." (*Smeltzley v. Nicholson Mfg. Co., supra,* 18 Cal. 3d 932, at p. 939, fns. omitted.) Nothing in this record suggests appellant was dilatory in amending his complaint. In fact, the trial court's order states that before March 30, 1982, "[appellant] had no basis for an action against the two defendants." Once he learned the facts giving him a cause of action against respondents on March 30, 1982, his first amended complaint naming respondents as defendants was promptly filed on May 18, 1982, within two months of discovery.

We conclude that, absent Streicher's defective substitution of respondents for the fictitiously named defendants, his first amended complaint relates back to the filing date of the original complaint under section 474, thus defeating the bar of the statute of limitations.

The issue remains whether the court abused its discretion in denying Streicher leave to amend the complaint to cure his failure to properly allege that respondents were being substituted for some of the fictitiously named defendants in the original complaint. Streicher argues this omission constituted a procedural error which was easily curable through amendment. We agree.

"It is axiomatic that if there is a reasonable possibility that a defect in the complaint can be cured by amendment or that the pleading liberally construed can state a cause of action, a demurrer should not be sustained without leave to amend. [Citations omitted.]" (*Minsky v. City of Los Angeles* (1974) 11 Cal. 3d 113, 118–119 [113 Cal. Rptr. 102, 520 P.2d 726].) We are satisfied the amended complaint's allegations sufficiently state a cause of action for products liability against respondents. Moreover, "[an] amendment substituting the true names of fictitious defendants is not a matter of substance because it does not change the cause of action nor affect the issues raised by the pleadings. [Citation omitted.]" (*Vincent v. Grayson* (1973) 30 Cal. App. 3d 899, 905, fn.2 [106 Cal. Rptr. 733].) Since the defect in the complaint does not affect the substance of its allegations and it is reasonably possible the defect can be cured by amendment, we conclude the trial court abused its discretion in dismissing the action without giving Streicher the opportunity to amend.

The judgment of dismissal is reversed.

Notes and Questions Regarding Doe Defendant Practice

(1) *Requirements for Use of Doe Defendant Practice.* Code of Civil Procedure sections 474 and 583.210 and the cases construing them set forth five requirements for the successful use of Doe defendant practice. *See* James E. Hogan, *California's Unique Doe Defendant Practice: A Fiction Stranger Than Truth*, 30 Stan. L. Rev. 51 (1977). First, the plaintiff must file the original complaint before the applicable statute of limitations has expired. Second, the plaintiff must be "ignorant of the name" of any defendant

designated by a fictitious name in the original complaint. Third, the plaintiff must plead this ignorance in the original complaint. Fourth, the plaintiff must allege a cause of action against the fictitious defendants in the original complaint based on the same general set of facts as the cause of action later asserted against the actually named defendants in the amended complaint. Fifth, the plaintiff must serve the amended complaint naming the actual defendants within the maximum period of three years of filing of the original complaint, and make return of service within 60 days after service of the complaint and summons.

(2) *Ignorance of the Defendant's "Name."* CCP § 474 specifies that the plaintiff must be "ignorant of the name" of any defendant designated in the complaint by a fictitious name. If the plaintiff does not possess the requisite ignorance when the original complaint is filed, the Doe defendant doctrine of § 474 does not apply. What does "ignorance" mean here? The words "ignorant of the name" in § 474 have not been construed literally:

(a) *Ignorance of the Defendant's Actual Name.* When the plaintiff knows the defendant's general identity, but does not know his name, the plaintiff is clearly "ignorant of the name" of the defendant within the meaning of CCP § 474 and can sue him as a Doe defendant. *Hoffman v. Keeton*, 132 Cal. 195, 64 P. 264 (1901). Likewise, § 474 would be applicable even if the plaintiff knows that the defendant exists, but does not know his name or even his general identity. *Gale v. McDaniel*, 72 Cal. 334, 13 P. 871 (1887). Such limited use of fictitious defendant pleading is typical of its use in many other states, as well as under Rule 15(c)(3) of the Federal Rules of Civil Procedure.

(b) *Ignorance of the Facts Giving Rise to the Cause of Action.* The court in *Larson v. Barnett*, 101 Cal. App. 2d 282, 225 P.2d 297 (1950), ruled that a plaintiff can still utilize CCP § 474 even when the plaintiff knew the individual's name and identity at the time the original complaint was filed. The court stated, as have numerous courts since then, that it is sufficient for purposes of § 474 that the plaintiff was ignorant of the facts giving plaintiff a cause of action against the individual at the time the original complaint was filed. *E.g., Barrows v. American Motors Corp.*, 144 Cal. App. 3d 1, 192 Cal. Rptr. 380 (1983); *Day v. Western Loan & Building Co.*, 42 Cal. App. 2d 226, 108 P.2d 702 (1940).

The court in *Day, supra,* stated that CCP § 474 does not require a plaintiff, when suing a fictitious defendant, to plead a description identifying the person intended to be sued. The court also rejected the theory that only names, and not defendants, may be fictitious. The court concluded that § 474 was applicable even though the plaintiff admittedly did not know the defendant's name, identity, or existence when the original complaint was filed. As the *Streicher* decision indicates, this broad use of "ignorance" is now established practice.

(c) *Ignorance That the Law Provides a Cause of Action.* A plaintiff can also utilize Doe defendant practice in circumstances where the substantive law did not provide a cause of action against the (unnamed) defendant at the time the original complaint was filed, but subsequently changed to authorize a cause of action. *See Marasco v.*

Wadsworth, 21 Cal. 3d 82, 145 Cal. Rptr. 843, 578 P.2d 90 (1978) (Plaintiff deemed "ignorant of the name" of the defendant even though she knew the defendant's name and all the facts but was unaware the law gave her a cause of action against the fictitiously named defendant and discovered that right by reason of a change in the relevant after the commencement of the action). However, § 474 is inapplicable where the plaintiff is ignorant of the law because she simply failed to discover that the existing substantive law provided a cause of action against the defendant at the time of the original complaint. *Von Gibson v. Estate of Lynch*, 197 Cal. App. 3d 725, 730, 243 Cal. Rptr. 50 (1988).

(3) *The Requirement of Actual Ignorance.* As the above discussion indicates, CCP § 474 has been construed quite broadly with respect to the requisite ignorance. However, as noted in *Streicher*, the ignorance must be genuine and not feigned. The plaintiff must actually be "ignorant" of the defendant's true name when the original complaint is filed. *See, e.g., Munoz v. Purdy*, 91 Cal. App. 3d 942, 154 Cal. Rptr. 472 (1979) (A plaintiff must actually be ignorant of the facts giving him a cause of action against a defendant, at the time of filing of the complaint). Is this requirement of actual ignorance based on a subjective or objective standard? Can a plaintiff be "ignorant" when a reasonable plaintiff would have easily determined the defendant's true name? Consider the following cases:

(a) In *Irving v. Carpentier*, 70 Cal. 23, 11 P. 391 (1886), the plaintiff filed a quiet title action against certain named defendants and several fictitious defendants who claimed an interest in disputed land. After the statute of limitations had run, plaintiff sought to amend the complaint to substitute the Pacific Improvement Company for one of the fictitious defendants. The defendant Company moved to dismiss the amended complaint on the grounds that plaintiff could have easily ascertained the company's name and existence before the original complaint was filed. If the plaintiff had searched the public records at the County Recorder's Office he would have readily found that the company claimed an interest in the disputed land. The Supreme Court rejected defendant's argument and allowed the amendment to relate back, stating that Section 474 applies when the plaintiff is actually ignorant of a certain fact, noting that "whether his ignorance is from misfortune or negligence, he is alike ignorant, and that is all the statute requires." *Irving, supra*, 70 Cal. at 26.

(b) In *Wallis v. Southern Pacific Transportation Co.*, 61 Cal. App. 3d 782, 132 Cal. Rptr. 631 (1976), plaintiff Wallis was injured while operating a door on a railroad car. His original complaint named several Doe defendants, and alleged that his injuries were caused by their negligent manufacture, operation, and maintenance of the box car. After the statute of limitations had apparently expired, plaintiff sought to amend his complaint to substitute the Transportation Company for a Doe defendant. Defendant Transportation Company moved to strike the amendment on the grounds that Wallis knew of defendant's existence when he filed the original complaint. The court rejected defendant's argument, stating that the fact that Wallis knew the defendant's existence "at the time of the commencement of the action is not controlling. . . . The question is whether he knew or reasonably should have known that he had a cause of action against respondent." * * * "The question as to whether the plaintiff has acted in good faith in his use of section 474 rests primarily with the trial court." *Wallis, supra*, 61 Cal. App. 3d at 786.

(c) More recently in *Parker v. Robert McKee, Inc.*, 3 Cal. App. 4th 512, 4 Cal. Rptr. 2d 347 (1992), the court considered the issue of whether § 474 is applicable where plaintiff knew the defendant's name and identity, but not the capacity in which the defendant acted. Plaintiff, a security guard, suffered personal injuries allegedly due to negligent accumulation of debris on stairs in a building being remodeled. Plaintiff timely filed a judicial council form complaint for general negligence and premises liability which named several contractors, including McKee, as defendants. Unable to locate McKee for service of process, plaintiff voluntarily dismissed McKee as a defendant. Two years later, plaintiff discovered that McKee was not simply one of the contractors involved in the remodeling, but was the general contractor on the project.

Plaintiff then filed an amended complaint pursuant to § 474, inserting McKee as a defendant in substitution for "Doe I." McKee demurred, contending that the amended complaint was barred by the one-year statute of limitation and that § 474 was inapplicable because the original complaint showed on its face that plaintiff was not ignorant of defendant McKee's name. The trial court sustained the demurrer, but the Court of Appeal reversed. The appellate court reasoned that the original complaint showed plaintiff was unaware defendant McKee was the general contractor rather than merely one of numerous subcontractors. The court then concluded that the previously unknown *fact* that defendant was the *general* contractor provides a proper new factual basis for a cause of action, and for use of § 474. The court viewed plaintiff's belated discovery that defendant was the general contractor as analogous to several cases, such as *Wallis*, where the plaintiff knew the defendant's identity but later learned the defendant acted in a different capacity than plaintiff knew at the time of filing the original complaint. *Parker, supra*, 3 Cal. App. 4th at 516–18.

Is the plaintiff's "ignorance" in *Parker* the same type of "ignorance" found in *Wallis*? Is *Parker* simply another application of the ignorance standard stated in *Wallis*, or something different? Is *Parker* consistent with *Wallis*? How can a plaintiff be "ignorant of the name of a defendant," when the plaintiff knows the defendant's identity and believes the defendant is *a* cause of plaintiff's injuries, and actually names that defendant in the original complaint? Is *Parker* an inappropriate extension of § 474? If plaintiff had not voluntarily dismissed McKee from the original complaint, would his amended complaint adding a cause of action against McKee as a general contractor be barred by the statute of limitation?

(d) What if the plaintiff's ignorance is due to his or her own negligence? In *Balon v. Drost*, 20 Cal. App. 4th 483, 25 Cal. Rptr. 2d 12 (1993), a divided court considered the plaintiff's forgetting of a defendant's previously known identity with no effort to refresh memory to be negligent ignorance, and held that negligent ignorance of the defendant's identity did not preclude adding that defendant under CCP § 474 after the statute of limitations expired. However, the court in *Woo v. Superior Court*, 75 Cal. App. 4th 169, 89 Cal. Rptr. 2d 20 (1999), disagreed with *Balon's* rule because it relieves forgetful plaintiffs of any obligation to refresh their memory with readily available information. Instead, the *Woo* court set forth what it perceived to be the better rule: If the plaintiff knows the defendant's identity and then forgets it at the time the complaint is filed, to use the § 474 relation back doctrine to avoid the bar of the statute of limitations the plaintiff must have at least reviewed readily available information likely to refresh his or her memory. *Woo, supra,* 75 Cal. App. 4th at 180. Do you agree that the *Woo* court's rule is the better rule? Why?

(4) *Doe Defendant Practice and the Delayed Discovery Rule.* As the above discussion indicates, there is no requirement in using CCP § 474 that a plaintiff must exercise reasonable diligence in discovering either the true identity of fictitious defendants or facts giving rise to a cause of action against such persons. *See also Joslin v. H.A.S. Ins. Broker,* 184 Cal. App. 3d 369, 228 Cal. Rptr. 878 (1986); *Munoz v. Purdy,* 91 Cal. App. 3d 942, 154 Cal. Rptr. 472 (1979). There is no such requirement *before* the original complaint is filed, nor *after* the original complaint is filed. *See, e.g., Streicher v. Tommy's Electric Co., supra; General Motors Corp. v. Superior Court,* 48 Cal. App. 4th 580, 55 Cal. Rptr. 2d 871 (1996).

Under the delayed discovery rule, the statute of limitations begins to run "when the plaintiff suspects or should suspect that her injury was caused by wrongdoing, that someone has done something wrong to her." *Jolly v. Eli Lilly & Co.* 44 Cal. 3d 1103, 1110, 245 Cal. Rptr. 658, 751 P.2d 923 (1988). Once the plaintiff has a suspicion of wrongdoing, and therefore an incentive to sue, she must decide whether to file suit or sit on her rights. "So long as a suspicion exists, it is clear that the plaintiff must go find the facts; she cannot wait for the facts to find her." *Jolly, supra,* 44 Cal. 3d at 1111. Ignorance of the legal significance of known facts or the identity of the wrongdoer will not delay the running of the statute. *Id.* at 1114.

How is the no-duty-of-diligence standard of California's Doe defendant practice consistent with duty-of-diligence requirement imposed by California's delayed discovery rule? *See General Motors Corp. v. Superior Court, supra,* 48 Cal. App. 4th at 595–96 (Discussing the delayed discovery rule and Doe defendant practice, and concluding that section 474 does not impose a duty of inquiry); *Munoz v. Purdy, supra,* 91 Cal. App. 3d at 947–48 (Observing that "the interjection of a discovery standard into section 474 would lead to the harmful practice in all litigation of requiring that all persons who might conceivably have some connection with the lawsuit be specifically named in order to avoid the sanctions of the failure to comply with the inquiry requirements of section 474").

(5) *Time Limits for Service of the Amended Complaint.* Under California's Doe defendant practice, the amended complaint must be served upon the (actual) defendant within the maximum period of three years from the date of the filing of the original complaint. CCP § 583.210. However, due to various state and local "fast track" rules adopted pursuant to the Trial Court Delay Reduction Act of 1986, Gov. Code § 68600 *et seq.,* the time within which to serve a complaint may be significantly less than three years. For example, Rule 3.110(b) of the California Rules of Court requires service of the complaint on all named defendants, and proofs of service filed, within 60 days

after the filing of the complaint, unless the court orders an extension of time. Rule 3.110(b) also provides that when a complaint is amended to add defendant, the added a defendant must be served within 30 days after the filing of the amended complaint. However, the current version of the Trial Court Delay Reduction Act provides that Doe defendants may not be dismissed prior to the conclusion of the introduction of evidence at trial, except on stipulation or motion of the parties. Gov. Code § 68616(h).

(6) *Federal Rule 15(c)(3) Compared.* Under Rule 15(c)(3) of the Federal Rules of Civil Procedure, an amended complaint adding a new party may relate back only if the newly named defendant had timely notice of the original complaint (*i.e.*, generally, within 90 days of filing of the original complaint) and knows his omission from the original complaint was due to a naming mistake by the plaintiff. How does federal Rule 15(c)(3) differ from California's Doe defendant practice? For a discussion of these differences, *see* Walter W. Heiser, *Relation Back of Amended Complaints: The California Courts Should Adopt a More Pragmatic Approach*, 44 Santa Clara L. Rev. 643, 678–83 (2004).

(7) *Federal Court Application.* Rule 15(c)(1) of the Federal Rules of Civil Procedure, added in 1991, authorizes relation back of an amended complaint in federal court whenever permitted "by the law that provides the statute of limitations applicable to the action." Essentially, if state law provides the controlling statute of limitations and affords a more forgiving principle of relation back than is provided under federal Rules 15(c)(2) and (3), the state doctrine should be available to save the cause of action. This means that where California law provides the statute of limitations applicable to a cause of action in federal court, the California fictitious ("Doe") defendant doctrine is authorized for that action. *See* David D. Siegel, *The Recent (Dec. 1, 1991) Changes in the Federal Rules of Civil Procedure*, 142 F.R.D. 359, 362–66 (1992).

C. Demurrers

1. General and Special Demurrers

A demurrer presents an objection to a complaint, cross-complaint, or answer when the ground for objection appears on the face of such pleading, and from any matter of which the court may take judicial notice. CCP § 430.30(a). When any ground for objection to a complaint or cross-complaint does not appear on the face of the pleading, the objection may be taken by answer. CCP § 430.30(b). A party objecting to a complaint or cross-complaint may demur and answer at the same time. § 430.30(c).

The grounds for objection to a complaint or cross-complaint are set forth in CCP § 430.10, which provides:

> The party against whom a complaint or cross-complaint has been filed may object, by demurrer or answer as provided in Section 430.30, to the pleading on any one or more of the following grounds:

(a) The court has no jurisdiction of the subject of the cause of action alleged in the pleading.

(b) The person who filed the pleading does not have the legal capacity to sue.

(c) There is another action pending between the same parties on the same cause of action.

(d) There is a defect or misjoinder of parties.

(e) The pleading does not state facts sufficient to constitute a cause of action.

(f) The pleading is uncertain. As used in this subdivision, "uncertain" includes ambiguous and unintelligible.

(g) In an action founded upon a contract, it cannot be ascertained from the pleading whether the contract is written, is oral, or is implied by conduct.

(h) No certificate was filed as required by Section 411.35 [Malpractice action against architect or engineer].

(i) No certificate was filed as required by Section 411.36 [Association action for negligence against licensed contractor].

Notes and Questions Regarding Demurrers

(1) *General and Specific Demurrers.* The statutes do not distinguish between "general" and "special" demurrers, but courts and attorneys usually do. *See* 5 Witkin, California Procedure, Pleading §§ 951–953 (5th ed. 2008) (citing cases). A demurrer on the ground that the pleading does not state facts sufficient to constitute a cause of action, CCP § 430.10(e), is typically referred to as a "general demurrer"; one based on any other ground stated in CCP § 430.10 as a "special demurrer."

(2) *Waiver.* A party must demur to a complaint or cross-complaint within 30 days after service, and to an answer within 10 days. CCP § 430.40. Failure to timely object to a pleading by demurrer or answer constitutes a waiver of all grounds for objection except an objection that the court lacks subject matter jurisdiction or that the pleading does not state facts sufficient to constitute a cause of action or a defense. CCP § 430.80; *see Collins v. Rocha*, 7 Cal. 3d 232, 239, 102 Cal. Rptr. 1, 497 P.2d 225 (1972) (Defendant's failure to raise uncertainty of complaint by a timely special demurrer deemed a waiver of such pleading defect). When a demurrer is sustained, the court must state in the order the specific grounds upon which the decision is based. CCP § 472d.

(3) *Standards for General Demurrers.* A demurrer does not test the truth of the allegations in a pleading, only the legal sufficiency of the pleading. *Committee on Children's Television, Inc. v. General Foods Corp.*, 35 Cal. 3d 197, 197 Cal. Rptr. 783, 673 P.2d 660 (1983). The court must "assume the truth of all properly pleaded material allegations of the complaint and give it a reasonable interpretation by reading it as a whole and its parts in their context." *Phillips v. Desert Hospital District*, 49 Cal. 3d 699, 702, 263 Cal. Rptr. 119, 780 P.2d 349 (1989). Consequently, a demurrer must be denied where the factual allegations state a cause of action but the defendant contests their accuracy. *See Committee on Children's Television, Inc., supra* (Defendants'

contention that the words and images of their television commercials were not misrepresentations, as plaintiffs had alleged in the complaint, framed a factual issue for resolution by trial, not demurrer).

(4) *Amendment after Sustained Demurrer.* An order sustaining a demurrer *without leave to amend* will constitute an abuse of discretion if there is any reasonable possibility that the defect can be cured by an amendment. *Cooper v. Leslie Salt Co.*, 70 Cal. 2d 627, 636, 75 Cal. Rptr. 766, 451 P.2d 406 (1969); *Goodman v. Kennedy*, 18 Cal. 3d 335, 349, 134 Cal. Rptr. 375, 556 P.2d 737 (1976). To meet the plaintiff's burden of showing abuse of discretion, the plaintiff must show how the complaint can be amended to state a cause of action. *Goodman v. Kennedy, supra.*

D. Answers

1. Introductory Note

A defendant served with a complaint has three principal choices: (1) do nothing and risk entry of default and a default judgment; (2) attack the complaint and seek a partial or complete dismissal of the action through use of the demurrer and other related motions; or (3) respond to the complaint on its own terms through the answer. Conceptually, preparing and filing an answer is the normal procedural response; whether in practice it is the most common response is not at all clear.

The answer is a pleading, just like the complaint, that responds to the allegations in the complaint. Except in those few instances where a defending party can file a general denial (*see* CCP § 431.40(a)), answers contain three types of responses. First, portions of the complaint may be admitted, either by express admission or by failure to deny. *See* CCP §§ 431.30(f), 431.20(a). Second, allegations in the complaint may be controverted by general or specific denial (§ 431.30(b)(1)), on the basis of information or belief (§ 431.30(d) & (f)), or on the ground of lack of information or belief (§ 431.30(d) & (e)). When the complaint is verified, the answer must also be verified. CCP § 446. Third, the answer may respond by stating defenses (usually called "affirmative defenses") that provide a defense to the complaint even if its allegations are true. *See* CCP § 431.30(b)(2) & (g).

Affirmative Relief. If the defending party seeks affirmative relief against the party filing the complaint, the defending party must proceed by separate cross-complaint. CCP §§ 431.30(c), 428.10(a), 428.40. The requirement of a separate cross-complaint differs from the federal practice that combines answers and counterclaims (but not third-party complaints, also called cross-complaints under California law) in the same pleading. *See* Rules 13 and 14, F.R.C.P.

Failure to Deny Constitutes an Admission. "Every material allegation of the complaint or cross-complaint, not controverted by the answer, shall, for purposes of the action, be taken as true." CCP § 431.20(a). Failure to properly deny a material allegation therefore constitutes an admission. *Valerio v. Andrew Youngquist Construction*, 103 Cal. App. 4th 1264, 1271–72, 127 Cal. Rptr. 2d 436 (2002).

2. Raising "New Matter"

An answer must contain a statement of any "new matter" constituting a defense. CCP § 431.30(b)(2). Each defense must be separately stated and separately numbered. CCP § 431.30(g); Rule 2.112, Cal. Rules of Ct.

Affirmative Defenses. New matter constituting an affirmative defense must be stated in the answer; failure to plead an affirmative defense waives that defense. *See, e.g., Hulsey v. Koehler,* 218 Cal. App. 3d 1150, 267 Cal. Rptr. 523 (1990) (Failure to assert a compulsory cross-complaint in prior action is a special defense which, like res judicata, is waived if not raised in the instant action); *Minton v. Cavaney,* 56 Cal. 2d 576, 581, 15 Cal. Rptr. 641, 364 P.2d 473 (1961) (Defendant waived statute of limitations defense by failing to plead that defense in the answer or by demurrer).

The reply is not recognized as a pleading in California. CCP § 411.10. Consequently, a plaintiff does not reply to affirmative defenses raised in defendant's answer to the complaint; affirmative defenses are deemed controverted and a plaintiff may introduce evidence on the issue at trial. CCP § 431.20(b); *see, e.g., Aerojet General Corp. v. Superior Court,* 177 Cal. App. 3d 950, 953, 223 Cal. Rptr. 249 (1986) (Plaintiff need not answer affirmative defense of statute of limitations raised in defendant's answer in order to contest this defense at trial).

What Constitutes "New Matter"? Under CCP § 431.30(b)(2), the answer to a complaint must include "[a] statement of any new matter constituting a defense." The phrase "new matter" refers to something relied on by a defendant which is not put in issue by the plaintiff. *State Farm Mutual Auto Ins. Co. v. Superior Court,* 228 Cal. App. 3d 721, 725, 279 Cal. Rptr. 116 (1991). Thus, where matters are not responsive to allegations of the complaint, they must be raised in the answer as "new matter." *Id.* Where, however, the answer sets forth facts showing some essential allegation of the complaint is not true, such facts are not "new matter" but only a traverse. *Id.* Accordingly, what is put in issue by a denial is limited to the allegations of the complaint.

Chapter IV

The Proper Court

A. Subject Matter Jurisdiction

1. California Trial Court Unification

Prior to 1998, California's trial courts consisted of superior and municipal courts, each with its own jurisdiction and number of judges fixed by the Legislature. In June of 1998, California voters approved Proposition 220 and thereby amended the California Constitution to permit superior and municipal courts within a county to consolidate their operations if approved by a majority of the superior court judges and a majority of the municipal court judges within that county. Cal. Const., Art. I, § 5(e) (1998). In counties that vote for unification, there will be only a superior court, Cal. Const., Art. I, § 5(e); the judgeships in each municipal court in that county are abolished and previously selected municipal court judges will become judges of the superior court in that county. Cal. Const., Art. 23, § 23(b). By March 2001, all 58 counties in California have voted to unify their municipal and superior courts into a single superior court.

Subsequently, in November of 2002, the California voters approved Proposition 48 and again amended the California Constitution, this time to eliminate references to the constitutional authority to vest judicial power in the municipal courts. Cal. Const. Art. VI, § 5 (repealed), § 6, § 8, § 16 & § 23. As a result of these constitutional amendments, the superior court now has jurisdiction in all matters that were previously under the jurisdiction of either the superior or municipal courts. Cal. Const., Art. VI, § 10. Even after unification, however, the jurisdictional differences between the superior courts and the former municipal courts remain relevant for purposes of certain trial court procedures, such as the size of the jury, and for purposes of the proper court for appellate review. Cal. Const., Art. I, § 16; Art. VI, § 11.

The Courts of Appeal have appellate jurisdiction as to the type of cases that were within the original jurisdiction of the superior courts on June 30, 1995, and in other cases as prescribed by statute. Cal. Const., Art. VI, § 11. As to all other cases, referred to in the legislation implementing Prop. 220 as "limited civil cases," the appellate division of the superior court has appellate jurisdiction. Cal. Const., Art. VI, § 11; CCP §§ 77–86, § 904.2. Under the current statutory scheme, the definition of "limited civil cases" corresponds to the type of cases that could only be heard in municipal court prior to unification, *i.e.*, generally, civil cases in which the amount in controversy is $25,000 or less. CCP § 86. The Legislature has the authority to change appellate jurisdiction of the Courts of Appeal, and therefore necessarily of the appellate division of the superior court, by changing the jurisdictional amount in controversy. Cal. Const., Art. VI, § 11.

2. "Limited" and "Unlimited" Civil Actions

Limited Civil Case. Generally speaking, a "limited civil case" is an action in which the amount in controversy does not exceed $25,000. CCP §§ 85(a), 86(a) (designating various specific actions as limited civil cases). An "unlimited civil case" is an action which seeks more than $25,000, CCP § 88; or one designated as an unlimited civil case by statute regardless of the amount in controversy. *See, e.g.,* Family Code §§ 200, 4900–4976, 8500–9206 (dissolution of marriage, adoption, and support proceedings); Probate Code §§ 2200, 7050 (guardianship, conservatorship, and probate proceedings); CCP § 1250.010 (eminent domain proceedings).

Although the procedural laws applicable to civil actions generally also apply to limited civil cases, CCP § 90; there are some provisions applicable only to limited civil cases. These include limitations on pleadings, CCP § 92; simplified discovery, CCP §§ 93–96; admissibility of affidavits or declarations in lieu of direct testimony, CCP § 98; lower filing fees, Gov. Code § 72055; and appeal to the appellate division of the superior court instead of the court of appeal, CCP § 904.2.

Reclassification. The clerk makes the initial jurisdictional classification of a civil case based on the plaintiff's classification designation in the caption of the complaint. CCP § 422.30(b); Rule 2.111(10), Cal. Rules of Ct. A party or the court on its own motion may move for reclassification of a case that is erroneously classified. CCP § 403.040. If a party files an amended pleading or a cross-complaint that causes the action to exceed the maximum amount in controversy or otherwise fail to satisfy the requirements for a limited civil case, and pays a reclassification fee, the clerk must change the jurisdictional classification from limited to unlimited. CCP §§ 403.020, 403.030. *See also* CCP § 403.050 (reclassification pursuant to parties' stipulation).

Amount in Controversy. The "amount in controversy" means the amount of the demand, or the recovery sought, or the value of the property, that is in controversy in an action, "exclusive of attorneys' fees, interest, and costs." CCP § 85(a). When a single plaintiff alleges multiple causes of action against a single defendant, the demands of all the claims are aggregated in computing the amount in controversy. *Hammell v. Superior Court,* 217 Cal. 5, 7–8, 17 P.2d 101 (1932).

Judgment Below Classification Minimum Amount. When a good faith demand in a complaint exceeds the amount necessary for classification as an unlimited civil case but the subsequent judgment is one that could have been rendered in a limited civil case, the court is not required to reclassify the action as a limited civil action but may refuse to award costs to the prevailing plaintiff. CCP §§ 403.040(e), 1033(a). When a plaintiff in a limited civil case recovers an amount within the jurisdictional limit of the small claims court, the court may deny costs to the prevailing plaintiff or may allow them in any amount it deems proper. CCP § 1033(b).

Small Claims Court. Each superior court must have a small claims division. CCP § 116.210. Generally speaking, the small claims court has jurisdiction in actions for recovery of money if the amount of the demand does not exceed $10,000 in an action brought by a natural person, and $5,000 with respect to actions brought by most other plaintiffs. CCP §§ 116.221, 116.220(a). In such actions, CCP § 116.220(b) also authorizes the court to grant equitable relief in the form of rescission, restitution, reformation, and specific performance. Is the small claims courts' jurisdiction exclusive or concurrent with the superior courts' on matters where the demand does not exceed $10,000? *See* CCP §§ 85(a), 86(a) and the discussion of "limited civil cases," *supra*.

A plaintiff who files an action in small claims court waives any damages above the jurisdictional limit. CCP § 116.220(d). A plaintiff who litigates in small claims court has no right to appeal the judgment on the plaintiff's claim. CCP § 116.710(a). However, the defendant with respect to the plaintiff's claim, and a plaintiff with respect to a claim of the defendant, may appeal the judgment to the superior court. CCP § 116.710(b). The appeal consists of a trial de novo before a superior court judge. CCP § 116.770.

B. Personal Jurisdiction

1. The California Long-Arm Statute

Unlike many states which limit the bases of their courts' personal jurisdiction by reference to specific statutory categories, the California long-arm statute, CCP § 410.10, broadly states that, "[a] court of this state may exercise jurisdiction on any basis not inconsistent with the Constitution of this state or of the United States." Section 410.10 manifests the intent that California courts exercise the broadest possible jurisdiction over nonresidents, limited only by constitutional considerations. *Sibley v. Superior Court*, 16 Cal. 3d 442, 445, 128 Cal. Rptr. 34, 546 P.2d 322 (1976).

2. Due Process: Minimum Contacts — General vs. Specific Jurisdiction

In *Vons Companies, Inc. v. Seabest Foods, Inc.*, 14 Cal. 4th 434, 58 Cal. Rptr. 2d 899, 926 P.2d 1085 (1996), the California Supreme Court attempted to clarify the personal jurisdiction concept of "specific jurisdiction" by defining the circumstances under which a cause of action "arises out of or relates to" a defendant's contacts with the forum. This was not an easy task — the court's discussion of this due process issue covers nearly 30 pages. *See Vons, supra*, 14 Cal. 4th at 446–75.

The main focus of the Court's analysis in *Vons* was on the nature of the nexus between the defendant's forum activities and the plaintiff's cause of action. The defendant in *Vons* had argued for the adoption of the proximate cause test formulated by the Court of Appeal, *i.e.*, unless the defendant's forum contacts *proximately caused* the occurrence that injured the plaintiff, the connection between the contacts and the claim is insufficient to permit the exercise of specific jurisdiction. *Vons, supra*, 14 Cal.

4th at 460–62. The Supreme Court rejected the proximate cause test as too narrow and as inconsistent with fairness rationale underlying the specific jurisdiction doctrine. *Id. at* 462–64. Likewise, the Supreme Court rejected as overly restrictive a similar test proffered by the defendant, referred to as the substantive relevance test. *Id.*

The plaintiff in *Vons* argued that the required relationship between the defendant's forum contacts and the plaintiff's cause of action should be determined by an expansive "but for" test, which focuses on whether the plaintiff's injury would have occurred "but for" the defendant's forum contacts. *Vons, supra,* 14 Cal. 4th at 464–66. The plaintiff pointed out that the U.S. Court of Appeals for the Ninth Circuit employed the "but for" test in its specific jurisdiction analysis in *Shute v. Carnival Cruise Lines,* 897 F.2d 377, 385 (9th Cir. 1990), and *Ballard v. Savage,* 65 F.3d 1495, 1500 (9th Cir. 1995). Despite the federal court precedent, the Supreme Court in *Vons* determined that the "but for" test was too broad and amorphous. *Vons, supra,* 14 Cal. 4th at 467–68. The *Vons* court wryly observed that "if the defendant is a lawyer who was received his or her legal education in the forum, that legal education may be said to be a 'but for' cause of any malpractice the lawyer commits anywhere in the nation, yet it hardly seems a sufficient basis for the forum to exercise jurisdiction." *Id.,* at 467.

The Supreme Court ultimately concluded in *Vons* that the appropriate inquiry for specific jurisdiction was whether the plaintiff's cause of action has a "substantial connection" with the defendant's forum activities, and defined "substantial connection" by reference to the facts of an earlier California Supreme Court decision, *Cornelison v. Chaney,* 16 Cal. 3d 143, 127 Cal. Rptr. 352, 545 P.2d 264 (1976):

> A claim need not arise directly from the defendant's forum contacts in order to be sufficiently related to the contact to warrant the exercise of specific jurisdiction. Rather, as long as the claim bears a substantial connection to the nonresident's forum contacts, the exercise of specific jurisdiction is appropriate. The due process clause is concerned with protecting nonresident defendants from being brought unfairly into court in the forum, on the basis of random contacts. That constitutional provision, however, does not provide defendants with a shield against jurisdiction when the defendant purposefully has availed himself or herself of benefits in the forum. The goal of fairness is well served by the standard we originally set out in *Cornelison, supra,* 16 Cal. 3d 143, that is, there must be a *substantial connection* between the forum contacts and the plaintiff's claim to warrant the exercise of specific jurisdiction. (*Id.* at p. 148.) * * *

> [I]n *Cornelison* . . . we held that a California resident could sue a Nebraska defendant in California for wrongful death in connection with an accident that occurred in Nevada. Because the defendant was engaged in the business of hauling goods by truck and made fairly frequent deliveries in California, and the accident occurred while he was en route to California for further deliveries, we found a "substantial nexus between plaintiff's cause of action and defendant's activities in California." (*Id.* at p. 149.) We explained that

the appropriate inquiry is whether the plaintiff's cause of action "arises out of or has a substantial connection with a business relationship defendant has purposefully established with California." (*Ibid.*) We commented that if, as we found, the defendant's activities are not so wide ranging as to justify general jurisdiction, "then jurisdiction depends upon the quality and nature of his activity in the forum *in relation* to the particular cause of action. In such a situation, the cause of action must arise out of an act done or transaction consummated in the forum, or defendant must perform some other act by which he purposefully avails himself of the privilege of conducting activities in the forum, thereby invoking the benefits and protections of its laws. Thus, as the relationship of the defendant with the state seeking to exercise jurisdiction over him grows more tenuous, the scope of jurisdiction also retracts, and fairness is assured by limiting the circumstances under which the plaintiff can compel him to appear and defend. The crucial inquiry concerns the character of defendant's activity in the forum, whether the cause of action *arises out of or has a substantial connection* with that activity, and upon the balancing of the convenience of the parties and the interests of the state in assuming jurisdiction." (*Id.* at pp. 147–148, fn. omitted, italics added, citing *Hanson v. Denckla* (1958) 357 U.S. 235, 250–253 [78 S. Ct. 1228, 2 L. Ed. 2d 1283, 1295–1298];....)

The Court of Appeal below focused on an asserted lack of relationship between [plaintiff] Vons, on the one hand, and [defendants] Seabest and WRMI, on the other. The court suggested this lack of relationship was critical in determining whether the claim was sufficiently related to the forum contacts to permit the exercise of specific jurisdiction in California. Contrary to the Court of Appeal's thesis, however, the defendant's forum activities need not be directed at the plaintiff in order to give rise to specific jurisdiction. (*See, e.g., Keeton v. Hustler Magazine, Inc.* (1984) 465 U.S. 770, 775 [104 S. Ct. 1473, 79 L. Ed. 2d 790, 798] [publisher that distributes magazines to the public in a distant state may be held accountable in that forum for damage to victim of defamation]; *Cornelison, supra*, 16 Cal. 3d 143 [jurisdiction found although the defendant's business activities in California were not directed at the accident victim]; ...)

The United States Supreme Court has stated more than once that the nexus required to establish specific jurisdiction is between the defendant, *the forum*, and the litigation (*Helicopteros [Nacionales de Columbia v. Hall]*, *supra*, 466 U.S. at p. 411 [80 L. Ed. 2d at p. 409]; *Shaffer v. Heitner* (1977) 433 U.S. 186, 204 [97 S. Ct. 2569, 53 L. Ed. 2d 683, 697–698]) — not between the plaintiff and the defendant. For the purpose of deciding whether a defendant has minimum contacts or purposefully has availed itself of forum benefits, the relevant contacts are said to be with *the forum*, because it is the defendant's choice to take advantage of opportunities that exist in the forum that subjects it to jurisdiction. (*Asahi Metal Industry Co. v. Superior Court*

(1987) 480 U.S. 102, 112 [107 S. Ct. 1026, 94 L. Ed. 2d 92, 104–105] (plur. opn. by O'Connor, J.); *Burger King [Corp. v. Rudzewics], supra,* 471 U.S. at pp. 475, 479 [85 L. Ed. 2d at pp. 542, 545]; *Helicopteros, supra,* 466 U.S. at p. 414 [80 L. Ed. 2d at p. 409]; *Shaffer v. Heitner, supra,* 433 U.S. at p. 204 [53 L. Ed. 2d at pp. 697–698].)

Vons, supra, 14 Cal. 4th at 457–58 (italics in original).

Notes and Questions Regarding Vons

(1) General jurisdiction refers to those cases in which the plaintiff's cause of action did not "arise out of or relate to" the defendant's forum activities, and therefore requires that the defendant's affiliations with the forum state are so "continuous and systematic" as to render the defendant essentially at home in the forum state. *See Daimler AG v. Bauman,* 571 U.S. 117, 134 S. Ct. 746, 187 L. Ed. 2d 624 (2014) (noting that for an individual, the paradigm forum for the exercise of general jurisdiction is the individual's domicile; for a corporation, the place of incorporation and the principle place of business). In light of the liberal definition of specific jurisdiction in *Vons,* under what circumstances must a plaintiff in a California court rely (only) on the concept of general jurisdiction?

(2) The recent United States Supreme Court decision in *Bristol-Myers Squibb Co. v. Superior Court,* 582 U.S. ___, 137 S. Ct. 1773, 198 L. Ed. 2d 395 (2017), casts doubt on the propriety of the liberal definition of specific jurisdiction adopted by the California Supreme Court in *Vons.* In *Bristol-Myers Squibb,* a group of plaintiffs—consisting of 86 California residents and 592 from 33 other states—asserted a variety of state law claims based on personal injuries allegedly caused by defendant Bristol-Myers Squibb's drug Plavix, a prescription blood thinner. The nonresident plaintiffs did not allege that they obtained Plavix through California physicians or from any other California source; nor did they claim that they were injured by Plavix, or were treated for their injuries, in California.

The defendant filed a motion to quash based on lack of personal jurisdiction with respect to the nonresident plaintiffs, which the Superior Court denied. The California Supreme Court affirmed, applying a sliding scale approach to specific jurisdiction. Under the California approach, the strength of the requisite "substantial connection" between the forum and the plaintiff's claims was relaxed if the defendant had extensive forum contacts unrelated to those claims. *See Bristol-Myers Squibb Co. v. Superior Court,* 1 Cal. 5th 783, 806 (quoting *Vons, supra,* 14 Cal. 4th at 455), *rev'd,* 137 S. Ct. 1773 (2017). The United States Supreme Court rejected this "sliding scale" approach, with the following explanation:

> In order for a court to exercise specific jurisdiction over a claim, there must be an "affiliation between the forum and the underlying controversy, principally, [an] activity or an occurrence that takes place in the forum State." * * * When there is no such connection, specific jurisdiction is lacking regardless of the extent of a defendant's unconnected activities in the State. * * *

For this reason, the California Supreme Court's "sliding scale approach" is difficult to square with our precedents. Under the California approach, the strength of the requisite connection between the forum and the specific claims at issue is relaxed if the defendant has extensive forum contacts that are unrelated to those claims. Our cases provide no support for this approach, which resembles a loose and spurious form of general jurisdiction. For specific jurisdiction, a defendant's general connections with the forum are not enough. As we have said, "[a] corporation's 'continuous activity of some sorts within a state . . . is not enough to support the demand that the corporation be amenable to suits unrelated to that activity.'" * * *

The present case illustrates the danger of the California approach. The State Supreme Court found that specific jurisdiction was present without identifying any adequate link between the State and the nonresidents' claims. As noted, the nonresidents were not prescribed Plavix in California, did not purchase Plavix in California, did not ingest Plavix in California, and were not injured by Plavix in California. The mere fact that other plaintiffs were prescribed, obtained, and ingested Plavix in California–and allegedly sustained the same injuries as did the nonresidents–does not allow the State to assert specific jurisdiction over the nonresidents' claims. * * * What is needed–and what is missing here–is a connection between the forum and the specific claims at issue.

In today's case,[t]he relevant plaintiffs are not California residents and do not claim to have suffered harm in that State. In addition, . . . all the conduct giving rise to the nonresidents' claims occurred elsewhere. It follows that the California courts cannot claim specific jurisdiction. * * * The judgment of the California Supreme Court is reversed.

Bristol-Myers Squibb, supra, 137 S. Ct. at 1781–82. Is the exercise of specific jurisdiction in *Vons* consistent with holding in *Bristol-Myers Squibb*? How about the exercise of specific jurisdiction in *Cornelison*? Can these two California Supreme Court cases be distinguished from *Bristol-Myers Squibb* based on the facts of each case? How so?

(3) More recently in *Ford Motor Co. v. Montana Eighth Judicial District Court*, ___ U.S. ___, 141 S. Ct. 1017, 209 L. Ed. 2d 225 (2021), the United States Supreme Court again applied the doctrine of specific (or "case-linked") jurisdiction in a products liability action. *Ford Motor* involved two single-car accidents involving Ford vehicles. One accident occurred in Montana, causing the death of the plaintiff, a Montana resident. The other occurred in Minnesota, seriously injuring a Minnesota resident. Each plaintiff sued Ford Motor in a state court of the state where the accident occurred (and the state of his/her residence). Defendant Ford moved to dismiss the two suits for lack of personal jurisdiction, on the grounds that the vehicles were not designed or manufactured, and the two vehicles involved in the accidents were not sold to the plaintiffs, in the forum states. Ford conceded that it does substantial business in the two forum states thereby purposely availing itself of the privilege of

conducting activities in each state, but that these activities were not sufficiently connected to plaintiffs' suits. The Supreme Court rejected Ford's arguments, and in doing so distinguished *Bristol-Myers*, 582 U.S. ___, 137 S. Ct. 1773, 198 L. Ed. 2d 395 (2017), with the following explanation:

> * * * Ford's causation-only approach finds no support in this Court's requirement of a "connection" between a plaintiff's suit and a defendant's activities. That rule indeed serves to narrow the class of claims over which a state court may exercise specific jurisdiction. But not quite so far as Ford wants. None of our precedents has suggested that only a strict causal relationship between the defendant's in-state activity and the litigation will do. As just noted, our most common formulation of the rule demands that the suit "arise out of *or relate to* the defendant's contacts with the forum." The first half of that standard asks about causation; but the back half, after the "or," contemplates that some relationships will support jurisdiction without a causal showing. That does not mean anything goes. In the sphere of specific jurisdiction, the phrase "relate to" incorporates real limits, as it must to adequately protect defendants foreign to a forum. But again, we have never framed the specific jurisdiction inquiry as always requiring proof of causation—*i.e.*, proof that the plaintiff's claim came about because of the defendant's in-state conduct.
> * * *

And indeed, this Court has stated that specific jurisdiction attaches in cases identical to the ones here—when a company like Ford serves a market for a product in the forum State and the product malfunctions there. In *World-Wide Volkswagen [Corp. v. Woodson]*, the Court held that an Oklahoma court could not assert jurisdiction over a New York car dealer just because a car it sold later caught fire in Oklahoma. 444 U. S., at 295, 100 S. Ct. 559, 62 L. Ed. 2d 490. But in so doing, we contrasted the dealer's position to that of two other defendants—Audi, the car's manufacturer, and Volkswagen, the car's nationwide importer (neither of which contested jurisdiction):

> "[I]f the sale of a product of a manufacturer or distributor such as Audi or Volkswagen is not simply an isolated occurrence, but arises from the efforts of the manufacturer or distributor to serve, directly or indirectly, the market for its product in [several or all] other States, it is not unreasonable to subject it to suit in one of those States if its allegedly defective merchandise has there been the source of injury to its owner or to others." *Id.*, at 297, 100 S. Ct. 559, 62 L. Ed. 2d 490.

* * * [I]n *World-Wide Volkswagen*, the Court did not limit jurisdiction to where the car was designed, manufactured, or first sold. * * *

Now turn to how [defendant Ford's] Montana- and Minnesota-based conduct relates to the claims in these cases, brought by state residents in Montana's and Minnesota's courts. Each plaintiff's suit, of course, arises from a car accident in one of those States. In each complaint, the resident-plaintiff alleges that a defective Ford vehicle—an Explorer in one, a Crown Victoria in the other—caused the crash and resulting harm. * * * Ford had advertised, sold, and serviced those two car models in both States for many years. In other words, Ford had systematically served a market in Montana and Minnesota for the very vehicles that the plaintiffs allege malfunctioned and injured them in those States. So there is a strong "relationship among the defendant, the forum, and the litigation"—the "essential foundation" of specific jurisdiction. That is why this Court has used this exact fact pattern (a resident-plaintiff sues a global car company, extensively serving the state market in a vehicle, for an in-state accident) as an illustration—even a paradigm example—of how specific jurisdiction works. * * *

Ford says of *Bristol-Myers* that it "squarely foreclose[s]" jurisdiction. In that case, non-resident plaintiffs brought claims in California state court against Bristol-Myers Squibb, the manufacturer of a nationally marketed prescription drug called Plavix. The plaintiffs had not bought Plavix in California; neither had they used or suffered any harm from the drug there. Still, the California Supreme Court thought it could exercise jurisdiction because Bristol-Myers Squibb sold Plavix in California and was defending there against identical claims brought by the State's residents. This Court disagreed, holding that the exercise of jurisdiction violated the Fourteenth Amendment. In Ford's view, the same must be true here. Each of these plaintiffs, like the plaintiffs in *Bristol-Myers*, alleged injury from a particular item (a car, a pill) that the defendant had sold outside the forum State. Ford reads *Bristol-Myers* to preclude jurisdiction when that is true, even if the defendant regularly sold "the same kind of product" in the State.

But that reading misses the point of our decision. We found jurisdiction improper in *Bristol-Myers* because the forum State, and the defendant's activities there, lacked any connection to the plaintiffs' claims. See 582 U.S., at ___, 137 S. Ct. 1773, 198 L. Ed. 2d 395, 405 ("What is needed—and what is missing here—is a connection between the forum and the specific claims at issue"). The plaintiffs, the Court explained, were not residents of California. They had not been prescribed Plavix in California. They had not ingested Plavix in California. And they had not sustained their injuries in California. In short, the plaintiffs were engaged in forum-shopping—suing in California because it was thought plaintiff-friendly, even though their cases had no tie to the State. That is not at all true of the cases before us. Yes, Ford sold the specific products in other States, as Bristol-Myers Squibb had. But here, the plaintiffs are residents of the forum States. They used the allegedly defective products in the forum States. And they suffered injuries when those products malfunctioned in the forum States. In sum, each of the plaintiffs brought suit in the most natural State—based on an "affiliation between the forum and the underlying controversy, principally, [an] activity or an occurrence that t[ook] place" there. *Bristol-Myers*, 137 S. Ct. 1773, 198 L. Ed. 2d 395, 399, 403–404 (internal quotation marks omitted). So Bristol-Myers does not bar jurisdiction. * * *

Ford Motor, *supra*, 141 S. Ct. at 1026–1031. Is the exercise of specific jurisdiction in Vons consistent with the holding in *Ford Motor*? How about the exercise of specific jurisdiction in *Cornelison*?

3. Due Process: The "Effects" Test

Pavlovich v. Superior Court

Supreme Court of California

29 Cal. 4th 262, 127 Cal. Rptr. 2d 329, 58 P.3d 2 (2002)

BROWN, JUSTICE.

[T]he so-called Internet revolution has spawned a host of new legal issues as courts have struggled to apply traditional legal frameworks to this new communication medium. Today, we join this struggle and consider the impact of the Internet on the determination of personal jurisdiction. In this case, a California court exercised personal jurisdiction over a defendant based on a posting on an Internet Web site. Under the particular facts of this case, we conclude the court's exercise of jurisdiction was improper.

I.

Digital versatile discs (DVD's) "provide high quality images, such as motion pictures, digitally formatted on a convenient 5-inch disc. . . ." Before the commercial release of DVD's containing motion pictures, the Content Scrambling System (CSS), a system used to encrypt and protect copyrighted motion pictures on DVD's, was developed. The CSS technology prevents the playing or copying of copyrighted motion pictures on DVD's without the algorithms and keys necessary to decrypt the data stored on the disc.

[Plaintiff] DVD Copy Control Association, Inc. (DVD CCA) is a nonprofit trade association organized under the laws of the State of Delaware with its principal place of business in California. The DVD industry created DVD CCA in December 1998 to control and administer licensing of the CSS technology. In September 1999, DVD CCA hired its staff, and, in December 1999, it began administering the licenses. Soon thereafter, DVD CCA acquired the licensing rights to the CSS technology and became the sole licensing entity for this technology in the DVD video format.

[Defendant] Matthew Pavlovich is currently a resident of Texas and the president of Media Driver, LLC, a technology consulting company in Texas. . . . Pavlovich does not reside or work in California. He has never had a place of business, telephone listing, or bank account in California and has never owned property in California. Neither Pavlovich nor his company has solicited any business in California or has any business contacts in California.

... Pavlovich was the founder and project leader of the LiVid video project (LiVid), which operated a Web site located at "livid.on.openprojects.net." The site consisted of a single page with text and links to other Web sites. The site only provided information; it did not solicit or transact any business and permitted no interactive exchange of information between its operators and visitors.

According to Pavlovich, the goal of LiVid was "to improve video and DVD support for Linux and to ... combine the resources and the efforts of the various individuals that were working on related things. . . ." To reach this goal, the project sought to defeat the CSS technology and enable the decryption and copying of DVD's containing motion pictures. Consistent with these efforts, LiVid posted the source code of a program named DeCSS on its Web site as early as October 1999. DeCSS allows users to circumvent the CSS technology by decrypting data contained on DVD's and enabling the placement of this decrypted data onto computer hard drives or other storage media.

At the time LiVid posted DeCSS, Pavlovich knew that DeCSS "was derived from CSS algorithms" and that reverse engineering these algorithms was probably illegal. He had also "heard" that "there was an organization which you had to file for or apply for a license" to the CSS technology. He did not, however, learn that the organization was DVD CCA or that DVD CCA had its principal place of business in California until after DVD CCA filed this action.

In its complaint, DVD CCA alleged that Pavlovich misappropriated its trade secrets by posting the DeCSS program on the LiVid Web site. . . . The complaint sought injunctive relief but did not seek monetary damages. In response, Pavlovich filed a motion to quash service of process, contending that California lacked jurisdiction over his person. DVD CCA opposed, contending that jurisdiction was proper because Pavlovich "misappropriated DVD CCA's trade secrets knowing that such actions would adversely impact an array of substantial California business enterprises—including the motion picture industry, the consumer electronics industry, and the computer industry." In a brief order, the trial court denied Pavlovich's motion, citing *Calder v. Jones* (1984) 465 U.S. 783, 104 S. Ct. 1482, 79 L. Ed. 2d 804 (*Calder*), and *Panavision Intern., L.P. v. Toeppen* (9th Cir. 1998) 141 F.3d 1316 (*Panavision*).

Pavlovich petitioned the Court of Appeal for a writ of mandate. The Court of Appeal . . . issued a published opinion denying the petition. Because Pavlovich knew that posting DeCSS on the LiVid Web site would harm the movie and computer industries in California and because "the reach of the Internet is also the reach of the extension of the poster's presence," the court found that he purposefully availed himself of forum benefits under the *Calder* effects test. The court also concluded that the exercise of jurisdiction over Pavlovich was reasonable.

We granted review to determine whether the trial court properly exercised jurisdiction over Pavlovich's person based solely on the posting of the DeCSS source code on the LiVid Web site. We conclude it did not.

II.

California courts may exercise personal jurisdiction on any basis consistent with the Constitutions of California and the United States. (Code Civ. Proc., § 410.10.) The exercise of jurisdiction over a nonresident defendant comports with these Constitutions "if the defendant has such minimum contacts with the state that the assertion of jurisdiction does not violate '"traditional notions of fair play and substantial justice."' (*Vons Companies, Inc. v. Seabest Foods, Inc.* (1996) 14 Cal. 4th 434, 444, 58 Cal. Rptr. 2d 899, 926 P.2d 1085 (*Vons*), quoting *Internat. Shoe Co. v. Washington* (1945) 326 U.S. 310, 316, 66 S. Ct. 154, 90 L. Ed. 95 (*Internat. Shoe*).) * * *

A court may exercise specific jurisdiction over a nonresident defendant only if: (1) "the defendant has purposefully availed himself or herself of forum benefits" (*Vons, supra*, 14 Cal. 4th at p. 446); (2) "the 'controversy is related to or "arises out of" [the] defendant's contacts with the forum'" (*ibid.*, quoting *Helicopteros, supra*, 466 U.S. at p. 414); and (3) "'the assertion of personal jurisdiction would comport with 'fair play and substantial justice'" (*Vons, supra*, 14 Cal. 4th at p. 447, quoting *Burger King Corp. v. Rudzewicz* (1985) 471 U.S. 462, 472–473, 105 S. Ct. 2174, 85 L. Ed. 2d 528 (*Burger King*)) * * *

In the defamation contest, the United States Supreme Court has described an "effects test" for determining purposeful availment. In *Calder*, a reporter in Florida wrote an article for the National Enquirer about Shirley Jones, a well-known actress who lived and worked in California. The president and editor of the National Enquirer reviewed and approved the article, and the National Enquirer published the article. Jones sued, among others, the reporter and editor (individual defendants) for libel in California. The individual defendants moved to quash service of process, contending they lacked minimum contacts with California. (*Calder, supra*, 465 U.S. at pp. 785–786.)

The United States Supreme Court disagreed and held that California could exercise jurisdiction over the individual defendants "based on the 'effects' of their Florida conduct in California." (*Calder, supra*, 465 U.S. at p. 789.) The court found jurisdiction proper because "California [was] the focal point both of the story and of the harm suffered." (*Ibid.*) "The allegedly libelous story concerned the California activities of a California resident. It impugned the professionalism of an entertainer whose television career was centered in California . . . and the brunt of the harm, in terms both of [Jones's] emotional distress and the injury to her professional reputation, was suffered in California." (*Id.* 465 U.S. at pp. 788–789, fn. omitted.) The court also noted that the individual defendants wrote or edited "an article that they knew would have a potentially devastating impact upon [Jones]. And they knew that the brunt of that injury would be felt by [Jones] in the State in which she lives and works and in which the National Enquirer has its largest circulation." (*Id.* 465 U.S. at pp. 789–790.)

Although *Calder* involved a libel claim, courts have applied the effects test to other intentional torts, including business torts. (*See IMO Industries, Inc. v. Kiekert AG* (3d

Cir. 1998) 155 F.3d 254, 259–260, 261 (*IMO*) [courts must consider Calder in intentional tort cases]; . . .) Application of the test has, however, been less than uniform. Indeed, courts have "struggled somewhat with *Calder's* import, recognizing that the case cannot stand for the broad proposition that a foreign act with foreseeable effects in the forum state always gives rise to specific jurisdiction." (*Bancroft & Masters, Inc. v. Augusta Nat. Inc.* (9th Cir. 2000) 223 F.3d 1082, 1087 (*Bancroft*).)

Despite this struggle, most courts agree that merely asserting that a defendant knew or should have known that his intentional acts would cause harm in the forum state is not enough to establish jurisdiction under the effects test. * * * Indeed, virtually every jurisdiction has held that the *Calder* effects test requires intentional conduct *expressly aimed at or targeting* the forum state in addition to the defendant's knowledge that his intentional conduct would cause harm in the forum. [W]e . . . join with those jurisdictions that require additional evidence of express aiming or intentional targeting. * * *

We now consider whether Pavlovich's contacts with California meet the effects test. "The plaintiff has the initial burden of demonstrating facts justifying the exercise of jurisdiction." (*Vons, supra,* 14 Cal. 4th at p. 449.) If the plaintiff meets this initial burden, then the defendant has the burden of demonstrating "that the exercise of jurisdiction would be unreasonable." (*Ibid.*) In reviewing a trial court's determination of jurisdiction, we will not disturb the court's factual determinations "if supported by substantial evidence." (*Ibid.*) "When no conflict in the evidence exists, however, the question of jurisdiction is purely one of law and the reviewing court engages in an independent review of the record." (*Ibid.*) Applying these standards, we conclude that the evidence in the record fails to show that Pavlovich expressly aimed his tortious conduct at or intentionally targeted California.

In this case, Pavlovich's sole contact with California is LiVid's posting of the DeCSS source code containing DVD CCA's proprietary information on an Internet Web site accessible to any person with Internet access. Pavlovich never worked in California. He owned no property in California, maintained no bank accounts in California, and had no telephone listings in California. Neither Pavlovich nor his company solicited or transacted any business in California. The record also contains no evidence of any LiVid contacts with California.

Although we have never considered the scope of personal jurisdiction based solely on Internet use, other courts have considered this issue, and most have adopted a sliding scale analysis. "At one end of the spectrum are situations where a defendant clearly does business over the Internet. If the defendant enters into contracts with residents of a foreign jurisdiction that involve the knowing and repeated transmission of computer files over the Internet, personal jurisdiction is proper. [Citation.] At the opposite end are situations where a defendant has simply posted information on an Internet Web site which is accessible to users in foreign jurisdictions. A passive Web site that does little more than make information available to those who are interested in it is not grounds for the exercise of personal jurisdiction. [Citation.]

The middle ground is occupied by interactive Web sites where a user can exchange information with the host computer. In these cases, the exercise of jurisdiction is determined by examining the level of interactivity and commercial nature of the exchange of information that occurs on the Web site." (*Zippo Manufacturing Co. v. Zippo Dot Com, Inc.* (W.D. Pa. 1997) 952 F. Supp. 1119, 1124.)

Here, LiVid's Web site merely posts information and has no interactive features. There is no evidence in the record suggesting that the site targeted California. Indeed, there is no evidence that any California resident ever visited, much less downloaded the DeCSS source code from, the LiVid Web site. Thus, Pavlovich's alleged "conduct in ... posting [a] passive Web site[ ] on the Internet is not," by itself, "sufficient to subject" him "to jurisdiction in California." (*Jewish Defense Organization, Inc. v. Superior Court* (1999) 72 Cal. App. 4th 1045, 1060, 85 Cal. Rptr. 2d 611, fn. omitted (*JDO*) [refusing to exercise jurisdiction under the effects test even though the defendant had "passive Web sites on the Internet"]; [refusing to exercise jurisdiction under the effects test even though the defendant posted infringing material on its Web site]; ...) "'Creating a site, like placing a product into the stream of commerce, may be felt nationwide—or even worldwide—but, without more, it is not an act purposefully directed toward the forum state.'" (*Cybersell, Inc. v. Cybersell, Inc.* (9th Cir. 1997) 130 F.3d 414, 418, quoting *Bensusan Restaurant Corp. v. King* (S.D.N.Y. 1996) 937 F. Supp. 295, 301, *affd.* (2d Cir. 1997) 126 F.3d 25.) Otherwise, "personal jurisdiction in internet-related cases would almost always be found in any forum in the country." Such a result would "vitiate long-held and inviolate principles of" personal jurisdiction.

Nonetheless, DVD CCA contends posting the misappropriated source code on an Internet Web site is sufficient to establish purposeful availment in this case because Pavlovich knew the posting would harm not only a licensing entity but also the motion picture, computer and consumer electronics industries centered in California. According to DVD CCA, this knowledge establishes that Pavlovich intentionally targeted California and is sufficient to confer jurisdiction under the *Calder* effects test. Although the question is close, we disagree.

As an initial matter, DVD CCA's reliance on Pavlovich's awareness that an entity owned the licensing rights to the CSS technology is misplaced. Although Pavlovich knew about this entity, he did not know that DVD CCA was that entity or that DVD CCA's primary place of business was California until *after* the filing of this lawsuit. More importantly, Pavlovich could not have known this information when he allegedly posted the misappropriated code in October 1999, because DVD CCA only began administering licenses to the CSS technology in December 1999—*approximately* two months later. Thus, even assuming Pavlovich should have determined who the licensor was and where that licensor resided before he posted the misappropriated code, he would not have discovered that DVD CCA was that licensor.[4] Because

---

4. At oral argument, DVD CCA claimed that Pavlovich had received a cease-and-desist letter from the Motion Picture Association (MPA), and contended his receipt of this letter established purposeful availment. Although the complaint alleged that MPA sent such a letter to various Web sites and

Pavlovich could not have known that his tortious conduct would harm DVD CCA in California when the misappropriated code was first posted, his knowledge of the existence of a licensing entity cannot establish express aiming at California.

Thus, the only question in this case is whether Pavlovich's knowledge that his tortious conduct may harm certain industries centered in California—i.e., the motion picture, computer, and consumer electronics industries—is sufficient to establish express aiming at California. As explained below, we conclude that this knowledge, by itself, cannot establish purposeful availment under the effects test.

First, Pavlovich's knowledge that DeCSS could be used to illegally pirate copyrighted motion pictures on DVD's and that such pirating would harm the motion picture industry in California does not satisfy the express aiming requirement. As an initial matter, we question whether these effects are even relevant to our analysis, because DVD CCA does not assert a cause of action premised on the illegal pirating of copyrighted motion pictures. In any event, "the mere 'unilateral activity of those who claim some relationship with a nonresident defendant cannot satisfy the requirement of contact with the forum State.'" (*World-Wide Volkswagen, supra*, 444 U.S. at p. 298, . . .) Thus, the foreseeability that third parties may use DeCSS to harm the motion picture industry cannot, by itself, satisfy the express aiming requirement. Because nothing in the record suggests that Pavlovich encouraged Web site visitors to use DeCSS to illegally pirate copyrighted motion pictures, his mere "awareness" they might do so does not show purposeful availment.

Second, Pavlovich's knowledge of the effects of his tortious conduct on the consumer electronics and computer industries centered in California is an even more attenuated basis for jurisdiction. According to DVD CCA, Pavlovich knew that posting DeCSS would harm the consumer electronics and computer industries in California, because many licensees of the CSS technology resided in California. The record, however, indicates that Pavlovich did not know that any of DVD CCA's licensees resided in California. At most, the record establishes that Pavlovich should have guessed that these licensees resided in California because there are many consumer electronic and computer companies in California. DVD CCA's argument therefore boils down to the following syllogism: jurisdiction exists solely because Pavlovich's tortious conduct had a foreseeable effect in California. But mere foreseeability is not enough for jurisdiction. Otherwise, the commission of any intentional tort affecting industries in California would subject a defendant to jurisdiction in California. We decline to adopt such an expansive interpretation of the effects test.

Indeed, such a broad interpretation of the effects test would effectively eliminate the purposeful availment requirement in the intentional tort context for select

---

Internet service providers, the record contains no copy of this letter. Moreover, nothing in the record indicates that such a letter was sent to Pavlovich or that he received or even knew about the letter. Accordingly, DVD CCA's unsubstantiated allusion to a cease-and-desist letter cannot support a finding of jurisdiction. In any event, DVD CCA made no mention of this letter to the trial court and Court of Appeal or in its briefs to this court. Thus, it has waived the issue.

plaintiffs. In most, if not all, intentional tort cases, the defendant is or should be aware of the industries that may be affected by his tortious conduct. Consequently, any plaintiff connected to industries centered in California—i.e., the motion picture, computer, and consumer electronics industries—could sue an out-of-state defendant in California for intentional torts that *may* harm those industries. For example, any creator or purveyor of technology that enables copying of movies or computer software—including a student in Australia who develops a program for creating backup copies of software and distributes it to some of his classmates or a store owner in Africa who sells a device that makes digital copies of movies on videotape—would be subject to suit in California because they should have known their conduct may harm the motion picture or computer industries in California. Indeed, DVD CCA's interpretation would subject any defendant who commits an intentional tort affecting the motion picture, computer, or consumer electronics industries to jurisdiction in California even if the plaintiff was not a California resident. Under this logic, plaintiffs connected to the auto industry could sue any defendant in Michigan, plaintiffs connected to the financial industry could sue any defendant in New York, and plaintiffs connected to the potato industry could sue any defendant in Idaho. Because finding jurisdiction under the facts in this case would effectively subject all intentional tortfeasors whose conduct may harm industries in California to jurisdiction in California, we decline to do so.

We, however, emphasize the narrowness of our decision. A defendant's knowledge that his tortious conduct may harm industries centered in California is undoubtedly relevant to any determination of personal jurisdiction and may support a finding of jurisdiction. We merely hold that this knowledge *alone* is insufficient to establish express aiming at the forum state as required by the effects test. Because the only evidence in the record even suggesting express aiming is Pavlovich's knowledge that his conduct may harm industries centered in California, due process requires us to decline jurisdiction over his person.

In addition, we are not confronted with a situation where the plaintiff has no other forum to pursue its claims and therefore do not address that situation. DVD CCA has the ability and resources to pursue Pavlovich in another forum such as Indiana or Texas. Our decision today does not foreclose it from doing so. Pavlovich may still face the music—just not in California.

III.

Accordingly, we reverse the judgment of the Court of Appeal and remand for further proceedings consistent with this opinion.

WE CONCUR: KENNARD, J.; WERDEGAR, J.; MORENO,
J. BAXTER, JUSTICE, DISSENTING.

I respectfully dissent. That this case involves a powerful new medium of electronic communication, usable for good or ill, should not blind us to the essential facts and principles. The record indicates that, by intentionally posting an unlicensed decryption code for the Content Scrambling System (CSS) on their Internet Web sites, defendant and his network of "open source" associates sought to undermine and defeat the very purposes of the licensed CSS encryption technology, i.e., *copyright protection* for movies recorded on digital versatile discs (DVD's) and *limitation of playback* to operating systems licensed to unscramble the encryption code. The intended targets of this effort were not individual persons or businesses, but entire industries. Defendant knew at least two of the intended targets—the movie industry and the computer industry involved in producing the licensed playback systems—either were centered in California or maintained a particularly substantial presence here. Thus, the record amply supports the trial court's conclusion, for purposes of specific personal jurisdiction, that defendant's intentional act, even if committed outside California, was "expressly aimed" at California. (*See Calder v. Jones* (1984) 465 U.S. 783, 788–790, 104 S. Ct. 1482, 79 L. Ed. 2d 804 (*Calder*).)

In the particular circumstances, it cannot matter that defendant may not have known or cared about the *exact identities* or *precise locations* of each individual target, or that he happened to employ a so-called passive Internet Web site, or whether any California resident visited the site. By acting with the broad intent to harm *industries he knew were centered or substantially present in this state*, defendant forged sufficient "minimum contacts" with *California* "that he should reasonably anticipate being haled into court [*here*]" (*World-Wide Volkswagen Corp. v. Woodson* (1980) 444 U.S. 286, 297, 100 S. Ct. 559, 62 L. Ed. 2d 490 (*World-Wide Volkswagen*)) for litigation "'arising out of'" forum-related conduct (*Vons Companies, Inc. v. Seabest Foods, Inc.* (1996) 14 Cal. 4th 434, 451, 926 P.2d 1085 (*Vons*)).

The majority ascribe undue significance to the fact that Pavlovich acted through a new and rapidly burgeoning medium of interstate and international communication—the Internet. They assert that the mere posting of information on a passive Internet Web site, which is accessible from anywhere but is directed at no particular audience, cannot be an action targeted at a particular forum. Otherwise, they worry, mere use of the Internet would subject the user to personal jurisdiction in any forum where the site was accessible.

I agree that *mere* operation of an Internet Web site cannot expose the operator to suit in any jurisdiction where the site's contents might be read, or where resulting injury might occur. Communication by a universally accessible Internet Web site cannot be equated with "express aiming" at the entire world.

However, defendants who aim conduct at particular jurisdictions, expecting and intending that injurious effects will be felt in those specific places, cannot shield themselves from suit there simply by using the Internet, or some other generalized medium of communication, as the means of inflicting the harm. (*See, e.g., Calder, supra,* 465 U.S. 783, 789–790 [significant California circulation of nationwide newspaper supports California defamation suit by California resident against Florida residents who wrote and edited defamatory article]; *Keeton v. Hustler Magazine, Inc.* (1984) 465 U.S. 770, 773–780 [104 S. Ct. 1473, 79 L. Ed. 2d 790] [significant regular circulation of nationwide magazine in New Hampshire supports New Hampshire defamation suit against magazine by well-known New York resident]; . . .) * * * In such circumstances, the defendant is not exposed to universal and unpredictable jurisdiction. He faces suit only in a particular forum where he directed his injurious conduct, and where he must reasonably anticipate being called to account. * * *

It is true that one cannot be sued in another forum simply because his or her conduct has *foreseeable* effects there. A number of lower court decisions suggest further that, absent other indicia of activity purposefully directed at the forum, even the defendant's intent to injure a forum resident, standing alone, is not sufficient to satisfy the test of *Calder, supra,* 465 U.S. 783. And several cases have held that alleged trademark infringement on an Internet Web site cannot alone, under *Calder,* establish minimum contacts with the forum in which the trademark's owner resides.

Nonetheless, I believe that the unusual and unprecedented facts of this case demonstrate *purposeful activity* directed toward this forum sufficient to establish minimum contacts under the *Calder* test. As a result of his actions, defendant Pavlovich should reasonably have anticipated being haled into court in this state, and recognition of California's jurisdiction thus meets constitutional standards of fairness.

The posting of the DeCSS source code on Pavlovich's LiViD Web site was done with the *specific goal* of negating, by illegal means, the licensed CSS technology Pavlovich knew had been jointly developed by the movie and DVD industries for their mutual protection. Pavlovich's immediate aim, he acknowledged, was to promote development of alternative DVD playback systems not dependent on CSS licensor. However, he also knew CSS was intended to afford crucial copyright protection to DVD movies. He has denied any personal desire to pirate movies, or to encourage others to do so. But by deciding to display the DeCSS source code without restriction on the universally accessible Web site, Pavlovich offered visitors to the site the patent opportunity to exploit this information as they chose.

By taking this calculated action, Pavlovich thus not only foresaw, but must have *intended,* the natural and probable consequences he knew would befall the affected industries. These consequences included *both* the competitive injury Pavlovich admitted he intended to inflict upon the DVD industry, which is substantially present in California, *and* the loss of copyright protection to the movie industry he knew is primarily associated with this state.

This lawsuit, brought by the agent of these affected industries, seeks to forestall just such damage by enjoining Pavlovich, and other members of his network, from continuing to display the DeCSS source code on their Web sites. (Civ. Code, § 3426.2, subd. (a).) For purposes of such an action, it is irrelevant whether Pavlovich himself exploited DeCSS for commercial benefit. The instant suit is predicated on the inherent harm to California-centered industries caused by Pavlovich's intentional, knowing, and allegedly improper "disclosure" of their trade secret. (*Id.,* § 3426.1, subd. (b) (2).) Pavlovich knew he was targeting those industries when he acted. He proceeded despite his assumption that DeCSS was likely "illegal." He thus had every reason to expect — indeed, he effectively invited — responsive litigation.

For purposes of this particular action, therefore, he established sufficient connection with this state that he must "reasonably anticipate" being haled into a *California* court to account for his conduct. (*World-Wide Volkswagen, supra,* 444 U.S. 286, 297; *see Burger King, supra,* 471 U.S. 462, 474.) Because of the minimum contacts he forged by his intentional conduct directed toward this state, maintenance of a related suit against him in this forum does not offend traditional notions of fair play and substantial justice. (*Calder, supra,* 465 U.S. 783, 787–788; *see Internat. Shoe Co., supra,* 326 U.S. 310, 316, 320; . . .)

I see no reason why the result should differ simply because Pavlovich targeted entire industries within the forum, rather than a single individual or business. The majority suggest there is no case "where a court exercised jurisdiction under the effects test based solely on the defendant's knowledge of industry-wide effects in the forum state." By the same token, however, no decision has held that the defendant's efforts to target an entire industry *cannot* form a basis for specific personal jurisdiction. Jurisdiction is appropriate under *Calder* whenever a foreign defendant expressly aimed injurious actions toward *the forum,* with the intent and understanding that the brunt of the harm would be felt there. (*Calder, supra,* 465 U.S. 783, 788–790.) While targeting of an individual forum resident certainly meets that test, the aiming is no less specific, and jurisdiction no less proper, when the effort is directed, with equal purpose and precision, at one or more entire industries located there. * * *

Nor, in my view, is it fatal that individual members of the industries Pavlovich targeted are not based *exclusively* within California. When, as here, one purposefully directs injurious conduct against entire industries, with *actual knowledge* that they are *primarily or substantially* present in a particular forum, his contacts with that state are no more attenuated, random, or fortuitous, than if, by unusual happenstance, they were solely concentrated there. The actor must reasonably anticipate that litigation generated by his intentional conduct will originate in a forum where, as he knows, the industry or industries he sought to injure are primarily or substantially located. Otherwise, one who acted from a remote location against an entire multistate or multinational industry, as opposed to a single enterprise, could rest secure that he was immune from suit in *every* jurisdiction where members of that industry were located.

Indeed, that is the unfortunate result, and the glaring flaw, of the majority's holding. Under the majority's rule, the California-centered industries directly targeted by Pavlovich and his numerous Internet colleagues have no recourse for their alleged injury but to pursue a multiplicity of individual suits against each defendant in his or her separate domicile. Nothing in the basic principles of long-arm jurisdiction compels such an illogical and unfair outcome. I therefore conclude that Pavlovich purposefully established minimum contacts with California sufficient to permit litigation related to those contacts to proceed against him here.

Of course, "once it has been decided that a defendant purposefully established minimum contacts within the forum State, these contacts [must] be considered in light of other factors to determine whether the assertion of personal jurisdiction would comport with 'fair play and substantial justice.' [Citations omitted.] Thus courts in 'appropriate cases' may evaluate 'the burden on the defendant,' 'the forum state's interest in adjudicating the dispute,' 'the plaintiff's interest in obtaining convenient and effective relief,' 'the interstate judicial system's interest in obtaining the most efficient resolution of controversies,' and the 'shared interests of the several states in furthering fundamental substantive social policies.' [Citations omitted.]" (*Burger King, supra*, 471 U.S. 462, 476–477; *see also Asahi Metal Industry Co., supra*, 480 U.S. 102, 113; *World-Wide Volkswagen, supra*, 444 U.S. 286, 292.)

"These considerations sometimes serve to establish the reasonableness of jurisdiction upon a *lesser showing of minimum contacts* than would otherwise be required. [Citations omitted.]" (*Burger King, supra*, 471 U.S. 462, 477, italics added.) Moreover, "where a defendant who purposefully has directed his activities at forum residents seeks to defeat jurisdiction, he must present a *compelling case* that the presence of some other considerations would render jurisdiction unreasonable." (*Ibid.*, italics added.)

Though Pavlovich argues otherwise, he has failed to make such a compelling case here. On the contrary, as the Court of Appeal concluded, the factors bearing on the overall reasonableness of California jurisdiction weigh strongly on the side of such jurisdiction.

The first of these factors, the burden on the defendant, favors Pavlovich the most, since he would presumably be required to travel from his current home in Texas to defend the suit. We cannot discount the significant time, expense, and inconvenience this may entail.

But such concerns are present whenever jurisdiction away from the defendant's residence is at issue. Here, the travel required is domestic, not international, and Pavlovich is not disadvantaged by the alien judicial system of a foreign nation. (Compare, e.g., *Asahi Metal Industry Co., supra*, 480 U.S. 102, 114; . . .) The distance between Texas and California is not extreme under modern conditions. Pavlovich cites his youth and represents in his brief that his current income is relatively low, but he does not otherwise suggest any unusual hardship.

Moreover, as indicated above, Pavlovich assumed the DeCSS source code was an illegal infringement of the licensed CSS technology, yet a decision was made to post it on the LiViD Web site anyway. Pavlovich thus had reason to anticipate a responsive lawsuit from somewhere. According to his deposition, he has already voluntarily appeared outside his home state as an expert witness in related litigation. Thus, the burden is not constitutionally unreasonable in this case.

On the other hand, the interests of the plaintiff, the forum, and the interstate judicial system all strongly favor jurisdiction in this state. For several reasons, California is a logical forum for convenient, efficient, and effective relief. The industries affected by Pavlovich's conduct are centered or substantially present here. Their licensing agent DVD CCA, the plaintiff in this suit, has its headquarters here. As indicated above, California has a natural interest, reflected by the reach of its long-arm statute, in redressing the effects of an act within its territory, even though the act was done elsewhere. California has also evidenced a more specific interest in the type of injury at issue here. California's adoption of the Uniform Trade Secrets Act reflects both its common concern with regulating trade secret infringements and its special interest in providing effective remedies for such infringements committed against its own residents.

Finally, and importantly, both DVD CCA and the interstate judicial system have a strong interest in efficient resolution of DVD CCA's dispute, involving common issues of fact and law, with *all* of the many defendants named in its complaint. That interest is not served by requiring DVD CCA to pursue individual defendants in separate fora, if a single suit in one fair and logical forum is possible. For the reasons already stated, California is such a forum in this case. In fact, I submit, California's specific interests, reinforced by the interest in efficient dispute resolution, are so strong here that "the reasonableness of [California] jurisdiction [may be established] upon a lesser showing of minimum contacts that would otherwise be required." (*Burger King, supra,* 471 U.S. 462, 477.) For these reasons, I am amply persuaded that California's assertion of personal jurisdiction over Pavlovich, for purposes of this specific litigation, is constitutionally fair and reasonable.

Though the majority imply otherwise, the result I propose does not signal a broad new rule that California jurisdiction is proper over any foreign defendant who causes foreseeable effects in this state. On the contrary, I base my conclusions on the specific facts of this case. These facts indicate that defendant Pavlovich engaged in intentional conduct purposefully targeted at interests he knew were centered or substantially present in California, with knowledge they would suffer harm here, such that he must reasonably have anticipated being called to account in this state. Pavlovich thus forged minimum contacts with California, and it is otherwise fair and reasonable to assert personal jurisdiction over him here for purposes of related litigation. For these reasons, and these reasons alone, I conclude that his motion to quash was properly denied.

I would affirm the judgment of the Court of Appeal.

WE CONCUR: GEORGE, C.J.; CHIN, J.

Notes and Questions Regarding Pavlovich *and the Effects Test*

(1) The *Pavlovich* majority emphasized that its purposeful availment decision was a narrow one, based on the particular facts of this case. What factual changes might cause the majority to conclude that defendant Pavlovich had expressly aimed his tortious conduct at, or intentionally targeted, California? What if Pavlovich had in fact received the cease-and-desist letter from the Motion Picture Association, referred to in footnote 4, *before* he posted the misappropriated code on his web site? What if Pavlovich had know DVD CCA was the entity that owned the licensing rights to CSS technology *before* he posted the misappropriated code? What if he also knew that DVD CCA's principal place of business was in California? Or he knew DVD CCA's licensees resided in California?

(2) Defendant Pavlovich's knowledge at the time he posted the misappropriated code on his web site was very important to the court in determining whether he expressly aimed at or targeted California within the meaning of the "effects" test. Should this inquiry into the defendant's knowledge be based on a subjective (*i.e.*, what did the defendant actually know) or an objective (*i.e.*, what should the defendant have known) standard? What standard did the *Pavlovich* majority employ? The dissent?

(3) The *Pavlovich* majority viewed the defendant's web site as "passive" because it merely posts information and has no interactive features. The dissent also agreed that the mere operation of a web site cannot expose the operator to suit in any jurisdiction where the site's content might be read. How is the determination of whether a web site is "passive" relevant to the application of the "effects" test?

(4) The *Pavlovich* majority viewed the "effects" test question as "close," yet did not consider whether California's assertion of personal jurisdiction would comport with "fair play and substantial justice." In light of the U.S. Supreme Court's statement in *Burger King Corp. v. Rudzewicz*, 471 U.S. 462, 476–78, 105 S. Ct. 2174, 85 L. Ed. 2d 528 (1985), that these considerations sometimes serve to establish the reasonableness of jurisdiction "upon a lesser showing of minimum contacts than would otherwise be required," was the majority's failure to consider the reasonableness of California jurisdiction a misapplication of the due process requirements? In contrast, did the *Pavlovich* dissent place too much weight on these reasonableness factors?

(5) Recently, in *Walden v. Fiore*, 571 U.S. 277, 134 S. Ct. 1115, 188 L. Ed. 2d 12 (2013), the U.S. Supreme Court held that a court in Nevada may not exercise personal jurisdiction over a defendant on the basis that he knew his allegedly tortious conduct in Georgia would delay the return of funds to plaintiffs with connections to Nevada. Defendant Walden, a Georgia police office working as a deputized DEA agent at a Georgia airport, seized a large amount of cash from the plaintiffs while they were catching a connecting flight to Nevada. After the plaintiffs returned to their Nevada residence, the defendant allegedly helped draft a false probable cause affidavit in support of the funds' forfeiture and forwarded it to the U.S. Attorney's Office in Georgia. In the end, no forfeiture complaint was filed and the funds were eventually returned to the plaintiffs in Nevada.

Plaintiffs then filed a tort suit against the defendant in a federal District Court in Nevada. The Ninth Circuit held that the District Court could properly exercise jurisdiction because the defendant had submitted the false probable cause affidavit with the knowledge that it would affect persons with significant Nevada connections. The Supreme Court reversed, explaining that under the *Calder* "effects" test "[t]he proper question is not where the plaintiff experienced a particular injury or effect but whether the defendant's conduct connects him to the forum in a meaningful way." *Walden*, 134 S. Ct. at 1125. Which opinion in *Pavlovich* is consistent with the *Walden* Court's interpretation of the "effects" test?

4. Raising the Personal Jurisdiction Defense

The California Legislature amended Code of Civil Procedure § 418.10, effective January 1, 2003, for the express purpose of conforming California practice with respect to challenging personal jurisdiction to the practice under Rule 12(b) of the Federal Rules of Civil Procedure, by adding new § 418.10(e), reproduced below.

CALIFORNIA CODE OF CIVIL PROCEDURE (2021)

Section 418.10. Motion to Quash Service of Summons or to Stay or Dismiss Actions; Procedure.

(a) A defendant, on or before the last day of his or her time to plead or within any further time that the court may for good cause allow, may serve and file a notice of motion for one or more of the following purposes:

(1) To quash service of summons on the ground of lack of jurisdiction of the court over him or her.

(2) To stay or dismiss the action on the ground of inconvenient forum.

(3) To dismiss the action pursuant to the applicable provisions of Chapter 1.5 (commencing with Section 583.110) of Title 8 [Dismissal based on lack of diligence in service or prosecution].

(b) The notice shall designate, as the time for making the motion, a date not more than 30 days after filing of the notice. The notice shall be served in the same manner, and at the same times, prescribed by subdivision (b) of Section 1005. The service and filing of the notice shall extend the defendant's time to plead until 15 days after service upon him or her of a written notice of entry of an order denying his or her motion, except that for good cause shown the court may extend the defendant's time to plead for an additional period not exceeding 20 days.

(c) If the motion is denied by the trial court, the defendant, within 10 days after service upon him or her of a written notice of an entry of an order of the court denying his or her motion, or within any further time not exceeding 20 days that the trial court may for good cause allow, and before pleading, may petition an appropriate reviewing court for a writ of mandate to require the trial court to enter its order quashing the service of summons or staying or dismissing the action. The defendant shall file or enter his or her responsive pleading in the trial court within the time prescribed by subdivision (b) unless, on or before the last day of the defendant's time to plead, he or she serves upon the adverse party and files with the trial court a notice that he or she has petitioned for a writ of mandate. The service and filing of the notice shall extend the defendant's time to plead until 10 days after service upon him or her of a written notice of the final judgment in the mandate proceeding. The time to plead may for good cause shown be extended by the trial court for an additional period not exceeding 20 days.

(d) No default may be entered against the defendant before expiration of his or her time to plead, and no motion under this section, or under Section 473 or 473.5

when joined with a motion under this section, or application to the court or stipulation of the parties for an extension of the time to plead, shall be deemed a general appearance by the defendant.

(e) A defendant or cross-defendant may make a motion under this section and simultaneously answer, demur, or move to strike the complaint or cross-complaint.

(1) Notwithstanding Section 1014, no act by a party who makes a motion under this section, including filing an answer, demurrer, or motion to strike constitutes an appearance, unless the court denies the motion made under this section. If the court denies the motion made under this section, the defendant or cross-defendant is not deemed to have generally appeared until entry of the order denying the motion.

(2) If the motion made under this section is denied and the defendant or cross-defendant petitions for a writ of mandate pursuant to subdivision (c), the defendant or cross-defendant is not deemed to have generally appeared until the proceedings on the writ petition have finally concluded.

(3) Failure to make a motion under this section at the time of filing a demurrer or motion to strike constitutes a waiver of the issues of lack of personal jurisdiction, inadequacy of process, inadequacy of service of process, inconvenient forum, and delay in prosecution.

Notes and Questions Regarding Raising the Personal Jurisdiction Defense

(1) *General Appearance.* A defendant must raise an objection to personal jurisdiction in the manner prescribed by CCP § 418.10. Pursuant to the 2003 amendment to § 418.10, the defendant need not raise the objection by a special appearance, but may simultaneously answer, demur, or move to strike, so long as the objection is raised in defendant's first appearance. CCP § 418.10 (e) (effective Jan. 1, 2003). If the defendant makes a general appearance, as defined in CCP § 1014, *before* filing a motion to quash objecting to personal jurisdiction, the defendant waives his right to contest the personal jurisdiction of the court. CCP § 418.10(e)(3).

Unlike the federal practice under Rule 12(b), F.R.C.P., CCP § 418.10 does not give a defendant the option to plead lack of jurisdiction as a defense and reserve determination of that issue until as late as trial. *Roy v. Superior Court*, 127 Cal. App. 4th 337, 25 Cal. Rptr. 3d 488 (2005). Section 418.10 continues to require a timely motion to quash as the means of challenging personal jurisdiction. A defendant may move to quash and simultaneously file an answer containing defenses to the action, but "the latter is not a substitute for the former." *Roy*, 127 Cal. App. 4th at 345.

(2) *Burden of Proof.* When a defendant moves to quash service of process on jurisdictional grounds, the plaintiff has the initial burden of demonstrating facts justifying the exercise of jurisdiction. *See, e.g., Vons Companies, Inc. v. Seabest Foods, Inc.*, 14 Cal. 4th 434, 449, 58 Cal. Rptr. 2d 899, 926 P.2d 1085 (1996); *Floveyor International,*

Ltd. v. Superior Court, 59 Cal. App. 4th 789, 69 Cal. Rptr. 2d 457 (1997) (Upholding a motion to quash because the plaintiff failed to produce any evidence that the defendant had any contacts with California). Once the facts showing "minimum contacts" with the forum state have been established, however, the burden to demonstrate that the exercise of jurisdiction would be "unreasonable" shifts to the defendant. *Vons, supra*, 14 Cal. 4th at 449.

5. Forum Selection Agreements

Forum Clauses, Generally. The California courts, like the federal courts and those of all but a handful of other states, will enforce a freely negotiated forum selection clause unless the resisting party shows that enforcement would be "unreasonable." *E.g., Smith, Valentino & Smith, Inc. v. Superior Court*, 17 Cal. 3d 491, 131 Cal. Rptr. 374, 551 P.2d 1206 (1976); *Cal-State Business Products & Services, Inc. v. Ricoh*, 12 Cal. App. 4th 1666, 16 Cal. Rptr. 2d 417 (1993). The test for reasonableness includes such factors as whether the forum selection clause is the result of unfair use of unequal bargaining power or fraud, the forum selected would be unavailable or unable to accomplish substantial justice, or would bring about a result contrary to the public policy of the forum. *Cal-State Business Products, supra.* However, neither inconvenience nor additional expense in litigating in the selected forum is part of this test. *Id.*

Validity of Forum Clauses in Consumer Contracts. The fact the forum selection clause is contained in a form consumer contract and was not the subject of bargaining does not defeat enforcement as a matter of law, where there is no evidence of unfair use of superior power to impose the contract upon the consumer and the consumer had adequate notice to the clause. *See, e.g., Intershop Communications AG v. Superior Court*, 104 Cal. App. 4th 191, 201–02, 127 Cal. Rptr. 2d 847 (2002) (Forum selection clause within an adhesion contract, which required plaintiff employee to litigate breach of stock options exchange agreement in Germany, will be enforced so long as the clause provided adequate notice to the plaintiff that he was agreeing to the jurisdiction cited in the contract); *Lu v. Dryclean-U.S.A of California, Inc.*, 11 Cal. App. 4th 1490, 14 Cal. Rptr. 2d 906 (1992) (Enforcing forum selection clause in franchise agreement requiring plaintiffs, individual franchisees, to litigate in Florida); *Bos Material Handling, Inc. v. Crown Controls Corp.*, 137 Cal. App. 3d 99, 186 Cal. Rptr. 740 (1982) (Enforcing forum clause in standardized contract which required arbitration in Ohio, even though contract deemed adhesive).

Legislative Limits on Enforcement. The California Legislature has recently added some protection for consumers with respect to enforcement of forum selection clauses in certain actions where the amount in controversy is less than $5,000. Pursuant to CCP § 116.225, an agreement entered into after January 1, 2003, establishing a forum outside California for an action arising from the provision of goods, services, property, or extensions of credit primarily for personal, family or household purposes that is otherwise within the jurisdiction of the small claims court of California is contrary to public policy and is void and unenforceable.

The Legislature has also placed some limits on forum clause enforcement in other specific types of contracts. *E.g.*, CCP § 410.42 (construction subcontracts); Commercial Code § 10106(b) (consumer leases); Corporations Code § 15627.5 (partnership agreements).

C. Venue

CALIFORNIA CODE OF CIVIL PROCEDURE (2021)

Section 395. County in which defendants reside; Personal injury; Family law matters; Contract to perform obligation in county; Contract involving goods for personal or family use.

(a) Except as otherwise provided by law and subject to the power of the court to transfer actions or proceedings as provided in this title, the superior court in the county where the defendants or some of them reside at the commencement of the action is the proper court for the trial of the action. If the action is for injury to person or personal property or for death from wrongful act or negligence, the superior court in either the county where the injury occurs or the injury causing death occurs or the county where the defendants, or some of them reside at the commencement of the action, is a proper court for the trial of the action. * * *

Subject to subdivision (b), if a defendant has contracted to perform an obligation in a particular county, the superior court in the county where the obligation is to be performed, where the contract in fact was entered into, or where the defendant or any defendant resides at the commencement of the action is a proper court for the trial of an action founded on that obligation, and the county where the obligation is incurred is the county where it is to be performed, unless there is a special contract in writing to the contrary.

If none of the defendants reside in the state or if they reside in the state and the county where they reside is unknown to the plaintiff, the action may be tried in the superior court in any county that the plaintiff may designate in his or her complaint, and, if the defendant is about to depart from the state, the action may be tried in the superior court in any county where either of the parties reside or service is made. If any person is improperly joined as a defendant or has been made a defendant solely for the purpose of having the action tried in the superior court in the county where he or she resides, his or her residence shall not be considered in determining the proper place for the trial of the action.

(b) Subject to the power of the court to transfer actions or proceedings as provided in this title, in an action arising from an offer or provision of goods, services, loans or extensions of credit intended primarily for personal, family or household use, other than an obligation described in Section 1812.10 or Section 2984.4 of the Civil Code, or an action arising from a transaction consummated as a proximate result of either an unsolicited telephone call made by a seller engaged in the business of consummating transactions of that kind or a telephone call or electronic transmission made by the buyer or lessee in response to a solicitation by the seller, the superior court in the county where the buyer or lessee in fact signed the contract, where the buyer or lessee resided at the time the contract was entered into, or where the buyer or lessee resides at the commencement of the action is the proper court for the trial of the action. * * *

(c) Any provision of an obligation described in subdivision (b) waiving that subdivision is void and unenforceable.

Notes and Questions Regarding Venue

(1) *General Venue Rules and Exceptions.* Various statutory provisions govern the determination of proper venue in California. These provisions often overlap in a conflicting manner, but may be reduced to one fundamental premise, as stated in CCP § 395: A defendant is entitled to have an action tried in the county of his residence unless the action falls within some statutory exception to this general venue rule. When there are multiple defendants, venue is generally proper in any county where at least one of them resides. CCP § 395. If none of the defendants resides in California, venue is generally proper in any county which plaintiff may designate in her complaint. CCP § 395. There are a number of statutory exceptions to these general rules of CCP § 395; these exceptions in turn may be subject to more specific exceptions. Some of the most common exceptions are discussed below.

(a) *Actions Involving Real Property.* The county in which real property, or some part of the property, is located is the proper venue for most actions for recovery of the property or some interest in the property. CCP § 392. The courts traditionally refer to such actions involving real property as "local actions"; and to all other actions as "transitory" actions. *E.g., Peiser v. Mettler*, 50 Cal. 2d 594, 328 P.2d 953 (1958); *Massae v. Superior Court*, 118 Cal. App. 3d 527, 173 Cal. Rptr. 527 (1981).

(b) *Personal injury actions.* In an action for "injury to person or personal property," or for wrongful death, the proper venue is either the county where the injury occurred or the county in which the defendants or some of them reside. CCP § 395. The courts have defined "injury to person" narrowly to include physical or bodily injury; but not injuries to character, reputation, mental or emotional distress. *E.g., Cacciaguidi v. Superior Court*, 226 Cal. App. 3d 181, 276 Cal. Rptr. 465 (1990) (Abuse of process action not one for "injury to person"); *Carruth v. Superior Court*, 80 Cal. App. 3d 215, 145 Cal. Rptr. 344 (1978) (Damage action for malicious prosecution); *Cubic Corp. v. Superior Court*, 186 Cal. App. 3d 622, 231 Cal. Rptr. 18 (1986) (Action for intentional infliction of emotional distress). Why did the courts narrowly construe "injury to person" in this manner? What venue provision governs in such actions if not this one?

(c) *Dissolution of Marriage.* In a dissolution of marriage proceeding, the proper venue is the county in which the petitioner has been resident for three months next preceding the commencement of proceedings. CCP § 395(a); Family Code § 2320.

(d) *Actions Against Corporations and Associations.* In an action against a corporation or association, the plaintiff has several venue options: The county where the contract was made or is to be performed, or where the obligation or liability arises, or where breach occurs, or of the corporation's principal place of business. CCP § 395.5. Although § 395.5 appears to only address contract actions, the courts construe it to govern tort actions as well. *See, e.g., Mission Imports, Inc. v. Superior Court,* 31 Cal. 3d 921, 928, 184 Cal. Rptr. 296, 647 P.2d 1075 (1982) (Collecting cases); *Black Diamond Asphalt, Inc. v. Superior Court,* 109 Cal. App. 4th 166, 134 Cal. Rptr. 2d 510 (2003) (Holding § 394 is also applicable to statutory liability cases). The purpose of § 395.5 is to permit a wider choice of venue in suits against a corporation than is permitted in suits against an individual defendant. *Mission Imports, supra.* Why this purpose?

(e) *Contract Actions.* In a contract action, the plaintiff has many venue options: The county where the obligation is to be performed or in which the contract was entered into, where any defendant resides; or, in certain contracts for sale of goods or services, where the buyer or lessee resided at the time of the contract or at the time of commencement of the action. CCP § 395(a) & (b).

(2) *Residence Defined.* Pursuant to Government Code § 244(a), the residence of an individual is defined as the one place where a person remains and to which he or she returns in seasons of repose. The residence of a corporation is its principal place of business. *See* CCP § 395.2. What factors determine a corporation's principal place of business? *See Rosas v. Superior Court,* 25 Cal. App. 4th 671, 30 Cal. Rptr. 2d 609 (1994) (For purposes of venue, corporation deemed bound by its designation of a principal place of business in corporate documents filed with the Secretary of State).

(3) *Mixed Action Rules.* The general statutory venue rules and exceptions often overlap and conflict when a lawsuit involves multiple parties or causes of actions. Such "mixed actions" may occur when plaintiffs permissively join transitory and local actions or multiple transitory actions, governed by conflicting venue statutes; and when one cause of action is brought but different forms of relief, some local and others transitory, are sought. Because the venue statutes do not provide any general approach for resolving these conflicts, the courts have developed their own general rules. As you might expect with venue analysis, however, these general court-made rules may be subject to exceptions in specific cases. *See generally* Arvo Van Alstyne, *Venue of Mixed Actions in California,* 44 Cal. L. Rev. 685 (1956).

(a) *The "Main Relief" Rule.* When a complaint alleges a single cause of action but seeks both local and transitory relief, the court will ascertain the primary object or "main relief" sought by the action to establish proper venue. *E.g., Massae v. Superior Court,* 118 Cal. App. 3d 527, 173 Cal. Rptr. 527 (1981) (In action by trustors under deed of trust seeking declaratory relief, reformation, and damages, court determined main relief to be for reformation and therefore the action local and governed by CCP § 392 for venue purposes); *Peiser v. Mettler,* 50 Cal. 2d 594, 603–06, 328 P.2d 953 (1958) (In action by lessor for breach of farm lease seeking return of improvements and damages for loss of use and waste, court determined that main relief sought was transitory for venue purposes).

(b) *Venue follows the transitory cause of action.* When a complaint joins local and transitory causes of action against a defendant, the courts usually disregard the local causes of action to establish proper venue. *E.g.*, *Peiser v. Mettler, supra*; *Smith v. Smith*, 88 Cal. 572, 26 P. 356 (1891); *Turlock Theatre Co. v. Laws*, 12 Cal. 2d 573, 86 P.2d 345 (1939). Why did the courts adopt this approach?

(c) *Mixed action rules: Multiple causes and single defendant.* Where there are multiple transitory causes of action subject to conflicting venue provisions, generally the court must grant a change of venue on the entire complaint whenever the defendant is entitled to a change of venue on any one cause of action. *See Brown v. Superior Court*, 37 Cal. 3d 477, 208 Cal. Rptr. 724, 691 P.2d 272 (1984), and cases cited therein. However, this judicial approach is subject to exceptions. *See Brown, supra* (Although the mixed action venue rule recognizes a preference for trial in the county of a defendant's residence, that preference is outweighed by the strong countervailing policy expressed in the special venue provision of the California Fair Employment and Housing Act which favors a plaintiff's choice of venue).

(d) *Mixed action rules: Multiple defendants and causes of actions.* In cases involving multiple defendants and causes of action, when venue is proper in the county in which one of the defendants resides as to one cause of action, venue is proper in that county as to all properly joined causes of action and defendants. *See, e.g., Monogram Co. v. Kingsley*, 38 Cal. 2d 28, 237 P.2d 265 (1951); *Tutor-Saliba-Perini Joint Venture v. Superior Court*, 233 Cal. App. 3d 736, 742, 285 Cal. Rptr. 1 (1991). Plaintiff's venue selection may not be defeated even if all the defendants concur in a motion to change venue to a county in which another defendant resides. *Tutor-Saliba-Perini, supra.* This approach applies even if some of the causes of action name only nonresidents of the county selected by plaintiff, so long as a resident defendant is named in others. *Id.*

This approach becomes more complicated when the action includes individual and corporate defendants. *See, e.g., Brown v. Superior Court, supra*, 37 Cal. 3d at 482, n.6; *Mosby v. Superior Court*, 43 Cal. App. 3d 219, 226, 117 Cal. Rptr. 588 (1974) (When a plaintiff brings an action against several defendants, both individual and corporate, in a county which is neither the residence nor principal place of business of any defendant, an individual defendant may change venue to the county of his residence even though venue initially laid may otherwise be proper on one of the alternative grounds provided in § 395.5).

(4) *Motion to Transfer.* A defendant who wishes to contest the plaintiff's choice of venue as not the proper county must "at the time he or she answers, demurs, or moves to strike, or, at his or her option, without answering, demurring, or moving to strike and within the time otherwise allowed to respond to the complaint," move to transfer the action to the proper court. CCP § 396b. Otherwise, the defendant's objection to improper venue is waived, and the action may be tried in the court where commenced. *Id.*

D. Service of Process

1. Introductory Note on Manner of Service

Code of Civil Procedure § 413.10 provides:

Except as otherwise provided by statute, a summons shall be served on a person:

(a) Within this state, as provided in this chapter.

(b) Outside this state but within the United States, as provided in this chapter or as prescribed by the law of the place where the person is served.

(c) Outside the United States, as provided in this chapter or as directed by the court in which the action is pending, or, if the court before or after service finds that the service is reasonably calculated to give actual notice, as prescribed by the law of the place where the person is served or as directed by the foreign authority in response to a letter rogatory. These rules are subject to the provisions of the Convention on the "Service Abroad of Judicial and Extrajudicial Documents" in Civil or Commercial Matter (Hague Service Convention).

Together with proper personal and subject matter jurisdiction, proper service of the complaint and summons on the defendant is a prerequisite to a valid judgment. *See, e.g., Mullane v. Central Hanover Bank & Trust Co.*, 339 U.S. 306, 70 S. Ct. 652, 94 L. Ed. 865 (1950) (Constitutionally adequate notice is prerequisite to valid judgment); *Insurance Corp. of Ireland v. Compagnie des Bauxites de Guinee*, 456 U.S. 694, 701, 102 S. Ct. 2099, 72 L. Ed. 2d 492 (1982) (The validity of an order depends on the court having jurisdiction over both the subject matter and the parties).

The Jurisdiction and Service of Process Act enacted in 1969 governs service of process in the California courts. CCP § 410.10 *et seq.* Generally speaking, the proper manner of service, and the person upon whom service must be made, depends on the place where process is to be served (*i.e.*, within California, in another state, or outside the United States) and the type of party to be served (*e.g.* an individual defendant, a corporation or association, or a public entity). CCP §§ 413.10–417.40.

2. Service Within California

Personal Service. Personal delivery of a copy of the complaint and summons is the preferred manner of service upon defendants within California. CCP § 415.10 (individuals); CCP §§ 416.10–416.90 (corporations, associations, public entities, guardians).

Substituted Service On Individuals. The requirements for substituted service on a person are found in CCP § 415.20, which states:

(b) If a copy of the summons and of the complaint cannot with reasonable diligence be personally delivered to the person to be served as specified in Section 416.60, 416.70, 416.80, or 416.90, a summons may be served by leaving a copy of the summons and of the complaint at such person's dwelling house, usual place of abode, ususal place of business, . . . in the presence of a competent member of the household or a person apparently in charge of his or her office, place of business, . . . at least 18 years of age, who shall be informed of the contents thereof, and by thereafter mailing a copy of the summons and of the complaint (by first class mail, postage prepaid) to the person to be served at the place where a copy of the summons and of the complaint were left. Service of the summons in this manner is deemed complete on the 10th day after mailing.

(c) Notwithstanding subdivision (b), if the only address reasonably known for the person to be served is a private mailbox obtained through a commercial mail receiving agency, service of process may be effected on the first delivery attempt by leaving a copy of the summons and complaint with the commercial mail receiving agency in the manner described in subdivision (d) of Section 17538.5 of the Business and Professions Code [Requiring the commercial mail receiving agency to place a copy of the documents into the mail receiving customer's mailbox, and to mail the documents to the customer's last known home or personal address].

Substituted service on an individual defendant pursuant to CCP §§ 415.20(b) is authorized only when process cannot with "reasonable diligence" be personally delivered. What constitutes "reasonable diligence" in this context? *See Bein v. Brechtel-Jochim Group, Inc.,* 6 Cal. App. 4th 1387, 8 Cal. Rptr. 2d 351 (1992) (Ordinarily, two or three attempts at personal service at a proper place should fully satisfy the requirement of reasonable diligence and allow substituted service to be made). Two or three attempts at personal service at a proper place? *Compare Espindola v. Nunez,* 199 Cal. App. 3d 1389, 245 Cal Rptr. 596 (1988) (Three unsuccessful attempts within four days to personally serve defendant at home constituted reasonable diligence sufficient to uphold substituted service on defendant's wife at home) *with Evartt v. Superior Court,* 89 Cal. App. 3d 795, 152 Cal. Rptr. 836 (1979) (Three unsuccessful attempts within two days to personally serve defendant at home while defendant is on short vacation insufficient to uphold substituted service on defendant's housesitter where plaintiff made no attempt to personally serve defendant, a long-time resident, until three days before expiration of three-year period within which plaintiff must effect service).

Substituted Service on Entities. When the defendant is a corporation, an unincorporated association, or a public entity, attempted personal service on the designated agent or officer is not a prerequisite to substitute service on someone in charge of the office during usual office hours. CCP § 415.20 (a). Why is a reasonable attempt at personal service a prerequisite to substitute service with respect to individual defendants, but not as to entity defendants?

Federal Rules Compared. Rule 4(e) of the Federal Rules of Civil Procedure authorizes substitute service on someone residing at an individual defendant's place of abode as an unqualified alternative to personal service. Likewise, the vast majority of states recognize substituted "abode" service as a primary method of service; only California and a few other states relegate it to a secondary method of service. *See* Philip Craig Starti, Note, *Substituted Service of Process on Individuals: Code of Civil Procedure Section 415.20 (b)*, 21 Hastings L. J. 1257, 1278 (1970) (Arguing that the requirement of reasonable diligence in CCP § 415.20 (b) unnecessarily restricts use of substituted service without significantly improving the likelihood that the defendant will actually receive notice). What policy considerations support the California view of substituted "abode" service? What ones support the federal or majority rule? *See id.* at 1274–80.

Constructive Service by Publication. Code of Civil Procedure § 415.50 permits constructive service by publication only where the court is satisfied that the party to be served cannot with "reasonable diligence" be served personally or by substituted service. The "reasonable diligence" necessary to uphold an order for service by publication under § 415.50 requires more exhaustive attempts to located the defendant than is sufficient to uphold substituted service on an individual defendant pursuant to § 415.20(b). *See Olvera v. Olvera*, 232 Cal. App. 3d 32, 283 Cal. Rptr. 271 (1991) (The standard of diligence required includes recent inquiries of all relatives, friends, and other persons likely to know defendant's whereabouts; searches of city directories, telephone directories, tax roles, and register of voters; and inquiries of occupants of all real estate involved in the litigation). A plaintiff must not only *exercise* due diligence as a prerequisite for an order of publication, but must *show* due diligence in the application to the court. CCP § 415.50.

Service by Mail Within California. Code of Civil Procedure § 415.30 authorizes a very limited form of service by mail within California. The plaintiff must mail copies of the complaint and summons, along with two copies of the "Notice of Acknowledgment," and a prepaid self-addressed return envelope, to the defendant. CCP § 415.30(b) specifies the required form and contents of this "Notice and Acknowledgment." *See also* Form POS-015, Judicial Council Forms. Service is not deemed complete unless the defendant executes and returns acknowledgment. § 415.30(c). Consequently, if the defendant fails to execute or return the acknowledgment form, the plaintiff must serve the defendant in some other proper method. The defendant may, however, be liable for reasonable expenses incurred by plaintiff in serving defendant by another method. § 415.30 (d). Rule 4(d) of the Federal Rules of Civil Procedure, as amended in 1993, authorizes a similar method of service by mail within the United States, referred to as a request for waiver of service. In what category of cases is this type of service by mail likely to be effective?

3. Service on Defendant Located in Another State

Service Options. A plaintiff has many options when required to serve a defendant located in another state. Code of Civil Procedure § 415.40 authorizes service of process on a defendant in another state in any manner provided by in the Jurisdiction and Service of Process Act for instate service, plus service by mail. Additionally, CCP § 413.10(b) authorizes service in another state in accordance with the law of the state where the defendant is to be served.

Service by Mail, Return Receipt Required. Code of Civil Procedure §415.40 and §417.20(b) authorize service by first-class mail, requiring a return receipt, on a person in another state when actual delivery is established by the signed return receipt or by "other evidence." What are some examples of sufficient "other evidence"? *See, e.g., In re Marriage of Tusinger*, 170 Cal. App. 3d 80, 215 Cal. Rptr. 838 (1985) (Letter written by defendant's attorney in Arkansas acknowledging defendant's receipt of complaint and summons constituted sufficient "other evidence"); *Taylor-Rush v. Multitech Corp.*, 217 Cal. App. 3d 103, 265 Cal. Rptr. 672 (1990) (While a return receipt signed by someone authorized by a nonresident defendant to sign for his mail is sufficient, the plaintiff must provide separate evidence establishing the authority of the person who signed the return receipt on defendant's behalf).

Substituted Service on Agent Within California. In a wide variety of situations, California statutes authorize substituted service on a designated agent of the defendant within California. For example, corporations, partnerships, and other entities doing business in California must designate an agent for service of process within the state. *E.g.*, Corp. Code §§1502–1505; 2105, 2107, 1701–1702, 2110–2111, 0210, and 8210–8212 (various domestic and foreign corporations); Corp. Code §15627 (partnerships); Insurance Code §§1600–1605 (insurance companies); CCP §§416.10–416.40. If no such agent for service of process is designated by the entity, substitute service may be made upon the California Secretary of State or other appropriate governmental agent. *E.g.*, Corp. Code §§1702, 2111, 15627(c).

Vehicle Code §17451 provides that ownership or operation of a motor vehicle within California by a nonresident is the equivalent to an appointment of the Director of the Department of Motor Vehicles as agent for service of process in any action arising from an accident resulting from operation of the motor vehicle in California. If the plaintiff serves process on the Director pursuant to this section, the plaintiff must also mail a copy to the defendant. Veh. Code §§17454, 17455.

Substituted service on a designated or implied agent is alternative to, not exclusive of, the other statutorily authorized methods of service on a defendant. *M. Lowenstein & Sons, Inc. v. Superior Court*, 80 Cal. App. 3d 762, 145 Cal. Rptr. 814 (1978) (Plaintiff serving nonresident corporation may serve designated agent pursuant to CCP §416.10 or, alternatively, may serve by mail pursuant to CCP §415.40); *Anderson v. Sherman*, 125 Cal. App. 3d 228, 235–37, 178 Cal. Rptr. 38 (1981) (Injured California resident may serve nonresident motorist pursuant to Veh. Code §§17454 & 17455, or CCP §415.40).

4. Service Outside the United States

Hague Service Convention. The United States has ratified two multilateral international agreements which govern service of process among signatory countries. One is the Hague Service Convention, ratified by the United States in 1969, which now includes such other signatories as Canada, Japan, the Peoples' Republic of China, the United Kingdom, Germany, and most of the other European countries. 20 U.S.T. 361–73, T.I.A.S. No. 6638, 658 U.N.T.S. 163. For a complete list of all parties to this

Convention, *see* the United States Code Annotated sections following Rule 4 of the Federal Rules of Civil Procedure.

Articles 2–9 and 19 of the Hague Service Convention authorize uniform procedures for extraterritorial service of judicial documents through a Central Authority designated by each country, through diplomatic channels, or by any method permitted by the internal law of the country where the service is made.

Article 10 authorizes additional extraterritorial service methods, including direct service by mail; but only if the receiving country has ratified and not objected to these alternative methods. *Water Splash v. Menon*, 581 U.S. ___, 137 S.Ct. 1504, 197 L. Ed. 2d 826 (2017). Consequently, a determination of the availability of these alternative methods requires an examination of the receiving country's accession to the Convention, as set forth in each country's "Declarations" concerning the Hague Service Convention. These Declarations are reprinted in the United States Code Annotated sections following Rule 4, F.R.C.P. The Declarations must also be consulted to determine each signatory country's requirements with respect to translation of documents to be served.

The U.S. Supreme Court in *Volkswagenwerk AG v. Schlunk*, 486 U.S. 694, 699, 108 S. Ct. 2104, 100 L. Ed. 2d 722 (1988), indicated in dicta that, by virtue of the Supremacy Clause, the Hague Service Convention preempts inconsistent methods of service prescribed by state law in all cases to which the Convention applies. CCP § 413.10(c) requires the same deference to the Convention in the California courts, as does Rule 4(f), F.R.C.P., in the federal courts.

By its terms, the Hague Service Convention applies only "where there is occasion to transmit a judicial or extrajudicial document for service abroad." Hague Service Convention, Art. 1. In other words, the Convention applies only when the law of the forum state requires formal service to be sent abroad. *Volkswagenwerk AG v. Schlunk*, *supra* (Holding Convention inapplicable where the sending forum, Illinois, did not require service abroad because its long-arm statute authorized domestic service through a subsidiary); *Rockefeller Technology Investments VII v. Changzhou SinoType Technology Co., Ltd.*, 9 Cal. 5th 125, 2020 Cal. Lexis 2091 (2020) (Concluding parties' agreement waiving formal service with respect to a company located in China in favor of informal notification constituted a waiver of formal service of process under California law, and therefore the Convention did not apply).

For commentary and analysis of the Hague Service Convention, *see* David Epstein and Jeffrey L. Snyder, *International Litigation: A Guide to Jurisdiction, Practice and Strategy*, §§ 4.01-4.05 (1993); Leonard A. Leo, Note, *The Interplay Between Domestic Rules Permitting Service Abroad by Mail and the Hague Convention on Service: Proposing an Amendment to the Federal Rules of Civil Procedure*, 22 Cornell Int'l L. J. 335 (1989); Pamela R. Parmalee, Note, *International Service of Process: A Guide to Serving Process Abroad Under the Hague Convention*, 39, Okla. L. Rev. 287 (1986).

Inter-American Convention. The United States ratified the Inter-American Convention on Letters Rogatory in 1986. This Convention, which includes Argentina, Guatemala, Mexico, Paraguay, Peru, the United States, and Uruguay among its signatories, authorizes international service of process by methods very similar to those of the Hague Service Convention. This Convention is reprinted in 14 Int'l Leg. Mat. 339 (1975), with additional Protocol reprinted in 18 Int'l Leg. Mat. 1238 (1979). For commentary on the Inter-American Convention; *see* Lucinda A. Low, *International Judicial Assistance among the American States — The Inter-American Conventions*, 18 Int'l Law. 705 (1984); Richard D. Kearney, *Developments in Private International Law*, 81 Am. J. Intl Law 724 (1987) (comparing Inter-American Convention and Hague Service Convention).

5. Procedures for Asserting Lack of Proper Service

Motion to Quash. A challenge to the validity of service of process must be made by filing a motion to quash on or before the last day to plead in response to the complaint. CCP § 418.10(a) & (b). Pursuant to a 2003 amendment to § 418.10, the defendant need not raise the objection by a special appearance, but may simultaneously answer, demur, or move to strike, so long as the objection is raised in defendant's first appearance. CCP § 418.10(e) (effective Jan. 1, 2003). If the defendant makes a general appearance, as defined in CCP § 1014, *before* filing a motion to quash objecting to lack of proper service, the defendant waives his right to contest the validity of the service. CCP § 418.10(e)(3).

Unlike the federal practice under Rule 12(b), F.R.C.P., CCP § 418.10 does not give a defendant the option to plead lack of proper service as a defense and reserve determination of that issue until as late as trial. *Roy v. Superior Court*, 127 Cal. App. 4th 337, 25 Cal. Rptr. 3d 488 (2005). Section 418.10 continues to require a timely motion to quash as the means of challenging validity of service of process. A defendant may move to quash and simultaneously file an answer containing defenses to the action, but "the latter is not a substitute for the former." *Roy*, 127 Cal. App. 4th at 345.

When a defendant properly moves to quash service of process, the burden is on the plaintiff to prove the facts establishing valid service. *Dill v. Berquist Construction Co.*, 24 Cal. App. 4th 1426, 1441–1443, 29 Cal. Rptr. 2d 746 (1994); *Taylor-Rush v. Multitech Corp.*, 217 Cal. App. 3d 103, 265 Cal. Rptr. 672 (1990). However, the return of a process server registered pursuant to § 22350 *et seq.* of the Business and Professions Code establishes a presumption, affecting the burden of producing evidence, of the truth of the facts stated in the return. Evidence Code § 647. This presumption arises only if the proof a service complies with the statutory requirements regarding such proofs. *See Dill v. Berquist Construction Co.*, supra (Proof of service which showed that the complaint was mailed to the wrong corporate officer raised no presumption of proper service).

If a motion to quash is granted, the service is quashed but the action is not dismissed. The plaintiff may attempt to perfect the court's jurisdiction by obtaining valid service, subject to applicable time limits for service such as those of CCP §§ 583.210–583.250. *Roberts v. Home Insurance Indemnity Co.*, 48 Cal. App. 3d 313, 317, 121 Cal. Rptr. 862 (1975). If a motion to quash is denied, the defendant may obtain immediate appellate review by a writ of mandate. CCP § 418.10(c).

6. Time Limits on Service of Process

Mandatory Dismissal. The complaint and summons must be served upon a defendant within three years after the action is commenced against the defendant. CCP §§ 583.210(a), 583.110. Return of summons or other proof of service must be made within 60 days after the time the summons and complaint must be served upon the defendant. § 583.210(b). These time-for-service requirements do not apply if the defendant enters into a written stipulation or does another act which constitutes a general appearance. § 583.220. Other exceptions and time exclusions are set forth in CCP § 583.230 and § 583.240. Failure to serve within the prescribed time will result in mandatory dismissal of the action. § 583.250.

Discretionary Dismissal. Service not made within two years after the action is commenced against the defendant may result in discretionary dismissal for delay in prosecution pursuant to CCP §§ 583.410, 583.420(a)(1) and Rules 3.1340 & 3.1342, Cal. Rules of Ct.

Court Rules. Rule 3.110 requires service of the complaint on all named defendants, and proofs of service filed, within 60 days after the filing of the complaint, unless the court orders an extension of time. Rule 3.110(b) & (e), Cal. Rules of Ct.

7. Process Servers

A summons and complaint may be served by any person who is at least 18 years of age and not a party to the action. CCP § 414.10. Consequently, although state laws also authorize a sheriff (Gov. Code § 26608), marshall (Gov. Code § 26665), constable (Gov. Code § 27820), or registered process server (Bus. & Prof. Code §§ 22350–22358) to serve the complaint and summons; the plaintiff has the option to select any adult individual to serve these documents.

8. Proof of Service

After a summons has been served, the summons must be returned together with proof of service as defined in CCP § 417.10 and § 417.20. CCP § 417.30(a); *see* Judicial Council Form POS-010. Actual service of process vests a court with jurisdiction to act in a matter rather than proof of service. *Oats v. Oats*, 148 Cal. App. 3d 416, 420, 196 Cal. Rptr. 20 (1983); *Willen v. Boggs*, 21 Cal. App. 3d 520, 523–24, 97 Cal. Rptr. 917 (1971). Proof and return of service, however, must be made within the required time limits of CCP § 583.210 to avoid mandatory dismissal. *Johnson & Johnson v. Superior Court*, 38 Cal. 3d 243, 211 Cal. Rptr. 517, 695 P.2d 1058 (1985).

E. Forum Non Conveniens

1. Relevant Factors Under the California Doctrine

Private and Public Interest Factors. The California doctrine of forum non conveniens is virtually identical to the federal doctrine applied by the U.S. Supreme Court in *Piper Aircraft Co. v. Reyno*, 454 U.S. 235, 259–261, 102 S. Ct. 252, 70 L. Ed. 2d 419,

437–439 (1981) and *Gulf Oil Corp. v. Gilbert*, 330 U.S. 501, 507–509, 67 S. Ct. 839, 91 L. Ed. 1055, 1061–1063 (1947). In *Stangvik v. Shiley Inc.*, 54 Cal. 3d 744, 751, 1 Cal. Rptr. 2d 556, 819 P.2d 14 (1991), the California Supreme Court describes the California doctrine in the following manner:

> In determining whether to grant a motion based on forum non conveniens, a court must first determine whether the alternate forum is a "suitable" place for trial. If it is, the next step is to consider the private interests of the litigants and the interests of the public in retaining the action for trial in California. The private interest factors are those that make trial and the enforceability of the ensuing judgment expeditious and relatively inexpensive, such as the ease of access to sources of proof, the cost of obtaining attendance of witnesses, and the availability of compulsory process for attendance of unwilling witnesses. The public interest factors include avoidance of overburdening local courts with congested calendars, protecting the interests of potential jurors so that they are not called upon to decide cases in which the local community has little concern, and weighing the competing interests of California and the alternate jurisdiction in the litigation. (*Piper Aircraft Co. v. Reyno* (1981) 454 U.S. 235, 259–261 [102 S. Ct. 252, 70 L. Ed. 2d 419, 437–439]; *Gulf Oil Corp. v. Gilbert* (1947) 330 U.S. 501, 507–509 [91 L. Ed. 1055, 1061–63, 67 S. Ct. 839].)

Like the federal doctrine, the possibility of an unfavorable change in the law is not accorded any weight in deciding a motion provided, however, that "some remedy is afforded." *Stangvik, supra*, 34 Cal. 3d at 753, n. 5.

Effect of Plaintiff's Residency. The effect of the plaintiff's residence in deciding a motion to dismiss for forum non conveniens under the California doctrine is essentially the same as under the federal doctrine. Although a trial court must accord substantial deference to a resident plaintiff's choice of a California court, a non-resident plaintiff's choice of a California court is not a substantial factor in favor of retaining jurisdiction. *Stangvik, supra*, 34 Cal. 3d at 754–755. One area where the California and federal doctrines may differ is over the treatment of a resident plaintiff when the defendant seeks a *stay* as opposed to a *dismissal*, as discussed below.

Dismissal vs. Stay. A court that dismisses a suit on grounds of forum non conveniens loses jurisdiction over the action. A court that stays the action retains jurisdiction over the parties and the cause, and can protect the interests of the parties pending the final decision of the foreign court. *Archibald v. Cinerama Hotels*, 15 Cal. 3d 853, 126 Cal. Rptr. 811, 544 P.2d 947 (1976). Several recent decisions have relied on the distinction between a dismissal and a stay to affirm a forum non conveniens stay even though the plaintiffs are California residents. *E.g., Berg v. MTC Electronics Technologies Co.*, 61 Cal. App. 4th 349, 71 Cal. Rptr. 2d 523 (1998); *Century Indemnity Co. v. Bank of America, FSB*, 58 Cal. App. 4th 408, 68 Cal. Rptr. 2d 132 (1997). Other cases have found this distinction relevant to the threshold issue of whether there is a suitable alternative forum. *E.g., Hansen v. Owens-Corning Fiberglas Corp.*, 51 Cal. App. 4th 753, 59 Cal. Rptr. 2d 229 (1996) (Moving party seeking a forum non conveniens *stay* not required to show all defendants are subject to personal jurisdiction in a particular alternative forum); *American Cemwood Corp. v. American Home Assurance Co.*, 87 Cal. App. 4th 431, 104 Cal. Rptr. 2d 670 (2001) (Failure of the moving party to demonstrated that all defendants are subject to jurisdiction in British Columbia precluded a forum non conveniens *dismissal*; *Hansen* was inapposite because there the moving party only sought a *stay*).

Chapter V

Joinder of Parties and Claims

A. Joinder of Parties and Claims, Generally

1. Permissive Joinder of Parties

Permissive Joinder of Plaintiffs. Code of Civil Procedure § 378 permits joinder of plaintiffs if they assert any right to relief "arising out of the same transaction, occurrence, or series of transactions or occurrences and if any question of law or fact common to all these persons will arise in the action. . . ." The courts liberally construe this statutory standard so as to permit joinder of plaintiffs. *See, e.g., Anaya v. Superior Court,* 160 Cal. App. 3d 228, 206 Cal. Rptr. 520 (1984) (Numerous employees of oil company permitted to join in one lawsuit seeking damages for exposure to toxic chemicals over the course of 20 years); *State Farm Fire & Casualty Co. v. Superior Court,* 45 Cal. App. 4th 1093, 53 Cal. Rptr. 2d 229 (1996) (Group of insured homeowners, whose homes were destroyed by an earthquake, were properly joined as plaintiffs).

Permissive Joinder of Defendants. Permissive joinder of defendants is proper where the complaint asserts against them any right to relief "arising out of the same transaction, occurrence, or series of transactions or occurrences and if any question of law or fact common to all defendants will arise in the action. . . ." CCP § 379; *see Farmers Ins. Exchange v. Adams,* 170 Cal. App. 3d 712, 216 Cal. Rptr. 287 (1985) (Joinder of 300 homeowners as defendants in action by plaintiff insurance company to declare plaintiff not liable for storm damage held inappropriate because claims did not arise from the "same transaction or occurrence").

There are important advantages to joining all co-defendants in one lawsuit where each defendant blames another defendant for the plaintiff's injuries. A typical example is a tort case where each defendant denies negligence, but argues that the plaintiff's injuries were caused by another defendant's negligence. If the plaintiff pursues separate actions against each defendant, there is a risk that the plaintiff will recover nothing even though the jury finds that her injuries were caused by *some* defendant's negligence. How so? What are the other advantages of joining several co-defendants into one action? What are the disadvantages?

Federal Rule 20(a) compared. The broad permissive joinder test of CCP § and § 379 is essentially the same as that of Rule 20(a) of the Federal Rules of Civil Procedure. *See Cal. Law Revision Comm'n Comments—1971 Amendments.*

2. Permissive Joinder of Claims

Code of Civil Procedure § 427.10 provides that a plaintiff who alleges a cause of action against one or more defendants "may unite with such cause any other causes which he has . . . against any such defendants." This provision effectively eliminates misjoinder of claims as a defense so long as joinder of parties is proper. *See Landau v. Salam*, 4 Cal. 3d 901, 905, 95 Cal. Rptr. 46, 484 P.2d 1390 (1971). The unlimited joinder of claims authorized by CCP § 427.10 is the same as that of Rule 18(a) of the Federal Rules of Civil Procedure.

3. Compulsory Joinder of Parties

Code of Civil Procedure § 389, which conforms substantially to Rule 19 of the Federal Rules of Civil Procedure, sets forth the criteria for compulsory joinder of parties. Section 389 requires joinder of any person who is subject to service of process and whose joinder will not deprive the court of subject matter jurisdiction, and who meets one of the criteria stated in § 389(a). In such circumstances, the trial court should not dismiss, but should order joinder of the missing person. *See, e.g., Conrad v. Unemployment Insurance Appeals Bd.*, 47 Cal. App. 3d 237, 241, 120 Cal. Rptr. 803 (1975).

If joinder is not possible, then the trial court must consider factors such as those contained in section 389(b) to determine whether, as an exercise of equitable discretion, the action should proceed with the existing parties or should be dismissed. *See, e.g., Deltakeeper v. Oakdale Irrigation Dist.*, 94 Cal. App. 4th 1092, 115 Cal. Rptr. 2d 244 (2001) (In a writ proceeding challenging an environmental impact report for a project involving a joint district water purchase agreement, trial court erred in dismissing the writ petition for failure to join all of the water purchasers as indispensable parties because the nonjoined parties' interests were adequately represented by the existing parties and there was no adequate remedy if the action is dismissed as the statute of limitations had run for joining more parties); *People ex rel. Lungren v. Community Redevelopment Agency*, 56 Cal. App. 4th 868, 65 Cal. Rptr. 2d 786 (1997) (Trial court abused its discretion in dismissing a complaint filed by the Attorney General against a city's community redevelopment agency to set aside a contract between the agency and an American Indian tribe under which the agency would transfer real property to the tribe for development of a gaming casino, where the tribe could not be joined because of its sovereign immunity).

Only if the trial court determines dismissal appropriate is the absent person regarded as "indispensable." *See, e.g., Save Our Bay, Inc. v. San Diego Unified Port Dist.*, 42 Cal. App. 4th 686, 49 Cal. Rptr. 2d 847 (1996) (Affirming dismissal of a mandate proceeding brought by an environmental organization challenging the adequacy of an environmental impact report for a marine project where the landowner, whose land had to be acquired to complete the project, was an indispensable party who could not be joined because a statutory 30-day limitation period for joining the landowner had expired).

B. Cross-Complaints

1. Cross-Complaints, Generally

The California cross-complaint is a multi-purpose pleading device which permits a party defending against a cause of action to assert her own affirmative cause of action against an opposing party, a co-party, or some other person not already a party to the action. CCP §§ 428.10–428.80. The California cross-complaint serves the same functions as the familiar counterclaim, cross-claim, and third-party impleader in federal court. *See* Rules 13 and 14, Federal Rules of Civil Procedure. The California legislature opted for the one-term-fits-all approach in 1971 when it eliminated technical limitations of prior methods of countersuits and replaced them with a single form of pleading. *See, e.g.,* CCP § 428.80 (Counterclaims abolished and deemed cross-complaints); Jack H. Friedenthal, *Joinder of Claims, Counterclaims, and Cross-Complaints: Suggested Revisions of the California Provisions*, 23 Stan. L. Rev. 1, 17–39 (1970); *1970 Law Revision Commission Report*, pp. 518–551.

The cross-complaint is one of the four types of pleadings allowed in civil actions, CCP § 422.10; and is the only pleading other than a complaint that can demand affirmative relief. *See* CCP § 431.30(c) (affirmative relief cannot be claimed in an answer). A cross-complaint must be filed and served as a separate document, and must comply with the same form and content rules applicable to a complaint. *See* CCP §§ 425.10, 428.40–428.60. A cross-complaint must, within 30 days after service, be responded to in the same manner as an original complaint. CCP § 432.10. Dismissal of the underlying complaint does not constitute a dismissal of a cross-complaint. *See* CCP § 581(i).

2. Compulsory Cross-Complaints

Code of Civil Procedure §§ 426.10 and 426.30 set forth the general preclusion rules for failure to plead a compulsory cross-complaint. Section 426.30(a) states:

> Except as otherwise provided by statute, if a party against whom a complaint has been filed and served fails to allege in a cross-complaint any related cause of action which (at the time of serving his answer to the complaint) he has against the plaintiff, such party may not thereafter in any other action assert against the plaintiff the related cause of action not pleaded.

Section 426.10(a) defines "complaint" to mean a complaint or cross-complaint; § 426.10(b) defines "plaintiff" to mean a person who files a complaint or a cross-complaint. Section 426.10(c) then provides:

> "Related cause of action" means a cause of action which arises out of the same transaction, occurrences, or series of transactions or occurrences as the cause of action which the plaintiff alleges in his complaint.

Section 426.10(c) utilizes the same type of "transactional" standard in defining a compulsory cross-complaint as is utilized by Rule 13(a) of the Federal Rules of Civil

Procedure in defining a compulsory counterclaim. *See Currie Medical Specialties, Inc. v. Newell Bowen*, 136 Cal. App. 3d 774, 186 Cal. Rptr. 543 (1982) (Both the federal and California courts apply the expansive "logical relationship" test when interpreting the transactional standard).

3. Cross-Complaints, Equitable Indemnity, and Good Faith Settlements

Cross-Complaints and Equitable Indemnity. California follows the tort rule of comparative negligence, under which an injured individual's recovery is proportionately diminished, rather than completely eliminated, when the injured individual is partially responsible for the injury. *Li v. Yellow Cab Co.*, 13 Cal. 3d 804, 119 Cal. Rptr. 858, 532 P.2d 1226 (1975). Subject to some important statutory exceptions, such as those expressed in Civil Code §§ 1431–1431.5, California also follows the doctrine of "joint and several liability," whereby which each tortfeasor whose negligence is a proximate cause of an indivisible injury remains individually liable for all compensable damages attributed to that injury. *Summers v. Tice*, 33 Cal. 2d 80, 199 P.2d 1 (1948). This doctrine recognizes that the wronged party may sue one or all of such concurrent (or "joint") tortfeasors to obtain recovery for his injuries, but that the tortfeasors should be left to determine the allocation of loss among themselves. *Id.* In apportioning liability among concurrent tortfeasors, California permits partial equitable indemnity, under which liability among multiple tortfeasors is apportioned on a comparative fault basis. *American Motorcycle Ass'n v. Superior Court*, 20 Cal. 3d 578, 146 Cal. Rptr. 182, 578 P.2d 899 (1978).

A typical use of the cross-complaint joinder device is to assert a claim for partial equitable indemnity against an existing co-defendant or against a new, third-party defendant. This use permits a court to resolve all potential liability issues between plaintiffs and defendants, and among defendants, in one lawsuit. For example, assume that plaintiff sues defendants A and B and C for injuries caused by defendants' concurrent negligence. The defendants file cross-complaints for equitable indemnity against each other. The jury awards $100,000 in damages and allocates fault as follows: Plaintiff (10%), defendant A (10%), defendant B (30%), and defendant C (50%). Based on comparative negligence, the plaintiff is entitled to recover $90,000 from the defendants. Under the doctrine of joint and several liability, the plaintiff can recover the entire $90,000 from one (or more) of the defendants. If defendant A pays the entire $90,000 to plaintiff, how much can defendant A then recover from defendant B based on defendant A's cross-complaint for partial equitable indemnity? From defendant C?

Good Faith Settlement. When a settlement is entered into between the plaintiff and one of several joint tortfeasors prior to trial, and is determined by the court to be a "good faith" settlement within the meaning of CCP §§ 877 and 877.6, that settlement bars any other joint tortfeasor from any further claims against the settling tortfeasor for equitable comparative indemnity. CCP § 877.6(c). Also, in those cases where the doctrine of joint and several liability applies, the plaintiff's recovery from the nonsettling tortfeasor is reduced by the amount of the good faith settlement. CCP § 877(a); *see American Motorcycle Ass'n v. Superior Court, supra.*

The court will declare that a settlement was made in "good faith" if, after following the hearing procedures set forth in CCP § 877.6 and applying the relevant standards set forth in *Tech-Bilt, Inc. v. Woodward-Clyde & Associates*, 38 Cal. 3d 488, 499–500, 213 Cal. Rptr. 256, 698 P.2d 159 (1985), it concludes "the amount of the settlement is within the reasonable range of the settling tortfeasor's proportional share of comparative liability for the plaintiff's injuries." *Tech-Bilt, supra*, 38 Cal. 3d at 499. In other words, a defendant's settlement figure must not be grossly disproportionate to what a reasonable person, at the time of the settlement, would estimate the settling defendant's liability to be. *Id.* Why require a settling defendant to settle "in the ballpark" of estimated liability in order to gain immunity from comparative indemnity?

The Effect of a Good Faith Settlement. The following hypothetical demonstrates the effect of a good faith settlement. Assume plaintiff sues three joint tortfeasors for injuries caused by their alleged negligence, and that the doctrine of joint and several liability applies. Plaintiff settles with defendant A for $50,000 prior to trial, and the settlement is determined to be in good faith within the meaning of CCP § 877.6. Defendants file cross-complaints for equitable indemnity against each other. Following a trial, the jury awards plaintiff $250,000, allocating fault as follows: Defendant A (10%), defendant B (30%), and defendant C (60%).

How much is the plaintiff entitled to recover from the non-settling defendants? If defendant B pays plaintiff that entire amount, how much is B entitled to recover from defendant A? From defendant C? How much is defendant A entitled to recover from defendant B? From defendant C?

The Fair Responsibility Act. The voter-approved Fair Responsibility Act of 1986 (Prop. 51), Civil Code §§ 1431–1431.5, modifies the common law rule of joint and several liability by making each defendant's liability for "non-economic" damages several and not joint in comparative fault cases. "Each defendant shall be liable only for the amount of non-economic damages allocated to that defendant in direct proportion to that defendant's percentage of fault." Civil Code § 1431.2(a). "Non-economic damages" are defined in Civil Code § 1431.2(b) to mean objectively verifiable monetary losses, such as medical expenses and loss of earnings; "economic damages" to mean subjective, non-monetary losses such as pain, suffering, loss of consortium, and injury to reputation.

The Fair Responsibility Act complicates the apportionment calculations in a "good faith" settlement situation. *See, e.g., Espinoza v. Machonga*, 9 Cal. App. 4th 268, 11 Cal. Rptr. 498 (1992) (Applying the following formula for calculating offsets from a good faith settlement: The portion of the settlement which may be set off from a judgment of economic damages is determined by application of the percentage of the economic damages awarded in relation to the total award of damages); *Hackett v. John Crane, Inc.*, 98 Cal. App. 4th 1233, 120 Cal. Rptr. 2d 662 (2002) (Applying the *Espinoza* formula in a wrongful death action).

Try your hand at answering the questions in the following simple hypothetical. Assume plaintiff sues defendants A, B, and C for personal injuries caused by defendants' alleged joint negligence. Plaintiff settles with defendant A for $300,000 before trial. The jury renders a verdict for plaintiff against all defendants for a total amount of $1 million in economic damages and another $1 million in non-economic damages. The special verdict allocates fault as follows: defendant A (60%), defendant B (30%), and defendant C (10%). How much is plaintiff entitled to recover from defendant B? From defendant C?

C. Intervention

1. Permissive Intervention

Bustop v. Superior Court

Court of Appeal of California, Second Appellate District

69 Cal. App. 3d 66, 137 Cal. Rptr. 793 (1977)

THE COURT.

In August of 1963, the case of "Mary Ellen Crawford, a minor, by Ellen Crawford, her guardian ad litem, et al, Plaintiffs, vs. Board of Education of the City of Los Angeles,[1] Defendant," (No. C 822 854) was instituted in the Superior Court of Los Angeles County. That action was aimed at correcting the alleged existence of racial segregation in the defendant school district.

In 1976, the California Supreme Court filed its opinion in that case (*Crawford v. Board of Education*, 17 Cal. 3d 280 [130 Cal. Rptr. 724, 551 P.2d 28]) affirming the trial court's determination that the defendant district was in fact segregated. The court also affirmed the trial court's order directing the defendant to prepare and implement "a reasonably feasible desegregation plan."

Subsequently defendant district undertook the political process of developing a "Plan for the Integration of Pupils in the Los Angeles Unified School District" (the Plan). The record before us does not delineate in detail the procedural steps in that process but we are informed by the parties that citizen as well as staff participation was involved and that divergent recommendations were received and considered.

The ultimate responsibility for promulgating the Plan was that of the elected members of the school board and the wisdom of their proposal is, of course, in the political process subject to the scrutiny and reactions of their constituents. The adequacy of the Plan vis-a-vis the mandate of the court is subject to the scrutiny of the court.

The Plan was submitted to the Superior Court of Los Angeles County on March 18, 1977, and the issue of its adequacy is currently being litigated. Again we are not provided with the details of the Plan except to the extent that the parties concede that the Plan contemplates a certain amount of mandatory reassignment of students to

---

1. The defendant later became the Los Angeles Unified School District.

schools other than their so-called "neighborhood schools," i.e., schools in the area in which they reside.

Prior to the presentation of the Plan petitioner Bustop, a nonprofit corporation, petitioned for leave to intervene in the action pursuant to section 387 of the Code of Civil Procedure. That section provides in part that "At any time before trial, any person, who has an interest in the matter in litigation, or in the success of either of the parties, *or an interest against both*, may intervene in the action or proceeding." (Italics added.)

Bustop is an organization with a membership of 65,000 parents, predominantly white, residing within the Los Angeles Unified School District. The organization's prime objective is the prevention of mandatory reassignment of students to schools other than those which they now attend or choose to attend.

The trial court by minute order entered March 14, 1977, denied Bustop's petition. Bustop petitioned this court for a writ of mandate to compel the trial court to permit intervention. We granted an alternative writ.

Bustop's proposed complaint in intervention alleges, and correctly so, that the Supreme Court in its opinion in *Crawford, supra,* did not require mandatory reassignment of students as a necessary element of any plan.

For that matter the court did not set forth any specific requirements but did state at page 306: "In our view, reliance on the judgment of local school boards in choosing between alternative desegregation strategies holds society's best hope for the formulation and implementation of desegregation plans which will actually achieve the ultimate constitutional objective. . . ."

Plaintiffs and the defendant district both oppose intervention by Bustop. They concede, and we agree, that Bustop represents a point of view which is entitled to and which should be heard and considered. The point of departure is the forum in which that hearing and consideration should take place.

The district's contention is that that point of view was considered in the political process of formulating the Plan but that now the issue is whether the Plan will satisfy the court and not whether the Plan is acceptable to the various elements that make up the district's constituency.

The trial court's order denying intervention followed the position of the district. That order recites as follows:

"This case is now on remand to this Court with the specific direction that it first look to the plans that were to be formulated by the Board to insure that the plans presented and filed with this Court by the respondent have met the constitutional standards in response to the mandate.

"Therefore, within that frame of reference, the stated function of this Court in this portion of the proceedings is limited. There is not, at the present time, the necessity or requirement that the broad equity powers inherent in this Court for the enforcement of injunction or mandate decrees should be called into play. . . ."

The trial court's order further says that it is entered "without prejudice to renew the motions if at a later stage the function of the Court should be radically changed, . . ."

The district's objection to intervention is further based on the arguments that (1) the district represents all of the residents of the district, and (2) that to permit Bustop to intervene would open the way for a multitude of other individuals and groups to also intervene.

For their part plaintiffs argue that the requirements of Code of Civil Procedure section 387 are not met by Bustop in that that organization has no "direct interest" in the outcome since no student has a "right" to remain assigned to any particular school and that any reassignment as a result of this litigation would only be an indirect consequence of an order designed to protect the interest of the minority students. We are of the opinion that facially Bustop satisfied the requirements of Code of Civil Procedure section 387 in its petition to intervene. Its members and the persons whom it purports to represent do have an interest in the litigation.

As was stated in *Johnson v. San Francisco Unified School District* (9th Cir. 1974) 500 F.2d 349, at p. 353, "[All] students and parents, whatever their race, have an interest in a sound educational system and in the operation of that system in accordance with the law. That interest is surely no less significant where, as here, it is entangled with the constitutional claims of a racially defined class."

Certainly the reassignment of students to schools distant from their residences would have a direct social, educational and economic impact on the students so reassigned and their parents.

This interest of those persons represented by Bustop is not presently represented by the parties to the action. The plaintiffs admittedly represent only the interests of specific minority students. Counsel for the district frankly admitted on oral argument that the district opposes intervention because Bustop's interpretation of the *Crawford* decision is contrary to that of the district's interpretation and in effect the position of the two are opposing. While conceding that *Crawford* does not mandate reassignment or "busing" of students the district contends as a practical matter that compliance with the court mandate requires it. Bustop disagrees.

In *Johnson v. San Francisco Unified School District, supra,* parents of elementary school children of Chinese ancestry sought to intervene in an action involving the compulsory reassignment of students in San Francisco to schools outside the area of their residences in order to achieve integration of black students into predominantly white schools. They claimed that such reassignment would impinge on the cultural and educational interests of the Chinese community and that they should be entitled to participate in fashioning any "desegregation" decree. The United States Circuit Court of Appeals agreed. We find that case on principle to be indistinguishable from the case before us.

In answer to the argument that the school board represented all of the district, the court there said at page 354: "[We] cannot agree . . . that the school district, which is charged with the representation of all parents within the district and which authored the very plan which appellants claim impairs their interest, adequately represents appellants."

The district's fear that Bustop's intervention may lead to a proliferation of interveners is unfounded. Further intervention can easily be limited by permitting additional intervention only by persons or groups whose interest is presently unrepresented in the action.

Nor would the intervention of Bustop necessitate any duplication of evidence or repetition of proceedings heretofore conducted. While Bustop may recall witnesses for cross-examination or present its own evidence, it must take the proceedings as it finds them at the time of intervention. This includes the qualification of the trial judge and precludes any right to disqualify him pursuant to Code of Civil Procedure section 170.6.[2]

Bustop does not and has not challenged the original finding in this case that the schools of the district are "segregated." Nor does it seek to challenge the principle that the district has a legal responsibility to take action to alleviate that condition. Hence the "trial" of the matter for all practical purposes began with the proceedings aimed at obtaining court approval of the Plan. Bustop's petition to intervene was filed prior to that time and was therefore timely.

Finally we reach the issue of the trial court's discretion in refusing to permit intervention. We agree with the trial court's statements in its minute order which delineates a limited role for the court in these proceedings and which opines that the input of various constituencies should be confined to the political process. As we view it the single issue before the trial court at this time is whether the Plan satisfies the requirements of the decision of the *California Supreme Court ruling in Crawford*.

Apropos of that concept is the Supreme Court's language in *Crawford v. Board of Education, supra,* 17 Cal. 3d 280, at pages 305 and 306: "[So] long as a local school board initiates and implements reasonably feasible steps to alleviate school segregation in its district, and so long as such steps produce meaningful progress in the alleviation of such segregation, and its harmful consequences, we do not believe the judiciary should intervene in the desegregation process. Under such circumstances, a court thus should not step in even if it believes that alternative desegregation techniques may produce more rapid desegregation in the school district."

So long as the litigation remains in the posture envisioned by the trial judge the role of Bustop as an intervener may be limited by rulings on the admissibility of proffered evidence.

However, lurking in the background is the language of *Crawford*, at page 307: "If, however, a court finds that a local school board has not implemented such a course

---

2. Bustop has stipulated to waive the provisions of Code of Civil Procedure section 170.6 as a condition of intervention.

of action, the court is left with no alternative but to intervene. . . . Faced with a recalcitrant or intractable school board, a trial court may exercise broad equitable powers in formulating and supervising a plan. . . ."

The history of performance of trial and appellate courts in this country in involvement with the operation of schools and school districts unfortunately has too often been one of overinvolvement rather than restraint. We have no way of predicting what turn the present litigation may take and while the trial court's order is a model of judicial restraint, it suggests the possibility that down stream the picture may change.

In the interest of fairness and to insure the maximum involvement by all responsible interested and affected persons, we believe that the proper exercise of discretion would have been to permit Bustop, representing as it does a proper and legitimate interest, to participate in the fashioning of any decree which may result in the mandatory reassignment and busing of students.

Let a peremptory writ of mandate issue directing the trial court to grant Bustop's petition to intervene. The alternative writ is discharged.

Notes and Questions Regarding Permissive Intervention

(1) *Direct Interest.* Code of Civil Procedure § 387(a) provides that any "interested" person may intervene in an action. The California courts interpret this broad authority to permit intervention to include several limitations. One is that the intervener's interest must not already be represented by existing parties. *E.g., Bustop v. Superior Court, supra.* Another is that the intervener's interest must be "direct and immediate," and not "indirect and consequential." In other words, as one court explained, the interest "must be of such direct and immediate character that the intervener will either gain or lose by the direct legal operation and effect of the judgment." *Knight v. Alefosio*, 158 Cal. App. 3d 716, 721, 205 Cal. Rptr. 42 (1984). Whether the intervener's interest is sufficiently direct must be decided on the facts of each case. *See, e.g., Simpson Redwood Co. v. State of California*, 196 Cal. App. 3d 1192, 1200, 242 Cal. Rptr. 447 (1987) (Analyzing several factors and holding that a group interested in preservation of old growth redwoods should be permitted to intervene in quiet title action regarding boundaries of state park); *Highland Development Co. v. City of Los Angeles*, 170 Cal. App. 3d 169, 179–180, 215 Cal. Rptr. 881 (1985) (Concluding that some, but not all, groups opposed to the construction of an apartment building adjacent to an historic district possessed the requisite direct interest for intervention in litigation between the developer and the city over the right to a city construction permit). However, the intervener need neither claim a pecuniary interest nor a specific legal or equitable interest in the subject matter of the litigation. *Simpson, supra.* And CCP § 387(a) should be liberally construed in favor of litigation. *Id.*

(a) The *Bustop* court held that a group of white parents opposed to mandatory busing of students had sufficient interest "in a sound educational system and in the operation of that system in accordance with the law" to permit intervention in an action where a school district was required to formulate a desegregation plan. Such plan would have a "direct social, educational and economic impact" on all students and parents in the district. *Id.* Based on this broad view of "direct and immediate interest," what other political action groups could be permitted to intervene in this desegregation litigation? What limitations are there on intervention by such groups?

(b) After the appellate ruling in *Bustop*, another organization entitled BEST (Better Education for Students Today) also sought intervention in the trial court. BEST's complaint in intervention disavowed any position toward any integration plan, but asserted that its members were well-intentioned citizens who would certainly have developed positions on the issues by the time they got to court. Should BEST be permitted to intervene? For a criticism of the reasoning in *Bustop* as an improper extension of the permissive intervention statute, *see* Stephen C. Yeazell, *Intervention and the Idea of Litigation: A Commentary on the Los Angeles School Case*, 25 U.C.L.A. L. Rev. 244 (1977).

(2) *Discretion.* Granting or denying leave to intervene under § 387(a) is in the discretion of the trial court. *See, e.g., Bustop, supra; Lincoln National Life Insurance Co. v. State Board of Equalization*, 30 Cal. App. 4th 1411, 36 Cal. Rptr. 2d 397 (1994) (Unless a special statute prohibits intervention, the trial court's discretion to permit intervention should be liberally construed in favor of intervention). Even if an applicant establishes the requisite interest in the litigation, a trial court may deny permissive intervention. What factors did the court in *Bustop* consider in exercising this discretion? How did it apply these factors?

2. Intervention of Right

In 1977, the Legislature amended CCP § 387 to authorize intervention of right in addition to traditional permissive intervention. After rewording in 2017, section 387(d)(1) provides:

> The court shall, upon timely application, permit a nonparty to intervene in the action or proceeding if either of the following conditions is satisfied: (A) A provision of law confers an unconditional right to intervene. (B) The person seeking intervention claims an interest relating to the property or transaction that is the subject of the action and that person is so situated that the disposition of the action may impair or impede that person's ability to protect that interest, unless that person's interest is adequately represented by one or more of the existing parties.

Section 387(d)(1) is modeled after Rule 24(a) of the Federal Rules of Civil Procedure.

D. Class Actions

1. No Comprehensive Class Action Statute

The class action is the ultimate joinder device. One or more named plaintiffs may represent the interests of thousands of absentee class members, and may obtain a class judgment that will bind those absentees by res judicata. E.g., *Daar v. Yellow Cab Co.*, 67 Cal. 2d 695, 63 Cal. Rptr. 724, 433 P.2d 732 (1967) (Class action by taxicab customer against taxicab company on behalf of all others similarly situated to recover excessive charges would be res judicata on thousands of class members); *Lazar v. Hertz Corp.*, 143 Cal. App. 3d 128, 191 Cal. Rptr. 849 (1983) (Class action on behalf of approximately 5,000,000 rental car customers); *Cartt v. Superior Court*, 50 Cal. App. 3d 960, 124 Cal. Rptr. 376 (1975) (Consumer class action on behalf of over 700,000 credit card holders).

Despite the obvious importance of the class actions and their concomitant potential for procedural problems, the California Legislature has yet to enact a comprehensive statute which specifically governs all applications of the class action device. The courts rely on CCP § 382 as the general authority for class actions and on Civil Code § 1781 for procedural guidelines. In the absence of controlling California authority, the California Supreme Court has suggested that trial courts utilize the class action procedures of Rule 23 of the Federal Rules of Civil Procedure. *City of San Jose v. Superior Court*, 12 Cal. 3d 447, 453, 115 Cal. Rptr. 797, 525 P.2d 701 (1974) (Trial courts should be procedurally innovative and incorporate class action procedures from outside sources, specifically Rule 23, F.R.C.P.); *La Sala v. American Savings & Loan Assn.*, 5 Cal. 3d 864, 872, 97 Cal. Rptr. 849, 489 P.2d 1113 (1971). Consequently, the California courts often cite federal court interpretations of Federal Rule 23 as authority when determining state court class action procedural issues. E.g., *Bell v. American Title Ins. Co.*, 226 Cal. App. 3d 1589, 277 Cal. Rptr. 583 (1991); *Frazier v. City of Richmond*, 184 Cal. App. 3d 1491, 228 Cal. Rptr. 376 (1986). You might therefore expect that the California courts' treatment of the class action device would be identical to that of the federal courts. In most applications, that expectation is reality. But in a few important procedural areas, discussed below, the California courts' approach differs markedly from that of the federal courts.

2. General California Prerequisites

The party seeking certification as a class action representative must establish the existence of an "ascertainable class" and a "well-defined community of interest" among the class members. *Richmond v. Dart Industries, Inc.*, 29 Cal. 3d 462, 174 Cal. Rptr. 515, 629 P.2d 23 (1981); *Daar v. Yellow Cab Co.*, 67 Cal. 2d 695, 704, 63 Cal. Rptr. 724, 433 P.2d 732 (1967). The "community of interest" requirement embodies three factors: (1) common questions of law or fact must predominate over individual issues; (2) class representatives must have claims or defenses typical of the class; and (3) class representatives must adequately represent the interests of the class. *See Richmond v. Dart*

Industries, supra, 29 Cal. 3d at 470; *Lockheed Martin Corp. v. Superior Court*, 29 Cal. 4th 1096, 1104, 131 Cal. Rptr. 2d 1, 63 P.3d 913 (2003); Civil Code § 1781(b)(2)–(4).

In *Brinker Restaurant Corp. v. Superior Court*, 53 Cal. 4th 1004, 139 Cal. Rptr. 3d 315, 273 P.3d 513 (2012), the California Supreme Court discussed the requirement that common questions must predominate over individual issues to certify a wage and hour class action. Citing numerous lower court cases, the Supreme Court noted that "[c]laims alleging a uniform policy consistently applied to a group of employees is in violation of the wage and hour laws are the sort routinely, and properly, found suitable for class treatment." *Brinker*, 53 Cal. 4th at 1033. In another wage and hour class action, *Duran v. U.S. Bank National Association*, 59 Cal. 4th 1, 172 Cal. Rptr. 3d 371, 325 P.3d 916 (2014), the California Supreme Court further discussed this requirement, observing that a finding that group, rather than individual, issues predominate "does not preclude consideration of individual issues at trial when those issues legitimately touch upon relevant aspects of the case being litigated." *Id.* at 28.

However, where individual issues regarding liability and damages substantially predominate over common factual questions, class action treatment is rarely appropriate. *City of San Jose v. Superior Court*, 12 Cal. 3d 447, 115 Cal. Rptr. 797, 525 P.2d 701 (1974). This common questions factor usually precludes class certification of mass tort actions for personal injuries. *See, e.g., Lockheed Martin Corp. v. Superior Court, supra* (Reversing certification of a medical monitoring class consisting of over 50,000 residents of Redlands, California who had consumed drinking water allegedly contaminated by the defendants' discharges of toxic chemicals over several decades because plaintiffs failed to demonstrate by substantial evidence that these common issues of causation and damages *predominate* over the individual ones); *Jolly v. Eli Lilly & Co.*, 44 Cal. 3d 1103, 1123, 245 Cal. Rptr. 658, 751 P.2d 923 (1988) (Mass tort actions for personal injury are rarely appropriate for class certification because their major elements — liability, proximate cause, and damages — may vary widely as to each individual claimant).

Whether a class is ascertainable may be determined by examining the class definition, the size of the class, and the means available for identifying class members. *Reyes v. San Diego County Bd. of Supervisors*, 196 Cal. App. 3d 1263, 1274, 242 Cal. Rptr. 339 (1987); *Miller v. Woods*, 148 Cal. App. 3d 862, 873, 196 Cal. Rptr. 69 (1983). If the existence of an ascertainable class has been shown, however, there is no need to identify its individual members in order to bind all members by the judgment. *Daar v. Yellow Cab Co.*, 67 Cal. 2d 695, 706, 63 Cal. Rptr. 724, 433 P.2d 732 (1967).

3. Class Action Procedures

Because few generally applicable state statutes or rules exist to govern class action procedures, the California courts usually follow the procedural provisions of the Consumers Legal Remedies Act, Civil Code § 1781(c)–(g), in all civil actions. *Vasquez v. Superior Court*, 4 Cal. 3d 800, 817–821, 94 Cal. Rptr. 796, 484 P.2d 964 (1971). And in the absence of relevant state precedents, the courts often utilize the procedures prescribed in Rule 23 of the Federal Rules of Civil Procedure. *See, e.g., City of San Jose v. Superior Court, supra,* 12 Cal. 3d at 453; *Green v. Obledo,* 29 Cal. 3d 126, 145–146, 172 Cal. Rptr. 206, 624 P.2d 256 (1981).

Management Rules. Newly adopted California Rules of Court now govern the management of class actions, including motions to certify or decertify a class, case conferences, notice to class members, orders in the conduct of class actions, discovery from unnamed class members, and settlement and dismissals of class actions. *See* Rules 3.760–3.771, Cal. Rules of Ct.

Appellate review. A trial court order denying class certification to an entire class is an immediately appealable order. *Daar v. Yellow Cab Co., supra,* 67 Cal. 2d at 699 (Order held appealable because it effectively terminated the entire action as to all members of the class); *Richmond v. Dart Industries, Inc., supra,* 29 Cal. 3d at 470; *see In re Baycol Cases I & II,* 51 Cal. 4th 751, 122 Cal. Rptr. 3d 153, 248 P.3d 681 (2011) (explaining that an order terminating class claims but not individual claims is immediately appealable under the death knell doctrine; however an order terminating both class claims and individual claims is not immediately appealable, but the subsequent final judgment is appealable). An order which denies class certification as to some causes of action but grants it as to others is not appealable as a matter of right, but may be reviewed by discretionary extraordinary writ. *See, e.g., Vasquez v. Superior Court, supra; Blue Chip Stamps v. Superior Court,* 18 Cal. 3d 381, 134 Cal. Rptr. 393, 556 P.2d 755 (1976) (Writ of mandamus issued directing trial court to vacate order which certified class against defendant).

4. Notice to Class Members

Code of Civil Procedure § 382 is silent on the issue of notice to class members. Generally, the California courts follow federal Rule 23(b) to determine whether a certified class is the type which requires mandatory notice to the absentee members of the class. E.g., *Bell v. American Title Insurance Co.,* 226 Cal. App. 3d 1589, 277 Cal. Rptr. 583 (1991); *Frazier v. City of Richmond,* 184 Cal. App. 3d 1491, 228 Cal. Rptr. 376 (1986). Consequently, mandatory notice to members of the class is required for those classes which satisfy only the definitions of Rule 23(b)(3); any notice is discretionary as to Rule 23(b)(1) and (b)(2) classes. Rule 23(c)(2) & (d), F.R.C.P.

When a California court determines that *some* notice to the class as certified is required, the court does not necessarily follow federal Rule 23(c) to determine the precise nature of the class notice. E.g., *Cartt v. Superior Court,* 50 Cal. App. 3d 960, 124 Cal. Rptr. 376 (1975); *Cooper v. American Savings & Loan Ass'n,* 55 Cal. App. 3d 274, 127 Cal. Rptr. 579 (1976). Instead, the court would apply the manner of notice requirements of Civil Code § 1781(d), which authorizes notice by publication if personal notification is unreasonably expensive, and Civil Code § 1781(e), which governs the content of class notice with respect to requests for exclusion. E.g., *Cartt, supra; Cooper, supra.*

Newly adopted Rule 3.766 of the California Rule of Court now provides some guidance on the procedures and content of notice to class members in all class actions.

With respect to the manner of giving notice, Rule 3.766(e) requires the court to consider:

> (1) The interests of the class; (2) The type of relief requested; (3) The stake of the individual class members; (4) The cost of notifying class members; (5) The resources of the parties; (6) The possible prejudice to class members who do not receive notice; and (7) The res judicata effect on class members.

Rule 3.766(f) then authorizes the court to consider these factors when ordering the means of notice:

> If personal notification is unreasonably expensive or the stake of the individual class members is insubstantial, or if it appears that all members of the class cannot be notified personally, the court may order a means of notice reasonably calculated to apprise the class members of the pendency of the action—for example, publication in a newspaper or magazine; broadcasting on television, radio, or the Internet; or posting or distribution through a trade or professional association, union, or public interest group.

5. Who Pays the Cost of Notice

The California Legislature has specifically authorized trial courts in consumer class actions to impose the cost of notice to the class upon either the plaintiff or the defendant. Civil Code § 1781(d). The Supreme Court extended this rule to all class actions in *Civil Service Employees Ins. Co. v. Superior Court*, 22 Cal. 3d 362, 374–381, 149 Cal. Rptr. 360, 584 P.2d 497 (1978), where it held that California trial courts clearly possess the authority to impose notice costs on either party in a class action. The Court also held that the imposition of class notice costs on a defendant was consistent with due process if, prior to the trial court order, the defendant had a full hearing on the issue of who should bear the cost of notifying the class during the pendency of the suit. *Id.* at 379–381. *See also* Rule 3.766, Cal. Rules of Ct.

Cost Allocation Factors. What factors are relevant to this allocation of class notice cost decision? The trial court's preliminary view of the strength of the plaintiff's claim? The cost of class notice in relation to the amount of the potential recovery for each individual class member? Which party is more capable of affording the financial burden of notice? *See Civil Service Employees Insurance Co. v. Superior Court, supra*, 22 Cal. 3d at 380–381; *Cartt v. Superior Court, supra*, 50 Cal. App. 3d at 974–975.

Federal Rule Compared. In contrast to the California rule, the Federal Rules of Civil Procedure do not authorize a federal court to impose the cost of class notice on the defendant. The U.S. Supreme Court in *Eisen v. Carlisle & Jacquelin*, 417 U.S. 156, 177–179, 94 S. Ct. 2140, 40 L. Ed. 2d 732 (1974), held that federal Rule 23 does not authorize departure from the usual rule that a plaintiff must initially bear the cost of notice to the class. The California Supreme Court in *Civil Service Employees* refused to follow *Eisen*, finding *Eisen* not binding on the California courts. Was this refusal proper? Why?

The issue of whether a trial court may impose the cost of class notice on the defendant is extremely important in many class actions. Why? What are the criticisms of the federal court rule? The California rule? For more discussion of these contrasting rules, *see* James R. McCall, *Due Process and Consumer Protection: Concepts and Realities in Procedure and Substance—Class Action Issues*, 25 Hastings L.J. 1351 (1974).

Appellate Review. A trial court order allocating the cost of class notice between plaintiff and defendant is not an appealable order, *Steen v. Fremont Cemetery Corp.*, 9 Cal. App. 4th 1221, 11 Cal. Rptr. 2d 780 (1992); although appellate review may be obtained through the discretionary extraordinary writ process. *E.g.*, *Civil Service Employees Insurance Co., supra*; *Cartt v. Superior Court, supra*.

6. Right to Opt Out of Class

The main purpose of providing proper notice of the pendency of a class action is to advise class members of their options: (1) To remain members of the class represented by plaintiff's counsel and become bound by a favorable or unfavorable judgment in the action, or (2) to intervene in the action through counsel of their own choosing, or (3) to "opt out" of the class action and pursue their own independent actions. *Home Savings & Loan Ass'n v. Superior Court*, 42 Cal. App. 3d 1006, 1010, 117 Cal. Rptr. 485 (1974); Civil Code § 1781(e); Rule 23(c)(2), F.R.C.P. A class member will be bound by the class action judgment unless that member affirmatively requests exclusion. Rule 23(c)(2), F.R.C.P.; Civil Code § 1781(e).

Due Process Concerns. An individual class member has no right to opt out of a class action certified under Rule 23(b)(1) or (b)(2). *See Bell v. American Title Insurance Co.*, 226 Cal. App. 3d 1589, 277 Cal. Rptr. 583 (1991). Why not? An individual class member does have the right to opt out of a Rule 23(b)(3) class action. Why?

A broader constitutional issue is whether an individual class member has a due process right to opt out of any class action which seeks money damages on behalf of the class. *Phillips Petroleum Co. v. Shutts*, 472 U.S. 797, 105 S. Ct. 2965, 86 L. Ed. 2d 628 (1985). Most courts determine whether class members are entitled to notice and the right to opt out based on whether the appropriate relief sought by the class action is exclusively or predominantly for money damages. E.g., *Shutts, supra*, 472 U.S. at 811–12; *Bell, supra*, 226 Cal. App. 3d at 1605–09; *Frazier, supra*, 184 Cal. App. 3d at 1501. However, the U.S. Court of Appeals for the Ninth Circuit in *Brown v. Ticor Title Insurance Co.*, 982 F.2d 386 (9th Cir. 1992), *cert. dismissed*, 511 U.S. 117, 114 S. Ct. 1359, 128 L. Ed. 2d 33 (1994), held that in order to bind an absentee class member concerning a claim for money damages, the court must provide the class member with an opportunity to opt out of the class action. The court, relying on *Shutt's* due process analysis, declined to extend res judicata to a prior class judgment for money damages where that class had been certified under federal Rule 23(b)(1) and (b)(2) and provided no right to opt out.

7. Settlement

Court Approval Required. A class action shall not be dismissed without approval of the court. CCP § 581(k); Civil Code § 1781(f); Rule 3.769 & 3.770, Cal. Rules of Ct. A trial court has broad discretion to determine whether a class action settlement is fair, but should consider the following relevant factors, identified in *Dunk v. Ford Motor Co.*, 48 Cal. App. 4th 1794, 1801, 56 Cal. Rptr. 2d 483 (1996):

> The strength of plaintiffs' case, the risk, expense, complexity and likely duration of further litigation, the risk of maintaining class action status through trial, the amount offered in settlement, the extent of discovery completed and the state of the proceedings, the experience and views of counsel, the presence of a governmental participant, and the reaction of the class members to the proposed settlement. The list of factors is not exhaustive and should be tailored to each case. Due regard should be given to what is otherwise a private consensual agreement between the parties.

The court in *Dunk, supra,* applied these factors and upheld the settlement of a nationwide class action brought against Ford Motor Company for alleged defects in the doors of certain cars, under which each class member would receive a coupon redeemable for $400 off the price of any new Ford vehicle. *See also 7-Eleven Owners for Fair Franchising v. Southland Corp.*, 85 Cal. App. 4th 1135, 102 Cal. Rptr. 2d 777 (2000) (Applying the fairness factors identified in *Dunk*, and affirming the trial court's approval of the settlement of a national class); *Wershba v. Apple Computer, Inc.*, 91 Cal. App. 4th 224, 110 Cal. Rptr. 2d 145 (2001) (Application of the four factors identified in *Dunk* lead to presumption that settlement of national class action was fair, a presumption the objectors failed to overcome).

Notice Requirement. Dismissal of class actions is one area where generally applicable state law exists to guide litigants and trial courts. Code of Civil Procedure § 581(k) requires notice to the class and court approval prior to dismissal of an action determined to be a class action under CCP § 382. Newly adopted Rules 3.769 and 3.770 also govern settlement and dismissal of class actions, including the manner of notice to class members of a proposed class settlement or dismissal. *See Wershba v. Apple Computer, Inc.*, 91 Cal. App. 4th 224, 110 Cal. Rptr. 2d 145 (2001) (Affirming settlement of a nationwide class action alleging that defendant Apple Computer had rescinded its policy of free technical phone support to its customers in violation of California's consumer protection law, and approving methods of notice which included notice e-mailed directly to more than 2.4 million class members and also published in *USA Today* and *MacWorld*, as well as the posting of notice by Apple on its internet homepage).

8. Class Action Remedies

Fluid Class Recovery. A trial court in a class action has the same authority to award the full range of legal and equitable remedies as the court would have in an individual action. In addition, the California courts have authority to award "fluid class" relief in appropriate cases. In *State v. Levi Strauss & Co.*, 41 Cal. 3d 460, 472–476, 224 Cal. Rptr. 605, 715 P.2d 564 (1986), the California Supreme Court endorsed the propriety of fluid recovery in consumer class actions, and stated guidelines for its use:

> The implementation of fluid recovery involves three steps. First, the defendant's total damage liability is paid over to a class fund. Second, individual class members are afforded an opportunity to collect their individual shares by proving their particular damages, usually according to a lowered standard of proof. Third, any residue remaining after individual claims have been paid is distributed by one of several practical procedures that have been developed by the courts.

> In order to assess the propriety of the fluid recovery method selected by the trial court in the present case, it is necessary to review briefly the available alternatives. The principal methods include a rollback of the defendant's prices, escheat to a governmental body for either specified or general purposes, establishment of a consumer trust fund, and claimant fund sharing. All of these methods promote the policies of disgorgement and deterrence by ensuring that the residue of the recovery does not revert to the wrongdoer. However, they differ substantially in their compensatory effect and in their suitability for particular cases.

> In determining which method to employ, the courts should consider: (1) the amount of compensation provided to class members, including nonclaiming (or "silent") members; (2) the proportion of class members sharing in the recovery; (3) the extent to which benefits will "spill over" to nonclass members and the degree to which the spillover benefits will effectuate the purposes of the underlying substantive law; and (4) the costs of administration.

In 1993 the Legislature enacted CCP § 384, which specifically endorses the concept of fluid class recovery. As amended in 2018 and 2019, section 384(a) states that it is the policy of the State of California "to ensure that the unpaid cash residue and unclaimed or abandoned funds in class action litigation are distributed, to the fullest extent possible, in a manner designed either to further the purposes of the underlying class action or causes of action, or to promote justice for all Californians."

Section 384(b) provides the general guidelines for distribution of any unpaid or unclaimed funds:

> [T]he court shall amend the judgment to direct the defendant to pay the sum of the unpaid residue or unclaimed or abandoned class member funds, plus any interest that has accrued thereon, to nonprofit organizations or foundations to support projects that will benefit the class or similarly situated persons, or that promote the law consistent with the objectives and purposes of the underlying cause of action, to child advocacy programs, or to nonprofit organizations providing civil legal services to the indigent.

Section 384 does not apply to any class action brought against a public entity or against a public employee. CCP § 384(c).

Most federal courts have disapproved of the use of fluid class recovery as a possible remedy in class actions. E.g., *Eisen v. Carlisle & Jacquelin*, 479 F.2d 1005, 1017–18 (2d Cir. 1973), *vacated on other grounds*, 417 U.S. 156 (1974). The fluid class recovery concept remains very controversial. Why? What are the objections to this type of relief? Do any of these objections have a constitutional basis? How so? Why is the potential of fluid class recovery so important to plaintiffs and plaintiffs' attorneys in consumer litigation?

Attorney Fees. The class action attorney may obtain payment of attorney fees from a portion of a class action settlement. *See Rebney v. Wells Fargo Bank*, 220 Cal. App. 3d 1117, 269 Cal. Rptr. 844 (1990). Any such attorney fees agreement must be disclosed to the members of the class, and approved by the court as part of the settlement process. *Id.*; *see* Rule 3.769(b), Cal. Rules of Ct. If the class action is not settled but proceeds to trial, a successful class attorney may be entitled to an award of statutory attorney fees in an amount which reflects the nature of the class-wide services rendered. *See Rebney v. Wells Fargo Bank, supra*; *Miller v. Woods*, 148 Cal. App. 3d 862, 875, 196 Cal. Rptr. 69 (1983); CCP § 1021.5. What are the advantages and disadvantages to a plaintiff of proceeding as a class action as opposed to an individual action? To a defendant? To the attorney for the plaintiff?

Chapter VI

Discovery

A. Coverage and Scope of Civil Discovery Statutes

In 1986, the California Legislature adopted the Civil Discovery Act, which clarified the original Discovery Act of 1956, incorporated existing case law construing the 1956 Act, and implemented many recommendations to bring California discovery principles closer to those of the Federal Rules of Civil Procedure.

General Coverage of Discovery Act. The Civil Discovery Act applies to all civil actions pending in the superior court (except the small claims division), CCP §§ 2016.010–.070, 2017.010–.020; including family court proceedings, *Schnabel v. Superior Court*, 5 Cal. 4th 704, 21 Cal. Rptr. 2d 200, 854 P.2d 1117 (1993). It does not apply to administrative proceedings, *Shively v. Stewart*, 65 Cal. 2d 475, 55 Cal. Rptr. 217, 421 P.2d 65 (1966); nor to juvenile court proceedings, *Joe Z. v. Superior Court*, 3 Cal. 3d 797, 91 Cal. Rptr. 594, 478 P.2d 26 (1970).

Limited Civil Cases. In limited civil cases — generally, cases in which the amount in controversy does not exceed $25,000 — numerical restrictions control the use of depositions, interrogatories, inspection demands, and requests for admissions. To promote affordable litigation in such cases the law limits the parties to one deposition per adverse party. CCP § 94(b). As to interrogatories, inspection demands, and requests for admission, the combined total permitted is 35 per adverse party. § 94(a). Additional discovery is allowed by stipulation or court order. § 95(a) & (b).

Scope of Discovery. Unless otherwise limited by an order of the court, "any party may obtain discovery regarding any matter, not privileged, that is relevant to the subject matter involved in the pending action or to the determination of any motion made in that action." CCP § 2017.010. The scope of discovery encompasses relevant matter that "either is itself admissible in evidence or appears to be reasonably calculated to lead to the discovery of admissible evidence." *Id.* In accordance with the liberal policies underlying the discovery procedures, "doubts as to relevance should generally be resolved in favor of permitting discovery." *Pacific Telephone & Telegraph v. Superior Court*, 2 Cal. 3d 161, 173, 84 Cal. Rptr. 718, 465 P.2d 854 (1970). The trial court may exercise control over the scope, frequency, or extent of use of discovery methods pursuant to a motion for a protective order when the court determines the discovery sought is unreasonably burdensome, expensive, or intrusive. CCP §§ 2017.020, 2019.030.

Insurance. In addition to providing broad guidelines, CCP §§ 2017.020–.740 directly address certain controversial discovery issues. Specifically, § 2017.210 expressly allows discovery of insurance coverage. A party may obtain discovery of the existence and contents of insurance policies including the identity of the carrier, the nature and limits of the coverage, and whether the insurance carrier is disputing coverage of the claim involved in the action. *Id.* Discovery of this information, however, does not make it admissible at trial. *Id.* Why is pretrial discovery of insurance information authorized but not its admission at trial?

B. Protection of Privileged Information

1. Privilege, Generally

Code of Civil Procedure § 2017.010 limits the scope discovery to matters which are not privileged. The laws of privilege are not set out in the Civil Discovery Act but are provided by the California Constitution, the Evidence Code, other statutes, and decisional law. Essentially, any privilege that protects against disclosure at trial also applies to discovery. While the term "privilege" is used generally to refer to information protected from disclosure, it is more accurate to divide the subject into (1) those matters which are truly privileged and entitled to absolute protection and (2) those matters which are entitled to qualified protection and subject to compelled disclosure in the interests of justice.

With respect to the assertion of a claim of privilege in discovery proceedings, the failure to object on the grounds of privilege will operate as a waiver of the privilege. CCP §§ 2025.460(a), 2028.050(a), and 2030.290(a). *See* 2 Hogan and Weber, California Civil Discovery §§ 12.1–13.20 (2005 & 2015 Supp.). Conversely, the assertion of a privilege during discovery may bar introduction at trial of the evidence withheld. *See Xebec Development Partners, Ltd. v. National Union Fire Ins. Co.*, 12 Cal. App. 4th 501, 15 Cal. Rptr. 2d 726 (1993) (Plaintiff who asserted attorney-client privilege as to certain billing materials during discovery can not waive the privilege at trial to prove amount of recoverable attorneys' fees because too late to cure prejudice to defendant).

2. Absolute Privileges

The Evidence Code codifies the absolute privileges which include: the privilege against self incrimination (§ 940 *et seq.*); the attorney-client privilege (§ 952 *et seq.*); the spousal privilege (§ 970 *et seq.*); the physician-patient privilege (§ 992 *et seq.*); the psychotherapist-patient privilege (§ 1012 *et seq.*); the clergyman-penitent privilege (§ 1030); the sexual assault victim-counselor privilege (§ 1035); the official information privilege (§ 1040 *et seq.*); and the mediation privilege (§§ 703.5, 1119, 1121). Unless some statutory exception applies or the privilege is waived, information covered by these privileges is protected from disclosure regardless of its relevance to the issues and the need for disclosure. *Rittenhouse v. Superior Court*, 235 Cal. App. 3d 1584, 1 Cal. Rptr. 2d 595 (1991). *See* 2 Hogan and Weber, California Civil Discovery § 12.1.

The Attorney-Client Privilege. Confidential communications between client and lawyer are privileged from disclosure. Evid. Code § 954. However, this absolute privilege is subject to several statutory exceptions. For example, Evidence Code § 956 provides an exception where the client consults the attorney to obtain advice in perpetrating a crime or fraud, and Evidence Code § 958 provides an exception where the attorney is sued for malpractice. Moreover, the attorney-client privilege is waived "if any holder of the privilege, without coercion, has disclosed a significant part of the communication or has consented to such disclosure made by anyone." Evid. Code § 912(a). And, of course, although the attorney-client privilege protects the communication between the attorney and the client, it does not prevent discovery of the underlying facts that are the subject of the communication. *See, e.g., Costco Wholesale Corp. v. Superior Court,* 47 Cal. 4th 725, 736, 101 Cal. Rptr. 3d 758, 219 P.3d 736 (2009); *Aerojet-General Corp. v. Transport Indemnity Ins.,* 18 Cal. App. 4th 996, 1004, 22 Cal. Rptr. 2d 862 (1993).

Attorney-Client Privilege Extends to Experts. The attorney-client privilege extends to experts who are retained as advisors or consultants to evaluate some aspect of the client's case. *See* 2 Hogan & Weber, California Civil Discovery § 12.11 (collecting cases). If the expert is later designated as a trial expert, the privilege will be waived. *Id.* at § 12.12. *But see Shooker v. Superior Court,* 111 Cal. App. 4th 923, 4 Cal. Rptr. 2d 334 (2003) (Designation of a party as an expert trial witness is not an implied waiver of the attorney-client privilege if the designation is withdrawn before the party discloses a significant part of a privileged communication).

3. Qualified Privileges

In addition to these absolute privileges, certain sensitive information may be protected from discovery unless the interests of justice compel disclosure. These qualified areas of protection include: the newsgatherer's immunity (Evid. Code § 1070 *et seq.*); the medical staff privilege (Evid. Code § 1157); the trade secret privilege (Evid. Code § 1060); the taxpayer's privilege (Civil Code § 4700.7); and the constitutional protection of privacy (Cal. Const., Art I, § 1).

Right of Privacy. A frequently invoked qualified privilege is the right to privacy protected by the Article I, section 1, of the California Constitution. In determining whether to require disclosure of information protected by this privilege, a court must balance the right of a civil litigant to discover relevant facts with the right of the information possessor to maintain reasonable privacy. *See, e.g., John B. v. Superior Court,* 38 Cal. 4th 1177, 45 Cal. Rptr. 3d 316, 137 P.3d 153 (2006) (Balancing husband's right of privacy against wife's right to discover relevant facts, and concluding that husband's medical records and prior sexual history were discoverable in order to confirm or refute wife's allegations that husband knowingly or negligently infected wife with HIV); *Valley Bank of Nevada v. Superior Court,* 15 Cal. 3d 652, 125 Cal. Rptr. 553, 542 P.2d 977 (1975) (Balancing interests of litigants and of nonparty bank customers with respect to discovery of customers' bank records); *Johnson v. Superior Court,* 80 Cal.

App. 4th 1050, 95 Cal. Rptr. 2d 864 (2000) (Donor's right of privacy in his identity and medical history outweighed by public policy interest in health of children, in action by parents and their children against sperm bank alleging transmission of kidney disease to the children by the sperm donor). For an example of the right to privacy applied in the context of a mental examination ordered pursuant to the Civil Discovery Act, CCP § 2032.020, *see Vinson v. Superior Court*, 43 Cal. 3d 833, 239 Cal. Rptr. 292, 740 P.2d 404 (1987), reproduced *infra*.

4. Work Product Protection

Coito v. Superior Court

Supreme Court of California

54 Cal. 4th 480, 278 P.3d 860, 142 Cal. Rptr. 3d 607 (2012)

LIU, JUSTICE.

In California, an attorney's work product is protected by statute. (Code Civ. Proc., § 2018.010 et seq.; all further unlabeled statutory references are to the Code of Civ. Proc.) Absolute protection is afforded to writings that reflect "an attorney's impressions, conclusions, opinions, or legal research or theories." (§ 2018.030, subd. (a).) All other work product receives qualified protection; such material "is not discoverable unless the court determines that denial of discovery will unfairly prejudice the party seeking discovery in preparing that party's claim or defense or will result in an injustice." (§ 2018.030, subd. (b).)

In this case, we decide what work product protection, if any, should be accorded two items: first, recordings of witness interviews conducted by investigators employed by defendant's counsel, and second, information concerning the identity of witnesses from whom defendant's counsel has obtained statements. Defendant objected to plaintiff's requests for discovery of these items, invoking the work product privilege. The trial court sustained the objection, concluding as a matter of law that the recorded witness interviews were entitled to absolute work product protection and that the other information sought was work product entitled to qualified protection. A divided Court of Appeal reversed, concluding that work product protection does not apply to any of the disputed items. The Court of Appeal issued a writ of mandate directing the trial court to grant the motion to compel discovery.

We conclude that the Court of Appeal erred. In light of the legislatively declared policy and the legislative history of the work product privilege, we hold that the recorded witness statements are entitled as a matter of law to at least qualified work product protection. The witness statements may be entitled to absolute protection if defendant can show that disclosure would reveal its "attorney's impressions, conclusions, opinions, or legal research or theories." (§ 2018.030, subd. (a).) If not, then the items may be subject to discovery if plaintiff can show that "denial of discovery will unfairly prejudice [her] in preparing [her] claim . . . or will result in an injustice." (§ 2018.030, subd. (b).)

As to the identity of witnesses from whom defendant's counsel has obtained statements, we hold that such information is not automatically entitled as a matter of law to absolute or qualified work product protection. In order to invoke the privilege, defendant must persuade the trial court that disclosure would reveal the attorney's tactics, impressions, or evaluation of the case (absolute privilege) or would result in opposing counsel taking undue advantage of the attorney's industry or efforts (qualified privilege).

We reverse the judgment of the Court of Appeal and remand the matter for further proceedings, consistent with our opinion, to determine whether the disputed materials should be produced.

I

On March 9, 2007, 13-year-old Jeremy Wilson drowned in the Tuolumne River in Modesto, California. His mother, Debra Coito, filed a complaint for wrongful death naming several defendants, including the State of California. The Department of Water Resources (DWR) is the agency defending the action for the state, represented by the Attorney General.

Six other juveniles witnessed what happened. There were allegations that all of the juveniles, including the decedent, were engaged in criminal conduct immediately before the drowning. On November 12, 2008, after codefendant City of Modesto had noticed the depositions of five of the six juvenile witnesses, counsel for the state sent two investigators, both special agents from the Bureau of Investigation of the Department of Justice, to interview four of the juveniles. The state's counsel provided the investigators with questions he wanted asked. Each interview was audio-recorded and saved on a separate compact disc.

On January 27, 2009, the City of Modesto began its deposition of one of the four interviewed witnesses. The state's counsel used the content of the witness's recorded interview in questioning the witness at the deposition.

On February 5, 2009, plaintiff served the state with supplemental interrogatories and document demands. The interrogatories included Judicial Council form interrogatory No. 12.3, which sought the names, addresses, and telephone numbers of individuals from whom written or recorded statements had been obtained. The document demands sought production of the audio recordings of the four witness interviews. The state objected to the requested discovery based on the work product privilege.

Plaintiff filed a motion to compel an answer to form interrogatory No. 12.3 and the production of the recorded interviews. In support of the motion, plaintiff filed declarations from two of the interviewed witnesses asserting that they had not intended their statements to be confidential. The state opposed the motion, relying primarily on *Nacht & Lewis Architects, Inc. v. Superior Court* (1996) 47 Cal.App.4th 214, 217 [54 Cal. Rptr. 2d 575] (*Nacht & Lewis*), which held that recorded witness statements are entitled to absolute work product protection and that information sought by form interrogatory No. 12.3 is entitled to qualified work product protection.

After an April 10, 2009 hearing, and without having reviewed the audio recordings, the trial court issued a written order that relied on *Nacht & Lewis* in denying plaintiff's motion except as to the recording used by the state to examine the witness during the January 27, 2009 deposition. As to that recording, the court reasoned that the state had waived the work product privilege by using the interview to examine the witness during the deposition.

Plaintiff petitioned for a writ of mandate that the Court of Appeal granted. The majority, relying on *Greyhound Corp. v. Superior Court* (1961) 56 Cal.2d 355 [15 Cal. Rptr. 90, 364 P.2d 266] (*Greyhound*) and expressly declining to follow *Nacht & Lewis*, concluded that witness interviews and the information sought by form interrogatory No. 12.3 are not entitled as a matter of law to absolute or qualified work product protection. Because defendant's attorney made no showing of entitlement to work product protection in the specific context of this case, the Court of Appeal directed the trial court to compel discovery. Justice Kane wrote a concurring and dissenting opinion. While agreeing that the trial court's order denying discovery should be vacated, he concluded that the recorded interviews were entitled as a matter of law to at least qualified work product protection, whereas the information sought by form interrogatory No. 12.3 must be produced unless the objecting party has made an adequate showing to support a claim of qualified privilege.

We granted review. As with all matters of statutory construction, our review of the Court of Appeal's interpretation of the work product statute is de novo. (*Imperial Merchant Services, Inc. v. Hunt* (2009) 47 Cal. 4th 381, 387 [97 Cal. Rptr. 3d 464, 212 P.3d 736].)

II

California's civil work product privilege is codified in section 2018.030. Subdivision (a) provides absolute protection to any "writing that reflects an attorney's impressions, conclusions, opinions, or legal research or theories." (§ 2018.030, subd. (a).) Such a writing "is not discoverable under any circumstances." (*Ibid.*) The term "writing" includes any form of recorded information, including audio recordings. (§ 2016.020, subd. (c) [adopting the definition set forth in Evid. Code, § 250].) Section 2018.030, subdivision (b) provides qualified protection for all other work product. Such material "is not discoverable unless the court determines that denial of discovery will unfairly prejudice the party seeking discovery in preparing that party's claim or defense or will result in an injustice." (§ 2018.030, subd. (b).) Here, we address the work product privilege in the civil context only, as criminal discovery is regulated by a different statute. (Pen. Code, § 1054 et seq.)

The language of section 2018.030 does not otherwise define or describe "work product." Courts have resolved whether particular materials constitute work product on a case-by-case basis (*City of Long Beach v. Superior Court* (1976) 64 Cal. App. 3d 65, 71 [134 Cal. Rptr. 468]), although they have sometimes taken different approaches. Some courts have attempted to answer the question by distinguishing between "derivative" or "nonderivative" material, or between "interpretative" and "evidentiary" material. (E.g., *Fellows v. Superior Court* (1980) 108 Cal.App.3d 55, 68-69 [166 Cal. Rptr. 274] (*Fellows*); *Rodriguez v. McDonnell Douglas Corp.* (1978) 87 Cal.App.3d 626, 647 [151 Cal. Rptr. 399] (*Rodriguez*); *Mack v. Superior Court* (1968) 259 Cal.App.2d 7, 10-11 [66 Cal. Rptr. 280] (*Mack*).) These cases have concluded that only derivative or interpretive material—material created by or derived from an attorney's work reflecting the attorney's evaluation of the law or facts—constitutes work product. Examples of such material include "diagrams prepared for trial, audit reports, appraisals, and other expert opinions, developed as a result of the initiative of counsel in preparing for trial." (*Mack*, at p. 10.) Nonderivative material—material that is only evidentiary in nature—does not constitute work product. Examples of such material include the identity and location of physical evidence or witnesses. (*Ibid.*; *City of Long Beach*, at p. 73.)

Other courts, instead of distinguishing between derivative and nonderivative material, have determined the scope of protected work product by relying primarily upon the policies underlying the work product statute and its legislative history. (E.g., *Dowden v. Superior Court* (1999) 73 Cal.App.4th 126, 130-133, 135 [86 Cal. Rptr. 2d 180] (*Dowden*).) Because those policies and the legislative history are instructive in resolving the instant case, we begin by reviewing the origins and development of California's work product privilege.

A

The idea that an attorney's work product should receive protection from discovery was first recognized by the United States Supreme Court in *Hickman v. Taylor* (1947) 329 U.S. 495 [91 L. Ed. 451, 67 S. Ct. 385] (*Hickman*). There, the defendant's counsel interviewed and took statements from the surviving crewmembers of a tugboat accident. The plaintiff sought the production of any written or oral statements taken from the crewmembers. After concluding that the statements were not covered by the attorney-client privilege, the court nonetheless affirmed the denial of the plaintiff's request. The court explained that the plaintiff's request was "simply an attempt, without purported necessity or justification, to secure written statements, private memoranda and personal recollections prepared or formed by an adverse party's counsel in the course of his legal duties." (*Id.* at p. 510.)

The court continued: "In performing his various duties, . . . it is essential that a lawyer work with a certain degree of privacy, free from unnecessary intrusion by opposing parties and their counsel. Proper preparation of a client's case demands that he assemble information, sift what he considers to be the relevant from the irrelevant facts, prepare his legal theories and plan his strategy without undue and needless interference. That is the historical and the necessary way in which lawyers act within the framework of our system of jurisprudence to promote justice and to protect their clients' interests. This work is reflected, of course, in interviews, statements, memoranda, correspondence, briefs, mental impressions, personal beliefs, and countless other tangible and intangible ways—aptly though roughly termed by the Circuit Court of Appeals in this case as the 'work product of the lawyer.' Were such materials open to opposing counsel on mere demand, much of what is now put down in writing would remain unwritten. An attorney's thoughts, heretofore inviolate, would not be his own. Inefficiency, unfairness and sharp practices would inevitably develop in the giving of legal advice and in the preparation of cases for trial. The effect on the legal profession would be demoralizing. And the interests of the clients and the cause of justice would be poorly served.

"We do not mean to say that all written materials obtained or prepared by an adversary's counsel with an eye toward litigation are necessarily free from discovery in all cases. Where relevant and non-privileged facts remain hidden in an attorney's file and where production of those facts is essential to the preparation of one's case, discovery may properly be had. Such written statements and documents might, under certain circumstances, be admissible in evidence or give clues as to the existence or location of relevant facts. Or they might be useful for purposes of impeachment or corroboration. And production might be justified where the witnesses are no longer available or can be reached only with difficulty. . . . But the general policy against invading the privacy of an attorney's course of preparation is so well recognized and so essential to an orderly working of our system of legal procedure that a burden rests on the one who would invade that privacy to establish adequate reasons to justify production through a subpoena or court order." (*Hickman, supra,* 329 U.S. at pp. 510–512.)

At the time *Hickman* was decided, California law protected work product only through the attorney-client privilege. * * * Against this statutory backdrop, this court in 1961 concluded that neither the attorney-client privilege nor the work product doctrine protected nonparty witness statements from discovery. (*Greyhound, supra,* 56 Cal.2d at pp. 399, 401.) * * * In response to *Greyhound,* the State Bar Committee proposed an amendment the following year with the purpose of codifying a work product privilege. [Here the court discusses the legislative history relevant to enactment of former section 2016 in 1963.]

Although the work product privilege was moved first from former section 2016 to former section 2018 and then from former section 2018 to its present location, the current text is virtually identical to the version first enacted in 1963. Section 2018.020 declares: "It is the policy of the state to do both of the following: [¶] (a) Preserve the rights of attorneys to prepare cases for trial with that degree of privacy necessary to encourage them to prepare their cases thoroughly and to investigate not only the favorable but the unfavorable aspects of those cases. [¶] (b) Prevent attorneys from taking undue advantage of their adversary's industry and efforts." Toward that end, section 2018.030 provides: "(a) A writing that reflects an attorney's impressions, conclusions, opinions, or legal research or theories is not discoverable under any circumstances. [¶] (b) The work product of an attorney, other than a writing described in subdivision (a), is not discoverable unless the court determines that denial of discovery will unfairly prejudice the party seeking discovery in preparing that party's claim or defense or will result in an injustice." As noted, section 2018.030, subdivision (a) provides absolute protection for certain work product, while subdivision (b) provides qualified protection for all other work product.

B

In light of the origins and development of the work product privilege in California, we conclude that witness statements obtained as a result of interviews conducted by an attorney, or by an attorney's agent at the attorney's behest, constitute work product protected by section 2018.030.

As mentioned, the Legislature in enacting section 2018.030 did not define "work product" and instead left the term open to judicial interpretation. From the very inception of judicial recognition of the concept, attorney work product has been understood to include witness statements obtained through an interview conducted by an attorney. The high court in *Hickman* specifically referred to "statements" and "interviews" in its nonexclusive enumeration of items comprising the "'work product of [a] lawyer.'" (*Hickman, supra*, 329 U.S. at p. 511.) And *Hickman* held that the district court in that case improperly ordered the defendant's attorney "to produce *all written statements of witnesses*" and other items that the attorney had obtained through his own interviews. (*Id.* at p. 509, italics added; see *id.* at p. 508 [plaintiff sought "discovery as of right of oral and *written statements of witnesses* whose identity is well known and whose availability to [plaintiff] appears unimpaired" (italics added)].)

The closest we have come to examining the applicability of section 2018.030 to witness statements is our decision in *Rico v. Mitsubishi Motors Corp.* (2007) 42 Cal.4th 807 [68 Cal. Rptr. 3d 758, 171 P.3d 1092] (*Rico*). There, we held that work product "protection extends to an attorney's written notes about a witness's statements" and that "[w]hen a witness's statement and the attorney's impressions are inextricably intertwined," the entire document receives absolute protection. (*Id.* at p. 814.) The question in *Rico* was not whether a witness's statement is itself protected work product, and the document at issue was not "a verbatim record of the [witnesses'] statements" but rather a summary prepared at the request of the defendant's attorney. (*Id.* at p. 815.) *Rico* thus did not speak to the issue now before us.

Nevertheless, in finding the document protected, *Rico*'s observation that "'its very existence is owed to the lawyer's thought process'" (*Rico, supra*, 42 Cal.4th at p. 815 [quoting trial court]) provides a useful touchstone for our present inquiry. There is no dispute that a statement independently prepared by a witness does not become protected work product simply upon its transmission to an attorney. (See *Wellpoint Health Networks, Inc. v. Superior Court* (1997) 59 Cal.App.4th 110, 119 [68 Cal. Rptr. 2d 844]; *Nacht & Lewis, supra*, 47 Cal. App. 4th at p. 218.) The issue here is what protection, if any, should be afforded where the witness's statement has been obtained through an attorney-directed interview. "In such situations," the Court of Appeal correctly observed, "it can surely be said that the witness statement is in part the product of the attorney's work." The witness statement would not exist but for the attorney's initiative, decision, and effort to obtain it. This essential fact informs our analysis of whether absolute or qualified work product privilege applies to such witness statements.

Absolute privilege. It is not difficult to imagine that a recorded witness interview may, in some instances, reveal the "impressions, conclusions, opinions, or legal research or theories" of the attorney and thus be entitled to absolute protection. (§ 2018.030, subd. (a).) This may occur not only when a witness's statements are "inextricably intertwined" with explicit comments or notes by the attorney stating his or her impressions of the witness, the witness's statements, or other issues in the case. (*Rico, supra,* 42 Cal. 4th at p. 814.) It also may occur when the questions that the attorney has chosen to ask (or not ask) provide a window into the attorney's theory of the case or the attorney's evaluation of what issues are most important. Lines of inquiry that an attorney chooses to pursue through followup questions may be especially revealing. In such situations, redaction of the attorney's questions may sometimes be appropriate and sufficient to protect privileged material. At other times, however, it may not do to simply redact the questions from the record, as the witness's statements will reveal what questions were asked. Moreover, in some cases, the very fact that the attorney has chosen to interview a particular witness may disclose important tactical or evaluative information, perhaps especially so in cases involving a multitude of witnesses. These are circumstances where absolute work product protection may apply.

We cannot say, however, that witness statements procured by an attorney will always reveal the attorney's thought process. The Court of Appeal below posited a scenario in which an attorney collects statements from witnesses to an accident with no particular foresight, strategy, selectivity, or planning: "What, for example, of the situation in which an attorney sends an investigator to interview all witnesses listed in a police report, and the investigator asks few if any questions while taking the witnesses' statements? Clearly, these statements would reveal nothing significant about the attorney's impressions, conclusions, or opinions about the case." For this reason (and such scenarios do not seem uncommon), we hold that witness statements procured by an attorney are not automatically entitled as a matter of law to absolute work product protection. Instead, the applicability of absolute protection must be determined case by case. An attorney resisting discovery of a witness statement based on absolute privilege must make a preliminary or foundational showing that disclosure would reveal his or her "impressions, conclusions, opinions, or legal research or theories." (§ 2018.030, subd. (a).) Upon an adequate showing, the trial court should then determine, by making an in camera inspection if necessary, whether absolute work product protection applies to some or all of the material.

Qualified privilege. Although witness statements obtained through an attorney-directed interview may or may not reveal the attorney's thought process, we believe such statements necessarily implicate two other interests that the Legislature sought to protect in enacting the work product privilege. Based on these interests, we conclude that witness statements procured by an attorney are entitled as a matter of law to at least qualified work product protection under section 2018.030, subdivision (b).

First, when an attorney obtains through discovery a witness statement obtained by opposing counsel through his or her own initiative, such discovery undermines the Legislature's policy to "[p]revent attorneys from taking undue advantage of their adversary's industry and efforts." (§ 2018.020, subd. (b).) Even when an attorney exercises no selectivity in determining which witnesses to interview, and even when the attorney simply records each witness's answer to a single question ("What happened?"), the attorney has expended time and effort in identifying and locating each witness, securing the witness's willingness to talk, listening to what the witness said, and preserving the witness's statement for possible future use. An attorney who seeks to discover what a witness knows is not without recourse. The attorney is free to interview the witness for himself or herself to find out what information the witness has that is relevant to the litigation. * * * Absent a showing that a witness is no longer available or accessible, or some other showing of unfair prejudice or injustice (§ 2018.030, subd. (b)), the Legislature's declared policy is to prevent an attorney from free riding on the industry and efforts of opposing counsel (§ 2018.020, subd. (b)).

Second, a default rule authorizing discovery of witness statements procured by an attorney would impede the Legislature's intent "to encourage [attorneys] to prepare their cases thoroughly and to investigate not only the favorable but the unfavorable aspects of those cases." (§ 2018.020, subd. (a).) If attorneys must worry about discovery whenever they take a statement from a witness, it is reasonably foreseeable that fewer witness statements will be recorded and that adverse information will not be memorialized. As Justice Kane observed below, without work product protection, "no meaningful privacy exists within which an attorney may have sufficient confidence to thoroughly investigate and record potentially *unfavorable* matters." This result would derogate not only from an attorney's duty and prerogative to investigate matters thoroughly, but also from the truth-seeking values that the rules of discovery are intended to promote. Accordingly, we hold that a witness statement obtained through an attorney-directed interview is, as a matter of law, entitled to at least qualified work product protection.

C

The protection afforded by section 2018.030, subdivision (b) to the witness statements in this case is essentially the same protection that the high court afforded to the witness statements in *Hickman*. There, the court held the statements protected and placed the burden on the party seeking discovery "to establish adequate reasons to justify production," such as unavailability or inaccessibility of the witnesses. (*Hickman, supra*, 329 U.S. at p. 512.) Qualified protection of this sort, the court said, is necessary if a lawyer is to discharge his duty "to work for the advancement of justice while faithfully protecting the rightful interests of his clients." (*Id.* at p. 510.)

In reaching a contrary conclusion, the Court of Appeal below relied primarily on *Greyhound*'s conclusion that witness statements are not protected by the work product privilege. Such reliance on *Greyhound* is misplaced. As previously discussed, the Legislature's 1963 amendments to the Discovery Act were intended as a corrective to *Greyhound*. * * *

The Court of Appeal also cited several cases suggesting that witness statements made to an attorney do not constitute work product. (E.g., *Fellows, supra*, 108 Cal.

App.3d at p. 69; *People v. Williams* (1979) 93 Cal.App.3d 40, 63-64 [155 Cal. Rptr. 414]; *Rodriguez, supra*, 87 Cal.App.3d at p. 647; *Kadelbach v. Amaral* (1973) 31 Cal. App. 3d 814, 822 [107 Cal. Rptr. 720].) But those cases address the issue in a conclusory manner without discussing the legislatively declared policy or the history of the work product privilege. * * *

Underlying these assertions that witness statements do not constitute work product is the notion that such writings are nonderivative or noninterpretative material that is wholly evidentiary in nature. (*Fellows, supra*, 108 Cal.App.3d at p. 69; *People v. Williams, supra*, 93 Cal.App.3d at pp. 63–64; *Rodriguez, supra*, 87 Cal.App.3d at p. 647.) However, . . . a witness statement taken by an attorney possesses both derivative characteristics (i.e., an attorney must put time and effort, and possibly thought and planning, into conducting the interview) and nonderivative characteristics (i.e., the statement may contain information regarding events provable at trial or the identity or location of physical evidence, or it may be useful for impeachment or refreshing the witness's recollection). * * *

In sum, we disapprove *Fellows v. Superior Court, supra*, 108 Cal.App.3d 55, *People v. Williams, supra*, 93 Cal.App.3d 40, *Rodriguez v. McDonnell Douglas Corp., supra*, 87 Cal.App.3d 626, and *Kadelbach v. Amaral, supra*, 31 Cal.App.3d 814 to the extent they suggest that a witness statement taken by an attorney does not, as a matter of law, constitute work product. In addition, *Greyhound, supra*, 56 Cal.2d 355, which was decided before the Legislature codified the work product privilege, should not be read as supporting such a conclusion. At the same time, we reject the dicta in *Nacht & Lewis, supra*, 47 Cal.App.4th at page 217 that said "recorded statements taken by defendants' counsel would be protected by the absolute work product privilege because they would reveal counsel's 'impressions, conclusions, opinions, or legal research or theories' . . . ." Instead, we hold that a witness statement obtained through an attorney-directed interview is entitled as a matter of law to at least qualified work product protection. A party seeking disclosure has the burden of establishing that denial of disclosure will unfairly prejudice the party in preparing its claim or defense or will result in an injustice. (§ 2018.030, subd. (b).) If the party resisting discovery alleges that a witness statement, or portion thereof, is absolutely protected because it "reflects an attorney's impressions, conclusions, opinions, or legal research or theories" (§ 2018.030, subd. (a)), that party must make a preliminary or foundational showing in support of its claim. The trial court should then make an in camera inspection to determine whether absolute work product protection applies to some or all of the material.

In the present case, we remand the matter for consideration of whether absolute privilege applies to all or part of the recorded witness interviews. If any or all of the interviews are not absolutely protected, the trial court should consider whether plaintiff can make a sufficient showing of unfair prejudice or injustice under section 2018.030, subdivision (b) to permit discovery. We do not disturb the trial court's conclusion that the state waived the work product privilege as to the recording used to examine a witness during the January 27, 2009 deposition.

D

In addition to the witness statements, plaintiff sought to compel defendant to answer form interrogatory No. 12.3, which asked: "Have YOU OR ANYONE ACTING ON YOUR BEHALF obtained a written or recorded statement from any individual concerning the INCIDENT?" For any such statement, the interrogatory requested (among other things) the name, address, and telephone number of the witness and the date the statement was obtained. * * *

The issue here is whether disclosure of a list of witnesses from whom an attorney took recorded statements at his or her own initiative implicates the work product privilege. Parties in litigation typically know the full universe of witnesses, not least because Judicial Council form interrogatory No. 12.1 requires parties to provide a list of all known witnesses. Thus, form interrogatory No. 12.3 specifically aims to reveal which witnesses an attorney for one party saw fit to ask for a recorded statement.

As discussed above, disclosing a list of witnesses from whom an attorney has taken recorded statements may, in some instances, reveal the attorney's impressions of the case. Take, for example, a bus accident involving 50 surviving passengers and an allegation that the driver fell asleep at the wheel. If an attorney for one of the passengers took recorded statements from only 10 individuals, disclosure of the list may well indicate the attorney's evaluation or conclusion as to which witnesses were in the best position to see the cause of the accident. (See *Hickman, supra*, 329 U.S. at p. 511 ["Proper preparation of a client's case demands that [the attorney] . . . sift what he considers to be the relevant from the irrelevant facts . . . ."].) Such information may be entitled to absolute privilege under section 2018.030, subdivision (a). If absolute privilege were inapplicable, such a list may still be entitled to qualified privilege under section 2018.030, subdivision (b) to the extent it reflects the attorney's industry and effort in selecting which witnesses to ask for a recorded statement. Perhaps the attorney devoted significant effort to tracking down bus tickets and passenger logs in order to determine which passengers sat in which seats, and then decided to take recorded statements from the 10 passengers closest to the driver. Even without obtaining the witness statements themselves, the bus company's lawyer would gain valuable information by free riding on the attorney's identification of the most salient witnesses. Such undue advantage taking is precisely what the Legislature intended the work product privilege to prevent. (§ 2018.020, subd. (b).)

At the same time, however, we cannot say that it will always or even often be the case that a witness list responsive to form interrogatory No. 12.3 reflects counsel's premeditated and carefully considered selectivity as in the scenario above. As Justice Kane posited in his separate opinion below: "Take, for example, a typical automobile accident. The police report may disclose the existence of several witnesses. If the attorney for one party obtains witness statements from one or more of those individuals whom everyone in the case knows are percipient witnesses, that fact does not show anything definite about the attorney's evaluation of the strengths and weaknesses of the case, attorney strategy or tactics, or even the relative strength of any particular witness. . . . Indeed, a particular witness statement might be in an attorney's file for a host of reasons, including that the person happened to be available when the attorney sent out an investigator." Although the witness statements themselves reflect the attorney's time and effort in taking the statements and are therefore qualified work product, disclosing the list of such witnesses in Justice Kane's scenario does not implicate the problem of one attorney free riding on the work of another, as no significant work or selectivity went into creating the list.

The instant case presents another scenario in which the work product privilege may be inapplicable. Where it appears that an attorney has sought to take recorded statements from all or almost all of the known witnesses to the incident, compelling a response to form interrogatory No. 12.3 is unlikely to violate the work product privilege. As Justice Kane observed: "In our case, DWR's attorney sent an investigator to interview the eyewitnesses to the drowning. There were six eyewitnesses, although it appears only five were known at the time the statements were sought. DWR's investigator succeeded in interviewing four eyewitnesses and generated four recorded statements. These facts, had they been disclosed in a response to form interrogatory No. 12.3, would have revealed nothing of consequence regarding DWR's evaluation of the case, one way or the other." Nor would it have implicated any time or effort expended by DWR's attorney in selecting the witnesses to interview, as it does not appear that any meaningful selection occurred.

Because it is not evident that form interrogatory No. 12.3 implicates the policies underlying the work product privilege in all or even most cases, we hold that information responsive to form interrogatory No. 12.3 is not automatically entitled as a matter of law to absolute or qualified work product privilege. Instead, the interrogatory usually must be answered. However, an objecting party may be entitled to protection if it can make a preliminary or foundational showing that answering the interrogatory would reveal the attorney's tactics, impressions, or evaluation of the case, or would result in opposing counsel taking undue advantage of the attorney's industry or efforts. Upon such a showing, the trial court should then determine, by making an in camera inspection if necessary, whether absolute or qualified work product protection applies to the material in dispute. Of course, a trial court may also have to consider nonparty witnesses' privacy concerns.

CONCLUSION

We reverse the judgment of the Court of Appeal and remand the matter for further proceedings, consistent with our opinion, to determine whether the disputed materials should be produced.

Notes and Questions Regarding Work Product Protection

(1) *Absolute Work Product Protection.* Code of Civil Procedure § 2018.030 provides both absolute and conditional work product protection. Absolute protection is provided to "[a]ny writing that reflects an attorney's impression, conclusions, opinions, or legal research or theories." CCP § 2018.030(a). There are (only) three recognized exceptions to this absolute privilege: The State Bar may discover attorney work product where disciplinary charges are pending, CCP § 2018.070; no privilege exists in an

action between an attorney and her client if work product is relevant to the attorney's alleged breach of duty, CCP § 2018.080; and, when an attorney is suspected of knowingly participating in a crime or fraud, there is no work product protection in any official investigation by a law enforcement agency or by a public prosecutor if the services of the lawyer were obtained to aid anyone to commit a crime or fraud. CCP § 2018.050. However, no crime-fraud exception to this absolute privilege applies in private civil litigation. *Rico v. Mitsubishi Motors Corp.*, 42 Cal. 4th 807, 820–21, 68 Cal. Rptr. 3d 758, 171 P.3d 1092 (2007).

(2) *Qualified Work Product Protection.* Conditional protection is afforded to any other attorney work product, which is only discoverable where "the court determines that denial of discovery will unfairly prejudice the party seeking discovery in preparing that party's claim or defense or will result in an injustice." CCP § 2018.030(b). The Civil Discovery Act does not define "work product" for purposes of this qualified privilege. How is "work product" defined in *Coito v. Superior Court*? The California Supreme Court did not announce a black-letter rule. Instead, it indicated that whether material constitutes "work product" should be decided on a case-by-case basis by relying upon the policies underlying the work product statute. The main policies are stated in CCP § 2018.020(a) & (b): (1) To prevent attorneys from taking undue advantage of their adversary's industry and efforts, and (2) to encourage attorneys to prepare their cases thoroughly and to investigate not only the favorable but the unfavorable aspects of those cases. Obviously, this is a very flexible test.

C. Individual Discovery Devices

The Civil Discovery Act authorizes the following individual discovery devices: Interrogatories, inspections, medical examinations, expert witness disclosures, depositions, and requests for admissions. However, unlike Rule 26(a)(1) of the Federal Rules of Civil Procedure, the Civil Discovery Act does not automatically require parties to provide initial disclosures of information that the disclosing party may use to support its claims or defenses.

1. Interrogatories

Discovery by written interrogatories to a party is authorized by Code of Civil Procedure §§ 2030.010–.310. Section § 2030.030 imposes a presumptive limit of 35 specially prepared interrogatories in addition to any number of official form interrogatories. To ensure that the presumptive limit is not evaded by clever drafting, CCP § 2030.060(f) prohibits subparts, compound, conjunctive or disjunctive special interrogatories. Interrogatories exceeding the statutory limit should be accompanied by a declaration showing a greater number is warranted. § 2030.050. To accommodate the need to update information as trial approaches, § 2030.070 permits a limited number of supplemental interrogatories before trial which do not count against the presumptive limit. Section 2030.010 also codifies certain judicial interpretations of the prior law, including approval of "contention interrogatories" whose answers involve opinions that relate to fact or the application of law to fact. § 2030.010(b).

Continuing Interrogatories. While contention interrogatories are expressly allowed, continuing interrogatories that ask the responding party to update the answers with information acquired in the future are expressly prohibited. CCP § 2030.060(g). Unlike Rule 26(e) of the Federal Rules of Civil Procedure, the Discovery Act prohibits placing this burden on the responding party and requires instead that the propounding party seek updated information through supplemental interrogatories. CCP § 2030.070.

Responses. The responding party's obligations and options are set out in CCP § 2030.210–.310. The responding party "shall respond in writing under oath separately to each interrogatory by (1) an answer containing the information sought to be discovered, (2) an exercise of the party's option to produce writings, or (3) an objection to the particular interrogatory." Under this subsection each answer "shall be as complete and straightforward as the information reasonably available to the responding party permits."

Time Limit. Unless the 30-day time limit to respond is extended by court order or stipulation, serious consequences flow from failure to serve a timely response. Specifically, a nonresponding party waives the right to exercise the option of producing writings and waives any objections, including privilege. CCP § 2030.290(a). The court may grant relief from a waiver where (1) the party has since served a proper response and (2) the failure to timely respond resulted from "mistake, inadvertence, or excusable neglect." *Id.* Within the 30-day limit, the responding party may seek a protective order on the grounds of "unwarranted annoyance, embarrassment, oppression, or undue burden or expense." CCP § 2030.090(b).

2. Inspections

Discovery by inspections of documents, things, and places is governed by two sets of statutes: CCP §§ 2031.010–.510, which apply to parties; and CCP §§ 2020.010–.510, which apply to nonparties.

Demands for Inspections of Items Controlled by a Party. Section 2031.010 provides that any party may obtain discovery by inspecting documents, tangible things, land, and other property in the possession, custody, or control of any other party. Within 30 days after service of the inspection demand, the party to whom the demand has been directed shall respond to each item or category of item sought to be inspected. CCP §§ 2031.210 & .260.

Any documents produced in response to an inspection demand must be identified with the specific request number to which the documents respond. § 2031.280(a). The responding party may respond by serving (1) a statement of compliance, (2) a representation of inability to comply, or (3) an objection. § 2031.210. Alternatively, the responding party may seek a protective order which, if granted, may direct that some of the items need not be produced, that the inspection be made on specified terms and conditions, that a trade secret or other confidential commercial information be protected, or may provide other appropriate restrictions. CCP § 2031.060.

The consequences of a failure to serve a timely response are significant. Specifically, the responding party waives any objection to the demand, including one based on privilege or work product protection. However, the court may relieve a party from the consequences of this waiver on a proper showing. CCP § 2031.300(a). The party making the demand may move for an order compelling a response. § 2031.300(b). If the responding party disobeys an order compelling a response, further appropriate sanctions may be ordered. § 2031.310.

In addition to any other sanctions imposed, monetary sanctions of $250 are mandatory for any party, person, or attorney who did not respond in good faith to a request for production of documents, who produced requested documents within seven days of a scheduled hearing on a motion to compel production of records, or who failed to meet and confer with the requesting party in a reasonable and good faith attempt to informally resolve a dispute concerning a request. CCP § 2023.050 (eff. Jan. 1, 2020).

Discovery of Electronically Stored Information. Information stored electronically, such as computer files and e-mail messages, are subject to inspection. *See Dodge, Warren & Peters Ins. Services, Inc. v. Riley*, 105 Cal. App. 4th 1414, 130 Cal. Rptr. 2d 385 (2003) (Affirming preliminary injunction that required the preservation of defendant's electronic evidence and allowed expert to copy all of it, including computer hard drives and disks, to recover deleted files); *R.S. Creative, Inc. v. Creative Cotton, Ltd.*, 75 Cal. App. 4th 486, 89 Cal. Rptr. 2d 353 (1999) (Affirming dismissal of plaintiff's complaint as sanction for repeated efforts to thwart discovery, including the deliberate destruction of evidence by deletion of plaintiff's computer files). *See also* CCP §§ 2017.710–.740 (Authorizing the use of electronic communication in conducting discovery in complex cases or by stipulation).

In 2009, the Legislature adopted the Electronic Discovery Act, thereby amending the Civil Discovery Act in order to modernize California's discovery law with respect to electronically stored information. These new provisions provide comprehensive procedures for the handling of demands for the inspection, copying, testing, or sampling of electronically stored information. CCP §§ 2031.010-2031.320. With respect to the important issue of whether the requesting party should pay the expense of information retrieval and production in a usable form, the Act provides: "If the court finds good cause for the production of electronically stored information from a source that is not reasonably accessible, the court may set conditions for the discovery of the electronically stored information, including allocation of the expense of discovery." CCP §§ 2031.060(e), 2031.310(e).

Moreover, a court must limit the frequency or extent of discovery of electronically stored information, even from a source that is reasonably accessible, if the court determines that any of the following conditions exist:

(1) It is possible to obtain the information from some other source that is more convenient, less burdensome, or less expensive.

(2) The discovery sought is unreasonably cumulative or duplicative.

(3) The party seeking discovery has had ample opportunity by discovery in the action to obtain the information sought.

(4) The likely burden or expense of the proposed discovery outweighs the likely benefit, taking into account the amount in controversy, the resources of the parties, the importance of the issues in the litigation, and the importance of the requested discovery in resolving the issues.

CCP §§ 2031.060(f), 2031.310(f).

Inspections of Items Not Controlled by a Party. The Discovery Act specifically provides for discovery from a nonparty. CCP § 2020.010-.510. These sections may be used to compel nonparties to permit inspection of records, documents, and tangible things, but not land or property. This inspection takes place in connection with an oral deposition and is initiated by a "deposition subpoena." § 2025.420. As an alternative to a deposition subpoena, § 2020.410 permits a party to serve a records only deposition subpoena for business records. When personal records are sought, the person who is the subject of the records must be notified and provided an opportunity to object to the production. CCP § 1985.3 and § 2020.410.

3. Depositions

Code of Civil Procedure sections 2025.010–.620 provide for oral depositions in California. Other depositions are covered in the following sections: CCP § 2026.010, oral depositions in another state; § 2027.010, oral depositions in another country; and §§ 2028.010–.080, written depositions. Section 2025.330 provides for stenographic, audiotaped, and videotaped depositions. However, unless the parties agree otherwise, the testimony must be recorded stenographically and that recording must be transcribed. CCP §§ 2025.330 & .510. In addition to answering questions, a deponent may be compelled to perform a re-enactment of an incident during a videotape deposition. *Emerson Electric Co. v. Superior Court*, 16 Cal. 4th 1101, 68 Cal. Rptr. 2d 883, 946 P.2d 841 (1997).

Objections. Section 2025.460 limits the requirements for objecting to deposition questions. In short, a party must object on the grounds of (1) privilege or work product protection, (2) curable matters including the oath administered and the form of any question or answer. CCP § 2025.460. Failure to object on these grounds results in waiver of the right to object. *Id.* On the other hand, certain other objections are statutorily unnecessary: "Objections to the competency of the deponent, or to the relevancy, materiality, or admissibility at trial of the testimony or of the materials produced are unnecessary and are not waived by failure to make them before or during the taking of the deposition." § 2025.460(c).

Where an issue of privilege arises and the deposing attorney persists with that line of questioning, a party may move to terminate or limit a deposition under CCP § 2025.470. This motion is also available in other circumstances where "the examination is being conducted in bad faith or in a manner that unreasonably annoys, embarrasses, or oppresses" the person being deposed. *Id.* To protect confidential or sensitive information, the court may enter a protective order providing "that the deposition be sealed and thereafter opened only on order of the court." CCP § 2025.420(b)(15); *see also* Rules 2.550 & 2.551, Cal. Rules of Ct. Such restrictions on the use of discovery information have withstood First Amendment challenges. *Seattle Times Co. v. Rhinehart*, 467 U.S. 20, 104 S. Ct. 2199, 81 L. Ed. 2d 17 (1984).

Use of Depositions at Trial. Section 2025.620 sets out the rules governing the use of depositions at trial. Specifically, unless another use is authorized by the Evidence Code, the deposition of a nonparty is generally only used to impeach or contradict live testimony. CCP § 2025.620(a). However, the deposition of a party or party-affiliated deponent may be used by the opponent for any purpose—either as substantive evidence or for impeachment—regardless of whether the deponent testifies at trial. § 2025.620(b). Finally, the deposition of any deponent (party, party-affiliated, or nonparty) may be used at trial where the deponent is unavailable or other exceptional circumstances justify its use. § 2025.620(c).

4. Medical Examinations

Code of Civil Procedure § 2032.020 provides for discovery by physical and mental examination of a party, an agent of a party, or a person in the custody or control of a party where that person's mental or physical condition is in controversy in a civil action. Section 2032.020(b) specifies the required qualifications of the examiner. The procedures for obtaining a medical examination fall into two categories: (1) those for the routine examination of a plaintiff in a personal injury action, and (2) those for other examinations by court order.

Noticed Examination of Plaintiff in a Personal Injury Action. The major innovation of the Civil Discovery Act of 1986 with respect to examinations is the simplified procedure for the defendant in a personal injury action to obtain an examination of the plaintiff without obtaining a prior court order. Under § 2032.220, "any defendant may demand one physical examination of the plaintiff, provided the examination does not include any diagnostic test or procedure that is painful, protracted, or intrusive, and is conducted at a location within 75 miles of the residence of the examinee."

After an examination, the party submitting to or producing someone to be examined may demand in writing "(1) a copy of a detailed written report setting out the history, examinations, findings, including the results of all tests made, diagnoses, prognoses, and conclusions of the examiner, and (2) a copy of reports of all earlier examinations of the same condition of the examinee made by that or any other examiner." CCP § 2032.610. The statute also provides that the report, if demanded, "shall be delivered within 30 days after service of the demand, or within 15 days of trial, whichever is earlier." *Id.* Failure to comply with these requirements will support a motion to compel and the imposition of sanctions. *Id.*

Court Ordered Examinations. Except for the initial routine physical examination in a personal injury action, a party who desires to obtain discovery by a medical examination must obtain leave of court. CCP § 2032.310. Alternatively, the parties may agree in writing to any examination. § 2016.030.

Vinson v. Superior Court

Supreme Court of California

43 Cal. 3d 833, 239 Cal. Rptr. 292, 740 P.2d 404 (1987)

Mosk, Justice.

The plaintiff in a suit for sexual harassment and intentional infliction of severe emotional distress petitions for a writ of mandate and/or prohibition to direct respondent court to forbid her pending psychiatric examination, or in the alternative to protect her from any inquiry into her sexual history, habits, or practices. She also requests that her attorney be allowed to attend the examination if it is held. We conclude that the examination should be permitted but that a writ should issue to restrict its scope. We further conclude that her counsel should not be present.

I. *The Appropriateness of a Mental Examination*

Plaintiff first contends the psychiatric examination should not be permitted because it infringes on her right to privacy. Before we can entertain this constitutional question, we must determine the statutory scope of the discovery laws. [Because the discovery was initiated under the old law, it is governed by the old law. However, many of the new provisions produce the same result.]

Code of Civil Procedure section 2032, subdivision (a), permits the mental examination of a party in any action in which the mental condition of that party is in controversy. Plaintiff disputes that her mental condition is in controversy.

In the case at bar, plaintiff haled defendants into court and accused them of causing her various mental and emotional ailments. Defendants deny her charges. As a result, the existence and extent of her mental injuries is indubitably in dispute. In addition, by asserting a causal link between her mental distress and defendants' conduct, plaintiff implicitly claims it was not caused by a preexisting mental condition, thereby raising the question of alternative sources for the distress. We thus conclude that her mental state is in controversy.

We emphasize that our conclusion is based solely on the allegations of emotional and mental damages in this case. A simple sexual harassment claim asking compensation for having to endure an oppressive work environment or for wages lost following an unjust dismissal would not normally create a controversy regarding the plaintiff's mental state. To hold otherwise would mean that every person who brings such a suit implicitly asserts he or she is mentally unstable, obviously an untenable proposition.

Determining that the mental or physical condition of a party is in controversy is but the first step in our analysis. In contrast to more pedestrian discovery procedures, a mental or physical examination requires the discovering party to obtain a court order. The court may grant the motion only for good cause shown. (§ 2032, subd. (a).)[5]

Section 2036 defines a showing of "good cause" as requiring that the party produce specific facts justifying discovery and that the inquiry be relevant to the subject matter of the action or reasonably calculated to lead to the discovery of admissible evidence.[6] The requirement of a court order following a showing of good cause is doubtless designed to protect an examinee's privacy interest by preventing an examination from becoming an annoying fishing expedition. While a plaintiff may place his mental state in controversy by a general allegation of severe emotional distress, the opposing party may not require him to undergo psychiatric testing solely on the basis of speculation that something of interest may surface.

Plaintiff in the case at bar asserts that she continues to suffer diminished self-esteem, reduced motivation, sleeplessness, loss of appetite, fear, lessened ability to help others, loss of social contacts, anxiety, mental anguish, loss of reputation, and severe emotional distress. In their motion defendants pointed to these allegations. Because the truth of these claims is relevant to plaintiff's cause of action and justifying facts have been shown with specificity, good cause as to these assertions has been demonstrated. Subject to limitations necessitated by plaintiff's right to privacy, defendants must be allowed to investigate the continued existence and severity of plaintiff's alleged damages.

II. *Privacy Limitations on the Scope of a Mental Examination*

If we find, as we do, that an examination may be ordered, plaintiff urges us to circumscribe its scope to exclude any probing into her sexual history, habits, or practices. Such probing, she asserts, would intrude impermissibly into her protected sphere of privacy. Furthermore, it would tend to contravene the state's strong interest in eradicating sexual harassment by means of private suits for damages. An examination into a plaintiff's past and present sexual practices would inhibit the bringing of meritorious sexual harassment actions by compelling the plaintiff—whose privacy has already been invaded by the harassment—to suffer another intrusion into her private life.

A right to privacy was recognized in the seminal case *of Griswold v. Connecticut* (1965) 381 U.S. 479, [85 S. Ct. 1678, 14 L. Ed. 2d 510]. It protects both the marital relationship (*ibid.*) and the sexual lives of the unmarried (*Eisenstadt v. Baird* (1972) 405 U.S. 438, [92 S. Ct. 1029, 31 L. Ed. 2d 349]). More significantly, California accords privacy the constitutional status of an "inalienable right," on a par with defending life and possessing property. (Cal. Const., art. I, § 1; *White v. Davis* (1975) 13 Cal. 3d 757,

---

5. After July 1, 1987, this requirement is contained in section 2032, subdivision (d).

6. This section has been repealed and has apparently not been replaced by equivalent language. There is no indication, however, that the Legislature intended repeal of former section 2036 to change the requirements for good cause in regard to mental examinations.

[120 Cal. Rptr. 94, 533 P.2d 222].) California's privacy protection similarly embraces sexual relations.

Defendants acknowledge plaintiff's right to privacy in the abstract but maintain she has waived it for purposes of the present suit.

Plaintiff's present mental and emotional condition is directly relevant to her claim and essential to a fair resolution of her suit; she has waived her right to privacy in this respect by alleging continuing mental ailments. But she has not, merely by initiating this suit for sexual harassment and emotional distress, implicitly waived her right to privacy in respect to her sexual history and practices. Defendants fail to explain why probing into this area is directly relevant to her claim and essential to its fair resolution. Plaintiff does not contend the alleged acts were detrimental to her present sexuality. Her sexual history is even less relevant to her claim. We conclude that she has not waived her right to sexual privacy.

But even though plaintiff retains certain unwaived privacy rights, these rights are not necessarily absolute. On occasion her privacy interests may have to give way to her opponent's right to a fair trial. Thus courts must balance the right of civil litigants to discover relevant facts against the privacy interests of persons subject to discovery.

Before proceeding, we note the Legislature recently enacted a measure designed to protect the privacy of plaintiffs in cases such as these. Section 2036.1 (operative until July 1, 1987; presently, substantially the same provision is contained in § 2017, subdivision (d)), provides that in a civil suit alleging conduct that constitutes sexual harassment, sexual assault, or sexual battery, any party seeking discovery concerning the plaintiff's sexual conduct with individuals other than the alleged perpetrator must establish specific facts showing good cause for that discovery, and that the inquiry is relevant to the subject matter and reasonably calculated to lead to the discovery of admissible evidence. We must determine whether the general balancing of interests embodied in this new legislation has obviated the need for us to engage in an individualized balancing of privacy with discovery in the case at bar.

In enacting the measure, the Legislature took pains to declare that "The discovery of sexual aspects of complainant's [sic] lives, as well as those of their past and current friends and acquaintances, has the clear potential to discourage complaints and to annoy and harass litigants . . . without protection against it, individuals whose intimate lives are unjustifiably and offensively intruded upon might face the 'Catch-22' of invoking their remedy only at the risk of enduring further intrusions into the details of their personal lives in discovery. . . . [¶] . . . Absent extraordinary circumstances, inquiry into those areas should not be permitted, either in discovery or at trial." (Stats. 1985, ch. 1328, § 1.)

Nowhere do defendants establish specific facts justifying inquiry into plaintiff's zone of sexual privacy or show how such discovery would be relevant. Rather they make only the most sweeping assertions regarding the need for wide latitude in the examination. Because good cause has not been shown, discovery into this area of plaintiff's life must be denied.

Section 2036.1, thus amply protects plaintiff's privacy interests. We anticipate that in the majority of sexual harassment suits, a separate weighing of privacy against discovery will not be necessary. It should normally suffice for the court, in ruling on whether good cause exists for probing into the intimate life of a victim of sexual harassment, sexual battery, or sexual assault, to evaluate the showing of good cause in light of the legislative purpose in enacting this section and the plaintiff's constitutional right to privacy.

III. *Presence of Counsel*

In the event a limited psychiatric examination is proper, plaintiff urges us to authorize the attendance of her attorney. She fears that the examiner will stray beyond the permitted area of inquiry. Counsel would monitor the interview and shield her from inappropriate interrogation. And depicting the examination as an "alien and frankly hostile environment," she asserts that she needs her lawyer to provide her with aid and comfort.

Defendants, joined by amici California Psychiatric Association and Northern California Psychiatric Association, counter that a meaningful mental examination cannot be conducted with an attorney interposing objections. And if plaintiff's counsel is present, defense counsel would also seek to attend. Defendants maintain these adversaries would likely convert the examination into a chaotic deposition.

We contemplated whether counsel must be allowed to attend the psychiatric examination of a client in *Edwards v. Superior Court* (1976) 16 Cal. 3d 905, [130 Cal. Rptr. 14, 549 P.2d 846]. The plaintiff in *Edwards* alleged that because of the defendant school district's failure to properly instruct and supervise users of school equipment, she sustained physical and emotional injuries. The trial court granted a motion compelling her to undergo a psychiatric examination alone. Holding that the plaintiff could not insist on the presence of her counsel, a majority of this court denied her petition for a peremptory writ.

The plaintiff in *Edwards* raised many of the points urged upon us here. She asserted that her attorney should be present to protect her from improper inquiries. We were skeptical that a lawyer, unschooled in the ways of the mental health profession, would be able to discern the psychiatric relevance of the questions. And the examiner should have the freedom to probe deeply into the plaintiff's psyche without interference by a third party. (*Id.* at p. 911.) The plaintiff further suggested counsel should be present to lend her comfort and support in an inimical setting. We responded that an examinee could view almost any examination of this sort, even by her own expert, as somewhat hostile. Whatever comfort her attorney's handholding might afford was substantially outweighed by the distraction and potential disruption caused by the presence of a third person. (*Ibid.*) Finally, we concluded counsel's presence was not necessary to ensure accurate reporting. Verbatim transcription might inhibit the examinee, preventing an effective examination. Furthermore, other procedural devices—pretrial discovery of the examiner's notes or cross-examination, for example—were available for the plaintiff's protection. (*Id.* at pp. 911–912.)

[The Court reviews federal decisions addressing this issue.] These cases suggest that in the federal courts a mental examinee has no absolute right to the presence of an attorney; but when the circumstances warrant it, the courts may fashion some means of protecting an examinee from intrusive or offensive probing.

[W]e conclude that a reconsideration of [the *Edwards*] decision—which is barely 10 years old—is not justified.[9] We emphasize, however, that *Edwards* should be viewed as standing for the proposition that the presence of an attorney is not required during a mental examination. In light of their broad discretion in discovery matters, trial courts retain the power to permit the presence of counsel or to take other prophylactic measures when needed.

Plaintiff makes no showing that the court abused its discretion in excluding her counsel from the examination. Her fears are wholly unfounded at this point; not a shred of evidence has been produced to show that defendants' expert will not respect her legitimate rights to privacy or might disobey any court-imposed restrictions. Plaintiff's apprehension appears to derive less from the reality of the proposed analysis than from the popular image of mental examinations.

Plaintiff's interests can be adequately protected without having her attorney present. In the first place, section 2032 requires the court granting a physical or mental examination to specify its conditions and scope. We must assume, absent evidence to the contrary, that the examiner will proceed in an ethical manner, adhering to these constraints. And if plaintiff truly fears that the examiner will probe into impermissible areas, she may record the examination on audio tape. This is an unobtrusive measure that will permit evidence of abuse to be presented to the court in any motion for sanctions.

Plaintiff refers us to the history of psychiatric examinations for victims of sexual assault. Such examinations were widely viewed as inhibiting prosecutions for rape by implicitly placing the victim on trial, leading to a legislative prohibition of examinations to assess credibility. The victim of sexual harassment is analogous to the prosecutrix in a rape case, plaintiff asserts, and she points to legislative findings that discovery of sexual aspects of complainants' lives "has the clear potential to discourage complaints." (Stats. 1985, ch. 1328, § 1.) If we conclude on the basis of general considerations that a mental examination is appropriate and that it should occur without the presence of counsel, plaintiff urges us to adopt a special rule exempting those who bring harassment charges from either or both of these requirements.

---

9. Section 2032, subdivision (g) (operative July 1, 1987), now specifically provides for the attendance of an attorney at a physical examination. (*See Sharff v. Superior Court* (1955) 44 Cal. 2d 508, 282 P.2d 896.) Subdivision (g)(2) states, however, that nothing in the discovery statutes shall be construed to alter, amend, or affect existing case law with respect to the presence of counsel or other persons during a mental examination by agreement or court order. Had the Legislature felt it desirable to have counsel present at psychiatric examinations, it would certainly have provided for this in its thorough revision of the section. Indeed, in the course of that revision the Legislature considered and rejected a provision that would have annulled our decision in *Edwards* by permitting counsel to attend a mental examination.

We believe that in these circumstances such a special rule is unwarranted. In the first place, we should be guided by the maxim that *entia non sunt multiplicanda praeter necessitatem*: we should carve out exceptions from general rules only when the facts require it. The state admittedly has a strong interest in eradicating the evil of sexual harassment, and the threat of a mental examination could conceivably dampen a plaintiff's resolve to bring suit. But we have seen that those who allege harassment have substantial protection under existing procedural rules. In general it is unlikely that a simple sexual harassment suit will justify a mental examination. Such examinations may ordinarily be considered only in cases in which the alleged mental or emotional distress is said to be ongoing. When an examination is permitted, investigation by a psychiatrist into the private life of a plaintiff is severely constrained, and sanctions are available to guarantee those restrictions are respected.

Finally, the mental examination in this case largely grows out of plaintiff's emotional distress claim. We do not believe the state has a greater interest in preventing emotional distress in sexual harassment victims than it has in preventing such distress in the victims of any other tort.

The judgment of the Court of Appeal is reversed with directions to issue a peremptory writ of mandate compelling respondent court to limit the scope of the mental examination in accordance with the views expressed herein.

Notes and Questions Regarding Examinations

(1) A personal injury plaintiff seeking damages for mental and emotional injuries may be ordered to submit to a mental examination. CCP §§ 2032.020, 2032.310 (leave of court required), 2032.320(a) (showing of good cause required). This examination may be avoided by (1) disclaiming extraordinary mental and emotional suffering and (2) agreeing not to introduce expert testimony on these issues at trial. § 2032.320(c).

(2) In contrast to physical examinations, neither counsel nor court reporters are generally allowed to attend mental examinations. *Edwards v. Superior Court*, 16 Cal. 3d 905, 910, 130 Cal. Rptr. 14, 549 P.2d 846 (1976). However, as *Vinson* suggests, the court has discretion to permit counsel to attend if there is some showing of special need. *See* CCP § 2032.530(b).

(3) Since neither counsel nor a court reporter may be present at a mental examination, § 2032.530(a) authorizes the recording of the entire examination by audio technology. Both the examiner and the examinee have the right to record the entire examination. *Id.*

5. Exchange of Information About Trial Experts

One of the major changes of the Civil Discovery Act of 1986 is reflected in Code of Civil Procedure § 2034.210, which provides for the compulsory exchange of the identity of expert witnesses who will testify at trial and of the general nature of their testimony. After the initial trial date is set, this exchange may be initiated by either side.

CCP § 2034.210(a). Section 2034.210 provides for the timely exchange of information to permit the opposing party to depose the designated expert and to designate additional experts if necessary.

Expert Witness Disclosures. The disclosure required by section 2034.210 is limited to experts who will be called to testify at trial. For such "retained experts" (*i.e.*, experts retained by a party for the purpose of expressing an opinion at trial), the disclosure must include an expert witness declaration setting out the expert's qualifications, the general substance of the expected testimony, a representation that the expert is ready to testify, and a statements of the expert's fees for deposition testimony. CCP § 2034.260. For treating physicians who are regarded as percipient witnesses, the identity must be disclosed if they will be called to express an opinion, but an expert declaration is not required. *See* § 2034.210; *Schreiber v. Estate of Kiser*, 22 Cal. 4th 31, 91 Cal. Rptr. 2d 293, 989 P.2d 720 (1999) (Failure of treating physician to submit an expert witness declaration did not preclude physician's opinion testify at trial regarding cause of plaintiff's injuries).

The identities and opinions of consulting experts who will not be called to testify at trial are protected work product under CCP § 2018.030. *See* Kennedy & Martin, California Expert Witness Guide §§ 8.18 & 10.6 (2d ed. 2015) (collecting cases). However, once a witness is designated as a trial expert the work product privilege may be waived as to earlier reports by that expert, even those tendered while the witness was only a consultant. *National Steel Products Co. v. Superior Court*, 164 Cal. App. 3d 476, 210 Cal. Rptr. 535 (1985); 2 Hogan & Weber, California Civil Discovery § 12.12 (2005 & 2015 Supp.).

Failure to Comply with Expert Witness Disclosure Requirements. If a party has unreasonably failed to comply with the requirements for expert disclosure under § 2034.210 with respect to a witness, the trial court upon objection is required to exclude from evidence the expert testimony of that witness. CCP § 2034.300. This rule applies where a party fails to list an expert, fails to submit a required declaration, fails to produce discoverable reports, or fails to make the expert available for the deposition. *Id.* Failure to submit an adequate expert declaration may also be grounds for excluding that expert's testimony. *Bonds v. Roy*, 20 Cal. 4th 140, 83 Cal. Rptr. 2d 289, 973 P.2d 66 (1999) (Expert witness precluded from testifying at trial on a subject whose general subject was not previously described in his expert witness declaration).

Testimony of Undesignated Experts. In a limited number of circumstances, a party may call an expert who the party has not designated. First, pursuant to CCP 2034.310(a), a party may call an expert to testify who has been designated by some other party to the case so long as the witness has been deposed. *Powell v. Superior Court*, 211 Cal. App. 3d 441, 259 Cal. Rptr. 390 (1989). Second, an undesignated expert may be called as a rebuttal witness for the purpose of "impeachment." CCP § 2034.310(b). For purposes of this statute, the term "impeachment" has been narrowly construed:

> [T]his impeachment may include testimony pertaining to the falsity or non-existence of any fact used as the foundation for any opinion by any other

party's expert witness, but may not include testimony that contradicts the opinion. Hence, an undisclosed expert may testify to facts which contradict the factual basis for the opinions of other experts but may not give opinion testimony which contradicts the opinions of other experts.

Fish v. Guevara, 12 Cal. App. 4th 142, 145, 15 Cal. Rptr. 2d 329 (1993)

6. Requests for Admissions

Under CCP §§ 2033.010–.420, a party may serve any other party a request to admit the genuineness of a document, the truth of specific factual matters, or opinions relating to fact. A party who has been served a set of requests for admissions has two basic options: either seek a protective order or respond. CCP §§ 2033.080 & .210. Unless the responding party moves for a protective order, that party must respond in writing under oath separately to each request within 30 days after service of the requests. §§ 2033.210–.250. The response must set out an answer or an objection to each request. § 2033.210. The effect of an admission is dramatic: Any admitted matter is conclusively established against the party making the admission for the purpose of the pending action. § 2033.410. A party may only amend or withdraw an admission with leave of the court after notice to all parties. § 2033.300.

A failure to serve timely responses operates as a waiver of all objections to the requests, including privilege and work product objections. CCP § 2033.280. If a party to whom requests for admission have been directed fails to serve a timely response, the requesting party may move for an order that the matters specified in the requests be deemed admitted, as well as for a monetary sanction. § 2033.280. If the delinquent party does not serve a proposed response to the admission requests prior to the hearing on the motion, the trial court must order that the matters be deemed admitted. *Id.* The court must also impose a monetary sanction on the delinquent party or attorney, even where a proposed response is served before the motion hearing. *Id.*

Under section 2033.300, a party may be permitted to withdraw or amend an admission, regardless of whether the admission was contained in an actual response or was deemed admitted for failure to respond. *Wilcox v. Birtwhistle*, 21 Cal. 4th 973, 90 Cal. Rptr. 2d 260, 987 P.2d 727 (1999). This provision imposes a heavy burden on the party seeking relief who must show: (1) mistake, inadvertence or excusable neglect; and (2) lack of prejudice to the requesting party. § 2033.300.

If a party denies the truth of a matter specified in a request for admission and the requesting party later proves the truth of that matter at trial, the requesting party may move the court to recover the attorney fees and other expenses incurred in making that proof. CCP § 2033.420. Section 2033.420 further provides that unless the admission sought was of no substantial importance, the denial or objection had a reasonable basis, or there was some other good reason for the failure to admit, the court must grant this motion. *See Wimberly v. Derby Cycle Corp.*, 56 Cal. App. 4th 618, 638, 65 Cal. Rptr. 2d 532 (1997) (Plaintiff was entitled to recover attorney fees and costs under § 2033.420 because the defendant was not reasonable in denying plaintiff's requests for admissions that the fork assembly on a bicycle was defective and that the defect was the proximate cause of plaintiff's injuries).

7. Initial Disclosures

Effective January 1, 2020, the Civil Discovery Act now authorizes the trial court, upon stipulation of all the parties, to order the exchange of initial disclosures by all parties, without a triggering discovery request. CCP § 2016.090. Similar in scope to Rule 26(b)(1) of the Federal Rules of Civil Procedure, this new discovery device requires disclosures of information regarding witnesses and documents, with a continuing duty to supplement. § 2016.090(1) & (3).

D. Enforcement of Discovery Requests

1. Motion to Compel Discovery

The sections of the Civil Discovery Act providing for specific discovery devices also provide for protective orders, motions to compel, and sanctions. These provisions follow the same general scheme. First, the parties are required to meet and confer to attempt to informally resolve the dispute. If the parties fail to attempt an informal resolution, monetary sanctions are mandatory. CCP § 2023.010(i). If the informal negotiation is unsuccessful, the dissatisfied party has 45 days (60 days for oral depositions) to move to compel discovery by court order, with the losing party being subject to mandatory monetary sanctions unless the court finds "substantial justification" for that party's position or other circumstances which would make the imposition of sanctions unjust. CCP §§ 2025.480, 2030.290 & .300, 2031.300 & .310, 2032.240 & .250, 2033.290 & 2034.730. Finally, disobedience of a court order compelling discovery can lead to the imposition of additional sanctions. §§ 2023.010–.040, 2025.480, 2030.290, 2031.320 & 2032.420.

The Civil Discovery Act requires that, prior to the initiation of a motion to compel, the moving party declare that he or she has made a serious attempt to obtain "an informal resolution of each issue." CCP §§ 2016.040. 2025.450, 2031.310. The Act requires that counsel undertake a reasonable and good faith attempt to talk the matter over, compare their views, consult, and deliberate. *See Townsend v. Superior Court*, 61 Cal. App. 4th 1431, 72 Cal. Rptr. 2d 333 (1998) (A good faith attempt at informal resolution entails something more than bickering with deponent's counsel at a deposition, and therefore directing the trial court to set aside an order compelling answers to deposition questions). A 2017 amendment to the Civil Discovery Act adds another possible avenue for informal resolution of discovery disputes. If a resolution is not reached by the parties after they "meet and confer," the court may conduct an informal discovery conference upon request by a party or on the court's own motion for the purpose of discussing the discovery dispute. CCP § 2016.080. If an informal discovery conference is granted or ordered, the court may toll the deadline for filing a discovery motion or make any other appropriate discovery order.

2. Discovery Sanctions

In addition to the specific statutes for each discovery device, CCP §§ 2023.010–.040 generally address sanctions for discovery misuse. These sections catalogue common misuses of the discovery process, § 2023.010; and the sanctions available, § 2023.030(b). In addition to monetary sanctions, § 2023.030(b) authorizes an issue sanction establishing certain facts in the action; an evidence sanction prohibiting the introduction of certain evidence; a terminating sanction striking a pleading, dismissing an action or rendering default judgment; and a contempt sanction treating the misuse as contempt of court.

Generally, a drastic sanction should not be appropriate in the first instance where a party has failed to respond to a discovery demand because that would be a disproportionate punishment. 2 HOGAN & WEBER, CALIFORNIA CIVIL DISCOVERY § 15.4 (2005 & 2015 Supp.). "Accordingly, under the approach taken in the new Discovery Act, an initial failure to provide discovery, whether in the form of no response at all or in the form of an inadequate response, can result in the first instance only in the imposition of the relatively mild 'monetary' sanction." *Id.* The more drastic sanctions are available after the general obligation to participate in discovery has been transformed into a court order. *Id.*

Several appellate decisions have emphasized the need for the trial court to tailor the sanction to fit the misconduct. For example, one court held that for failure to appear at a deposition an issue or evidence sanction would be appropriate, not a terminating sanction. *McArthur v. Bockman*, 208 Cal. App. 3d 1076, 256 Cal. Rptr. 522 (1989). For other examples of the imposition of an evidence and an issue sanction tailored to specific discovery misuse, *see Juarez v. Boy Scouts of America, Inc.*, 81 Cal. App. 4th 377, 97 Cal. Rptr. 2d 12 (2000)) (Plaintiff prohibited from producing at trial the evidence he repeatedly refused to produce during discovery); *Vallbona v. Springer*, 43 Cal. App. 4th 1525, 1541–1549, 51 Cal. Rptr. 2d 311 (1996) (Defendants prohibited from introducing certain documents into evidence, and certain admissions imposed, where the defendants willfully failed to respond to the plaintiff's request for production of documents); *Pate v. Channel Lumber Co.*, 51 Cal. App. 4th 1447, 59 Cal. Rptr. 2d 919 (1997) (Evidence sanction proper where the defendant repeatedly assured the plaintiff that all relevant documentation had been produced and then attempted mid-trial to introduce documents not discovered by plaintiff).

However, several cases also demonstrate that the imposition of case-terminating sanctions may be appropriate where lessor sanctions would not bring about compliance with discovery orders. *See, e.g., American Home Assurance Co. v. Societe Commerciale Toutelectric*, 104 Cal. App. 4th 406, 435–37, 128 Cal. Rptr. 2d 430 (2002) (Order striking defendant's answer and entering a $25 million default judgment upheld as sanction for willful failure to meet discovery obligations); *Lang v. Hochman*, 77 Cal. App. 4th 1225, 92 Cal. Rptr. 2d 322 (2000) (Default against defendants and dismissal of defendants' cross-complaint upheld as sanctions for inexcusable failure to comply with three discovery orders, where trial court had progressively sanctioned defendants but defendants still did not produce requested documents); *R.S. Creative, Inc. v. Creative Cotton, Ltd.*, 75 Cal. App. 4th 486, 89 Cal. Rptr. 2d 353 (1999) (Dismissal of plaintiff's complaint affirmed as sanction for repeated efforts to thwart discovery, including the violation of two discovery orders and deliberate destruction of evidence by deletion of plaintiff's computer files); *TMS, Inc. v. Aihara*, 71 Cal. App. 4th 377, 83 Cal. Rptr. 2d 834 (1999) (Defendant's willful disobedience of trial court's order to answer post-judgment interrogatories, designed to secure information to aid in enforcement of a money judgment entered against defendant, justified dismissal of defendant's appeal from that judgment).

Chapter VII

Resolution of Cases Before Trial

A. Summary Judgment

1. Summary Judgment, Generally

California practice employs the motion for summary judgment, which includes a motion for summary adjudication, as a potentially powerful procedural device to probe beneath the pleadings. Pleading motions have limited utility—they accept the facts, or at least the well-pleaded facts, contained in the pleadings as true in testing the sufficiency of claims. Except for novel or badly pleaded causes of action, a technically skillful pleader will state proper causes of action. Nevertheless, the claim or defenses made to the claim in the pleadings may not be factually substantial enough to warrant a full trial. Summary judgment is the means for weeding out causes of action and defenses that lack merit because they are factually unsupportable. "The purpose of summary judgment is to penetrate evasive language and adept pleading and to ascertain . . . the presence or absence of triable issues of fact." *Molko v. Holy Spirit Ass'n*, 46 Cal. 3d 1092, 1107, 252 Cal. Rptr. 122, 762 P.2d 46 (1988).

As in the case of its federal rule equivalent, Rule 56, F.R.C.P., California's motion for summary judgment is extensively regulated by statute. The awkwardly numbered section 437c of the Code of Civil Procedure now takes up almost three pages of an unannotated code book, all in fine print. The statute has been regularly, almost annually, amended, but its principal standards have remained constant:

> (a) Any party may move for summary judgment in any action or proceeding if it is contended that the action has no merit or that there is no defense to the action or proceeding. . . . (b) The motion shall be supported by affidavits, declarations, admissions, answers to interrogatories, depositions, and matters of which judicial notice shall or may be taken. . . . (c) The motion for summary judgment shall be granted if all the papers submitted show that there is no triable issue as to any material fact and that the moving party is entitled to a judgment as a matter of law . . . .

The corollary motion for summary adjudication is used to test the merits of one or more specific causes of action, one or more affirmative defenses, one or more claims for damages, or one or more issues of duty. *See* CCP § 437c. The relationship between the motion for summary judgment and the motion for summary adjudication is roughly equivalent to the relationship between the general demurrer and the motion to strike at the pleading stage.

2. California's Burden-Shifting Approach

Moving Party's Initial Burden. Pursuant to a trio of recent California Supreme Court decisions, summary judgment practice in California now conforms, largely if not completely, to its federal counterpart Rule 56 of the Federal Rules of Civil Procedure. *See Saelzler v. Advanced Group 400*, 25 Cal. 4th 763, 107 Cal. Rptr. 2d 617, 23 P.3d 1143 (2001); *Aguilar v. Atlantic Richfield Co.*, 25 Cal. 4th 826, 107 Cal. Rptr. 2d 841, 24 P.3d 493 (2001); *Guz v. Bechtel National, Inc.*, 24 Cal. 4th 317, 100 Cal. Rptr. 2d 352, 8 P.3d 1089 (2000). In *Saelzler v. Advanced Group 400, supra*, the Supreme Court described the burden-shifting approach to summary judgment after the 1992 and 1993 amendments to CCP § 473c as follows:

> Under the current version of the summary judgment statute, a moving defendant need not support his motion with affirmative evidence negating an essential element of the responding party's case. Instead, the moving defendant may . . . point to *the absence of evidence to support the plaintiff's case.* When that is done, the burden shifts to the plaintiff to present evidence showing there is a triable issue of material fact. If the plaintiff is unable to meet her burden of proof regarding an essential element of her case, all other facts are rendered immaterial.

Saelzler, supra, 25 Cal. 4th at 780–81 (quoting *Leslie G. v. Perry & Associates*, 43 Cal. App. 4th 472, 482, 50 Cal. Rptr. 2d 785 (1996) (italics in original).

Subsequently, in *Aguilar v. Atlantic Richfield, supra*, the Supreme Court again endorsed the burden-shifting approach to summary judgment described in *Saelzer. Aguilar, supra*, 25 Cal. 4th at 849–51. However, the *Aguilar* court further explained that the summary judgment law in California now conforms "largely but not completely" to its federal counterpart:

> [S]ummary judgment law in this state [no] longer require[s] a defendant moving for summary judgment to conclusively negate an element of the plaintiff's cause of action. In this particular too, it now accords with federal law. All that the defendant need do is to "show[ ] that one or more elements of the cause of action . . . cannot be established" by the plaintiff. (Code Civ. Proc., § 437c, subd. (o)(2).) In other words, all that the defendant need do is to show that the plaintiff cannot establish at least one element of the cause of action — for example, that the plaintiff cannot prove element X. Although he remains free to do so, the defendant need not himself conclusively negate any such element — for example, himself prove *not* X. This is in line with the purpose of the 1992 and 1993 amendments, which was to liberalize the granting of motions for summary judgment. * * * The defendant has shown that the plaintiff cannot establish at least one element of the cause of action by showing that the plaintiff does not possess, and cannot reasonably obtain, needed evidence: The defendant must show that the plaintiff *does not possess* needed evidence, because otherwise the plaintiff might be able to establish the elements of the cause of action; the defendant must also show that the

plaintiff *cannot reasonably obtain* needed evidence, because the plaintiff must be allowed a reasonable opportunity to oppose the motion (Code Civ. Proc., §437c, subd. (h)). * * *

Summary judgment law in this state, however, continues to require a defendant moving for summary judgment to present evidence, and not simply point out that the plaintiff does not possess, and cannot reasonably obtain, needed evidence. In this particular at least, it still diverges from federal law. For the defendant *must* "support []" the "motion" with evidence including "affidavits, declarations, admissions, answers to interrogatories, depositions, and matters of which judicial notice" must or may "be taken." (Code Civ. Proc., §437c, subd. (b).) The defendant may, but need not, present evidence that conclusively negates an element of the plaintiff's cause of action. The defendant may also present evidence that the plaintiff does not possess, and cannot reasonably obtain, needed evidence—as through admissions by the plaintiff following extensive discovery to the effect that he has discovered nothing. But, as *Fairbank v. Wman Cato Johnson* (9th Cir. 2000) 212 F.3d 528 concludes, the defendant *must* indeed present evidence": Whereas, federal law, "pointing out through argument" (*id.* at p. 532) may be sufficient, state law, it is not.

Aguilar, supra, 25 Cal. 4th at 853–55.

How significant is this difference between requiring a moving defendant to "present evidence" as opposed to "simply pointing out through argument," identified by the *Aguilar* court? For a discussion of this question, as well as a review of California summary judgment law after the Supreme Court's decisions in *Aguilar, Saelzler*, and *Guz, see* Glenn S. Koppel, *The California Supreme Court Speaks Out on Summary Judgment in Its Own "Trilogy" of Decisions: Has the Celotex Era Arrived?*, 42 Santa Clara Law Review 483 (2002). *See also Kids' Universe v. In2Labs*, 95 Cal. App. 4th 870, 116 Cal. Rptr. 2d 158 (2002) (Discussing the burden of production language in *Aguilar*).

Burden Shifting and "Factually Devoid" Discovery Responses. Several cases have held that a defendant may rely on "factually devoid" discovery responses to sustain its burden as the moving party on summary judgment. *See, e.g., Union Bank v. Superior Court*, 31 Cal. App. 4th 573, 37 Cal. Rptr. 2d 653 (1995) (Summary judgment for defendant appropriate where plaintiffs' answer to interrogatory requesting all facts that would support plaintiffs' fraud claim merely stated plaintiffs "believed" defendant had engaged in fraudulent conduct); *McGonnell v. Kaiser Gypsum Co.*, 98 Cal. App. 4th 1098, 120 Cal. Rptr. 2d 23 (2002) (Defendant met its summary judgment burden in wrongful death action for occupational exposure to asbestos based on deposition of plaintiffs' decedent showing plaintiffs could not establish causation); *Rio Linda Unified School Dist. v. Superior Court*, 52 Cal. App. 4th 732, 60 Cal. Rptr. 2d 710 (1997) (Summary judgment for defendant school district was appropriate in a personal injury action because, disregarding the inadmissable hearsay in a deposition to which the defendant objected, the plaintiff produced no evidence that minor plaintiff had in fact fallen from a slide on school property).

The extent to which a defendant may rely on "factually devoid" discovery responses to sustain its summary judgment burden was clarified in *Scheiding v. Dinwiddie Construction Co.*, 69 Cal. App. 4th 64, 81 Cal. Rptr. 2d 360 (1999), a decision quoted with approval by the Supreme Court in *Saelzler v. Advanced Group 400, supra*, 25 Cal. 4th at 768. After extensive analysis of the recent amendments to §437c, the *Scheiding* court concluded that the defendant must "show" from the plaintiff's discovery responses that the only reasonable inference is that there is no further evidence available to oppose the motion. In other words, defendant's initial burden is not met by merely showing that, based on the discovery responses currently in the record, there are no facts to support an essential element of plaintiff's claim. Instead, the defendant must "show" that the discovery questions were directed to an essential element of plaintiff's claim and, based on the plaintiff's discovery answers, the only reasonable inference is that the plaintiff can produce no further evidence to support this essential element. *Scheiding, supra*, 69 Cal. App. 4th at 75–84. *See also Gaggero v. Yura*, 108 Cal. App. 4th 884, 134 Cal. Rptr. 2d 313 (2003) (Defendant failed to meet its summary judgment burden based on deposition of plaintiff where plaintiff refused to answer questions about an essential element of plaintiff's cause of action).

3. Summary Judgment Procedure

Summary judgment motions are permissible 60 days after a general appearance of the party against whom the motion is brought. CCP §437c(a). Notice of the motion and supporting papers must be served 75 days before the hearing date (subject to extension when service is made by mail); opposition papers must be served 14 days before the hearing, and reply papers five days before the hearing §437c(b).

The procedure for supporting and opposing papers is elaborately set out in section 437c(b): There must be separate statements setting forth "plainly and concisely all material facts which the moving party contends are undisputed;" each such fact must be followed by a reference to the supporting evidence. The opposing party must provide a separate statement that responds to each of the moving party's undisputed facts, agreeing or disagreeing with the characterization; it must set forth any other material facts that the opposing party contends are undisputed, along with references to the evidence. If either party has evidentiary objections to the other's summary judgment evidence, they must be made at the hearing or they are waived. CCP §473c(b) (5). For a detailed explanation of the form and format requirements for summary judgment and summary adjudication motions, *see* Rules 3.1350 and 3.1354 of the California Rules of Court.

B. Default Judgment

1. Default Judgments, Generally

A plaintiff may obtain a judgment by default against a defendant, properly served with a complaint and summons, or a cross-complaint, who fails to timely file an appropriate responsive paper. CCP §§ 585, 586. Likewise, a defendant may obtain a default judgment against another defendant or a plaintiff, properly served with a cross-complaint, who fails to timely file an appropriate responsive paper. §§ 585(e), 587.5. An appropriate responsive paper CCP § 585 includes such items as an answer or demurrer, and a notice of motion to strike, to transfer, to quash service of summons, or to stay or dismiss for inconvenient forum.

Relief Limited to Demand in Complaint. Default judgments entered against defendants for failure to timely answer properly served complaints are commonplace. Most such default judgments involve routine procedural issues easily resolved by reference to the appropriate code section. Code of Civil Procedure § 580, for example, directs that "[t]he relief granted to the plaintiff, if there is no answer, cannot exceed that which he or she shall have demanded in his or her complaint." Section 580 embodies a fundamental due process notice requirement, *Marriage of Lippel*, 51 Cal. 3d 1160, 1166, 276 Cal. Rptr. 290, 801 P.2d 1041 (1990); a default judgment greater than the amount specifically demanded is void as beyond the court's jurisdiction. *Greenup v. Rodman*, 42 Cal. 3d 822, 231 Cal. Rptr. 220, 726 P.2d 1295 (1986); *Becker v. S.P.V. Construction Co.*, 27 Cal. 3d 489, 165 Cal. Rptr. 825, 612 P.2d 915 (1980).

2. General Procedures

The procedures utilized to obtain default judgments are also fairly routine in most cases. After the applicable time specified in the summons for responding to the served complaint has expired (within 30 days after completion of service in most actions, CCP § 412.20(a)(3)) the plaintiff must make written application to the clerk or the court for an entry of default. CCP §§ 585(a)–(c). The plaintiff must complete and file the "Request for Entry of Default" form (CIV-100) adopted for use by the Judicial Council of California, along with the proof of service and return of the original summons. CCP §§ 585(a)–(c); 417.10–.30.

Entry of Default. Generally, the procedural scheme set forth in CCP § 585(a)–(c), an "entry of default" is a prerequisite to a "default judgment." These two concepts are often lumped together, but are actually two different steps in the default process. When a defendant (or cross-defendant) has not filed the appropriate responsive paper within the prescribed time, the plaintiff (or cross-plaintiff) may request the court clerk to enter the default. Until the time of such entry, the defendant may ordinarily file a belated response without consequence. But the entry of default terminates the defendant's right to file an answer or take any other affirmative steps in the litigation until either the default is set aside or a default judgment entered. *See, e.g., Devlin v. Kearny Mesa AMC/Jeep/Renault, Inc.*, 155 Cal. App. 3d 381, 385, 202 Cal. Rptr. 204 (1984) (Entry of default precluded defendant from participating in subsequent proceedings to determine amount of punitive damages); *Forbes v. Cameron Petroleums, Inc.*, 83 Cal. App. 3d 257, 263, 147 Cal. Rptr. 766 (1978) (Demurrer or answer filed after entry of default was a legal nullity).

Obtaining Default Judgments. After entry of default by the clerk, the plaintiff (or cross-plaintiff) may apply for entry of a default judgment. In some actions, the court clerk has statutory authority to enter the default judgment, such as an action on a contract that provides for a definite fixed amount of damages ascertainable from the contract, and then only if a defendant has been served other than by publication. CCP § 585(a). In all other cases, a plaintiff must apply to the court for a default judgment. This includes all actions not based on contract or on a judgment, CCP § 585(b); actions based on a contract or a judgment where the damages or the attorneys' fees are not fixed, § 585(a); and all actions where service of the summons was by publication, § 585(c). Why does § 585 require a court judgment, as opposed to a clerk's judgment, in these types of actions?

Procedures for Court's Default Judgment. Section 585, as supplemented by local court rules, specifies the procedure by which a plaintiff may obtain a court's judgment. The plaintiff must apply for the relief demanded in the complaint; and "the court shall hear the evidence offered by the plaintiff, and shall render judgment in his or her favor for such sum not exceeding the amount stated in the complaint, in the statement required by § 425.11, or in the statement provided for by § 425.115, as appears by such evidence to be just." CCP §§ 585(b)&(c).

To "prove-up" the default for the court, the plaintiff need only introduce evidence sufficient to establish a prima facie case. *Morehouse v. Wanzo*, 266 Cal. App. 2d 846, 853–54, 72 Cal. Rptr. 607 (1968); *Csordas v. United Slate Tile & Composition Roofers*, 177 Cal. App. 2d 184, 185–86, 2 Cal. Rptr. 133 (1960). Where the complaint states a cause of action and the evidence introduced establishes a prima facie case, the court must enter the default judgment. *Morehouse v. Wanzo, supra*; *see Taliaferro v. Hoogs*, 219 Cal. App. 2d 559, 33 Cal. Rptr. 415 (1963) (Court properly refused to enter default where plaintiff offered no proof of damages sustained).

3. Procedures in Personal Injury Actions

In an action brought in superior court to recover actual or punitive damages for personal injury or wrongful death, the process of obtaining an entry of default is a little more complex. Complications may arise in such actions because the plaintiff is statutorily precluded from stating in the complaint the dollar amount of actual and punitive damages demanded. CCP § 425.10(b); Civil Code § 3295(e). Consequently, the plaintiff must serve on the defendant a statement of damages "setting forth the nature and amount of damages being sought," before a default may be taken. CCP § 425.11 (personal injury damages), § 425.115 (punitive damages). This statement should be served a reasonable (usually 30 days) time before entry of defendant's default, and must be served in the same manner as a summons. CCP §§ 425.11(d), 425.115(g). Failure to comply with these requirements precludes the entry of a default. *Schwab v. Rondel Homes, Inc.*, 53 Cal. 3d 428, 280 Cal. Rptr. 83, 808 P. 2d 226 (1991).

Does a complaint which specifies the amount of personal injury or punitive damages in contravention of CCP § 425.10 provide the requisite notice for a default judgment? *See, e.g., Uva v. Evans*, 83 Cal. App. 3d 356, 147 Cal. Rptr. 795 (1978) (Upholding validity of default judgment where plaintiff's complaint specifically requested $30,000 general damages for personal injuries, contrary to § 425.10, despite failure to serve a statement of damages); *Cummings Medical Corp. v. Occupational Medical Corp.*, 10 Cal. App. 4th 1291, 13 Cal. Rptr. 2d 585 (1992) (Upholding a default judgment entered for the amount of punitive damages alleged in a cross-complaint).

4. Statutory Restrictions on Default Judgments

Various specific statutes impose additional procedural restrictions on the entry of certain default judgments. For example, CCP § 764.010 prohibits entry of a default judgment in a quiet title action unless the court hears evidence of the plaintiff's title and of the claims of any defendants. Section 1088 prohibits the granting of a writ of mandamus or prohibition by default and requires such cases be heard by the court whether or not the adverse party appears. Family Code § 2336 prohibits a default judgment in a dissolution of marriage or legal separation proceeding, and requires proof of the grounds alleged presented to the court by affidavit or personal appearance.

Certain persons are also statutorily protected against judgment by default, regardless of the nature of the action. The most notable such protection is the federal Soldiers' and Sailors' Civil Relief Act of 1940, 50 U.S.C. App. § 501 *et seq.*, which generally seeks to prevent the entry of a default judgment against a defendant who is in the military service. 50 U.S.C. App. § 520; *see, e.g., Interinsurance Exchange v. Collins*, 30 Cal. App. 4th 1445, 37 Cal. Rptr. 2d 126 (1994) (Court clerk's refusal to enter a default on ground that plaintiff did not submit a signed declaration of defendant's nonmilitary status held improper; federal Act protected military personnel from default judgments but not from defaults).

5. Relief from Default Judgments

A defendant (or cross-defendant), unhappy with a default judgment entered for failure to timely file a responsive paper, often has a myriad of procedural options available for requesting relief. Precisely which option the defendant should select depends on the reason for the default and on how promptly the defendant seeks relief.

Martin Potts & Associates, Inc. v. Corsair, LLC

Court of Appeal of California, Second Appellate District

244 Cal. App. 4th 432, 197 Cal. Rptr. 3d 856 (2016)

HOFFSTADT, JUSTICE.

A trial court is required by statute to vacate a default, default judgment, or dismissal that is "in fact" caused by an attorney's "mistake, inadvertence, surprise, or neglect" if the attorney files a sworn affidavit "attesting" to such. (Code Civ. Proc., § 473, subd. (b).). Must the attorney's affidavit also disclose the reasons for his mistake, inadvertence, surprise, or neglect? We conclude the answer is "no." Although such a statement of reasons will be helpful, and may sometimes be relevant to prove the causal link between the attorney's conduct and the default, default judgment, or dismissal, a statement of reasons is not required. We accordingly affirm the trial court's order setting aside the default and default judgment in this case.

FACTS AND PROCEDURAL BACKGROUND

In 2011, defendant Corsair, LLC (Corsair), was developing a real estate project known as the Gran Plaza Outlets. In December 2011, Corsair hired plaintiff Martin Potts and Associates, Inc. (plaintiff), to provide management services for this project. When Corsair stopped paying plaintiff for those services in August 2013, plaintiff sued Corsair in February 2014 for the outstanding amount owed under theories of (1) account stated, (2) open book, and (3) breach of contract. Corsair never filed a responsive pleading. On March 25, 2014, the trial court entered an order of default against Corsair. On August 15, 2014, the court entered a default judgment awarding plaintiff $101,760.

On October 1, 2014, Corsair moved to set aside the default and default judgment pursuant to section 473, subdivision (b). As support, Corsair submitted an affidavit from Corsair's managing member and two affidavits from an attorney named Nicholas Klein (Klein). These affidavits stated the following facts: Klein had provided legal representation to Corsair "for over 15 years." Corsair's managing member, who was plaintiff's primary contact at Corsair, had received plaintiff's complaint and other filings in this case. As he had done many times before, the managing member had his assistant forward those documents to Klein. Klein received these documents, but took no action with respect to the lawsuit. Klein admitted that "[i]t was these failures on my part, as counsel for [Corsair] that allowed the Default and Default Judgment to be entered in this matter," and that "my failure to protect the interest of [Corsair], as its counsel, is the sole reason the default was allowed to occur." Klein declined to "discuss the reasons for my failure to act in this matter." Plaintiff opposed Corsair's motion.

The trial court set aside the default and default judgment. The court found that "the default and default judgment . . . were caused by . . . Klein's mistake, inadvertence, surprise or neglect"—namely, that Klein did not "fil[e] a responsive pleading on behalf of [Corsair]" and did not "advis[e] [Corsair] to file a responsive pleading." The court also ordered Corsair to file a responsive pleading within 30 days, and directed Klein to pay $5,267.83 to plaintiff as "reasonable compensatory legal fees and costs." Plaintiff timely appeals.

DISCUSSION

Plaintiff argues that the trial court erred in setting aside the default and default judgment because (1) section 473, subdivision (b) requires an attorney to explain the reasons behind his "mistake, inadvertence, surprise, or neglect," and (2) Corsair did not provide this explanation or otherwise meet the requirements for relief from default and default judgment. The meaning of section 473, subdivision (b) is a question of statutory interpretation we review de novo. Whether section 473, subdivision (b)'s requirements have been satisfied in any given case is a question we review for substantial evidence where the evidence is disputed and de novo where it is undisputed. (*Carmel, Ltd. v. Tavoussi* (2009) 175 Cal.App.4th 393, 399 [95 Cal. Rptr. 3d 694]

(*Carmel*) [disputed facts]; *SJP Limited Partnership v. City of Los Angeles* (2006) 136 Cal.App.4th 511, 516 [39 Cal. Rptr. 3d 55] (*SJP Limited*) [undisputed facts].)

I. Requirements of Section 473, Subdivision (b)'s Mandatory Relief Provision

Prior to 1989, section 473, subdivision (b) granted a trial court the discretion to relieve a party "from a judgment, dismissal, order, or other proceeding taken against him" if (1) that action was due to the party's or lawyer's "mistake, inadvertence, surprise, or excusable neglect" and (2) the request for relief was "made within a reasonable time [and] in no case exceeding six months." (§ 473, subd. (b).) In 1988, our Legislature added a second basis for relief under section 473, subdivision (b). As amended further in 1992, this additional provision provides that a "court shall, whenever an application for relief is made no more than six months after entry of judgment, is in proper form, and is accompanied by an attorney's sworn affidavit attesting to his or her mistake, inadvertence, surprise, or neglect, vacate any (1) resulting default entered by the clerk against his or her client, . . . or (2) resulting default judgment or dismissal entered against his or her client, unless the court finds that the default or dismissal was not in fact caused by the attorney's mistake, inadvertence, surprise, or neglect." (Ibid.)

Thus, section 473, subdivision (b) "contains two distinct provisions for relief from default" (*Even Zohar Construction & Remodeling, Inc. v. Bellaire Townhouses, LLC* (2015) 61 Cal.4th 830, 838 [189 Cal. Rptr. 3d 824, 352 P.3d 391] (*Even Zohar*)) — one makes relief discretionary with the court; the other makes it mandatory. (*Todd v. Thrifty Corp.* (1995) 34 Cal.App.4th 986, 991 [40 Cal. Rptr. 2d 727] (*Todd*).) The two provisions differ in several other respects: (1) the mandatory relief provision is narrower in scope insofar as it is only available for defaults, default judgments, and dismissals, while discretionary relief is available for a broader array of orders (e.g., *Henderson v. Pacific Gas & Electric Co.* (2010) 187 Cal.App.4th 215, 228–229 [113 Cal. Rptr. 3d 692] (*Henderson*) [mandatory relief not available to set aside summary judgment order]; *Leader v. Health Industries of America, Inc.* (2001) 89 Cal.App.4th 603, 620 [107 Cal. Rptr. 2d 489] [listing types of dismissals falling outside the scope of the mandatory relief provision]); (2) the mandatory relief provision is broader in scope insofar as it is available for inexcusable neglect (*Rodrigues v. Superior Court* (2005) 127 Cal.App.4th 1027, 1033 [26 Cal. Rptr. 3d 194] (*Rodrigues*)), while discretionary relief is reserved for "excusable neglect" (§ 473, subd. (b), italics added; see *Carmel, supra*, 175 Cal.App.4th at pp. 399–400 [inexcusable attorney misconduct falling short of "total abandonment" not a basis for discretionary relief]); and (3) mandatory relief comes with a price — namely, the duty to pay "reasonable compensatory legal fees and costs to opposing counsel or parties" (§ 473, subd. (b)).

Plaintiff argues that the trial court's duty to grant relief from a default, default judgment, or dismissal under the mandatory relief provision is triggered only when the attorney's affidavit includes the reasons for the attorney's "mistake, inadvertence, surprise, or neglect." We reject this argument for several reasons.

To begin, the text of section 473, subdivision (b) does not require an explication of reasons as a prerequisite to mandatory relief. "Statutory analysis begins with the plain language of [a] statute, and if that language is unambiguous, the inquiry ends there" as well. (*KB Home Greater Los Angeles, Inc. v. Superior Court* (2014) 223 Cal. App.4th 1471, 1476 [168 Cal. Rptr. 3d 142].) As noted above, section 473, subdivision (b) makes relief mandatory only if the request for relief "is accompanied by an attorney's sworn affidavit attesting to his or her mistake, inadvertence, surprise, or neglect." (§ 473, subd. (b).) As this text indicates, what must be attested to is the mistake, inadvertence, surprise, or neglect — not the reasons for it. (Accord, *State Farm Fire & Casualty Co. v. Pietak* (2001) 90 Cal.App.4th 600, 609 [109 Cal. Rptr. 2d 256] (*Pietak*) [attorney affidavit must include "admission by counsel for the moving party that his error resulted in the entry of a default or dismissal" or a "real concession of error"].)

Even if we were to go beyond the text of section 473, subdivision (b) and consider its purpose (*Lorenz v. Commercial Acceptance Ins. Co.* (1995) 40 Cal.App.4th 981, 990 [47 Cal. Rptr. 2d 362] (*Lorenz*) [noting how courts may look to our Legislature's intent in construing statutes]), that purpose is served without requiring attorneys to spell out the reasons for their omission. The purpose of section 473, subdivision (b) generally is "to promote the determination of actions on their merits." (*Even Zohar, supra*, 61 Cal.4th at p. 839, citing *Zamora v. Clayborn Contracting Group, Inc.* (2002) 28 Cal.4th 249, 255–256 [121 Cal. Rptr. 2d 187, 47 P.3d 1056].) More specifically, section 473, subdivision (b)'s mandatory relief provision has three purposes: (1) "to relieve the innocent client of the consequences of the attorney's fault" (*Solv-All v. Superior Court* (2005) 131 Cal.App.4th 1003, 1009 [32 Cal. Rptr. 3d 202] (*Solv-All*); see *Generale Bank Nederland v. Eyes of the Beholder Ltd.* (1998) 61 Cal.App.4th 1384, 1397 [72 Cal. Rptr. 2d 188] [noting purpose is "to alleviate the hardship on parties who lose their day in court due solely to an inexcusable failure to act on the part of their attorneys"]); (2) "to place the burden on counsel" (*Solv-All*, at p. 1009); and (3) "to discourage additional litigation in the form of malpractice actions by the defaulted client against the errant attorney" (*ibid.*).

These purposes are advanced as long as mandatory relief is confined to situations in which the attorney, rather than the client, is the cause of the default, default judgment, or dismissal. (See *Metropolitan Service Corp. v. Casa de Palms, Ltd.* (1995) 31 Cal.App.4th 1481, 1487 [37 Cal. Rptr. 2d 575] (*Metropolitan Service*) [fault of attorney sufficient]; *SJP Limited, supra*, 136 Cal.App.4th at p. 517 [fault of attorney who is not attorney of record sufficient]; *Hu v. Fang* (2002) 104 Cal.App.4th 61, 64 [127 Cal. Rptr. 2d 756] (*Hu*) [fault of paralegal supervised by attorney sufficient]; cf. *Todd, supra*, 34 Cal.App.4th at pp. 991–992 [fault of client; not sufficient].) In other words, the purpose of the mandatory relief provision under section 473, subdivision (b) is achieved by focusing on who is to blame, not why.

Indeed, in many cases, the reasons for the attorney's mistake, inadvertence, surprise, or neglect will be irrelevant; that is because, as noted above, the mandatory relief provision entitles a party to relief even when his or her attorney's error is inexcusable. (*Graham v. Beers* (1994) 30 Cal.App.4th 1656, 1660 [36 Cal. Rptr. 2d 765] (*Graham*); *Solv-All, supra*, 131 Cal.App.4th at p. 1010 [attorney's conscious decision not to file an answer is grounds for mandatory relief]; cf. *Jerry's Shell v. Equilon Enterprises, LLC* (2005) 134 Cal.App.4th 1058, 1073–1074 [36 Cal. Rptr. 3d 637] [attorney's strategic decision to err with intent to have client later invoke § 473, subd. (b)'s mandatory relief provision precludes resort to mandatory relief].) We are reluctant to construe section 473, subdivision (b), to require in every case the production of information that will in many cases be of no use in deciding whether to grant relief.

The case law reinforces our reading of the text and purpose of section 473, subdivision (b), because the courts have thus far eschewed any rule making mandatory relief contingent upon a disclosure of reasons. In *Hu, supra,* 104 Cal.App.4th 61, the court disclaimed any requirement that "evidence" beyond the attorney's affidavit is necessary to substantiate the attorney's "mistake, inadvertence, surprise, or neglect." (*Hu,* at p. 65.) And the court in *Graham, supra,* 30 Cal.App.4th 1656 noted the following in dicta: "[C]ounsel need not show that his or her mistake, inadvertence, surprise or neglect was excusable. No reason need be given for the existence of one of these circumstances. Attestation that one of these reasons existed is sufficient to obtain relief, unless the trial court finds that the dismissal did not occur because of these reasons." (*Graham,* at p. 1660); see *Avila v. Chua* (1997) 57 Cal.App.4th 860, 869 [67 Cal. Rptr. 2d 373] [same]; *Yeap v. Leake* (1997) 60 Cal.App.4th 591, 601 [70 Cal. Rptr. 2d 680] (*Yeap*) [same]; see also *Pietak, supra,* 90 Cal.App.4th at p. 609 [noting that mandatory relief is triggered by an "indispensable admission by counsel . . . that his error resulted in the entry of default or dismissal"].) The language in these cases is irreconcilable with plaintiff's contention that the reasons for an attorney's error must always be given as a precursor to mandatory relief.

Plaintiff proffers five reasons why the reasons for the attorney's mistake, inadvertence, surprise, or neglect must nevertheless be set forth in the attorney's affidavit before relief under section 473, subdivision (b) becomes mandatory. None is persuasive.

First, plaintiff argues that the mandatory relief provision of section 473, subdivision (b) employs language similar to that used in its discretionary relief provision; thus, plaintiff reasons, we must "presume that the Legislature intended the same construction." (*Estate of Griswold* (2001) 25 Cal.4th 904, 915–916 [108 Cal. Rptr. 2d 165, 24 P.3d 1191].) However, this maxim of statutory construction is inapplicable. By its very terms, the maxim applies when the language of two provisions is the same; as described in detail above, however, the statutory language creating the mandatory and discretionary relief provisions of section 473, subdivision (b) is significantly different. Moreover, this maxim does not apply when "a contrary intent clearly appears." (*Griswold,* at pp. 915–916.) Here, it does. The whole point of creating the mandatory relief provision was to make it easier to set aside a default, default judgment, or other dismissal due to attorney error, and the Legislature did so by supplementing the discretionary relief provision that required a showing of an attorney's "total abandonment" (*Carmel, supra,* 175 Cal.App.4th at pp. 399–400) with a provision that made relief automatic upon a showing of any error, excusable or not. Construing the two provisions to mean the same thing would fly in the face of this legislative intent.

Second, plaintiff argues that a requirement that an attorney state his or her reasons is more consistent with "the strong policy favoring the finality of judgments." (*Kulchar v. Kulchar* (1969) 1 Cal.3d 467, 470 [82 Cal. Rptr. 489, 462 P.2d 17].) But the Legislature enacted both provisions of section 473, subdivision (b) as an exception to this more general policy and as a means of "promot[ing] the determination of actions on their merits" (*Even Zohar, supra*, 61 Cal.4th at p. 839).

Third, plaintiff asserts that precedent supports its construction of section 473, subdivision (b)'s mandatory relief provision. Plaintiff cites language in *Even Zohar, supra*, 61 Cal.4th 840 stating that "[a]n attorney who candidly and fully acknowledges under oath the errors that have led a client into default will rarely have anything to add in a renewed motion" (*Even Zohar*, at p. 842), and in *Pietak, supra*, 90 Cal.App.4th 600 requiring a "straightforward admission of fault" (*Pietak*, at p. 610). These passages at most demand an attorney's candid, full, and straightforward acknowledgment of his or her error; they do not speak to the reasons for those errors. Plaintiff also cites a number of cases in which a party seeking relief under section 473, subdivision (b) has submitted an attorney affidavit that sets forth the reasons for the attorney's error. However, an attorney's decision in any particular case to offer more information than is statutorily required does not somehow cause that information to be statutorily required. Because none of the cases plaintiff cites holds or, for that matter even comments in passing, that the additional information offered in the attorney affidavit was required by section 473, subdivision (b), these cases lend little if any support to plaintiff's argument. [citations to these cases omitted]

Fourth, plaintiff contends that the reasons underlying the attorney's "mistake, inadvertence, surprise, or neglect" may be relevant to prove that the error was the attorney's fault rather than the client's. Plaintiff is right. As noted above, mandatory relief is available only if the default or dismissal "was . . . in fact caused by the attorney's mistake, inadvertence, surprise, or neglect." (§ 473, subd. (b).) Such relief is not available when the error is the client's alone (*Todd, supra*, 34 Cal.App.4th at pp. 991–992); the courts are still divided as to whether it is available when the error lies partly at the client's feet and partly at the attorney's (compare *Lang v. Hochman* (2000) 77 Cal. App.4th 1225, 1248 [92 Cal. Rptr. 2d 322] (*Lang*) [relief available only if client is "totally innocent of any wrongdoing"]; *In re Marriage of Hock, supra*, 80 Cal.App.4th at p. 1446 [same]; *Carmel, supra*, 175 Cal.App.4th at p. 400 [same] with *Benedict v. Danner Press* (2001) 87 Cal.App.4th 923, 932 [104 Cal. Rptr. 2d 896] [relief available as long as client did not engage in intentional misconduct]; *SJP Limited, supra*, 136 Cal.App.4th at p. 520 [same]; see generally *Gutierrez v. G & M Oil Co., Inc.* (2010) 184 Cal.App.4th 551, 557–558 [108 Cal. Rptr. 3d 864] [detailing split of authority]).

Where the cause of the default or dismissal is in dispute, the attorney's affidavit can serve as "a causation testing device" (*Milton, supra*, 53 Cal.App.4th at p. 867, quoting *Cisneros v. Vueve* (1995) 37 Cal.App.4th 906, 912 [44 Cal. Rptr. 2d 682]), and a statement of reasons may be quite probative regarding who is at fault (see, e.g., *Todd*, at pp. 991–992 [looking to attorney's affidavit]; *Johnson v. Pratt & Whitney Canada, Inc.* (1994) 28 Cal.App.4th 613, 621–623 [34 Cal. Rptr. 2d 26] [same]; *Lang*, at pp. 1248–1252 [same]). Because it is often unknown at the time a motion for mandatory relief is filed whether causation will be disputed, an attorney would be well served to include the reasons for his or her "mistake, inadvertence, surprise, or neglect" in the affidavit of fault. This is no doubt why practice guides so recommend. (E.g., Weil & Brown, Cal. Practice Guide: Civil Procedure Before Trial (The Rutter Group 2015) ¶ 5:390.1, p. 5–109 [recommending that attorney "include detailed factual explanations as to how the claimed 'mistake' or 'neglect' occurred" (some italics omitted)].) But the fact that it may be a very good idea to include an explanation of attorney fault does not mean it is a requirement of section 473, subdivision (b)'s mandatory relief provision. For the reasons noted above, it is not.

Lastly, plaintiff argues that an attorney affidavit of fault lacking an explanation of the reason for that fault is nothing more than an "affidavit[] or declaration[] setting forth only conclusions, opinions or ultimate facts," which is "insufficient" as a matter of law. [citations omitted] We disagree. To be sure, it is not enough for the attorney to attest, "My client is entitled to relief under section 473, subdivision (b)"; that would be an impermissible conclusion of ultimate fact. But an attorney's admission of his mistake, inadvertence, surprise, or neglect is not an impermissible ultimate fact because it is precisely what section 473, subdivision (b) calls for—namely, a "sworn affidavit attesting to [the attorney's] mistake, inadvertence, surprise, or neglect" (§ 473, subd. (b)).

For all these reasons, we conclude that an attorney affidavit of fault under the mandatory relief provisions of section 473, subdivision (b) need not include an explanation of the reasons for the attorney's mistake, inadvertence, surprise, or neglect.

II. Review of the Affidavit in This Case

As explained above, a trial court is obligated to set aside a default, default judgment, or dismissal if the motion for mandatory relief (1) is filed within six months of the entry of judgment, (2) "is in proper form," (3) is accompanied by the attorney affidavit of fault, and (4) demonstrates that the default or dismissal was "in fact caused by the attorney's mistake, inadvertence, surprise, or neglect." (§ 473, subd. (b).) Plaintiff concedes that Corsair has met the first and second requirements, but disputes the last two.

Plaintiff challenges the sufficiency of Klein's affidavit. Specifically, he argues that Klein's affidavit is deficient because (1) Klein does not set forth the reasons for his neglect, (2) Klein's recitations are oblique and obtuse (that is, they contain statements attesting to what Klein did not do rather than to what he did), and (3) Klein's admissions that he failed to file a responsive pleading do not sufficiently attest to a mistake, inadvertence, surprise or neglect.

These arguments lack merit. We have rejected the first, statute-based argument. We also reject plaintiff's second contention. Although an affidavit more directly spelling out an attorney's actions might be more easily understood, Klein's declarations nevertheless unequivocally spell out that he was Corsair's lawyer; he received plaintiff's filings from Corsair; he did nothing with those papers; and his decision to do so was his and his alone. Lastly, Klein sufficiently admitted his neglect. "Neglect" includes an "omission" (*Barragan v. County of Los Angeles* (2010) 184 Cal.App.4th 1373, 1382–1383 [109 Cal. Rptr. 3d 501]), including the failure to give "proper attention to a person or thing, whether inadvertent, negligent, or willful" (*In re Ethan C.* (2012) 54 Cal.4th 610, 627 [143 Cal. Rptr. 3d 565, 279 P.3d 1052], quoting Black's Law Dictionary (8th ed. 2004)). Klein's acknowledgment that he received plaintiff's lawsuit filings from Corsair and did nothing with them qualifies as not giving them proper attention, and thus as neglect. Because we are dealing with the mandatory relief provision, it does not matter whether Klein's neglect was excusable or inexcusable.

Plaintiff also challenges the trial court's finding that Klein's neglect caused the default. In particular, plaintiff argues that it is possible that Corsair directed Klein to stall by not responding to plaintiff's filings—thus making the default Corsair's fault—because (1) the affidavits from Klein and Corsair's managing member did not absolutely preclude the possibility that someone else at Corsair (other than the managing member) so directed Klein and (2) plaintiff presented evidence that a corporation with a similar name (Corsairs LLC) was formed days after plaintiff filed suit. However, as detailed above, those affidavits also detail Klein's failure to take any action and include his admission that it was "failures on [his] part . . . that allowed the Default . . . to be entered." As such, the affidavits constitute substantial evidence that Klein's neglect was the sole cause of the default. Because a conflict in the evidence does not render it insubstantial (e.g., *People v. Panah* (2005) 35 Cal.4th 395, 489 [25 Cal. Rptr. 3d 672, 107 P.3d 790]), we have no basis to disturb the court's factual finding regarding causation.

DISPOSITION

The order granting relief from default and default judgment is affirmed. Corsair is entitled to costs on appeal.

Notes and Questions Regarding Relief from Default Judgments

(1) *Mandatory Relief When Accompanied by Attorney's Affidavit of Neglect.* As *Martin Potts & Associates, Inc. v. Corsair, LLC* demonstrates, the 1988 amendments to CCP § 473 broadened the grounds for relief from default to now include attorney mistake or neglect, even when the neglect is inexcusable. If the application is accompanied by the attorney's sworn affidavit attesting to his or her mistake or neglect, the court must vacate the default or default judgment. CCP § 473(b). However, the court must direct the attorney to pay reasonable compensatory legal fees and costs to opposing counsel or parties; but cannot condition the relief from default on the attorney's payment of such fees, costs, or other sanctions and penalties. § 473(b). What are the policy reasons for prohibiting conditional grants of relief in such attorney neglect situations? The 1992 amendments to § 473, which extended this mandatory provision to relief from most involuntary dismissal orders, are discussed in § 12.03, Involuntary Dismissals, *infra*.

(a) Section 473(b)'s attorney affidavit provision mandates relief "unless the court finds that the default . . . as not in fact caused by the attorney's . . . neglect." This provision requires the trial court to assess both credibility and causation in determining whether the default was due to attorney error. *See, e.g., Stafford v. Mach*, 64 Cal. App. 4th 1174, 75 Cal. Rptr. 2d 809 (1998) (concluding any mistake that may have contributed to the entry of default was the fault of the insurer and not any attorney, and therefore the mandatory provisions of § 473 were inapplicable); *Milton v. Perceptual Dev. Corp.*, 53 Cal. App. 4th 861, 62 Cal. Rptr. 2d 98 (1997) (upholding order vacating entry of defaults and default judgments where substantial evidence supported the trial court's finding that the attorney's admitted misconduct proximately caused both the defaults and default judgments); *Cisneros v. Vueve*, 37 Cal. App. 4th 906, 44 Cal. Rptr. 2d 682 (1995) (ruling because the attorney was not representing the defendants at the time the default was entered, he was not the proximate cause of the entry of default as required by the mandatory relief provision of § 473).

(b) *Incentives to Attorneys?* What incentives are there for an attorney to prepare and file an affidavit of neglect in support of a § 473 motion to set aside a default? If the attorney refuses to sign an affidavit of neglect, what must a defaulting party prove in order to convince the court, in its discretion, to grant relief from default under § 473? What are the policy reasons behind the different treatment afforded defaulting parties under § 473 in cases where the request for relief is accompanied by the attorney's affidavit of neglect, as opposed to those cases where no such affidavit is available? Is this difference in treatment wise policy? Why?

(2) *Discretionary Relief for Excusable Neglect Sought Within Six Months.* As indicated in *Martin Potts & Associates*, prior to a 1988 amendment CCP § 473(b) only authorized *discretionary relief* from default for *excusable* neglect or mistake. Seeking relief under the pre-amendment statute proved to be time-consuming for the parties and the courts, and often involved appellate review for abuse of discretion. Moreover, because the distinction between "excusable" versus "inexcusable" neglect proved difficult to apply, relief from default was uncertain and unpredictable. The significance of the 1988 amendment to CCP § 473(b) is that it makes this distinction irrelevant and makes relief mandatory, so long as the defaulting party's attorney submits a proper affidavit of neglect. Consequently, where a defaulting party's request satisfies the prerequisites for mandatory relief, there simply is no reason to rely on § 473's discretionary grounds for relief. The discretionary approach is only necessary in those few instances where mandatory relief is unavailable, such as where the request for relief does not satisfy the attorney causation requirement or involves an order not governed by the scope of the mandatory relief provision.

(a) *Excusable vs. Inexcusable Neglect or Mistake.* To determine whether a mistake or neglect is excusable, the court inquires whether "a reasonably prudent person under the same or similar circumstances might have made the same error." *Zamora v. Clayborn Contracting Grp., Inc.*, 28 Cal. 4th 249, 258, 121 Cal. Rptr. 2d 187, 47 P. 3d 1056 (2002); *see Fasuyi v. Permatex, Inc.*, 167 Cal. App. 4th 681, 84 Cal. Rptr. 3d 351 (2008) (discussing the general principles applicable to the trial court's discretion to set aside a default judgment under CCP § 473). "Unless inexcusable neglect is clear, the policy favoring trial on the merits prevails" and doubts should be resolved in favor of the request for relief from default. *Elston v. City of Turlock*, 38 Cal. 3d 227, 235, 211 Cal.

Rptr. 416, 695 P.2d 713 (1985). Courts often note that "when the moving party promptly seeks relief and there is no prejudice to the opposing party, very slight evidence is required to justify relief" from a default judgment. *See, e.g., Rogalski v. Nabers Cadillac*, 11 Cal. App. 4th 816, 821, 14 Cal. Rptr. 2d 286 (1992); *Mink v. Superior Court*, 2 Cal. App. 4th 1338, 1343, 4 Cal. Rptr. 2d 195 (1992).

(b) Examples of circumstances where the court has found excusable neglect sufficient to grant relief under § 473 include cases where settlement discussions lulled defendants into a false sense of security, *Beard v. Beard*, 16 Cal. 2d 645, 648, 107 P.2d 385 (1940); default was due to disability or illness of defendant or defendant's attorney, *e.g., Stone v. McWilliams*, 43 Cal. App. 490, 492, 185 P. 478 (1919); where the default was due to attorney's change in personnel and consequent misplacement and lack of knowledge of court papers, *Elston v. City of Turlock*, 38 Cal. 3d 227, 234–35, 211 Cal. Rptr. 416, 695 P.2d 713 (1985); *but see Henderson v. Pac. Gas & Elec. Co.*, 187 Cal. App. 4th 215, 229–252, 113 Cal. Rptr. 3d 692 (2010) (ruling attorney's failure to file timely opposition to summary judgment motion, the preparation of which the attorney delegated to his paralegal, was inexcusable neglect because attorney failed to supervise his employee). For more examples of excusable and inexcusable neglect under § 473, see 8 Witkin, California Procedure, Attack on Judgment in Trial Court §§ 160–169 (5th ed. 2008) and 2 CEB, Civil Procedure Before Trial § 38.82 (4th ed. 2017).

(c) Even though the policy of the law favors trial on the merits, some showing of excusable neglect or mistake and of meritorious defense is necessary to set aside a default judgment under the discretionary grounds in CCP § 473. For example, relief from default has been denied where the party or his attorney deliberately refused to take timely and adequate steps to avoid default, *e.g., Elms v. Elms*, 72 Cal. App. 2d 508, 513, 164 P.2d 936 (1948); where the attorney's explanation for failure to respond to the complaint and to promptly seek relief from default was that his girlfriend was hospitalized for four days, *Beeman v. Burling*, 216 Cal. App. 3d 1586, 265 Cal. Rptr. 719 (1990); where the defendant's attorney mistakenly assumed that his unanswered requests to opposing counsel for an extension of time to file an answer was a grant of the extension, *Iott v. Franklin*, 206 Cal. App. 3d 521, 531, 253 Cal. Rptr. 635 (1988); and where the defendant's attorney mistakenly believed that the clerk's default was not conclusive, *Barragan v. Banco BCH*, 188 Cal. App. 3d 283, 301, 232 Cal. Rptr. 758 (1986).

(3) *Inexcusable Neglect of Attorney Not Imputed to Client When Positive Misconduct.* The inexcusable neglect of an attorney is imputed to the client, and is not grounds for § 473 relief in the absence of the attorney's affidavit of fault. *Carroll v. Abbott Laboratories, Inc.*, 32 Cal. 3d 892, 898, 187 Cal. Rptr. 592, 654 P.2d 775 (1982). As *Beeman* suggests, however, when the attorney's neglect is of such an extreme degree that it amounts to "positive misconduct"—an abandonment by the lawyer of his client, and a de facto severance of the attorney-client relationship—the client should not be charged with the attorney's negligence. *Carroll v. Abbott Laboratories, Inc., supra; Daley v. County of Butte*, 227 Cal. App. 2d 380, 38 Cal. Rptr. 693 (1964).

(a) What are the policy reasons for this "positive misconduct" rule? Is the distinction between attorney "positive misconduct" (grounds for relief from default) and attorney "inexcusable neglect" (not grounds for relief from default) a reasonable one? A workable one? A fair one? Do you agree with the *Beeman* court's finding of inexcusable neglect and no positive misconduct by the defendant's attorney? Why?

(b) Does this rule encourage negligent attorneys to totally abandon their clients in order to rescue their clients from defaults and themselves from malpractice? Despite the *Carroll* court's attempt to limit this abandonment rule, does this rule still benefit parties who choose the most negligent attorneys? For a criticism of the Carroll court's restriction of the "positive misconduct" rule, *see* Thomas N. Thrasher and Gary T. Blake, *Positive Misconduct: Excusing an Attorney's Inexcusable Neglect*, 15 Western St. U. L. Rev. 667 (1988).

(4) *Relief Sought After Six Months.* After the six-month period has passed, relief from default is no longer available based on the statutory grounds of CCP § 473. Independent of this statutory authority, however, a court has the inherent equity power to grant relief from a default judgment where there has been "extrinsic fraud or mistake." *Rappleyea v. Campbell*, 8 Cal. 4th 975, 35 Cal. Rptr. 2d 669, 884 P. 2d 126 (1994); *Marriage of Park*, 27 Cal. 3d 337, 342, 165 Cal. Rptr. 792, 612 P.2d 882 (1980).

(a) *Extrinsic Fraud or Mistake.* Extrinsic fraud or mistake is a broad concept that tends to encompass almost any set of extrinsic circumstances which deprive a party of a fair adversary hearing. *Marriage of Modnick*, 33 Cal. 3d 897, 905, 191 Cal. Rptr. 629, 663 P. 2d 187 (1983). The particular circumstances need not qualify as fraudulent or mistaken in the strict legal sense. *Marriage of Park, supra.* The clearest examples of extrinsic fraud are in cases where the aggrieved party is kept in ignorance of the proceeding or is in some other way induced not to appear. *Estate of Sanders*, 40 Cal. 3d 607, 614, 221 Cal. Rptr. 432, 710 P.2d 232 (1985). The equity power to grant relief from a default based on extrinsic fraud or mistake is similar to the statutory power to vacate for excusable fraud or neglect CCP § 473, although the equity power is usually considered narrower. *See, e.g., Carroll v. Abbott Laboratories, Inc., supra*, 32 Cal. 3d at 901, fn.8; *Rappleyea v. Campbell, supra.*

(b) *Intrinsic Fraud or Mistake.* By contrast, intrinsic fraud or mistake exists where a party has been given notice of the action and has not been prevented from participating therein, but unreasonably neglected to do so. *Kulchar v. Kulchar*, 1 Cal. 3d 467, 471, 82 Cal. Rptr. 489, 462 P.2d 17 (1969); *Marriage of Stevenot*, 154 Cal. App. 3d 1051, 1069–70, 202 Cal. Rptr. 116 (1984). A party's mistake as to the law or the facts is usually an insufficient basis to set aside a default judgment if the party could have reasonably discovered the mistake. *Marriage of Stevenot, supra; Heyman v. Franchise Mortgage Acceptance Corp.*, 107 Cal. App. 4th 921, 132 Cal. Rptr. 2d 465 (2003) (Although value of company was the very subject of the lawsuit, defendant's alleged misrepresentations about company's financial condition were intrinsic where plaintiff conducted no investigation or discovery into the financial condition); *Home Ins. Co. v. Zurich Ins. Co.*, 96 Cal. App. 4th 17, 116 Cal. Rptr. 2d 583 (2002) (Misrepresentation by insurer's attorney that policy limits were $15,000 instead of $500,000, which induced injured party to settle lying suit for $15,000 after conducting no discovery, held intrinsic because a reasonable investigation and use of discovery would have disclosed the true extent of insurance coverage).

(c) *Viability of the Extrinsic/Intrinsic Distinction.* The courts have criticized the distinction between extrinsic and intrinsic fraud as "quite nebulous" and "hopelessly blurred." *E.g., Marriage of Stevenot, supra,* 154 Cal. App. 3d at 1060; *Marriage of Baltins,* 212 Cal. App. 3d 66, 82, 260 Cal. Rptr. 403 (1989). The Restatement Second of Judgments (1982), § 68, does not distinguish between extrinsic and intrinsic fraud; nor does Rule 60(b) of the Federal Rules of Civil Procedure, which expressly abandoned the distinction.

(d) *Policy Reasons.* What are the policy reasons for the California extrinsic-intrinsic fraud distinction? Is this a reasonable distinction? A workable one? Are the difficulties in applying this extrinsic-intrinsic fraud distinction less evident in cases where a party seeks relief from a default judgment as opposed to a judgment after an adversarial hearing? Why? Should the courts simply ignore this distinction when considering requests for relief from default judgments, but apply it to requests for relief from other judgments?

(5) *Void Judgments.* A default judgment can be void for lack of personal or subject matter jurisdiction, *Forbes v. Hyde,* 31 Cal. 342, 355 (1866); or for the granting of relief which the trial court had no power to grant. *Becker v. S.P.V. Construction Co.,* 27 Cal. 3d 489, 493, 165 Cal. Rptr. 825, 612 P.2d 915 (1980). A trial court has the inherent power to set aside a judgment void on its face at any time. *Reid v. Balter,* 14 Cal. App. 4th 1186, 1194, 18 Cal. Rptr. 2d 287 (1993); *Stevenson v. Turner,* 94 Cal. App. 3d 315, 318, 156 Cal. Rptr. 499 (1979). A default judgment in excess of the amount stated in the complaint or statement of damages, for example, can be collaterally attacked after the six-month period has expired, *Becker v. S.P.V. Construction Co., supra;* and may even be challenged for the first time on appeal. *National Diversified Services, Inc. v. Bernstein,* 168 Cal. App. 3d 410, 417, 214 Cal. Rptr. 113 (1985); *Petty v. Manpower, Inc.,* 94 Cal. App. 3d 794, 798, 156 Cal. Rptr. 622 (1979).

C. Involuntary Dismissals

1. Introductory Note

If a party's lawyer fails to prosecute an action diligently, the action may be dismissed. Statutes provide for both mandatory and discretionary dismissal, CCP §§ 583.110– 583.430; and apply to complaints, cross-complaints, and other initial pleadings, CCP § 583.110(b). Their purpose is to promote the trial of cases before evidence is lost or witnesses have forgotten the facts, and to protect defendants from the annoyance of an unmeritorious action remaining undecided for an indefinite period of time. *Moran v. Superior Court,* 35 Cal. 3d 229, 237, 197 Cal. Rptr. 546, 673 P.2d 216 (1983). A significant percentage of civil dispositions in the California superior courts are dismissals for delay in prosecution: 5.6% in fiscal year 2012–13. *See* Judicial Council of California, *2014 Court Statistics Report*.

A dismissal for lack of prosecution before trial is without prejudice. §581(b)(3). Because such dismissals are not on the merits, they have no res judicata effect. *Wilson v. Bittick*, 63 Cal. 2d 30, 35–36, 45 Cal. Rptr. 31, 403 P.2d 159 (1965). Consequently, if a cause of action is not barred by the applicable statute of limitations, a party may again litigate it after a dismissal by commencement of a new lawsuit. *See, e.g., Gonsalves v. Bank of America*, 16 Cal. 2d 169, 172–73, 105 P.2d 118 (1940); *Nassif v. Municipal Court*, 214 Cal. App. 3d 1294, 263 Cal. Rptr. 195 (1989).

In addition to the statutory diligence requirements, state and local rules provide for involuntary dismissal. The most important are the state and local "fast track" rules implementing the Trial Court Delay Reduction Act, which frequently impose shorter time limits than the state statutes and also authorize sanctions for failure to comply. Gov. Code §§68608 & 68616; CCP §§575.1 & 575.2. In addition, a court has inherent authority to dismiss an action for severe misconduct. *Lyons v. Wickhorst*, 42 Cal. 3d 911, 915, 231 Cal. Rptr. 738, 727 P.2d 1019 (1986).

2. Mandatory Dismissals for Lack of Prosecution

Dismissal is mandatory if a plaintiff fails to meet any one of three statutory deadlines: (1) Failure to serve the action within three years of filing, CCP §§583.110, 583.210; (2) failure to bring the case to trial within five years, CCP §583.310; and (3) failure to bring a case to a new trial within three years, CCP §583.320.

Failure to Serve the Action Within Three Years of Filing. CCP §583.210(a), dismissal is mandatory if the action is not served within three years of filing of the complaint. Because return of service is required within 60 days of actual service, the plaintiff has an additional 60 days after the three-year period to file the proof of service. §583.210(b). This provision applies both to named defendants and to fictitious defendants. *See Nelson v. A.H. Robins Co.*, 149 Cal. App. 3d 862, 197 Cal. Rptr. 179 (1983); *Lesko v. Superior Court*, 127 Cal. App. 3d 476, 179 Cal. Rptr. 595 (1982).

Statutory Tolling Provisions. Although dismissal for failure to serve within three years is mandatory, the plaintiff can avoid dismissal on a proper showing of tolling or excuse. Specifically, in computing the time in which service must be made, the time during which any of the following conditions existed is excluded: (a) The defendant was not amenable to service; (b) the prosecution of the action was stayed; (c) the parties were litigating the validity of service; or (d) service was "impossible, impracticable, or futile due to causes beyond plaintiff's control." CCP §583.240. what circumstances is a defendant "not amenable to the process of the court" within the meaning of CCP §583.240(b)? When the defendant is absent from, or concealed within, the state, and his whereabouts unknown? *See Watts v. Crawford*, 10 Cal. 4th 743, 42 Cal. Rptr. 2d 81, 896 P.2d 807 (1995) (The relevant inquiry is whether the party was subject to being served applicable constitutional and statutory provisions, not whether the defendant was reasonably available as a practical matter for service of process); *Perez v.*

Smith, 19 Cal. App. 4th 1595, 24 Cal. Rptr. 2d 186 (1993) (A defendant is amenable to service even though only method of service is by publication).

Extensions of the Three-Year Limit. In addition to these tolling provisions, statutory exceptions to the three-year requirement apply when the parties extend the period by written stipulation, CCP § 583.220; when the parties extend the period by oral stipulation in open court, § 583.230; and when the defendant makes a general appearance, § 583.220. Finally, estoppel may bar the dismissal where a defendant has induced the plaintiff to delay service. § 583.140.

Failure to Bring the Case to Trial within Five Years. CCP § 583.310, dismissal is mandatory if the action is not brought to trial within five years after it is commenced. The burden is on plaintiff to ensure that the action is brought to trial within the five-year period. *See Howard v. Thrifty Drug & Discount Stores*, 10 Cal. 4th 424, 41 Cal. Rptr. 2d 362, 895 P.2d 469 (1995). As the deadline approaches, the plaintiff must move for preference CCP § 36(e) or to specially set the case for trial Rule 3.1335 of the California Rules of Court. *See Wale v. Rodriguez*, 206 Cal. App. 3d 129, 253 Cal. Rptr. 382 (1988). Failure to seek a preference may in itself show plaintiff's lack of diligence. *See Tejada v. Blas*, 196 Cal. App. 3d 1335, 242 Cal. Rptr. 538 (1987); *Westinghouse Electric Corp. v. Superior Court*, 143 Cal. App. 3d 95, 107, 191 Cal. Rptr. 549 (1983).

Even where the plaintiff brings such a motion, the court has no mandatory duty to provide a preferential trial date and may decline to do so where the plaintiff has failed to show due diligence in prosecuting the action. *See, e.g., Howard, supra*, 10 Cal. 4th at 440–41 (Motion for preferential trial setting raises essentially the same issues as a motion for discretionary dismissal; court should consider factors listed in Rule 3.1342(e), Cal. Rules of Ct.); *Salas v. Sears, Roebuck & Co.*, 42 Cal. 3d 342, 228 Cal. Rptr. 504, 721 P.2d 590 (1986) (No mandatory duty to set a preferential trial date; trial court should consider such discretionary factors as the condition of court calendar, dilatory conduct by plaintiff, and prejudice to defendant of an accelerated trial date); *Nye v. 20th Century Ins. Co.*, 225 Cal. App. 3d 1041, 275 Cal. Rptr. 319 (1990) (Trial court did not abuse its discretion in refusing to set case for trial before expiration of five-year period; plaintiffs who have failed to act diligently will not be allowed to cut in line ahead of diligent litigants).

Statutory Exceptions to Mandatory Dismissal. Although the dismissal for failure to bring a case to trial within five years is mandatory, a few statutory exceptions do apply. First, the time may be extended by written stipulation or oral stipulation in open court. CCP § 583.330(a)–(b). Second, the time will be extended where the court's jurisdiction is suspended or prosecution is stayed. §§ 583.340(a)–(b). Third, the time will be extended where bringing the action to trial was "impossible, impracticable, or futile." § 583.340(c); *see Coe v. City of Los Angeles*, 25 Cal. App. 4th 88, 29 Cal. Rptr. 2d 297 (1994) (Trial court abused discretion in dismissing action; five-year statute must be tolled by aggregate of court-ordered continuances based upon courtroom unavailability). The burden is on the plaintiff to make this showing, which requires proof that the plaintiff has exercised reasonable diligence in prosecuting the case. *Moran, supra,* 35 Cal. 3d at 238. Finally, the time will be extended on a showing of waiver or estoppel. § 583.140.

Failure to Bring the Case to New Trial within Three Years. CCP § 583.320, dismissal is mandatory if the plaintiff fails to bring an action to trial within three years after a mistrial, hung jury, order for new trial, or appellate remand. *See, e.g., Finnie v. District No. 1-Pacific Coast District Ass'n.,* 9 Cal. App. 4th 1311, 12 Cal. Rptr. 2d 348 (1992). However, this section does not apply where the initial five-year period for bringing an action to trial has not yet expired; the plaintiff gets the benefit of the five-year statute. § 583.320(d). A plaintiff is entitled to an extension of the three-year deadline on the same grounds as allowed for an extension of the initial five-year period. §§ 583.310–583.360.

3. Discretionary Dismissals for Lack of Prosecution

Discretionary dismissal is permitted when a plaintiff fails to meet any one of three statutory deadlines: Failure to serve defendant within two years, CCP § 583.420(a)(1); failure to bring the case to trial within two years, CCP § 583.420(a)(2) and Rule 3.1340, Cal. Rules of Ct.; and failure to bring a case to new trial within two years, CCP § 583.420(a)(3). *See Eliceche v. Federal Land Bank Ass'n,* 103 Cal. App. 4th 1349, 128 Cal. Rptr. 2d 200 (2002) (Affirming discretionary dismissal for failure to prosecute 18 days short of the date set for trial).

Rule 3.1342(e) of the California Rules of Court governs the court's exercise of discretion in ordering dismissals on these grounds and requires the court to be guided by the policies favoring the rights of parties to make stipulations and the disposition of actions on their merits. Moreover, before entering a discretionary dismissal, Rule 3.1342(e) requires a court to consider: the entire court file; the availability of parties for service of process; the plaintiff's diligence in effecting service; the extent of settlement discussions; the parties' diligence in discovery and pretrial proceedings; the nature and complexity of the case; the applicable law; the pendency of related litigation; the nature of extensions of time; the condition of the court's calendar; the availability of an earlier trial date; the interests of justice; and any other relevant facts or circumstances.

4. Relief from Dismissals

An amendment to CCP § 473 requires a court to vacate a "dismissal" when an application for relief is made within six months of the dismissal and is accompanied by an attorney's affidavit attesting that the dismissal was the result of the attorney's mistake or neglect. By express limitation, this provision of § 473 cannot lengthen the mandatory five-year period for bringing a case to trial in CCP § 583.310. *See also Bernasconi Commercial Real Estate v. St. Joseph's Regional Healthcare System,* 57 Cal. App. 4th 1078, 1080, 67 Cal. Rptr. 2d 475 (1997) (CCP § 473(b) does not mandate relief from a dismissal CCP § 583.210 for failure to serve a complaint within three years). Should this mandatory § 473 relief based on an attorney's affidavit of neglect apply to discretionary dismissals? *See Peltier v. McCloud River R.R. Co.*, 34 Cal. App. 4th 1809, 41 Cal. Rptr. 2d 182 (1995) (Mandatory relief provision in § 473 intended to reach only those dismissals which occur through attorney's failure to oppose a discretionary dismissal motion); *Graham v. Beers*, 30 Cal. App. 4th 1656, 36 Cal. Rptr. 2d 765 (1994) (Mandatory relief § 473 held inapplicable to discretionary dismissal statutes).

5. Involuntary Dismissals State and Local "Fast Track" Rules

Trial Court Delay Reduction Act. the Trial Court Delay Reduction Act (the Act), Government Code §§ 68600–68620, the Judicial Council has established the following time goals for disposition of unlimited civil cases assigned to the case management ("fast track") program: 75% should be disposed within 12 months of filing, 85% within 18 months, and 100% within 24 months. Rule 3.714 (b)(1), Cal. Rules of Ct.; Standards of Judicial Admin., Cal. Rules of Ct. App., § 2.2(f)(1). Similar goals apply to limited civil cases: 90% should be disposed of within 12 months of filing, 98% within 18 months, and 100% within 24 months. Rule 3.714 (b)(2); Standards, § 2.2(f)(2).

The Trial Court Delay Reduction Act was enacted in 1986 as a pilot project. *See Wagner v. Superior Court*, 12 Cal. App. 4th 1314, 1318, 16 Cal. Rptr. 2d 534 (1993) (discussing history of current Act). The Legislature intended to "grant to the project courts the Act wide procedural latitude in developing their own rules and procedures to implement the Act in 'response to the urgent public need to reduce litigation delays that have reached, in some counties, scandalous proportions.'" *Laborers' International Union of North America v. El Dorado Landscape Co.*, 208 Cal. App. 3d 993, 1001, 256 Cal. Rptr. 632 (1989).

After substantial revision in 1988, the Legislature in 1990 repealed the original Act and enacted the new Trial Court Delay Reduction Act effective January 1, 1991. The new Act continued many of the basic policies and goals of the original Act, Gov. Code §§ 68603 & 68607; and applies in all superior courts to all civil actions except juvenile, probate, and domestic relations, and to all limited civil cases except in small claims and unlawful detainer actions. Gov. Code §§ 68605.5, 68620. The new Act also continues the emphasis on delay reduction implementation through state and local rules, Gov. Code § 68616; but established minimum time periods for certain steps in the litigation process that cannot be shortened by local rule:

CALIFORNIA GOVERNMENT CODE (2021)

Section 68616. Minimum time periods for certain actions.

Delay reduction rules shall not require shorter time periods than as follows:

(a) Service of the complaint within 60 days after filing. Exceptions, for longer periods of time, (1) may be granted as authorized by local rule and (2) shall be granted on a showing that service could not reasonably be achieved within the time required with the exercise of due diligence consistent with the amount in controversy.

(b) Service of responsive pleadings within 30 days after service of the complaint. The parties may stipulate to an additional 15 days. Exceptions, for longer periods of time, may be granted as authorized by local rule.

(c) Time for service of notice or other paper Sections 1005 and 1013 of the Code of Civil Procedure and time to plead after service of summons Section 412.20 of the Code of Civil Procedure shall not be shortened except as provided in those sections.

(d) Within 30 days of service of the responsive pleadings, the parties may, by stipulation filed with the court, agree to a single continuance not to exceed 30 days. It is the intent of the Legislature that these stipulations not detract from the efforts of the courts to comply with standards of timely disposition. * * *

(e) A status conference, or similar event, other than a challenge to the jurisdiction of the court, shall not be required to be conducted sooner than 30 days after service of the first responsive pleadings, or 30 days after expiration of a stipulated continuance, if any, pursuant to subdivision (d).

(f) Title 4 (commencing with Section 2016.010) of Part 4 of the Code of Civil Procedure shall govern discovery, except in arbitration proceedings.

(g) A case shall not be referred to arbitration prior to 210 days after filing of the complaint, exclusive of the stipulated period provided for in subdivision (d). Any rule adopted pursuant to this article shall not contravene Sections 638 and 639 of the Code of Civil Procedure.

(h) Unnamed (DOE) defendants shall not be dismissed or severed prior to the conclusion of the introduction of evidence at trial, except upon stipulation or motion of the parties.

Case Management Rules. In practice, the critical rules are the state-wide case management rules adopted by the Judicial Council, Rules 3.700–3.750, 3.1380–3.1385, Cal. Rules of Ct.; as well as the local delay reduction rules adopted by each superior court pursuant to Government Code § 68612 and CCP § 575.1. These rules establish time periods that are often dramatically shorter than those set out in the mandatory and discretionary dismissal statutes. For example, CCP § 583.210 provides that dismissal is mandatory if an action is not served within three years of filing; but Rule 3.110, a complaint must be served on all named defendants within 60 days after filing, unless extended by the court. Rule 3.110(b)&(e), Cal. Rules of Ct.

In addition to authorizing shorter time limits, the Act reflects a different policy toward stipulations extending time than the dismissal statutes. The dismissal statutes favor the right of parties to make stipulations in their own interests. *See* CCP § 583.130. In contrast, the Act discourages continuances by stipulation of the parties. Gov. Code § 68607(g); *see also* Rule 3.1332, Cal. Rules of Ct. (setting forth good cause standards for continuance of trial date). To promote the efficient resolution of litigation, the Act limits the parties to a single continuance not to exceed 30 days. Gov. Code § 68616(d).

The new Act also authorizes the Judicial Council to adopt rules establishing a "case differentiation classification system." Gov. Code § 68603(c). The implementing rules require a trial court to evaluate each case based on relevant factors, and assign each case to a case-management plan with a specified case-disposition time goal. Rules 3.714 & 3.715, Cal. Rules of Ct. These rules also authorize a court to exempt certain cases involving exceptional circumstances from case-disposition time goals, in the interests of justice. Rule 3.714(c).

Dismissal and Other "Fast Track" Sanctions. The teeth in the Trial Court Delay Reduction Act are provided by its sanctions provisions. Government Code § 60608(b) authorizes a judge to impose a variety of sanctions for failure to comply with fast track rules, including the power to dismiss actions or strike pleadings if it appears that less severe sanctions would not be effective. *See also* Rule 2.30, Cal. Rules of Ct.

During the height of reliance on local rules to implement the Act, an issue arose as to whether Government Code § 60608(b) preempted CCP § 575.2, which only authorizes the imposition of sanctions that "adversely affect the party's cause of action or defense" if the failure to comply with local rules is the fault of the party and not the party's attorney. *Compare Intel Corp. v. USAIR, Inc.*, 228 Cal. App. 3d 1559, 279 Cal. Rptr. 569 (1991) (Trial court properly imposed dismissal of plaintiff's complaint as a sanction for plaintiff counsel's repeated failure to comply with local "fast track" rules) *with Moyal v. Lanphear*, 208 Cal. App. 3d 491, 256 Cal. Rptr. 296 (1989) (Monetary sanctions affirmed, but dismissal sanction held improper because no showing that client was the cause of counsel's failure to comply with local fast track rules). The Supreme Court subsequently resolved this issue in *Garcia v. McCutchen*, 16 Cal. 4th 469, 66 Cal. Rptr. 2d 319, 940 P.2d 906 (1997), where it held that the limitations on the power to impose case-dispositive sanctions expressed in CCP § 572.2 were applicable to violations of all types of local rules, including local "fast track" rules designed to implement the mandates of the Trial Court Delay Reduction Act.

D. Offer of Judgment

CALIFORNIA CODE OF CIVIL PROCEDURE (2021)

Section 998. Withholding or augmenting costs following rejection or acceptance of offer to allow judgment.

(a) The costs allowed Sections 1031 and 1032 shall be withheld or augmented as provided in this section.

(b) Not less than 10 days prior to commencement of trial or arbitration (as provided in Section 1281 or 1295) of a dispute to be resolved by arbitration, any party may serve an offer in writing upon any other party to the action to allow judgment to be taken or an award to be entered in accordance with the terms and conditions stated at that time. The written offer shall include a statement of the offer, containing the terms and conditions of the judgment or award, and a provision that allows the accepting party to indicate acceptance of the offer by signing a statement that the offer is accepted. Any acceptance of the offer, whether made on the document containing the offer or on a separate document of acceptance, shall be in writing and shall be signed by counsel for the accepting party or, if not represented by counsel, by the accepting party.

(1) If the offer is accepted, the offer with proof of acceptance shall be filed and the clerk or the judge shall enter judgment accordingly. In the case of an arbitration, the offer with proof of acceptance shall be filed with the arbitrator or arbitrators who shall promptly render an award accordingly.

(2) If the offer is not accepted prior to trial or arbitration or within 30 days after it is made, whichever occurs first, it shall be deemed withdrawn, and cannot be given in evidence upon the trial or arbitration.

(3) For purposes of this subdivision, a trial or arbitration shall be deemed to be actually commenced at the beginning of the opening statement of the plaintiff or counsel, or if there is no opening statement, at the time of the administering of the oath or affirmation to the first witness, or the introduction of any evidence.

(c) (1) If an offer made by a defendant is not accepted and the plaintiff fails to obtain a more favorable judgment or award, the plaintiff shall not recover his or her postoffer costs and shall pay the defendant's costs from the time of the offer. In addition, in any action or proceeding other than an eminent domain action, the court or arbitrator, in its discretion, may require the plaintiff to pay a reasonable sum to cover postoffer costs of the services of expert witnesses, who are not regular employees of any party, actually incurred and reasonably necessary in either, or both, preparation for trial or arbitration, or during trial or arbitration, of the case by the defendant.

(2) (A) In determining whether the plaintiff obtains a more favorable judgment, the court or arbitrator shall exclude the postoffer costs.

(B) It is the intent of the Legislature in enacting subparagraph (A) to supersede the holding in *Encinitas Plaza Real v. Knight*, 209 Cal.App.3d 996, that attorney's fees awarded to the prevailing party were not costs for purposes of this section but were part of the judgment.

(d) If an offer made by a plaintiff is not accepted and the defendant fails to obtain a more favorable judgment or award in any action or proceeding other than an eminent domain action, the court or arbitrator, in its discretion, may require the defendant to pay a reasonable sum to cover postoffer costs of the services of expert witnesses, who are not regular employees of any party, actually incurred and reasonably necessary in either, or both, preparation for trial or arbitration, or during trial or arbitration, of the case by the plaintiff, in addition to plaintiff's costs.

(e) If an offer made by a defendant is not accepted and the plaintiff fails to obtain a more favorable judgment or award, the costs this section, from the time of the offer, shall be deducted from any damages awarded in favor of the plaintiff. If the costs awarded this section exceed the amount of the damages awarded to the plaintiff the net amount shall be awarded to the defendant and judgment or award shall be entered accordingly.

(f) Police officers shall be deemed to be expert witnesses for the purposes of this section. For purposes of this section, "plaintiff" includes a cross-complainant and "defendant" includes a cross-defendant. Any judgment or award entered pursuant to this section shall be deemed to be a compromise settlement.

(g) This chapter does not apply to either of the following:

(1) An offer that is made by a plaintiff in an eminent domain action.

(2) Any enforcement action brought in the name of the people of the State of California by the Attorney General, a district attorney, or a city attorney, acting as a public prosecutor.

(h) The costs for services of expert witnesses for trial subdivisions (c) and (d) shall not exceed those specified in Section 68092.5 of the Government Code.

(i) This section shall not apply to labor arbitrations filed pursuant to memoranda of standing the Ralph C. Dills Act (Chapter 10.3 (commencing with Section 3512) of Division 4 of Title 1 of the Government Code).

Notes and Questions Regarding Offers of Judgment

(1) *Consequences of Failure to Obtain a More Favorable Judgment.* The purpose of statutory offers to compromise authorized by CCP § 998 is to encourage the settlement of lawsuits before trial by penalizing a party who fails to accept a reasonable offer from another party. *T.M. Cobb Co. v. Superior Court*, 36 Cal. 3d 273, 280, 204 Cal. Rptr. 143, 682 P.2d 338 (1984).

(a) *Effect on Award of Costs and Expert Witness Expenses.* The penalty for failing to obtain a judgment more favorable than the unaccepted offer is the withholding or augmenting of allowable costs, as specified in §§ 998(c)–(e). Costs affected by § 998 include those items recoverable pursuant to CCP § 1032 and allowable § 1033.5; and therefore include attorney fees when authorized by contract, statute, or law. CCP § 1033.5(a) (10). Section 998 also authorizes the trial court in its discretion to require the offeree who fails to obtain a more favorable judgment to pay the postoffer expenses for certain expert witnesses of the offeror. § 998(c)&(d). *See Regency Outdoor Advertising, Inc. v. City of Los Angeles*, 39 Cal. 4th 507, 531–34, 46 Cal. Rptr. 3d 742, 139 P. 3d 119 (2006).

(b) *Prejudgment Interest.* A defendant's rejection of a § 998 offer in a personal injury tort action has another consequence if the plaintiff subsequently obtains a more favorable judgment. Pursuant to Civil Code § 3291, the judgment shall bear interest of 10% calculated from the date of the plaintiff's first § 998 offer and accrue until satisfaction of judgment. *See, e.g., Lakin v. Watkins Associated Industries*, 6 Cal. 4th 644, 656–64, 25 Cal. Rptr. 2d 109, 863 P.2d 179 (1993) (Civil Code § 3291 authorized courts to award prejudgment interest only on damages attributable to personal injury); *Gourley v. State Farm Mutual Automobile Insurance Co.*, 53 Cal. 3d 121, 3 Cal. Rptr. 2d 666, 822 P.2d 374 (1991) (Prejudgment interest award Civil Code § 3291 held improper where § 998 offer rejected by defendant in insurance bad faith action because action was for interference with property rights, not for personal injury damages).

(2) *What Constitutes "A More Favorable Judgment"?* One of the more difficult issues faced by courts applying CCP § 998 is the determination of whether a party has failed to obtain a "more favorable judgment" than the pretrial offer. What items should be included or deleted from the amount of a verdict in making this determination can be quite complicated.

(a) *Are Court Costs Added to the Verdict?* the current version of § 998, reproduced above, court costs awarded to the prevailing party pursuant to CCP § 1032(b) and § 1033.5(a) are added to the plaintiff's verdict when the § 998 offer was made by the plaintiff and rejected by the defendant. *Stallman v. Bell*, 235 Cal. App. 3d 740, 286 Cal. Rptr. 755 (1991); *Hoch v. Allied-Signal, Inc.*, 24 Cal. App. 4th 48, 29 Cal. Rptr. 2d 615 (1994). However, when the offer was made by the defendant and rejected by the plaintiff, only the plaintiff's pre-offer costs are added to the verdict. CCP § 998(c)(2)(A). What is the policy reason for this difference in treatment based on who made the offer? *See Stallman, supra*, 235 Cal App. 3d at 747–49.

(b) *Are Attorney Fees Added to the Verdict?* A more troublesome question had been whether an award of attorney fees should be added to a verdict when making the § 998 favorability determination. In *Encinitas Plaza Real v. Knight*, 209 Cal. App. 3d 996, 257 Cal. Rptr. 646 (1989), the court held that an award of attorney fees pursuant to a contract was not an item of costs within the meaning of then-existing CCP § 1032 and § 1033.5(a)(10), and consequently could not be included in determining a "more favorable judgment" § 998. The soundness of the *Encinitas Plaza* holding became doubtful after a 1990 amendment to CCP § 1033.5(a)(10) which specifically made attorney fees authorized by contract, statute, or law an item of costs recoverable by a prevailing party. Subsequently, a 1997 amendment to § 998 superceded the holding in *Encinitas Plaza Real v. Knight, supra*. CCP § 998(c)(2). Accordingly, the current version of § 998, an award of attorney fees to the plaintiff as a prevailing party will be added to the verdict in the same manner as court costs.

(3) *Revocability of Offer.* An unaccepted offer made pursuant to CCP § 998 may be revoked by the offeror prior to the expiration of the statutory period. *T.M. Cobb Co. v. Superior Court*, 36 Cal. 3d. 273, 204 Cal. Rptr. 143, 682 P. 2d 338 (1984). However, a § 998 offer is not revoked by a counteroffer and may be accepted by the offeree during the statutory period unless the offer has been revoked by the offeror. *Poster v. Southern California Rapid Transit Dist.*, 52 Cal. 3d 266, 276 Cal. Rptr. 321, 801 P. 2d 1072 (1990). Also, a later offer of compromise does not extinguish a previous offer made by the same party for purposes of CCP § 998's cost-shifting provisions. *See Martinez v. Brownco Construction Co.*, 56 Cal. 4th 1014, 157 Cal. Rptr. 3d 558, 301 P.3d 1167 (2013) (concluding that where a plaintiff makes two successive statutory offers and the defendant fails to obtain a judgment more favorable than *either* offer, allowing recovery of expert witness fees incurred from the date of the first offer is consistent with § 998's language and best promotes the statutory purpose to encourage settlements).

(4) *Offers of Judgment in Federal Court.* Rule 68 of the Federal Rules of Civil Procedure authorizes an offer of judgment process for federal courts analogous to that of CCP § 998. However, federal Rule 68, only "a party defending against a claim" may serve an offer of judgment on the adverse party, and the other remains operative for 10 days. The consequence of rejecting an offer is also more limited than CCP § 998. Rule 68 provides that "[i]f the judgment finally obtained by the offeree is not more favorable than the offer, the offeree must pay the costs incurred after making the offer." The U.S. Supreme Court construed this language to encompass only a judgment in favor of an offeree and not a judgment against the offeree. *Delta Air Lines, Inc. v. August,* 450 U.S. 346, 101 S. Ct. 1146, 67 L. Ed. 2d 287 (1981). Rule 68 is simply inapplicable in a case where the plaintiff-offeree lost at trial because the defendant-offeror obtained the judgment. *Id.* at 351–52.

Chapter VIII

Trial and Post-Trial Motions

A. Disqualification of Trial Judge

1. Challenge for Cause: Disqualification for Actual or Perceived Bias

The Code of Civil Procedure specifies the grounds for disqualification of judges. *See* CCP §§ 170.1–170.9. Disqualification is required, for example, where the judge has personal knowledge of disputed evidentiary facts, served as a lawyer in the case, has a financial interest in the subject of the proceeding, has some relationship with a party or a lawyer, or has a physical inability to properly conduct the proceeding. CCP § 170.1(a), 170.2, 170.5. A disqualified judge must not further participate in a proceeding, except for certain limited power to act as specified in § 170.4 pending the assignment of another judge. CCP § 170.3(a)(1); *Geldermann, Inc. v. Bruner*, 229 Cal. App. 3d 662, 280 Cal. Rptr. 264 (1991) (Judge who disqualified himself after trial and announcement of tentative decision precluded from issuance of statement of decision).

A judge must also be disqualified where "a person aware of the facts might reasonably entertain a doubt that the judge would be able to be impartial." CCP § 170.1(a)(6)(c). This potentially broad ground for recusal was interpreted in *United Farm Workers of America v. Superior Court*, 170 Cal. App. 3d 97, 104–05, 216 Cal. Rptr. 4 (1985), to incorporate an objective standard: A judge faced with a potential ground for disqualification "ought to consider how his participation in a given case looks to the average person on the street." Of course, the average person on the street does not determine whether a judge must be disqualified. That decision is initially made by the judge himself or herself. § 170.3. If a judge who should disqualify himself fails to do so, any party may challenge that judge by a written verified statement of objection setting forth the facts constituting the grounds for disqualification. § 170.3(c)(1). If the judge still refuses to recuse himself, the question of disqualification must be heard and determined by another judge. § 170.3(c)(5).

2. Peremptory Challenge

Code of Civil Procedure § 170.6(a)(1) directs that no judge shall try a civil action when it is established that the judge is prejudiced against any party or attorney. Section 170.6(a)(2) then provides that any party or attorney may establish this prejudice by an oral or written motion without notice supported by an affidavit which simply states that the judge before whom the action is pending "is prejudiced against any party or attorney or the interest of the party or attorney so that the party or attorney cannot or believes that he or she cannot have a fair and impartial trial or hearing before the judge." If this motion is made according to the time limits and procedures contained in § 170.6(a)(2), then, "without any further act or proof," some other judge must be assigned to try the proceeding. CCP § 170.6(a)(3). The recommended form and content of this peremptory challenge is set forth in § 170.6(a)(5).

A party is permitted to make only one such challenge to a judge in any one action. CCP § 170.6(a)(3); *but see* CCP § 170.6(a)(2) (Authorizing party who filed an appeal and obtained reversal of a trial court's decision to exercise peremptory challenge if the same judge assigned to new trial, regardless of whether that party has previously exercised a peremptory challenge). Why would a party bother to challenge a judge for cause when a peremptory challenge is permitted? Are there circumstances where a challenge for cause is the only procedure available to disqualify a judge? What are these likely circumstances?

B. Trial by Jury

1. Right to Trial By Jury

C & K Engineering Contractors v. Amber Steel Co.

Supreme Court of California

23 Cal. 3d 1, 151 Cal. Rptr. 323, 587 P.2d 1136 (1978)

RICHARDSON, JUSTICE.

The issue posed by this case is whether or not defendant was improperly denied its constitutional right to a jury trial. (Cal. Const., art. I, § 16.) * * *

Plaintiff, a general contractor, solicited bids from defendant and other subcontractors for the installation of reinforcing steel in the construction of a waste water treatment plant in Fresno County. Plaintiff included defendant's bid in its master bid, which was ultimately accepted by the public sanitation district, the proposed owner of the plant. After defendant refused to perform in accordance with its bid on the subcontract, plaintiff brought the present action to recover $102,660 in damages for defendant's alleged breach of contract.

The allegations of plaintiff's first cause of action may be summarized: defendant submitted a written bid of $139,511 for the work; defendants gave a subsequent "verbal promise" that the work would be performed for the bid price; plaintiff "reasonably relied" on defendant's bid and promise in submitting its master bid; defendant knew or should have known that plaintiff would submit a master bid based upon defendant's bid; defendant refused to perform in accordance with its bid; plaintiff was required to expend $242,171 to perform the reinforcing steel work; as a result plaintiff was damaged in the amount of $102,660; and "Injustice can be avoided only by enforcement of defendant's promise to perform. . . ."

Defendant's answer to the complaint alleged its bid was the result of an "honest mistake" in calculation; plaintiff knew of the mistake but failed to notify defendant or permit it to revise its bid as is customary in the industry; and plaintiff's conduct in this regard should bar it from recovering damages.

Defendant demanded a jury trial. The trial court, deeming the case to be essentially in equity, denied the request but empaneled an advisory jury to consider the sole issue of plaintiff's reasonable reliance on defendant's promise. The jury found that plaintiff reasonably relied to its detriment on defendant's bid. The trial court adopted this finding and entered judgment in plaintiff's favor for $102,620, the approximate amount of its prayer, together with interest and costs. Defendant appeals.

Defendant's primary contention is that it was improperly denied a jury trial of plaintiff's action for damages. In resolving this contention we first review the nature and derivation of the doctrine of promissory estoppel. Thereafter, we discuss certain authorities governing the right to jury trial in this state. * * *

1. *Promissory Estoppel*

The elements of the doctrine of promissory estoppel, as described concisely in section 90 of the Restatement of Contracts, are as follows: "A promise which the promisor should reasonably expect to induce action or forbearance of a definite and substantial character on the part of the promisee and which does induce such action or forbearance is binding if injustice can be avoided only by enforcement of the promise." The foregoing rule has been judicially adopted in California and it applies to actions, such as the present case, to enforce a subcontractor's bid. (*Drennan v. Star Paving Co.*, [(1958)] 51 Cal. 2d 409, 413–415 [333 P.2d 757].) It is undisputed that plaintiff's complaint in the matter before us relies exclusively upon the doctrine to enforce defendant's alleged promise to perform its bid. In fact, the language of the complaint, summarized above, paraphrases that of section 90 in asserting that "Injustice can be avoided only by enforcement of defendant's promise to perform . . . ."

We have recently characterized promissory estoppel as "a doctrine which employs *equitable* principles to satisfy the requirement that consideration must be given in exchange for the promise sought to be enforced. [Citations omitted.]" (*Raedeke v. Gibraltar Sav. & Loan Assn.* (1974) 10 Cal. 3d 665, 672 [111 Cal. Rptr. 693, 517 P.2d 1157], italics added; *see Seymour v. Oelrichs* (1909) 156 Cal. 782, 794–800 [106 P. 88]; *Klein v. Farmer* (1948) 85 Cal. App. 2d 545, 552–553 [194 P.2d 106].) * * *

Treatise writers and commentators have confirmed the generally *equitable* nature of promissory estoppel in enforcing a promise which otherwise would be unenforceable. (*See* 3 Pomeroy, Equity Jurisprudence (5th ed. 1941) § 808b, at pp. 211–216; 1 Williston, Contracts (3d ed. 1957) § 140, pp. 618–619, fn. 6; Seavey, *Reliance Upon Gratuitous Promises or Other Conduct* (1951) 64 Harv. L. Rev. 913, 925; Henderson, *Promissory Estoppel and Traditional Contract Doctrine* (1969) 78 Yale L.J. 343, 379–380; Ames, *The History of Assumpsit* (1888) 2 Harv. L. Rev. 1, 14.) As expressed by Professor Henderson, "[Promissory] estoppel is *a peculiarly equitable doctrine* designed to deal with situations which, in total impact, necessarily call into play discretionary powers, . . ." (78 Yale L.J., *supra*, at pp. 379–380, italics added.) One distinguished commentator has observed that promissory estoppel derives from both "the decisions of the courts of common law from the very beginnings of the action of assumpsit [as well as] the decrees of courts of equity making a very flexible use of the doctrine of 'estoppel,' . . ." (1A Corbin, Contracts (1963) § 194, at p. 193, fn. omitted; *see also id.*, § 195.) The available authorities generally concur, however, that as of 1850 assumpsit would not lie to enforce a gratuitous promise, where the promisee's detrimental reliance was not requested by the promisor. (Ames, *supra*, 2 Harv. L. Rev. at p. 14; Seavey, *supra*, 64 Harv. L. Rev. at p. 913; Shattuck, *Gratuitous Promises — A New Writ* (1937) 35 Mich. L. Rev. 908, 909–914; 1 Williston, *supra*, at pp. 618–619, fn. 6; 8 Holdsworth, A History of English Law (1966) p. 10.).

The equitable character of promissory estoppel is confirmed by a close scrutiny of the purpose of the doctrine, namely, that "*injustice* can be avoided only by enforcement of the promise." (Rest., Contracts, *supra*, § 90, italics added.) As expressed by us in a similar subcontractor bid case, once the prerequisites of the doctrine are met, ". . . *it is only fair* that plaintiff should have at least an opportunity to accept defendant's bid after the general contract has been awarded to him." (*Drennan v. Star Paving Co.*, *supra*, 51 Cal. 2d at p. 415, italics added; *see also* Seavey, *supra*, 64 Harv. L. Rev. at p. 925; Henderson, *supra*, 78 Yale L.J. at p. 379 ["The specific concern of Section 90 with 'injustice,' standing alone, contemplates broad judicial discretion to make use of equitable principles"].) * * *

We conclude, accordingly, that the doctrine of promissory estoppel is essentially equitable in nature, developed to provide a remedy (namely, enforcement of a gratuitous promise) which was not generally available in courts of law prior to 1850. We now move to an examination of the authorities on the subject of the right to a jury trial, to determine whether the equitable nature of plaintiff's action precluded a jury trial as a matter of right.

2. Right to Jury Trial

The right to a jury trial is guaranteed by our Constitution. (Cal. Const., art. I, § 16.) We have long acknowledged that the right so guaranteed, however, is the right as it existed at common law in 1850, when the Constitution was first adopted, "and what that right is, is a purely historical question, a fact which is to be ascertained like any other social, political or legal fact." (*People v. One 1941 Chevrolet Coupe* (1951) 37 Cal. 2d 283, 287 [231 P.2d 832]; accord *Southern Pac. Transportation Co. v. Superior Court* (1976) 58 Cal. App. 3d 433, 436 [129 Cal. Rptr. 912]; . . .) As a general proposition, "[The] jury trial is a matter of right in a civil action at law, but not in equity." (*Southern Pac. Transportation Co. v. Superior Court*, *supra*, 58 Cal. App. 3d at p. 436; . . .)

As we stated in *People v. One 1941 Chevrolet Coupe*, *supra*, 37 Cal. 2d 283, "'If the action has to deal with ordinary common-law rights cognizable in courts of law, it is to that extent an action at law. In determining whether the action was one triable by a jury at common law, the court is not bound by the form of the action but rather by the nature of the rights involved and the facts of the particular case — the *gist* of the action. A jury trial must be granted where the *gist* of the action is legal, where the action is in reality cognizable at law.'" (P. 299, fn. omitted, italics added.) On the other hand, if the action is essentially one in equity and the relief sought "depends upon the application of equitable doctrines," the parties are not entitled to a jury trial. (E.g., *Hartman v. Burford* (1966) 242 Cal. App. 2d 268, 270 [51 Cal. Rptr. 309] [enforcement of promise to make a will]; *Tibbitts v. Fife* (1958) 162 Cal. App. 2d 568, 572 [328 P.2d 212] [establishment of constructive trust].) Although we have said that "the legal or equitable nature of a cause of action ordinarily is determined by the mode of relief to be afforded" (*Raedeke v. Gibraltar Sav. & Loan Assn., supra,* 10 Cal. 3d 665, 672), the prayer for relief in a particular case is not conclusive. Thus, "The fact that damages is one of a full range of possible remedies does not guarantee . . . the right to a jury. . . ." (*Southern Pac. Transportation Co. v. Superior Court, supra,* 58 Cal. App. 3d at p. 437.)

In the present case, the complaint purports to seek recovery of damages for breach of contract, in form an action at law in which a right to jury trial ordinarily would exist. (*Raedeke, supra,* 10 Cal. 3d at p. 671; Code Civ. Proc., § 592.) As we have seen, however, the complaint seeks relief which was available only in equity, namely, the enforcement of defendant's gratuitous promise to perform its bid through application of the equitable doctrine of promissory estoppel. Although there is no direct authority on point, several cases have held that actions based upon the analogous principle of equitable estoppel may be tried by the court without a jury. (*Jaffe v. Albertson Co.* (1966) 243 Cal. App. 2d 592, 607–608 [53 Cal. Rptr. 25] [estoppel to bar reliance on statute of frauds]; *Moss v. Bluemm* (1964) 229 Cal. App. 2d 70, 72–73 [40 Cal. Rptr. 50] [estoppel to bar statute of limitations defense]; *Richard v. Degen & Brody, Inc.* (1960) 181 Cal. App. 2d 289, 295 [5 Cal. Rptr. 263] [estoppel as defense to unlawful detainer action]; . . .)

Defendant responds by relying primarily upon . . . *Raedeke, supra,* which also concerned an action based on promissory estoppel. The *Raedeke* complaint alleged *dual* theories of traditional breach of contract and promissory estoppel. We stressed that the "resolution of the instant case did not depend entirely upon the application of equitable principles; the doctrine of promissory estoppel was only one of two alternative theories of recovery." Accordingly, we held in *Raedeke* that plaintiffs were entitled to a jury trial, and that the trial court erred in treating the jury's findings and verdict as advisory only. * * *

The foregoing general principles do not alter our conclusion that the present action is, essentially, one recognized only in courts of equity and, despite plaintiff's request for damages, is not an "action at law" involving, to use the *Raedeke* language, the "incidental adoption of equitable sounding measures." Defendant before us has argued that because plaintiff sought to recover damages rather than to compel defendant to perform its bid, plaintiff requested relief which is available at common law. Yet, as we have seen, damages at law were unavailable in actions for breach of a gratuitous promise. The only manner in which damages have been recognized in such cases of gratuitous promises is by application of the equitable doctrine of promissory estoppel which renders such promises legally binding. Without the employment of this doctrine, essentially equitable, there was no remedy at all. As illustrated by the express language of section 90 of the Restatement of Contracts, promissory estoppel is used to avoid injustice "by *enforcement* of the promise." (Italics added.)

Furthermore, the addition, in such cases, of a prayer for damages does not convert what is essentially an equitable action into a legal one for which a jury trial would be available. This was demonstrated in a recent case, *Southern Pac. Transportation Co. v. Superior Court, supra*, 58 Cal. App. 3d 433, wherein plaintiff sought damages as a good faith improver of land owned by another person. (*See* Code Civ. Proc., § 871.1 et seq.) The appellate court rejected the contention that plaintiff's request for damages necessarily identified the action as one at law. The court first noted that since the good faith improver statute had no counterpart in English common law, "classification of the action as either legal or equitable depends upon characterization of the nature of the relief sought."

The *Southern Pac. Transportation* court properly observed that under the statute, the trial court must "effect such an adjustment of the rights, equities, and interests" of the parties as was consistent with substantial justice. (Code Civ. Proc., § 871.5.) Thus, the action was essentially one calling for the exercise of equitable principles. The court added, "The fact that damages is one of a full range of possible remedies does not guarantee real parties the right to a jury," since "there is no possibility of severing the legal from the equitable. The trier of fact must determine whether to quiet title in the improver on the condition he pay to the landowner the value of the unimproved land, or whether and in what amount, to award damages to the improver, or whether to require a completely different form of relief.... Such a determination is not susceptible of division into one component to be resolved by the court and another component to be determined by a jury. Only one decision can be made, and it must make a proper adjustment of the 'rights, equities, and interests' of all the parties involved." The court concluded that in view of the various equitable considerations involved, it would be resolve the dispute.

Similarly, in the present case, the trier of fact is called upon to determine whether "injustice can be avoided only by enforcement of [defendant's] promise." (Rest., Contracts, § 90.) The "gist" of such an action is equitable. Both historically and functionally, the task of weighing such equitable considerations is to be performed by the trial court, not the jury. We conclude that the trial court properly treated the action as equitable in nature, to be tried by the court with or without an advisory jury as the court elected.

The judgment is affirmed.

NEWMAN, JUSTICE, dissenting.

I dissent. The Chancery Court in England sometimes created rights, sometimes remedies. When California courts decide whether a jury trial should be assured, I believe that they should focus not on rights but on remedies. A plaintiff who seeks damages should be entitled to a jury. One who seeks specific performance or an injunction or quiet title, etc. (plus supplementary damages or "damages in lieu" that would have been allowed in Chancery) is not entitled to a jury.

The majority opinion here discusses "promissory estoppel," "equitable estoppel," "equitable principles," "equitable doctrine," "equitable nature," and even "injustice." To pretend that words like those enable us to isolate "ordinary common-law rights cognizable in courts of law" or that "the *gist* of the action" governs (quoting from *People v. One 1941 Chevrolet Coupe* (1951) 37 Cal. 2d 283, 299 [231 P.2d 832]) seems to me to be uninstructive fictionalizing. We are told that courts deal with "a purely historical question, a fact which is to be ascertained like any other social, political or legal fact." Yet how often, I wonder, do (or should) California judges instead decide whether the wisdom of a Corbin, in 1963, outweighs comments by Ames, Seavey, Shattuck, and Williston written during the period from 1888 to 1957?

In fact, most rights that are now enforced via a jury were created not by courts but by legislatures. We look at the *remedy* sought, not at the judicial or legislative history of the *right*, to decide whether the trial is to be "legal" or "equitable." There are troubling borderlines, but the basic rule should be that no jury is required when plaintiff seeks equitable relief rather than "legal" damages. That approach requires no complex, historical research regarding when and by whom certain rights were created. It also requires less reliance on the anomalies of England's unique juridical history. Courts thus may focus on a basic policy concern; that is, the typically more continuing and more personalized involvement of the trial judge in specific performance and injunctive decrees than in mere judgments for damages.

Plaintiff in this case sought damages for an alleged breach of contract. He did not seek equitable relief. Thus defendant should have been granted the jury trial he requested.

Notes and Questions Regarding Right to Jury Trial

(1) *The Legal/Equitable Dichotomy.* Article I, Section 16, of the California Constitution preserves the right to jury trial in those actions in which there was a right to a jury at common law at the time the California Constitution was first adopted. *Crouchman v. Superior Court*, 45 Cal. 3d 1167, 1175, 248 Cal. Rptr. 626, 755 P.2d 1075 (1988). Consequently, as *C & K Engineering* illustrates, the determination of the constitutional guarantee must turn on an historical analysis. The basic inquiry is whether the gist of the action is "legal" (*i.e.*, triable by a jury at common law), or "equitable" and therefore to be resolved by the court sitting without a jury. *Id.*

Most typical civil actions, such as those for damages based on traditional breach of contract or negligence on the one hand, or suits for injunctive relief only on the other, readily fall into one historical category or the other. Occasionally, as *C & K Engineering* illustrates, an action is not so easily classified. *See, e.g., Arciero Ranches v. Meza*, 17 Cal. App. 4th 114, 21 Cal. Rptr. 2d 127 (1993) (Defendants entitled to jury trial on cross-complaint seeking injunction to enforce prescriptive easement because gist of such action was considered legal and not equitable in 1850); *Beasley v. Wells*

Fargo Bank, 235 Cal. App. 3d 1383, 1 Cal. Rptr. 2d 446 (1991) (Although plaintiff entitled to jury determination of the amount of damages in breach of contract action, a sub-issue of the validity of a liquidated damages provision must be determined by the judge); *Van de Kamp v. Bank of America*, 204 Cal. App. 3d 819, 862–65, 251 Cal. Rptr. 530 (1988) (Gist of beneficiaries' action for damages against trustee was based on equitable principle of an accounting, and therefore no right to jury trial).

Are you satisfied with the "gist of the action" historical approach? What is the source of that approach? Would a better analytical approach be to focus on the remedy sought, not on the history of the right, and to require no jury when a party seeks equitable relief rather that "legal" damages? Why do the California courts not utilize this simpler analytical approach?

(2) *Actions Involving Both Legal and Equitable Issues.* Where legal and equitable claims are joined in the same action, the parties are entitled to a jury trial on the legal issues. *See, e.g., Connell v. Bowes*, 19 Cal. 2d 870, 871, 123 P.2d 456 (1942); *Arciero Ranches v. Meza*, 17 Cal. App. 4th 114, 124, 21 Cal. Rptr. 2d 127 (1993) (citing cases). Ordinarily, the court will resolve the equitable issues first and then, if any legal issues remain, the jury will resolve them. *See Arciero Ranches v. Meza, supra; A-C Co. v. Security Pacific National Bank*, 173 Cal. App. 3d 462, 219 Cal. Rptr. 62 (1985). Is this "equity first" rule consistent with the "gist of the action" approach? How so?

(3) *Waiver of Right to Trial by Jury.* The California Constitution permits the waiver of jury trial in a civil action "by the consent of the parties expressed as prescribed by statute." Cal. Const., Art I, § 16. Code of Civil Procedure § 631 specifies the ways a jury trial may be waived. These include written consent or oral consent in open court; failure to appear at trial; and failure to announce that a jury is required, at the time the cause is first set for trial. CCP § 631(d)(1)–(4). A party may also waive the right to a jury trial by operation of law by failing to deposit with the clerk certain jury fees in advance of the date set for trial, or additional jury fees as they subsequently become due. § 631(d)(5)–(6). If trial by jury is demanded by either party and that party later waives a jury trial, § 631(b) & (c) provides that any other party with the opportunity to promptly demand a jury trial.

(4) *Expedited Jury Trials.* After a civil action is filed, the parties may consent to an "expedited jury trial" as authorized by the recently adopted Expedited Jury Trials Act, CCP §§ 630.01-630.12. *See* Rules 3.1545–3.1552, Cal. Rules of Ct. (specifying pretrial and trial procedures for expedited jury trials). An expedited jury trial consists of 8 or fewer jurors with no alternates, allows only 3 peremptory challenges for each side, and limits each side to 3 hours to present its case. CCP §§ 630.03(e)(2), 630.04. The parties also agree to waive all rights to appeal or to make any post-trial motions, except for the very limited grounds specified in the Act. CCP §§ 630.03(e)(2)(A); 630.08-630.09. A key element of this summary trial is the "high/low agreement," defined as a written agreement entered into by the parties that specifies a minimum amount of damages a plaintiff is guaranteed to receive from the defendant, and a

maximum amount of damages that the defendant will be liable for, regardless of the ultimate verdict returned by the jury. CCP § 630.01(b). The high/low agreement is not disclosed to the jury. *Id.*

2. Jury Selection

Selection of Trial Jury Panel. The Trial Jury Selection and Management Act, CCP §§ 190–237, governs the selection and formation of trial juries for both civil and criminal cases. CCP § 192. The jury commissioner for each county must create a master list of persons potentially qualified for jury service. §§ 195–196. All persons selected for jury service must be selected at random, from sources inclusive of a representative cross-section of the area served by the court. §§ 197 & 198. Approved sources are a combined list of registered voters and DMV licensed drivers, and may also include customer mailing lists, telephone directories, and utility company lists. *Id.* The jury commissioner must also utilize random selection to create qualified juror lists from the master list, and to select jurors for trial jury panels to be sent to courtrooms for voir dire. § 219. The clerk in each courtroom must randomly select names of jurors for voir dire from these panels, unless the jury commissioner provides the court with the trial jury panel list in random order, in which case the court must seat the prospective jurors in the same order as in the list. CCP § 222.

A party may challenge the entire trial jury panel for failure to include a representative cross-section. CCP § 225(a). The random selection processes make such challenges difficult to establish in civil cases. *See, e.g., People v. Breaux,* 1 Cal. 4th 281, 3 Cal. Rptr. 2d 81, 821 P.2d 585 (1991) (Criminal defendant must show intentional and systematic exclusion of a particular race, religion, economic class, or other cognizable group).

Voir Dire in Civil Jury Trials. To select a fair and impartial jury, the trial judge initially examines prospective jurors in civil jury trial. CCP § 222.5(a); Rule 3.1540, Cal. Rules of Ct. The Standards of Judicial Administration recommended by the Judicial Council set forth the areas of inquiry the trial judge's examination should cover. Standard 3.25. Upon completion of the judge's initial examination, counsel for each party has the right to examine, by oral and direct questioning, any prospective jurors in order to enable counsel to intelligently exercise both peremptory challenges and challenges for cause. CCP § 222.5(b)(1). The trial judge should permit liberal and probing examination calculated to discover bias or prejudice with regard to the circumstances of a particular case; the fact that a topic was included in the judge's examination should not preclude additional nonduplicative questioning in the same area by counsel. § 222.5(b)(1). The judge must not impose unreasonable or arbitrary time limits on counsels' voir dire examination. § 222.5(b)(2).

Generally speaking, counsel in civil jury trials are given considerable freedom and latitude to directly voir dire prospective jurors, unless a particular counsel engages in improper questioning. Section 222.5 defines an "improper question" as "any question that, as it dominant purpose, attempts to precondition the prospective jurors to a particular result, indoctrinate the jury, or question the prospective jurors concerning the pleadings or the applicable law." *See also* Standards of Judicial Administration 3.25(f).

3. Challenges to Individual Jurors

Challenges for Cause. A party may challenge an individual juror for cause for a general disqualification, for an implied bias, or for an actual bias. CCP §§ 225–230. Challenges for general disqualification are limited to two grounds: lack of an eligibility qualification to be a competent juror as defined in §228. A challenge for implied bias may be taken when the juror possesses some type of relationship to a party or interest in the action which makes the juror inappropriate for that particular case as a matter of law, as specified in §229. By contrast, actual bias is "the existence of a state of mind on the part of the juror in reference to the case, or to any of the parties, which will prevent the juror from acting with entire impartiality, and without prejudice to the substantial rights of any party." §225(b)(1)(c). How might actual bias be demonstrated during voir dire in a civil case?

Peremptory Challenges. In civil cases, each party is entitled to six peremptory challenges. CCP §231(c). If there are more than two parties, each side is entitled to eight peremptory challenges; and if more than two sides, the court may allot additional challenges. *Id.* The procedure for exercising peremptory challenges is specified by statute. §231(d) & (e). Peremptory challenges are taken or passed by the sides alternately, commencing with the plaintiff. *Id.* Each party is entitled to have a full panel of jurors before exercising any peremptory challenge; the number of challenges remaining with a side is not diminished by any passing. *Id.* When each side passes consecutively the jury selection process is complete, and the jury is then sworn. *Id.*

Constitutional Limitations on Exercise of Peremptory Challenges. Traditionally, a peremptory challenge may be exercised for any reason and no explanation is necessary. CCP §226(b). However, recent decisions applying the Fourteenth Amendment to the U.S. Constitution hold that a party to a civil lawsuit may not use peremptory challenges to exclude jurors on account of their race or gender. *Edmonson v. Leesville Concrete Co.*, 500 U.S. 614, 111 S. Ct. 2077, 114 L. Ed. 2d 660 (1991) (Race-based exclusion in civil actions violates equal protection rights of challenged jurors).

In 2002, the Legislature added CCP §231.5, which provides that a party "may not use a peremptory challenge to remove a prospective juror on the basis of an assumption that the prospective juror is biased merely because of his or her race, color, religion, sex, national origin, sexual orientation, or similar grounds."

4. Putting the Case to the Jury

Sabella v. Southern Pacific Company

Supreme Court of California

70 Cal. 2d 311, 74 Cal. Rptr. 534, 449 P.2d 750 (1969)

Mosk, Justice.

Defendant appeals from a judgment in favor of plaintiff under the Federal Employers' Liability Act. The jury brought in a verdict of $115,500, but by remittitur to which plaintiff consented the award was reduced to $80,000. Defendant cites as error the trial court's refusal to admit evidence of a disability pension, and purported misconduct by plaintiff's counsel. We conclude that the judgment must be affirmed.

Plaintiff Mike Sabella was injured while working as a "carman cutter" for defendant railroad. Among other duties, it was his task to cut damaged freight cars into scrap. While doing so, plaintiff fell from the roof of a car he was cutting and sustained severe back injuries. He alleged that his fall was caused by the negligence of defendant's crane operator in moving the roof section, which had been attached to the crane preparatory to lifting the section off, while plaintiff was still walking on it; and by the failure of defendant to provide a reasonably safe place in which to work. The defense was based on a denial of negligence and an allegation of contributory negligence, which may reduce an F.E.L.A. award.

At the conclusion of the trial, and following the verdict in favor of plaintiff, defendant moved for a new trial on multiple grounds: (1) insufficiency of the evidence; (2) excessive damages; (3) disregard by the jury of the court's instructions as to contributory negligence; (4) error in law in excluding evidence of a disability pension received by plaintiff; and (5) misconduct by plaintiff's counsel. The court made an order finding "That the evidence is insufficient to sustain the verdict of the jury; and [that there] was error in law, occurring at the trial and excepted to by defendant, and that such error was prejudicial. . . ." A new trial was denied, however, on the condition that plaintiff consent to a reduction of the verdict from $115,500 to $80,000. Plaintiff agreed and does not now challenge the propriety of the reduction.

We turn now to defendant's . . . contention . . . that plaintiff's counsel was guilty of prejudicial misconduct. The alleged misconduct consisted, among other things, of repeated references, both direct and indirect, to defendant as "inhuman" and heartless, sending plaintiff "down the tubes" and casting him on the "human trash pile;" as "cheapskates" attempting to put up a "smokescreen" by perjury and deceit, so as to deprive plaintiff of his just due and put the money instead into defendant's "coffers." Reference was also made to the disparity in wealth between plaintiff and defendant, combined with an appeal to the jurors' personal sympathies.[4] It is unnecessary to detail any further the precise language used or to make a phrase-by-phrase comparison between this and other exemplars of misconduct since it is only the record as a whole, and not specific phrases out of context, that can reveal the nature and effect of such tactics. Upon review of the entire record we conclude that plaintiff's counsel was guilty of deplorable misconduct which might well have been prejudicial. However, in view

---

4. In recent years a number of personal injury lawyers have written books suggesting a variety of somewhat deceptive means of eliciting sympathy for litigants appearing before a jury. (*See* Prosser, 43 Cal. L. Rev. 556 (1955), reviewing Belli, Modern Trials (1954); R. M. Mosk, 16 U.C.L.A. L.Rev. 216 (1968), reviewing Appleman, Preparation and Trial (1967).) Such tactics are not part of the repertoire of the ethical professional man.

of defendant's failure to take proper steps to preserve the latter issue of prejudice on appeal, we find it unnecessary to reach it on the merits.[5]

Assuming counsel's conduct was both improper and prejudicial, and further assuming for purposes of discussion that such misconduct went to the issue of liability and so could not be cured by remittitur, we examine the record before us in light of the applicable legal principles.

"Generally a claim of misconduct is entitled to no consideration on appeal unless the record shows a timely and proper objection and a request that the jury be admonished." (*Horn v. Atchison, T. & S. F. Ry. Co.* (1964) 61 Cal. 2d 602, 610 [39 Cal. Rptr. 721, 394 P.2d 561].) "'As the effect of misconduct can ordinarily be removed by an instruction to the jury to disregard it, it is generally essential, in order that such act be reviewed on appeal, that it shall first be called to the attention of the trial court at the time, to give the court an opportunity to so act in the premises, if possible, as to correct the error and avoid a mistrial. Where the action of the court is not thus invoked, the alleged misconduct will not be considered on appeal, if an admonition to the jury would have removed the effect.'" (*Cope v. Davison* (1947) *supra*, 30 Cal. 2d at p. 202.) "'It is only in extreme cases that the court, when acting promptly and speaking clearly and directly on the subject, cannot, by instructing the jury to disregard such matters, correct the impropriety of the act of counsel and remove any effect his conduct or remarks would otherwise have.' (*Tingley v. Times-Mirror Co.*, 151 Cal. 1, 23 [89 P. 1097].) . . . [We] are aware of no California case wherein a plaintiff's verdict was reversed for misconduct during his counsel's argument in the lack of timely objections and a request that the jury be admonished where such admonition could be effective." (*Horn v. Atchison, T. & S.F. Ry. Co.* (1964) *supra*, 61 Cal. 2d at pp. 610–611.)

This case is neither precisely like *Horn, supra,* in which no objection or request for admonition was made until after conclusion of the closing argument (and relief was thus denied); nor like *Hoffman v. Brandt* (1966) 65 Cal. 2d 549 [55 Cal. Rptr. 417, 421 P.2d 425], in which an admonition, especially as there given by the trial court, could not have been effective under the circumstances; nor like *Love v. Wolf* (1964) 226 Cal. App. 2d 378 [38 Cal. Rptr. 183], in which admonition of the jury was requested several times but disregarded by the trial court. Here defendant remained silent as to all but one line of argument, and as to the latter he objected but failed at any time to request an admonition of the jury to disregard the remarks. Under the circumstances we conclude that defendant must be denied relief.

The record indicates that while plaintiff's counsel accused witnesses of perjury, made reference to defendant's wealth and plaintiff's lack of resources, and appealed, though indirectly, to the jurors to place themselves in plaintiff's position, all of which tactics are improper and to be condemned (*see, e.g., Hoffman v. Brandt* (1966) *supra,*

---

5. In any event, the trial court impliedly found no misconduct, or at least no prejudice, when ruling on the motion for new trial. "A trial judge is in a better position than an appellate court to determine whether a verdict resulted wholly, or in part, from the asserted misconduct of counsel and his conclusion in the matter will not be disturbed unless, under all the circumstances, it is plainly wrong." (*Cope v. Davison* (1947) 30 Cal. 2d 193, 203 [180 P.2d 873, 171 A.L.R. 667].)

65 Cal. 2d 549; *Horn v. Atchison, T. & S.F. Ry. Co.* (1964) *supra*, 61 Cal. 2d 602; *Love v. Wolf* (1964) *supra*, 226 Cal. App. 2d 378), defendant did not once object to such remarks, much less request an admonition to the jury. "In the absence of a timely objection the offended party is deemed to have waived the claim of error through his participation in the atmosphere which produced the claim of prejudice." (*Horn v. Atchison, T. & S.F. Ry. Co.* (1964) *supra*, 61 Cal. 2d at p. 610.)

Defendant did object, however, to one distinct line of argument by his adversary. As discussed earlier, defendant challenged references to turning its back on plaintiff and refusing to help him or to give him a job and generally being out to defeat his claim. This was, in fact, perhaps the mildest and least prejudicial of the alleged instances of misconduct. Although counsel used improper language, the question of defendant's treatment of plaintiff appears to have been put in issue, at least in part, by defendant when it asserted during opening statement that there was work plaintiff could do on the railroad. However, even assuming that the entire line of argument was misconduct, defendant remained silent when during opening argument plaintiff's counsel at least twice alluded to defendant's denial of a job and of hospitalization to plaintiff, and when during the trial he used such terms as "cheapskates" in referring to defendant. It was not until closing argument, after defendant had attempted to counter the "unfairness" argument with evidence of plaintiff's disability pension, rather than by means of the long established procedure of admonishing the jury,[6] that defendant finally objected, but even at that tardy point counsel did not request an admonition. Certainly as to this particular line of argument an admonition would have been effective, especially if requested at the outset. One of the primary purposes of admonition at the beginning of an improper course of argument is to avoid repetition of the remarks and thus obviate the necessity of a new trial. (*Horn v. Atchison, T. & S.F. Ry. Co.* (1964) *supra*, 61 Cal. 2d at p. 610.) Except perhaps in cases of highly emotional or inflammatory language or reference to extremely prejudicial circumstances not in evidence, a jury must be deemed capable, if so instructed, of ignoring references to a litigant's personal or corporate virtues and confining itself to the merits of the case.[7]

Defendant urges us to ignore the rules of procedure relating to the "magic words" of proper objection and admonition. But the procedure outlined above is not a

---

6. Defendant asserts that it did not know at the outset how heavily this line of argument would be emphasized, although during one objection defendant claimed that it had been "anticipating" such an argument and meant to counter it by evidence of the disability pension. Obviously, the fact that this counterevidence was subsequently excluded cannot alone excuse the failure to object if in fact the argument was improper. It was not the exclusion of the pension evidence that determined the propriety of the language and allusions employed by plaintiff's counsel.

7. Defendant was apparently not unaware of the tactical availability and desirability of an admonition to the jury. When plaintiff attempted to argue damages on a "per diem" basis, defendant objected strenuously and asked for and received an admonition that the jury disregard this line of argument. (As to the propriety of that ruling, *see Beagle v. Vasold* (1966) 65 Cal. 2d 166 [53 Cal. Rptr. 129, 417 P.2d 673].) It is signifi cant that far more questionable statements made at the same time, which defendant now cites as misconduct, were not alluded to in the "per diem" objection.

meaningless ritual; it has been designed through judicial experience to prevent by timely words of caution the very problem with which we are here concerned.

We emphasize again that the particular language used by counsel and the form or lack of objection by defendant in this case are not meant to serve as invariable guidelines for future reference. Each case must ultimately rest upon a court's view of the overall record, taking into account such factors, inter alia, as the nature and seriousness of the remarks and misconduct, the general atmosphere, including the judge's control,[8] of the trial, the likelihood of prejudicing the jury, and the efficacy of objection or admonition under all the circumstances.

Our conclusions should in no way be interpreted as condoning the deplorable conduct of plaintiff's counsel.[9] However, punishment of counsel to the detriment of his client is not the function of the court. Intemperate and unprofessional conduct by counsel as is here involved runs a grave and unjustifiable risk of sacrificing an otherwise sound case for recovery, and as such is a disservice to a litigant. These same tactics, in another context, would likely result in a reversal. However, under the facts and circumstances of this case, we conclude that the award to plaintiff, as modified by the remittitur, is justified.

The judgment is affirmed.

Traynor, Chief Justice, dissenting.

I dissent.

I would reverse the judgment on the ground that the misconduct of counsel for plaintiff deprived defendant of its right to a fair trial.

In his opening statement, counsel for plaintiff made a preliminary appeal to the sympathy of the jury by stressing that plaintiff had left school after the seventh grade to go to work and had worked for defendant for 36 years. Thereafter in the course of the trial, counsel deliberately sought to implant prejudice in the jury against defendant. He insinuated without offering any evidence to prove it, that defense counsel had withheld photographs favorable to plaintiff. He referred to defendant and its attorneys as "cheapskates." He asked rhetorical questions calculated to convey the impression that defense witnesses were not honest in their testimony. Nor was that all. After several days of trial, when a trial court is normally reluctant to grant a mistrial, he used his closing argument to intensify his appeal to the passion and prejudice of the jury. The appeal was the more insidious because it followed upon a fulsome declaration of his great trust in the jury system. His trust was such that he urged a verdict on

---

8. While it cannot be said that the trial court here "lost control" of the proceedings (cf. *Love v. Wolf* (1964) *supra*, 226 Cal. App. 2d 378, 391), a court should on its own initiative intercede to prevent potentially prejudicial conduct of counsel. Such action here, directed either at counsel or to the jury, not only might have mitigated the prejudice here alleged, but it would have enhanced the dignity and demeanor of the proceedings.

9. Counsel's law firm has been the subject of judicial condemnation in at least two other recent instances of comparable misconduct. (*Horn v. Atchison*, T. & S.F. Ry. Co., *supra*, 61 Cal. 2d 602; *Love v. Wolf, supra*, 226 Cal. App. 2d 378.)

issues extraneous to the merits. Approximately a third of his argument consisted of emotional attacks on defendant, its counsel, and its witnesses for defendant. He called upon the jury to "tell the Southern Pacific in that verdict it is high time to quit treating their employees that way."

There is no question that his conduct was on its face prejudicial. The question to be resolved is whether or not defendant waived its right to complain even though it repeatedly made objections at the trial.[1] The objections were more than enough to alert the trial

---

1. Counsel for defendant objected ten times during the closing argument for plaintiff. The appeals to prejudice and the corresponding objections are tallied below:*First*: "Now, ladies and gentlemen, I know that before you folks sat here, that you came here on January 25th, 1964, and I know in your hearts, as in my heart, after you saw the presentation of this case, that I'll bet you are amazed and stunned beyond belief. This isn't really 1964 at all. This goes back to the early stages of man's inhumanity to man long before they were savages, because I submit, and I will discuss with you folks this afternoon, never in the history of man could anyone have been taken down the tubes or down the drain like one Mike Sabella was.

"And I say to you, ladies and gentlemen, that the conduct of his employer, the Southern Pacific Company in this case, is about as reprehensible in 1956 [*sic*] —

"MR. PHELPS [counsel for defendant]: Your Honor, I am going to object to this line of argument and assign it as misconduct, particularly in view of Your Honor's ruling that is keeping out of evidence the matter that I wanted to introduce, the matter that I — the argument is along the lines I was anticipating and I could have met and did want to meet by evidence, and I will object and cite it as misconduct and ask for a mistrial.

"THE COURT: Well, the motion for a mistrial will be denied; and I suggest, Mr. Teerlink, that you confine yourself to the evidence and such reasonable implications as you may draw therefrom.

"MR. TEERLINK: Yes, Your Honor."

Second: "Did they even agree to pick up $11.50 a month to see that the poor guy got his hospitalization? No.

"MR. PHELPS: If Your Honor please, I am going to object in view of the offer of proof I made in chambers as to what this man's actual situation was and the election he made, and I think it is misconduct to encroach in the manner that has been done.

"MR. TEERLINK: The stipulation, as I understand, Your Honor, was that the railroad company tendered the right to pick up his hospital benefits, and they declined; that was the stipulation that you entered.

"MR. PHELPS: I understand that, but you are arguing something that prevents me from answering.

"THE COURT: Let's not go beyond the stipulation."

Third: "They cut off — no more hospital benefits, no more out-patient, by the time of December —

"MR. PHELPS: I make the same objection, Your Honor please, in view of the situation, my hands having been tied —

"MR. TEERLINK: I say there are no benefits payable after December. That is the evidence.

"MR. PHELPS: What did the Southern Pacific Company do when you —

"THE COURT: Let's —

"MR. PHELPS: — I object to that and assign it as misconduct.

"MR. TEERLINK: That is the evidence, Your Honor. He had no benefits after December.

"THE COURT: I know, but you are going beyond that.

"MR. PHELPS: You foreclosed me.

court. The court itself sought to call a halt to the objectionable conduct by admonishing counsel for plaintiff to "confine yourself to the evidence and such reasonable

---

"THE COURT: Let's stay within the confines."

Fourth: "Do you think that was strategy? This is the way they play the ball game. They don't know how to play it fair. The last witness, ladies and gentlemen, is, lo and behold, McLaughlin —

"MR. PHELPS: I object and assign that as misconduct: 'They don't know how to play it fair.' There is a case that this very firm has been reversed for, argument of a similar nature, and I assign it as misconduct and ask for a mistrial.

"THE COURT: Motion denied."

Fifth: "They employ 45,000 people, and they couldn't make room for him to do anything — maybe even delivering the messages down at 65 Market Street; you mean to tell me, ladies and gentlemen, if you have got the good will of your employee at stake that you won't at least call him up and say —

"MR. PHELPS: I am going to object to this on the same ground and cite it as misconduct. Your Honor knows what the situation is. Your Honor knows what I was foreclosed from, and I think that this is improper argument.

"THE COURT: Just a moment.

"MR. PHELPS: Your Honor knows what the situation was.

"THE COURT: Let's keep it within the confines of the evidence."

Sixth: "Now, ladies and gentlemen, isn't it interesting to you, when they've got all these pictures, where is that claims man with the rest of the pictures they didn't show? He has been around here for two weeks, and we haven't seen or heard from him.

"MR. PHELPS: Just a moment. He is implying — You told me you didn't want him this morning.

"MR. TEERLINK: Only —

"MR. PHELPS: You told me you didn't want him. I had him here at your request.

"MR. TEERLINK: Sit down and let me finish my argument.

"THE COURT: All right, gentlemen; we have a time limit. Please."

Seventh: "Does it seem ironical to you, ladies and gentlemen, that they can take aerial photographs —

"MR. PHELPS: I —

"MR. TEERLINK: Will you keep out of my argument — that they can take aerial photographs within a few hours or less than that? Imagine getting an airplane and camera equipment and start shooting photographs to defeat a claim — and rulers, when all they would have had to do — ' "

(The photographs were not taken from an airplane.)

Eighth: "Mike Sabella was lying on his back with a busted back thinking maybe they were going to do something decent for him, maybe once in a life the friendly Southern Pacific could be friendly. No, sir. All we get is a second best, a lousy evidence that they decide to bring in.

"You see, all the pictures that may show it to his advantage, you don't see them.

"MR. PHELPS: Now —

"MR. TEERLINK: They are not here.

"MR. PHELPS: I will object to that and assign it as misconduct. This is, again, characteristic of the defense, and without any evidence, without justification, and the type of thing that the Courts have said is not proper, and I object to it.

"THE COURT: Go ahead."

implications as you may draw therefrom." When counsel for plaintiff nevertheless made fresh appeals to the passion and prejudice of the jury, and defense counsel continued to object, the court once again admonished counsel for plaintiff to "stay within the confines." When counsel for plaintiff persisted in his misconduct, in the face not only of defendant's objections and motions for mistrial but also of the admonitions of the court, he evinced a studied determination to ride roughshod over any and all objections or admonitions.

Though he threw one caution after another to the wind, he now contends that defendant waived objection to any misconduct by not supplementing his repeated objections with a request that the trial court admonish the jury to disregard the misconduct.[2] No admonition, however, could cure the prejudicial effect of such misconduct as prevailed throughout this case. Accordingly, defendant's failure to request admonitions to the jury does not preclude it from challenging the misconduct on appeal. (*Hoffman v. Brandt* (1966) 65 Cal. 2d 549, 553 [55 Cal. Rptr. 417, 421 P.2d 425]; *Horn v. Atchison, T. & S. F. R.R. Co.* (1964) 61 Cal. 2d 602, 611 [39 Cal. Rptr. 721, 394 P.2d 561]; *Love v. Wolf* (1964) 226 Cal. App. 2d 378, 392 [38 Cal. Rptr. 183].) Plaintiff's counsel can hardly claim that his repeated appeals to passion and prejudice were of such little appeal that they could have been simply erased by admonitions.

Counsel for plaintiff offers a brace of alternative contentions, namely, that there was no misconduct but only colorful argument, and that in the event of any error, it was cured by the trial court's remittitur. These contentions cannot be sustained. It is

---

Ninth: "Now, what about poor Mr. Medina [a witness for defendant]? What do you think poor Mr. Medina must think when he sees and he knows what they are doing to Mike? What would happen to poor Medina if he didn't go along with it? Ever think about that? When they see how they threw him on the human trash pile, how quick would they give it to Medina if he didn't go along—

"MR. PHELPS: I object again and cite this as misconduct in view of the fact I was foreclosed from proving that isn't the fact as to what we did or what was done for this man, and I cannot stand still and listen to this, knowing what the facts are."

Tenth: "[You] can look at the sorrowful look in a man's eyes when you are taking his deposition, and they cry out to you, 'I would like to help you, Mr. Teerlink, but I can't; I've got to send him down the tubes; it is him or me,' and that is the way you see it.

"MR. PHELPS: If Your Honor please, 'down the tubes,' when this man is down—the situation is such, Your Honor please, I am foreclosed from saying t—

"MR. TEERLINK: You've said that about 14 times.

"MR. PHELPS: The ruling—

"MR. TEERLINK: You haven't given him a job; that is for sure.

"MR. PHELPS: That is just—Now, there we go again.

"If Your Honor please, instruct Mr. Teerlink to desist from that. I assign it again as misconduct and move for a mistrial in view of the offers that I made of proof.

"THE COURT: Denied. Proceed."

2. It is at least debatable that implicit in any objection to misconduct is a request that the jury be admonished to disregard it. Thus, in *Hoffman v. Brandt* (1966) 65 Cal. 2d 549, 553 [55 Cal. Rptr. 417, 421 P.2d 425], counsel objected but did not request an admonition. The trial court, however, admonished the jury on its own motion. We nevertheless held that the admonition did not cure the error.

misconduct to compare the wealth of plaintiff and defendant (*Hoffman v. Brandt, supra,* 65 Cal. 2d 549, 553; *Love v. Wolf, supra,* 226 Cal. App. 2d 378, 388–389); counsel for plaintiff did so.[3] It is misconduct to accuse defendant and defendant's counsel of suborning perjury (*Love v. Wolf, supra,* 226 Cal. App. 2d 378, 391); counsel for plaintiff did so. It is misconduct to accuse defense counsel of withholding evidence (*Keena v. United Railroads* (1925) 197 Cal. 148, 158–160 [239 P. 1061]); counsel for plaintiff did so. It is misconduct to suggest to the jurors that they measure damages by what they would take to endure plaintiff's suffering (*Horn v. Atchison, T. & S. F. R.R. Co., supra,* 61 Cal. 2d 602, 609; *Zibbell v. Southern Pac. Co.* (1911) 160 Cal. 237, 255 [116 P. 513]); counsel for plaintiff did so.[6] It is misconduct to suggest facts not in evidence that counsel knows could be contradicted by evidence that the court had excluded (*Hoffman v. Brandt, supra,* 65 Cal. 2d 549, 554); counsel for plaintiff did so.

The line of argument that defendant refused to give plaintiff a job is contradicted by the fact that plaintiff did not attempt to return to work but applied for a pension instead. We may assume, without deciding, that evidence of the pension was inadmissible.

The courtroom is a forum for the presentation of evidence and rational argument, not a stage for over mellow drama. The responsibility of a lawyer is to raise issues, not scenes, and to reason about them in nontheatrical terms. Invective, with all its theatrics, has no place in the language of the law.

When appeals to passion and prejudice may have influenced a verdict, they may have influenced it on the issue of liability as well as on the issue of damages. Hence, in such a case remittitur cannot cure the error. There is no cure but reversal for an error that impairs the right to a fair trial. The right to a fair trial includes the right to an impartial trier of fact and the correlative right to a trial free of appeals to passion and prejudice.

We take great care to excuse prospective jurors who may be subject to emotional appeals. We take great care to instruct jurors not to discuss the case with outsiders or to read about it, so that they will remain beyond the reach of influence outside the courtroom. It is a minimum propriety to guard against calculated attempts to prejudice the jury inside the courtroom, for they do violence to the substantial rights of a litigant. Still worse, they would in the long run so debase the judicial process that no one could enter a courtroom confident of a fair trial.

---

3. Referring to plaintiff, counsel said: "You saw what they did to him. You saw the thanks he got. He got just exactly what they give to any poor guy with a seventh grade education: he got nothing." About defendant, he said: "They employ 45,000 people, and they wouldn't even make room for him to do anything—maybe even delivering the messages down at 65 Market Street."

6. "And as to that 6570 days of misery he has got left, there isn't a soul in this world that would put up with what Mike Sabella is going to have to put up with, the hopelessness of it all, for a measly figure we have got down there."

Notes and Questions Regarding Putting the Case to the Jury

(1) *Closing Argument.* Upon conclusion of the evidence at trial, the attorneys have the right to present closing arguments to the jury. CCP §607(7). As *Sabella* indicates, vigorous and forceful argument is not only expected, but is proper and desirable. An attorney has the right to express opinions based upon fair deductions and reasonable inferences from the evidence given at trial. The argument need not be absolutely logical, but must be based on facts in evidence. The difference between proper and improper argument is difficult to define. Misstatements of the law or facts during argument are clearly improper, but beyond that the line is less clear. The general standards—such as the prohibition on appeals to prejudice, passions, or sympathy of the jury—provide minimal guidance at best.

An attorney has an ethical obligation to represent the interests of his or her client zealously within the bounds of the law. *See* ABA Model Rules of Professional Conduct, comment to Rule 1.3. The California Rules of Professional Conduct provide that a lawyer "shall not intentionally, recklessly, with gross negligence, or repeatedly fail to perform legal services with competence" and "with reasonable diligence in representing a client." Rule 1.1(a), 1.3(a), Cal. Rules of Prof. Conduct. "Competence" in any legal service means to apply the "(i) learning and skill, and (ii) mental, emotional, and physical ability reasonably necessary for the performance of such service." Rule 1.1(b). "Reasonable diligence" means that a lawyer acts with "commitment and dedication to the interests of the client and does not neglect or disregard . . . a legal matter entrusted to the lawyer. Rule 1.3(b). Other rules require an attorney, in presenting a matter to a tribunal, to employ such means as are only consistent with the truth and not to mislead the judge or jury by an artifice or false statement of fact or law. Bus. & Prof. Code § 6068(d); Rule 3.3, Cal. Rules of Prof. Conduct.

Did the attorney for the plaintiff is *Sabella* breach these rules? Did the attorney for the defendant? If both attorneys in *Sabella* breached ethical duties, whose conduct was less professional?

(2) *Jury Instructions.* A party is entitled upon request to correct nonargumentative jury instructions as to the law on every theory of the case which is supported by substantial evidence, whether or not that evidence was considered persuasive by the trial court. *Soule v. General Motors Corp.*, 8 Cal. 4th 548, 572, 34 Cal. Rptr. 2d 607, 882 P.2d 298 (1994). The refusal to give a jury instruction adequately covering a party's theory, where that theory is supported by substantial evidence, may be considered prejudicial error. *See Soule, supra* (collecting cases).

Jury instructions must accurately and completely state the applicable legal principles; and must not be slanted, unduly repetitious, or argumentative. The pattern jury instructions adopted by the Judicial Council and set forth in *California Civil Jury Instructions* ("CACI") are the official, approved instructions in California. *See* Rule 2.1050(e), Cal. Rules of Ct. When CACI does not contain an instruction on a point, the judge may modify a CACI instruction to submit the issue properly or use a special instruction submitted by a party, but the instruction given should be simple, brief, impartial, free from argument, and accurate.

Generally speaking, counsel for the respective parties must deliver proposed jury instructions to the trial judge, and serve them upon opposing counsel, before the first witness is sworn. CCP § 607a. Thereafter, but before commencement of closing arguments, counsel may deliver additional proposed instructions upon questions of law developed by the evidence and not disclosed by the pleadings. *Id.* Before commencement of the closing arguments, the court upon request must determine whether to give, refuse, or modify the proposed instructions; must decide what additional instructions will be given; and must advise counsel of all instructions to be given. §§ 607a, 609. Upon the jury retiring for deliberation, the trial court may, and if requested by the jury, shall, supply the jury with a written copy of the instructions. § 612.5.

(3) *Comments by Trial Judge.* A trial court judge has the authority to call and interrogate witnesses, Evidence Code § 775; and to comment on the testimony and credibility of any witness, Cal. Const., art VI, § 10. However, a judge's power to comment on the evidence is not unlimited. The judge "cannot withdraw material evidence from the jury or distort the testimony" and "must inform the jurors that they are the exclusive judges of all questions of fact and of the credibility of witnesses." *Lewis v. Bill Robertson & Sons, Inc.*, 162 Cal. App. 3d 650, 654, 208 Cal. Rptr. 699 (1984).

5. Jury Verdicts

Nonunanimous Verdicts. The jury in a civil case must consist of twelve persons, unless the parties agree upon a lesser number, but may consist of eight persons in a limited civil case if the Legislature so provides, or a lesser number if agreed upon by the parties. Cal. Const., Art. I, § 16. The California Constitution does not require a unanimous jury in civil cases; a verdict rendered by three-fourths of the jury is permitted. Cal. Const., Art. I, § 16; CCP § 618. Prior to *Resch v. Volkswagen of America, Inc.*, 36 Cal. 3d 676, 205 Cal. Rptr. 827, 685 P.2d 1178 (1984), the same nine jurors had to agree on all elements of the ultimate verdict when returning special verdicts. *See Earl v. Times-Mirror Co.*, 185 Cal. 165, 182, 196 P. 57 (1921). The *Resch* court repudiated this identical-nine rule, and requires only that any nine jurors agree on each special verdict comprising the ultimate verdict.

General Verdicts vs. Special Verdicts. The verdict of a jury must be either a general or a special verdict. CCP § 624. Unlike a general verdict, which merely implies findings on all issues in favor of the plaintiff or defendant, a special verdict presents to the jury each ultimate fact in the case. *Falls v. Superior Court*, 194 Cal. App. 3d 851, 854–55, 239 Cal. Rptr. 862 (1987). The jury must resolve all of the ultimate facts presented to it in the special verdict, so that "nothing shall remain to the court but to draw from them conclusions of law." § 624.

When Special Verdicts Are Recommended or Required. Generally, the decision whether to submit a general verdict or special verdicts to the jury is entirely in the discretion of the trial court. CCP § 625; *Hurlbut v. Sonora Community Hospital*, 207 Cal. App. 3d 388, 403, 254 Cal. Rptr. 840 (1989); *Stone v. Foster*, 106 Cal. App. 3d 334,

350, 164 Cal. Rptr. 901 (1980). Use of special verdicts is required by CCP § 625, however, in all cases in which issues of punitive damages are presented to the jury so that findings of punitive damages are separate from compensatory damages. Use of special verdicts, or of a general verdict accompanied by special findings, may be necessary in other situations. *See, e.g., Gorman v. Leftwich*, 218 Cal. App. 3d 141, 266 Cal. Rptr. 671 (1990) (Trial court abused its discretion by refusing to use requested special verdict forms with respect to calculation of past and future damages by the jury in a medical malpractice case, where the case involved the possibility of substantial future damages which under CCP § 667.7 must be paid periodically and not in a lump sum); *Daly v. General Motors Corp.*, 20 Cal. 3d 725, 743, 144 Cal. Rptr. 380, 575 P.2d 1162 (1978) (Recommending the use of special verdicts when jury is asked to apportion fault on a comparative basis).

C. Taking the Case from the Jury

1. Nonsuit, Directed Verdict, and Judgment Notwithstanding the Verdict (JNOV)

A defendant may move for a judgment of nonsuit upon completion of the plaintiff's opening statement or of the presentation of plaintiff's evidence in a jury trial. CCP § 581c(a). If the motion is granted, the judgment on nonsuit operates as an adjudication on the merits unless the court specifies otherwise. § 581c(c). If the motion is denied, the defendant still has the right to offer evidence. § 581c(a). After all parties have completed the presentation of all their evidence in a jury trial, any party may move for an order directing entry of a verdict in its favor. § 630(a). Except for this difference in timing, a directed verdict is equivalent to a nonsuit. After a jury verdict, the judge or a party against whom the verdict was rendered may move for a judgment notwithstanding the verdict. CCP § 629.

The test for entering a nonsuit, directing a verdict, and granting a motion for judgment notwithstanding the verdict, is the same, as explained in *Hauter v. Zogarts*, 14 Cal. 3d 104, 110–11, 120 Cal. Rptr. 681, 534 P.2d 377 (1975):

> The trial judge's power to grant a judgment notwithstanding the verdict is identical to his power to grant a directed verdict. The trial judge cannot reweigh the evidence, or judge the credibility of witnesses. If the evidence is conflicting or if several reasonable inferences may be drawn, the motion for judgment notwithstanding the verdict should be denied. "A motion for judgment notwithstanding the verdict of a jury may properly be granted only if it appears from the evidence, viewed in the light most favorable to the party securing the verdict, that there is no substantial evidence to support the verdict. If there is any substantial evidence, or reasonable inferences to be drawn therefrom, in support of the verdict, the motion should be denied." (*Brandenburg v. Pac. Gas & Elec. Co.* (1946) 28 Cal. 2d 282, 284 [169 P.2d 909].)

2. Motion for New Trial

The most frequently employed post-trial motion is the motion for a new trial. If granted, a new trial order authorizes a de novo trial as if the first trial never occurred, and permits a reexamination of an issue of fact in the same court after a trial and decision by a jury, court, or referee. CCP § 656. The grounds and procedures for new trial motions are set forth in CCP §§ 657–663.2. Because the right to move for a new trial is a creature of statute, the procedural steps prescribed by these statutes must be strictly followed. *Linhart v. Nelson*, 18 Cal. 3d 641, 644, 134 Cal. Rptr. 813, 557 P.2d 104 (1976). The permissible grounds for a new trial are set forth in CCP § 657, which is reproduced below.

CALIFORNIA CODE OF CIVIL PROCEDURE (2021)

Section 657. Grounds for new trial; Requisites of order granting new trial for insufficiency of evidence.

The verdict may be vacated and any other decision may be modified or vacated, in whole or in part, and a new or further trial granted on all or part of the issues, on the application of the party aggrieved, for any of the following causes, materially affecting the substantial rights of such party:

1. Irregularity in the proceedings of the court, jury or adverse party, or any order of the court or abuse of discretion by which either party was prevented from having a fair trial.

2. Misconduct of the jury; and whenever any one or more of the jurors have been induced to assent to any general or special verdict, or to a finding on any question submitted to them by the court, by a resort to the determination of chance, such misconduct may be proved by the affidavit of any one of the jurors.

3. Accident or surprise, which ordinary prudence could not have guarded against.

4. Newly discovered evidence, material for the party making the application, which he could not, with reasonable diligence, have discovered and produced at the trial.

5. Excessive or inadequate damages.

6. Insufficiency of the evidence to justify the verdict or other decision, or the verdict or other decision is against law.

7. Error in law, occurring at the trial and excepted to by the party making the application.

When a new trial is granted, on all or part of the issues, the court shall specify the ground or grounds upon which it is granted and the court's reason or reasons for granting the new trial upon each ground stated.

A new trial shall not be granted upon the ground of insufficiency of the evidence to justify the verdict or other decision, nor upon the ground of excessive or inadequate damages, unless after weighing the evidence the court is convinced from the entire record, including reasonable inferences therefrom, that the court or jury clearly should have reached a different verdict or decision.

The order passing upon and determining the motion must be made and entered as provided in Section 660 and if the motion is granted must state the ground or grounds relied upon by the court, and may contain the specification of reasons. If an order granting such motion does not contain such specification of reasons, the court must, within 10 days after filing such order, prepare, sign and file such specification of reasons in writing with the clerk. The court shall not direct the attorney for a party to prepare either or both said order and said specification of reasons.

On appeal from an order granting a new trial the order shall be affirmed if it should have been granted upon any ground stated in the motion, whether or not specified in the order or specification of reasons, except that (a) the order shall not be affirmed upon the ground of the insufficiency of the evidence to justify the verdict or other decision, or upon the ground of excessive or inadequate damages, unless such ground is stated in the order granting the motion and (b) on appeal from an order granting a new trial upon the ground of the insufficiency of the evidence to justify the verdict or other decision, or upon the ground of excessive or inadequate damages, it shall be conclusively presumed that said order as to such ground was made only for the reasons specified in said order or said specification of reasons, and such order shall be reversed as to such ground only if there is no substantial basis in the record for any of such reasons.

Notes and Questions Regarding New Trial Motions

(1) *Motion for New Trial: Statutory Grounds Exclusive.* Section 657 sets forth the exclusive grounds upon which a trial court may grant a new trial. *Linhart v. Nelson*, 18 Cal. 3d 641, 134 Cal. Rptr. 813, 557 P.2d 104 (1976). These enumerated grounds encompass both procedural errors (*e.g.*, jury misconduct and other irregularities in the proceedings) and substantive errors (*e.g.*, insufficiency of the evidence, excessive damages, and error in law) occurring during trial. A new trial may not be granted, of course, unless the error materially affects the substantial rights of the moving party—in other words, unless the error is prejudicial and not harmless. Cal. Const., Art. VI, § 13 ("No judgment shall be set aside, or new trial granted . . . unless, after an examination of the entire cause, including the evidence, the court shall be of the opinion that theerror complained of has resulted in a miscarriage of justice").

(2) *Aggrieved Party Must File Motion for New Trial.* Code of Civil Procedure sections 657 and 660 impose several limitations and requirements on motions for new trials. The power of the trial court to grant a new trial may be exercised only by following the statutory procedure and is conditioned upon the timely filing of a motion for new trial, the court being without power to order a new trial *sua sponte. Sanchez-Corea v. Bank of America*, 38 Cal. 3d 892, 215 Cal. Rptr. 679, 701 P.2d 826 (1985).

An aggrieved party must file a written notice of intention to move for a new trial within 15 days of the date of mailing of the notice of entry of judgment by the clerk or by a party, or within 180 days after entry of judgment, whichever is earliest. CCP § 659, Rule 3.1600, Cal. Rules of Court. This notice must designate the grounds upon which the motion is made. § 659. The motion for new trial can only be granted on a ground specified in the notice of intention to move for a new trial. *Malkasian v. Irwin,* 61 Cal. 2d 738, 745, 40 Cal. Rptr. 78, 394 P.2d 822 (1964); *Wagner v. Singleton,* 133 Cal. App. 3d 69, 183 Cal. Rptr. 631 (1982) (Order granting new trial on ground of misconduct of counsel held void when motion only specified ground of insufficiency of the evidence); *Neal v. Montgomery Elevator Co.,* 7 Cal. App. 4th 1194, 1198, 9 Cal. Rptr. 2d 497 (1992) (New trial granted due to material error of law ruled procedurally proper where error of law listed as one of the grounds in plaintiff's notice of motion, although not urged by plaintiff in moving papers or at oral argument).

(3) *The New Trial Order Must State Grounds and Specify Reasons.* If a motion for new trial is granted, CCP § 657 requires the trial judge to state the grounds upon which the motion was granted in the new trial order, and to specify the reasons within 10 days after the order. *See Oakland Raiders v. National Football League,* 41 Cal. 4th 624, 634–35, 61 Cal. Rptr. 3d 634, 161 P. 3d 151 (2007) (Defining "grounds" and "reasons") A new trial order which does not state grounds or specify reasons is defective but not void. *Sanchez-Corea, supra,* 38 Cal. 3d at 900. Under such circumstances, an appellate court is precluded by § 657 from affirming the order on the grounds of insufficiency of the evidence or excessive damages. *Id.,* at 905; *but see La Manna v. Stewart,* 13 Cal. 3d 413, 118 Cal. Rptr. 761, 530 P.2d 1073 (1975) (Appellate court properly considered ground of insufficiency of evidence to justify verdict despite trial court's failure to state any grounds in new trial order, where motion for new trial made solely on ground that one ground). An appellate court is also precluded from considering any other ground not designated in the motion for new trial. CCP § 657; *see Neal, supra,* 7 Cal. App. 4th at 1198.

(4) *Seventy-Five Day Limit on Trial Court's Power to Decide Motion.* Code of Civil Procedure § 660 imposes a time limit on the trial court's power to rule on a motion for new trial. After an amendment in 2018, which increased this limit from 60 to 75 days, § 660(c) provides in pertinent part:

> [T]he power of the court to rule on a motion for a new trial shall expire 75 days after the mailing of notice of entry of judgment by the clerk of the court . . . or 75 days after service on the moving party by any party of written notice of entry of judgment, whichever is earlier, or if that notice has not been given, 75 days after the filing of the first notice of intention to move for a new trial. If the motion is not determined within the 75-day period . . . the effect shall be a denial of the motion without further order of the court.

A trial court lacks jurisdiction to decide a new trial motion after the 75-day limitation imposed by CCP § 660. *Siegal v. Superior Court,* 68 Cal. 2d 97, 101, 65 Cal. Rptr. 311, 436 P.2d 311 (1968). If no determination is made within the 75-day period, the motion is deemed to have been denied. §660. A trial court also lacks jurisdiction to file the statement of grounds after the 75-day period, even though the trial court decided the motion within the 75-day limitation. *See Sanchez-Corea, supra,* 38 Cal. 3d at 901–05.

(5) *Motion an Exercise of Discretion.* Regardless of whether the grounds asserted in support of a new trial motion would constitute procedural or substantive error, the determination of the motion is addressed to the trial court's discretion. *See, e.g., Romero v. Riggs,* 24 Cal. App. 4th 117, 121, 29 Cal. Rptr. 2d 219 (1994) (Abuse of discretion standard applied to new trial granted because of insufficiency of the evidence); *Neal v. Farmers Insurance Exchange,* 21 Cal. 3d 910, 933, 148 Cal. Rptr. 389, 582 P.2d 980 (1978) (Appellant court will not reverse a proper order granting a new trial on grounds of excessive damages, or requiring a reduction of the amount as a condition of denying one, unless trial court clearly abused its discretion); *Hand Electronics, Inc. v. Snowline Joint Unified School Dist.,* 21 Cal. App. 4th 862, 871, 26 Cal. Rptr. 2d 446 (1994) (On appeal from an order granting a new trial because of misleading jury instruction, sole question is whether trial court abused its discretion).

A new trial order will not be disturbed on appeal "unless a manifest and unmistakable abuse of discretion clearly appears." *Jiminez v. Sears, Roebuck & Co.,* 4 Cal. 3d 379, 387, 93 Cal. Rptr. 769, 482 P.2d 681 (1971) (So long as a reasonable or even fairly debatable justification under law is shown for an order granting a new trial, the order will not be set aside). Why is the determination of a new trial motion asserting grounds of substantive error a matter for the trial court's discretion? Should it be? In what sense is such a motion not a matter of trial court discretion?

(6) *Insufficiency of the Evidence.* When a trial court determines a motion for new trial made upon the ground of insufficiency of the evidence, CCP §657 requires the judge to weigh the evidence and judge the credibility of witnesses. *See Dominguez v. Pantalone,* 212 Cal. App. 3d 201, 260 Cal. Rptr. 431 (1989). In so doing, the court may disbelieve witnesses and draw inferences contrary to those supporting the verdict. *Locksley v. Ungureanu,* 178 Cal. App. 3d 457, 463, 223 Cal. Rptr. 737 (1986); *Widener v. Pacific Gas & Electric Co.,* 75 Cal. App. 3d 415, 440, 142 Cal. Rptr. 304 (1977). The court may grant a new trial even though there is sufficient evidence to sustain the jury's verdict on appeal. *Candido v. Huitt,* 151 Cal. App. 3d 918, 923, 199 Cal. Rptr. 41 (1984). Nonetheless, a new trial cannot be granted "unless after weighing the evidence the court is convinced from the entire record, including reasonable inferences therefrom, that the court or jury clearly should have reached a different verdict or decision." CCP §657.

How is the standard a trial judge must employ when determining a new trial motion for insufficiency of the evidence under CCP §657 different from the standard applicable to a motion for judgment notwithstanding the verdict under CCP §629? *See Fountain Valley Chateau Blanc Homeowner's Assn. v. Department of Veterans Affairs,* 67 Cal. App. 4th 743, 79 Cal. Rptr. 2d 248 (1998). Why are these two standards different? If a trial court grants a new trial motion for insufficiency of the evidence, must it also grant an accompanying JNOV motion? If the court denies a party's new trial motion on the ground of insufficiency of the evidence, must it also deny that party's JNOV motion?

What is the standard applicable to appellate review of a trial court order granting a new trial on the basis of insufficient evidence to support the jury verdict? The Supreme Court answered this question, and several others with respect to new trial orders under CCP § 657, in *Lane v. Hughes Aircraft Co.*, 22 Cal. 4th 405, 93 Cal. Rptr. 2d 60, 993 P.2d 388 (2000). An order granting a new trial based on insufficiency of the evidence "must be sustained on appeal unless the opposing party demonstrates that no reasonable finder of fact could have found for the movant on [the trial court's] theory." *Lane, supra,* 22 Cal. 4th at 409. The reason for this deference is that the trial court, in ruling on the new trial motion, sits as an independent trier of fact. *Id.* at 412. "Therefore, the trial court's factual determinations, reflected in its decision to grant a new trial, are entitled to the same deference that an appellate court would ordinarily accord a jury's factual determinations." *Id.* The Supreme Court emphasized that "so long as the outcome is uncertain at the close of trial—that is, so long as the evidence can support a verdict if favor of either party—a properly constructed new trial order is not subject to reversal on appeal." *Id.* at 414.

(7) *Excessive Damages and Conditional New Trial Orders (Remittitur).* Section 657 also requires a trial judge to weigh the evidence and judge the credibility of witnesses when determining a motion for new trial based upon the ground of excessive or inadequate damages. In ruling on a motion for a new trial for excessive damages, the trial court does not sit in an appellate capacity "but as an independent trier of fact." *Neal v. Farmers Insurance Exchange*, 21 Cal. 3d 910, 933, 148 Cal. Rptr. 389, 582 P.2d 980 (1978) (Trial court did not abuse discretion in granting new trial motion for excessive damages where the evidence bearing on damages issue was in substantial conflict).

The trial court may, in its discretion, order a new trial limited to the issue of damages and may condition its order so that the motion is denied if the party in whose favor the verdict has been rendered consents to such reduction of damages "as the court in its independent judgment determines from the evidence to be fair and reasonable." CCP § 662.5. Such a conditional new trial procedure, commonly referred to as "remittitur," is expressly authorized by CCP § 662.5(b). Section 662.5(a) authorizes the corresponding process of "additur" for inadequate damages. *See, e.g., Marshall v. Department of Water & Power*, 219 Cal. App. 3d 1124, 1137, 268 Cal. Rptr. 559 (1990) (Jury award of $1 increased by means of additur to $100,001 after plaintiff moved for new trial).

Trial courts often utilize remittitur when damages are properly awarded but the amount is excessive, and a new trial can be avoided if the nonmoving party consents to a reduction. *See, e.g., Hasson v. Ford Motor Co.*, 32 Cal. 3d 388, 418–21, 185 Cal. Rptr. 654, 650 P.2d 1171 (1982) (Trial court required plaintiff to consent to a $1,650,000 reduction in damage award in order to avoid a new trial); *Neal v. Farmers Insurance Exchange, supra* (Jury verdict of $1.5 million remitted to $750,000); *Grimshaw v. Ford*

Motor Co., 119 Cal. App. 3d 757, 174 Cal. Rptr. 348 (1981) (Trial court required plaintiff to remit all but $3.5 million of $125 million punitive damage verdict as a condition of denial of defendant's new trial motion).

(8) *Newly Discovered Evidence.* In *Marriage of Liu*, 197 Cal. App. 3d 143, 153–54, 242 Cal. Rptr. 649 (1987), the court expressed the narrow construction typically given this ground: "In making a motion for new trial on this ground, the party seeking relief has the burden to prove that he exercised reasonable diligence to discover and produce the evidence at trial. If the party does not make this showing, the motion must be denied. Moreover, a general averment of diligence is insufficient. The moving party must state the particular acts or circumstances which establish diligence." In *Liu*, the appellant contended that a new trial should be granted because she only discovered after trial that a previously uncooperative key expert witness was now willing to testify. The court found appellant's newly discovered evidence argument meritless because she failed to explain why she could not have discovered this prior to or during trial. *Id.* at 154.

Even where the moving party successfully proves the requisite exercise of diligence, the party must also show that the newly discovered evidence is "material in the sense that it is likely to produce a different result" at the trial. *Sherman v. Kinetic Concepts, Inc.*, 67 Cal. App. 4th 1152, 79 Cal. Rptr. 2d 641 (1998); *National Elevator Services, Inc. v. Department of Industrial Relations*, 136 Cal. App. 3d 131, 138–39, 186 Cal. Rptr. 165 (1982). How might a party demonstrate the requisite "materiality" of newly discovered evidence?

(9) *Accident or Surprise.* The courts apply this ground quite narrowly to preclude a new trial based on mistake, inadvertence, or neglect by a party or her attorney. *See, e.g., In re Marriage of Liu, supra*, 197 Cal. App. 3d at 155 (citing cases).

(10) *Misconduct During Trial.* Misconduct during trial—either by the jury, judge, or the opposing counsel—is often asserted as a ground when moving for a new trial. *See, e.g., Sabella v. Southern Pacific Co.*, 70 Cal. 2d 311, 74 Cal. Rptr. 534, 449 P.2d 750 (1969) (Attorney misconduct); *Lewis v. Bill Robertson & Sons, Inc.*, 162 Cal. App. 3d 650, 208 Cal. Rptr. 699 (1984) (Improper commenting on the evidence by judge in jury trial); *Krouse v. Graham*, 19 Cal. 3d 59, 137 Cal. Rptr. 863, 562 P.2d 1022 (1977) (Juror misconduct). Any irregularities which deprive a party of a fair and impartial trial may constitute grounds for a new trial under CCP § 657(1).

(11) *Impeachment of Verdict for Juror Misconduct.* Code of Civil Procedure § 657 authorizes a new trial where the substantial rights of a party are materially affected by misconduct or irregularity in the proceedings of the jury. CCP § 657(1) & (2). Evidence Code § 1150(a), quoted below, imposes a fundamental restriction on the impeachment of a verdict for juror misconduct:

Upon an inquiry as to the validity of a verdict, any otherwise admissible evidence may be received as to statements made, or conduct, conditions, or events occurring, either within or without the jury room, of such a character as is likely to have influenced the verdict improperly. No evidence is admissible to show the effect of such statement, conduct, condition, or event upon a juror either in influencing him to assent to or dissent from the verdict or concerning the mental processes by which it was determined.

(a) *The Basic Objective/Subjective Distinction.* The distinction in Evidence Code § 1150 between proof of objectively ascertainable facts and proof of the subjective mental processes of jurors is the basic starting point with respect to impeachment of verdicts for juror misconduct. Juror declarations which describe objectively verifiable acts of misconduct are admissible to impeach a verdict; but declarations which describe individual or collective juror subjective mental process, purporting to show how the verdict was reached, are inadmissible. *People v. Hutchinson,* 71 Cal. 2d 342, 349–50, 78 Cal. Rptr. 196, 455 P.2d 132 (1969); *Maple v. Cincinnati, Inc.,* 163 Cal. App. 3d 387, 394, 209 Cal. Rptr. 451 (1985).

(b) How clear is this distinction? Does the distinction permit prejudicial error to go unremedied, even where the jurors have admitted to serious misconduct? What are the policy reasons for this distinction?

(c) Is a declaration of the foreperson admissible which evidenced a discussion among the jurors to inflate their verdict to compensate for attorney fees and income taxes? *See Tramell v. McDonnell Douglas Corp.,* 163 Cal. App. 3d 157, 172–73, 209 Cal. Rptr. 427 (1984) (Juror declarations properly admitted). Are affidavits from several jurors admissible which establish that the jury foreman advised the jury not to worry about the size of the verdict they might return because the trial judge had the power to reduce any excessive award? *See DiRosario v. Havens,* 196 Cal. App. 3d 1224, 1235–38, 242 Cal. Rptr. 423 (1987) (Juror declarations held inadmissible). Are declarations from multiple jurors admissible where they state that two jurors, who had relatives with an injury similar to that suffered by the plaintiff, discussed their relatives' injuries and rehabilitation? *See Maple v. Cincinnati, Inc.,* 163 Cal. App. 3d 387, 209 Cal. Rptr. 451 (1985) (reversing new trial order because trial court improperly admitted jury declarations). Where three of these jurors also stated that they had made up their minds about the case before deliberations? *See id.*

(d) *The Objective/Subjective Distinction and "Deliberative Error."* Juror declarations are inadmissible where they describe juror misunderstanding and misinterpretation of the law—"deliberative error" in the jury's subjective reasoning process. *See, e.g., Mesecher v. County of San Diego,* 9 Cal. App. 4th 1677, 1683, 12 Cal. Rptr. 279 (1992) (Several juror declarations which essentially stated that the jurors used a definition of battery in their deliberations which was more favorable to the plaintiff than the trial court's instructions held inadmissible); *Ford v. Bennacka,* 226 Cal. App. 3d 330, 276 Cal. Rptr. 513 (1990) (Five juror declarations that showed jury misapplied concept of comparative negligence held inadmissible).

(e) *Impeachment for Reliance on Juror Expertise or Other Outside Evidence.* Another ground frequently asserted to impeach a verdict is that the jury was improperly influenced by outside information or by jurors' recounting their own outside experiences or expertise. *See, e.g., Glage v. Hawes Firearms Co.*, 226 Cal. App. 3d 314, 276 Cal. Rptr. 430 (1990) (Juror's reference to a dictionary for the definition of a term used in an instruction constitutes misconduct); *Elsworth v. Beech Aircraft Corp.*, 37 Cal. 3d 540, 208 Cal. Rptr. 874, 691 P.2d 630 (1984) (New trial properly denied in wrongful death action against manufacturer of light plane that crashed where submitted declarations stated two jurors had remarked that they had watched, shortly before commencement of deliberations that lead to large verdict for plaintiffs, a television broadcast of a program criticizing the safety record of light aircraft); *McDonald v. Southern Pacific Transportation Co.*, 71 Cal. App. 4th 256, 83 Cal. Rptr. 2d 734 (1999) (In an action by a train brakeman for injuries suffered in a train yard, trial court erred in denying plaintiff's motion for a new trial where a juror declaration stated that another juror, a professional transportation consultant, commented at length during deliberations as to why the plaintiff's theory of how due care could have made this workplace safer was unrealistic and impractical); *Lankster v. Alpha Beta Co.*, 15 Cal. App. 4th 678, 18 Cal. Rptr. 923 (1993) (Independent investigation of facts by juror constituted misconduct).

(f) The courts often struggle with the vexing problem of to what extent should a verdict be impeachable when jurors relate their personal experiences during deliberations. Compare *Enyart v. City of Los Angeles*, 76 Cal. App. 4th 499, 90 Cal. Rptr. 2d 502 (1999) (Trial court improperly denied defendants' motion for a new trial of a negligence action based on juror misconduct where the declarations of several jurors indicated that three jurors during deliberations had expressed negative generalizations about the conduct and veracity of the defendants City and Los Angeles Police Department; declarations demonstrated that the jurors' negative attitudes were not based solely on the evidence, were the product of bias, and were prejudicial) *with Iwekaogwu v. City of Los Angeles*, 75 Cal. App. 4th 803, 89 Cal. Rptr. 2d 505 (1999) (Affirming denial of defendant City's new trial motion in an employment discrimination action, where juror declarations revealed that during deliberations one juror gave emotional descriptions of instances of discrimination he had seen as a reserve police officer).

(g) *Juror Inattentiveness.* Courts are reluctant to overturn jury verdicts on the ground of inattentiveness during trial. The Supreme Court in *Hasson v. Ford Motor Co.*, 32 Cal. 3d 388, 185 Cal. Rptr. 654, 650 P.2d 1171 (1982), surveyed numerous cases of such alleged jury misconduct—jurors falling asleep during trial, reading newspapers during trial, consuming alcoholic beverages prior to hearing evidence—and observed that not one reported case granted a new trial on that ground. *Hasson, supra*, 32 Cal. 3d at 411–12. The Hasson court itself concluded that misconduct of three jurors consisting of reading a novel and working crossword puzzles during trial proceedings was not sufficiently prejudicial so as to overturn the verdict of $11.5 million awarded plaintiffs. *Id.* at 417–18. Why are the courts so reluctant to overturn a jury verdict on the ground of juror inattentiveness, even where proven by objectively ascertainable evidence of misconduct?

(h) *Presumption of Prejudice When Jury Misconduct Proven.* Proof of jury misconduct does not automatically require a new trial. The complaining party must also establish prejudice as a result of the misconduct. *Hasson v. Ford Motor Co., supra.* "Prejudice exists if it is reasonably probable that a result more favorable to the complaining party would have been achieved in the absence of the misconduct." *Id.* at 415. Proof of juror misconduct does, however, give rise to a presumption of prejudice. This presumption "may be rebutted by an affirmative evidentiary showing that prejudice does not exist or by a reviewing court's examination of the entire record to determine whether there is a reasonable probability of actual harm to the complaining party resulting from the misconduct." *Id.* at 417 (citing cases). Some of the factors to be considered "are the strength of the evidence that the misconduct occurred, the nature and seriousness of the misconduct, and the probability that actual prejudice may have ensued." *Id.*

(i) *Juror Misconduct During Voir Dire.* The intentional concealment during voir dire of bias, belief, or state of mind which prevents a juror from following the court's instructions and acting in an impartial manner constitutes misconduct. *See, e.g., Weathers v. Kaiser Foundation Hospitals,* 5 Cal. 3d 98, 95 Cal. Rptr. 516, 485 P.2d 1132 (1971) (Intentional concealment of racial prejudice against plaintiffs and bias in favor of defendant hospital held misconduct); *Wiley v. Southern Pacific Transportation Co.,* 220 Cal. App. 3d 177, 269 Cal. Rptr. 240 (1990) (Intentional concealment of juror's status as the defendant in similar lawsuit held misconduct); *Tapia v. Barker,* 160 Cal. App. 3d 761, 206 Cal. Rptr. 803 (1984) (Concealed prejudice against plaintiffs Mexican background and against awarding damages for pain and suffering, both of which were biases the jurors had denied on voir dire, constituted misconduct); *Smith v. Covell,* 100 Cal. App. 3d 947, 954–55, 161 Cal. Rptr. 377 (1980) (Juror's silence concealed his bias against high verdicts).

(j) *No-Knowledge Declaration.* A party who moves for a new trial on the ground of juror improprieties must file a "no-knowledge" declaration which states that neither the attorney nor the client was aware of the alleged misconduct prior to the verdict. *Weathers v. Kaiser Foundation Hospitals,* 5 Cal. 3d 98, 103, 95 Cal. Rptr. 516, 485 P.2d 1132 (1971); *Wiley v. Southern Pacific Transportation Co.,* 220 Cal. App. 3d 177, 186–87, 269 Cal. Rptr. 240 (1990) (citing cases). What is the purpose of this "no-knowledge" declaration?

(12) *Federal Court Grounds for New Trial Motions Compared.* Rule 59(a) of the Federal Rules of Civil Procedure authorizes a federal trial judge to grant a new trial "for any reason for which a new trial has heretofore been granted in an action at law in federal court." This broad authority permits a federal district court to order a new trial on grounds such as insufficiency of the evidence to support the verdict, excessive damages, newly discovered evidence, misconduct of jury or opposing counsel, and other prejudicial irregularities in the proceedings. *See generally* Wright, Miller, and Kane, *Federal Practice and Procedure: Civil* 2d §§ 2805–2810 (1995 & 2011 Supp.).

(a) The federal district courts commonly employ some variant of the "verdict-against-the-great-weight-of-the-evidence" standard when determining the insufficiency of the evidence to support a verdict. *See, e.g., Eyre v. McDonough Power Equipment, Inc.*, 755 F.2d 416, 420 (5th Cir. 1985) (District court empowered to grant motion for new trial when "verdict is against the great—but not merely the greater—weight of the evidence"); *Brown v. McGraw-Edison Co.*, 736 F.2d 609, 616–17 (10th Cir. 1984) (New trial standard is whether the verdict is "clearly, decidedly, or overwhelmingly against the weight of the evidence"). How, and why, is this different than the California standard?

(b) The federal courts may also grant a new trial on the ground of excessive damages, and may condition this new trial upon a remittitur. *See, e.g., Gumbs v. Pueblo International, Inc.*, 823 F.2d 768 (3d Cir. 1987); *United States v. 47.14 Acres of Land*, 674 F.2d 722 (8th Cir. 1982); *see also* Irene Sann, Note, *Remittitur Practice in the Federal Courts*, 76 Colum. L. Rev. 299 (1976). However, federal judges lack the authority to grant a new trial for inadequate damages conditioned upon the defendant's consent to an increase in damages, because such an additur is viewed as an impermissible invasion of the province of the jury and therefore precluded by the Seventh Amendment to the U.S. Constitution. *See Dimick v. Schiedt*, 293 U.S. 474, 55 S. Ct. 296, 79 L. Ed. 603 (1935).

(13) *Federal Procedures for New Trial Compared.* There are some significant differences in the procedures governing new trial motions in the federal courts as opposed to in the California state courts. A party has 28 days after entry of judgment to serve a motion for new trial in federal court under federal Rule 59(b), as opposed to 15 days under CCP § 659. More importantly, a federal district judge has power to order a new trial of its own initiative within this 28-day period. Rule 59(d), F.R.C.P. When a party has made a timely motion, the court may order a new trial for a reason not raised in the motion. *Id.* In such circumstances, federal Rule 59(d) requires the district judge to specify the grounds upon which the new trial is granted, although apparently with less particularity than CCP § 657 requires of a state court judge for new trial orders generally. *See Gilliland v. Lyons*, 278 F.2d 56, 59 (9th Cir. 1960) (As a general rule, no reasons need be stated by the trial court in an order granting a party's motion for new trial). Unlike the 75-day period in CCP § 660, federal Rule 59 does not impose any time limit on the district court's power to rule on a party's new trial motion.

Chapter IX

Appeals and Writs

A. Appeals

1. Appealable Judgments and Orders

CALIFORNIA CODE OF CIVIL PROCEDURE (2021)

Section 904.1. Judgments and orders that may be appealed.

(a) An appeal, other than in a limited civil case, is to the court of appeal. An appeal, other than in a limited civil case, may be taken from any of the following:

(1) From a judgment, except (A) an interlocutory judgment, other than as provided in paragraphs (8), (9), and (11), or (B) a judgment of contempt that is made final and conclusive by Section 1222.

(2) From an order made after a judgment made appealable by paragraph (1).

(3) From an order granting a motion to quash service of summons or granting a motion to stay the action on the ground of inconvenient forum, or from a written order of dismissal under Section 581d following an order granting a motion to dismiss the action on the ground of inconvenient forum.

(4) From an order granting a new trial or denying a motion for judgment notwithstanding the verdict.

(5) From an order discharging or refusing to discharge an attachment or granting a right to attach order.

(6) From an order granting or dissolving an injunction, or refusing to grant or dissolve an injunction.

(7) From an order appointing a receiver.

(8) From an interlocutory judgment, order, or decree, hereafter made or entered in an action to redeem real or personal property from a mortgage thereof, or a lien thereon, determining the right to redeem and directing an accounting.

(9) From an interlocutory judgment in an action for partition determining the rights and interests of the respective parties and directing partition to be made.

(10) From an order made appealable by the provisions of the Probate Code or the Family Code.

(11) From an interlocutory judgment directing payment of monetary sanctions by a party or an attorney for a party if the amount exceeds five thousand dollars ($5,000).

(12) From an order directing payment of monetary sanctions by a party or an attorney for a party if the amount exceeds five thousand dollars ($5,000).

(13) From an order granting or denying a special motion to strike under Section 425.16.

(14) From a final order or judgment in a bifurcated proceeding regarding child custody or visitation rights.

(b) Sanction orders or judgments of five thousand dollars ($5,000) or less against a party or an attorney for a party may be reviewed on an appeal by that party after entry of final judgment in the main action, or, at the discretion of the court of appeal, may be reviewed upon petition for an extraordinary writ.

Notes and Questions Regarding Appealable Decisions

(1) Generally speaking, the right to appeal is governed by statute. Code of Civil Procedure § 904.1, reproduced above, sets forth the statutory authority for appeals from a superior court in unlimited civil cases. Section 904.2 delineates when an appeal may be taken to the appellate division of the superior court in a limited civil case; § 904.5, by reference to §§ 116.710–.795, indicates when an appeal may be taken from a small claims court; §§ 1294 and 1294.2 specify appealable orders in arbitration; and a few other statutes contain special appeal provisions, *e.g.*, Family Code § 2025; CCP § 597. However, the statement often repeated by the courts — that "the right to appeal is wholly statutory," e.g., *UAP-Columbus JV 326132 v. Nesbitt*, 234 Cal. App. 3d 1028, 1034, 285 Cal. Rptr. 856 (1991); Kinoshita v. Horio, 186 Cal. App. 3d 959, 962, 231 Cal. Rptr. 241 (1986) — is misleading. The California courts permit appeals in certain circumstances despite the lack of statutory authority. These nonstatutory bases for appeal are discussed below.

(2) *The One-Final-Judgment-Rule.* California supposedly follows the one-final-judgment-rule, the essence of which is that an appeal lies only from a final judgment which terminates the proceeding in the lower court by completely disposing of the matter in controversy. *See, e.g.,* *Kinoshita v. Horio*, 186 Cal. App. 3d 959, 963, 231 Cal. Rptr. 241 (1986); *Bank of America National Trust & Savings Ass'n v. Superior Court*, 20 Cal. 2d 697, 701, 128 P.2d 357 (1942). Essentially, a judgment is "final," so as to be appealable, when no further judicial action by the court is essential to the final determination of the rights of the parties to the action. *UAP-Columbus JV 326132 v. Nesbitt*, 234 Cal. App. 3d 1028, 1035, 285 Cal. Rptr. 856 (1991). "It is not the form of the decree but the substance and effect of the adjudication which is determinative. As a general test, which must be adapted to the particular circumstances of the individual case, it may be said that where no issue is left for future consideration except the fact of compliance or noncompliance with the terms of the first decree, that decree is final. . . ." *Lyon v. Goss*, 19 Cal. 2d 659, 670, 123 P.2d 11 (1942).

As a general test of whether a trial court's decree is appealable or not, the one-final-judgment-rule is obviously inaccurate. Code of Civil Procedure § 904.1 authorizes appeals from several non-final (or "interlocutory") orders, such as orders granting or refusing to grant a preliminary injunction and certain sanction orders. CCP § 904.1(a) (6), (8)–(12). Moreover, as discussed below, the California courts have developed significant nonstatutory exceptions to the rule.

(3) *Judge-Made Exceptions to Statutory One-Final-Judgment-Rule.* There are at least two judicially created exceptions to the one-final-judgment-rule.

(a) *Ruling on Collateral Matter.* Perhaps the most frequently utilized exception is a ruling on a collateral matter, which has been defined by the California Supreme Court as follows: "When a court renders an interlocutory order collateral to the main issue, dispositive of the rights of the parties in relation to the collateral matter, and directing payment of money or performance of an act, direct appeal may be taken. . . . This constitutes a necessary exception to the one final judgment rule. Such a determination is substantially the same as a final judgment in an independent proceeding." *In re Marriage of Skelley*, 18 Cal. 3d 365, 368, 134 Cal. Rptr. 197, 556 P.2d 297 (1976).

The courts have applied this exception to permit immediate appeal of interlocutory orders in a variety of circumstances, including certain orders for payment of money sanctions, *I.J. Weinrot & Son, Inc. v. Jackson*, 40 Cal. 3d 327, 331, 220 Cal. Rptr. 103, 708 P.2d 682 (1985); and orders reducing temporary spousal support, *In re Marriage of Skelly, supra.* Some courts do not always require, for this exception to apply, that the collateral order direct the payment of money or the performance of an act. *See, e.g., Truck Ins. Exchange v. Fireman's Fund Ins. Co.*, 6 Cal. App. 4th 1050, 1052–53, n.1, 8 Cal. Rptr. 2d 228 (1992) (Order disqualifying attorney is immediately appealable as collateral matter); *Meehan v. Hopps*, 45 Cal. 2d 213, 216–17, 288 P.2d 267 (1955).

But most courts conclude that judicially compelled payment of money or performance of an act was an essential prerequisite. *See, e.g, Conservatorship of Rich*, 46 Cal. App. 4th 1233, 54 Cal. Rptr. 2d 459 (1996) (A superior court order refusing to allow substitution of attorneys was not appealable under the collateral matter doctrine); *Ponce-Bran v. Trustees of the California State Univ. and Colleges*, 48 Cal. App. 4th 1656, 56 Cal. Rptr. 2d 358 (1996) (Trial court's order denying a motion to appoint counsel was not appealable under the collateral order doctrine because the order did not direct the payment of money or the performance of an act); *Samuel v. Stevedoring Services*, 24 Cal. App. 4th 414, 418, 29 Cal. Rptr. 2d 420 (1994) (After surveying prior Supreme Court decisions, collateral order doctrine held limited to situations where trial court orders either payment of money or performance of some act).

(b) *Judgment Final as to One Party.* When litigation involves multiple parties and a judgment is entered which leaves no issue to be determined as to one party, that party may immediately appeal that judgment even though the litigation is not final as to other parties. E.g., *Justus v. Atchison*, 19 Cal. 3d 564, 568, 139 Cal. Rptr. 97, 565 P.2d 122 (1977) (Dismissal of all causes of action pleaded by one of two plaintiffs constitutes appealable judgment even though remaining plaintiff had joined in some of these causes of action), *disapproved on another point*, *Ochoa v. Superior Court*, 39 Cal. 3d 159, 171, 216 Cal. Rptr. 661, 703 P.2d 1 (1985); *Hydrotech Systems, Ltd. v. Oasis*

Waterpark, 52 Cal. 3d 988, 993, n.3, 277 Cal. Rptr. 517, 803 P.2d 370 (1991) (Order dismissing fewer than all defendants from an action is a final judgment as to them, and thus is appealable). This exception to the one-final-judgment-rule apparently is the rationale for numerous holdings that an order denying a motion to certify a class action is appealable. E.g., *Richmond v. Dart Industries, Inc.*, 29 Cal. 3d 462, 470, 174 Cal. Rptr. 515, 629 P.2d 23 (1981); *Daar v. Yellow Cab Co.*, 67 Cal. 2d 695, 699, 63 Cal. Rptr. 724, 433 P.2d 732 (1967) (Demurrer sustained as to class action allegations "is tantamount to a dismissal of the action as to all members of the class other than plaintiff").

(4) *Stays Pending Appeal.* Code of Civil Procedure § 916(a) states that the perfecting of an appeal (*i.e.*, the timely filing the notice of appeal) automatically stays enforcement of the trial court's judgment. However, the numerous exceptions contained in CCP §§ 917.1–917.9 swallow up this general rule. For example, a judgment for money damages will not be stayed pending appeal "unless an undertaking is given." § 917.1(a). An "undertaking" means the furnishing of some type of authorized security, such as a bond by a surety insurer pursuant to CCP § 995.310, or depositing money or negotiable instruments into court pursuant to CCP § 995.710. The amount of the required security is 1½ to 2 times the amount of the money judgment, depending on the type of security furnished. § 917.1(b). The filing of a notice of appeal does automatically stay enforcement of several common types of judgments under the general rule, including appeals from mandatory injunctions and, pursuant to CCP § 995.220, judgments against public entities and public officers.

2. Time Limitations for Appeals

General Time Limits. Rules 8.104(a)–(f) of the California Rules of Court set forth the general time limitations for civil appeals from superior court:

(a) *Normal time.*

    (1) Unless a statute or rules 8.108, 8.702, or 8.712 provides otherwise, a notice of appeal must be filed on or before the earliest of:

        (A) 60 days after the superior court clerk serves the party filing the notice of appeal with a document entitled "Notice of Entry" of judgment or a filed-endorsed copy of the judgment, showing the date either was served;

        (B) 60 days after the party filing the notice of appeal serves or is served by a party with a document entitled "Notice of Entry" of judgment or a filed-endorsed copy of the judgment, accompanied by proof of service; or

        (C) 180 days after entry of judgment.

    (2) Service under (1)(A) and (B) may be by any method permitted by the Code of Civil Procedure, including electronic service when permitted under Code of Civil Procedure section 1010.6 and rules 2.250–2.261.

    (3) If the parties stipulated in the trial court under Code of Civil Procedure section 1019.5 to waive notice of the court order being appealed, the time to appeal under (1)(C) applies unless the court or a party serves notice of entry

of judgment or a filed-endorsed copy of the judgment to start the time period under (1)(A) or (B).

(b) *No extension of time; late notice of appeal.* * * * If a notice of appeal is filed late, the reviewing court must dismiss the appeal.

* * *

(d) *Premature notice of appeal.* (1) A notice of appeal file after judgment is rendered but before it is entered is valid and is treated as filed immediately after entry of judgment. (2) The reviewing court may treat a notice of appeal file before the superior court has announced its intended ruling, but before it has rendered judgment, as filed immediately after entry of judgment.

(e) *Appealable order.* As used in subdivision (a) and (d), "judgment" includes an appealable order if appeal is from an appealable order.

In the usual civil case where a party serves the notice of entry of judgment, Rule 8.104(a)(1)(B) provides the relevant time limitation. Rule 8.104(a)(1)(A) is more likely to apply in dissolution of marriage cases, where superior court clerks are required to serve the notice of entry. *See* CCP § 664.5; Rule 5.413, Cal. Rules of Ct. Rule 8.104(c) contains specific definitions of what constitutes entry of judgment or an appealable order based on the procedure followed by the trial court, and should be read closely.

Late Appeals. The time for taking an appeal is mandatory. An appellate court has no jurisdiction to consider an appeal taken after the applicable limitation period has expired. Rule 8.104(b); *see Sharp v. Union Pacific Railroad Co.*, 8 Cal. App. 4th 357, 361, 9 Cal. Rptr. 2d 925 (1992) ("[N]either mistake, inadvertence, accident, misfortune, estoppel nor waiver can afford relief from the jurisdictional necessity of filing a timely notice of appeal"); *Delmonico v. Laidlaw Waste Systems, Inc.*, 5 Cal. App. 4th 81, 6 Cal. Rptr. 2d 599 (1992) (Appeal untimely when not filed within 60 days after service of notice of entry of judgment, pursuant to Rule 8.104(a)(2), despite fact that notice stated incorrect date of entry of judgment). The time limits for filing a notice of appeal set forth Rule 8.104(a) must be closely observed, and will only be extended as provided by Rule 8.108 or an applicable statute.

Extensions for Postjudgment Motions. Rule 8.108 provides extensions of time in which to file a notice of appeal when a party challenges a judgment by filing a notice of intention to move for a new trial or to vacate a judgment, moves for a judgment notwithstanding the verdict, or moves to reconsider an appealable order. Revised Rule 8.108 must be read closely to determine the various circumstances in which the time to appeal is increased due to the filing of certain postjudgment motions.

Cross-Appeals. The first appeal filed in a case is the "appeal;" any subsequent appeals by any party are "cross-appeals." *See* Rule 8.108(g), Cal. Rules of Ct. Rule 8.108(g), which deals with cross-appeals, provides as follows:

(1) If an appellant timely appeals from a judgment or appealable order, the time for any other party to appeal from the same judgment or order is extended until 20 days after the superior court clerk serves notification of the first appeal. (2) If an appellant timely appeals from an order granting a motion

for new trial, an order granting—within 150 days after entry of judgment—a motion to vacate the judgment, or a judgment notwithstanding the verdict, the time for any other party to appeal from the original judgment or from an order denying a motion for judgment notwithstanding the verdict is extended until 20 days after the clerk serves notification of the first appeal.

3. Preserving Error for Appeal

The appellant has the responsibility for preserving an error for appeal by making necessary objections or taking other appropriate actions during the trial court proceedings. Generally, an issue must be raised in the trial court to be argued on appeal. *See, e.g., North Coast Business Park v. Nielsen Construction Co.*, 17 Cal. App. 4th 22, 28–32, 21 Cal. Rptr. 2d 104 (1993). Likewise, the theory upon which a case is tried must be adhered to on appeal. *See, e.g., Id.*; *Ernst v. Searle*, 218 Cal. 233, 240–41, 22 P.2d 715 (1933); *Frink v. Prod*, 31 Cal. 3d 166, 170, 181 Cal. Rptr. 893, 643 P.2d 476 (1982). One major but ill-defined exception is that issues of law, or new legal theories based on undisputed facts, may be raised for the first time on appeal. E.g., *Ward v. Taggart*, 51 Cal. 2d 736, 742, 336 P.2d 534 (1959) (Although facts pleaded and proved by plaintiff do not sustain the judgment on the theory of tort advanced in the trial court, they are sufficient under the quasi-contract unjust enrichment theory advanced on appeal); *Fisher v. City of Berkeley*, 37 Cal. 3d 644, 654, n.3, 209 Cal. Rptr. 682, 693 P.2d 261 (1984) (Supreme Court considers antitrust issues with respect to validity of rent control ordinance even though raised for first time on appeal, because based on undisputed facts and involves question of great public importance).

Not only must an issue be raised in the trial court, but error must be preserved for appellate review by an appropriate challenge during the trial proceedings. *Doers v. Golden Gate Bridge District*, 23 Cal. 3d 180, 184–85, n.3, 151 Cal. Rptr. 837, 588 P.2d 1261 (1979) (Appellate courts will not consider procedural errors where an objection could have been but was not presented to the lower court, or where acquiescence constitutes waiver or estoppel). Failure to register a timely objection in the proper manner generally waives the issue for appeal. *Id.*; CCP § 353(a) (No appellate consideration of erroneous admission of evidence unless record contains objection with specific grounds); *but see, e.g.,* CCP § 647 (List of trial court orders to which exception is deemed to be made); *Myers Building Industries, Ltd. v. Interface Technology, Inc.*, 13 Cal. App. 4th 949, 957, n.3, 17 Cal. Rptr. 2d 242 (1993) (Court raises issue regarding special verdicts on own motion because of due process consideration, despite lack of objection); *Consolidated Theatres, Inc. v. Theatrical Stage Employees Union*, 69 Cal. 2d 713, 721, 73 Cal. Rptr. 213, 447 P.2d 325 (1968) (Failure to object to subject matter jurisdiction in the trial court does not preclude raising it for first time on appeal).

Some trial errors require additional procedural steps, such as a motion to strike, to preserve them for appeal. E.g., *Sabella v. Southern Pacific Co.*, 70 Cal. 2d 311, 74

Cal. Rptr. 534, 449 P.2d 750 (1969) (Party must both object and request that jury be admonished to preserve for appeal issues of attorney misconduct during closing argument); CCP § 657(5) (Claim of excessive or inadequate damages cannot be reviewed on appeal unless first urged as error in a timely motion for new trial); CCP § 437c(b) & (d) (Objections to form and competency of declarations, and other evidentiary objections, deemed waived unless made at summary judgment hearing).

4. Standards of Appellate Review

The term "appellate standard of review" refers to the degree of deference an appellate court must grant a particular type of trial court ruling. Generally, an appellate court must apply one of three available standards of review in assessing the correctness of a trial court determination: the substantial evidence rule, independent (de novo) review, or abuse of discretion.

Substantial Evidence Rule. An appellate court must apply the "substantial evidence rule" when reviewing a trial court's determination of an issue of fact, whether in a jury or nonjury trial, based on whether there was sufficient evidence to support the determination. E.g., *Alderson v. Alderson*, 180 Cal. App. 3d 450, 465, 225 Cal. Rptr. 610 (1986); *Tillery v. Richland*, 158 Cal. App. 3d 957, 962–63, 205 Cal. Rptr. 191 (1984). This standard is usually stated as follows:

> In reviewing the evidence on . . . appeal all conflicts must be resolved in favor of the respondent, and all legitimate and reasonable inferences indulged in to uphold the verdict if possible. It is an elementary, but often overlooked principle of law, that when a verdict is attacked as being unsupported, the power of the appellate court begins and ends with a determination as to whether there is any substantial evidence, contradicted or uncontradicted, which will support the conclusion reached by the jury. When two or more inferences can be reasonably deduced from the facts, the reviewing court is without power to substituted its deductions for those of the trial court.

Crawford v. Southern Pacific Co., 3 Cal. 2d 427, 429, 45 P.2d 183 (1935).

Independent (De Novo) Review. An appellate court gives no deference to a trial court's determination of a pure question of law, but must engage in an independent ("de novo") review of the issue. *See, e.g., Parsons v. Bristol Development Co.*, 62 Cal. 2d 861, 865–66, 44 Cal. Rptr. 767, 402 P.2d 839 (1965); *Stratton v. First National Life Insurance Co.*, 210 Cal. App. 3d 1071, 1083, 258 Cal. Rptr. 721 (1989). What constitutes a pure question of law? How can an appellant persuade the reviewing court that an issue is one of law as opposed to one of fact? What factors will the court consider in making this distinction? Why is it important for an appellant to have the appellate court characterize an issue as one of law?

Abuse of Discretion. A wide variety of decisions are, by law, committed to the discretion of the trial court. The appropriate standard of appellate review of such decisions is "abuse of discretion." What, precisely, does this standard mean? A typical general definition was stated in *Shamblin v. Brattain*, 44 Cal. 3d 474, 478–79, 243 Cal. Rptr. 902, 749 P.2d 339 (1988): "The appropriate test for abuse of discretion is whether the trial court exceeded the bounds of reason. When two or more inferences can reasonably be deduced from the facts, the reviewing court has no authority to substitute its decision for that of the trial court." The abuse of discretion standard may overlap with the other appellate standards of review. Why?

In making a discretionary decision, a trial court must apply the correct legal standards and follow the proper procedure. *See, e.g., Dockery v. Hyatt*, 169 Cal. App. 3d 830, 215 Cal. Rptr. 488 (1985); *Bartling v. Glendale Adventist Medical Center*, 184 Cal. App. 3d 97, 228 Cal. Rptr. 847 (1986). The factual bases for the trial court's exercise of discretion must be supported by substantial evidence. *See, e.g., Westside Community for Independent Living, Inc. v. Obledo*, 33 Cal. 3d 348, 188 Cal. Rptr. 873, 657 P.2d 365 (1983); *Marriage of Connolly*, 23 Cal. 3d 590, 598, 153 Cal. Rptr. 423, 591 P.2d 911 (1979). Likewise, for example, although the trial court's determination of the balance of harm for a preliminary injunction is reviewed on appeal for abuse of discretion, the trial court's interpretation of a statute is a matter of law reviewed de novo. *See, e.g., Department of Fish & Game v. Anderson-Cottonwood Irrigation Dist.*, 8 Cal. App. 4th 1554, 11 Cal. Rptr. 2d 222 (1992); *Thornton v. Carlson*, 4 Cal. App. 4th 1249, 6 Cal. Rptr. 2d 375 (1992).

5. The Prejudicial Error Rule

A judgment or order is presumed to be correct; error must be affirmatively shown by the appellant. *Denham v. Superior Court*, 2 Cal. 3d 557, 564, 86 Cal. Rptr. 65, 468 P.2d 193 (1970). Even where error is proven on appeal a reversal is not automatic. The appellate court will reverse or modify only for "prejudicial" error (as opposed to "harmless" error). Consequently, an appellant not only has the burden to prove error, but must also demonstrate that the error is prejudicial. E.g., *Soule v. General Motors Corp.*, 8 Cal. 4th 548, 34 Cal. Rptr. 2d 607, 882 P.2d 298 (1994) (Erroneous refusal of proffered jury instruction not automatically reversible error); *Pool v. City of Oakland*, 42 Cal. 3d 1051, 1069, 232 Cal. Rptr. 528, 728 P.2d 1163 (1986) (Defendant must prove instructional error caused prejudice).

Prejudicial Error Rule. The "prejudicial error" rule is based on Article VI, § 13, of the California Constitution, as well as statutes such as Code of Civil Procedure § 475 and Evidence Code §§ 353, 354. The most common judicial statement of the rule comes from *People v. Watson*, 46 Cal. 2d 818, 836, 299 P.2d 243 (1953), quoting portions of Article VI, § 13:

> A "miscarriage of justice" should be declared only when the court, "after an examination of the entire cause, including the evidence," is of the opinion that it is reasonably probable that a result more favorable to the appealing party would have been reached in the absence of the error.* * * The test is necessarily based upon reasonable probabilities rather than upon mere

possibilities; otherwise the entire purpose of the constitutional provision would be defeated.

What constitutes "prejudicial," as opposed to "harmless," error? What factors should an appellate court consider in determining whether it is "reasonably probable" that a trial judge or jury would have reached a result more favorable to the appealing party in the absence of error?

Prejudice Per Se. A few types of error are considered "reversible per se" such that prejudice is conclusively presumed and need not be proven. These include denial of the right to a jury trial, e.g., *Selby Constructors v. McCarthy*, 91 Cal. App. 3d 517, 527, 154 Cal. Rptr. 164 (1979) (Denial of right to jury trial is reversible error per se, without the need to demonstrate actual prejudice); undue restriction on right of cross-examination, e.g., *Fremont Indemnity Co. v. Workers' Compensation Appeals Bd.*, 153 Cal. App. 3d 965, 971, 200 Cal. Rptr. 762 (1984); erroneous sustaining of demurrer without leave to amend, e.g., *Deeter v. Angus*, 179 Cal. App. 3d 241, 251, 224 Cal. Rptr. 801 (1986); and an award of punitive damages entered without evidence of the defendant's financial condition. *See Adams v. Murakami*, 54 Cal. 3d 105, 284 Cal. Rptr. 318, 813 P.2d 1348 (1991).

6. Stipulated Reversals

Prior to 2000, an appellate court's power to reverse or vacate a trial court's judgment when the parties reached a stipulation as a condition of a proposed settlement of a pending appeal was governed by the judicial rule set forth in *Neary v. Regents of the University of California*, 3 Cal. 4th 273, 10 Cal. Rptr. 2d 859, 834 P.2d 119 (1992). The *Neary* court had held that "when the parties to an action agree to settle their dispute and as a part of their settlement stipulate to a reversal of the trial court judgment, the Court of Appeal should grant their request for the stipulated reversal absent a showing of extraordinary circumstances that warrant an exception to this general rule." *Id.* at 284. The *Neary* court emphasized that this presumption in favor of stipulated reversal to effectuate settlement was strong, and that the extraordinary circumstances exception was narrow. *Id.*

However, the judicial rule set forth in *Neary* has been superceded by the Legislature. Effective January 1, 2000, CCP § 128(a)(8) was amended to read:

An appellate court shall not reverse or vacate a duly entered judgment upon an agreement or stipulation of the parties unless the court finds both of the following: (A) There is no reasonable possibility that the interests of non-parties or the public will be adversely affected by the reversal. (B) the reasons of the parties for requesting reversal outweigh the erosion of public trust that may result from the nullification of a judgment and the risk that the availability of stipulated reversal will reduce the incentive for pretrial settlement.

The express purpose of amended CCP § 128(a)(8) was to overrule the *Neary* rule and to instead follow the federal court view of stipulated reversals set forth in *U.S. Bancorp Co. v. Bonner Mall Partnership*, 513 U.S. 18, 115 S. Ct. 386, 130 L. Ed. 2d 233 (1994). *See* Assembly Committee on Judiciary, *Analysis of Assembly Bill 1676 (1999–2000 Reg. Sess.)*. In *Bancorp*, the U.S. Supreme Court held that, in the absence of exceptional circumstances, settlement during appeal does not justify vacatur of the judgment under review. The court specifically ruled that the requisite "exceptional circumstances do not include the mere fact that the settlement provides for a vacatur." *Bancorp, supra*, 513 U.S. at 29. The court noted that judicial precedents are valuable to the legal community as a whole, and "are not merely the property of private litigants and should stand unless a court concludes that the public interest would be served by a vacatur." *Id.* at 26. The *Bancorp* court also rejected facilitation of settlement as a policy justification for stipulated vacatur. *Id.* at 27–29.

B. Extraordinary Writs

Omaha Indemnity Co. v. Superior Court

Court of Appeal of California, Second Appellate District

209 Cal. App. 3d 1266, 258 Cal. Rptr. 66 (1989)

GILBERT, JUSTICE.

An attorney files a writ petition with the Court of Appeal pointing out an apparent error of the trial court. The Court of Appeal summarily denies the petition. The bewildered attorney asks, "Why?"

If this case does not answer the question, we hope the following rule will at least assuage counsel's frustration: Error by the trial judge does not of itself ensure that a writ petition will be granted. A remedy will not be deemed inadequate merely because additional time and effort would be consumed by its being pursued through the ordinary course of the law.

In this action, plaintiffs are suing defendants for negligence. They are also suing defendants' insurance company in a cause of action for declaratory relief. Plaintiffs claim that they are third party beneficiaries of this insurance contract. The trial court has denied the motion of the insurance company to sever the declaratory relief cause of action, and the insurance company therefore seeks relief by way of extraordinary writ. We initially denied the writ, but after our Supreme Court directed us to issue an alternative writ, we shall now grant a writ of mandate.

BACKGROUND

Real parties Frank and Margaret Greinke owned rental property in the City of Santa Maria. In July of 1980, the Greinkes leased the premises to K. R. Trefts and Patricia M. Trefts. The lease agreement required the Trefts to purchase a general liability insurance policy for the mutual benefit of landlord and tenant. In July of 1982, Omaha

Indemnity Company, an insurance company, issued a general liability policy to the Trefts.

The Greinkes claim that, on or about July 17, 1986, they became aware of damage to their property caused by an oil spill. They contend that the oil spill occurred during the Trefts' occupation of the property. The Greinkes demanded that Omaha compensate them, under the terms of the insurance policy, for the damage to the property. Omaha has purportedly denied coverage under the policy.

On March 14, 1988, the Greinkes sued the Trefts for damage resulting from the oil spill. They also sued Omaha for declaratory relief of their rights under the terms of the insurance contract.

Omaha demurred to the declaratory relief cause of action. In its demurrer it asserted that the Greinkes were not parties to the contract of insurance and, therefore, had no standing to pursue a claim for declaratory relief. It contended that the Greinkes had alleged neither interest in the insurance policy nor a denial of coverage. Thus, Omaha reasoned that there is no case or controversy pending against it.

The trial court was correct in overruling the demurrer. The Greinkes allege that they are the intended beneficiaries of the insurance policy and that Omaha had denied them coverage. In such instances, an action for declaratory relief is appropriate.

In the alternative, Omaha moved to sever the declaratory relief action from the tort lawsuit. Omaha claimed that it would suffer prejudice should the lawsuit against both itself and the Trefts go forward. Further, it pointed out that severance would promote judicial economy in that there would be no need to try the declaratory relief action should the tenants be found not liable.

Although Omaha has requested our review of this ruling, it has neglected to supply us with a copy of the reporter's transcript. This did not simplify our task of review.

On August 2, 1988, we denied a petition for writ of mandate. On September 29, 1988, the Supreme Court granted a petition for review. It then ordered the case retransferred to us with the direction to issue an alternative writ in light of Evidence Code section 1155 and *Moradi-Shalal v. Fireman's Fund Ins. Companies* (1988) 46 Cal. 3d 287, 306 [250 Cal. Rptr. 116, 758 P.2d 58].

DISCUSSION

A. *Motion to Sever*

Code of Civil Procedure section 1048, subdivision (b) states, in pertinent part: "The court, in furtherance of convenience or to avoid prejudice, or when separate trials will be conducive to expedition and economy, may order a separate trial of any cause of action...."

In a negligence action, Evidence Code section 1155 precludes the use of evidence that a tortfeasor has insurance for the injury that he has allegedly caused. "The evidence [of a party being insured] is regarded as both irrelevant and prejudicial to the defendant." (1 Witkin, Cal. Evidence (3d ed. 1986) § 417, p. 391.)

Our Supreme Court has stated that the suing of an insured for negligence and the insurer for bad faith in the same lawsuit "'. . . obviously [violates] both the letter and spirit of [Evid. Code, § 1155].' [*Royal Globe Ins. Co. v. Superior Court* (1979) 23 Cal. 3d 880, 891 (153 Cal. Rptr. 842, 592 P.2d 329).] . . . '. . . [*Until*] *the liability of the insured is first determined*, the defense of the insured may be seriously hampered by discovery initiated by the injured claimant against the insurer.' [Citations omitted.]" (*Moradi-Shalal v. Fireman's Fund Ins. Companies, supra*, 46 Cal. 3d at p. 306, italics in original.)

"It is within the discretion of the court to order a severance and separate trials of such actions [citations omitted], and the exercise of such discretion will not be interfered with on appeal except when there has been a manifest abuse thereof. [Citation.]" (*McLellan v. McLellan* (1972) 23 Cal. App. 3d 343, 353 [100 Cal. Rptr. 258].) Although we find that the trial court abused its discretion when it denied Omaha's motion to sever, relief by way of extraordinary writ should not be considered a foregone conclusion.

B. *Relief by Way of Extraordinary Writ — Why It Is Hard to Get, and Why We Initially Denied the Petition*

Approximately 90 percent of petitions seeking extraordinary relief are denied. (*See* Cal. Civil Writ Practice (Cont. Ed. Bar 1987) § 2.2, p. 50.) Only rarely does the court give detailed reasons for its rejection of a petition. Instead, counsel is usually notified in a terse minute order or postcard that the petition is denied. (*See* Cal. Civil Writ Practice, *supra*, at § 10.27, p. 408; 8 Witkin, Cal. Procedure (3d ed. 1985) Extraordinary Writs, § 165, p. 801.)

Although, as a rule, the court states no reason for its denial of a petition, it will on occasion refer to an authority in support of its order of denial. This oblique message, ostensibly designed to enlighten, often has the opposite effect and promotes anxiety among those attorneys unable to tolerate either uncertainty or ambiguity.

Case law has done little to explain why appellate courts deny writ petitions. The subject is most commonly broached in those cases in which relief has been granted. The appellate court in dicta will briefly explain why extraordinary relief is typically not available. The discussion primarily centers on the unique circumstances of the case at hand that were found to warrant extraordinary relief. (*See, e.g., Cianci v. Superior Court* (1985) 40 Cal. 3d 903, 908, fn.2 [221 Cal. Rptr. 575, 710 P.2d 375].)

Just as case law has been disappointing as a source of information concerning the mysteries of the writ, so have attempts to impart information by hierophants of appellate practice. Those who have tried to extract a coherent set of rules from cases and treatises on writs have found it easier to comprehend a "washing bill in Babylonic cuneiform." (Gilbert & Sullivan, Pirates of Penzance (1879).)

The large number of rejections of writ petitions demonstrates that courts will not use their scarce resources to second-guess every ruling and order of the trial court, particularly when to do so would save neither time nor aid in the resolution of a lawsuit.

Writ relief, if it were granted at the drop of a hat, would interfere with an orderly administration of justice at the trial and appellate levels. Reviewing courts have been cautioned to guard against the tendency to take "'. . . too lax a view of the "extraordinary" nature of prerogative writs . . .'" (8 Witkin, *supra*, at § 141, pp. 782–783) lest they run the risk of fostering the delay of trials, vexing litigants and trial courts with multiple proceedings, and adding to the delay of judgment appeals pending in the appellate court. (*Babb v. Superior Court* (1971) 3 Cal. 3d 841, 851 [92 Cal. Rptr. 179, 479 P.2d 379];. . . .)

"If the rule were otherwise, in every ordinary action a defendant whenever he chose could halt the proceeding in the trial court by applying for a writ of prohibition to stop the ordinary progress of the action toward a judgment until a reviewing tribunal passed upon an intermediate question that had arisen. If such were the rule, reviewing courts would in innumerable cases be converted from appellate courts to nisi prius tribunals." (*Mitchell v. Superior Court* (1958) 50 Cal. 2d 827, 833–834 [330 P.2d 48] (conc. opn. of McComb, J.).)

Particularly today, "in an era of excessively crowded lower court dockets, it is in the interest of the fair and prompt administration of justice to discourage piecemeal litigation." (*Kerr v. United States District Court* (1976) 426 U.S. 394, 403 [96 S. Ct. 2119, 48 L. Ed. 2d 725, 732].)

Were reviewing courts to treat writs in the same manner as they do appeals, these courts would be trapped in an appellate gridlock. This in turn would cause ordinary appeals, waiting for review, to be shunted to the sidelines. One writer sees a writ petition as being a device used to "cut into line" ahead of those litigants awaiting determination of postjudgment appeals. (Davis, *Tips for Obtaining a Civil Writ* (Aug. 1985) Cal. Law. 55.)

The Court of Appeal is generally in a far better position to review a question when called upon to do so in an appeal instead of by way of a writ petition. When review takes place by way of appeal, the court has a more complete record, more time for deliberation and, therefore, more insight into the significance of the issues. "Unlike the ordinary appeal which moves in an orderly, predictable pattern onto and off the appellate court's calendar, writ proceedings follow no set procedural course." (Chernoff & Watson, *Writ Lore* (1981) 56 State Bar J. 12.)

Further, some issues may diminish in importance as a case proceeds towards trial. Petitioners seeking extraordinary writs do not always consider that a purported error of a trial judge may (1) be cured prior to trial, (2) have little or no effect upon the outcome of trial, or (3) be properly considered on appeal. (*Hogya v. Superior Court* (1977) 75 Cal. App. 3d 122, 128 [142 Cal. Rptr. 325].)

An unrestrained exercise of the power to grant extraordinary writs carries the potential to undermine the relationship between trial and appellate courts. Writ petitions "'have the unfortunate consequence of making the judge a litigant, obliged to obtain personal counsel or to leave his defense to one of the litigants [appearing] before him' in the underlying case. [Citations omitted.]" (*Kerr v. United States District Court, supra*, 426 U.S. at pp. 402–403 [48 L. Ed. 2d at p. 732].) Judges should be umpires rather than players.

In order to confine the use of mandamus to its proper office, the Supreme Court, in various cases, has stated general criteria for determining the propriety of an extraordinary writ: (1) the issue tendered in the writ petition is of widespread interest (*Brandt v. Superior Court* (1985) 37 Cal. 3d 813, 816 [210 Cal. Rptr. 211, 693 P.2d 796]) or presents a significant and novel constitutional issue (*Britt v. Superior Court* (1978) 20 Cal. 3d 844, 851–852 [143 Cal. Rptr. 695, 574 P.2d 766]); (2) the trial court's order deprived petitioner of an opportunity to present a substantial portion of his cause of action (*Brandt, supra*, at p. 816; *Vasquez v. Superior Court* (1971) 4 Cal. 3d 800, 807 [94 Cal. Rptr. 796, 484 P.2d 964, 53 A.L.R.3d 513]); (3) conflicting trial court interpretations of the law require a resolution of the conflict (*Greyhound Corp. v. Superior Court* (1961) 56 Cal. 2d 355, 378 [15 Cal. Rptr. 90, 364 P.2d 266]); (4) the trial court's order is both clearly erroneous as a matter of law and substantially prejudices petitioner's case (*Babb v. Superior Court, supra*, 3 Cal. 3d at p. 851; *Schweiger v. Superior Court* (1970) 3 Cal. 3d 507, 517 [90 Cal. Rptr. 729, 476 P.2d 97]); (5) the party seeking the writ lacks an adequate means, such as a direct appeal, by which to attain relief (*Phelan v. Superior Court* (1950) 35 Cal. 2d 363, 370–372 [217 P.2d 951]); and (6) the petitioner will suffer harm or prejudice in a manner that cannot be corrected on appeal (*Valley Bank of Nevada v. Superior Court* (1975) 15 Cal. 3d 652 [125 Cal. Rptr. 553, 542 P.2d 977]; *Roberts v. Superior Court* (1973) 9 Cal. 3d 330 [107 Cal. Rptr. 309, 508 P.2d 309]). The extent to which these criteria apply depends on the facts and circumstances of the case. (*Hogya v. Superior Court, supra*, 75 Cal. App. 3d at pp. 127–130.)

To adequately and intelligently decide the issues in this case or any other case, the court must have a complete record. Here, we did not have a copy of the reporter's transcript, and consequently did not know whether the court had even denied the motion to sever. The minute order states only that the court did not grant the demurrer.

After the Supreme Court remanded the matter to this court, at oral argument the parties stipulated that respondent court had denied the motion to sever. This was helpful, but we still do not know upon what grounds the trial judge made his decision.

It is true that mandate, in certain instances, provides a more effective remedy than does appeal for the purpose of reviewing an order denying severance. If, however, the trial court here denied the motion for severance without prejudice to bring the motion at a later time, writ relief would be inappropriate.

Under such circumstances, the failure to order severance would not meet the definition of an "irreparable injury." It would constitute, at best, an "irreparable inconvenience." (*Ordway v. Superior Court* (1988) 198 Cal. App. 3d 98, 101, fn.1 [243 Cal. Rptr. 536].) Upon proper application at a later time, Omaha may have succeeded in obtaining an order for severance. A trial court is entitled to change its mind before judgment and may vacate a prior order for consolidation and order severance.

Here, however, there is no indication that the motion was denied without prejudice. The Supreme Court's order directing that an alternative writ be issued constitutes a determination that, in the ordinary course of the law, the petitioner is without an adequate remedy. (*Payne v. Superior Court* (1976) 17 Cal. 3d 908, 925 [132 Cal. Rptr. 405, 553 P.2d 565].)

Let a writ of mandate issue ordering respondeat superior court to grant the motion to sever. The stay of proceedings is dissolved.

Sav-On Drugs, Inc. v. Superior Court

Supreme Court of California

15 Cal. 3d 1, 123 Cal. Rptr. 283, 538 P.2d 739 (1975)

RICHARDSON, JUSTICE.

Preliminarily, it may be observed that the [extraordinary] writ is not the favored method of reviewing discovery orders. Ordinarily the aggrieved party must raise the issue on direct appeal from a final judgment. (*Pacific Tel. & Tel. Co. v. Superior Court*, 2 Cal. 3d 161, 169 [84 Cal. Rptr. 718, 465 P.2d 854]; *Oceanside Union School Dist. v. Superior Court*, 58 Cal. 2d 180, 185–186, fn. 4 [23 Cal. Rptr. 375, 373 P.2d 439].) The premise upon which this general policy rests is that in the great majority of cases the delay due to interim review of discovery orders is likely to result in greater harm to the judicial process by reason of protracted delay than is the enforcement of a possibly improper discovery order. (2 Cal. 3d at p. 170.) Nonetheless, we have concluded that the instant case comes within an exception recognized in *Pacific Tel., supra*, 2 Cal. 3d at page 170, footnote 11 and more recently in *Roberts v. Superior Court*, 9 Cal. 3d 330, 335–336 [107 Cal. Rptr. 309, 508 P.2d 309], to the effect that we may properly entertain a petition for extraordinary relief when the petitioning party asserts, as here, that to compel an answer would violate a privilege.

Notes and Questions Regarding Extraordinary Writs

(1) *Extraordinary Writs, Generally.* Extraordinary writs provide a mechanism for potential immediate appellate review on non-appealable interlocutory decisions of trial tribunals. Writs are extraordinary remedies in the sense that they are speedy and discretionary and, unlike appeals, do not require appellate review as a matter of right. As *Omaha Indemnity Co. v. Superior Court, supra*, demonstrates, writs involve foundational prerequisites not necessary for an appeal. Generally speaking, an extraordinary writ allows a higher court to review actions of a lower tribunal when review by appeal is inadequate. *See, e.g.*, CCP §§ 1085, 1086, 1094.5; Rules 8.485, 8.486, 8.930–8.934, Cal. Rules of Ct.

(2) *Primer on Extraordinary Writ Practice.* A "writ" is an order entered by a higher court directed at an inferior court, administrative agency, or individual. When a writ is sought from the Court of Appeal, for example, the process is referred to as "petitioning" for a writ. The "petition" is a set of documents which resembles a combina-

tion of a complaint and a brief. *See* CEB, *California Writ Practice, Initiating a Writ Proceeding in the Court of Appeals* §§ 18.5–18.60 (4th ed. 2011). Usually there are three parties to a writ proceeding: the petitioner, the respondent, and the real party in interest. The "petitioner" is the party seeking relief from the appellate court, and the "respondent" is the inferior tribunal (usually a trial court) whose decision is being challenged by the petitioner. The "real party in interest" is the party who prevailed in the decision by the trial court. Generally the real party in interest, not the respondent, is expected to respond to the petition.

(3) *"Alternative" and "Peremptory" Writs.* Writs of mandate and of prohibition may issue as either "alternative" or "peremptory" writs. CCP §§ 1087, 1104.

(a) *Alternative Writ.* An "alternative writ" is essentially an order to show cause. This writ, when issued, commands the respondent inferior court or agency to grant the requested relief or to show cause why such relief should not be granted. CCP §§ 1087 & 1104. The issuance of an alternative writ usually constitutes a determination that the petitioner has satisfied the general procedural prerequisites to extraordinary writ review, but is not necessarily a decision for petitioner on the merits of the petition. E.g., *Civil Service Employees Ins. Co. v. Superior Court*, 22 Cal. 3d 362, 149 Cal. Rptr. 360, 584 P.2d 497 (1978) (Superior court issued alternative writ, but subsequently denied peremptory writ); *Diamond v. Allison*, 8 Cal. 3d 736, 106 Cal. Rptr. 13, 505 P.2d 205 (1973).

When an alternative writ is issued, the requested relief may be imposed on the respondent if no response is filed by the real party in interest. If the real party in interest wishes to contest the proposed relief, the real party should file a response (or "return") to the alternative writ by way of demurrer, verified answer, or both. CCP §§ 1089, 1105; Rule 8.487, Cal. Rules of Ct. This may be followed by a reply (or "replication") from the petitioner, and each party may be entitled to present oral argument. CCP §§ 1093–1094, 1105, 1108. If the appellate court then grants the requested relief, a "peremptory writ" will issue and the alternative writ will be discharged. E.g., *Brandt v. Superior Court*, 37 Cal. 3d 813, 210 Cal. Rptr. 211, 693 P.2d 796 (1985).

(b) *Peremptory Writ.* A "peremptory writ" is the reviewing court's ultimate order that the respondent must grant the relief requested in the writ petition. CCP §§ 1087, 1097, 1104. As indicated above, a peremptory writ (of mandate or prohibition) may issue after the issuance of, and hearing on, an alternative writ. CCP §§ 1087, 1104. However, a peremptory writ may be "issued in the first instance"—without first requesting or granting an alternative writ—upon due notice. CCP §§ 1088, 1105; *see Palma v. U.S. Industrial Fasteners, Inc.*, 36 Cal. 3d 171, 203 Cal. Rptr. 626, 681 P.2d 893 (1984) (Holding that a peremptory writ should not issue in the first instance unless the respondent and the real party in interest have received notice that such a procedure is being considered and have either filed a response on the merits or been given an opportunity to do so).

(4) *"Statutory" Writs.* Certain extraordinary writs are referred to as "statutory" writs, as opposed to "common law" writs. Unlike the distinctions between "alternative" and "peremptory," or "mandate" and "prohibition," this classification carries little legal

significance. A "statutory" writ is not a distinct type of writ, but is simply one where writ review is specifically authorized for a particular situation by a special statute. Such special statutory authorization for writ review usually contains specific time limitations for filing the writ petition, which may be jurisdictional and should be scrupulously followed. Writ review specifically authorized by statute applies to some very important interlocutory decisions, including denial of a motion to quash service of process, CCP § 418.10(a)(1) and (c) (Petition for writ of mandate within 10 days after notice to parties of the decision), and review of decisions on motions to change venue, CCP § 400 (Petition for writ of mandate within 20 days after service of notice of decision). Review by mandate is the exclusive remedy here, is it not? Why? *See McCorkle v. City of Los Angeles*, 70 Cal. 2d 252, 256–60, 74 Cal. Rptr. 389, 449 P.2d 453 (1969); *Hennigan v. Boren*, 243 Cal. App. 2d 810, 814–15, 52 Cal. Rptr. 748 (1966).

(5) *Types of Extraordinary Writs.* There are a number of different types of writs recognized in California. The two most frequently requested appellate writs are the "writ of mandate" (also referred to by the traditional name of "mandamus") authorized by CCP §§ 1084–1094, and the "writ of prohibition" authorized by CCP §§ 1102–1105, 1107–1108. Other appellate writs include the "writ of certiorari" (or "writ of review"), CCP §§ 1067–1077; "supersedeas," CCP §§ 923, Rules 8.112, 8.116, Cal. Rules of Ct.; and "habeas corpus," Penal Code §§ 1473–1508. The California courts are fairly understanding and flexible when it comes to selecting the appropriate writ; rarely will they refuse relief solely because the petitioner requested the wrong type of writ. *See, e.g., Anton v. San Antonio Community Hospital*, 19 Cal. 3d 802, 813–14, 140 Cal. Rptr. 442, 567 P.2d 1162 (1977) (Petition brought as traditional mandamus pursuant to CCP § 1085 properly treated as one for administrative mandamus under § 1094.5); *Babb v. Superior Court*, 3 Cal. 3d 841, 850, 92 Cal. Rptr. 179, 479 P.2d 379 (1971) (Petitioner sought writ of prohibition and Supreme Court issued an alternative writ of prohibition; Supreme Court then found mandate more appropriate and treated petition as one for mandate, issued peremptory writ).

(6) *Basic Writ Prerequisites.* As *Omaha Indemnity* indicates, extraordinary writs are discretionary. The reviewing court is not required to decide the merits of a writ petition or even state a reason for denying an alternative writ. There are some basic statutory prerequisites common to all writs of mandate, prohibition, and certiorari.

(a) *Inadequate Remedy at Law.* First, the petitioner must have no "plain, speedy, and adequate remedy in the ordinary course of law." CCP §§ 1068, 1086, 1103. Generally, writ review is inappropriate if the challenged decision is immediately appealable. *In re Marriage of Skelley*, 18 Cal. 3d 365, 369, 134 Cal. Rptr. 197, 556 P.2d 297 (1976); *Phelan v. Superior Court*, 35 Cal. 2d 363, 370, 217 P.2d 951 (1950). An appeal is usually viewed as "adequate" even though it involves far greater expense and time than review by writ. *Rescue Army v. Municipal Court*, 28 Cal. 2d 460, 466, 171 P.2d 8 (1946); *Hogya v. Superior Court*, 75 Cal. App. 3d 122, 128–29, 142 Cal. Rptr. 325 (1977).

(b) *Irreparable Injury.* A second general prerequisite to writ review, similar to inadequacy of remedy at law, is that the petitioner will suffer "irreparable injury" if the writ is not granted. This prerequisite encompasses several related inquiries, but the main concern is whether the nature of the harm or prejudice is such that it cannot be corrected on appeal. *See, e.g., Roberts v. Superior Court,* 9 Cal. 3d 330, 336, 107 Cal. Rptr. 309, 508 P.2d 309 (1973) (Use of extraordinary writ held proper in discovery cases where trial court's order allegedly violated a privilege; person seeking to exercise privilege must either succumb to court's order and disclose privileged information or subject himself to contempt for refusal to obey court's order pending appeal); *Barrett v. Superior Court,* 222 Cal. App. 3d 1176, 1183, 272 Cal. Rptr. 304 (1990) (Writ appropriate because if trial court's order is determined incorrect on an appeal, a second trial would be required).

Although generally the courts will not find "irreparable injury" based on the fact that if the trial court's ruling is wrong the petitioner will unnecessarily incur the time and expense of going to trial, *see, e.g., Ordway v. Superior Court,* 198 Cal. App. 3d 98, 101 n.1, 243 Cal. Rptr. 536 (1988); sometimes the courts will find writ review necessary to prevent an expensive trial and ultimate reversal, *see, e.g., City of Glendale v. Superior Court,* 18 Cal. App. 4th 1768, 1776, 23 Cal. Rptr. 2d 305 (1993) (Bifurcated trial); *Smith v. Superior Court,* 10 Cal. App. 4th 1033, 13 Cal. Rptr. 2d 133 (1992) (Writ review of trial court's denial of motion to strike emotional distress and punitive damage allegations from complaint held proper because delay and expense of a trial made remedy of appeal inadequate and significant legal issue of importance involved).

Chapter X

The Preclusive Effects
of Prior Judgments

A. California's Claim Preclusion
(Res Judicata) Doctrine

Sawyer v. First City Financial Corp.

Court of Appeal of California, Fourth Appellate District

124 Cal. App. 3d 390, 177 Cal. Rptr. 398 (1981)

FROELICH, JUSTICE.

Plaintiffs appeal from adverse summary judgment rulings in favor of all defendants. An understanding of the litigation requires an analysis of two separate cases involving essentially the same parties, of which the present appeal relates specifically to the second. For reference purposes these two cases will be called Sawyer I and Sawyer II. Each case arises from the same general factual background.

Factual Background

The principal parties to both cases are the plaintiffs Sawyer, owners and sellers of land; the defendants First City Financial Corporation, Ltd. (First City) and its subsidiaries, purchasers and encumbrancers of the land who sought to develop it; and Toronto Dominion Bank of California, the development lender to First City's subsidiary. The broad brush of facts is that in May of 1974 the Sawyers sold 32 acres of land in La Jolla, California, to the subsidiary of First City—F. C. Financial Associates, Ltd.—for $1,180,000 consisting of $510,000 in cash and a note secured by deed of trust in the sum of $670,000. Concurrently with the sale, F. C. Financial Associates committed to borrow $1.8 million in the form of a development loan from Toronto Dominion Bank. This loan was guaranteed by First City and was secured by a first deed of trust on the realty, the Sawyers specifically subordinating their deed of trust to the new encumbrance. The Sawyers as part of the sales documents specifically waived any deficiency judgment with respect to their note and deed of trust, with the result that after the sales and refinancing escrows closed their sole resource for collection of their $670,000 note was foreclosure on their deed of trust, now subordinate to a $1.8 million first deed of trust to the Bank.

Early in 1975, F. C. Financial Associates discontinued payments on the note to Toronto Dominion Bank, asserting that it could not proceed further with development of the land because the construction bids it had received were excessively high. Total amounts owed on the note at that time approximated $900,000. Toronto Dominion Bank commenced nonjudicial foreclosure proceedings on April 1, 1975, and purchased the land at foreclosure sale in September 1975, for its bid of $650,000. The land was ultimately transferred in December 1976 to Lexington Properties, Inc., a corporation owned by one Richard Ehrlich, for a purchase price of some $800,000.

The Sawyers contend in pleadings and other documentation that at the time of the foreclosure sale Toronto Dominion Bank had agreed to resell the realty to First City for a price equal to the bank's total investment in it, but that this transfer was delayed until the sale to Ehrlich and his corporation could be arranged, so that neither First City nor its subsidiary again appeared as record titleholder. Ehrlich and his corporation obtained development funds for the property from a corporation called Lomitas Properties, Inc., which is a corporation owned and controlled by the majority stockholders, directors and officers of First City, and which derived its funds from First City.

Appellant's view of the facts, therefore, is that the Sawyers were induced to take a nonrecourse note for more than half the consideration involved in the sale of their land, the security for which note was made subject to a large development loan. The development borrower then defaulted on the note and arranged with the development lender to foreclose, to buy in at the foreclosure sale, and to resell to the development borrower for the amount of the foreclosure sales price plus the balance of the loan guarantee. The practical effect of this transaction, it is alleged, was to wipe out the obligation to the Sawyers and permit First City to proceed with sale or development of the land without having to pay $650,000 of the purchase price. In order to avoid airing the mechanics of the transaction, the agreement between the Toronto Dominion Bank and First City was kept secret, and the resale to First City was not recorded, the ultimate purchaser being a puppet of First City set up in an apparently independent corporation, borrowing funds from a new and anonymous lending company, but actually deriving development funds indirectly from First City. We are alert to caution that the above construction of the facts from and after the foreclosure sale is that alleged by the plaintiffs, who seek the opportunity of proving same in a full-scale evidentiary trial.

Legal Proceedings

Sawyer I

Sawyer I was commenced in July of 1975. The defendants were F. C. Financial Associates, its parent First City, and, later, another subsidiary of First City (all sometimes called herein Financial); and Toronto Dominion Bank of California (Bank). The several causes of action all were based upon contractual theories. Reference was made to the land acquisition and development loan agreement executed between Financial and Bank, which provided for the construction of a planned residential development in accordance with an existing permit. The Sawyers alleged that they were third party beneficiaries of that agreement and had been damaged by the failure of Financial to perform in accordance with it. The breach is alleged not only as a simple breach of contract, but as a breach by the defendants of "a contractual duty of good faith and fair dealing." A separate cause of action asks for declaratory relief with respect to the contractual commitments; and a final cause of action seeks judicial foreclosure of the Sawyer note. The monetary relief prayed for was the amount of the note ($674,500) plus attorney fees.

The case was tried in February of 1978. By stipulation the issues were severed for trial and dispositive issues were presented to a judge, sitting without jury. The judgment rendered in March of 1978, focused upon the issue of the validity of the waiver by Sawyers of their right to a deficiency judgment. This waiver was found to be effective and judgment was rendered in favor of all defendants on all causes of action. Following affirmance on appeal, the judgment became final in December of 1979.

Sawyer II

Sawyer II was filed in January of 1978. Entitled "Complaint for Damages Based Upon Conspiracy and Fraud," it joined as defendants all of the parties named in Sawyer I and in addition the ultimate purchaser Ehrlich and his corporation, Lexington Properties; the new financier of the development, Lomitas Properties; and a number of officers and directors of the Financial companies and the Bank. Three of the causes of action of this new lawsuit are based upon an alleged conspiracy among the defendants to cause a default in the Bank's note and trust deed, hold a sham sale, and take other action for the purpose of eliminating the obligation to the Sawyers. The only essential difference in the three causes of action is the date of commencement of the alleged conspiracy—one alleging the evil motives from the very start of the land acquisition transaction, a second alleging commencement of the conspiracy when Financial defaulted on its note payments, and a third alleging commencement of the conspiracy at the time of the foreclosure sale. The fourth cause of action uses the same factual allegations as the basis for a claim of intentional interference with contractual relation (Financial's note obligation to the Sawyers). Damages alleged are the same as in Sawyer I except that additional punitive damages are sought.

The procedural history of Sawyer II is detailed as follows:

1. Promptly upon filing Sawyer II, counsel sought to consolidate with Sawyer I, and moved for a continuance of the trial of Sawyer I. This motion was opposed by the defendants, who objected because the issues and causes of action of Sawyer II were different from those of Sawyer I, and also because the case, then pending for two and one-half years, was scheduled for trial nine days later. The court denied a motion to continue the trial of Sawyer I, and it was tried without consolidation with Sawyer II.

2. In January of 1980, the Bank and its officers moved for summary judgment in Sawyer II upon the ground of the res judicata effect of Sawyer I, and also upon the basis of a written release which had been executed in favor of the Bank in Sawyer I—removing the Bank from the case before its trial. The Honorable Douglas Woodworth denied the motion based upon res judicata, but granted the motion as to

the Bank only, upon the ground of the written waiver. The bank officers moved for reconsideration on the theory that the waiver should be construed to cover them as well as the Bank, and this motion was taken under submission by the judge in March of 1980. On July 24, 1980, Judge Woodworth denied the motions by written minute order.

3. In May of 1980, a separate motion for summary judgment was filed by the Financial corporations on the ground that Sawyer I was res judicata to the issues of Sawyer II—that the plaintiffs had split their cause of action by attempting to relitigate the same issues in a second lawsuit. The bank officers (whose motion for reconsideration was then pending before Judge Woodworth) joined in this motion, and it was set for hearing before the Honorable Franklin B. Orfield. On July 25, 1980, Judge Orfield ruled in favor of all defendants on the ground of res judicata and the enforceability of the Bank's written release in Sawyer I.

The Appeal

Appellants appeal from the summary judgments of both Judge Woodworth (dismissing the Bank) and Judge Orfield (dismissing all parties). . . . Many bases of appeal are urged: The central and most important issue, however, is the question of res judicata. As reviewed in 3 Witkin, California Procedure (2d ed. 1971) Pleading, section 32 et seq., page 1715, a single cause of action cannot be split and made the subject of several suits. If a primary right is so split, determination of the issues in the first suit will be res judicata to the attempt to relitigate them in the second suit. Where the plaintiff has several causes of action, however, even though they may arise from the same factual setting, and even though they might have been joined in one suit under permissive joinder provisions, the plaintiff is privileged to bring separate actions based upon each separate cause.

Res Judicata Issue

A valid final judgment on the merits in favor of a defendant serves as a complete bar to further litigation on the same cause of action. (*Slater v. Blackwood* (1975) 15 Cal. 3d 791, 795 [126 Cal. Rptr. 225, 543 P.2d 593].) The question in this and similar cases, of course, is whether the attempted second litigation involves the "same cause of action." A "cause of action" is conceived as the remedial right in favor of a plaintiff for the violation of one "primary right." That several remedies may be available for violation of one "primary right" does not create additional "causes of action." However, it is also true that a given set of facts may give rise to the violation of more than one "primary right," thus giving a plaintiff the potential of two separate lawsuits against a single defendant. (*See* 3 Witkin, *supra*, p. 1707 et seq.)

The theoretical discussion of what constitutes a "primary right" is complicated by historical precedent in several well-litigated areas establishing the question of "primary rights" in a manner perhaps contrary to the result that might be reached by a purely logical approach. For instance, the primary right to be free from personal injury has been construed as to embrace all theories of tort which might have given rise to the injury. In *Panos v. Great Western Packing Co.* (1943) 21 Cal. 2d 636 [134 P.2d 242], the plaintiff was injured in a meat packing house. His first cause of action was based upon alleged negligence of the packing house in permitting third parties to come upon the premises and operate equipment. A defense judgment was then held to bar a second suit based upon an entirely different factual theory of negligence — that the defendant itself had negligently operated the equipment. In *Slater v. Blackwood, supra*, 15 Cal. 3d 791, a defense judgment in a suit based upon violation of the guest statute (intoxication or willful misconduct) was held to bar a second suit (after the guest statute was held unconstitutional) based upon allegations of ordinary negligence.

Other examples of torts resulting in easily conceptualized types of damages have been settled, one way or the other, by precedent. While one act of tortious conduct might well be deemed to violate only one "primary right" — the right to be free from the particular unlawful conduct — the resultant (1) injury to person and (2) damage to property have been deemed creative of separate causes of action. On the other hand, one course of wrongful conduct which damages several pieces of property traditionally gives rise to only one cause of action. (*See* 3 Witkin, *supra*, at pp. 1720–1721, and cases cited therein.)

Other classes of litigation, however, with perhaps less historical or precedential background, are not so well defined in terms of deciding how many "primary rights" derive from a single factual transaction. The tort in *Agarwal v. Johnson* (1979) 25 Cal. 3d 932 [160 Cal. Rptr. 141, 603 P.2d 58], was unfair treatment of a minority race employee by an employer. Plaintiff's first action was in federal court for back wages under the authority of the federal Civil Rights Act. The state Supreme Court determined this was no bar to a second suit in superior court for general and punitive damages for defamation and intentional infliction of emotional distress. Although the same set of facts is presented in each claim, one primary right is created by the federal statute prohibiting discriminatory employment practices; and the second primary right is grounded in state common law. Also, the "harm suffered" was deemed separable — damages for lost wages in the federal action, and damages for injury to reputation and peace of mind in the state case. Compare *Mattson v. City of Costa Mesa* (1980) 106 Cal. App. 3d 441 [164 Cal. Rptr. 913], where the actionable facts consisted of an unlawful arrest of the plaintiff and his abuse in confinement. His first action in federal court under the authority of the Civil Rights Act was held to be a bar to a subsequent suit in state court for negligence, assault and battery. The court found that the "primary rights" giving rise to the state common law tort action were the same as those reflected in the Civil Rights Act, and that the civil rights action was "simply a different way of expressing an invasion of the same primary rights or the assertion of a different legal theory for recovery." (*Id.*, at pp. 447–448.) In *City of Los Angeles v. Superior Court* (1978) 85 Cal. App. 3d 143, 153 [149 Cal. Rptr. 320], a federal civil rights action followed by a superior court common law tort action, both involving wrongful seizure of personal property, the appellate court reached the same conclusion and applied the bar of res judicata on the ground that "the civil rights action was designed to vindicate precisely the same interests in . . . personal property that (the plaintiff) seeks to vindicate in the matter before us."

One would assume that the question of litigation of claims arising from one transaction first on the basis of contract, and then on alleged tort theories, would have received substantial appellate attention. The authorities, however, are surprisingly sparce. The Restatement of the Law, Judgments (1942) chapter 3, section 63, page 261, provides several illustrations involving actions to cancel a deed. A failure to sustain the first action on contractual grounds (i.e., failure of execution or delivery of the deed) is held to bar a subsequent action based upon fraudulent procurement — thus suggesting that the "primary right" is the right to cancel the deed (as applied to our case, to validate the note) and that this gives rise to only one cause of action, whether it be framed in contract or tort.

Respondents rely upon two cases which purport to be illustrative of contract actions followed by separate tort actions, arising from the same transaction: *Olwell v. Hopkins* (1946) 28 Cal. 2d 147 [168 P.2d 972]; and *Steiner v. Thomas* (1949) 94 Cal. App. 2d 655 [211 P.2d 321]. The plaintiff's claim in *Olwell* resulted from farming operations carried on by a joint venture which included a Washington corporation. In the first suit the action was dismissed without a trial of the substantive issues on the ground that the corporation had never qualified to do business in California with the result that the contract upon which the suit was based was "void." A second suit based upon the same transaction alleged fraudulent concealment of facts and prayed that the defendants be declared constructive trustees of certain realty. While this scenario would seem to pose a problem similar to that of the case before us, it was resolved without addressing the issue of the existence of separate causes of action in contract and for fraud. The court assumed (and presumably counsel did not argue to the contrary) that there was only one cause of action, and that the second suit was merely an alternative statement of that one cause of action. (*See Olwell v. Hopkins, supra,* 28 Cal. 2d at pp. 149, 150.) The question directly addressed by the court was the effect of dismissal of the first suit without a trial on the merits, and whether such dismissal on procedural grounds would operate as a bar to a second action, recognizing that in order to constitute a bar, the dismissal must have been following "'an adjudication of the merits of the controversy, . . .'" (*Id.,* at p. 149.)

In *Steiner,* two successive actions were brought against an administrator of a decedent's estate for the purpose of recovering a certain parcel of real property which had been transferred to the decedent by the plaintiff before the decedent's death. The first action was for rescission based upon fraud, alleging that the realty had been transferred so as to permit the decedent to collect rents and that the decedent had promised to reconvey the property at a later date. The second lawsuit was based upon an alleged breach of an agreement to devise the property to the plaintiff, as evidenced by two letters from the decedent to the plaintiff. The court resolved the question of res judicata against the plaintiff, focusing on the identity or similarity of facts litigated in the first suit as compared to those in issue at the second suit. The court stated: "The fact is that in the former action the merits of all the facts were determined and relief was denied. . . . Upon presentation of the special plea in the instant action the court had merely to decide whether the facts alleged in the first suit for rescission of the contract were substantially those alleged in the second action for breach of the same contract." (*Steiner v. Thomas, supra*, 94 Cal. App. 2d at p. 658.) The court thus construed the situation as one in which alternative remedies in contract were successively brought — related to the same contract — rather than a case in which an action on contract was followed by an action for an intentional tort related to or as part of the transaction giving rise to the contract. Neither *Orwell* nor *Steiner* appears controlling.

The case before us is not one in which the same factual structure is characterized in one complaint as a breach of contract and in another as a tort. The first action is solely on contract and is based upon the note, deed of trust, and loan and development agreement. At the time of trial the principal issue litigated was the effectiveness of the waiver of deficiency judgment, and this issue was presented in the context of contractual theories. There was no contention and no evidence was presented relating to a possible invalidation of the waiver on grounds of fraud, misrepresentation or any other tort.

Sawyer II, of course, had as its object collection of the same promissory note which was the subject matter of Sawyer I; but the basis of the claim is completely different, and rests upon a completely separate set of facts. The complaint assumes and admits that the forms of the waiver of deficiency and the subordination are technically appropriate and enforceable. The pleading reaches beyond these documents, however, to highlight other conduct of the parties alleged to be tortious. The core of the alleged wrongful conduct is an agreement among the parties to conduct what is characterized as a sham foreclosure sale, the only substantive effect of which would be secretly to discharge the obligation to Sawyer, leaving all other parties in essentially the same position as prior to the sale. Surely one's breach of contract by failing to pay a note violates a "primary right" which is separate from the "primary right" not to have the note stolen. That the two causes of action might have been joined in one lawsuit under our permissive joinder provisions (*see* 3 Witkin, *supra*, at p. 1915) does not prevent the plaintiff from bringing them in separate suits if he elects to do so. While the monetary loss may be measurable by the same promissory note amount, and hence in a general sense the same "harm" has been done in both cases, theoretically the plaintiffs have been "harmed" differently by tortious conduct destroying the value of the note, than by the contractual breach of simply failing to pay it. We conclude, therefore, that Sawyer II is based upon a separate and severable cause of action from that litigated in Sawyer I, and that it was error to grant summary judgment on the ground of res judicata.

Estoppel

A second prong to appellant's argument about the summary judgment ruling as respects res judicata is that the moving parties were estopped to deny the separate nature of the two causes of action because they had earlier opposed a motion to consolidate the two cases. Appellants rely upon *United Bank & Trust Co. v. Hunt* (1934) 1 Cal. 2d 340 [34 P.2d 1001], where the court at page 345 stated:

> Where counsel by timely notice call to a court's attention the pendency of other proceedings covering kindred matters and strive to have the same embraced within the scope of the inquiry, and such attempt is successfully blocked by opposing counsel and the trial proceeds to the investigation of the specific issue before the court, counsel who were successful in preventing the consolidation of the issues cannot be heard later to object to a trial of the related matters upon the ground of *res judicata*. The course pursued by the court and counsel . . . was tantamount to an express determination on the part of the court with the consent of opposing counsel to reserve the issues involved for future adjudication. [Citations omitted.] Litigants cannot successfully assume such inconsistent positions.

The inconsistent position asserted to have been taken by defense counsel was at the time of the hearing of a motion to continue the trial of Sawyer I.* * *

At the hearing of the motion for continuance on February 6, counsel for the defendants did argue that the case should not be continued to permit consideration of a consolidation motion because consolidation would be improper by virtue of the different theories and causes of action in Sawyer II. However, no express argument was made about, nor consideration given, to the question of the res judicata effect of the prior trial of Sawyer I. In light of the long period of preparation for trial and the then once-continued trial date impending only nine days hence, the trial court presumably considered further continuance to be prejudicial to the rights of the defendants. A court is not required to grant a continuance of a trial when the pleadings have been completed, adequate time for discovery has been provided, the issues are joined, and one side is ready for trial, even though the moving party alleges newly discovered facts or newly found issues which suggest more discovery or an amendment to the pleadings.

The reasonable interpretation to be derived from a review of the record in Sawyer I was that the court denied the motion for continuance because Sawyer I was ready for trial, had been delayed previously and should not be delayed further. Therefore, while we have determined that the motion for summary judgment should not have been granted on the ground of res judicata, we must agree with the trial court that the moving parties were not estopped by their prior conduct from making the motion.

STANIFORTH, ACTING PRESIDING JUDGE, concurs.
WIENER, JUSTICE, Concurring.

. . . I conclude defendants, except for the Toronto Dominion Bank and its officers, are estopped from raising the defense of res judicata. Accordingly, I agree with the result reached by the majority.

Plaintiffs filed their first case (No. 369573) in July 1975; their second (No. 409803) on January 11, 1978. On January 13, 1978, plaintiffs moved to consolidate both cases because some of the parties and certain of the issues were the same. Unable to serve all defendants, plaintiffs' motion to consolidate was reset beyond February 15, 1978, the trial date in case No. 369573. Pending hearing on that motion, plaintiffs moved to continue the trial to allow the court to consider the motion for consolidation. Counsel for First City defendants in Sawyer I, one of whom is appellate counsel here, opposed the motion for continuance by saying there was no basis for consolidation, arguing further that "[plaintiffs] are pursuing theories of action for conspiracy and fraud in Case No. 409803, whereas in the above-captioned action plaintiffs are pursuing theories for breach of contract, declaratory relief and judicial foreclosure. *The issues raised in the two cases are necessarily and substantially different.*" (Italics supplied.)

If defendants' counsel made the tactical decision to oppose the continuance on the assumption that if successful they would then be able to prevent litigation in the second case on the basis of res judicata, it would have been simple enough for them to tell the court that res judicata was involved. If they had done so the judge considering the motion would then have been able to evaluate all relevant factors affecting his decision before exercising discretion in making his ruling. In light of the language which defendants selected to oppose the motion for the continuance the ruling on which prevented the court from ever considering the merits of plaintiffs' request for consolidation, it was reasonable for both the court and plaintiffs' counsel to conclude defendants' opposition to the continuance would not prevent a trial of the second case in which the issues were represented to be "necessarily and substantially different." Accordingly, reasonably interpreted, defendants' actions fall within the narrow rule of *United Bank & Trust Co. v. Hunt, supra.* Once having represented to the court there were two different actions with different issues, they may not now stop plaintiffs from having a full trial on those "different issues."

Notes and Questions Regarding Claim Preclusion

(1) *Primary Rights Theory.* The primary rights theory was developed by Professor John Norton Pomeroy in the nineteenth century, and adopted by the California Supreme Court as early as 1887. *See Hutchinson v. Ainsworth*, 73 Cal. 452, 455, 15 P. 82 (1887). Under the primary rights theory advanced by Pomeroy, a "cause of action" consists of a "primary right" possessed by the plaintiff, a corresponding "primary duty" of the defendant, and a wrongful act by the defendant constituting a breach of that duty. *See Crowley v. Katleman*, 8 Cal. 4th 666, 34 Cal. Rptr. 2d 386, 881 P.2d 1083, 1090 (Cal. 1994); J. POMEROY, REMEDIES AND REMEDIAL RIGHTS § 453, at 487 (1876). For an historical analysis of the primary rights theory and res judicata, *see* Walter W. Heiser, *California's Unpredictable Res Judicata (Claim Preclusion) Doctrine*, 35 San Diego L. Rev. 559, 571–76 (1998).

(2) *"Cause of Action."* The central feature of California's claim preclusion doctrine, as *Sawyer* illustrates, is that a single cause of action cannot be split and made the subject of separate lawsuits. Where a plaintiff has more than one cause of action against a defendant, however, the plaintiff may join them in one lawsuit but is not required to

do so either by rules of joinder or of res judicata. In other words, a plaintiff who has two causes of action against a defendant may proceed with two separate lawsuits. A judgment in one lawsuit will have no claim preclusive effect on the other.

(a) *Primary Right.* This makes the definition of "cause of action" of central importance. As *Sawyer* illustrates, the California courts define a "cause of action" for purposes of claim preclusion according to the "primary rights" theory, *i.e.*, the violation of each separate "primary right" gives rise to a separate cause of action and, potentially, a separate lawsuit against the same defendant.

(b) *Harm Suffered Approach.* How is "primary right" defined? More importantly, how do the courts determine whether a set of facts gives rise to only one primary right as opposed to multiple primary rights? The most frequently quoted response to these questions is from *Agarwal v. Johnson*, 25 Cal. 3d 932, 954, 160 Cal. Rptr. 141, 603 P.2d 58 (1979): "Under the 'primary rights' theory adhered to in California it is true there is only a single cause of action for the invasion of one primary right. . . . But the significant factor is the harm suffered; that the same facts are involved in both suits is not conclusive." How significant was this "harm suffered" factor in *Sawyer v. First City Financial Corp.*?

(3) *Primary Rights Determined by Precedent.* Despite the general uncertainty in defining a "primary right," some applications of the theory are (relatively) settled by precedent. Litigants can feel reasonably comfortable in determining whether one or two lawsuits are permissible in such circumstances. Perhaps the most frequently encountered application involves a tort victim who simultaneously suffers both personal injury and property damage caused by the defendant's single act. A typical example is negligence litigation arising out of the crash of two cars, where one driver sues the other. The resulting personal injury to the plaintiff driver is a separate primary right from the property damage to the plaintiff's car, and may be pursued in two separate lawsuits. *See Holmes v. David H. Bricker, Inc.*, 70 Cal. 2d 786, 76 Cal. Rptr. 431, 452 P.2d 647 (1969). However, a breach of contract that results in injury to person and property violates only one primary right, and therefore gives rise to only one cause of action. *Id.*

Other areas (relatively) settled by precedent are also suggested in *Sawyer*. One wrongful act which results in injury to several pieces of property traditionally gives rise to only one cause of action, as does one wrongful act which results in multiple personal injuries to a plaintiff. *See Sawyer* and cases cited therein; *Swartzendruber v. City of San Diego*, 3 Cal. App. 4th 896, 904, 5 Cal. Rptr. 2d 64 (1992) (Consequential damages did not support a second cause of action).

(4) *Declaratory Judgment Exception.* Under the Declaratory Judgment Act, a party may ask the court for a binding declaration of rights and duties. CCP § 1060. This Act also provides an exception from the bar of res judicata (claim preclusion) for declaratory judgments, stating "no judgment under this chapter shall preclude any party from obtaining additional relief based on the same facts." CCP § 1062. In *Mycogen*

Corp. v. Monsanto Co., 28 Cal. 4th 888, 123 Cal. Rptr. 2d 432, 51 P.3d 297 (2002), the Supreme Court construed the Act's exception to claim preclusion as applicable only where the plaintiff's initial action seeks *pure* declaratory relief, and not where the action seeks both declaratory relief and additional coercive relief such as damages, specific performance, or an injunction. *Id.* at 897–902. Because plaintiff Mycogen sought and received both declaratory and coercive relief in the form of specific performance in its prior breach of contract action, res judicata precluded Mycogen from seeking additional relief in the form of damages for the same breach of contract in a subsequent action. *Id.* at 903–04.

(5) *Final Judgment on the Merits.* The doctrine of res judicata applies only to "final" judgments and orders. *American Enterprise, Inc. v. Van Winkle*, 39 Cal. 2d 210, 218, 246 P.2d 935 (1952); Restatement (Second) of Judgments § 13 (1982). What constitutes a final judgment under the California doctrine? The California rule is that a judgment is not final for purposes of res judicata if it is still open to direct attack by appeal or otherwise. *Agarwal v. Johnson*, 25 Cal. 3d 932, 954 n.11, 160 Cal. Rptr. 141, 603 P.2d 58 (1979). Consequently, an order or judgment is not final under the California rule for res judicata purposes during the pendency of an appeal; and, even though no appeal has yet been taken, until the time for appeal has expired. *See Agarwal v. Johnson, supra*; CCP § 1049.

(a) In order to have a res judicata effect, a judgment must not only be final but must also be rendered "on the merits." *Wilson v. Bittick*, 63 Cal. 2d 30, 35, 45 Cal. Rptr. 31, 403 P.2d 159 (1965); § 19, Restatement (Second) of Judgments (1982). The paradigm "judgment on the merits" is one entered after a full trial of the issues of fact and law, rendered by a judge or jury. Restatement, *supra*, § 19, cmt. a. This includes a judgment rendered on a directed verdict and a judgment notwithstanding the verdict. *Id.*, cmt. h.

(b) When a judgment is rendered without a full trial on the facts, the question of whether it is on the merits becomes a little more complicated. When not dealing with the paradigm, a particular judgment must be closely scrutinized to determine whether it is or is not an adjudication on the merits. For example, although a default judgment is "on the merits," *English v. English*, 9 Cal. 2d 358, 70 P.2d 625 (1937); a summary judgment is only if based on a determination of the merits as opposed to some other ground, such as statute of limitations. *Koch v. Rodlin Enterprises, Inc.*, 223 Cal. App. 3d 1591, 1595–97, 273 Cal. Rptr. 438 (1990).

(6) *Affirmative Defense.* Res judicata must be properly pleaded or proved at trial, or it is waived. *See, e.g., Wolfsen v. Hathaway*, 32 Cal. 2d 632, 638, 198 P.2d 1 (1948); *Parker v. Walker*, 5 Cal. App. 4th 1173, 1191, 6 Cal. Rptr. 2d 908 (1992); *see also* CCP §§ 456, 1908.5. The normal and appropriate method of raising res judicata is by an affirmative defense. *See, e.g., Parker v. Walker, supra.*

B. California's Issue Preclusion (Collateral Estoppel) Doctrine

1. Collateral Estoppel Doctrine, Generally

The California courts usually follow the Restatement (Second) of Judgments when deciding questions of issue preclusion. *See* Walter W. Heiser, *California's Confusing Collateral Estoppel (Issue Preclusion) Doctrine*, 35 San Diego L. Rev. 509, 528–32 (1998). Court opinions often quote extensively from relevant sections of the Restatement, as well as from the explanations contained in the various section "comments." E.g., *Lucido v. Superior Court*, 51 Cal. 3d 335, 272 Cal. Rptr. 767, 795 P.2d 1223 (1990); *In re Nathaniel P.*, 211 Cal. App. 3d 660, 259 Cal. Rptr. 555 (1989) (quoting § 28(4)); *Barker v. Hull*, 191 Cal. App. 3d 221, 226, 236 Cal. Rptr. 285 (1987) (quoting § 27, cmt. d); *Sandoval v. Superior Court*, 140 Cal. App. 3d 932, 190 Cal. Rptr. 29 (1983) (relying on § 29 and comments thereunder).

Although California courts do generally rely on the Restatement definitions in resolving collateral estoppel questions, the most common general statement of the California doctrine is as follows:

> The doctrine of collateral estoppel precludes relitigation of an issue previously adjudicated if: (1) the issue necessarily decided in the previous suit is identical to the issue sought to be relitigated; (2) there was a final judgment on the merits of the previous suit; and (3) the party against whom the plea is asserted was a party, or in privity with a party, to the previous suit. *Producers Dairy Delivery Co. v. Sentry Ins. Co.*, 41 Cal. 3d 903, 910, 226 Cal. Rptr. 558, 718 P.2d 920 (1986); *Bernhard v. Bank of America*, 19 Cal. 2d 807, 122 P.2d 892 (1942).

The California Supreme Court has restated these basic prerequisites, and distinguished between the "threshold requirements" and the public policy considerations of collateral estoppel, in *Lucido v. Superior Court*, 51 Cal. 3d 335, 341–43, 272 Cal. Rptr. 767, 795 P.2d 1223 (1990):

> Collateral estoppel precludes relitigation of issues argued and decided in prior proceedings.* * * Traditionally, we have applied the doctrine only if several threshold requirements are fulfilled. First, the issue sought to be precluded from relitigation must be identical to that decided in a former proceeding. Second, this issue must have been actually litigated in the former proceeding. Third, it must have been necessarily decided in the former proceeding. Fourth, the decision in the former proceeding must be final and on the merits. Finally, the party against whom preclusion is sought must be the same as, or in privity with, the party to the former proceeding.* * *
>
> Even assuming all the threshold requirements are satisfied, however, our analysis is not at an end. We have repeatedly looked to the public policies underlying the doctrine before — concluding that collateral estoppel should

be applied in a particular setting.* * * Accordingly, the public policies underlying collateral estoppel — preservation of the integrity of the judicial system, promotion of judicial economy, and protection of litigants from harassment by vexatious litigation — strongly influence whether its application in a particular circumstance would be fair to the parties and constitutes sound judicial policy.

In *Lucido*, the Supreme Court refused to apply collateral estoppel even though the threshold requirements were satisfied, because to do so would be inconsistent with these public policies.

2. Mutuality Doctrine Rejected

The California Supreme Court rejected the mutuality doctrine in the landmark case of *Bernhard v. Bank of America*, 19 Cal. 2d 807, 122 P.2d 892 (1942). The court noted that the criteria for determining *who may assert* collateral estoppel differ fundamentally from the criteria for determining *against whom* a plea of collateral estoppel may be asserted. *Bernhard, supra*, 19 Cal. 2d at 811, 812. "There is no compelling reason . . . for requiring that a party asserting a plea of [collateral estoppel] must have been a party, or in privity with a party, to the earlier litigation." *Id.* at 812. The court then articulated the now familiar inquiries for application of collateral estoppel: "Was the issue decided in the prior adjudication identical with the one presented in the action in question? Was there a final judgment on the merits? Was the party *against whom* the plea is asserted a party or in privity with a party to the prior adjudication?" *Id.* at 813.

The *Bernhard* decision involved application of defensive nonmutual collateral estoppel, where the prior judgment is invoked defensively in a second action against a plaintiff bringing suit on an issue that the plaintiff litigated and lost as plaintiff against a different defendant in a prior action. The California courts also recognize the more controversial doctrine of offensive nonmutual collateral estoppel, where a plaintiff seeks to foreclose the defendant from litigating an issue the defendant has litigated unsuccessfully in a prior action with another party. *See, e.g., Imen v. Glassford*, 201 Cal. App. 3d 898, 247 Cal. Rptr. 514 (1988); *White Motor Corp. v. Teresinski*, 214 Cal. App. 3d 754, 263 Cal. Rptr. 26 (1989).

3. Privity

Generally, issue and claim preclusion can only be applied against parties who was also parties in the prior lawsuit. However, not only are actual parties bound by a prior judgment, but also nonparties who are "in privity" with the actual parties. Although traditional applications of privity were quite limited, the modern California doctrine is much broader. Privity now extends to any relationship between the party to be estopped and the unsuccessful party in the prior litigation which is "sufficiently close" so as to justify application of the doctrine of res judicata or collateral estoppel. *See Clemmer v. Hartford Ins. Co.*, 22 Cal. 3d 865, 875, 151 Cal. Rptr. 285, 587 P.2d 1098 (1978). This is a very flexible standard which is limited, however, by the requirements of due process.

California's modern doctrine of privity was explained in *Dyson v. State Personnel Board*, 213 Cal. App. 3d 711, 723–25, 262 Cal. Rptr. 112 (1989):

The privity requirement has undergone an evolution in the law. "Traditionally it has been held to refer to an interest in the subject matter of litigation acquired after rendition of the judgment through or under one of the parties, as by inheritance, succession or purchase. (*Bernhard v. Bank of America* (1942) 19 Cal. 2d 807, 811 [122 P.2d 892].). The concept has also been expanded to refer to a mutual or successive relationship to the same rights of property, or to such an identification in interest of one person with another as to represent the same legal rights and, more recently, to a relationship between the party to be estopped and the unsuccessful party in the prior litigation which is 'sufficiently close' so as to justify application of the doctrine of collateral estoppel" (*Clemmer v. Hartford Ins. Co.* (1978) 22 Cal. 3d 865, 875 [151 Cal. Rptr. 285, 587 P.2d 1098].).

As one commentator has noted, the determination whether a party is in privity with another for purposes of collateral estoppel is a policy decision. "[T]he term 'privity' in itself does not state a reason for either including or excluding a person from the binding effect of a prior judgment, but rather it represents a legal conclusion that the relationship between the one who is a party on the record and the non-party is sufficiently close to afford application of the principle of preclusion. The emphasis in the analysis is upon the policy of ending litigation where there has been a fair trial of one's interests, as it has been observed that 'the doctrine of res judicata is primarily one of public policy and only secondarily of private benefit to individual litigants.'" (Vestal, *Preclusion/Res Judicata Variables: Parties* (1964) 50 Iowa L. Rev. 27, 45, fn. omitted . . .)

However, the expanded notions of privity notwithstanding, collateral estoppel may be applied only if the requirements of due process are satisfied. (*Clemmer v. Hartford Ins., supra*, 22 Cal. 3d at p. 875.) "In the context of collateral estoppel, due process requires that the party to be estopped must have had an identity or community of interest with, and adequate representation by, the losing party in the first action as well as that the circumstances must have been such that the party to be estopped should reasonably have expected to be bound by the prior adjudication. [Citations omitted]. Thus, in deciding whether to apply collateral estoppel, the court must balance the rights of the party to be estopped against the need for applying collateral estoppel in the particular case, in order to promote judicial economy by minimizing repetitive litigation, to prevent inconsistent judgments which undermine the integrity of the judicial system, or to protect against vexatious litigation. [Citations omitted]." (*Ibid.*)

Notes and Questions Regarding Privity

(1) Is "sufficiently close" a workable test, or simply a conclusion? How is "sufficiently close" defined? Do the due process requirements provide a clearer definition of "sufficiently close?"

(2) California courts have found privity to exist in a variety of relationships, such as:

(a) Successors in interest. *See, e.g., Brown v. Rahman*, 231 Cal. App. 3d 1458, 282 Cal. Rptr. 815 (1991) (Heirs of deceased in wrongful death action held in privity with deceased who, in earlier personal injury action prior to death, lost on issues of causation and liability against same defendant); *Garcia v. Rehrig International, Inc.*, 99 Cal. App. 4th 869, 877–79, 121 Cal. Rptr. 2d 723 (2002);

(b) Persons represented by a fiduciary. E.g., *Armstrong v. Armstrong*, 15 Cal. 3d 942, 951, 126 Cal. Rptr. 805, 544 P.2d 941 (1976);

(c) Persons who have a proprietary or financial interest in and control of the conduct of a lawsuit may be bound by the result even though not a party. E.g., *George F. Hillenbrand, Inc. v. Insurance Co. Of North America*, 104 Cal. App. 4th 784, 824–27, 128 Cal. Rptr. 2d 586 (2002) (Agent in privity with employer where agent controlled when and how employer prosecuted prior lawsuit); *Aronow v. LaCroix*, 219 Cal. App. 3d 1039, 1050–52, 268 Cal. Rptr. 866 (1990), *cert. denied*, 498 U.S. 1105, 111 S. Ct. 1009, 112 L. Ed. 2d 1091 (1991) (Plaintiff, an attorney who served as co-counsel and a witness for a physician in a prior unsuccessful malicious prosecution action, had sufficient interest in and control of prior action to be in privity with respect to plaintiff's identical malicious prosecution claim against same defendants);

(d) Individual members of a homeowner association may be in privity with the association. *Kirkpatrick v. City of Oceanside*, 232 Cal. App. 3d 267, 280–81, 283 Cal. Rptr. 191 (1991); and

(e) A Governmental entity may be in privity with the individual claimants it represents. *See, e.g., Rynsburger v. Dairymen's Fertilizer Cooperative, Inc.*, 266 Cal. App. 2d 269, 72 Cal. Rptr. 102 (1968) (Property owner residents held bound by adverse judgment against city which represented their interests); *Citizens For Open Access to Sand and Tide, Inc. v. Seadrift Ass'n*, 60 Cal. App. 4th 1053, 1069–74, 71 Cal. Rptr. 2d 77 (1998) (Private public interest group concerned with the recreational access to beaches was in privity with state agencies in prior lawsuit and therefore bound by a settlement agreement reached between the state agencies and various beachfront homeowners); *but see Payne v. National Collection Systems, Inc.*, 91 Cal. App. 4th 1037, 111 Cal. Rptr. 2d 260 (2001) (Judgment in an action brought by the Attorney General on behalf of the People of the State of California against defendants under the unfair competition law does not preclude private suits against the defendants under the same law by individuals who did not receive restitution as a result of the Attorney General's litigation); *Victa v. Merle Norman Cosmetics, Inc.*, 19 Cal. App. 4th 454, 24

Cal. Rptr. 2d 117 (1993) (EEOC represented public interest rather than individual's in prior age discrimination action and was not in privity with individual plaintiff; injunctive consent decree in prior EEOC action therefore did not preclude individual plaintiff's age discrimination action against same defendant).

Part Two

Federal Civil Procedure Materials

Appendix 1

Federal Rules

FEDERAL RULES OF CIVIL PROCEDURE

I.   FEDERAL RULES OF CIVIL PROCEDURE

TITLE I.   SCOPE OF RULES; FORM OF ACTION

RULE 1.   SCOPE OF AND PURPOSE.

These rules govern the procedure in all civil actions and proceedings in the United States district courts, except as stated in Rule 81. They should be construed, administered, and employed by the court and the parties to secure the just, speedy, and inexpensive determination of every action and proceeding.

[*Adopted Dec. 20, 1937, effective Sept. 16, 1938; amended April 29, 2015, effective Dec. 1, 2015.*]

RULE 2.   ONE FORM OF ACTION.

There is one form of action—the civil action.

[*Adopted Dec. 20, 1937, effective Sept. 16, 1938; amended April 30, 2007, effective Dec. 1, 2007.*]

TITLE II.   COMMENCING AN ACTION; SERVICE OF PROCESS, PLEADINGS, MOTIONS, AND ORDERS

RULE 3.   COMMENCEMENT OF ACTION.

A civil action is commenced by filing a complaint with the court.

[*Adopted Dec. 20, 1937, effective Sept. 16, 1938; amended April 30, 2007, effective Dec. 1, 2007.*]

RULE 4.   SUMMONS.

(a) **Contents; Amendments.**

(1) *Contents.*

A summons must:

(A) name the court and the parties;

(B) be directed to the defendant;

(C) state the name and address of the plaintiff's attorney or—if unrepresented—of the plaintiff;

(D) state the time within which the defendant must appear and defend;

(E) notify the defendant that a failure to appear and defend will result in a default judgment against the defendant for the relief demanded in the complaint;

(F) be signed by the clerk; and

(G) bear the court's seal.

(2) *Amendments.*

The court may permit a summons to be amended.

(b) Issuance.

On or after filing the complaint, the plaintiff may present a summons to the clerk for signature and seal. If the summons is properly completed, the clerk must sign, seal, and issue it to the plaintiff for service on the defendant. A summons—or a copy of a summons that is addressed to multiple defendants—must be issued for each defendant to be served.

(c) Service.

(1) *In General.*

A summons must be served with a copy of the complaint. The plaintiff is responsible for having the summons and complaint served within the time allowed by Rule 4(m) and must furnish the necessary copies to the person who makes service.

(2) *By Whom.*

Any person who is at least 18 years old and not a party may serve a summons and complaint.

(3) *By a Marshal or Someone Specially Appointed.*

At the plaintiff's request, the court may order that service be made by a United States marshal or deputy marshal or by a person specially appointed by the court. The court must so order if the plaintiff is authorized to proceed in forma pauperis under 28 U.S.C. § 1915 or as a seaman under 28 U.S.C. § 1916.

(d) Waiving Service.

(1) *Requesting a Waiver.*

An individual, corporation, or association that is subject to service under Rule 4(e), (f), or (h) has a duty to avoid unnecessary expenses of serving the summons. The plaintiff may notify such a defendant that an action has been commenced and request that the defendant waive service of a summons. The notice and request must:

(A) be in writing and be addressed:

(i) to the individual defendant; or

(ii) for a defendant subject to service under Rule 4(h), to an officer, a managing or general agent, or any other agent authorized by appointment or by law to receive service of process;

(B) name the court where the complaint was filed;

(C) be accompanied by a copy of the complaint, two copies of the waiver form appended to this Rule 4, and a prepaid means for returning the form;

(D) inform the defendant, using the form appended to this Rule 4, of the consequences of waiving and not waiving service;

(E) state the date when the request is sent;

(F) give the defendant a reasonable time of at least 30 days after the request was sent—or at least 60 days if sent to the defendant outside any judicial district of the United States—to return the waiver; and

(G) be sent by first-class mail or other reliable means.

(2) *Failure to Waive.*

If a defendant located within the United States fails, without good cause, to sign and return a waiver requested by a plaintiff located within the United States, the court must impose on the defendant:

(A) the expenses later incurred in making service; and

(B) the reasonable expenses, including attorney's fees, of any motion required to collect those service expenses.

(3) *Time to Answer After a Waiver.*

A defendant who, before being served with process, timely returns a waiver need not serve an answer to the complaint until 60 days after the request was sent—or until 90 days after it was sent to the defendant outside any judicial district of the United States.

(4) *Results of Filing a Waiver.*

When the plaintiff files a waiver, proof of service is not required and these rules apply as if a summons and complaint had been served at the time of filing the waiver.

(5) *Jurisdiction and Venue Not Waived.*

Waiving service of a summons does not waive any objection to personal jurisdiction or to venue.

(e) Serving an Individual Within a Judicial District of the United States.

Unless federal law provides otherwise, an individual—other than a minor, an incompetent person, or a person whose waiver has been filed—may be served in a judicial district of the United States by:

(1) following state law for serving a summons in an action brought in courts of general jurisdiction in the state where the district court is located or where service is made; or

(2) doing any of the following:

(A) delivering a copy of the summons and of the complaint to the individual personally;

(B) leaving a copy of each at the individual's dwelling or usual place of abode with someone of suitable age and discretion who resides there; or

(C) delivering a copy of each to an agent authorized by appointment or by law to receive service of process.

(f) Serving an Individual in a Foreign Country.

Unless federal law provides otherwise, an individual—other than a minor, an incompetent person, or a person whose waiver has been filed—may be served at a place not within any judicial district of the United States:

(1) by any internationally agreed means of service that is reasonably calculated to give notice, such as those authorized by the Hague Convention on the Service Abroad of Judicial and Extrajudicial Documents;

(2) if there is no internationally agreed means, or if an international agreement allows but does not specify other means, by a method that is reasonably calculated to give notice:

(A) as prescribed by the foreign country's law for service in that country in an action in its courts of general jurisdiction;

(B) as the foreign authority directs in response to a letter rogatory or letter of request; or

(C) unless prohibited by the foreign country's law, by:

(i) delivering a copy of the summons and of the complaint to the individual personally; or

(ii) using any form of mail that the clerk addresses and sends to the individual and that requires a signed receipt; or

(3) by other means not prohibited by international agreement, as the court orders.

(g) Serving a Minor or an Incompetent Person.

A minor or an incompetent person in a judicial district of the United States must be served by following state law for serving a summons or like process on such a defendant in an action brought in the courts of general jurisdiction of the state where service is made. A minor or an incompetent person who is not within any judicial district of the United States must be served in the manner prescribed by Rule 4(f)(2)(A), (f)(2)(B), or (f)(3).

(h) Serving a Corporation, Partnership, or Association.

Unless federal law provides otherwise or the defendant's waiver has been filed, a domestic or foreign corporation, or a partnership or other unincorporated association that is subject to suit under a common name, must be served:

(1) in a judicial district of the United States:

    (A) in the manner prescribed by Rule 4(e)(1) for serving an individual; or

    (B) by delivering a copy of the summons and of the complaint to an officer, a managing or general agent, or any other agent authorized by appointment or by law to receive service of process and—if the agent is one authorized by statute and the statute so requires—by also mailing a copy of each to the defendant; or

(2) at a place not within any judicial district of the United States, in any manner prescribed by Rule 4(f) for serving an individual, except personal delivery under (f)(2)(C)(i).

(i) Serving the United States and Its Agencies, Corporations, Officers, or Employees.

    (1) *United States.*

To serve the United States, a party must:

    (A) (i)deliver a copy of the summons and of the complaint to the United States attorney for the district where the action is brought—or to an assistant United States attorney or clerical employee whom the United States attorney designates in a writing filed with the court clerk—or

        (ii) send a copy of each by registered or certified mail to the civil-process clerk at the United States attorney's office;

    (B) send a copy of each by registered or certified mail to the Attorney General of the United States at Washington, D.C.; and

    (C) if the action challenges an order of a nonparty agency or officer of the United States, send a copy of each by registered or certified mail to the agency or officer.

    (2) *Agency; Corporation; Officer or Employee Sued in an Official Capacity.*

To serve a United States agency or corporation, or a United States officer or employee sued only in an official capacity, a party must serve the United States and also send a copy of the summons and of the complaint by registered or certified mail to the agency, corporation, officer, or employee.

    (3) *Officer or Employee Sued Individually.*

To serve a United States officer or employee sued in an individual capacity for an act or omission occurring in connection with duties performed on the United States' behalf (whether or not the officer or employee is also sued in an official capacity), a party must serve the United States and also serve the officer or employee under Rule 4(e), (f), or (g).

(4) *Extending Time.*

The court must allow a party a reasonable time to cure its failure to:

(A) serve a person required to be served under Rule 4(i)(2), if the party has served either the United States attorney or the Attorney General of the United States; or

(B) serve the United States under Rule 4(i)(3), if the party has served the United States officer or employee.

(j) Serving a Foreign, State, or Local Government.

(1) *Foreign State.*

A foreign state or its political subdivision, agency, or instrumentality must be served in accordance with 28 U.S.C. § 1608.

(2) *State or Local Government.*

A state, a municipal corporation, or any other state-created governmental organization that is subject to suit must be served by:

(A) delivering a copy of the summons and of the complaint to its chief executive officer; or

(B) serving a copy of each in the manner prescribed by that state's law for serving a summons or like process on such a defendant.

(k) Territorial Limits of Effective Service.

(1) *In General.*

Serving a summons or filing a waiver of service establishes personal jurisdiction over a defendant:

(A) who is subject to the jurisdiction of a court of general jurisdiction in the state where the district court is located;

(B) who is a party joined under Rule 14 or 19 and is served within a judicial district of the United States and not more than 100 miles from where the summons was issued;

(C) when authorized by a federal statute.

(2) *Federal Claim Outside State-Court Jurisdiction.*

For a claim that arises under federal law, serving a summons or filing a waiver of service establishes personal jurisdiction over a defendant if:

(A) the defendant is not subject to jurisdiction in any state's courts of general jurisdiction; and

(B) exercising jurisdiction is consistent with the United States Constitution and laws.

(l) Proving Service.

(1) *Affidavit Required.*

Unless service is waived, proof of service must be made to the court. Except for service by a United States marshal or deputy marshal, proof must be by the server's affidavit.

(2) *Service Outside the United States.*

Service not within any judicial district of the United States must be proved as follows:

> (A) if made under Rule 4(f)(1), as provided in the applicable treaty or convention; or

> (B) if made under Rule 4(f)(2) or (f)(3), by a receipt signed by the addressee, or by other evidence satisfying the court that the summons and complaint were delivered to the addressee.

(3) *Validity of Service; Amending Proof.*

Failure to prove service does not affect the validity of service. The court may permit proof of service to be amended.

(m) Time Limit for Service.

If a defendant is not served within 90 days after the complaint is filed, the court—on motion or on its own after notice to the plaintiff—must dismiss the action without prejudice against that defendant or order that service be made within a specified time. But if the plaintiff shows good cause for the failure, the court must extend the time for service for an appropriate period. This subdivision (m) does not apply to service in a foreign country under Rule 4(f), 4(h)(2), or 4(j)(1), or to service of a notice under Rule 71.1(d)(3)(A).

(n) Asserting Jurisdiction over Property or Assets.

(1) *Federal Law.*

The court may assert jurisdiction over property if authorized by a federal statute. Notice to claimants of the property must be given as provided in the statute or by serving a summons under this rule.

(2) *State Law.*

On a showing that personal jurisdiction over a defendant cannot be obtained in the district where the action is brought by reasonable efforts to serve a summons under this rule, the court may assert jurisdiction over the defendant's assets found in the district. Jurisdiction is acquired by seizing the assets under the circumstances and in the manner provided by state law in that district.

[*Adopted Dec. 20, 1937, effective Sept. 16, 1938; as amended April 27, 2017, effective Dec. 1, 2017.*]

Rule 4 Notice of a Lawsuit and Request to Waive Service of a Summons.

(Caption)

To (*name the defendant or—if the defendant is a corporation, partnership, or association—name an officer or agent authorized to receive service*):

Why are you getting this?

A lawsuit has been filed against you, or the entity you represent, in this court under the number shown above. A copy of the complaint is attached.

This is not a summons, or an official notice from the court. It is a request that, to avoid expenses, you waive formal service of a summons by signing and returning the enclosed waiver. To avoid these expenses, you must return the signed waiver within (*give at least 30 days or at least 60 days if the defendant is outside any judicial district of the United States*) from the date shown below, which is the date this notice was sent. Two copies of the waiver form are enclosed, along with a stamped, self-addressed envelope or other prepaid means for returning one copy. You may keep the other copy.

What happens next?

If you return the signed waiver, I will file it with the court. The action will then proceed as if you had been served on the date the waiver is filed, but no summons will be served on you and you will have 60 days from the date this notice is sent (see the date below) to answer the complaint (or 90 days if this notice is sent to you outside any judicial district of the United States).

If you do not return the signed waiver within the time indicated, I will arrange to have the summons and complaint served on you. And I will ask the court to require you, or the entity you represent, to pay the expenses of making service.

Please read the enclosed statement about the duty to avoid unnecessary expenses. I certify that this request is being sent to you on the date below.

Date: _____

_____
[Signature of the attorney or unrepresented party]

_____
[Printed name]

_____
[Address]

_____
[E-mail address]

_____
[Telephone number]

Rule 4 Waiver of the Service of Summons.

(Caption)

To: [*Name of the plaintiff's attorney or the unrepresented plaintiff*]

I have received your request to waive service of a summons in this action along with a copy of the complaint, two copies of this waiver form, and a prepaid means of returning one signed copy of the form to you.

I, or the entity I represent, agree to save the expense of serving a summons and complaint in this case.

I understand that I, or the entity I represent, will keep all defenses or objections to the lawsuit, the court's jurisdiction, and the venue of the action, but that I waive any objections to the absence of a summons or of service.

I also understand that I, or the entity I represent, must file and serve an answer or a motion under Rule 12 within 60 days from, the date when this request was sent (or 90 days if it was sent outside the United States). If I fail to do so, a default judgment will be entered against me or the entity I represent.

Date: _____

[Signature of the attorney or unrepresented party]

[Printed name]

[Address]

[E-mail address]

[Telephone number]

(Attach the following)

Duty to Avoid Unnecessary Expenses of Serving a Summons

Rule 4 of the Federal Rules of Civil Procedure requires certain defendants to cooperate in saving unnecessary expenses of serving a summons and complaint. A defendant who is located in the United States and who fails to return a signed waiver of service requested by a plaintiff located in the United States will be required to pay the expenses of service, unless the defendant shows good cause for the failure.

"Good cause" does not include a belief that the lawsuit is groundless, or that it has been brought in an improper venue, or that the court has no jurisdiction over this matter or over the defendant or the defendant's property.

If the waiver is signed and returned, you can still make these and all other defenses and objections, but you cannot object to the absence of a summons or of service.

If you waive service, then you must, within the time specified on the waiver form, serve an answer or a motion under Rule 12 on the plaintiff and file a copy with the court. By signing and returning the waiver form, you are allowed more time to respond than if a summons had been served.

NOTES OF ADVISORY COMMITTEE ON 2015 AMENDMENT TO RULE 4

Subdivision (d). Abrogation of Rule 84 and the other official forms requires that former Forms 5 and 6 be directly incorporated into Rule 4.

Subdivision (m). The presumptive time for serving a defendant is reduced from 120 days to 90 days. This change, together with the shortened times for issuing a scheduling order set by amended Rule 16(b)(2), will reduce delay at the beginning of litigation.

Shortening the presumptive time for service will increase the frequency of occasions to extend the time. More time may be needed, for example, when a request to waive service fails, a defendant is difficult to serve, or a marshal is to make service in an in forma pauperis action. The final sentence is amended to make it clear that the reference to Rule 4 in Rule 71.1(d)(3)(A) does not include Rule 4(m). Dismissal under Rule 4(m) for failure to make timely service would be inconsistent with the limits on dismissal established by Rule 71.1(i)(1)(C).

Shortening the time to serve under Rule 4(m) means that the time of the notice required by Rule 15(c)(1)(C) for relation back is also shortened.

NOTES OF ADVISORY COMMITTEE ON 1993 AMENDMENTS TO RULES

SPECIAL NOTE: Mindful of the constraints of the Rules Enabling Act, the Committee calls the attention of the Supreme Court and Congress to new subdivision (k)(2). Should this limited extension of service be disapproved, the Committee nevertheless recommends adoption of the balance of the rule, with subdivision (k)(1) becoming simply subdivision (k). The Committee Notes would be revised to eliminate references to subdivision (k)(2).

Purposes of Revision. The general purpose of this revision is to facilitate the service of the summons and complaint. The revised rule explicitly authorizes a means for service of the summons and complaint on any defendant. While the methods of service so authorized always provide appropriate notice to persons against whom claims are made, effective service under this rule does not assure that personal jurisdiction has been established over the defendant served.

First, the revised rule authorizes the use of any means of service provided by the law not only of the forum state, but also of the state in which a defendant is served, unless the defendant is a minor or incompetent.

Second, the revised rule clarifies and enhances the cost-saving practice of securing the assent of the defendant to dispense with actual service of the summons and complaint. This practice was introduced to the rule in 1983 by an act of Congress authorizing "service-by-mail," a procedure that effects economic service with the cooperation of the defendant. Defendants that magnify costs of service by requiring expensive service not necessary to achieve full notice of an action brought against them are required to bear the wasteful costs. This provision is made available in actions against defendants who cannot be served in the districts in which the actions are brought.

Third, the revision reduces the hazard of commencing an action against the United States or its officers, agencies, and corporations. A party failing to effect service on all the offices of the United States as required by the rule is assured adequate time to cure defects in service.

Fourth, the revision calls attention to the important effect of the Hague Convention and other treaties bearing on service of documents in foreign countries and favors the use of internationally agreed means of service. In some respects, these treaties have facilitated service in foreign countries but are not fully known to the bar.

Finally, the revised rule extends the reach of federal courts to impose jurisdiction over the person of all defendants against whom federal law claims are made and who can be constitutionally subjected to the jurisdiction of the courts of the United States. The present territorial limits on the effectiveness of service to subject a defendant to the jurisdiction of the court over the defendant's person are retained for all actions in which there is a state in which personal jurisdiction can be asserted consistently with state law and the Fourteenth Amendment. A new provision enables district courts to exercise jurisdiction, if permissible under the Constitution and not precluded by statute, when a federal claim is made against a defendant not subject to the jurisdiction of any single state.

* * *

Subdivision (b). Revised subdivision (b) replaces the former subdivision (a). The revised text makes clear that the responsibility for filling in the summons falls on the plaintiff, not the clerk of the court. If there are multiple defendants, the plaintiff may secure issuance of a summons for each defendant, or may serve copies of a single original bearing the names of multiple defendants if the addressee of the summons is effectively identified.

Subdivision (c). Paragraph (1) of revised subdivision (c) retains language from the former subdivision (d)(1). Paragraph (2) retains language from the former subdivision (a), and adds an appropriate caution regarding the time limit for service set forth in subdivision (m).

The 1983 revision of Rule 4 relieved the marshals' offices of much of the burden of serving the summons. Subdivision (c) eliminates the requirement for service by the marshal's office in actions in which the party seeking service is the United States. The United States, like other civil litigants, is now permitted to designate any person who is 18 years of age and not a party to serve its summons.

The court remains obligated to appoint a marshal, a deputy, or some other person to effect service of a summons in two classes of cases specified by statute: action brought *in forma pauperis* or by a seaman. 28 U.S.C. §§ 1915, 1916. The court also retains discretion to appoint a process server on motion of a party. If a law enforcement presence appears to be necessary or advisable to keep the peace, the court should appoint a marshal or deputy or other official person to make the service. The Department of Justice may also call upon the Marshals Service to perform services in actions brought by the United States. 28 U.S.C. § 651.

Subdivision (d). This text is new, but is substantially derived from the former subdivisions (c)(2)(C) and (D), added to the rule by Congress in 1983. The aims of the provision are to eliminate the costs of service of a summons on many parties and to foster cooperation among adversaries and counsel. The rule operates to impose upon the defendant those costs that could have been avoided if the defendant had cooperated reasonably in the manner prescribed. This device is useful in dealing with defendants who are furtive, who reside in places not easily reached by process servers, or who are outside the United States and can be served only at substantial and unnecessary expense. Illustratively, there is no useful purpose achieved by requiring a plaintiff to comply with all the formalities of service in a foreign country, including costs of translation, when suing a defendant manufacturer, fluent in English, whose products are widely distributed in the United States. *See Bankston v. Toyota Motor Corp.*, 889 F.2d 172 (8th Cir. 1989).

The former text described this process as service-by-mail. This language misled some plaintiffs into thinking that service could be effected by mail without the affirmative cooperation of the defendant. *E.g., Gulley, v. Mayo Foundation*, 886 F.2d 161 (8th Cir. 1989). It is more accurate to describe the communication sent to the defendant as a request for a waiver of formal service.

The request for waiver of service may be sent only to defendants subject to service under subdivision (e), (f), or (h). The United States is not expected to waive service for the reason that its mail receiving facilities are inadequate to assure that the notice is actually received by the correct person in the Department of Justice. The same principle is applied to agencies, corporations, and officers of the United States and to other governments and entities subject to service under subdivision (j). Moreover, there are policy reasons why governmental entities should not be confronted with the potential for bearing costs of service in cases in which they ultimately prevail. Infants or incompetent persons likewise are not called upon to waive service because, due to their presumed inability to understand the request and its consequences, they must generally be served through fiduciaries.

*   *   *

The opportunity for waiver has distinct advantages to a foreign defendant. By waiving service, the defendant can reduce the costs that may ultimately be taxed against it if unsuccessful in the lawsuit, including the sometimes substantial expense of translation that may be wholly unnecessary for defendants fluent in English. Moreover, a foreign defendant that waives service is afforded substantially more time to defend against the action than if it had been formally served: under Rule 12, a defendant ordinarily has only 20 days after service in which to file its answer or raise objections by motion, but by signing a waiver it is allowed 90 days after the date the request for waiver was mailed in which to submit its defenses. Because of the additional time needed for mailing and the unreliability of some foreign mail services, a period of 60 days (rather than the 30 days required for domestic transmissions) is provided for a return of a waiver sent to a foreign country.

It is hoped that, since transmission of the notice and waiver forms is a private non-judicial act, does not purport to effect service, and is not accompanied by any summons or directive from a court, use of the procedure will not offend foreign sovereignties, even those that have withheld their assent to formal service by mail or have objected to the "service-by-mail" provisions of the former rule. Unless the addressee consents, receipt of the request under the revised rule does not give rise to any obligation to answer the lawsuit, does not provide a basis for default judgment, and does not suspend the statute of limitations in those states where the period continues to run until service. Nor are there any adverse consequences to a foreign defendant, since the provisions for shifting the expense of service to a defendant that declines to waive service apply only if the plaintiff and defendant are both located in the United States.

With respect to a defendant located in a foreign country like the United Kingdom, which accepts documents in English, whose Central Authority acts promptly in effecting service, and whose policies discourage its residents from waiving formal service, there will be little reason for a plaintiff to send the notice and request under subdivision (d) rather than use convention methods. On the other hand, the procedure offers significant potential benefits to a plaintiff when suing a defendant that, though fluent in English, is located in a country where, as a condition to formal service under a convention, documents must be translated into another language or where formal service will be otherwise costly or time-consuming.

Paragraph (1) is explicit that a timely waiver of service of a summons does not prejudice the right of a defendant to object by means of a motion authorized by Rule 12(b)(2) to the absence of jurisdiction over the defendant's person, or to assert other defenses that may be available. The only issues eliminated are those involving the sufficiency of the summons or the sufficiency of the method by which it is served.

*   *   *

Paragraph (2)(A) is explicit that a request for waiver of service by a corporate defendant must be addressed to a person qualified to receive service. The general mail rooms of large organizations cannot be required to identify the appropriate individual recipient for an institutional summons.

Paragraph (2)(B) permits the use of alternatives to the United States mails in sending the Notice and Request. While private messenger services or electronic communications may be more expensive than the mail, they may be equally reliable and on occasion more convenient to the parties. Especially with respect to transmissions to foreign countries, alternative means may be desirable, for in some countries facsimile transmission is the most efficient and economical means of communication. If electronic means such as facsimile transmission are employed, the sender should maintain a record of the transmission to assure proof of transmission if receipt is denied, but a party receiving such a transmission has a duty to cooperate and cannot avoid liability for the resulting cost of formal service if the transmission is prevented at the point of receipt.

A defendant failing to comply with a request for waiver shall be given an opportunity to show good cause for the failure, but sufficient cause should be rare. It is not a good cause for failure to waive service that the claim is unjust or that the court lacks jurisdiction. Sufficient cause not to shift the cost of service would exist, however, if the defendant did not receive the request or was insufficiently literate in English to understand it. It should be noted that the provisions for shifting the cost of service apply only if the plaintiff and the defendant are both located in the United States, and accordingly a foreign defendant need not show "good cause" for its failure to waive service.

Paragraph (3) extends the time for answer if, before being served with process, the defendant waives formal service. The extension is intended to serve as an inducement to waive service and to assure that a defendant will not gain any delay by declining to waive service and thereby causing the additional time needed to effect service. By waiving service, a defendant is not called upon to respond to the complaint until 60 days from the date the notice was sent to it-90 days if the notice was sent to a foreign country-rather than within the 20 day period from date of service specified in Rule 12.

Paragraph (4) clarifies the effective date of service when service is waived; the provision is needed to resolve an issue arising when applicable law requires service of process to toll the statute of limitations. *E.g., Morse v. Elmira Country Club*, 752 F.2d 35 (2d Cir. 1984). *Cf. Walker v. Armco Steel Corp.*, 446 U.S. 740 (1980).

The provisions in former subdivision (c)(2)(C)(ii) of this rule may have been misleading to some parties. Some plaintiffs, not reading the rule carefully, supposed that receipt by the defendant of the mailed complaint had the effect both of establishing the jurisdiction of the court over the defendant's person and of tolling the statute of limitations in actions in which service of the summons is required to toll the limitations period. The revised rule is clear that, if the waiver is not returned and filed, the limitations period under such a law is not tolled and the action will not otherwise proceed until formal service of process is effected.

Some state limitations laws may toll an otherwise applicable statute at the time when the defendant receives notice of the action. Nevertheless, the device of requested waiver of service is not suitable if a limitations period which is about to expire is not tolled by filing the action. Unless there is ample time, the plaintiff should proceed directly to the formal methods for service identified in subdivisions (e), (f), or (h).

The procedure of requesting waiver of service should also not be used if the time for service under subdivision (m) will expire before the date on which the waiver must be returned. While a plaintiff has been allowed additional time for service in that situation, *e.g., Prather v. Raymond Constr. Co.*, 570 F. Supp. 278 (N.D. Ga. 1983), the court could refuse a request for additional time unless the defendant appears to have evaded service pursuant to subdivision (e) or (h). It may be noted that the presumptive time limit for service under subdivision (m) does not apply to service in a foreign country.

Paragraph (5) is a cost-shifting provision retained from the former rule. The costs that may be imposed on the defendant could include, for example, the cost of the time of a process server required to make contact with a defendant residing in a guarded apartment house or residential development. The paragraph is explicit that the costs of enforcing the cost-shifting provision are themselves recoverable from a defendant who fails to return the waiver. In the absence of such a provision, the purpose of the rule would be frustrated by the cost of its enforcement, which is likely to be high in relation to the small benefit secured by the plaintiff.

Some plaintiffs may send a notice and request for waiver and, without waiting for return of the waiver, also proceed with efforts to effect formal service on the defendant. To discourage this practice, the cost-shifting provisions in paragraphs (2) and (5) are limited to costs of effecting service incurred after the time expires for the defendant to return the waiver. Moreover, by returning the waiver within the time allowed and before being served with process, a defendant receives the benefit of the longer period for responding to the complaint afforded for waivers under paragraph (3).

Subdivision (e). This subdivision replaces former subdivisions (c)(2)(C)(i) and (d) (1). It provides a means for service of summons on individuals within a judicial district of the United States. Together with subdivision (f), it provides for service on persons anywhere, subject to constitutional and statutory constraints.

Service of the summons under this subdivision does not conclusively establish the jurisdiction of the court over the person of the defendant. A defendant may assert the territorial limits of the court's reachset forth in subdivision (k), including the constitutional limitations that may be imposed by the Due Process Clause of the Fifth Amendment.

Paragraph (1) authorizes service in any judicial district in conformity with state law. This paragraph sets forth the language of former subdivision (c)(2)(C)(i), which authorized the use of the law of the state in which the district court sits, but adds as an alternative the use of the law of the state in which the service is effected.

Paragraph (2) retains the text of the former subdivision (d)(1) and authorizes the use of the familiar methods of personal or abode service or service on an authorized agent in any judicial district.

*   *   *

Subdivision (f). This subdivision provides for service on individuals who are in a foreign country, replacing the former subdivision (i) that was added to Rule 4 in 1963.

*   *   *

Paragraph (1) gives effect to the Hague Convention on the Service Abroad of Judicial and Extrajudicial Documents, which entered into force for the United States on February 10, 1969. See 28 U.S.C.A., Fed. R. Civ. P. 4 (Supp. 1986). This Convention is an important means of dealing with problems of service in a foreign country. *See generally* 1 B. Ristau, *International Judicial Assistance* §§ 4-1-1 to 4-5-2 (1990). Use of the Convention procedures, when available, is mandatory if documents must be transmitted aboard to effect service. *See Volkswagenwerk Aktiengesellschaft v. Schlunk,* 486 U.S. 694 (1988) (noting that voluntary use of these procedures may be desirable even when service could constitutionally be effected in another manner); J. Weis, *The Federal Rules and the Hague Conventions: Concerns of Conformity and Comity,* 50 U. Pitt. L. Rev. 903 (1989). Therefore, this paragraph provides that, when service is to be effected outside a judicial district of the United States, the methods of service appropriate under an applicable treaty shall be employed if available and if the treaty so requires.

* * *

Paragraph (2) provides alternative methods for use when internationally agreed methods are not intended to be exclusive, or where there is no international agreement applicable. It contains most of the language formerly set forth in subdivision (i) of the rule. Service by methods that would violate foreign law is not generally authorized. Subparagraphs (A) and (B) prescribe the more appropriate methods for conforming to local practice or using a local authority. Subparagraph (C) prescribes other methods authorized by the former rule.

Paragraph (3) authorizes the court to approve other methods of service not prohibited by international agreements. The Hague Convention, for example, autho- rizes special forms of service in cases of urgency if convention methods will not permit service within the time required by the circumstances. Other circumstances that might justify the use of additional methods include the failure of the foreign country's Central Authority to effect service within the six-month period provided by the Convention, or the refusal of the Central Authority to serve a complaint seeking punitive damages or to enforce the antitrust laws of the United States. In such cases, the court may direct a special method of service not explicitly authorized by international agreement if not prohibited by the agreement. Inasmuch as our Constitution requires that reasonable notice be given, an earnest effort should be made to devise a method of communication that is consistent with due process and minimizes offense to foreign law. A court may in some instances specially authorize use of ordinary mail. Cf. Levin v. Ruby Trading Corp., 248 F. Supp. 537 (S.D.N.Y. 1965).

Subdivision (g). This subdivision retains the text of former subdivision (d)(2). Provision is made for service upon an infant or incompetent person in a foreign country.

Subdivision (h). This subdivision retains the text of former subdivision (d)(3), with changes reflecting those made in subdivision (e). It also contains the provisions for service on a corporation or association in a foreign country, as formerly found in subdivision (i).

Frequent use should be made of the Notice and Request procedure set forth in subdivision (d) in actions against corporations. Care must be taken, however, to address the request to an individual officer or authorized agent of the corporation. It is not effective use of the Notice and Request procedure if the mail is sent undirected to the mail room of the organization.

Subdivision (i). This subdivision retains much of the text of former subdivisions (d)(4) and (d)(5). Paragraph (1) provides for service of a summons on the United States; it amends former subdivision (d)(4) to permit the United States attorney to be served by registered or certified mail. The rule does not authorize the use of the Notice and Request procedure of revised subdivision (d) when the United States is the defendant. To assure proper handling of mail in the United States attorney's office, the authorized mail service must be specifically addressed to the civil process clerk of the office of the United States attorney.

Paragraph (2) replaces former subdivision (d)(5). Paragraph (3) saves the plaintiff from the hazard of losing a substantive right because of failure to comply with the complex requirements of multiple service under this subdivision. That risk has proved to be more than nominal. *E.g., Whale v. United States*, 792 F.2d 951 (9th Cir. 1986). This provision should be read in connection with the provisions of subdivision (c) of Rule 15 to preclude the loss of substantive rights against the United States or its agencies, corporations, or officers resulting from a plaintiff's failure to correctly identify and serve all the persons who should be named or served.

Subdivision (j). This subdivision retains the text of former subdivision (d)(6) without material change. The waiver-of-service provision is also inapplicable to actions against governments subject to service pursuant to this subdivision. The revision adds a new paragraph (1) referring to the statute governing service of a summons on a foreign state and its political subdivisions, agencies, and instrumentalities, the Foreign Sovereign Immunities Act of 1976, 28 U.S.C. § 1608. The caption of the subdivision reflects that change.

Subdivision (k). This subdivision replaces the former subdivision (f), with no change in the title. Paragraph (1) retains the substance of the former rule in explicitly authorizing the exercise of personal jurisdiction over persons who can be reached under state long-arm law, the "100-mile bulge" provision added in 1963, or the federal interpleader act. Paragraph (1)(D) is new, but merely calls attention to federal legislation that may provide for nationwide or even world-wide service of process in cases arising under particular federal laws. Congress has provided for nationwide service of process and full exercise of territorial jurisdiction by all district courts with respect to specified federal actions. *See* 1 R. Casad, *Jurisdiction in Civil Actions* (2d Ed.) chap. 5 (1991).

Paragraph (2) is new. It authorizes the exercise of territorial jurisdiction over the person of any defendant against whom is made a claim arising under any federal law if that person is subject to personal jurisdiction in no state. This addition is a companion to the amendments made in revised subdivisions (e) and (f).

This paragraph corrects a gap in the enforcement of federal law. Under the former rule, a problem was presented when the defendant was a non-resident of the United States having contacts with the United States sufficient to justify the application of United States law and to satisfy federal standards of forum selection, but having insufficient contact with any single state to support jurisdiction under state long-arm legislation or meet the requirements of the Fourteenth Amendment limitation on state court territorial jurisdiction. In such cases, the defendant was shielded from the enforcement of federal law by the fortuity of a favorable limitation on the power of state courts, which was incorporated into the federal practice by the former rule. In this respect, the revision responds to the suggestion of the Supreme Court made in *Omni Capital Int'l v. Rudolf Wolff & Co. Ltd.,* 484 U.S. 97, 111 (1987).

There remain constitutional limitations on the exercise of territorial jurisdiction by federal courts over persons outside the United States. These restrictions arise from the Fifth Amendment rather than from the Fourteenth Amendment, which limits state-court reach and which was incorporated into federal practice by the reference to state law in the text of the former subdivision (e) that is deleted by this revision. The Fifth Amendment requires that any defendant have affiliating contacts with the United States sufficient to justify the exercise of personal jurisdiction over that party. *Cf. Wells Fargo & Co. v. Wells Fargo Express Co.,* 556 F.2d 406, 418 (9th Cir. 1977). There also may be a further Fifth Amendment constraint in that a plaintiff's forum selection might be so inconvenient to a defendant that it would be a denial of "fair play and substantial justice" required by the due process clause, even though the defendant had significant affiliating contacts with the United States. *See DeJames v. Magnifi- cence Carriers,* 654 F.2d 280, 286 n.3 (3rd Cir.), *cert. denied,* 454 U.S. 1085 (1981).

Compare World-Wide Volkswagen Corp. v. Woodson, 444 U.S. 286, 293–294 (1980); *Insurance Corp. of Ireland v. Compagnie des Bauxites de Guinee,* 456 U.S. 694, 702–03 (1982); *Burger King Corp. v. Rudzewicz,* 471 U.S. 462, 476–78 (1985); *Asahi Metal Indus. v. Superior Court of Cal., Solano County,* 480 U.S. 102, 108–13 (1987). *See generally* R. Lusardi, *Nationwide Service of Process: Due Process Limitations on the Power of the Sovereign,* 33 *Vill. L. Rev.* 1 (1988).

This provision does not affect the operation of federal venue legislation. *See generally* 28 U.S.C. § 1391. Nor does it affect the operation of federal law providing for the change of venue. 28 U.S.C. §§ 1404, 1406. The availability of transfer for fairness and convenience under § 1404 should preclude most conflicts between the full exercise of territorial jurisdiction permitted by this rule and the Fifth Amendment requirement of "fair play and substantial justice."

*   *   *

The district court should be especially scrupulous to protect aliens who reside in a foreign country from forum selections so onerous that injustice could result. "[G]reat care and reserve should be exercised when extending our notions of personal juris- diction into the international field." *Asahi Metal Indus. v. Superior Court of Cal., Solano County,* 480 U.S. 102, 115 (1987), quoting *United States v. First Nat'l City Bank,* 379 U.S. 378, 404 (1965) (Harlan, J., dissenting).

This narrow extension of the federal reach applies only if a claim is made against the defendant under federal law. It does not establish personal jurisdiction if the only claims are those arising under state law or the law of another country, even though there might be diversity or alienage subject matter jurisdiction as to such claims. If, however, personal jurisdiction is established under this paragraph with respect to a federal claim, then 28 U.S.C. § 1367(a) provides supplemental jurisdiction over related claims against that defendant, subject to the court's discretion to decline exercise of that jurisdiction under 28 U.S.C. § 1367(c).

Subdivision (l). This subdivision assembles in one place all the provisions of the present rule bearing on proof of service. No material change in the rule is effected. The provision that proof of service can be amended by leave of court is retained from the former subdivision (h). *See generally* 4A Wright & Miller, *Federal Practice and Procedure* § 1132 (2d ed. 1987).

Subdivision (m). This subdivision retains much of the language of the present subdivision (j).

The new subdivision explicitly provides that the court shall allow additional time if there is good cause for the plaintiff's failure to effect service in the prescribed 120 days, and authorizes the court to relieve a plaintiff of the consequences of an application of this subdivision even if there is no good cause shown. Such relief formerly was afforded in some cases, partly in reliance on Rule 6(b). Relief may be justified, for example, if the applicable statute of limitations would bar the refiled action, or if the defendant is evading service or conceals a defect in attempted service. *E.g., Ditkof v. Owens- Illinois, Inc.,* 114 F.R.D. 104 (E.D. Mich. 1987). A specific instance of good cause is set forth in paragraph (3) of this rule, which provides for extensions if necessary to correct oversights in compliance with the requirements of multiple service in actions against the United States or its officers, agencies, and corporations. The district court should also take care to protect *pro se* plaintiffs from consequences of confusion or delay attending the resolution of an *in forma pauperis* petition. *Robinson v. America's Best Contacts & Eyeglasses,* 876 F.2d 596 (7th Cir. 1989).

The 1983 revision of this subdivision referred to the "party on whose behalf such service was required," rather than to the "plaintiff," a term used generically elsewhere in this rule to refer to any party initiating a claim against a person who is not a party to the action. To simplify the text, the revision returns to the usual practice in the rule of referring simply to the plaintiff even though its principles apply with equal force to defendants who may assert claims against non-parties under Rules 13(h), 14, 19, 20, or 21.

＊　＊　＊

RULE 4.1.   SERVING OTHER PROCESS.

(a) In General.

Process—other than a summons under Rule 4 or a subpoena under Rule 45—must be served by a United States marshal or deputy marshal or a person specially appointed for that purpose. It may be served anywhere within the territorial limits of the state where the district court is located and, if authorized by a federal statute, beyond those limits. Proof of service must be made under Rule 4(l).

(b) Enforing Orders; Committing for Civil Contempt.

An order committing a person for civil contempt of a decree or injunction issued to enforce federal law may be served and enforced in any district. Any other order in a civil contempt proceeding may be served only in the state where the issuing court is located or elsewhere in the United States within 100 miles where the order was issued.

[Adopted Apr. 22, 1993, effective Dec. 1, 1993; amended April 30, 2007, effective Dec. 1., 2007.]

RULE 5. SERVING AND FILING PLEADINGS AND OTHER PAPERS.

(a) Service: When Required.

(1) *In General.*

Unless these rules provide otherwise, each of the following papers must be served on every party:

(A) an order stating that service is required;

(B) a pleading filed after the original complaint, unless the court orders otherwise under Rule 5(c) because there are numerous defendants;

(C) a discovery paper required to be served on a party, unless the court orders otherwise;

(D) a written motion, except one that may be heard ex parte; and

(E) a written notice, appearance, demand, or offer of judgment, or any similar paper.

(2) *If a Party Fails to Appear.*

No service is required on a party who is in default for failing to appear. But a pleading that asserts a new claim for relief against such a party must be served on that party under Rule 4.

(3) *Seizing Property.*

If an action is begun by seizing property and no person is or need be named as a defendant, any service required before the filing of an appearance, answer, or claim must be made on the person who had custody or possession of the property when it was seized.

(b) Service: How Made.

(1) *Serving an Attorney.*

If a party is represented by an attorney, service under this rule must be made on the attorney unless the court orders service on the party.

(2) *Service in General.* A paper is served under this rule by:

(A) handing it to the person;

(B) leaving it:

(i) at the person's office with a clerk or other person in charge or, if no one is in charge, in a conspicuous place in the office; or

(ii) if the person has no office or the office is closed, at the person's dwelling or usual place of abode with someone of suitable age and discretion who resides there;

(C) mailing it to the person's last known address—in which event service is complete upon mailing;

(D) leaving it with the court clerk if the person has no known address;

(E) sending it to a registered user by filing it with the court's electronic-filing system or sending it by other electronic means that the person consented to in writing—in either of which events service is complete upon filing or sending, but is not effective if the filer or sender learns that it did not reach the person to be served; or

(F) delivering it by any other means that the person consented to in writing—in which event service is complete when the person making service delivers it to the agency designated to make delivery.

(3) *Using Court Facilities.*

[Abrogated (Apr. 26, 2018, eff. Dec. 1, 2018)]

(c) Serving Numerous Defendants.

(1) *In General.*

If an action involves an unusually large number of defendants, the court may, on motion or on its own, order that:

(A) defendants' pleadings and replies to them need not be served on other defendants;

(B) any crossclaim, counterclaim, avoidance, or affirmative defense in those pleadings and replies to them will be treated as denied or avoided by all other parties; and

(C) filing any such pleading and serving it on the plaintiff constitutes notice of the pleading to all parties.

(2) *Notifying Parties.*

A copy of every such order must be served on the parties as the court directs.

(d) Filing.

(1) *Required Filings; Certificate of Service.*

(A) *Papers after the Complaint.* Any paper after the complaint that is required to be served must be filed no later than a reasonable time after service. But disclosures under Rule 26(a) or (2) and the following discovery requests and responses must not be filed until they are used in the proceeding or the court orders filing: depositions, interrogatories, requests for documents or tangible things or to permit entry onto land, and requests for admission.

(B) *Certificate of Service.* No certificate of service is required when a paper is served by filing it with the court's electronic-filing system. When a paper that is required to be served is served by other means:

(i) if the paper is filed, a certificate of service must be filed with it or within a reasonable time after service; and

(ii) if the paper is not filed, a certificate of service need not be filed unless filing is required by court order or by local rule.

(2) *Nonelectronic Filing.*

A paper not filed electronically is filed by delivering it:

(A) to the clerk; or

(B) to a judge who agrees to accept it for filing, and who must then note the filing date on the paper and promptly send it to the clerk.

(3) *Electronic Filing and Signing.*

(A) *By a Represented Person—Generally Required; Exceptions.* A person represented by an attorney must file electronically, unless nonelectronic filing is allowed by the court for good cause or is allowed or required by local rule.

(B) *By an Unrepresented Person—When Allowed or Required.* A person not represented by an attorney:

(i) may file electronically only if allowed by court order or by local rule; and

(ii) may be required to file electronically only by court order, or by a local rule that includes reasonable exceptions.

(C) *Signing.* A filing made through a person's electronic-filing account and authorized by that person, together with that person's name on a signature block, constitutes the person's signature.

(D) *Same as a Written Paper.* A paper filed electronically is a written paper for purposes of these rules.

(4) *Acceptance by the Clerk.*

The clerk must not refuse to file a paper solely because it is not in the form prescribed by these rules or by a local rule or practice.

[Adopted Dec. 20, 1937, effective Sept. 16, 1938; as amended Apr. 26, 2018, effective Dec. 1, 2018.]

ADVISORY COMMITTEE'S NOTE TO 2006 AMENDMENT

Amended Rule 5(e) acknowledges that many courts have required electronic filing by means of a standing order, procedures manual, or local rule. These local practices reflect the advantages that courts and most litigants realize from electronic filing. Courts that mandate electronic filing recognize the need to make exceptions when requiring electronic filing imposes a hardship on a party. Under amended Rule 5(e), a local rule that requires electronic filing must include reasonable exceptions, but Rule 5(e) does not define the scope of those exceptions. Experience with the local rules that have been adopted and that will emerge will aid in drafting new local rules and will facilitate gradual convergence on uniform exceptions, whether in local rules or in an amended Rule 5(e).

ADVISORY COMMITTEE'S NOTE TO 2001 AMENDMENT

Rule 5(b) is restyled.

Rule 5(b)(1) makes it clear that the provision for service on a party's attorney applies only to service made under Rules 5(a) and 77(d). Service under Rules 4, 4.1, 45(b), and 71A(d)(3) — as well as rules that invoke those rules — must be made as provided in those rules.

Subparagraphs (A), (B), and (C) of Rule 5(b)(2) carry forward the method-of-service provisions of former Rule 5(b).

Subparagraph (D) of Rule 5(b)(2) is new. It authorizes service by electronic means or any other means, but only if consent is obtained from the person served. The consent must be express, and cannot be implied from conduct. Early experience with electronic filing as authorized by Rule 5(d) is positive, supporting service by electronic means as well. Consent is required, however, because it is not yet possible to assume universal entry into the world of electronic communication. Subparagraph (D) also authorizes service by nonelectronic means. The Rule 5(b)(2)(B) provision making mail service complete on mailing is extended in subparagraph (D) to make service by electronic means complete on transmission; transmission is effected when the sender does the last act that must be performed by the sender. Service by other agencies is complete on delivery to the designated agency.

Finally, subparagraph (D) authorizes adoption of local rules providing for service through the court. Electronic case filing systems will come to include the capacity to make service by using the court's facilities to transmit all documents filed in the case. It may prove most efficient to establish an environment in which a party can file with the court, making use of the court's transmission facilities to serve the filed paper on all other parties. Transmission might be by such means as direct transmission of the paper, or by transmission of a notice of filing that includes an electronic link for direct access to the paper. Because service is under subparagraph (D), consent must be obtained from the persons served.

Consent to service under Rule 5(b)(2)(D) must be in writing, which can be provided by electronic means. Parties are encouraged to specify the scope and duration of the consent. The specification should include at least the persons to whom service should be made, the appropriate address or location for such service — such as the e-mail address or facsimile machine number, and the format to be used for attachments. A district court may establish a registry or other facility that allows advance consent to service by specified means for future actions.

Rule 6(e) is amended to allow additional time to respond when service is made under Rule 5(b)(2)(D). The additional time does not relieve a party who consents to service under Rule 5(b)(2)(D) of the responsibilities to monitor the facility designated for receiving service and to provide prompt notice of any address change.

Paragraph (3) addresses a question that may arise from a literal reading of the provision that service by electronic means is complete on transmission. Electronic communication is rapidly improving, but lawyers report continuing failures of transmission, particularly with respect to attachments. Ordinarily the risk of non- receipt falls on the person being served, who has consented to this form of service. But the risk should not extend to situations in which the person attempting service learns that the attempted service in fact did not reach the person to be served. Given actual knowledge that the attempt failed, service is not effected. The person attempting service must either try again or show circumstances that justify dispensing with service.

Paragraph (3) does not address the similar questions that may arise when a person attempting service learns that service by means other than electronic means in fact did not reach the person to be served. Case law provides few illustrations of circumstances in which a person attempting service actually knows that the attempt failed but seeks to act as if service had been made. This negative history suggests there is no need to address these problems in Rule 5(b)(3). This silence does not imply any view on these issues, nor on the circumstances that justify various forms of judicial action even though service has not been made.

ADVISORY COMMITTEE'S NOTE TO 2000 AMENDMENT

Subdivision (d). Rule 5(d) is amended to provide that disclosures under Rule 26(a)(1) and (2), and discovery requests and responses under Rules 30, 31, 33, 34, and 36 must not be filed until they are used in the action. "Discovery requests" includes deposition notices and "discovery responses" includes objections. The rule supersedes and invalidates local rules that forbid, permit, or require filing of these materials before they are used in the action. The former Rule 26(a)(4) requirement that disclosures under Rule 26(a)(1) and (2) be filed has been removed. Disclosures under Rule 26(a)(3), however, must be promptly filed as provided in Rule 26(a)(3). Filings in connection with Rule 35 examinations, which involve a motion proceeding when the parties do not agree, are unaffected by these amendments.

* * *

The amended rule provides that discovery materials and disclosures under Rule 26(a)(1) and (a)(2) must not be filed until they are "used in the proceeding." This phrase is meant to refer to proceedings in court. This filing requirement is not triggered by "use" of discovery materials in other discovery activities, such as depositions. In connection with proceedings in court, however, the rule is to be interpreted broadly; any use of discovery materials in court in connection with a motion, a pretrial conference under Rule 16, or otherwise, should be interpreted as use in the proceeding.

Once discovery or disclosure materials are used in the proceeding, the filing requirements of Rule 5(d) should apply to them. But because the filing requirement applies only with regard to materials that are used, only those parts of voluminous materials that are actually used need be filed. Any party would be free to file other pertinent portions of materials that are so used. *See* Fed. R. Evid. 106; *cf.* Rule 32(a) (4). If the parties are unduly sparing in their submissions, the court may order further filings. By local rule, a court could provide appropriate direction regarding the filing of discovery materials, such as depositions, that are used in proceedings.

"Shall" is replaced by "must" under the program to conform amended rules to current style conventions when there is no ambiguity.

RULE 5.1.   CONSTITUTIONAL CHALLENGE TO A STATUTE — NOTICE, CERTIFICATION, AND INTERVENTION.

(a) Notice by a Party.

A party that files a pleading, written motion, or other paper drawing into question the constitutionality of a federal or state statute must promptly:

(1) file a notice of constitutional question stating the question and identifying the paper that raises it, if:

(A) a federal statute is questioned and the parties do not include the United States, one of its agencies, or one of its officers or employees in an official capacity; or

(B) a state statute is questioned and the parties do not include the state, one of its agencies, or one of its officers or employees in an official capacity; and

(2) serve the notice and paper on the Attorney General of the United States if a federal statute is questioned—or on the state attorney general if a state statute is questioned—either by certified or registered mail or by sending it to an electronic address designated by the attorney general for this purpose.

(b) Certification by the Court.

The court must, under 28 U.S.C. § 2403, certify to the appropriate attorney general that a statute has been questioned.

(c) Intervention; Final Decision on the Merits.

Unless the court sets a later time, the attorney general may intervene within 60 days after the notice is filed or after the court certifies the challenge, whichever is earlier. Before the time to intervene expires, the court may reject the constitutional challenge, but may not enter a final judgment holding the statute unconstitutional.

(d) No Forfeiture.

A party's failure to file and serve the notice, or the court's failure to certify, does not forfeit a constitutional claim or defense that is otherwise timely asserted.

[*Adopted April 12, 2006, Dec. 1, 2006; amended April 30, 2007, effective Dec. 1, 2007.*]

RULE 5.2.   PRIVACY PROTECTION FOR FILINGS MADE WITH THE COURT.

(a) Redacted Filings.

Unless the court orders otherwise, in an electronic or paper filing with the court that contains an individual's social-security number, taxpayer-identification number, or birth date, the name of an individual known to be a minor, or a financial-account number, a party or nonparty making the filing may include only:

(1) the last four digits of the social-security number and taxpayer-identification number;

(2) the year of the individual's birth;

(3) the minor's initials; and

(4) the last four digits of the financial-account number.

(b) Exemptions from the Redaction Requirement.

The redaction requirement does not apply to the following:

(1) a financial-account number that identifies the property allegedly subject to forfeiture in a forfeiture proceeding;

(2) the record of an administrative or agency proceeding;

(3) the official record of a state-court proceeding;

(4) the record of a court or tribunal, if that record was not subject to the redaction requirement when originally filed;

(5) a filing covered by Rule 5.2(c) or (d); and

(6) a pro se filing in an action brought under 28 U.S.C. §§ 2241, 2254, or 2255.

(c) Limitations on Remote Access to Electronic Files; Social-Security Appeals and Immigration Cases.

Unless the court orders otherwise, in an action for benefits under the Social Security Act, and in an action or proceeding relating to an order of removal, to relief from removal, or to immigration benefits or detention, access to an electronic file is authorized as follows:

(1) the parties and their attorneys may have remote electronic access to any part of the case file, including the administrative record;

(2) any other person may have electronic access to the full record at the courthouse, but may have remote electronic access only to:

(A) the docket maintained by the court; and

(B) an opinion, order, judgment, or other disposition of the court, but not any other part of the case file or the administrative record.

(d) Filings Made Under Seal.

The court may order that a filing be made under seal without redaction. The court may later unseal the filing or order the person who made the filing to file a redacted version for the public record.

(e) Protective Orders.

For good cause, the court may by order in a case:

(1) require redaction of additional information; or

(2) limit or prohibit a nonparty's remote electronic access to a document filed with the court.

(f) Option for Additional Unredacted Filing Under Seal.

A person making a redacted filing may also file an unredacted copy under seal. The court must retain the unredacted copy as part of the record.

(g) Option for Filing a Reference List.

A filing that contains redacted information may be filed together with a reference list that identifies each item of redacted information and specifies an appropriate identifier that uniquely corresponds to each item listed. The list must be filed under seal and may be amended as of right. Any reference in the case to a listed identifier will be construed to refer to the corresponding item of information.

(h) Waiver of Protection of Identifiers.

A person waives the protection of Rule 5.2(a) as to the person's own information by filing it without redaction and not under seal.

[*Adopted April 30, 2007, effective Dec. 1, 2007.*]

ADVISORY COMMITTEE NOTES TO 2007 ADOPTION

The rule is adopted in compliance with section 205(c)(3) of the E-Government Act of 2002, Public Law 107–347. Section 205(c)(3) requires the Supreme Court to prescribe rules "to protect privacy and security concerns relating to electronic filing of documents and the public availability . . . of documents filed electronically." The rule goes further than the E-Government Act in regulating paper filings even when they are not converted to electronic form. But the number of filings that remain in paper form is certain to diminish over time. Most districts scan paper filings into the electronic case file, where they become available to the public in the same way as documents initially filed in electronic form. It is electronic availability, not the form of the initial filing, that raises the privacy and security concerns addressed in the E- Government Act.

The rule is derived from and implements the policy adopted by the Judicial Conference in September 2001 to address the privacy concerns resulting from public access to electronic case files. *See* http://www.privacy.uscourts.gov/Policy.htm. The Judicial Conference policy is that documents in case files generally should be made available electronically to the same extent they are available at the courthouse, provided that certain "personal data identifiers" are not included in the public file.

While providing for the public filing of some information, such as the last four digits of an account number, the rule does not intend to establish a presumption that this information never could or should be protected. For example, it may well be necessary in individual cases to prevent remote access by nonparties to any part of an account number or social security number. It may also be necessary to protect information not covered by the redaction requirement — such as driver's license numbers and alien registration numbers — in a particular case. In such cases, protection may be sought under subdivision (d) or (e). Moreover, the Rule does not affect the protection available under other rules, such as Civil Rules 16 and 26(c), or under other sources of protective authority.

Parties must remember that any personal information not otherwise protected by sealing or redaction will be made available over the internet. Counsel should notify clients of this fact so that an informed decision may be made on what information is to be included in a document filed with the court.

The clerk is not required to review documents filed with the court for compliance with this rule. The responsibility to redact filings rests with counsel and the party or nonparty making the filing.

Subdivision (c) provides for limited public access in Social Security cases and immigration cases. Those actions are entitled to special treatment due to the prevalence of sensitive information and the volume of filings. Remote electronic access by nonparties is limited to the docket and the written dispositions of the court unless the court orders otherwise. The rule contemplates, however, that nonparties can obtain full access to the case file at the courthouse, including access through the court's public computer terminal.

Subdivision (d) reflects the interplay between redaction and filing under seal. It does not limit or expand the judicially developed rules that govern sealing. But it does reflect the possibility that redaction may provide an alternative to sealing.

Subdivision (e) provides that the court can by order in a particular case for good cause require more extensive redaction than otherwise required by the Rule. Nothing in this subdivision is intended to affect the limitations on sealing that are otherwise applicable to the court.

Subdivision (f) allows a person who makes a redacted filing to file an unredacted document under seal. This provision is derived from section 205(c)(3)(iv) of the E-Government Act.

Subdivision (g) allows the option to file a register of redacted information. This provision is derived from section 205(c)(3)(v) of the E-Government Act, as amended in 2004. In accordance with the E-Government Act, subdivision (g) refers to "redacted" information. The term "redacted" is intended to govern a filing that is prepared with abbreviated identifiers in the first instance, as well as a filing in which a personal identifier is edited after its preparation.

Subdivision (h) allows a person to waive the protections of the rule as to that person's own personal information by filing it unsealed and in unredacted form. One may wish to waive the protection if it is determined that the costs of redaction outweigh the benefits to privacy. If a person files an unredacted identifier by mistake, that person may seek relief from the court.

Trial exhibits are subject to the redaction requirements of Rule 5.2 to the extent they are filed with the court. Trial exhibits that are not initially filed with the court must be redacted in accordance with the rule if and when they are filed as part of an appeal or for other reasons.

RULE 6.   COMPUTING AND EXTENDING TIME; TIME FOR MOTION PAPERS.

(a) Computing Time.

The following rules apply in computing any time period specified in these rules, in any local rule or court order, or in any statute that does not specify a method of computing time.

(1) *Period Stated in Days or a Longer Unit.*

When the period is stated in days or a longer unit of time:.

> (A) exclude the day of the event that triggers the period;

> (B) count every day, including intermediate Saturdays, Sundays, and legal holidays; and

> (C) include the last day of the period, but if the last day is a Saturday, Sunday, or legal holiday, the period continues to run until the end of the next day that is not a Saturday, Sunday, or legal holiday.

(2) *Period Stated in Hours.*

When the period is stated in hours:

> (A) begin counting immediately on the occurrence of the event that triggers the period;

> (B) count every hour, including hours during intermediate Saturdays, Sundays, and legal holidays; and

> (C) if the period would end on a Saturday, Sunday, or legal holiday, the period continues to run until the same time on the next day that is not a Saturday, Sunday, or legal holiday.

(3) *Inaccessibility of the Clerk's Office.*

Unless the court orders otherwise, if the clerk's office is inaccessible:

> (A) on the last day for filing under Rule 6(a)(1), then the time for filing is extended to the first accessible day that is not a Saturday, Sunday, or legal holiday; or

> (B) during the last hour for filing under Rule 6(a)(2), then the time for filing is extended to the same time on the first accessible day that is not a Saturday, Sunday, or legal holiday.

(4) *"Last Day" Defined.*

Unless a different time is set by a statute, local rule, or court order, the last day ends:

> (A) for electronic filing, at midnight in the court's time zone; and

> (B) for filing by other means, when the clerk's office is scheduled to close.

(5) *"Next Day" Defined.*

The "next day" is determined by continuing to count forward when the period is measured after an event and backward when measured before an event.

(6) *"Legal Holiday" Defined.*

"Legal holiday" means:

(A) the day set aside by statute for observing New Year's Day, Martin Luther King Jr.'s Birthday, Washington's Birthday, Memorial Day, Independence Day, Labor Day, Columbus Day, Veterans' Day, Thanksgiving Day, or Christmas Day;

(B) any day declared a holiday by the President or Congress; and

(C) for periods that are measured after an event, any other day declared a holiday by the state where the district court is located.

(b) Extending Time.

(1) *In General.*

When an act may or must be done within a specified time, the court may, for good cause, extend the time:

(A) with or without motion or notice if the court acts, or if a request is made, before the original time or its extension expires; or

(B) on motion made after the time has expired if the party failed to act because of excusable neglect.

(2) *Exceptions.*

A court must not extend the time to act under Rules 50(b) and (d), 52(b), 59(b), (d), and (e), and 60(b).

(c) Motions, Notices of Hearing, and Affidavits.

(1) *In General.*

A written motion and notice of the hearing must be served at least 14 days before the time specified for the hearing, with the following exceptions:

(A) when the motion may be heard ex parte;

(B) when these rules set a different time; or

(C) when a court order — which a party may, for good cause, apply for ex parte — sets a different time.

(2) *Supporting Affidavit.*

Any affidavit supporting a motion must be served with the motion. Except as Rule 59(c) provides otherwise, any opposing affidavit must be served at least 1 day before the hearing, unless the court permits service at another time.

(d) Additional Time After Certain Kinds of Service.

When a party may or must act within a specified time after being served and service is made under Rule 5(b)(2)(C) (mail), (D) (leaving with clerk), or (F) (other means consented to), 3 days are added after the period would otherwise expire under Rule 6(a).

[*Adopted Dec. 20, 1937, effective Sept. 16, 1938; as amended April 28, 2016, effective Dec. 1, 2016.*]

TITLE III.   PLEADINGS AND MOTIONS

RULE 7.   PLEADINGS ALLOWED; FORM OF MOTIONS AND OTHER PAPERS.

(a) Pleadings.

Only these pleadings are allowed:

(1) a complaint;

(2) an answer to a complaint;

(3) an answer to a counterclaim designated as a counterclaim;

(4) an answer to a crossclaim;

(5) a third-party complaint;

(6) an answer to a third-party complaint; and

(7) if the court orders one, a reply to an answer.

(b) Motions and Other Papers.

(1) *In General.*

A request for a court order must be made by motion. The motion must:

(A) be in writing unless made during a hearing or trial;

(B) state with particularity the grounds for seeking the order; and

(C) state the relief sought.

(2) *Form.*

The rules governing captions and other matters of form in pleadings apply to motions and other papers.

[*Adopted Dec. 20, 1937, effective Sept. 16, 1938; amended Dec. 27, 1946, effective Mar. 19, 1948; Jan. 21, 1963, effective July 1, 1963; Apr. 28, 1983, effective Aug. 1, 1983; amended April 30, 2007, effective Dec. 1, 2007.*]

RULE 7.1.   DISCLOSURE STATEMENT.

(a) Who Must File; Contents.

A nongovernmental corporate party must file two copies of a disclosure statement:

(1) identifies any parent corporation and any publicly held corporation own-ing 10% or more of its stock; or

(2) states that there is no such corporation.

(b) Time to File; Supplemental Filing.

A party must:

(1) file the disclosure statement with its first appearance, pleading, petition, motion, response, or other request addressed to the court, and

(2) promptly file a supplemental statement if any required information changes. [*Adopted Apr. 29, 2002, effective Dec. 1, 2002; amended April 30, 2007, effective Dec. 1, 2007.*]

RULE 8.   GENERAL RULES OF PLEADING.

(a) Claim for Relief.

A pleading that states a claim for relief must contain:

(1) a short and plain statement of the grounds for the court's jurisdiction, unless the court already has jurisdiction and the claim needs no new jurisdictional support;

(2) a short and plain statement of the claim showing that the pleader is entitled to relief; and

(3) a demand for the relief sought, which may include relief in the alternative or different types of relief.

(b) Defenses; Admissions and Denials.

(1) *In General.*

In responding to a pleading, a party must:

(A) state in short and plain terms its defenses to each claim asserted against it; and

(B) admit or deny the allegations asserted against it by an opposing party.

(2) *Denials—Responding to the Substance.*

A denial must fairly respond to the substance of the allegation.

(3) *General and Specific Denials.*

A party that intends in good faith to deny all the allegations of a pleading—including the jurisdictional grounds—may do so by a general denial. A party that does not intend to deny all the allegations must either specifically deny designated allegations or generally deny all except those specifically admitted.

(4) *Denying Part of an Allegation.*

A party that intends in good faith to deny only part of an allegation must admit the part that is true and deny the rest.

(5) *Lacking Knowledge or Information.*

A party that lacks knowledge or information sufficient to form a belief about the truth of an allegation must so state, and the statement has the effect of a denial.

(6) *Effect of Failing to Deny.*

An allegation — other than one relating to the amount of damages — is admitted if a responsive pleading is required and the allegation is not denied. If a responsive pleading is not required, an allegation is considered denied or avoided.

(c) Affirmative Defenses.

(1) *In General.*

In responding to a pleading, a party must affirmatively state any avoidance or affirmative defense, including:

- accord and satisfaction;
- arbitration and award;
- assumption of risk;
- contributory negligence;
- duress;
- estoppel;
- failure of consideration;
- fraud;
- illegality;
- injury by fellow servant;
- laches;
- license;
- payment;
- release;
- res judicata;
- statute of frauds;
- statute of limitations; and
- waiver.

(2) *Mistaken Designation.*

If a party mistakenly designates a defense as a counterclaim, or a counterclaim as a defense, the court must, if justice requires, treat the pleading as though it were correctly designated, and may impose terms for doing so.

(d) Pleading to Be Concise and Direct; Alternative Statements; Inconsistency.

(1) *In General.*

Each allegation must be simple, concise, and direct. No technical form is required.

(2) *Alternative Statements of a Claim or Defense.*

A party may set out two or more statements of a claim or defense alternatively or hypothetically, either in a single count or defense or in separate ones. If a party makes alternative statements, the pleading is sufficient if any one of them is sufficient.

(3) *Inconsistent Claims or Defenses.*

A party may state as many separate claims or defenses as it has, regardless of consistency.

(e) Construing Pleadings.

Pleadings must be construed so as to do justice.

[*Adopted Dec. 20, 1937, effective Sept. 16, 1938; amended Feb. 28, 1966, effective July 1, 1966; Mar. 2, 1987, effective Aug. 1, 1987; amended April 30, 2007, effective Dec. 1, 2007; amended April 28, 2010, effective December 1, 2010.*]

RULE 9.   PLEADING SPECIAL MATTERS.

(a) Capacity or Authority to Sue; Legal Existence.

(1) *In General.*

Except when required to show that the court has jurisdiction, a pleading need not allege:

(A) a party's capacity to sue or be sued;

(B) a party's authority to sue or be sued in a representative capacity; or

(C) the legal existence of an organized association of persons that is made a party.

(2) *Raising Those Issues.*

To raise any of those issues, a party must do so by a specific denial, which must state any supporting facts that are peculiarly within the party's knowledge.

(b) Fraud or Mistake; Conditions of Mind.

In alleging fraud or mistake, a party must state with particularity the circumstances constituting fraud or mistake. Malice, intent, knowledge, and other conditions of a person's mind may be alleged generally.

(c) Conditions Precedent.

In pleading conditions precedent, it suffices to allege generally that all conditions precedent have occurred or been performed. But when denying that a condition precedent has occurred or been performed, a party must do so with particularity.

(d) Official Document or Act.

In pleading an official document or official act, it suffices to allege that the document was legally issued or the act legally done.

(e) Judgment.

In pleading a judgment or decision of a domestic or foreign court, a judicial or quasi-judicial tribunal, or a board or officer, it suffices to plead the judgment or decision without showing jurisdiction to render it.

(f) Time and Place.

An allegation of time or place is material when testing the sufficiency of a pleading.

(g) Special Damages.

If an item of special damage is claimed, it must be specifically stated.

(h) Admiralty or Maritime Claim.

(1) *How Designated.*

If a claim for relief is within the admiralty or maritime jurisdiction and also within the court's subject-matter jurisdiction on some other ground, the pleading may designate the claim as an admiralty or maritime claim for purposes of Rules 14(c), 38(e), and 82 and the Supplemental Rules for Admiralty or Maritime Claims and Asset Forfeiture Actions. A claim cognizable only in the admiralty or maritime jurisdiction is an admiralty or maritime claim for those purposes, whether or not so designated.

(2) *Designation for Appeal.*

A case that includes an admiralty or maritime claim within this subdivision (h) is an admiralty case within 28 U.S.C. § 1292(a)(3).

[*Adopted Dec. 20, 1937, effective Sept. 16, 1938; amended Feb. 28, 1966, effective July 1, 1966; Dec. 4, 1967, effective July 1, 1968; Mar. 30, 1970, effective July 1, 1970; Mar. 2, 1987, effective Aug. 1, 1987; Apr. 11, 1997, effective Dec. 1, 1997; April 12, 2006, effective December 1, 2006; amended April 30, 2007, effective Dec. 1, 2007.*]

RULE 10.   FORM OF PLEADINGS.

(a) Caption; Names of Parties.

Every pleading must have a caption setting forth the court's name, a title, a file number, and a Rule 7(a) designation. The title of the complaint must name all the parties; the title of other pleadings, after naming the first party on each side, may refer generally to other parties.

(b) Paragraphs; Separate Statements.

A party must state its claims or defenses in numbered paragraphs, each limited as far as practicable to a single set of circumstances. A later pleading may refer by number to a paragraph in an earlier pleading. If doing so would promote clarity, each claim founded upon a separate transaction or occurrence—and each defense other than a denial—must be stated in a separate count or defense.

(c) Adoption by Reference; Exhibits.

A statement in a pleading may be adopted by reference elsewhere in the same pleading or in another pleading or motion. A copy of any written instrument that is an exhibit to a pleading is a part of the pleading for all purposes.

[*Adopted Dec. 20, 1937, effective Sept. 16, 1938; amended April 30, 2007, effective Dec. 1, 2007.*]

RULE 11. SIGNING PLEADINGS, MOTIONS, AND OTHER PAPERS; REPRESENTATIONS TO COURT; SANCTIONS.

(a) Signature.

Every pleading, written motion, and other paper must be signed by at least one attorney of record in the attorney's name—or by a party personally if the party is unrepresented. The paper must state the signer's address, e-mail address, and telephone number. Unless a rule or statute specifically states otherwise, a pleading need not be verified or accompanied by affidavit. The court must strike an unsigned paper unless the omission is promptly corrected after being called to the attorney's or party's attention.

(b) Representations to the Court.

By presenting to the court pleading, written motion, or other paper—whether by signing, filing, submitting, or later advocating it—an attorney or unrepresented party certifies that to the best of the person's knowledge, information, and belief, formed after an inquiry reasonable under the circumstances:

(1) it is not being presented for any improper purpose, such as to harass, cause unnecessary delay, or needless increase the cost of litigation;

(2) the claims, defenses, and other legal contentions therein are warranted by existing law or by a nonfrivolous argument for the extending, modifying, or reversing existing law or for establishing new law;

(3) the factual contentions have evidentiary support or, if specifically so identified, will likely to have evidentiary support after a reasonable opportunity for further investigation or discovery; and

(4) the denials of factual contentions are warranted on the evidence or, if specifically so identified, are reasonably based on belief or a lack of information.

(c) Sanctions.

(1) *In General.*

If, after notice and a reasonable opportunity to respond, the court determines that Rule 11(b) has been violated, the court may impose an appropriate sanction on any attorney, law firm, or party that violated the rule or is responsible for the violation. Absent exceptional circumstances, a law firm must be held jointly responsible for a violation committed by its partner, associate, or employee.

(2) *Motion for Sanctions.*

A motion for sanctions must be made separately from any other motion and must describe the specific conduct that allegedly violates Rule 11(b). The motion must be served under Rule 5, but it must not be filed or be presented to the court if the challenged paper, claim, defense, contention, or denial is withdrawn or appropri- ately corrected within 21 days after service or within another time the court sets. If warranted, the court may award to the prevailing party the reasonable expenses, including attorney's fees, incurred for the motion.

(3) *On the Court's Initiative.*

On its own, the court may order an attorney, law firm, or party to show cause why conduct specifically described in the order has not violated Rule 11(b).

(4) *Nature of a Sanction.*

A sanction imposed under this rule must be limited to what suffices to deter repetition of the conduct or comparable conduct by others similarly situated. The sanction may include nonmonetary directives; an order to pay a penalty into court; or, if imposed on motion and warranted for effective deterrence, an order directing payment to the movant of part or all of the reasonable attorney's fees and other expenses directly resulting from the violation.

(5) *Limitations on Monetary Sanctions.*

The court must not impose a monetary sanction:

(A) against a represented party for violating Rule 11(b)(2); or

(B) on its own, unless it issued the show-cause order under Rule 11(c)(3) before voluntary dismissal or settlement of the claims made by or against the party that is, or whose attorneys are, to be sanctioned.

(6) *Requirements for an Order.*

An order imposing a sanction must describe the sanctioned conduct and explain the basis for the sanction.

(d) Inapplicability to Discovery.

This rule does not apply to disclosures and discovery requests, responses, objections, and motions under Rules 26 through 37.

[*Adopted Dec. 20, 1937, effective Sept. 16, 1938; amended Apr. 28, 1983, effective Aug. 1, 1983; Mar. 2, 1987, effective Aug. 1, 1987; Apr. 22, 1993, effective Dec. 1, 1993; amended April 30, 2007, effective Dec. 1, 2007.*]

NOTE OF ADVISORY COMMITTEE ON 1993 AMENDMENTS TO RULES

Purpose of revision. This revision is intended to remedy problems that have arisen in the interpretation and application of the 1983 revision of the rule. * * *

The rule retains the principle that attorneys and pro se litigants have an obligation to the court to refrain from conduct that frustrates the aims of Rule 1. The revision broadens the scope of this obligation, but places greater constraints on the imposition of sanctions and should reduce the number of motions for sanctions presented to the court. New subdivision (d) removes from the ambit of this rule all discovery requests, responses, objections, and motions subject to the provisions of Rule 26 through 37.

Subdivision (a). Retained in this subdivision are the provisions requiring signatures on pleadings, written motions, and other papers. Unsigned papers are to be received by the Clerk, but then are to be stricken if the omission of the signature is not corrected promptly after being called to the attention of the attorney or pro se litigant. Correction can be made by signing the paper on file or by submitting a duplicate that contains the signature. A court may require by local rule that papers contain additional identifying information regarding the parties or attorneys, such as telephone numbers to facilitate facsimile transmissions, though, as for omission of a signature, the paper should not be rejected for failure to provide such information.

The sentence in the former rule relating to the effect of answers under oath is no longer needed and has been eliminated. The provision in the former rule that signing a paper constitutes a certificate that it has been read by the signer also has been eliminated as unnecessary. The obligations imposed under subdivision (b) obviously require that a pleading, written motion, or other paper be read before it is filed or submitted to the court.

Subdivisions (b) and (c). These subdivisions restate the provisions requiring attorneys and pro se litigants to conduct a reasonable inquiry into the law and facts before signing pleadings, written motions, and other documents, and prescribing sanctions for violation of these obligations. The revision in part expands the responsibilities of litigants to the court, while providing greater constraints and flexibility in dealing with infractions of the rule. The rule continues to require litigants to "stop-and-think" before initially making legal or factual contentions. It also, however, emphasizes the duty of candor by subjecting litigants to potential sanctions for insisting upon a position after it is no longer tenable and by generally providing protection against sanctions if they withdraw or correct contentions after a potential violation is called to their attention.

The rule applies only to assertions contained in papers filed with or submitted to the court. It does not cover matters arising for the first time during oral presentations to the court, when counsel may make statements that would not have been made if there had been more time for study and reflection. However, a litigant's obligations with respect to the contents of these papers are not measured solely as of the time they are filed with or submitted to the court, but include reaffirming to the court and advocating positions contained in those pleadings and motions after learning that they cease to have any merit. For example, an attorney who during a pretrial conference insists on a claim or defense should be viewed as "presenting to the court" that contention and would be subject to the obligations of subdivision (b) measured as of that time. Similarly, if after a notice of removal is filed, a party urges in federal court the allegations of a pleading filed in state court (whether as claims, defenses, or in disputes regarding removal or remand), it would be viewed as "presenting"—and hence certifying to the district court under Rule 11—those allegations.

The certification with respect to allegations and other factual contentions is revised in recognition that sometimes a litigant may have good reason to believe that a fact is true or false but may need discovery, formal or informal, from opposing parties or third persons to gather and confirm the evidentiary basis for the allegation. Tolerance of factual contentions in initial pleadings by plaintiffs or defendants when specifically identified as made on information and belief does not relieve litigants from the obligation to conduct an appropriate investigation into the facts that is reasonable under the circumstances; it is not a license to join parties, make claims, or present defenses without any factual basis or justification. Moreover, if evidentiary support is not obtained after a reasonable opportunity for further investigation or discovery, the party has a duty under the rule not to persist with that contention. Subdivision (b) does not require a formal amendment to pleadings for which evidentiary support is not obtained, but rather calls upon a litigant not thereafter to advocate such claims or defenses.

The certification is that there is (or likely will be) "evidentiary support" for the allegation, not that the party will prevail with respect to its contention regarding the fact. That summary judgment is rendered against a party does not necessarily mean, for purposes of this certification, that it had no evidentiary support for its position. On the other hand, if a party has evidence with respect to a contention that would suffice to defeat a motion for contention that would suffice to defeat a motion for summary judgment based thereon, it would have sufficient "evidentiary support" for purposes of Rule 11.

Denials of factual contentions involve somewhat different considerations. Often, of course, a denial is premised upon the existence of evidence contradicting the alleged fact. At other times a denial is permissible because, after an appropriate investigation, a party has no information concerning the matter or, indeed, has a reasonable basis for doubting the credibility of the only evidence relevant to the matter. A party should not deny an allegation it knows to be true; but it is not required, simply because it lacks contradictory evidence, to admit an allegation that it believes is not true.

The changes in subdivisions (b)(3) and (b)(4) will serve to equalize the burden of the rule upon plaintiffs and defendants, who under Rule 8(b) are in effect allowed to deny allegations by stating that from their initial investigation they lack sufficient information to form a belief as to the truth of the allegation. If, after further investigation or discovery, a denial is no longer warranted, the defendant should not continue to insist on that denial. While sometimes helpful, formal amendment of the pleadings to withdraw an allegation or denial is not required by subdivision (b).

Arguments for extensions, modifications, or reversals of existing law or for creation of new law do not violate subdivision (b)(2) provided they are "nonfrivolous." This establishes an objective standard, intended to eliminate any "empty-head pure-heart" justification for patently frivolous arguments. However, the extent to which a litigant has researched the issues and found some support for its theories even in minority opinions, in law review articles, or through consultation with other attorneys should certainly be taken into account in determining whether paragraph (2) has been violated. Although arguments for a change of law are not required to be specifically so identified, a contention that is so identified should be viewed with greater tolerance under the rule.

The court has available a variety of possible sanctions to impose for violations, such as striking the offending paper; issuing an admonition, reprimand, or censure; requiring participation in seminars or other educational programs; ordering a fine payable to the court; referring the matter to disciplinary authorities (or, in the case of government attorneys, to the Attorney General, Inspector General, or agency head), etc. *See Manual for Complex Litigation, Second*, § 42.3. The rule does not attempt to enumerate the factors a court should consider in deciding whether to impose a sanction or what sanctions would be appropriate in the circumstances; but, for emphasis, it does specifically note that a sanction may be nonmonetary as well as monetary. Whether the improper conduct was willful, or negligent; whether it was part of a pattern of activity, or an isolated event; whether it infected the entire pleading, or only one particular count or defense; whether the person has engaged in similar conduct in other litigation; whether it was intended to injure; what effect it had on the litigation process in time or expense; whether the responsible person is trained in the law; what amount, given the financial resources of the responsible person, is needed to deter that person from repetition in the same case; what amount is needed to deter similar activity by other litigants: all of these may in a particular case be proper considerations. The court has significant discretion in determining what sanctions, if any, should be imposed for a violation, subject to the principle that the sanctions should not be more severe than reasonably necessary to deter repetition of the conduct by the offending person or comparable conduct by similarly situated persons.

Since the purpose of Rule 11 sanctions is to deter rather than to compensate, the rule provides that, if a monetary sanction is imposed, it should ordinarily be paid into court as a penalty. However, under unusual circumstances, particularly for (b)(1) violations, deterrence may be ineffective unless the sanction not only requires the person violating the rule to make a monetary payment, but also directs that some or all of this payment be made to those injured by the violation. Accordingly, the rule authorizes the court, if requested in a motion and if so warranted, to award attorney's fees to another party. Any such award to another party, however, should not exceed the expenses and attorneys' fees for the services directly and unavoidably caused by the violation of the certification requirement. If, for example, a wholly unsupportable count were included in a multi-count complaint or counterclaim for the purpose of needlessly increasing the cost of litigation to an impecunious adversary, any award of expenses should be limited to those directly caused by inclusion of the improper count, and not those resulting from the filing of the complaint or answer itself. The award should not provide compensation for services that could have been avoided by an earlier disclosure of evidence or an earlier challenge to the groundless claims or defenses. Moreover, partial reimbursement of fees may constitute a sufficient deterrent with respect to violations by persons having modest financial resources. In cases brought under statutes providing for fees to be awarded to prevailing parties, the court should not employ cost-shifting under this rule in a manner that would be inconsistent with the standards that govern the statutory award of fees, such as stated in *Christiansburg Garment Co. v. EEOC*, 434 U.S. 412 (1978).

The sanction should be imposed on the persons-whether attorneys, law firms, or parties-who have violated the rule or who may be determined to be responsible for the violation. The person signing, filing, submitting, or advocating a document has a nondelegable responsibility to the court, and in most situations is the person to be sanctioned for a violation. Absent exceptional circumstances, a law firm is to be held also responsible when, as a result of a motion under subdivision (c)(1)(A), one of its partners, associates, or employees is determined to have violated the rule. Since such a motion may be filed only if the offending paper is not withdrawn or corrected within 21 days after service of the motion, it is appropriate that the law firm ordinarily be viewed as jointly responsible under established principles of agency. This provision is designed to remove the restrictions of the former rule. *Cf. Pavelic & LeFlore v. Marvel Entertainment Group*, 493 U.S. 120 (1989) (1983 version of Rule 11 does not permit sanctions against law firm of attorney signing groundless complaint).

The revision permits the court to consider whether other attorneys in the firm, co-counsel, other law firms, or the party itself should be held accountable for their part in causing a violation. When appropriate, the court can make an additional inquiry in order to determine whether the sanction should be imposed on such persons, firms, or parties either in addition to or, in unusual circumstances, instead of the person actually making the presentation to the court. For example, such an inquiry may be appropriate in cases involving governmental agencies or other institutional parties that frequently impose substantial restrictions on the discretion of individual attorneys employed by it.

Sanctions that involve monetary awards (such as a fine or an award of attorney's fees) may not be imposed on a represented party for causing a violation of subdivision (b)(2), involving frivolous contentions of law. Monetary responsibility for such violations is more properly placed solely on the party's attorneys. With this limitation, the rule should not be subject to attack under the Rules Enabling Act. *See Willy v. Coastal Corp.*, 503 U.S. 131 (1992); *Business Guides, Inc. v. Chromatic Communications Enter. Inc.*, 498 U.S. 533 (1991). This restriction does not limit the court's power to impose sanctions or remedial orders that may have collateral financial consequences upon a party, such as dismissal of a claim, preclusion of a defense, or preparation of amended pleadings.

Explicit provision is made for litigants to be provided notice of the alleged violation and an opportunity to respond before sanctions are imposed. Whether the matter should be decided solely on the basis of written submissions or should be scheduled for oral argument (or, indeed, for evidentiary presentation) will depend on the circumstances. If the court imposes a sanction, it must, unless waived, indicate its reasons in a written order or on the record; the court should not ordinarily have to explain its denial of a motion for sanctions. Whether a violation has occurred and what sanctions, if any, to impose for a violation are matters committed to the discretion of the trial court; accordingly, as under current law, the standard for appellate review of these decisions will be for abuse of discretion. See Cooter & Gell v. Hartmarx Corp., 496 U.S. 384 (1990) (noting, however, that an abuse would be established if the court based its ruling on an erroneous view of the law or on a clearly erroneous assessment of the evidence).

The revision leaves for resolution on a case-by-case basis, considering the particular circumstances involved, the question as to when a motion for violation of Rule 11 should be served and when, if filed, it should be decided. Ordinarily the motion should be served promptly after the inappropriate paper is filed, and, if delayed too long, may be viewed as untimely. In other circumstances, it should not be served until the other party has had a reasonable opportunity for discovery. Given the "safe harbor" provisions discussed below, a party cannot delay serving its Rule 11 motion until conclusion of the case (or judicial rejection of the offending contention).

Rule 11 motions should not be made or threatened for minor, inconsequential violations of the standards prescribed by subdivision (b). They should not be employed as a discovery device or to test the legal sufficiency or efficacy of allegations in the pleadings; other motions are available for those purposes. Nor should Rule 11 motions be prepared to emphasize the merits of a party's position, to exact an unjust settlement, to intimidate an adversary into withdrawing contentions that are fairly debatable, to increase the costs of litigation, to create a conflict of interest between attorney and client, or to seek disclosure of matters otherwise protected by the attorney-client privilege or the work-product doctrine. As under the prior rule, the court may defer its ruling (or its decision as to the identity of the persons to be sanctioned) until final resolution of the case in order to avoid immediate conflicts of interest and to reduce the disruption created if a disclosure of attorney-client communications is needed to determine whether a violation occurred or to identify the person responsible for the violation.

The rule provides that requests for sanctions must be made as a separate motion, i.e., not simply included as an additional prayer for relief contained in another motion. The motion for sanctions is not, however, to be filed until at least 21 days (or such other period as the court may set) after being served. If, during this period, the alleged violation is corrected, as by withdrawing (whether formally or informally) some allegation or contention, the motion should not be filed with the court. These provisions are intended to provide a type of "safe harbor" against motions under Rule 11 in that a party will not be subject to sanctions on the basis of another party's motion unless, after receiving the motion, it refuses to withdraw that position or to acknowledge candidly that it does not currently have evidence to support a specified allegation. Under the former rule, parties were sometimes reluctant to abandon a questionable contention lest that be viewed as evidence of a violation of Rule 11; under the revision, the timely withdrawal of a contention will protect a party against a motion for sanctions.

To stress the seriousness of a motion for sanctions and to define precisely the conduct claimed to violate the rule, the revision provides that the "safe harbor" period begins to run only upon service of the motion. In most cases, however, counsel should be expected to give informal notice to the other party, whether in person or by a telephone call or letter, of a potential violation before proceeding to prepare and serve a Rule 11 motion.

As under former Rule 11, the filing of a motion for sanctions is itself subject to the requirements of the rule and can lead to sanctions. However, service of a cross motion under Rule 11 should rarely be needed since under the revision the court may award to the person who prevails on a motion under Rule 11 — whether the movant or the target of the motion — reasonable expenses, including attorney's fees, incurred in presenting or opposing the motion.

The power of the court to act on its own initiative is retained, but with the condition that this be done through a show cause order. This procedure provides the person with notice and an opportunity to respond. The revision provides that a monetary sanction imposed after a court-initiated show cause order be limited to a penalty payable to the court and that it be imposed only if the show cause order is issued before any voluntary dismissal or an agreement of the parties to settle the claims made by or against the litigant. Parties settling a case should not be subsequently faced with an unexpected order from the court leading to monetary sanctions that might have affected their willingness to settle or voluntarily dismiss a case. Since show cause orders will ordinarily be issued only in situations that are akin to a contempt of court, the rule does not provide a "safe harbor" to a litigant for withdrawing a claim, defense, etc., after a show cause order has been issued on the court's own initiative. Such corrective action, however, should be taken into account in deciding what-if any-sanction to impose if, after consideration of the litigant's response, the court concludes that a violation has occurred.

Subdivision (d). Rules 26(g) and 37 establish certification standards and sanctions that apply to discovery disclosures, requests, responses, objections, and motions. It is appropriate that Rules 26 through 37, which are specially designed for the discovery process, govern such documents and conduct rather than the more general provisions of Rule 11. Subdivision (d) has been added to accomplish this result.

Rule 11 is not the exclusive source for control of improper presentations of claims, defenses, or contentions. It does not supplant statutes permitting awards of attorney's fees to prevailing parties or alter the principles governing such awards. It does not inhibit the court in punishing for contempt, in exercising its inherent powers, or in imposing sanctions, awarding expenses, or directing remedial action authorized under other rules or under 28 U.S.C. § 1927. *See Chambers v. NASCO*, U.S. (1991). *Chambers* cautions, however, against reliance upon inherent powers if appropriate sanctions can be imposed under provisions such as Rule 11, and the procedures specified in Rule 11—notice, opportunity to respond, and findings—should ordinarily be employed when imposing a sanction under the court's inherent powers. Finally, it should be noted that Rule 11 does not preclude a party from initiating an independent action for malicious prosecution or abuse of process.

RULE 12. DEFENSES AND OBJECTIONS: WHEN AND HOW PRESENTED; MOTION FOR JUDGMENT ON THE PLEADINGS; CONSOLIDATING MOTIONS; WAIVING DEFENSES; PRETRIAL HEARING.

(a) **Time to Serve a Responsive Pleadings.**

(1) *In General.*

Unless another time is specified by this rule or a federal statute, the time for serving a responsive pleading is as follows:

(A) A defendant must serve an answer:

(i) within 21 days after being served with the summons and complaint; or

(ii) if it has timely waived service under Rule 4(d), within 60 days after the request for a waiver was sent, or within 90 days after it was sent to the defendant outside any judicial district of the United States.

(B) A party must serve an answer to a counterclaim or crossclaim within 21 days after being served with the pleading that states the counterclaim or crossclaim.

(C) A party must serve a reply to an answer within 21 days after being served with an order to reply, unless the order specifies a different time.

(2) *United States and Its Agencies, Officers, or Employees Sued in an Official Capacity.*

The United States, a United States agency, or a United States officer or employee sued only in an official capacity must serve an answer to a complaint, counterclaim, or crossclaim within 60 days after service on the United States attorney.

(3) *United States Officers or Employees Sued in an Individual Capacity.*

A United States officer or employee sued in an individual capacity for an act or omission occurring in connection with duties performed on the United States' behalf must serve an answer to a complaint, counterclaim, or crossclaim within 60 days after service on the officer or employee or service on the United States attorney, whichever is later.

(4) *Effect of a Motion.*

Unless the court sets a different time, serving a motion under this rule alters these periods as follows:

(A) if the court denies the motion or postpones its disposition until trial, the responsive pleading must be served within 14 days after notice of the court's action; or

(B) if the court grants a motion for a more definite statement, the responsive pleading must be served within 14 days after the more definite statement is served.

(b) How to Present Defenses.

Every defense to a claim for relief in any pleading must be asserted in the responsive pleading if one is required. But a party may assert the following defenses by motion:

(1) lack of subject-matter jurisdiction;

(2) lack of personal jurisdiction;

(3) improper venue;

(4) insufficient process; — *mistake in paperwork*

(5) insufficient service of process;

(6) failure to state a claim upon which relief can be granted; and

(7) failure to join a party under Rule 19. A motion asserting any of these defenses must be made before pleading if a responsive pleading is allowed. If a pleading sets out a claim for relief that does not require a responsive pleading, an opposing party may assert at trial any defense to that claim. No defense or objection is waived by joining it with one or more other defenses or objections in a responsive pleading or in a motion.

(c) Motion for Judgment on the Pleadings.

After the pleadings are closed—but early enough not to delay trial—a party may move for judgment on the pleadings.

(d) Result of Presenting Matters Outside the Pleadings.

If, on a motion under Rule 12(b)(6) or 12(c), matters outside the pleadings are presented to and not excluded by the court, the motion must be treated as one for summary judgment under Rule 56. All parties must be given a reasonable opportunity to present all the material that is pertinent to the motion.

(e) Motion for a More Definite Statement.

A party may move for a more definite statement of a pleading to which a responsive pleading is allowed but which is so vague or ambiguous that the party cannot reasonably prepare a response. The motion must be made before filing a responsive pleading and must point out the defects complained of and the details desired. If the court orders a more definite statement and the order is not obeyed within 14 days after notice of the order or within the time the court sets, the court may strike the pleading or issue any other appropriate order.

(f) Motion to Strike.

The court may strike from a pleading an insufficient defense or any redundant, immaterial, impertinent, or scandalous matter. The court may act:

(1) on its own; or

(2) on motion made by a party either before responding to the pleading or, if a response is not allowed, within 21 days after being served with the pleading.

(g) Joining Motions. *need to know*

(1) *Right to Join.*

A motion under this rule may be joined with any other motion allowed by this rule.

(2) *Limitation on Further Motions.*

Except as provided in Rule 12(h)(2) or (3), a party that makes a motion under this rule must not make another motion under this rule raising a defense or objection that was available to the party but omitted from its earlier motion.

(h) Waiving and Preserving Certain Defenses.

(1) *When Some Are Waived.*

A party waives any defense listed in Rule 12(b)(2)–(5) by:

(A) omitting it from a motion in the circumstances described in Rule 12(g)(2);

or

(B) failing to either:

(i) make it by motion under this rule; or

(ii) include it in a responsive pleading or in an amendment allowed by Rule 15(a)(1) as a matter of course.

(2) *When to Raise Others.*

Failure to state a claim upon which relief can be granted, to join a person required by Rule 19(b), or to state a legal defense to a claim may be raised:

(A) in any pleading allowed or ordered under Rule 7(a);

(B) by a motion under Rule 12(c); or

(C) at trial.

(3) *Lack of Subject-Matter Jurisdiction.*

If the court determines at any time that it lacks subject-matter jurisdiction, the court must dismiss the action.

(i) Hearing Before Trial.

If a party so moves, any defense listed in Rule 12(b)(1)–(7)—whether made in a pleading or by motion—and a motion under Rule 12(c) must be heard and decided before trial unless the court orders a deferral until trial.

[Adopted Dec. 20, 1937, effective Sept. 16, 1938; amended Dec. 27, 1946, effective Mar. 19, 1948; Jan. 21, 1963, effective July 1, 1963; Feb. 28, 1966, effective July 1, 1966; Mar. 2, 1987, effective Aug. 1, 1987; Apr. 22, 1993, effective Dec. 1, 1993; amended Apr. 17, 2000, effective Dec. 1, 2000; amended April 30, 2007, effective Dec. 1, 2007; amended March 26, 2009, effective Dec. 1, 2009.]

RULE 13.   COUNTERCLAIM AND CROSSCLAIM.

(a) Compulsory Counterclaim.

(1) *In General.*

A pleading must state as a counterclaim any claim that — at the time of its service — the pleader has against an opposing party if the claim:

> (A) arises out of the transaction or occurrence that is the subject matter of the opposing party's claim; and

> (B) does not require adding another party over whom the court cannot acquire jurisdiction.

(2) *Exceptions.*

The pleader need not state the claim if:

> (A) when the action was commenced, the claim was the subject of another pending action; or

> (B) the opposing party sued on its claim by attachment or other process that did not establish personal jurisdiction over the pleader on that claim, and the pleader does not assert any counterclaim under this rule.

(b) Permissive Counterclaim.

A pleading may state as a counterclaim against an opposing party any claim that is not compulsory.

(c) Relief Sought in a Counterclaim.

A counterclaim need not diminish or defeat the recovery sought by the opposing party. It may request relief that exceeds in amount or differs in kind from the relief sought by the opposing party.

(d) Counterclaim Against the United States.

These rules do not expand the right to assert a counterclaim — or to claim a credit — against the United States or a United States officer or agency.

(e) Counterclaim Maturing or Acquired After Pleading.

The court may permit a party to file a supplemental pleading asserting a counterclaim that matured or was acquired by the party after serving an earlier pleading.

(f)

[Abrogated.]

(g) Crossclaim Against a Coparty.

A pleading may state as a crossclaim any claim by one party against a coparty if the claim arises out of the transaction or occurrence that is the subject matter of the original action or of a counterclaim, or if the claim relates to any property that is the subject matter of the original action. The crossclaim may include a claim that the coparty is or may be liable to the crossclaimant for all or part of a claim asserted in the action against the crossclaimant.

(h) Joining Additional Parties.

Rules 19 and 20 govern the addition of a person as a party to a counterclaim or crossclaim.

(i) Separate Trials; Separate Judgments.

If the court orders separate trials under Rule 42(b), it may enter judgment on a counterclaim or crossclaim under Rule 54(b) when it has jurisdiction to do so, even if the opposing party's claims have been dismissed or otherwise resolved.

[*Adopted Dec. 20, 1937, effective Sept. 16, 1938; amended Dec. 27, 1946, effective Mar. 19, 1948; Jan. 21, 1963, effective July 1, 1963; Feb. 28, 1966, effective July 1, 1966; Mar. 2, 1987, effective Aug. 1, 1987; amended Apr. 17, 2000, effective Dec. 1, 2000; April 12, 2006, effective Dec. 1, 2006; amended April 30, 2007, effective Dec. 1, 2007; amended March 26, 2009, effective Dec. 1, 2009.*]

RULE 14.   THIRD-PARTY PRACTICE.

(a) When a Defending Party May Bring in a Third Party.

(1) *Timing of the Summons and Complaint.*

A defending party may, as third-party plaintiff, serve a summons and complaint on a nonparty who is or may be liable to it for all or part of the claim against it. But the third-party plaintiff must, by motion, obtain the court's leave if it files the third-party complaint more than 14 days after serving its original answer.

(2) *Third-Party Defendant's Claims and Defenses.*

The person served with the summons and third-party complaint — the "third-party defendant":

(A) must assert any defense against the third-party plaintiff's claim under Rule 12;

(B) must assert any counterclaim against the third-party plaintiff under Rule 13(a), and may assert any counterclaim against the third-party plaintiff under Rule 13(b) or any crossclaim against another third-party defendant under Rule 13(g);

(C) may assert against the plaintiff any defense that the third-party plaintiff has to the plaintiff's claim; and

(D) may also assert against the plaintiff any claim arising out of the transaction or occurrence that is the subject matter of the plaintiff's claim against the third-party plaintiff.

(3) *Plaintiff's Claims Against a Third-Party Defendant.*

The plaintiff may assert against the third-party defendant any claim arising out of the transaction or occurrence that is the subject matter of the plaintiff's claim against the third-party plaintiff. The third-party defendant must then assert any defense under Rule 12 and any counterclaim under Rule 13(a), and may assert any counterclaim under Rule 13(b) or any crossclaim under Rule 13(g).

(4) *Motion to Strike, Sever, or Try Separately.*

Any party may move to strike the third-party claim, to sever it, or to try it separately.

(5) *Third-Party Defendant's Claim Against a Nonparty.*

A third-party defendant may proceed under this rule against a nonparty who is or may be liable to the third-party defendant for all or part of any claim against it.

(6) *Third-Party Complaint In Rem.*

If it is within the admiralty or maritime jurisdiction, a third-party complaint may be in rem. In that event, a reference in this rule to the "summons" includes the warrant of arrest, and a reference to the defendant or third-party plaintiff includes, when appropriate, a person who asserts a right under Supplemental Rule C(6)(a)(i) in the property arrested.

(b) When a Plaintiff May Bring in a Third Party.

When a claim is asserted against a plaintiff, the plaintiff may bring in a third party if this rule would allow a defendant to do so.

(c) Admiralty or Maritime Claim.

(1) *Scope of Impleader.*

If a plaintiff asserts an admiralty or maritime claim under Rule 9(h), the defendant or a person who asserts a right under Supplemental Rule C(6)(a)(i) may, as a third-party plaintiff, bring in a third-party defendant who may be wholly or partly liable — either to the plaintiff or to the third-party plaintiff — for remedy over, contribution, or otherwise on account of the same transaction, occurrence, or series of transactions or occurrences.

(2) *Defending Against a Demand for Judgment for the Plaintiff.*

The third-party plaintiff may demand judgment in the plaintiff's favor against the third-party defendant. In that event, the third-party defendant must defend under Rule 12 against the plaintiff's claim as well as the third-party plaintiff's claim; and the action proceeds as if the plaintiff had sued both the third-party defendant and the third-party plaintiff.

[Adopted Dec. 20, 1937, effective Sept. 16, 1938; amended Dec. 27, 1946, effective Mar. 19, 1948; Jan. 21, 1963, effective July 1, 1963; Feb. 28, 1966, effective July 1, 1966; Mar. 2, 1987, effective Aug. 1, 1987; amended Apr. 17, 2000, effective Dec. 1, 2000; April 12, 2006, effective Dec. 1, 2006; amended April 30, 2007, effective Dec. 1, 2007; amended March 26, 2009, effective Dec. 1, 2009.]

RULE 15.   AMENDED AND SUPPLEMENTAL PLEADINGS.

(a) Amendments Before Trial.

(1) *Amending as a Matter of Course.*

A party may amend its pleading once as a matter of course:

(A) 21 days after serving it, or

(B) if the pleading is one to which a responsive pleading is required, 21 days after service of a responsive pleading or 21 days after service of a motion under Rule 12(b), (e), or (f), whichever is earlier.

(2) *Other Amendments.*

In all other cases, a party may amend its pleading only with the opposing party's written consent or the court's leave. The court should freely give leave when justice so requires.

(3) *Time to Respond.*

Unless the court orders otherwise, any required response to an amended pleading must be made within the time remaining to respond to the original pleading or within 14 days after service of the amended pleading, whichever is later.

(b) Amendments During and After Trial.

(1) *Based on an Objection at Trial.*

If, at trial, a party objects that evidence is not within the issues raised in the pleadings, the court may permit the pleadings to be amended. The court should freely permit an amendment when doing so will aid in presenting the merits and the objecting party fails to satisfy the court that the evidence would prejudice that party's action or defense on the merits. The court may grant a continuance to enable the objecting party to meet the evidence.

(2) *For Issues Tried by Consent.*

When an issue not raised by the pleadings is tried by the parties' express or implied consent, it must be treated in all respects as if raised in the pleadings. A party may move—at any time, even after judgment—to amend the pleadings to conform them to the evidence and to raise an unpleaded issue. But failure to amend does not affect the result of the trial of that issue.

(c) Relation Back of Amendments.

(1) *When an Amendment Relates Back.*

Does it relate back? How?

An amendment to a pleading relates back to the date of the original pleading when: *The Erie Doctrine*

> (A) the law that provides the applicable statute of limitations allows relation back;
>
> (B) the amendment asserts a claim or defense that arose out of the conduct, transaction, or occurrence set out — or attempted to be set out — in the original pleading; or
>
> (C) the amendment changes the party or the naming of the party against whom a claim is asserted, if Rule 15(c)(1)(B) is satisfied and if, within the period provided by Rule 4(m) for serving the summons and complaint, the party to be brought in by amendment:
>
>> (i) received such notice of the action that it will not be prejudiced in defending on the merits; and
>>
>> (ii) knew or should have known that the action would have been brought against it, but for a mistake concerning the proper party's identity.

(2) *Notice to the United States.*

When the United States or a United States officer or agency is added as a defendant by amendment, the notice requirements of Rule 15(c)(1)(C)(i) and (ii) are satisfied if, during the stated period, process was delivered or mailed to the United States attorney or the United States attorney's designee, to the Attorney General of the United States, or to the officer or agency.

(d) Supplemental Pleadings.

On motion and reasonable notice, the court may, on just terms, permit a party to serve a supplemental pleading setting out any transaction, occurrence, or event that happened after the date of the pleading to be supplemented. The court may permit supplementation even though the original pleading is defective in stating a claim or defense. The court may order that the opposing party plead to the supplemental pleading within a specified time.

[*Adopted Dec. 20, 1937, effective Sept. 16, 1938; amended Jan. 21, 1963, effective July 1, 1963; Feb. 28, 1966, effective July 1, 1966; Mar. 2, 1987, effective Aug. 1, 1987; Apr. 30, 1991, effective Dec. 1, 1991; Dec. 9, 1991; Apr. 22, 1993, effective Dec. 1, 1993; amended April 30, 2007, effective Dec. 1, 2007; amended March 26, 2009, effective Dec. 1, 2009.*]

ADVISORY COMMITTEE'S NOTE TO 1991 AMENDMENT OF RULE 15

The rule has been revised to prevent parties against whom claims are made from taking unjust advantage of otherwise inconsequential pleading errors to sustain a limitations defense.

Paragraph (c)(1). This provision is new. It is intended to make it clear that the rule does not apply to preclude any relation back that may be permitted under the applicable limitations law. Generally, the applicable limitations law will be state law. If federal jurisdiction is based on the citizenship of the parties, the primary reference is the law of the state in which the district court sits. *Walker v. Armco Steel Corp.*, 446 U.S. 740 (1980). If federal jurisdiction is based on a federal question, the reference may be to the law of the state governing relations between the parties. *E.g., Board of Regents v. Tomanio,* 446 U.S. 478 (1980). In some circumstances, the controlling limitations law may be federal law. *E.g., West v. Conrail, Inc.* 107 S. Ct. 1538 (1987). Cf. *Burlington Northern R. Co. v. Woods,* 480 U.S. 1 (1987); *Stewart Organization v. Ricoh,* 108 S. Ct. 2239 (1988). Whatever may be the controlling body of limitations law, if that law affords a more forgiving principle of relation back than the one provided in this rule, it should be available to save the claim. Accord, *Marshall v. Mulrenin,* 508 F.2d 39 (1st Cir. 1974). If *Schiavone v. Fortune,* 106 S. Ct. 2379 (1986) implies the contrary, this paragraph is intended to make a material change in the rule.

Paragraph (c)(3). This paragraph has been revised to change the result in *Schiavone v. Fortune, supra,* with respect to the problem of a misnamed defendant. An intended defendant who is notified of an action within the period allowed by Rule 4(m) for service of a summons and complaint may not under the revised rule defeat the action on account of a defect in the pleading with respect to the defendant's name, provided that the requirements of clauses (A) and (B) have been met. If the notice requirement is met within the Rule 4(m) period, a complaint may be amended at any time to correct a formal defect such as a misnomer or misidentification. On the basis of the text of the former rule, the Court reached a result in *Schiavone v. Fortune* that was inconsistent with the liberal pleading practices secured by Rule 8. See Bauer, Schiavone: *An Un-Fortune-ate Illustration of the Supreme Court's Role as Interpreter of the Federal Rules of Civil Procedure,* 63 NOTRE DAME L. REV. 720 (1988); Brussack, *Outrageous Fortune: The Case for Amending Rule 15(c) Again,* 61 S. CAL. L. REV. 671 (1988); Lewis, *The Excessive History of Federal Rule 15(c) and Its Lessons for Civil Rules Revision,* 86 Mich. L. Rev. 1507 (1987).

In allowing a name-correcting amendment within the time allowed by Rule 4(m), this rule allows not only the 120 days specified in that rule, but also any additional time resulting from any extension ordered by the court pursuant to that rule, as may be granted, for example, if the defendant is a fugitive from service of the summons.

RULE 16.   PRETRIAL CONFERENCES; SCHEDULING; MANAGEMENT.

(a) Purposes of a Pretrial Conference.

In any action, the court may order the attorneys and any unrepresented parties to appear for one or more pretrial conferences for such purposes as:

(1) expediting disposition of the action;

(2) establishing early and continuing control so that the case will not be protracted because of lack of management;

(3) discouraging wasteful pretrial activities;

(4) improving the quality of the trial through more thorough preparation; and

(5) facilitating settlement.

(b) Scheduling.

(1) *Scheduling Order.*

Except in categories of actions exempted by local rule, the district judge—or a magistrate judge when authorized by local rule—must issue a scheduling order:

(A) after receiving the parties' report under Rule 26(f); or

(B) after consulting with the parties' attorneys and any unrepresented parties at a scheduling conference.

(2) *Time to Issue.*

The judge must issue the scheduling order as soon as practicable, but unless the judge finds good cause for delay, the judge must issue it within the earlier of 90 days after any defendant has been served with the complaint or 60 days after any defendant has appeared.

(3) *Contents of the Order.*

(A) *Required Contents.*

The scheduling order must limit the time to join other parties, amend the pleadings, complete discovery, and file motions.

(B) *Permitted Contents.*

The scheduling order may:

(i) modify the timing of disclosures under Rules 26(a) and 26(e)(1);

(ii) modify the extent of discovery;

(iii) provide for disclosure, discovery, or preservation of electronically stored information;

(iv) include any agreements the parties reach for asserting claims of privilege or of protection as trial-preparation material after information is produced, including agreements reached under Federal Rule of Evidence 502;

(v) direct that before moving for an order relating to discovery, the movant must request a conference with the court;

(vi) set dates for pretrial conferences and for trial; and

(vii) include other appropriate matters.

(4) *Modifying a Schedule.*

A schedule may be modified only for good cause and with the judge's consent.

(c) Attendance and Matters for Consideration at a Pretrial Conference.

(1) *Attendance.*

A represented party must authorize at least one of its attorneys to make stipulations and admissions about all matters that can reasonably be anticipated for discussion at a pretrial conference. If appropriate, the court may require that a party or its representative be present or reasonably available by other means to consider possible settlement.

(2) *Matters for Consideration.*

At any pretrial conference, the court may consider and take appropriate action on the following matters:

(A) formulating and simplifying the issues, and eliminating frivolous claims or defenses;

(B) amending the pleadings if necessary or desirable;

(C) obtaining admissions and stipulations about facts and documents to avoid unnecessary proof, and ruling in advance on the admissibility of evidence;

(D) avoiding unnecessary proof and cumulative evidence, and limiting the use of testimony under Federal Rule of Evidence 702;

(E) determining the appropriateness and timing of summary adjudication under Rule 56;

(F) controlling and scheduling discovery, including orders affecting disclosures and discovery under Rule 26 and Rules 29 through 37;

(G) identifying witnesses and documents, scheduling the filing and exchange of any pretrial briefs, and setting dates for further conferences and for trial;

(H) referring matters to a magistrate judge or a master;

(I) settling the case and using special procedures to assist in resolving the dispute when authorized by statute or local rule;

(J) determining the form and content of the pretrial order;

(K) disposing of pending motions;

(L) adopting special procedures for managing potentially difficult or protracted actions that may involve complex issues, multiple parties, difficult legal questions, or unusual proof problems;

(M) ordering a separate trial under Rule 42(b) of a claim, counterclaim, crossclaim, third-party claim, or particular issue;

(N) ordering the presentation of evidence early in the trial on a manageable issue that might, on the evidence, be the basis for a judgment as a matter of law under Rule 50(a) or a judgment on partial findings under Rule 52(c);

(O) establishing a reasonable limit on the time allowed to present evidence; and

(P) facilitating in other ways the just, speedy, and inexpensive disposition of the action.

(d) Pretrial Orders.

After any conference under this rule, the court should issue an order reciting the action taken. This order controls the course of the action unless the court modifies it.

(e) Final Pretrial Conference and Orders.

The court may hold a final pretrial conference to formulate a trial plan, including a plan to facilitate the admission of evidence. The conference must be held as close to the start of trial as is reasonable, and must be attended by at least one attorney who will conduct the trial for each party and by any unrepresented party. The court may modify the order issued after a final pretrial conference only to prevent manifest injustice.

(f) Sanctions.

(1) *In General.*

On motion or on its own, the court may issue any just orders, including those authorized by Rule 37(b)(2)(A)(ii)–(vii), if a party or its attorney:

(A) fails to appear at a scheduling or other pretrial conference;

(B) is substantially unprepared to participate—or does not participate in good faith—in the conference; or

(C) fails to obey a scheduling or other pretrial order.

(2) *Imposing Fees and Costs.*

Instead of or in addition to any other sanction, the court must order the party, its attorney, or both to pay the reasonable expenses—including attorney's fees—incurred because of any noncompliance with this rule, unless the noncompliance was substantially justified or other circumstances make an award of expenses unjust.

[*Adopted Dec. 20, 1937, effective Sept. 16, 1938; amended April 12, 2006, effective Dec. 1, 2006; amended April 30, 2007, effective Dec. 1, 2007; amended April 29, 2015, effective Dec. 1, 2015.*]

ADVISORY COMMITTEE'S NOTE TO 2015 AMENDMENT OF RULE 16

The provision for consulting at a scheduling conference by "telephone, mail, or other means" is deleted. A scheduling conference is more effective if the court and parties engage in direct simultaneous communication. The conference may be held in person, by telephone, or by more sophisticated electronic means.

The time to issue the scheduling order is reduced to the earlier of 90 days (not 120 days) after any defendant has been served, or 60 days (not 90 days) after any defendant has appeared. This change, together with the shortened time for making service under

Rule 4(m), will reduce delay at the beginning of litigation. At the same time, a new provision recognizes that the court may find good cause to extend the time to issue the scheduling order. In some cases it may be that the parties cannot prepare adequately for a meaningful Rule 26(f) conference and then a scheduling conference in the time allowed. Litigation involving complex issues, multiple parties, and large organizations, public or private, may be more likely to need extra time to establish meaningful collaboration between counsel and the people who can supply the information needed to participate in a useful way. Because the time for the Rule 26(f) conference is geared to the time for the scheduling conference or order, an order extending the time for the scheduling conference will also extend the time for the Rule 26(f) conference. But in most cases it will be desirable to hold at least a first scheduling conference in the time set by the rule.

Three items are added to the list of permitted contents in Rule 16(b)(3)(B).

The order may provide for preservation of electronically stored information, a topic also added to the provisions of a discovery plan under Rule 26(f)(3)(C). Parallel amendments of Rule 37(e) recognize that a duty to preserve discoverable information may arise before an action is filed.

The order also may include agreements incorporated in a court order under Evidence Rule 502 controlling the effects of disclosure of information covered by attorney-client privilege or work-product protection, a topic also added to the provisions of a discovery plan under Rule 26(f)(3)(D).

Finally, the order may direct that before filing a motion for an order relating to discovery the movant must request a conference with the court. Many judges who hold such conferences find them an efficient way to resolve most discovery disputes without the delay and burdens attending a formal motion, but the decision whether to require such conferences is left to the discretion of the judge in each case.

ADVISORY COMMITTEE'S NOTE TO 2006 AMENDMENT OF RULE 16

The amendment to Rule 16(b) is designed to alert the court to the possible need to address the handling of discovery of electronically stored information early in the litigation if such discovery is expected to occur. Rule 26(f) is amended to direct the parties to discuss discovery of electronically stored information if such discovery is contemplated in the action. Form 35 is amended to call for a report to the court about the results of this discussion. In many instances, the court's involvement early in the litigation will help avoid difficulties that might otherwise arise.

Rule 16(b) is also amended to include among the topics that may be addressed in the scheduling order any agreements that the parties reach to facilitate discovery by minimizing the risk of waiver of privilege or work-product protection. Rule 26(f) is amended to add to the discovery plan the parties' proposal for the court to enter a case-management or other order adopting such an agreement. The parties may agree to various arrangements. For example, they may agree to initial provision of requested materials without waiver of privilege or protection to enable the party seeking production to designate the materials desired or protection for actual production, with the privilege review of only those materials to follow. Alternatively, they may agree that if privileged or protected information is inadvertently produced, the producing party may by timely notice assert the privilege or protection and obtain return of the materials without waiver. Other arrangements are possible. In most circumstances, a party who receives information under such an arrangement cannot assert that production of the information waived a claim of privilege or of protection as trial-preparation material.

An order that includes the parties' agreement may be helpful in avoiding delay and excessive cost in discovery. *See Manual for Complex Litigation* (4th) § 11.446. Rule 16(b)(6) recognizes the propriety of including such agreements in the court's order. The rule does not provide the court with authority to enter such a case-management or other order without party agreement, or limit the court's authority to act on motion.

TITLE IV.   PARTIES

Rule 17.   Parties Plaintiff and Defendant; Capacity.

(a) **Real Party in Interest.**

(1) *Designation in General.*

An action must be prosecuted in the name of the real party in interest. The following may sue in their own names without joining the person for whose benefit the action is brought:

> (A) an executor;
>
> (B) an administrator;
>
> (C) a guardian;
>
> (D) a bailee;
>
> (E) a trustee of an express trust;
>
> (F) a party with whom or in whose name a contract has been made for another's benefit; and
>
> (G) a party authorized by statute.

(2) *Action in the Name of the United States for Another's Use or Benefit.*

When a federal statute so provides, an action for another's use or benefit must be brought in the name of the United States.

(3) *Joinder of the Real Party in Interest.*

The court may not dismiss an action for failure to prosecute in the name of the real party in interest until, after an objection, a reasonable time has been allowed for the real party in interest to ratify, join, or be substituted into the action. After ratification, joinder, or substitution, the action proceeds as if it had been originally commenced by the real party in interest.

(b) Capacity to Sue or Be Sued.

Capacity to sue or be sued is determined as follows:

(1) for an individual who is not acting in a representative capacity, by the law of the individual's domicile;

(2) for a corporation, by the law under which it was organized; and

(3) for all other parties, by the law of the state where the court is located, except that:

(A) a partnership or other unincorporated association with no such capacity under that state's law may sue or be sued in its common name to enforce a substantive right existing under the United States Constitution or laws; and

(B) 28 U.S.C. §§ 754 and 959(a) govern the capacity of a receiver appointed by a United States court to sue or be sued in a United States court.

(c) Minor or Incompetent Person.

(1) *With a Representative.*

The following representatives may sue or defend on behalf of a minor or an incompetent person:

(A) a general guardian;

(B) a committee;

(C) a conservator; or

(D) a like fiduciary.

(2) *Without a Representative.*

A minor or an incompetent person who does not have a duly appointed representative may sue by a next friend or by a guardian ad litem. The court must appoint a guardian ad litem — or issue another appropriate order — to protect a minor or incompetent person who is unrepresented in an action.

(d) Public Officer's Title and Name.

A public officer who sues or is sued in an official capacity may be designated by official title rather than by name, but the court may order that the officer's name be added.

[*Adopted Dec. 20, 1937, effective Sept. 16, 1938; amended Dec. 27, 1946, effective Mar. 19, 1948; Dec. 29, 1948, effective Oct. 20, 1949; Feb. 28, 1966, effective July 1, 1966; Mar. 2, 1987, effective Aug. 1, 1987; Apr. 25, 1988, effective Aug. 1, 1988; Nov. 18, 1988; amended April 30, 2007, effective Dec. 1, 2007.*]

RULE 18. JOINDER OF CLAIMS.

(a) In General.

A party asserting a claim, counterclaim, crossclaim, or third-party claim may join, as independent or alternative claims, as many claims as it has against an opposing party.

(b) Joinder of Contingent Claims.

A party may join two claims even though one of them is contingent on the disposition of the other; but the court may grant relief only in accordance with the parties' relative substantive rights. In particular, a plaintiff may state a claim for money and a claim to set aside a conveyance that is fraudulent as to that plaintiff, without first obtaining a judgment for the money.

[*Adopted Dec. 20, 1937, effective Sept. 16, 1938; amended Feb. 28, 1966, effective July 1, 1966; Mar. 2, 1987, effective Aug. 1, 1987; amended April 30, 2007, effective Dec. 1, 2007.*]

RULE 19.   REQUIRED JOINDER OF PARTIES.

(a) Persons Required to Be Joined if Feasible.

(1) *Required Party.*

A person who is subject to service of process and whose joinder will not deprive the court of subject-matter jurisdiction must be joined as a party if:

> (A) in that person's absence, the court cannot accord complete relief among existing parties; or
>
> (B) that person claims an interest relating to the subject of the action and is so situated that disposing of the action in the person's absence may:
>
>> (i) as a practical matter impair or impede the person's ability to protect the interest; or
>>
>> (ii) leave an existing party subject to a substantial risk of incurring double, multiple, or otherwise inconsistent obligations because of the interest.

(2) *Joinder by Court Order.*

If a person has not been joined as required, the court must order that the person be made a party. A person who refuses to join as a plaintiff may be made either a defendant or, in a proper case, an involuntary plaintiff.

(3) *Venue.*

If a joined party objects to venue and the joinder would make venue improper, the court must dismiss that party.

(b) When Joinder Is Not Feasible.

If a person who is required to be joined if feasible cannot be joined, the court must determine whether, in equity and good conscience, the action should proceed among the existing parties or should be dismissed. The factors for the court to consider include:

> (1) the extent to which a judgment rendered in the person's absence might prejudice that person or the existing parties;
>
> (2) the extent to which any prejudice could be lessened or avoided by:

(A) protective provisions in the judgment;

(B) shaping the relief; or

(C) other measures;

(3) whether a judgment rendered in the person's absence would be adequate; and

(4) whether the plaintiff would have an adequate remedy if the action were dismissed for nonjoinder.

(c) Pleading the Reasons for Nonjoinder.

When asserting a claim for relief, a party must state:

(1) the name, if known, of any person who is required to be joined if feasible but is not joined; and

(2) the reasons for not joining that person.

(d) Exception for Class Actions.

This rule is subject to Rule 23.

[*Adopted Dec. 20, 1937, effective Sept. 16, 1938; amended Feb. 28, 1966, effective July 1, 1966; Mar. 2, 1987, effective Aug. 1, 1987; amended April 30, 2007, effective Dec. 1, 2007.*]

ADVISORY COMMITTEE'S NOTES TO 1966 AMENDMENT OF RULE 19
GENERAL CONSIDERATIONS

Whenever feasible, the persons materially interested in the subject of an action—see the more detailed description of these persons in the discussion of new subdivision

(a) below—should be joined as parties so that they may be heard and a complete disposition made. When this comprehensive joinder cannot be accomplished—a situation which may be encountered in Federal courts because of limitations on service of process, subject matter jurisdiction, and venue—the case should be examined pragmatically and a choice made between the alternatives of proceeding with the action in the absence of particular interested persons, and dismissing the action.

Even if the court is mistaken in its decision to proceed in the absence of an interested person, it does not by that token deprive itself of the power to adjudicate as between the parties already before it through proper service of process. But the court can make a legally binding adjudication only between the parties actually joined in the action. It is true that an adjudication between the parties before the court may on occasion adversely affect the absent person as a practical matter, or leave a party exposed to a later inconsistent recovery by the absent person. These are factors which should be considered in deciding whether the action should proceed, or should rather be dismissed; but they do not themselves negate the court's power to adjudicate as between the parties who have been joined.

THE AMENDED RULE

New *subdivision (a)* defines the persons whose joinder in the action is desirable. Clause (1) stresses the desirability of joining those persons in whose absence the court would be obliged to grant partial or "hollow" rather than complete relief to the parties before the court. The interests that are being furthered here are not only those of the parties, but also that of the public in avoiding repeated lawsuits on the same essential subject matter. Clause (2)(i) recognizes the importance of protecting the person whose joinder is in question against the practical prejudice to him which may arise through a disposition of the action in his absence. Clause (2)(ii) recognizes the need for considering whether a party may be left, after the adjudication, in a position where a person not joined can subject him to a double or otherwise inconsistent liability.

The subdivision (a) definition of persons to be joined is not couched in terms of the abstract nature of their interests—"joint," "united," "separable," or the like. . . . It should be noted particularly, however, that the description is not at variance with the settled authorities holding that a tortfeasor with the usual "joint-and-several" liability is merely a permissive party to an action against another with like liability. . . . Joinder of these tortfeasors continues to be regulated by Rule 20; compare Rule 14 on third-party practice.

If a person as described in subdivision (a)(1)–(2) is amenable to service of process and his joinder would not deprive the court of jurisdiction in the sense of competence over the action, he should be joined as a party; and if he has not been joined, the court should order him to be brought into the action. If a party joined has a valid objection to the venue and chooses to assert it, he will be dismissed from the action.

Subdivision (b). When a person as described in subdivision (a)(1)–(2) cannot be made a party, the court is to determine whether in equity and good conscience the action should proceed among the parties already before it, or should be dismissed. That this decision is to be made in the light of pragmatic considerations has often been acknowledged by the courts. . . . The subdivision sets out four relevant considerations drawn from the experience revealed in the decided cases. The factors are to a certain extent overlapping, and they are not intended to exclude other considerations which may be applicable in particular situations.

The *first factor* brings in a consideration of what a judgment in the action would mean to the absentee. Would the absentee be adversely affected in a practical sense, and if so, would the prejudice be immediate and serious, or remote and minor? The possible collateral consequences of the judgment upon the parties already joined are also to be appraised. Would any party be exposed to a fresh action by the absentee, and if so, how serious is the threat? . . .

The *second factor* calls attention to the measures by which prejudice may be averted or lessened. The "shaping of relief" is a familiar expedient to this end. See, *e.g.,* the award of money damages in lieu of specific relief where the latter might affect an absentee adversely. *Ward v. Deavers*, 203 F.2d 72 (D.C. Cir. 1953); *Miller & Lux, Inc. v. Nickel*, 141 F. Supp. 41 (N.D. Calif. 1956). On the use of "protectiveprovisions," see *Roos v. Texas Co., supra; Atwood v. Rhode Island Hosp. Trust Co.*, 275 Fed. 513, 519 (1st Cir. 1921), *cert. denied*, 257 U.S. 661 (1922); *cf. Stumpf v. Fidelity Gas Co.*, 294 F.2d 886 (9th Cir. 1961); and the general statement in *National Licorice Co. v. Labor Board*, 309 U.S. 350, 363 (1940).

Sometimes the party is himself able to take measures to avoid prejudice. Thus a defendant faced with a prospect of a second suit by an absentee may be in a position to bring the latter into the action by defensive interpleader. See *Hudson v. Newell*, 172 F.2d 848, 852, mod., 176 F.2d 546 (5th Cir. 1949); *Gauss v. Kirk*, 198 F.2d 83, 86 (D.C. Cir. 1952); *Abel v. Brayton Flying Service, Inc.*, 248 F.2d 713, 716 (5th Cir. 1957) (suggestion of possibility of counterclaim under Rule 13(h)). . . . So also the absentee may sometimes be able to avert prejudice to himself by voluntarily appearing in the action or intervening or an ancillary basis [Citations omitted]. The court should consider whether this, in turn, would impose undue hardship on the absentee. (For the possibility of the court's informing an absentee of the pendency of the action, see comment under subdivision (c) below.)

The *third factor* — whether an "adequate" judgment can be rendered in the absence of a given person-calls attention to the extent of the relief that can be accorded among the parties joined. It meshes with the other factors, especially the "shaping of relief" mentioned under the second factor. . . .

The *fourth factor*, looking to the practical effects of a dismissal, indicates that the court should consider whether there is any assurance that the plaintiff, if dismissed, could sue effectively in another forum where better joinder would be possible. . . .

The subdivision uses the word "indispensable" only in a conclusory sense, that is, a person is "regarded as indispensable" when he cannot be made a party and, upon consideration of the factors above-mentioned, it is determined that in his absence it would be preferable to dismiss the action, rather than to retain it.

A person may be added as a party at any stage of the action on motion or on the court's initiative (see Rule 21); and a motion to dismiss, on the ground that a person has not been joined and justice requires that the action should not proceed in his absence, may be made as late as the trial on the merits (see Rule 12(h)(2), as amended; *cf.* Rule 12(b)(7), as amended). However, when the moving party is seeking dismissal in order to protect himself against a later suit by the absent person (subdivision (a)(2) (ii)), and is not seeking vicariously to protect the absent person against a prejudicial judgment (subdivision (a)(2)(i)), his undue delay in making the motion can properly be counted against him as a reason for denying the motion. A joinder question should be decided with reasonable promptness, but decision may properly be deferred if adequate information is not available at the time. Thus the relationship of an absent person to the action, and the practical effects of an adjudication upon him and others, may not be sufficiently revealed at the pleading stage; in such a case it would be appropriate to defer decision until the action was further advanced. *Cf.* Rule 12(d).

The amended rule makes no special provision for the problem arising in suits against subordinate Federal officials where it has often been set up as a defense that some superior officer must be joined. Frequently this defense has been accompanied by or intermingled with defenses of sovereign immunity or lack of consent of the United States to suit. So far as the issue of joinder can be isolated from the rest, the new subdivision seems better adapted to handle it than the predecessor provision. See the discussion in *Johnson v. Kirkland*, 290 F.2d 440, 446–47 (6th Cir. 1961) (stressing the practical orientation of the decisions); *Shaughnessy v. Pedreiro*, 349 U.S. 48, 54 (1955). Recent legislation, P.L. 87-748, 76 Stat. 744, approved October 5, 1962, adding §§ 1361, 1391(e) to Title 28, U.S.C., vests original jurisdiction in the district courts over actions in the nature of mandamus to compel officials of the United States to perform their legal duties, and extends the range of service of process and liberalizes venue in these actions. If, then, it is found that a particular official should be joined in the action, the legislation will make it easy to bring him in.

Subdivision (c) parallels the predecessor subdivision (c) of Rule 19. In some situations it may be desirable to advise a person who has not been joined of the fact that the action is pending, and in particular cases the court in its discretion may itself convey this information by directing a letter or other informal notice to the absentee.

RULE 20. PERMISSIVE JOINDER OF PARTIES.

(a) Persons Who May Join or Be Joined.

(1) *Plaintiffs.*

Persons may join in one action as plaintiffs if:

(A) they assert any right to relief jointly, severally, or in the alternative with respect to or arising out of the same transaction, occurrence, or series of transactions or occurrences; and

(B) any question of law or fact common to all plaintiffs will arise in the action.

(2) *Defendants.*

Persons — as well as a vessel, cargo, or other property subject to admiralty process in rem — may be joined in one action as defendants if:

(A) *any right to relief is asserted against them jointly, severally, or in the alternative with respect to or arising out of the same transaction, occurrence, or series of transactions or occurrences; and*

(B) any question of law or fact common to all defendants will arise in the action.

(3) *Extent of Relief.*

Neither a plaintiff nor a defendant need be interested in obtaining or defending against all the relief demanded. The court may grant judgment to one or more plaintiffs according to their rights, and against one or more defendants according to their liabilities.

(b) Protective Measures.

The court may issue orders — including an order for separate trials — to protect a party against embarrassment, delay, expense, or other prejudice that arises from including a person against whom the party asserts no claim and who asserts no claim against the party.

[*Adopted Dec. 20, 1937, effective Sept. 16, 1938; amended Feb. 28, 1966, effective July1, 1966; Mar. 2, 1987, effective Aug. 1, 1987; amended April 30, 2007, effective Dec. 1, 2007.*]

RULE 21.   MISJOINDER AND NONJOINDER OF PARTIES.

Misjoinder of parties is not a ground for dismissing an action. On motion or on its own, the court may at any time, on just terms, add or drop a party. The court may also sever any claim against a party.

[*Adopted Dec. 20, 1937, effective Sept. 16, 1938; amended April 30, 2007, effective Dec. 1, 2007.*]

RULE 22.   INTERPLEADER.

(a) Grounds.

(1) *By a Plaintiff.*

Persons with claims that may expose a plaintiff to double or multiple liability may be joined as defendants and required to interplead. Joinder for interpleader is proper even though:

> (A) the claims of the several claimants, or the titles on which their claims depend, lack a common origin or are adverse and independent rather than identical; or

> (B) the plaintiff denies liability in whole or in part to any or all of the claimants.

(2) *By a Defendant.*

A defendant exposed to similar liability may seek interpleader through a cross-claim or counterclaim.

(b) Relation to Other Rules and Statutes.

This rule supplements — and does not limit — the joinder of parties allowed by Rule 20. The remedy this rule provides is in addition to — and does not supersede or limit — the remedy provided by 28 U.S.C. §§ 1335, 1397, and 2361. An action under those statutes must be conducted under these rules.

[*Adopted Dec. 20, 1937, effective Sept. 16, 1938; amended Dec. 29, 1948, effective Oct. 20, 1949; Mar. 2, 1987, effective Aug. 1, 1987; amended April 30, 2007, effective Dec. 1, 2007.*]

RULE 23. CLASS ACTIONS.

(a) Prerequisites.

One or more members of a class may sue or be sued as representative parties on behalf of all members only if:

(1) the class is so numerous that joinder of all members is impracticable;

(2) there are questions of law or fact common to the class;

(3) the claims or defenses of the representative parties are typical of the claims or defenses of the class; and

(4) the representative parties will fairly and adequately protect the interests of the class.

(b) Types of Class Actions.

A class action may be maintained if Rule 23(a) is satisfied and if:

(1) prosecuting separate actions by or against individual class members would create a risk of:

(A) inconsistent or varying adjudications with respect to individual class members that would establish incompatible standards of conduct for the party opposing the class; or

(B) adjudications with respect to individual class members that, as a practical matter, would be dispositive of the interests of the other members not parties to the individual adjudications or would substantially impair or impede their ability to protect their interests;

(2) the party opposing the class has acted or refused to act on grounds that apply generally to the class, so that final injunctive relief or corresponding declaratory relief is appropriate respecting the class as a whole; or

(3) the court finds that the questions of law or fact common to class members predominate over any questions affecting only individual members, and that a class action is superior to other available methods for fairly and efficiently adjudicating the controversy. The matters pertinent to these findings include:

(A) the class members' interests in individually controlling the prosecution or defense of separate actions;

(B) the extent and nature of any litigation concerning the controversy already begun by or against class members;

(C) the desirability or undesirability of concentrating the litigation of the claims in the particular forum; and

(D) the likely difficulties in managing a class action.

(c) Certification Order; Notice to Class Members; Judgment; Issues Classes; Subclasses.

(1) *Certification Order.*

(A) *Time to Issue.*

At an early practicable time after a person sues or is sued as a class representative, the court must determine by order whether to certify the action as a class action.

(B) *Defining the Class; Appointing Class Counsel.*

An order that certifies a class action must define the class and the class claims, issues, or defenses, and must appoint class counsel under Rule 23(g).

(C) *Altering or Amending the Order.*

An order that grants or denies class certification may be altered or amended before final judgment.

(2) *Notice.*

(A) *For (b)(1) or (b)(2) Classes.*

For any class certified under Rule 23(b)(1) or (b)(2), the court may direct appropriate notice to the class.

(B) *For (b)(3) Classes.*

For any class certified under Rule 23(b)(3)—or upon ordering notice under Rule 23(e)(1) to a class proposed to be certified for purposes of settlement under Rule 23(b)(3)—the court must direct to class members the best notice that is practicable under the circumstances, including individual notice to all members who can be identified through reasonable effort. The notice may be by one or more of the following: United States mail, electronic means, or other appropriate means. The notice must clearly and concisely state in plain, easily understood language:

(i) the nature of the action;

(ii) the definition of the class certified;

(iii) the class claims, issues, or defenses;

(iv) that a class member may enter an appearance through an attorney if the member so desires;

(v) that the court will exclude from the class any member who requests exclusion;

(vi) the time and manner for requesting exclusion; and

(vii) the binding effect of a class judgment on members under Rule 23(c)(3).

(3) *Judgment.*

Whether or not favorable to the class, the judgment in a class action must:

(A) for any class certified under Rule 23(b)(1) or (b)(2), include and describe those whom the court finds to be class members; and

(B) for any class certified under Rule 23(b)(3), include and specify or describe those to whom the Rule 23(c)(2) notice was directed, who have not requested exclusion, and whom the court finds to be class members.

(4) *Particular Issues.*

When appropriate, an action may be brought or maintained as a class action with respect to particular issues.

(5) *Subclasses.*

When appropriate, a class may be divided into subclasses that are each treated as a class under this rule.

(d) Conducting the Action.

(1) *In General.*

In conducting an action under this rule, the court may issue orders that:

(A) determine the course of proceedings or prescribe measures to prevent undue repetition or complication in presenting evidence or argument;

(B) require—to protect class members and fairly conduct the action—giving appropriate notice to some or all class members of:

(i) any step in the action;

(ii) the proposed extent of the judgment; or

(iii) the members' opportunity to signify whether they consider the representation fair and adequate, to intervene and present claims or defenses, or to otherwise come into the action;

(C) impose conditions on the representative parties or on intervenors;

(D) require that the pleadings be amended to eliminate allegations about representation of absent persons and that the action proceed accordingly; or

(E) deal with similar procedural matters.

(2) *Combining and Amending Orders.*

An order under Rule 23(d)(1) may be altered or amended from time to time and may be combined with an order under Rule 16.

(e) Settlement, Voluntary Dismissal, or Compromise.

The claims, issues, or defenses of a certified class—or a class proposed to be certified for purposes of settlement—may be settled, voluntarily dismissed, or compromised only with the court's approval. The following procedures apply to a proposed settlement, voluntary dismissal, or compromise:

(1) *Notice to the Class.*

(A) *Information That Parties Must Provide to the Court.*

The parties must provide the court with information sufficient to enable it to determine whether to give notice of the proposal to the class.

(B) *Grounds for a Decision to Give Notice.*

The court must direct notice in a reasonable manner to all class members who would be bound by the proposal if giving notice is justified by the parties' showing that the court will likely be able to:

(i) approve the proposal under Rule 23(e)(2); and

(ii) certify the class for purposes of judgment on the proposal.

(2) *Approval of the Proposal.*

If the proposal would bind class members, the court may approve it only after a hearing and only on finding that it is fair, reasonable, and adequate after considering whether:

(A) the class representatives and class counsel have adequately represented the class;

(B) the proposal was negotiated at arm's length;

(C) the relief provided for the class is adequate, taking into account:

(i) the costs, risks, and delay of trial and appeal;

(ii) the effectiveness of any proposed method of distributing relief to the class, including the method of processing class-member claims;

(iii) the terms of any proposed award of attorney's fees, including timing of payment; and

(iv) any agreement required to be identified under Rule 23(e)(3); and

(D) the proposal treats class members equitably relative to each other.

(3) *Identifying Agreements.*

The parties seeking approval must file a statement identifying any agreement made in connection with the proposal.

(4) *New Opportunity to Be Excluded.*

If the class action was previously certified under Rule 23(b)(3), the court may refuse to approve a settlement unless it affords a new opportunity to request exclusion to individual class members who had an earlier opportunity to request exclusion but did not do so.

(5) *Class-Member Objections.*

(A) *In General.*

Any class member may object to the proposal if it requires court approval under this subdivision (e). The objection must state whether it applies only to the objector, to a specific subset of the class, or to the entire class, and also state with specificity the grounds for the objection.

(B) *Court Approval Required for Payment in Connection with an Objection.* Unless approved by the court after a hearing, no payment or other consideration may be provided in connection with:

    (i) forgoing or withdrawing an objection, or

    (ii) forgoing, dismissing, or abandoning an appeal from a judgment approving the proposal.

(C) *Procedure for Approval After an Appeal.*

If approval under Rule 23(e)(5)(B) has not been obtained before an appeal is docketed in the court of appeals, the procedure of Rule 62.1 applies while the appeal remains pending.

(f) Appeals.

A court of appeals may permit an appeal from an order granting or denying class-action certification under this rule, but not from an order under Rule 23(e)(1). A party must file a petition for permission to appeal with the circuit clerk within 14 days after the order is entered or within 45 days after the order is entered if any party is the United States, a United States agency, or a United States officer or employee sued for an act or omission occurring in connection with duties performed on the United States' behalf. An appeal does not stay proceedings in the district court unless the district judge or the court of appeals so orders.

(g) Class Counsel.

(1) *Appointing Class Counsel.*

Unless a statute provides otherwise, a court that certifies a class must appoint class counsel. In appointing class counsel, the court:

    (A) must consider:

        (i) the work counsel has done in identifying or investigating potential claims in the action;

        (ii) counsel's experience in handling class actions, other complex litigation, and the types of claims asserted in the action;

        (iii) counsel's knowledge of the applicable law; and

        (iv) the resources that counsel will commit to representing the class;

    (B) may consider any other matter pertinent to counsel's ability to fairly and adequately represent the interests of the class;

    (C) may order potential class counsel to provide information on any subject pertinent to the appointment and to propose terms for attorney's fees and nontaxable costs;

    (D) may include in the appointing order provisions about the award of attorney's fees or nontaxable costs under Rule 23(h); and

(E) may make further orders in connection with the appointment.

(2) *Standard for Appointing Class Counsel.*

When one applicant seeks appointment as class counsel, the court may appoint that applicant only if the applicant is adequate under Rule 23(g)(1) and (4). If more than one adequate applicant seeks appointment, the court must appoint the applicant best able to represent the interests of the class.

(3) *Interim Counsel.*

The court may designate interim counsel to act on behalf of a putative class before determining whether to certify the action as a class action.

(4) *Duty of Class Counsel.*

Class counsel must fairly and adequately represent the interests of the class.

(h) Attorney's Fees and Nontaxable Costs.

In a certified class action, the court may award reasonable attorney's fees and non-taxable costs that are authorized by law or by the parties' agreement. The following procedures apply:

(1) A claim for an award must be made by motion under Rule 54(d)(2), subject to the provisions of this subdivision (h), at a time the court sets. Notice of the motion must be served on all parties and, for motions by class counsel, directed to class members in a reasonable manner.

(2) A class member, or a party from whom payment is sought, may object to the motion.

(3) The court may hold a hearing and must find the facts and state its legal conclusions under Rule 52(a).

(4) The court may refer issues related to the amount of the award to a special master or a magistrate judge, as provided in Rule 54(d)(2)(D).

[*Adopted Dec. 20, 1937, effective Sept. 16, 1938; amended Feb. 28, 1966, effective July 1, 1966; amended Mar. 27, 2003, effective Dec. 1, 2003; amended April 30, 2007, effective Dec. 1, 2007; amended March 26, 2009, eff. Dec. 1, 2009; amended April 26, 2018, effective Dec. 1, 2018*]

ADVISORY COMMITTEE'S NOTE TO 2003 AMENDMENT OF RULE 23

Subdivision (c). Subdivision (c) is amended in several respects. The requirement that the court determine whether to certify a class "as soon as practicable after commencement of an action" is replaced by requiring determination "at an early practicable time." The notice provisions are substantially revised.

Paragraph (1). Subdivision (c)(1)(A) is changed to require that the determination whether to certify a class be made "at an early practicable time." The "as soon as practicable" exaction neither reflects prevailing practice nor captures the many valid reasons that may justify deferring the initial certification decision. See Willging, Hooper & Niemic, *Empirical Study of Class Actions in Four Federal District Courts: Final Report to the Advisory Committee on Civil Rules 26–36* (Federal Judicial Center 1996).

Time may be needed to gather information necessary to make the certification decision. Although an evaluation of the probable outcome on the merits is not properly part of the certification decision, discovery in aid of the certification decision often includes information required to identify the nature of the issues that actually will be presented at trial. In this sense it is appropriate to conduct controlled discovery into the "merits," limited to those aspects relevant to making the certification decision on an informed basis. Active judicial supervision may be required to achieve the most effective balance that expedites an informed certification determination without forcing an artificial and ultimately wasteful division between "certification discovery" and "merits discovery." A critical need is to determine how the case will be tried. An increasing number of courts require a party requesting class certification to present a "trial plan" that describes the issues likely to be presented at trial and tests whether they are susceptible of class-wide proof. See Manual For Complex Litigation Third, § 21.213, p. 44; § 30.11, p. 214; § 30.12, p. 215.

Other considerations may affect the timing of the certification decision. The party opposing the class may prefer to win dismissal or summary judgment as to the individual plaintiffs without certification and without binding the class that might have been certified. Time may be needed to explore designation of class counsel under Rule 23(g), recognizing that in many cases the need to progress toward the certification determination may require designation of interim counsel under Rule 23(g)(2)(A).

Although many circumstances may justify deferring the certification decision, active management may be necessary to ensure that the certification decision is not unjustifiably delayed.

Subdivision (c)(1)(C) reflects two amendments. The provision that a class certification "may be conditional" is deleted. A court that is not satisfied that the requirements of Rule 23 have been met should refuse certification until they have been met. The provision that permits alteration or amendment of an order granting or denying class certification is amended to set the cut-off point at final judgment rather than "the decision on the merits." This change avoids the possible ambiguity in referring to "the decision on the merits." Following a determination of liability, for example, proceedings to define the remedy may demonstrate the need to amend the class definition or subdivide the class. In this setting the final judgment concept is pragmatic. It is not the same as the concept used for appeal purposes, but it should be flexible, particularly in protracted litigation.

The authority to amend an order under Rule 23(c)(1) before final judgment does not restore the practice of "one-way intervention" that was rejected by the 1966 revision of Rule 23. A determination of liability after certification, however, may show a need to amend the class definition. Decertification may be warranted after further proceedings.

If the definition of a class certified under Rule 23(b)(3) is altered to include members who have not been afforded notice and an opportunity to request exclusion, notice—including an opportunity to request exclusion—must be directed to the new class members under Rule 23(c)(2)(B).

Paragraph (2). The first change made in Rule 23(c)(2) is to call attention to the court's authority—already established in part by Rule 23(d)(2)—to direct notice of certification to a Rule 23(b)(1) or (b)(2) class. The present rule expressly requires notice only in actions certified under Rule 23(b)(3). Members of classes certified under Rules 23(b)(1) or (b)(2) have interests that may deserve protection by notice.

The authority to direct notice to class members in a (b)(1) or (b)(2) class action should be exercised with care. For several reasons, there may be less need for notice than in a (b)(3) class action. There is no right to request exclusion from a (b)(1) or (b)(2) class. The characteristics of the class may reduce the need for formal notice. The cost of providing notice, moreover, could easily cripple actions that do not seek damages. The court may decide not to direct notice after balancing the risk that notice costs may deter the pursuit of class relief against the benefits of notice.

When the court does direct certification notice in a (b)(1) or (b)(2) class action, the discretion and flexibility established by subdivision (c)(2)(A) extend to the method of giving notice. Notice facilitates the opportunity to participate. Notice calculated to reach a significant number of class members often will protect the interests of all. Informal methods may prove effective. A simple posting in a place visited by many class members, directing attention to a source of more detailed information, may suffice. The court should consider the costs of notice in relation to the probable reach of inexpensive methods.

If a Rule 23(b)(3) class is certified in conjunction with a (b)(2) class, the (c)(2)(B) notice requirements must be satisfied as to the (b)(3) class.

The direction that class-certification notice be couched in plain, easily understood language is a reminder of the need to work unremittingly at the difficult task of communicating with class members. It is difficult to provide information about most class actions that is both accurate and easily understood by class members who are not themselves lawyers. Factual uncertainty, legal complexity, and the complication of class-action procedure raise the barriers high. The Federal Judicial Center has created illustrative clear-notice forms that provide a helpful starting point for actions similar to those described in the forms.

Subdivision (e). Subdivision (e) is amended to strengthen the process of reviewing proposed class-action settlements. Settlement may be a desirable means of resolving a class action. But court review and approval are essential to assure adequate representation of class members who have not participated in shaping the settlement.

Paragraph (1). Subdivision (e)(1)(A) expressly recognizes the power of a class representative to settle class claims, issues, or defenses.

Rule 23(e)(1)(A) resolves the ambiguity in former Rule 23(e)'s reference to dismissal or compromise of "a class action." That language could be—and at times was—read to require court approval of settlements with putative class representatives that resolved only individual claims. See Manual for Complex Litigation Third, § 30.41. The new rule requires approval only if the claims, issues, or defenses of a certified class are resolved by a settlement, voluntary dismissal, or compromise.

Subdivision (e)(1)(B) carries forward the notice requirement of present Rule 23(e) when the settlement binds the class through claim or issue preclusion; notice is not required when the settlement binds only the individual class representatives. Notice of a settlement binding on the class is required either when the settlement follows class certification or when the decisions on certification and settlement proceed simultaneously.

Reasonable settlement notice may require individual notice in the manner required by Rule 23(c)(2)(B) for certification notice to a Rule 23(b)(3) class. Individual notice is appropriate, for example, if class members are required to take action—such as filing claims—to participate in the judgment, or if the court orders a settlement opt-out opportunity under Rule 23(e)(3).

Subdivision (e)(1)(C) confirms and mandates the already common practice of holding hearings as part of the process of approving settlement, voluntary dismissal, or compromise that would bind members of a class.

Subdivision (e)(1)(C) states the standard for approving a proposed settlement that would bind class members. The settlement must be fair, reasonable, and adequate. A helpful review of many factors that may deserve consideration is provided by *In re: Prudential Ins. Co. America Sales Practice Litigation Agent Actions*, 148 F.3d 283, 316–324 (3d Cir. 1998). Further guidance can be found in the Manual for Complex Litigation.

The court must make findings that support the conclusion that the settlement is fair, reasonable, and adequate. The findings must be set out in sufficient detail to explain to class members and the appellate court the factors that bear on applying the standard.

Settlement review also may provide an occasion to review the cogency of the initial class definition. The terms of the settlement themselves, or objections, may reveal divergent interests of class members and demonstrate the need to redefine the class or to designate subclasses. Redefinition of a class certified under Rule 23(b)(3) may require notice to new class members under Rule 23(c)(2)(B). See Rule 23(c)(1)(C).

Paragraph (2). Subdivision (e)(2) requires parties seeking approval of a settlement, voluntary dismissal, or compromise under Rule 23(e)(1) to file a statement identifying any agreement made in connection with the settlement. This provision does not change the basic requirement that the parties disclose all terms of the settlement or compromise that the court must approve under Rule 23(e)(1). It aims instead at related undertakings that, although seemingly separate, may have influenced the terms of the settlement by trading away possible advantages for the class in return for advantages for others. Doubts should be resolved in favor of identification.

Further inquiry into the agreements identified by the parties should not become the occasion for discovery by the parties or objectors. The court may direct the parties to provide to the court or other parties a summary or copy of the full terms of any agreement identified by the parties. The court also may direct the parties to provide a summary or copy of any agreement not identified by the parties that the court considers relevant to its review of a proposed settlement. In exercising discretion under this rule, the court may act in steps, calling first for a summary of any agreement that may have affected the settlement and then for a complete version if the summary does not provide an adequate basis for review. A direction to disclose a summary or copy of an agreement may raise concerns of confidentiality. Some agreements may include information that merits protection against general disclosure. And the court must provide an opportunity to claim work-product or other protections.

Paragraph (3). Subdivision (e)(3) authorizes the court to refuse to approve a settlement unless the settlement affords class members a new opportunity to request exclusion from a class certified under Rule 23(b)(3) after settlement terms are known. An agreement by the parties themselves to permit class members to elect exclusion at this point by the settlement agreement may be one factor supporting approval of the settlement. Often there is an opportunity to opt out at this point because the class is certified and settlement is reached in circumstances that lead to simultaneous notice of certification and notice of settlement. In these cases, the basic opportunity to elect exclusion applies without further complication. In some cases, particularly if settlement appears imminent at the time of certification, it may be possible to achieve equivalent protection by deferring notice and the opportunity to elect exclusion until actual settlement terms are known. This approach avoids the cost and potential confusion of providing two notices and makes the single notice more meaningful. But notice should not be delayed unduly after certification in the hope of settlement.

Rule 23(e)(3) authorizes the court to refuse to approve a settlement unless the settlement affords a new opportunity to elect exclusion in a case that settles after a certification decision if the earlier opportunity to elect exclusion provided with the certification notice has expired by the time of the settlement notice. A decision to remain in the class is likely to be more carefully considered and is better informed when settlement terms are known.

The opportunity to request exclusion from a proposed settlement is limited to members of a (b)(3) class. Exclusion may be requested only by individual class members; no class member may purport to opt out other class members by way of another class action.

The decision whether to approve a settlement that does not allow a new opportunity to elect exclusion is confided to the court's discretion. The court may make this decision before directing notice to the class under Rule 23(e)(1)(B) or after the Rule 23(e)(1)(C) hearing. Many factors may influence the court's decision. Among these are changes in the information available to class members since expiration of the first opportunity to request exclusion, and the nature of the individual class members' claims.

The terms set for permitting a new opportunity to elect exclusion from the proposed settlement of a Rule 23(b)(3) class action may address concerns of potential misuse. The court might direct, for example, that class members who elect exclusion are bound by rulings on the merits made before the settlement was proposed for approval. Still other terms or conditions may be appropriate.

Paragraph (4). Subdivision (e)(4) confirms the right of class members to object to a proposed settlement, voluntary dismissal, or compromise. The right is defined in relation to a disposition that, because it would bind the class, requires court approval under subdivision (e)(1)(C).

Subdivision (e)(4)(B) requires court approval for withdrawal of objections made under subdivision (e)(4)(A). Review follows automatically if the objections are withdrawn on terms that lead to modification of the settlement with the class. Review also is required if the objector formally withdraws the objections. If the objector simply abandons pursuit of the objection, the court may inquire into the circumstances.

Approval under paragraph (4)(B) may be given or denied with little need for further inquiry if the objection and the disposition go only to a protest that the individual treatment afforded the objector under the proposed settlement is unfair because of factors that distinguish the objector from other class members. Different considerations may apply if the objector has protested that the proposed settlement is not fair, reasonable, or adequate on grounds that apply generally to a class or subclass. Such objections, which purport to represent class-wide interests, may augment the opportunity for obstruction or delay. If such objections are surrendered on terms that do not affect the class settlement or the objector's participation in the class settlement, the court often can approve withdrawal of the objections without elaborate inquiry.

Once an objector appeals, control of the proceeding lies in the court of appeals. The court of appeals may undertake review and approval of a settlement with the objector, perhaps as part of appeal settlement procedures, or may remand to the district court to take advantage of the district court's familiarity with the action and settlement.

Subdivision (g). Subdivision (g) is new. It responds to the reality that the selection and activity of class counsel are often critically important to the successful handling of a class action. Until now, courts have scrutinized proposed class counsel as well as the class representative under Rule 23(a)(4). This experience has recognized the importance of judicial evaluation of the proposed lawyer for the class, and this new subdivision builds on that experience rather than introducing an entirely new element into the class certification process. Rule 23(a)(4) will continue to call for scrutiny of the proposed class representative, while this subdivision will guide the court in assessing proposed class counsel as part of the certification decision. This subdivision recognizes the importance of class counsel, states the obligation to represent the interests of the class, and provides a framework for selection of class counsel. The procedure and standards for appointment vary depending on whether there are multiple applicants to be class counsel. The new subdivision also provides a method by which the court may make directions from the outset about the potential fee award to class counsel in the event the action is successful.

Paragraph (1) sets out the basic requirement that class counsel be appointed if a class is certified and articulates the obligation of class counsel to represent the interests of the class, as opposed to the potentially conflicting interests of individual class members. It also sets out the factors the court should consider in assessing proposed class counsel.

Paragraph (1)(A) requires that the court appoint class counsel to represent the class. Class counsel must be appointed for all classes, including each subclass that the court certifies to represent divergent interests.

Paragraph (1)(A) does not apply if "a statute provides otherwise." This recognizes that provisions of the Private Securities Litigation Reform Act of 1995, Pub. L. No. 104-67, 109 Stat. 737 (1995) (codified in various sections of 15 U.S.C.), contain directives that bear on selection of a lead plaintiff and the retention of counsel. This subdivision does not purport to supersede or to affect the interpretation of those provisions, or any similar provisions of other legislation.

Paragraph (1)(B) recognizes that the primary responsibility of class counsel, resulting from appointment as class counsel, is to represent the best interests of the class. The rule thus establishes the obligation of class counsel, an obligation that may be different from the customary obligations of counsel to individual clients. Appointment as class counsel means that the primary obligation of counsel is to the class rather than to any individual members of it. The class representatives do not have an unfettered right to "fire" class counsel. In the same vein, the class representatives cannot command class counsel to accept or reject a settlement proposal. To the contrary, class counsel must determine whether seeking the court's approval of a settlement would be in the best interests of the class as a whole.

Paragraph (1)(C) articulates the basic responsibility of the court to appoint class counsel who will provide the adequate representation called for by paragraph (1)(B). It identifies criteria that must be considered and invites the court to consider any other pertinent matters. Although couched in terms of the court's duty, the listing also informs counsel seeking appointment about the topics that should be addressed in an application for appointment or in the motion for class certification.

The court may direct potential class counsel to provide additional information about the topics mentioned in paragraph (1)(C) or about any other relevant topic. For example, the court may direct applicants to inform the court concerning any agreements about a prospective award of attorney fees or nontaxable costs, as such agreements may sometimes be significant in the selection of class counsel. The court might also direct that potential class counsel indicate how parallel litigation might be coordinated or consolidated with the action before the court.

The court may also direct counsel to propose terms for a potential award of attorney fees and nontaxable costs. Attorney fee awards are an important feature of class action practice, and attention to this subject from the outset may often be a productive technique. Paragraph (2)(C) therefore authorizes the court to provide directions about attorney fees and costs when appointing class counsel. Because there will be numerous class actions in which this information is not likely to be useful, the court need not consider it in all class actions.

Some information relevant to class counsel appointment may involve matters that include adversary preparation in a way that should be shielded from disclosure to other parties. An appropriate protective order may be necessary to preserve confidentiality.

In evaluating prospective class counsel, the court should weigh all pertinent factors. No single factor should necessarily be determinative in a given case. For example, the resources counsel will commit to the case must be appropriate to its needs, but the court should be careful not to limit consideration to lawyers with the greatest resources.

If, after review of all applicants, the court concludes that none would be satisfactory class counsel, it may deny class certification, reject all applications, recommend that an application be modified, invite new applications, or make any other appropriate order regarding selection and appointment of class counsel.

Paragraph (2). This paragraph sets out the procedure that should be followed in appointing class counsel. Although it affords substantial flexibility, it provides the framework for appointment of class counsel in all class actions. For counsel who filed the action, the materials submitted in support of the motion for class certification may suffice to justify appointment so long as the information described in paragraph (g)(1)(C) is included. If there are other applicants, they ordinarily would file a formal application detailing their suitability for the position.

In a plaintiff class action the court usually would appoint as class counsel only an attorney or attorneys who have sought appointment. Different considerations may apply in defendant class actions.

The rule states that the court should appoint "class counsel." In many instances, the applicant will be an individual attorney. In other cases, however, an entire firm, or perhaps numerous attorneys who are not otherwise affiliated but are collaborating on the action will apply. No rule of thumb exists to determine when such arrangements are appropriate; the court should be alert to the need for adequate staffing of the case, but also to the risk of overstaffing or an ungainly counsel structure.

Paragraph (2)(A) authorizes the court to designate interim counsel during the pre- certification period if necessary to protect the interests of the putative class. Rule 23(c)(1)(B) directs that the order certifying the class include appointment of class counsel. Before class certification, however, it will usually be important for an attorney to take action to prepare for the certification decision. The amendment to Rule 23(c)(1) recognizes that some discovery is often necessary for that determination. It also may be important to make or respond to motions before certification. Settlement may be discussed before certification. Ordinarily, such work is handled by the lawyer who filed the action. In some cases, however, there may be rivalry or uncertainty that makes formal designation of interim counsel appropriate. Rule 23(g)(2)(A) authorizes the court to designate interim counsel to act on behalf of the putative class before the certification decision is made. Failure to make the formal designation does not prevent the attorney who filed the action from proceeding in it. Whether or not formally designated interim counsel, an attorney who acts on behalf of the class before certification must act in the best interests of the class as a whole. For example, an attorney who negotiates a pre-certification settlement must seek a settlement that is fair, reasonable, and adequate for the class.

Rule 23(c)(1) provides that the court should decide whether to certify the class "at an early practicable time," and directs that class counsel should be appointed in the order certifying the class. In some cases, it may be appropriate for the court to allow a reasonable period after commencement of the action for filing applications to serve as class counsel. The primary ground for deferring appointment would be that there is reason to anticipate competing applications to serve as class counsel. Examples might include instances in which more than one class action has been filed, or in which other attorneys have filed individual actions on behalf of putative class members. The purpose of facilitating competing applications in such a case is to afford the best possible representation for the class. Another possible reason for deferring appointment would be that the initial applicant was found inadequate, but it seems appropriate to permit additional applications rather than deny class certification.

Paragraph (2)(B) states the basic standard the court should use in deciding whether to certify the class and appoint class counsel in the single applicant situation —that the applicant be able to provide the representation called for by paragraph (1) B) in light of the factors identified in paragraph (1)(C).

If there are multiple adequate applicants, paragraph (2)(B) directs the court to select the class counsel best able to represent the interests of the class. This decision should also be made using the factors outlined in paragraph (1)(C), but in the multiple applicant situation the court is to go beyond scrutinizing the adequacy of counsel and make a comparison of the strengths of the various applicants. As with the decision whether to appoint the sole applicant for the position, no single factor should be dispositive in selecting class counsel in cases in which there are multiple applicants. The fact that a given attorney filed the instant action, for example, might not weigh heavily in the decision if that lawyer had not done significant work identifying or investigating claims. Depending on the nature of the case, one important consideration might be the applicant's existing attorney-client relationship with the proposed class representative.

Paragraph (2)(C) builds on the appointment process by authorizing the court to include provisions regarding attorney fees in the order appointing class counsel. Courts may find it desirable to adopt guidelines for fees or nontaxable costs, or to direct class counsel to report to the court at regular intervals on the efforts undertaken in the action, to facilitate the court's later determination of a reasonable attorney fee.

Subdivision (h). Subdivision (h) is new. Fee awards are a powerful influence on the way attorneys initiate, develop, and conclude class actions. Class action attorney fee awards have heretofore been handled, along with all other attorney fee awards, under Rule 54(d)(2), but that rule is not addressed to the particular concerns of class actions. This subdivision is designed to work in tandem with new subdivision (g) on appointment of class counsel, which may afford an opportunity for the court to provide an early framework for an eventual fee award, or for monitoring the work of class counsel during the pendency of the action.

Subdivision (h) applies to "an action certified as a class action." This includes cases in which there is a simultaneous proposal for class certification and settlement even though technically the class may not be certified unless the court approves the settlement pursuant to review under Rule 23(e). When a settlement is proposed for Rule 23(e) approval, either after certification or with a request for certification, notice to class members about class counsel's fee motion would ordinarily accompany the notice to the class about the settlement proposal itself.

This subdivision does not undertake to create new grounds for an award of attorney fees or nontaxable costs. Instead, it applies when such awards are authorized by law or by agreement of the parties. Against that background, it provides a format for all awards of attorney fees and nontaxable costs in connection with a class action, not only the award to class counsel. In some situations, there may be a basis for making an award to other counsel whose work produced a beneficial result for the class, such as attorneys who acted for the class before certification but were not appointed class counsel, or attorneys who represented objectors to a proposed settlement under Rule 23(e) or to the fee motion of class counsel. Other situations in which fee awards are authorized by law or by agreement of the parties may exist.

This subdivision authorizes an award of "reasonable" attorney fees and nontaxable costs. This is the customary term for measurement of fee awards in cases in which counsel may obtain an award of fees under the "common fund" theory that applies in many class actions, and is used in many fee-shifting statutes. Depending on the circumstances, courts have approached the determination of what is reasonable in different ways. In particular, there is some variation among courts about whether in "common fund" cases the court should use the lodestar or a percentage method of determining what fee is reasonable. The rule does not attempt to resolve the question whether the lodestar or percentage approach should be viewed as preferable.

Active judicial involvement in measuring fee awards is singularly important to the proper operation of the class-action process. Continued reliance on caselaw development of fee-award measures does not diminish the court's responsibility. In a class action, the district court must ensure that the amount and mode of payment of attorney fees are fair and proper whether the fees come from a common fund or are otherwise paid. Even in the absence of objections, the court bears this responsibility.

Courts discharging this responsibility have looked to a variety of factors. One fundamental focus is the result actually achieved for class members, a basic consideration in any case in which fees are sought on the basis of a benefit achieved for class members. The Private Securities Litigation Reform Act of 1995 explicitly makes this factor a cap for a fee award in actions to which it applies. See 15 U.S.C. §§ 77z-1(a)(6); 78u-4(a)(6) (fee award should not exceed a "reasonable percentage of the amount of any damages and prejudgment interest actually paid to the class"). For a percentage approach to fee measurement, results achieved is the basic starting point.

In many instances, the court may need to proceed with care in assessing the value conferred on class members. Settlement regimes that provide for future payments, for example, may not result in significant actual payments to class members. In this connection, the court may need to scrutinize the manner and operation of any applicable claims procedure. In some cases, it may be appropriate to defer some portion of the fee award until actual payouts to class members are known.

Settlements involving nonmonetary provisions for class members also deserve careful scrutiny to ensure that these provisions have actual value to the class. On occasion the court's Rule 23(e) review will provide a solid basis for this sort of evaluation, but in any event it is also important to assessing the fee award for the class.

At the same time, it is important to recognize that in some class actions the monetary relief obtained is not the sole determinant of an appropriate attorney fees award. *Cf. Blanchard v. Bergeron*, 489 U.S. 87, 95 (1989) (cautioning in an individual case against an "undesirable emphasis" on "the importance of the recovery of damages in civil rights litigation" that might "shortchange efforts to seek effective injunctive or declaratory relief").

Any directions or orders made by the court in connection with appointing class counsel under Rule 23(g) should weigh heavily in making a fee award under this subdivision.

Courts have also given weight to agreements among the parties regarding the fee motion, and to agreements between class counsel and others about the fees claimed by the motion. Rule 54(d)(2)(B) provides: "If directed by the court, the motion shall also disclose the terms of any agreement with respect to fees to be paid for the services for which claim is made." The agreement by a settling party not to oppose a fee application up to a certain amount, for example, is worthy of consideration, but the court remains responsible to determine a reasonable fee. "Side agreements" regarding fees provide at least perspective pertinent to an appropriate fee award.

In addition, courts may take account of the fees charged by class counsel or other attorneys for representing individual claimants or objectors in the case. In determining a fee for class counsel, the court's objective is to ensure an overall fee that is fair for counsel and equitable within the class. In some circumstances individual fee agreements between class counsel and class members might have provisions inconsistent with those goals, and the court might determine that adjustments in the class fee award were necessary as a result.

Finally, it is important to scrutinize separately the application for an award covering nontaxable costs. If costs were addressed in the order appointing class counsel, those directives should be a presumptive starting point in determining what is an appropriate award.

Paragraph (1). Any claim for an award of attorney fees must be sought by motion under Rule 54(d)(2), which invokes the provisions for timing of appeal in Rule 58 and Appellate Rule 4. Owing to the distinctive features of class action fee motions, however, the provisions of this subdivision control disposition of fee motions in class actions, while Rule 54(d)(2) applies to matters not addressed in this subdivision.

The court should direct when the fee motion must be filed. For motions by class counsel in cases subject to court review of a proposed settlement under Rule 23(e), it would be important to require the filing of at least the initial motion in time for inclusion of information about the motion in the notice to the class about the proposed settlement that is required by Rule 23(e). In cases litigated to judgment, the court might also order class counsel's motion to be filed promptly so that notice to the class under this subdivision (h) can be given.

Besides service of the motion on all parties, notice of class counsel's motion for attorney fees must be "directed to the class in a reasonable manner." Because members of the class have an interest in the arrangements for payment of class counsel whether that payment comes from the class fund or is made directly by another party, notice is required in all instances. In cases in which settlement approval is contemplated under Rule 23(e), notice of class counsel's fee motion should be combined with notice of the proposed settlement, and the provision regarding notice to the class is parallel to the requirements for notice under Rule 23(e). In adjudicated class actions, the court may calibrate the notice to avoid undue expense.

Paragraph (2). A class member and any party from whom payment is sought may object to the fee motion. Other parties—for example, nonsettling defendants—may not object because they lack a sufficient interest in the amount the court awards. The rule does not specify a time limit for making an objection. In setting the date objections are due, the court should provide sufficient time after the full fee motion is on file to enable potential objectors to examine the motion.

The court may allow an objector discovery relevant to the objections. In determining whether to allow discovery, the court should weigh the need for the information against the cost and delay that would attend discovery. See Rule 26(b)(2). One factor in determining whether to authorize discovery is the completeness of the material submitted in support of the fee motion, which depends in part on the fee measurement standard applicable to the case. If the motion provides thorough information, the burden should be on the objector to justify discovery to obtain further information.

Paragraph (3). Whether or not there are formal objections, the court must determine whether a fee award is justified and, if so, set a reasonable fee. The rule does not require a formal hearing in all cases. The form and extent of a hearing depend on the circumstances of the case. The rule does require findings and conclusions under Rule 52(a).

Paragraph (4). By incorporating Rule 54(d)(2), this provision gives the court broad authority to obtain assistance in determining the appropriate amount to award. In deciding whether to direct submission of such questions to a special master or magistrate judge, the court should give appropriate consideration to the cost and delay that such a process might entail.

ADVISORY COMMITTEE'S NOTE TO 1966 AMENDMENT OF RULE 23

*   *   *

The amended rule describes in more practical terms the occasions for maintaining class actions; provides that all class actions maintained to the end as such will result in judgments including those whom the court finds to be members of the class, whether or not the judgment is favorable to the class; and refers to the measures which can be taken to assure the fair conduct of these actions.

Subdivision (a) states the prerequisites for maintaining any class action in terms of the numerousness of the class making joinder of the members impracticable, the existence of questions common to the class, and the desired qualifications of the representative parties. . . . These are necessary but not sufficient conditions for a class action. . . . Subdivision (b) describes the additional elements which in varying situations justify the use of a class action.

Subdivision (b)(1). The difficulties which would be likely to arise if resort were had to separate actions by or against the individual members of the class here furnish the reasons for, and the principal key to, the propriety and value of utilizing the class-action device. The considerations stated under clauses (A) and (B) are compa- rable to certain of the elements which define the persons whose joinder in an action is desirable as stated in Rule 19(a), as amended. See amended Rule 19(a)(2)(i) and (ii), and the Advisory Committee's Note thereto; Hazard, *Indispensable Party: The Historical Origin of a Procedural Phantom,* 61 Colum. L. Rev. 1254, 1259–60 (1961). . . .

Clause (A): One person may have rights against, or be under duties toward, numerous persons constituting a class, and be so positioned that conflicting or varying adjudications in lawsuits with individual members of the class might establish incompatible standards to govern his conduct. The class action device can be used effectively to obviate the actual or virtual dilemma which would thus confront the party opposing the class. The matter has been stated thus: "The felt necessity for a class action is greatest when the courts are called upon to order or sanction the alteration of the status quo in circumstances such that a large number of persons are in a position to call on a single person to alter the status quo, or to complain if it is altered, and the possibility exists that [the] actor might be called upon to act in inconsistent ways." . . . To illustrate: Separate actions by individuals against a municipality to declare a bond issue invalid or condition or limit it, to prevent or limit the making of a particular appropriation or to compel or invalidate an assessment, might create a risk of inconsistent or varying determinations. In the same way, individual litigations of the rights and duties of riparian owners, or of landowners' rights and duties respecting a claimed nuisance, could create a possibility of incompatible adjudications. Actions by or against a class provide a ready and fair means of achieving unitary adjudication. . . .

Clause (B): This clause takes in situations where the judgment in a nonclass action by or against an individual member of the class, while not technically concluding the other members, might do so as a practical matter. The vice of an individual action would lie in the fact that the other members of the class, thus practically concluded, would have had no representation in the lawsuit. In an action by policy holders against a fraternal benefit association attacking a financial reorganization of the society, it would hardly have been practical, if indeed it would have been possible, to confine the effects of a validation of the reorganization to the individual plaintiffs. Consequently a class action was called for with adequate representation of all members of the class. . . . For much the same reason actions by shareholders to compel the declaration of a dividend, the proper recognition and handling of redemption or pre-emption rights, or the like (or actions by the corporation for corresponding declarations of rights), should ordinarily be conducted as class actions, although the matter has been much obscured by the insistence that each shareholder has an individual claim. . . . . These shareholders' actions are to be distinguished from derivative actions by shareholders dealt with in new Rule 23.1. The same reasoning applies to an action which charges a breach of trust by an indenture trustee or other fiduciary similarly affecting the members of a large class of security holders or other beneficiaries, and which requires an accounting or like measures to restore the subject of the trust. . . .

In various situations an adjudication as to one or more members of the class will necessarily or probably have an adverse practical effect on the interests of other members who should therefore be represented in the lawsuit. This is plainly the case when claims are made by numerous persons against a fund insufficient to satisfy all claims. A class action by or against representative members to settle the validity of the claims as a whole, or in groups, followed by separate proof of the amount of each valid claim and proportionate distribution of the fund, meets the problem. . . . The same reasoning applies to an action by a creditor to set aside a fraudulent convey-ance by the debtor and to appropriate the property to his claim, when the debtor's assets are insufficient to pay all creditors' claims. . . . Similar problems, however, can arise in the absence of a fund either present or potential. A negative or mandatory injunction secured by one of a numerous class may disable the opposing party from performing claimed duties toward the other members of the class or materially affect his ability to do so. An adjudication as to movie "clearances and runs" nominally affecting only one exhibitor would often have practical effects on all the exhibitors in the same territorial area. *Cf. United States v. Paramount Pictures, Inc.*, 66 F. Supp. 323, 341–46 (S.D.N.Y. 1946); 334 U.S. 131, 144–48 (1948). Assuming a sufficiently numerous class of exhibitors, a class action would be advisable. (Here representation of subclasses of exhibitors could become necessary; see subdivision (c)(3)(B).)

Subdivision (b)(2). This subdivision is intended to reach situations where a party has taken action or refused to take action with respect to a class, and final relief of an injunctive nature or of a corresponding declaratory nature, settling the legality of the behavior with respect to the class as a whole, is appropriate. Declaratory relief "corresponds" to injunctive relief when as a practical matter it affords injunctive relief or serves as a basis for later injunctive relief. The subdivision does not extend to cases in which the appropriate final relief relates exclusively or predominantly to money damages. Action or inaction is directed to a class within the meaning of this subdivision even if it has taken effect or is threatened only as to one or a few members of the class, provided it is based on grounds which have general application to the class.

Illustrative are various actions in the civil-rights field where a party is charged with discriminating unlawfully against a class, usually one whose members are incapable of specific enumeration. . . . Subdivision (b)(2) is not limited to civil-rights cases. Thus an action looking to specific or declaratory relief could be brought by a numerous class of purchasers, say retailers of a given description, against a seller alleged to have undertaken to sell to that class at prices higher than those set for other purchasers, say retailers of another description, when the applicable law forbids such a pricing differential. So also a patentee of a machine, charged with selling or licensing the machine on condition that purchasers or licensees also purchase or obtain licenses to use an ancillary unpatented machine, could be sued on a class basis by a numerous group of purchasers or licensees, or by a numerous group of competing sellers or licensors of the unpatented machine, to test the legality of the "tying" condition.

Subdivision (b)(3). In the situations to which this subdivision relates, class-action treatment is not as clearly called for as in those described above, but it may nevertheless be convenient and desirable depending upon the particular facts. Subdivision (b)(3) encompasses those cases in which a class action would achieve economies of time, effort, and expense, and promote uniformity of decision as to persons similarly situated, without sacrificing procedural fairness or bringing about other undesirable results. . . .

The court is required to find, as a condition of holding that a class action may be maintained under this subdivision, that the questions common to the class predominate over the questions affecting individual members. It is only where this predominance exists that economies can be achieved by means of the class-action device. In this view, a fraud perpetrated on numerous persons by the use of similar misrepresenta- tions may be an appealing situation for a class action, and it may remain so despite the need, if liability is found, for separate determination of the damages suffered by individuals within the class. On the other hand, although having some common core, a fraud case may be unsuited for treatment as a class action if there was material variation in the representations made or in the kinds or degrees of reliance by the persons to whom they were addressed. . . . A "mass accident" resulting in injuries to numerous persons is ordinarily not appropriate for a class action because of the likelihood that significant questions, not only of damages but of liability and defenses to liability, would be present, affecting the individuals in different ways. In these circumstances an action conducted nominally as a class action would degenerate in practice into multiple lawsuits separately tried. . . . Private damage claims by numerous individuals arising out of concerted antitrust violations may or may not involve predominating common questions. . . .

That common questions predominates is not itself sufficient to justify a class action under subdivision (b)(3), for another method of handling the litigious situation may be available which has greater practical advantages. Thus one or more actions agreed to by the parties as test or model actions may be preferable to a class action; or it may prove feasible and preferable to consolidate actions. . . . Even when a number of separate actions are proceeding simultaneously, experience shows that the burdens on the parties and the courts can sometimes be reduced by arrangements for avoiding repetitive discovery or the like.... To reinforce the point that the court with the aid of the parties ought to assess the relative advantages of alternative procedures for handling the total controversy, subdivision (b)(3) requires, as a further condition of maintaining the class action, that the court shall find that that procedure is "superior" to the others in the particular circumstances.

Factors (A)–(D) are listed, non-exhaustively, as pertinent to the findings. The court is to consider the interests of individual members of the class in controlling their own litigations and carrying them on as they see fit....

In this connection the court should inform itself of any litigation actually pending by or against the individuals. The interests of individuals in conducting separate lawsuits may be so strong as to call for denial of a class action. On the other hand, these interests may be theoretic rather than practical; the class may have a high degree of cohesion and prosecution of the action through representatives would be quite unobjectionable, or the amounts at stake for individuals may be so small that separate suits would be impractical. The burden that separate suits would impose on the party opposing the class, or upon the court calendars, may also fairly be considered. (See the discussion, under subdivision (c)(2) below, of the right of members to be excluded from the class upon their request.)

Also pertinent is the question of the desirability of concentrating the trial of the claims in the particular forum by means of a class action, in contrast to allowing the claims to be litigated separately in forums to which they would ordinarily be brought. Finally, the court should consider the problems of management which are likely to arise in the conduct of a class action.

Subdivision (c)(1). In order to give clear definition to the action, this provision requires the court to determine, as early in the proceedings as may be practicable, whether an action brought as a class action is to be so maintained. The determination depends in each case on satisfaction of the terms of subdivision (a) and the relevant provisions of subdivision (b).

*　　*　　*

Subdivision (c)(2) makes special provision for class actions maintained under subdivision (b)(3). As noted in the discussion of the latter subdivision, the interests of the individuals in pursuing their own litigations may be so strong here as to warrant denial of a class action altogether. Even when a class action is maintained under subdivision (b)(3), this individual interest is respected. Thus the court is required to direct notice to the members of the class of the right of each member to be excluded from the class upon his request. A member who does not request exclusion may, if he wishes, enter an appearance in the action through his counsel; whether or not he does so, the judgment in the action will embrace him.

The notice, setting forth the alternatives open to the members of the class, is to be the best practicable under the circumstances, and shall include individual notice to the members who can be identified through reasonable effort. (For further discussion of this notice, see the statement under subdivision (d)(2) below.)

Subdivision (c)(3). The judgment in a class action maintained as such to the end will embrace the class, that is, in a class action under subdivision (b)(1) or (b)(2), those found by the court to be class members; in a class action under subdivision (b)(3), those to whom the notice prescribed by subdivision (c)(2) was directed, excepting those who requested exclusion or who are ultimately found by the court not to be members of the class. The judgment has this scope whether it is favorable or unfavorable to the class. In a (b)(1) or (b)(2) action the judgment "describes" the members of the class, but need not specify the individual members; in a (b)(3) action the judgment "specifies" the individual members who have been identified and describes the others.

* * *

Although thus declaring that the judgment in a class action includes the class, as defined, subdivision (c)(3) does not disturb the recognized principle that the court conducting the action cannot predetermine the *res judicata* effect of the judgment; this can be tested only in a subsequent action. See Restatement, *Judgments* § 86, comment (h), § 116 (1942). The court, however, in framing the judgment in any suit brought as a class action, must decide what its extent or coverage shall be, and if the matter is carefully considered, questions of *res judicata* are less likely to be raised at a later time and if raised will be more satisfactorily answered. . . .

Subdivision (c)(4). This provision recognizes that an action may be maintained as a class action as to particular issues only. For example, in a fraud or similar case the action may retain its "class" character only through the adjudication of liability to the class; the members of the class may thereafter be required to come in individually and prove the amounts of their respective claims.

Two or more classes may be represented in a single action. Where a class is found to include subclasses divergent in interest, the class may be divided correspondingly, and each subclass treated as a class.

Subdivision (d) is concerned with the fair and efficient conduct of the action and lists some types of orders which may be appropriate.

The court should consider how the proceedings are to be arranged in sequence, and what measures should be taken to simplify the proof and argument. See subdivision (d)(1). The orders resulting from this—consideration, like the others referred to in subdivision (d), may be combined with a pretrial order under Rule 16, and are subject to modification as the case proceeds.

* * *

Subdivision (e) requires approval of the court, after notice, for the dismissal or compromise of any class action.

RULE 23.1. DERIVATIVE ACTIONS.

(a) Prerequisites.

This rule applies when one or more shareholders or members of a corporation or an unincorporated association bring a derivative action to enforce a right that the corporation or association may properly assert but has failed to enforce. The derivative action may not be maintained if it appears that the plaintiff does not fairly and adequately represent the interests of shareholders or members who are similarly situated in enforcing the right of the corporation or association.

(b) Pleading Requirements.

The complaint must be verified and must:

(1) allege that the plaintiff was a shareholder or member at the time of the transaction complained of, or that the plaintiff's share or membership later devolved on it by operation of law;

(2) allege that the action is not a collusive one to confer jurisdiction that the court would otherwise lack; and

(3) state with particularity:

(A) any effort by the plaintiff to obtain the desired action from the directors or comparable authority and, if necessary, from the shareholders or members; and

(B) the reasons for not obtaining the action or not making the effort.

(c) Settlement, Dismissal, and Compromise.

A derivative action may be settled, voluntarily dismissed, or compromised only with the court's approval. Notice of a proposed settlement, voluntary dismissal, or compromise must be given to shareholders or members in the manner that the court orders.

[*Adopted Feb. 28, 1966, effective July 1, 1966; amended Mar. 2, 1987, effective Aug. 1, 1987; amended April 30, 2007, effective Dec. 1, 2007.*]

RULE 23.2.   ACTIONS RELATING TO UNINCORPORATED ASSOCIATIONS.

This rule applies to an action brought by or against the members of an unincorpo- rated association as a class by naming certain members as representative parties. The action may be maintained only if it appears that those parties will fairly and adequately protect the interests of the association and its members. In conducting the action, the court may issue any appropriate orders corresponding with those in Rule 23(d), and the procedure for settlement, voluntary dismissal, or compromise must correspond with the procedure in Rule 23(e).

[*Adopted Feb. 28, 1966, effective July 1, 1966; amended April 30, 2007, effective Dec. 1, 2007.*]

RULE 24.   INTERVENTION.

(a) Intervention of Right.

On timely motion, the court must permit anyone to intervene who:

(1) is given an unconditional right to intervene by a federal statute; or

(2) claims an interest relating to the property or transaction that is the subject of the action, and is so situated that disposing of the action may as a practical

matter impair or impede the movant's ability to protect its interest, unless existing parties adequately represent that interest.

(b) Permissive Intervention.

(1) *In General.*

On timely motion, the court may permit anyone to intervene who:

(A) is given a conditional right to intervene by a federal statute; or

(B) has a claim or defense that shares with the main action a common question of law or fact.

(2) *By a Government Officer or Agency.*

On timely motion, the court may permit a federal or state governmental officer or agency to intervene if a party's claim or defense is based on:

(A) a statute or executive order administered by the officer or agency; or

(B) any regulation, order, requirement, or agreement issued or made under the statute or executive order.

(3) *Delay or Prejudice.*

In exercising its discretion, the court must consider whether the intervention will unduly delay or prejudice the adjudication of the original parties' rights.

(c) Notice and Pleading Required.

A motion to intervene must be served on the parties as provided in Rule 5. The motion must state the grounds for intervention and be accompanied by a pleading that sets out the claim or defense for which intervention is sought.

[*Adopted Dec. 20, 1937, effective Sept. 16, 1938; amended Dec. 27, 1946, effective Mar. 19, 1948; Dec. 29, 1948, effective Oct. 20, 1949; Jan. 21, 1963, effective July 1, 1963; Feb. 28, 1966, effective July 1, 1966; Mar. 2, 1987, effective Aug. 1, 1987; Apr. 30, 1991, effective Dec. 1, 1991; April 12, 2006, effective December 1, 2006; amended April 30, 2007, effective Dec. 1, 2007.*]

RULE 25.   SUBSTITUTION OF PARTIES.

(a) Death.

(1) *Substitution if the Claim Is Not Extinguished.*

If a party dies and the claim is not extinguished, the court may order substitution of the proper party. A motion for substitution may be made by any party or by the decedent's successor or representative. If the motion is not made within 90 days after service of a statement noting the death, the action by or against the decedent must be dismissed.

(2) *Continuation Among the Remaining Parties.*

After a party's death, if the right sought to be enforced survives only to or against the remaining parties, the action does not abate, but proceeds in favor of or against the remaining parties. The death should be noted on the record.

(3) *Service.*

A motion to substitute, together with a notice of hearing, must be served on the parties as provided in Rule 5 and on nonparties as provided in Rule 4. A statement noting death must be served in the same manner. Service may be made in any judicial district.

(b) Incompetency.

If a party becomes incompetent, the court may, on motion, permit the action to be continued by or against the party's representative. The motion must be served as provided in Rule 25(a)(3).

(c) Transfer of Interest.

If an interest is transferred, the action may be continued by or against the original party unless the court, on motion, orders the transferee to be substituted in the action or joined with the original party. The motion must be served as provided in Rule 25(a)(3).

(d) Public Officers; Death or Separation from Office.

An action does not abate when a public officer who is a party in an official capacity dies, resigns, or otherwise ceases to hold office while the action is pending. The officer's successor is automatically substituted as a party. Later proceedings should be in the substituted party's name, but any misnomer not affecting the parties' substantial rights must be disregarded. The court may order substitution at any time, but the absence of such an order does not affect the substitution.

[*Adopted Dec. 20, 1937, effective Sept. 16, 1938; amended Dec. 29, 1948, effective Oct. 20, 1949; Apr. 17, 1961, effective July 19, 1961; Jan. 21, 1963, effective July 1, 1963; Mar. 2, 1987, effective Aug. 1, 1987; amended April 30, 2007, effective Dec. 1, 2007.*]

TITLE V.   DISCLOSURES AND DISCOVERY

RULE 26.   DUTY TO DISCLOSE; GENERAL PROVISIONS GOVERNING DISCOVERY.

(a) Required Disclosures.

(1) *Initial Disclosure.*

(A) *In General.*

Except as exempted by Rule 26(a)(1)(B) or as otherwise stipulated or ordered by the court, a party must, without awaiting a discovery request, provide to the other parties:

(i) the name and, if known, the address and telephone number of each individual likely to have discoverable information—along with the subjects of that information—that the disclosing party may use to support its claims or defenses, unless the use would be solely for impeachment;

(ii) a copy—or a description by category and location—of all documents, electronically stored information, and tangible things that the disclosing party has in its possession, custody, or control and may use to support its claims or defenses, unless the use would be solely for impeachment;

(iii) a computation of each category of damages claimed by the disclosing party—who must also make available for inspection and copying as under Rule 34 the documents or other evidentiary material, unless privileged or protected from disclosure, on which each computation is based, including materials bearing on the nature and extent of injuries suffered; and

(iv) for inspection and copying as under Rule 34, any insurance agreement under which an insurance business may be liable to satisfy all or part of a possible judgment in the action or to indemnify or reimburse for payments made to satisfy the judgment.

(B) *Proceedings Exempt from Initial Disclosure.*

The following proceedings are exempt from initial disclosure:

(i) an action for review on an administrative record;

(ii) a petition for habeas corpus or any other proceeding to challenge a criminal conviction or sentence;

(iii) an action brought without an attorney by a person in the custody of the United States, a state, or a state subdivision;

(iv) an action to enforce or quash an administrative summons or subpoena;

(v) an action by the United States to recover benefit payments;

(vi) an action by the United States to collect on a student loan guaranteed by the United States;

(vii) a proceeding ancillary to a proceeding in another court; and

(viii) an action to enforce an arbitration award.

(C) *Time for Initial Disclosures—In General.*

A party must make the initial disclosures at or within 14 days after the parties' Rule 26(f) conference unless a different time is set by stipulation or court order, or unless a party objects during the conference that initial disclosures are not appropriate in this action and states the objection in the proposed discovery plan. In ruling on the objection, the court must determine what disclosures, if any, are to be made and must set the time for disclosure.

(D) *Time for Initial Disclosures—For Parties Served or Joined Later.*

A party that is first served or otherwise joined after the Rule 26(f) conference must make the initial disclosures within 30 days after being served or joined, unless a different time is set by stipulation or court order.

(E) *Basis for Initial Disclosure; Unacceptable Excuses.*

A party must make its initial disclosures based on the information then reasonably available to it. A party is not excused from making its disclosures because it has not fully investigated the case or because it challenges the sufficiency of another party's disclosures or because another party has not made its disclosures.

(2) *Disclosure of Expert Testimony.*

(A) *In General.*

In addition to the disclosures required by Rule 26(a)(1), a party must disclose to the other parties the identity of any witness it may use at trial to present evidence under Federal Rule of Evidence 702, 703, or 705.

(B) *Witnesses Who Must Provide a Written Report.*

Unless otherwise stipulated or ordered by the court, this disclosure must be accompanied by a written report—prepared and signed by the witness—if the witness is one retained or specially employed to provide expert testimony in the case or one whose duties as the party's employee regularly involve giving expert testimony. The report must contain:

(i) a complete statement of all opinions the witness will express and the basis and reasons for them;

(ii) the facts or data considered by the witness in forming them;

(iii) any exhibits that will be used to summarize or support them;

(iv) the witness's qualifications, including a list of all publications authored in the previous ten years;

(v) a list of all other cases in which, during the previous four years, the witness testified as an expert at trial or by deposition; and

(vi) a statement of the compensation to be paid for the study and testimony in the case.

(C) *Witnesses Who Do Not Provide a Written Report.*

Unless otherwise stipulated or ordered by the court, if the witness is not required to provide a written report, this disclosure must state:

(i) the subject matter on which the witness is expected to present evidence under Federal Rule of Evidence 702, 703, or 705; and

(ii) a summary of the facts and opinions to which the witness is expected to testify.

(D) *Time to Disclose Expert Testimony*

A party must make these disclosures at the times and in the sequence that the court orders. Absent a stipulation or a court order, the disclosures must be made:

(i) at least 90 days before the date set for trial or for the case to be ready for trial; or

(ii) if the evidence is intended solely to contradict or rebut evidence on the same subject matter identified by another party under Rule 26(a)(2)(B) or (C), within 30 days after the other party's disclosure.

(E) *Supplementing the Disclosure.*

The parties must supplement these disclosures when required under Rule 26(e).

(3) *Pretrial Disclosures.*

(A) *In General.*

In addition to the disclosures required by Rule 26(a)(1) and (2), a party must provide to the other parties and promptly file the following information about the evidence that it may present at trial other than solely for impeachment:

> (i) the name and, if not previously provided, the address and telephone number of each witness — separately identifying those the party expects to present and those it may call if the need arises;

> (ii) the designation of those witnesses whose testimony the party expects to present by deposition and, if not taken stenographically, a transcript of the pertinent parts of the deposition; and

> (iii) an identification of each document or other exhibit, including summaries of other evidence — separately identifying those items the party expects to offer and those it may offer if the need arises.

(B) *Time for Pretrial Disclosures; Objections.*

Unless the court orders otherwise, these disclosures must be made at least 30 days before trial. Within 14 days after they are made, unless the court sets a different time, a party may serve and promptly file a list of the following objections: any objections to the use under Rule 32(a) of a deposition designated by another party under Rule 26(a)(3)(A)(ii); and any objection, together with the grounds for it, that may be made to the admissibility of materials identified under Rule 26(a)(3)(A)(iii). An objection not so made — except for one under Federal Rule of Evidence 402 or 403 — is waived unless excused by the court for good cause.

(4) *Form of Disclosures.*

Unless the court orders otherwise, all disclosures under Rule 26(a) must be in writing, signed, and served.

(b) Discovery Scope and Limits.

(1) *Scope in General.*

Unless otherwise limited by court order, the scope of discovery is as follows: Parties may obtain discovery regarding any nonprivileged matter that is relevant to any party's claim or defense and proportional to the needs of the case, considering the importance of the issues at stake in the action, the amount in controversy, the parties' relative access to relevant information, the parties' resources, the importance of the discovery in resolving the issues, and whether the burden or expense of the proposed discovery outweighs its likely benefit. Information within this scope of discovery need not be admissible in evidence to be discoverable.

(2) *Limitations on Frequency and Extent.*

(A) *When Permitted.*

By order, the court may alter the limits in these rules on the number of depositions and interrogatories or on the length of depositions under Rule 30. By order or local rule, the court may also limit the number of requests under Rule 36.

(B) *Specific Limitations on Electronically Stored Information.*

A party need not provide discovery of electronically stored information from sources that the party identifies as not reasonably accessible because of undue burden or cost. On motion to compel discovery or for a protective order, the party from whom discovery is sought must show that the information is not reasonably accessible because of undue burden or cost. If that showing is made, the court may nonetheless order discovery from such sources if the requesting party shows good cause, considering the limitations of Rule 26(b)(2)(C). The court may specify conditions for the discovery.

(C) *When Required.*

On motion or on its own, the court must limit the frequency or extent of discovery otherwise allowed by these rules or by local rule if it determines that:

> (i) the discovery sought is unreasonably cumulative or duplicative, or can be obtained from some other source that is more convenient, less burdensome, or less expensive;

> (ii) the party seeking discovery has had ample opportunity to obtain the information by discovery in the action; or

> (iii) the proposed discovery is outside the scope permitted by Rule 26(b)(1).

(3) *Trial Preparation: Materials.*

(A) *Documents and Tangible Things.*

Ordinarily, a party may not discover documents and tangible things that are prepared in anticipation of litigation or for trial by or for another party or its representative (including the other party's attorney, consultant, surety, indemni- tor, insurer, or agent). But, subject to Rule 26(b)(4), those materials may be discovered if:

> (i) they are otherwise discoverable under Rule 26(b)(1); and

> (ii) the party shows that it has substantial need for the materials to prepare its case and cannot, without undue hardship, obtain their substantial equivalent by other means.

(B) *Protection Against Disclosure.*

If the court orders discovery of those materials, it must protect against disclosure of the mental impressions, conclusions, opinions, or legal theories of a party's attorney or other representative concerning the litigation.

(C) *Previous Statement.*

Any party or other person may, on request and without the required showing, obtain the person's own previous statement about the action or its subject matter. If the request is refused, the person may move for a court order, and Rule 37(a)(5) applies to the award of expenses. A previous statement is either:

> (i) a written statement that the person has signed or otherwise adopted or approved; or

> (ii) a contemporaneous stenographic, mechanical, electrical, or other recording—or a transcription of it—that recites substantially verbatim the person's oral statement.

(4) *Trial Preparation: Experts.*

(A) *Deposition of an Expert Who May Testify.*

A party may depose any person who has been identified as an expert whose opinions may be presented at trial. If Rule 26(a)(2)(B) requires a report from the expert, the deposition may be conducted only after the report is provided.

(B) *Trial-Preparation Protection for Draft Reports or Disclosures.*

Rules 26(b)(3)(A) and (B) protect drafts of any report or disclosure required under Rule 26(a)(2), regardless of the form in which the draft is recorded.

(C) *Trial-Preparation Protection for Communications Between a Party's Attorney and Expert Witnesses.*

Rules 26(b)(3)(A) and (B) protect communications between the party's attorney and any witness required to provide a report under Rule 26(a)(2)(B), regardless of the form of the communications, except to the extent that the communications:

> (i) relate to compensation for the expert's study or testimony;

> (ii) identify facts or data that the party's attorney provided and that the expert considered in forming the opinions to be expressed; or

> (iii) identify assumptions that the party's attorney provided and that the expert relied on in forming the opinions to be expressed.

(D) *Expert Employed Only for Trial Preparation*

Ordinarily, a party may not, by interrogatories or deposition, discover facts known or opinions held by an expert who has been retained or specially employed by another party in anticipation of litigation or to prepare for trial and who is not expected to be called as a witness at trial. But a party may do so only:

> (i) as provided in Rule 35(b); or

> (ii) on showing exceptional circumstances under which it is impracticable for the party to obtain facts or opinions on the same subject by other means.

(E) *Payment*

Unless manifest injustice would result, the court must require that the party seeking discovery:

(i) pay the expert a reasonable fee for time spent in responding to discovery under Rule 26(b)(4)(A) or (D); and

(ii) for discovery under (D), also pay the other party a fair portion of the fees and expenses it reasonably incurred in obtaining the expert's facts and opinions..

(5) *Claiming Privilege or Protecting Trial-Preparation Materials.*

(A) *Information Withheld.*

When a party withholds information otherwise discoverable by claiming that the information is privileged or subject to protection as trial-preparation material, the party must:

(i) expressly make the claim; and

(ii) describe the nature of the documents, communications, or tangible things not produced or disclosed—and do so in a manner that, without revealing information itself privileged or protected, will enable other parties to assess the claim.

(B) *Information Produced.*

If information produced in discovery is subject to a claim of privilege or of protection as trial preparation material, the party making the claim may notify any party that received the information of the claim and the basis for it. After being notified, a party must promptly return, sequester, or destroy the specified information and any copies it has; must not use or disclose the information until the claim is resolved; must take reasonable steps to retrieve the information if the party disclosed it before being notified; and may promptly present the information to the court under seal for a determination of the claim. The producing party must preserve the information until the claim is resolved.

(c) **Protective Orders.**

(1) *In General.*

A party or any person from whom discovery is sought may move for a protective order in the court where the action is pending—or as an alternative on matters relating to a deposition, in the court for the district where the deposition will be taken. The motion must include a certification that the movant has in good faith conferred or attempted to confer with other affected parties in an effort to resolve the dispute without court action. The court may, for good cause, issue an order to protect a party or person from annoyance, embarrassment, oppression, or undue burden or expense, including one or more of the following:

(A) forbidding the disclosure or discovery;

(B) specifying terms, including time and place or the allocation of expenses, for the disclosure or discovery;

(C) prescribing a discovery method other than the one selected by the party seeking discovery;

(D) forbidding inquiry into certain matters, or limiting the scope of disclosure or discovery to certain matters;

(E) designating the persons who may be present while the discovery is conducted;

(F) requiring that a deposition be sealed and opened only on court order;

(G) requiring that a trade secret or other confidential research, development, or commercial information not be revealed or be revealed only in a specified way; and

(H) requiring that the parties simultaneously file specified documents or information in sealed envelopes, to be opened as the court directs.

(2) *Ordering Discovery.*

If a motion for a protective order is wholly or partly denied, the court may, on just terms, order that any party or person provide or permit discovery.

(3) *Awarding Expenses.*

Rule 37(a)(5) applies to the award of expenses.

(d) Timing and Sequence of Discovery.

(1) *Timing.*

A party may not seek discovery from any source before the parties have conferred as required by Rule 26(f), except in a proceeding exempted from initial disclosure under Rule 26(a)(1)(B), or when authorized by these rules, by stipulation, or by court order.

(2) *Early Rule 34 Requests.*

(A) *Time to Deliver.* More than 21 days after the summons and complaint are served on a party, a request under Rule 34 may be delivered:

(i) to that party by any other party, and

(ii) by that party to any plaintiff or to any other party that has been served.

(B) *When Considered Served.* The request is considered to have been served at the first Rule 26(f) conference.

(3) *Sequence.* Unless the parties stipulate or the court orders otherwise for the parties' and witnesses' convenience and in the interests of justice:

(A) methods of discovery may be used in any sequence; and

(B) discovery by one party does not require any other party to delay its discovery.

(e) Supplementing Disclosures and Responses.

(1) *In General.*

A party who has made a disclosure under Rule 26(a) — or who has responded to an interrogatory, request for production, or request for admission — must supplement or correct its disclosure or response:

(A) in a timely manner if the party learns that in some material respect the disclosure or response is incomplete or incorrect, and if the additional or corrective information has not otherwise been made known to the other parties during the discovery process or in writing; or

(B) as ordered by the court.

(2) *Expert Witness.*

For an expert whose report must be disclosed under Rule 26(a)(2)(B), the party's duty to supplement extends both to information included in the report and to information given during the expert's deposition. Any additions or changes to this information must be disclosed by the time the party's pretrial disclosures under Rule 26(a)(3) are due.

(f) **Conference of the Parties; Planning for Discovery.**

(1) *Conference Timing.*

Except in a proceeding exempted from initial disclosure under Rule 26(a)(1)(B) or when the court orders otherwise, the parties must confer as soon as practicable—and in any event at least 21 days before a scheduling conference is to be held or a scheduling order is due under Rule 16(b).

(2) *Conference Content; Parties' Responsibilities.*

In conferring, the parties must consider the nature and basis of their claims and defenses and the possibilities for promptly settling or resolving the case; make or arrange for the disclosures required by Rule 26(a)(1); discuss any issues about preserving discoverable information; and develop a proposed discovery plan. The attorneys of record and all unrepresented parties that have appeared in the case are jointly responsible for arranging the conference, for attempting in good faith to agree on the proposed discovery plan, and for submitting to the court within 14 days after the conference a written report outlining the plan. The court may order the parties or attorneys to attend the conference in person.

(3) *Discovery Plan.*

A discovery plan must state the parties' views and proposals on:

(A) what changes should be made in the timing, form, or requirement for disclosures under Rule 26(a), including a statement of when initial disclosures were made or will be made;

(B) the subjects on which discovery may be needed, when discovery should be completed, and whether discovery should be conducted in phases or be limited to or focused on particular issues;

(C) any issues about disclosure, discovery, or preservation of electronically stored information, including the form or forms in which it should be produced;

(D) any issues about claims of privilege or of protection as trial-preparation materials, including—if the parties agree on a procedure to assert these claims after production—whether to ask the court to include their agreement in an order under Federal Rule of Evidence 502;

(E) what changes should be made in the limitations on discovery imposed under these rules or by local rule, and what other limitations should be imposed; and

(F) any other orders that the court should issue under Rule 26(c) or under Rule 16(b) and (c).

(4) *Expedited Schedule.*

If necessary to comply with its expedited schedule for Rule 16(b) conferences, a court may by local rule:

(A) require the parties' conference to occur less than 21 days before the scheduling conference is held or a scheduling order is due under Rule 16(b); and

(B) require the written report outlining the discovery plan to be filed less than 14 days after the parties' conference, or excuse the parties from submitting a written report and permit them to report orally on their discovery plan at the Rule 16(b) conference.

(g) Signing Disclosures and Discovery Requests, Responses, and Objections.

(1) *Signature Required; Effect of Signature.*

Every disclosure under Rule 26(a)(1) or (a)(3) and every discovery request, response, or objection must be signed by at least one attorney of record in the attorney's own name—or by the party personally, if unrepresented—and must state the signer's address, e-mail address, and telephone number. By signing, an attorney or party certifies that to the best of the person's knowledge, information, and belief formed after a reasonable inquiry:

(A) with respect to a disclosure, it is complete and correct as of the time it is made; and

(B) with respect to a discovery request, response, or objection, it is:

(i) consistent with these rules and warranted by existing law or by a nonfrivolous argument for extending, modifying, or reversing existing law, or for establishing new law;

(ii) not interposed for any improper purpose, such as to harass, cause unnecessary delay, or needlessly increase the cost of litigation; and

(iii) neither unreasonable nor unduly burdensome or expensive, considering the needs of the case, prior discovery in the case, the amount in controversy, and the importance of the issues at stake in the action.

(2) *Failure to Sign.*

Other parties have no duty to act on an unsigned disclosure, request, response, or objection until it is signed, and the court must strike it unless a signature is promptly supplied after the omission is called to the attorney's or party's attention.

(3) *Sanction for Improper Certification.*

If a certification violates this rule without substantial justification, the court, on motion or on its own, must impose an appropriate sanction on the signer, the party on whose behalf the signer was acting, or both. The sanction may include an order to pay the reasonable expenses, including attorney's fees, caused by the violation.

[*Adopted Dec. 20, 1937, effective Sept. 16, 1938; amended Dec. 27, 1946, effective Mar. 19, 1948; Jan. 21, 1963, effective July 1, 1963; Feb. 28, 1966, effective July 1, 1966; Mar. 30, 1970, effective July 1, 1970; Apr. 29, 1980, effective Aug. 1, 1980; Apr. 28, 1983, effective Aug. 1, 1983; Mar. 2, 1987, effective Aug. 1, 1987; Apr. 22, 1993, effective Dec. 1, 1993; amended Apr. 17, 2000, effective Dec. 1, 2000; April 12, 2006, effective Dec. 1, 2006; amended April 30, 2007, effective Dec. 1, 2007; amended April 28, 2010, effective Dec. 1, 2010; amended April 29, 2015, effective Dec. 1, 2015.*]

NOTES OF ADVISORY COMMITTEE ON 2015 AMENDMENTS TO RULE 26

Rule 26(b)(1) is changed in several ways.

Information is discoverable under revised Rule 26(b)(1) if it is relevant to any party's claim or defense and is proportional to the needs of the case. The considerations that bear on proportionality are moved from present Rule 26(b)(2)(C)(iii), slightly rearranged and with one addition.

Most of what now appears in Rule 26(b)(2)(C)(iii) was first adopted in 1983. The 1983 provision was explicitly adopted as part of the scope of discovery defined by Rule 26(b)(1). Rule 26(b)(1) directed the court to limit the frequency or extent of use of discovery if it determined that "the discovery is unduly burdensome or expensive, taking into account the needs of the case, the amount in controversy, limitations on the parties' resources, and the importance of the issues at stake in the litigation." At the same time, Rule 26(g) was added. Rule 26(g) provided that signing a discovery request, response, or objection certified that the request, response, or objection was "not unreasonable or unduly burdensome or expensive, given the needs of the case, the discovery already had in the case, the amount in controversy, and the importance of the issues at stake in the litigation." The parties thus shared the responsibility to honor these limits on the scope of discovery. * * *

The present amendment restores the proportionality factors to their original place in defining the scope of discovery. This change reinforces the Rule 26(g) obligation of the parties to consider these factors in making discovery requests, responses, or objections. Restoring the proportionality calculation to Rule 26(b)(1) does not change the existing responsibilities of the court and the parties to consider proportionality, and the change does not place on the party seeking discovery the burden of addressing all proportionality considerations. Nor is the change intended to permit the opposing party to refuse discovery simply by making a boilerplate objection that it is not proportional. The parties and the court have a collective responsibility to consider the proportionality of all discovery and consider it in resolving discovery disputes.

* * *

Restoring proportionality as an express component of the scope of discovery warrants repetition of parts of the 1983 and 1993 Committee Notes that must not be lost from sight. The 1983 Committee Note explained that "[t]he rule contemplates greater judicial involvement in the discovery process and thus acknowledges the reality that it cannot always operate on a self-regulating basis." The 1993 Committee Note further observed that "[t]he information explosion of recent decades has greatly increased both the potential cost of wide-ranging discovery and the potential for discovery to be used as an instrument for delay or oppression." What seemed an explosion in 1993 has been exacerbated by the advent of e-discovery. The present amendment again reflects the need for continuing and close judicial involvement in the cases that do not yield readily to the ideal of effective party management. It is expected that discovery will be effectively managed by the parties in many cases. But there will be important occasions for judicial management, both when the parties are legitimately unable to resolve important differences and when the parties fall short of effective, cooperative management on their own.

It also is important to repeat the caution that the monetary stakes are only one factor, to be balanced against other factors. The 1983 Committee Note recognized "the significance of the substantive issues, as measured in philosophic, social, or institu- tional terms. Thus the rule recognizes that many cases in public policy spheres, such as employment practices, free speech, and other matters, may have importance far beyond the monetary amount involved." Many other substantive areas also may involve litigation that seeks relatively small amounts of money, or no money at all, but that seeks to vindicate vitally important personal or public values.

So too, consideration of the parties' resources does not foreclose discovery requests addressed to an impecunious party, nor justify unlimited discovery requests addressed to a wealthy party. The 1983 Committee Note cautioned that "[t]he court must apply the standards in an even-handed manner that will prevent use of discovery to wage a war of attrition or as a device to coerce a party, whether financially weak or affluent."

The burden or expense of proposed discovery should be determined in a realistic way. This includes the burden or expense of producing electronically stored information. Computer-based methods of searching such information continue to develop, particularly for cases involving large volumes of electronically stored information. Courts and parties should be willing to consider the opportunities for reducing the burden or expense of discovery as reliable means of searching electronically stored information become available.

A portion of present Rule 26(b)(1) is omitted from the proposed revision. * * * The amendment deletes the former provision authorizing the court, for good cause, to order discovery of any matter relevant to the subject matter involved in the action. The Committee has been informed that this language is rarely invoked. Proportional discovery relevant to any party's claim or defense suffices, given a proper understanding of what is relevant to a claim or defense. The distinction between matter relevant to a claim or defense and matter relevant to the subject matter was introduced in 2000. The 2000 Note offered three examples of information that, suitably focused, would be relevant to the parties' claims or defenses. The examples were "other incidents of the same type, or involving the same product"; "information about organizational arrange- ments or filing systems"; and "information that could be used to impeach a likely witness." Such discovery is not foreclosed by the amendments. Discovery that is relevant to the parties' claims or defenses may also support amendment of the pleadings to add a new claim or defense that affects the scope of discovery.

The former provision for discovery of relevant but inadmissible information that appears "reasonably calculated to lead to the discovery of admissible evidence" is also deleted. The phrase has been used by some, incorrectly, to define the scope of discovery. As the Committee Note to the 2000 amendments observed, use of the "reasonably calculated" phrase to define the scope of discovery "might swallow any other limitation on the scope of discovery." The 2000 amendments sought to prevent such misuse by adding the word "Relevant" at the beginning of the sentence, making clear that "'relevant' means within the scope of discovery as defined in this subdivision . . ." The "reasonably calculated" phrase has continued to create problems, however, and is removed by these amendments. It is replaced by the direct statement that "Information within this scope of discovery need not be admissible in evidence to be discoverable." Discovery of nonprivileged information not admissible in evidence remains available so long as it is otherwise within the scope of discovery.

Rule 26(b)(2)(C)(iii) is amended to reflect the transfer of the considerations that bear on proportionality to Rule 26(b)(1). The court still must limit the frequency or extent of proposed discovery, on motion or on its own, if it is outside the scope permitted by Rule 26(b)(1).

Rule 26(c)(1)(B) is amended to include an express recognition of protective orders that allocate expenses for disclosure or discovery. Authority to enter such orders is included in the present rule, and courts already exercise this authority. Explicit recognition will forestall the temptation some parties may feel to contest this authority. Recognizing the authority does not imply that cost-shifting should become a common practice. Courts and parties should continue to assume that a responding party ordinarily bears the costs of responding.

Rule 26(d)(2) is added to allow a party to deliver Rule 34 requests to another party more than 21 days after that party has been served even though the parties have not yet had a required Rule 26(f) conference. Delivery may be made by any party to the party that has been served, and by that party to any plaintiff and any other party that has been served. Delivery does not count as service; the requests are considered to be served at the first Rule 26(f) conference. Under Rule 34(b)(2)(A) the time to respond runs from service. This relaxation of the discovery moratorium is designed to facilitate focused discussion during the Rule 26(f) conference. Discussion at the conference may produce changes in the requests. The opportunity for advance scrutiny of requests delivered before the Rule 26(f) conference should not affect a decision whether to allow additional time to respond. * * *

ADVISORY COMMITTEE'S NOTE TO 2010 AMENDMENT TO RULE 26

Rule 26. Rules 26(a)(2) and (b)(4) are amended to address concerns about expert discovery. The amendments to Rule 26(a)(2) require disclosure regarding expected expert testimony of those expert witnesses not required to provide expert reports and limit the expert report to facts or data (rather than "data or other information," as in the current rule) considered by the witness. Rule 26(b)(4) is amended to provide work-product protection against discovery regarding draft expert disclosures or reports and—with three specific exceptions—communications between expert witnesses and counsel.

In 1993, Rule 26(b)(4)(A) was revised to authorize expert depositions and Rule 26(a)(2) was added to provide disclosure, including—for many experts—an extensive report. Many courts read the disclosure provision to authorize discovery of all communications between counsel and expert witnesses and all draft reports. The Committee has been told repeatedly that routine discovery into attorney-expert communications and draft reports has had undesirable effects. Costs have risen. Attorneys may employ two sets of experts—one for purposes of consultation and another to testify at trial—because disclosure of their collaborative interactions with expert consultants would reveal their most sensitive and confidential case analyses. At the same time, attorneys often feel compelled to adopt a guarded attitude toward their interaction with testifying experts that impedes effective communication, and experts adopt strategies that protect against discovery but also interfere with their work.

Subdivision (a)(2)(B). Rule 26(a)(2)(B)(ii) is amended to provide that disclosure include all "facts or data considered by the witness in forming" the opinions to be offered, rather than the "data or other information" disclosure prescribed in 1993. This amendment is intended to alter the outcome in cases that have relied on the 1993 formulation in requiring disclosure of all attorney-expert communications and draft reports. The amendments to Rule 26(b)(4) make this change explicit by providing work-product protection against discovery regarding draft reports and disclosures or attorney-expert communications.

The refocus of disclosure on "facts or data" is meant to limit disclosure to material of a factual nature by excluding theories or mental impressions of counsel. At the same time, the intention is that "facts or data" be interpreted broadly to require disclosure of any material considered by the expert, from whatever source, that contains factual ingredients. The disclosure obligation extends to any facts or data "considered" by the expert in forming the opinions to be expressed, not only those relied upon by the expert.

Subdivision (a)(2)(C). Rule 26(a)(2)(C) is added to mandate summary disclosures of the opinions to be offered by expert witnesses who are not required to provide reports under Rule 26(a)(2)(B) and of the facts supporting those opinions. This disclosure is considerably less extensive than the report required by Rule 26(a)(2)(B).

Courts must take care against requiring undue detail, keeping in mind that these witnesses have not been specially retained and may not be as responsive to counsel as those who have.

This amendment resolves a tension that has sometimes prompted courts to require reports under Rule 26(a)(2)(B) even from witnesses exempted from the report requirement. An (a)(2)(B) report is required only from an expert described in (a)(2)(B).

A witness who is not required to provide a report under Rule 26(a)(2)(B) may both testify as a fact witness and also provide expert testimony under Evidence Rule 702, 703, or 705. Frequent examples include physicians or other health care professionals and employees of a party who do not regularly provide expert testimony. Parties must identify such witnesses under Rule 26(a)(2)(A) and provide the disclosure required under Rule 26(a)(2)(C). The (a)(2)(C) disclosure obligation does not include facts unrelated to the expert opinions the witness will present. * * *

Subdivision (b)(4). Rule 26(b)(4)(B) is added to provide work-product protection under Rule 26(b)(3)(A) and (B) for drafts of expert reports or disclosures. This protection applies to all witnesses identified under Rule 26(a)(2)(A), whether they are required to provide reports under Rule 26(a)(2)(B) or are the subject of disclosure under Rule 26(a)(2)(C). It applies regardless of the form in which the draft is recorded, whether written, electronic, or otherwise. It also applies to drafts of any supplementation under Rule 26(e); see Rule 26(a)(2)(E).

Rule 26(b)(4)(C) is added to provide work-product protection for attorney-expert communications regardless of the form of the communications, whether oral, written, electronic, or otherwise. The addition of Rule 26(b)(4)(C) is designed to protect counsel's work product and ensure that lawyers may interact with retained experts without fear of exposing those communications to searching discovery. The protection is limited to communications between an expert witness required to provide a report under Rule 26(a)(2)(B) and the attorney for the party on whose behalf the witness will be testifying, including any "preliminary" expert opinions. Protected "communications" include those between the party's attorney and assistants of the expert witness. The rule does not itself protect communications between counsel and other expert witnesses, such as those for whom disclosure is required under Rule 26(a)(2)(C). The rule does not exclude protection under other doctrines, such as privilege or independent development of the work-product doctrine.

The most frequent method for discovering the work of expert witnesses is by deposition, but Rules 26(b)(4)(B) and (C) apply to all forms of discovery.

Rules 26(b)(4)(B) and (C) do not impede discovery about the opinions to be offered by the expert or the development, foundation, or basis of those opinions. For example, the expert's testing of material involved in litigation, and notes of any such testing, would not be exempted from discovery by this rule. Similarly, inquiry about communications the expert had with anyone other than the party's counsel about the opinions expressed is unaffected by the rule. Counsel are also free to question expert witnesses about alternative analyses, testing methods, or approaches to the issues on which they are testifying, whether or not the expert considered them in forming the opinions expressed. These discovery changes therefore do not affect the gatekeeping functions called for by *Daubert v. Merrell Dow Pharmaceuticals, Inc.*, 509 U.S. 579 (1993), and related cases.

The protection for communications between the retained expert and "the party's attorney" should be applied in a realistic manner, and often would not be limited to communications with a single lawyer or a single law firm. For example, a party may be involved in a number of suits about a given product or service, and may retain a particular expert witness to testify on that party's behalf in several of the cases. In such a situation, the protection applies to communications between the expert witness and the attorneys representing the party in any of those cases. Similarly, communications with in-house counsel for the party would often be regarded as protected even if the in-house attorney is not counsel of record in the action. Other situations may also justify a pragmatic application of the "party's attorney" concept.

Although attorney-expert communications are generally protected by Rule 26(b) (4)(C), the protection does not apply to the extent the lawyer and the expert communicate about matters that fall within three exceptions. But the discovery authorized by the exceptions does not extend beyond those specific topics. Lawyer- expert communications may cover many topics and, even when the excepted topics are included among those involved in a given communication, the protection applies to all other aspects of the communication beyond the excepted topics.

First, under Rule 26(b)(4)(C)(i) attorney-expert communications regarding compensation for the expert's study or testimony may be the subject of discovery.

* * *

Second, under Rule 26(b)(4)(C)(ii) discovery is permitted to identify facts or data the party's attorney provided to the expert and that the expert considered in forming the opinions to be expressed. The exception applies only to communications "identifying" the facts or data provided by counsel; further communications about the potential relevance of the facts or data are protected.

Third, under Rule 26(b)(4)(C)(iii) discovery regarding attorney-expert communications is permitted to identify any assumptions that counsel provided to the expert and that the expert relied upon in forming the opinions to be expressed. For example, the party's attorney may tell the expert to assume the truth of certain testimony or evidence, or the correctness of another expert's conclusions. This exception is limited to those assumptions that the expert actually did rely on in forming the opinions to be expressed. More general attorney-expert discussions about hypotheticals, or exploring possibilities based on hypothetical facts, are outside this exception.

Under the amended rule, discovery regarding attorney-expert communications on subjects outside the three exceptions in Rule 26(b)(4)(C), or regarding draft expert reports or disclosures, is permitted only in limited circumstances and by court order. A party seeking such discovery must make the showing specified in Rule 26(b)(3)(A)(ii)—that the party has a substantial need for the discovery and cannot obtain the substantial equivalent without undue hardship. It will be rare for a party to be able to make such a showing given the broad disclosure and discovery otherwise allowed regarding the expert's testimony. A party's failure to provide required disclosure or discovery does not show the need and hardship required by Rule 26(b)(3)(A); remedies are provided by Rule 37.

In the rare case in which a party does make this showing, the court must protect against disclosure of the attorney's mental impressions, conclusions, opinions, or legal theories under Rule 26(b)(3)(B). But this protection does not extend to the expert's own development of the opinions to be presented; those are subject to probing in deposition or at trial. * * *

ADVISORY COMMITTEE'S NOTE TO 2006 AMENDMENT TO RULE 26

Subdivision (a). Rule 26(a)(1)(B) is amended to parallel Rule 34(a) by recognizing that a party must disclose electronically stored information as well as documents that it may use to support its claims or defenses. The term "electronically stored information" has the same broad meaning in Rule 26(a)(1) as in Rule 34(a). This amendment is consistent with the 1993 addition of Rule 26(a)(1)(B). The term "data compilations" is deleted as unnecessary because it is a subset of both documents and electronically stored information.

* 　 * 　 *

Subdivision (b)(2). The amendment to Rule 26(b)(2) is designed to address issues raised by difficulties in locating, retrieving, and providing discovery of some electronically stored information. Electronic storage systems often make it easier to locate and retrieve information. These advantages are properly taken into account in determining the reasonable scope of discovery in a particular case. But some sources of electroni- cally stored information can be accessed only with substantial burden and cost. In a particular case, these burdens and costs may make the information on such sources not reasonably accessible.

It is not possible to define in a rule the different types of technological features that may affect the burdens and costs of accessing electronically stored information. Information systems are designed to provide ready access to information used in regular ongoing activities. They also may be designed so as to provide ready access to information that is not regularly used. But a system may retain information on sources that are accessible only by incurring substantial burdens or costs. Subparagraph (B) is added to regulate discovery from such sources.

Under this rule, a responding party should produce electronically stored information that is relevant, not privileged, and reasonably accessible, subject to the (b)(2)(C) limitations that apply to all discovery. The responding party must also identify, by category or type, the sources containing potentially responsive information that it is neither searching nor producing. The identification should, to the extent possible, provide enough detail to enable the requesting party to evaluate the burdens and costs of providing the discovery and the likelihood of finding responsive information on the identified sources.

A party's identification of sources of electronically stored information as not reasonably accessible does not relieve the party of its common-law or statutory duties to preserve evidence. Whether a responding party is required to preserve unsearched sources of potentially responsive information that it believes are not reasonably accessible depends on the circumstances of each case. It is often useful for the parties to discuss this issue early in discovery.

The volume of—and the ability to search—much electronically stored information means that in many cases the responding party will be able to produce information from reasonably accessible sources that will fully satisfy the parties' discovery needs. In many circumstances the requesting party should obtain and evaluate the information from such sources before insisting that the responding party search and produce information contained on sources that are not reasonably accessible. If the requesting party continues to seek discovery of information from sources identified as not reasonably accessible, the parties should discuss the burdens and costs of accessing and retrieving the information, the needs that may establish good cause for requiring all or part of the requested discovery even if the information sought is not reasonably accessible, and conditions on obtaining and producing the information that may be appropriate.

If the parties cannot agree whether, or on what terms, sources identified as not reasonably accessible should be searched and discoverable information produced, the issue may be raised either by a motion to compel discovery or by a motion for a protective order. The parties must confer before bringing either motion. If the parties do not resolve the issue and the court must decide, the responding party must show that the identified sources of information are not reasonably accessible because of undue burden or cost. The requesting party may need discovery to test this assertion. Such discovery might take the form of requiring the responding party to conduct a sampling of information contained on the sources identified as not reasonably accessible; allowing some form of inspection of such sources; or taking depositions of witnesses knowledgeable about the responding party's information systems.

Once it is shown that a source of electronically stored information is not reasonably accessible, the requesting party may still obtain discovery by showing good cause, considering the limitations of Rule 26(b)(2)(C) that balance the costs and potential benefits of discovery. The decision whether to require a responding party to search for and produce information that is not reasonably accessible depends not only on the burdens and costs of doing so, but also on whether those burdens and costs can be justified in the circumstances of the case. Appropriate considerations may include: (1) the specificity of the discovery request; (2) the quantity of information available from other and more easily accessed sources; (3) the failure to produce relevant information that seems likely to have existed but is no longer available on more easily accessed sources; (4) the likelihood of finding relevant, responsive information that cannot be obtained from other, more easily accessed sources; (5) predictions as to the importance and usefulness of the further information; (6) the importance of the issues at stake in the litigation; and (7) the parties' resources.

The responding party has the burden as to one aspect of the inquiry—whether the identified sources are not reasonably accessible in light of the burdens and costs required to search for, retrieve, and produce whatever responsive information may be found. The requesting party has the burden of showing that its need for the discovery outweighs the burdens and costs of locating, retrieving, and producing the information. In some cases, the court will be able to determine whether the identified sources are not reasonably accessible and whether the requesting party has shown good cause for some or all of the discovery, consistent with the limitations of Rule 26(b)(2)(C), through a single proceeding or presentation. The good-cause determination, however, may be complicated because the court and parties may know little about what information the sources identified as not reasonably accessible might contain, whether it is relevant, or how valuable it may be to the litigation. In such cases, the parties may need some focused discovery, which may include sampling of the sources, to learn more about what burdens and costs are involved in accessing the information, what the information consists of, and how valuable it is for the litigation in light of information that can be obtained by exhausting other opportunities for discovery.

The good-cause inquiry and consideration of the Rule 26(b)(2)(C) limitations are coupled with the authority to set conditions for discovery. The conditions may take the form of limits on the amount, type, or sources of information required to be accessed and produced. The conditions may also include payment by the requesting party of part or all of the reasonable costs of obtaining information from sources that are not reasonably accessible. A requesting party's willingness to share or bear the access costs maybe weighed by the court in determining whether there is good cause. But the producing party's burdens in reviewing the information for relevance and privilege may weigh against permitting the requested discovery.

The limitations of Rule 26(b)(2)(C) continue to apply to all discovery of electronically stored information, including that stored on reasonably accessible electronic sources.

Subdivision (b)(5). The Committee has repeatedly been advised that the risk of privilege waiver, and the work necessary to avoid it, add to the costs and delay of discovery. When the review is of electronically stored information, the risk of waiver, and the time and effort required to avoid it, can increase substantially because of the volume of electronically stored information and the difficulty in ensuring that all information to be produced has in fact been reviewed. Rule 26(b)(5)(A) provides a procedure for a party that has withheld information on the basis of privilege or protection as trial-preparation material to make the claim so that the requesting party can decide whether to contest the claim and the court can resolve the dispute. Rule 26(b)(5)(B) is added to provide a procedure for a party to assert a claim of privilege or trial-preparation material protection after information is produced in discovery in the action and, if the claim is contested, permit any party that received the information to present the matter to the court for resolution.

Rule 26(b)(5)(B) does not address whether the privilege or protection that is asserted after production was waived by the production. The courts have developed principles to determine whether, and under what circumstances, waiver results from inadvertent production of privileged or protected information. Rule 26(b)(5)(B) provides a procedure for presenting and addressing these issues. Rule 26(b)(5)(B) works in tandem with Rule 26(f), which is amended to direct the parties to discuss privilege issues in preparing their discovery plan, and which, with amended Rule 16(b), allows the parties to ask the court to include in an order any agreements the parties reach regarding issues of privilege or trial-preparation material protection. Agreements reached under Rule 26(f)(4) and orders including such agreements entered under Rule 16(b)(6) may be considered when a court determines whether a waiver has occurred. Such agreements and orders ordinarily control if they adopt procedures different from those in Rule 26(b)(5)(B).

A party asserting a claim of privilege or protection after production must give notice to the receiving party. That notice should be in writing unless the circumstances preclude it. Such circumstances could include the assertion of the claim during a deposition. The notice should be as specific as possible in identifying the information and stating the basis for the claim. Because the receiving party must decide whether to challenge the claim and may sequester the information and submit it to the court for a ruling on whether the claimed privilege or protection applies and whether it has been waived, the notice should be sufficiently detailed so as to enable the receiving party and the court to understand the basis for the claim and to determine whether waiver has occurred. Courts will continue to examine whether a claim of privilege or protection was made at a reasonable time when delay is part of the waiver determination under the governing law.

After receiving notice, each party that received the information must promptly return, sequester, or destroy the information and any copies it has. The option of sequestering or destroying the information is included in part because the receiving party may have incorporated the information in protected trial-preparation materials. No receiving party may use or disclose the information pending resolution of the privilege claim. The receiving party may present to the court the questions whether the information is privileged or protected as trial-preparation material, and whether the privilege or protection has been waived. If it does so, it must provide the court with the grounds for the privilege or protection specified in the producing party's notice, and serve all parties. In presenting the question, the party may use the content of the information only to the extent permitted by the applicable law of privilege, protection for trial-preparation material, and professional responsibility.

If a party disclosed the information to nonparties before receiving notice of a claim of privilege or protection as trial-preparation material, it must take reasonable steps to retrieve the information and to return it, sequester it until the claim is resolved, or destroy it.

Whether the information is returned or not, the producing party must preserve the information pending the court's ruling on whether the claim of privilege or of protection is properly asserted and whether it was waived. As with claims made under Rule 26(b)(5)(A), there may be no ruling if the other parties do not contest the claim.

Subdivision (f). Rule 26(f) is amended to direct the parties to discuss discovery of electronically stored information during their discovery-planning conference. The rule focuses on "issues relating to disclosure or discovery of electronically stored information;" the discussion is not required in cases not involving electronic discovery, and the amendment imposes no additional requirements in those cases. When the parties do anticipate disclosure or discovery of electronically stored information, discussion at the outset may avoid later difficulties or ease their resolution.

When a case involves discovery of electronically stored information, the issues to be addressed during the Rule 26(f) conference depend on the nature and extent of the contemplated discovery and of the parties' information systems. It may be important for the parties to discuss those systems, and accordingly important for counsel to become familiar with those systems before the conference. With that information, the parties can develop a discovery plan that takes into account the capabilities of their computer systems. In appropriate cases identification of, and early discovery from, individuals with special knowledge of a party's computer systems may be helpful.

The particular issues regarding electronically stored information that deserve attention during the discovery planning stage depend on the specifics of the given case. *See Manual for Complex Litigation* (4th) § 40.25(2) (listing topics for discussion in a proposed order regarding meet-and-confer sessions). For example, the parties may specify the topics for such discovery and the time period for which discovery will be sought. They may identify the various sources of such information within a party's control that should be searched for electronically stored information. They may discuss whether the information is reasonably accessible to the party that has it, including the burden or cost of retrieving and reviewing the information. *See* Rule 26(b)(2)(B). Rule 26(f)(3) explicitly directs the parties to discuss the form or forms in which electronically stored information might be produced. The parties may be able to reach agreement on the forms of production, making discovery more efficient. Rule 34(b) is amended to permit a requesting party to specify the form or forms in which it wants electronically stored information produced. If the requesting party does not specify a form, Rule 34(b) directs the responding party to state the forms it intends to use in the production. Early discussion of the forms of production may facilitate the application of Rule 34(b) by allowing the parties to determine what forms of production will meet both parties' needs. Early identification of disputes over the forms of production may help avoid the expense and delay of searches or productions using inappropriate forms.

Rule 26(f) is also amended to direct the parties to discuss any issues regarding preservation of discoverable information during their conference as they develop a discovery plan. This provision applies to all sorts of discoverable information, but can be particularly important with regard to electronically stored information. The volume and dynamic nature of electronically stored information may complicate preservation obligations. The ordinary operation of computers involves both the automatic creation and the automatic deletion or overwriting of certain information. Failure to address preservation issues early in the litigation increases uncertainty and raises a risk of disputes.

The parties' discussion should pay particular attention to the balance between the competing needs to preserve relevant evidence and to continue routine operations critical to ongoing activities. Complete or broad cessation of a party's routine computer operations could paralyze the party's activities. Cf. Manual for Complex Litigation (4th) § 11.422 ("A blanket preservation order may be prohibitively expensive and unduly burdensome for parties dependent on computer systems for their day-to-day operations.") The parties should take account of these considerations in their discussions, with the goal of agreeing on reasonable preservation steps.

The requirement that the parties discuss preservation does not imply that courts should routinely enter preservation orders. A preservation order entered over objections should be narrowly tailored. Ex parte preservation orders should issue only in exceptional circumstances.

Rule 26(f) is also amended to provide that the parties should discuss any issues relating to assertions of privilege or of protection as trial-preparation materials, including whether the parties can facilitate discovery by agreeing on procedures for asserting claims of privilege or protection after production and whether to ask the court to enter an order that includes any agreement the parties reach. The Committee has repeatedly been advised about the discovery difficulties that can result from efforts to guard against waiver of privilege and work-product protection. Frequently parties find it necessary to spend large amounts of time reviewing materials requested through discovery to avoid waiving privilege. These efforts are necessary because materials subject to a claim of privilege or protection are often difficult to identify. A failure to withhold even one such item may result in an argument that there has been a waiver of privilege as to all other privileged materials on that subject matter. Efforts to avoid the risk of waiver can impose substantial costs on the party producing the material and the time required for the privilege review can substantially delay access for the party seeking discovery.

These problems often become more acute when discovery of electronically stored information is sought. The volume of such data, and the informality that attends use of e-mail and some other types of electronically stored information, may make privilege determinations more difficult, and privilege review correspondingly more expensive and time consuming. Other aspects of electronically stored information pose particular difficulties for privilege review. For example, production may be sought of information automatically included in electronic files but not apparent to the creator or to readers. Computer programs may retain draft language, editorial comments, and other deleted matter (sometimes referred to as "embedded data" or "embedded edits") in an electronic file but not make them apparent to the reader. Information describing the history, tracking, or management of an electronic file (sometimes called "metadata") is usually not apparent to the reader viewing a hard copy or a screen image. Whether this information should be produced may be among the topics discussed in the Rule 26(f) conference. If it is, it may need to be reviewed to ensure that no privileged information is included, further complicating the task of privilege review.

Parties may attempt to minimize these costs and delays by agreeing to protocols that minimize the risk of waiver. They may agree that the responding party will provide certain requested materials for initial examination without waiving any privilege or protection—sometimes known as a "quick peek." The requesting party then designates the documents it wishes to have actually produced. This designation is the Rule 34 request. The responding party then responds in the usual course, screening only those documents actually requested for formal production and assert- ing privilege claims as provided in Rule 26(b)(5)(A). On other occasions, parties enter agreements—sometimes called "clawback agreements"—that production without intent to waive privilege or protection should not be a waiver so long as the responding party identifies the documents mistakenly produced, and that the documents should be returned under those circumstances. Other voluntary arrangements may be appropriate depending on the circumstances of each litigation. In most circumstances, a party who receives information under such an arrangement cannot assert that production of the information waived a claim of privilege or of protection as trial-preparation material.

Although these agreements may not be appropriate for all cases, in certain cases they can facilitate prompt and economical discovery by reducing delay before the discovering party obtains access to documents, and by reducing the cost and burden of review by the producing party. A case-management or other order including such agreements may further facilitate the discovery process. Form 35 is amended to include a report to the court about any agreement regarding protections against inadvertent forfeiture or waiver of privilege or protection that the parties have reached, and Rule 16(b) is amended to recognize that the court may include such an agreement in a case-management or other order. If the parties agree to entry of such an order, their proposal should be included in the report to the court.

Rule 26(b)(5)(B) is added to establish a parallel procedure to assert privilege or protection as trial-preparation material after production, leaving the question of waiver to later determination by the court.

ADVISORY COMMITTEE'S NOTE TO 2000 AMENDMENT

Purposes of amendments. The Rule 26(a)(1) initial disclosure provisions are amended to establish a nationally uniform practice. The scope of the disclosure obligation is narrowed to cover only information that the disclosing party may use to support its position. In addition, the rule exempts specified categories of proceedings from initial disclosure, and permits a party who contends that disclosure is not appropriate in the circumstances of the case to present its objections to the court, which must then determine whether disclosure should be made. Related changes are made in Rules 26(d) and (f). * * *

Subdivision(a)(1). The amendments remove the authority to alter or opt out of the national disclosure requirements by local rule, invalidating not only formal local rules but also informal "standing" orders of an individual judge or court that purport to create exemptions from — or limit or expand — the disclosure provided under the national rule. *See* Rule 83. Case-specific orders remain proper, however, and are expressly required if a party objects that initial disclosure is not appropriate in the circumstances of the action. Specified categories of proceedings are excluded from initial disclosure under subdivision (a)(1)(E). In addition, the parties can stipulate to forgo disclosure, as was true before. But even in a case excluded by subdivision (a)(1)(E) or in which the parties stipulate to bypass disclosure, the court can order exchange of similar information in managing the action under Rule 16.

The initial disclosure obligation of subdivisions (a)(1)(A) and (B) has been narrowed to identification of witnesses and documents that the disclosing party may use to support its claims or defenses. "Use" includes any use at a pretrial conference, to support a motion, or at trial. The disclosure obligation is also triggered by intended use in discovery, apart from use to respond to a discovery request; use of a document to question a witness during a deposition is a common example. The disclosure obligation attaches both to witnesses and documents a party intends to use and also to witnesses and to documents the party intends to use if — in the language of Rule 26(a)(3) — "the need arises."

A party is no longer obligated to disclose witnesses or documents, whether favorable or unfavorable, that it does not intend to use. The obligation to disclose information the party may use connects directly to the exclusion sanction of Rule 37(c)(1). Because the disclosure obligation is limited to material that the party may use, it is no longer tied to particularized allegations in the pleadings. Subdivision (e)(1), which is unchanged, requires supplementation if information later acquired would have been subject to the disclosure requirement. As case preparation continues, a party must supplement its disclosures when it determines that it may use a witness or document that it did not previously intend to use.

The disclosure obligation applies to "claims and defenses," and therefore requires a party to disclose information it may use to support its denial or rebuttal of the allegations, claim, or defense of another party. It thereby bolsters the requirements of Rule 11(b)(4), which authorizes denials "warranted on the evidence," and disclosure should include the identity of any witness or document that the disclosing party may use to support such denials.

Subdivision (a)(3) presently excuses pretrial disclosure of information solely for impeachment. Impeachment information is similarly excluded from the initial disclosure requirement.

Subdivisions (a)(1)(C) and (D) are not changed. Should a case be exempted from initial disclosure by Rule 26(a)(1)(E) or by agreement or order, the insurance information described by subparagraph (D) should be subject to discovery, as it would have been under the principles of former Rule 26(b)(2), which was added in 1970 and deleted in 1993 as redundant in light of the new initial disclosure obligation.

New subdivision (a)(1)(E) excludes eight specified categories of proceedings from initial disclosure. The objective of this listing is to identify cases in which there is likely to be little or no discovery, or in which initial disclosure appears unlikely to contribute to the effective development of the case.

*   *   *

Subdivision (a)(3). The amendment to Rule 5(d) forbids filing disclosures under subdivisions (a)(1) and (a)(2) until they are used in the proceeding, and this change is reflected in an amendment to subdivision (a)(4). Disclosures under subdivision (a)(3), however, may be important to the court in connection with the final pretrial conference or otherwise in preparing for trial. The requirement that objections to certain matters be filed points up the court's need to be provided with these materials. Accordingly, the requirement that subdivision (a)(3) materials be filed has been moved from subdivision (a)(4) to subdivision (a)(3), and it has also been made clear that they—and any objections—should be filed "promptly."

*   *   *

Subdivision (b)(1).

*   *   *

The Committee intends that the parties and the court focus on the actual claims and defenses involved in the action. The dividing line between information relevant to the claims and defenses and that relevant only to the subject matter of the action cannot be defined with precision. A variety of types of information not directly pertinent to the incident in suit could be relevant to the claims or defenses raised in a given action. For example, other incidents of the same type, or involving the same product, could be properly discoverable under the revised standard. Information about organizational arrangements or filing systems of a party could be discoverable if likely to yield or lead to the discovery of admissible information. Similarly, information that could be used to impeach a likely witness, although not otherwise relevant to the claims or defenses, might be properly discoverable. In each instance, the determination whether such information is discoverable because it is relevant to the claims or defenses depends on the circumstances of the pending action.

The rule change signals to the court that it has the authority to confine discovery to the claims and defenses asserted in the pleadings, and signals to the parties that they have no entitlement to discovery to develop new claims or defenses that are not already identified in the pleadings. In general, it is hoped that reasonable lawyers can cooperate to manage discovery without the need for judicial intervention. When judicial intervention is invoked, the actual scope of discovery should be determined according to the reasonable needs of the action. The court may permit broader discovery in a particular case depending on the circumstances of the case, the nature of the claims and defenses, and the scope of the discovery requested.

* * *

Subdivision (f). As in subdivision (d), the amendments remove the prior authority to exempt cases by local rule from the conference requirement. The Committee has been informed that the addition of the conference was one of the most successful changes made in the 1993 amendments, and it therefore has determined to apply the conference requirement nationwide. The categories of proceedings exempted from initial disclosure under subdivision (a)(1)(E) are exempted from the conference requirement for the reasons that warrant exclusion from initial disclosure. The court may order that the conference need not occur in a case where otherwise required, or that it occur in a case otherwise exempted by subdivision (a)(1)(E). "Standing" orders altering the conference requirement for categories of cases are not authorized.

The rule is amended to require only a "conference" of the parties, rather than a "meeting." There are important benefits to face-to-face discussion of the topics to be covered in the conference, and those benefits may be lost if other means of conferring were routinely used when face-to-face meetings would not impose burdens. Never-the- less, geographic conditions in some districts may exact costs far out of proportion to these benefits. The amendment allows the court by case-specific order to require a face-to-face meeting, but "standing" orders so requiring are not authorized.

As noted concerning the amendments to subdivision (a)(1), the time for the conference has been changed to at least 21 days before the Rule 16 scheduling conference, and the time for the report is changed to no more than 14 days after the Rule 26(f) conference. This should ensure that the court will have the report well in advance of the scheduling conference or the entry of the scheduling order.

* * *

ADVISORY COMMITTEE'S NOTES TO 1993 AMENDMENTS TO RULES

Subdivision (a). Through the addition of paragraphs (1)–(4), this subdivision imposes on parties a duty to disclose, without awaiting formal discovery requests, certain basic information that is needed in most cases to prepare for trial or make an informed decision about settlement.

* * *

Paragraph (1). As the functional equivalent of court-ordered interrogatories, this paragraph requires early disclosure, without need for any request, of four types of information that have been customarily secured early in litigation through formal discovery. * * *

The initial disclosure requirements of subparagraphs (A) and (B) are limited to identification of potential evidence "relevant to disputed facts alleged with partic- ular- ity in the pleadings." There is no need for a party to identify potential evidence with respect to allegations that are admitted. Broad, vague, and conclusory allegations sometimes tolerated in notice pleading—for example, the assertion that a product with many component parts is defective in some unspecified manner—should not impose upon responding parties the obligation at that point to search for and iden- tify all persons possibly involved in, or all documents affecting, the design, manufacture, and assembly of the product. The greater the specificity and clarity of the allegations in the pleadings, the more complete should be the listing of potential witnesses and types of documentary evidence. Although paragraphs (1)(A) and (1)(B) by their terms refer to the factual disputes defined in the pleadings, the rule contemplates that these issues would be informally refined and clarified during the meeting of the parties under subdivision (f) and that the disclosure obligations would be adjusted in the light of these discussions. The disclosure requirements should, in short, be applied with com- mon sense in light of the principles of Rule 1, keeping in mind the salutary purposes that the rule is intended to accomplish. The litigants should not indulge in games- manship with respect to the disclosure obligations.

Subparagraph (C) imposes a burden of disclosure that includes the functional equivalent of a standing Request for Production under Rule 34. A party claiming dam- ages or other monetary relief must, in addition to disclosing the calculation of such damages, make available the supporting documents for inspection and copying as if a request for such materials had been made under Rule 34. This obligation applies only with respect to documents then reasonably available to it and not privileged or protected as work product. Likewise, a party would not be expected to provide a calculation of damages which, as in many patent infringement actions, depends on information in the possession of another party or person.

Subparagraph (D) replaces subdivision (b)(2) of Rule 26, and provides that liability insurance policies be made available for inspection and copying. The last two sen- tences of that subdivision have been omitted as unnecessary, not to signify any change of law. The disclosure of insurance information does not thereby render such information admissible in evidence. See Rule 411, Federal Rules of Evidence. Nor does subparagraph (D) require disclosure of applications for insurance, though in par- ticular cases such information may be discoverable in accordance with revised subdi- vision (a)(5).

* * *

Before making its disclosures, a party has the obligation under subdivision (g)(1) to make a reasonable inquiry into the facts of the case. The rule does not demand an exhaustive investigation at this stage of the case, but one that is reasonable under the circumstances, focusing on the facts that are alleged with particularity in the pleadings. The type of investigation that can be expected at this point will vary based upon such factors as the number and complexity of the issues; the location, nature, number, and availability of potentially relevant witnesses and documents; the extent of past working relationships between the attorney and the client, particularly in handling related or similar litigation; and of course how long the party has to conduct an investigation, either before or after filing of the case. As provided in the last sentence of subdivision (a)(1), a party is not excused from the duty of disclosure merely because its investigation is incomplete. The party should make its initial disclosures based on the pleadings and the information then reasonably available to it. As its investigation continues and as the issues in the pleadings are clarified, it should supplement its disclosures as required by subdivision (e)(1). A party is not relieved from its obligation of disclosure merely because another party has not made its disclosures or has made an inadequate disclosure.

*   *   *

Paragraph (2). This paragraph imposes an additional duty to disclose information regarding expert testimony sufficiently in advance of trial that opposing parties have a reasonable opportunity to prepare for effective cross examination and perhaps arrange for expert testimony from other witnesses. * * *

Paragraph (2)(B) requires that persons retained or specially employed to provide expert testimony, or whose duties as an employee of the party regularly involve the giving of expert testimony, must prepare a detailed and complete written report, stating the testimony the witness is expected to present during direct examination, together with the reasons therefore. * * * Rule 26(a)(2)(B) does not preclude counsel from providing assistance to experts in preparing the reports, and indeed, with experts such as automobile mechanics, this assistance may be needed. Nevertheless, the report, which is intended to set forth the substance of the direct examination, should be written in a manner that reflects the testimony to be given by the witness and it must be signed by the witness. * * *

Revised subdivision (b)(4)(A) authorizes the deposition of expert witnesses. Since depositions of experts required to prepare a written report may be taken only after the report has been served, the length of the deposition of such experts should be reduced, and in many cases the report may eliminate the need for a deposition. Revised subdivision (e)(1) requires disclosure of any material changes made in the opinions of an expert from whom a report is required, whether the changes are in the written report or in testimony given at a deposition.

For convenience, this rule and revised Rule 30 continue to use the term "expert" to refer to those persons who will testify under Rule 702 of the Federal Rules of Evidence with respect to scientific, technical, and other specialized matters. The requirement of a written report in paragraph (2)(B), however, applies only to those experts who are retained or specially employed to provide such testimony in the case or whose duties as an employee of a party regularly involve the giving of such testimony. A treating physician, for example, can be deposed or called to testify at trial without any requirement for a written report. By local rule, order, or written stipulation, the requirement of a written report may be waived for particular experts or imposed upon additional persons who will provide opinions under Rule 702.

Paragraph (3). This paragraph imposes an additional duty to disclose, without any request, information customarily needed in final preparation for trial. These disclosures are to be made in accordance with schedules adopted by the court under Rule 16(b) or by special order. If no such schedule is directed by the court, the disclosures are to be made at least 30 days before commencement of the trial. By its terms, rule 26(a)(3) does not require disclosure of evidence to be used solely for impeachment purposes; however, disclosure of such evidence—as well as other items relating to conduct of trial—may be required by local rule or a pretrial order.

Subparagraph (A) requires the parties to designate the persons whose testimony they may present as substantive evidence at trial, whether in person or by deposition. Those who will probably be called as witnesses should be listed separately from those who are not likely to be called but who are being listed in order to preserve the right to do so if needed because of developments during trial. Revised Rule 37(c)(1) provides that only persons so listed may be used at trial to present substantive evidence. This restriction does not apply unless the omission was "without substantial justification" and hence would not bar an unlisted witness if the need for such testimony is based upon developments during trial that could not reasonably have been anticipated—*e.g.*, a change of testimony.

Listing a witness does not obligate the party to secure the attendance of the person at trial, but should preclude the party from objecting if the person is called to testify by another party who did not list the person as a witness.

Subparagraph (B) requires the party to indicate which of these potential witnesses will be presented by deposition at trial. A party expecting to use at trial a deposition not recorded by stenographic means is required by revised Rule 32 to provide the court with a transcript of the pertinent portions of such depositions. This rule requires that copies of the transcript of a nonstenographic deposition be provided to other parties in advance of trial for verification, an obvious concern since counsel often utilize their own personnel to prepare transcripts from audio or video tapes. By order or local rule, the court may require that parties designate the particular portions of steno- graphic depositions to be used at trial.

Subparagraph (C) requires disclosure of exhibits, including summaries (whether to be offered in lieu of other documentary evidence or to be used as an aid in understanding such evidence), that may be offered as substantive evidence. The rule requires a separate listing of each such exhibit, though it should permit voluminous items of a similar or standardized character to be described by meaningful categories. For example, unless the court has otherwise directed, a series of vouchers might be shown collectively as a single exhibit with their starting and ending dates. As with witnesses, the exhibits that will probably be offered are to be listed separately from those which are unlikely to be offered but which are listed in order to preserve the right to do so if needed because of developments during trial. Under revised Rule 37(c)(1) the court can permit use of unlisted documents the need for which could not reasonably have been anticipated in advance of trial.

Upon receipt of these final pretrial disclosures, other parties have 14 days (unless a different time is specified by the court) to disclose any objections they wish to preserve to the usability of the deposition testimony or to the admissibility of the documentary evidence (other than under Rules 402 and 403 of the Federal Rules of Evidence). Similar provisions have become commonplace either in pretrial orders or by local rules, and significantly expedite the presentation of evidence at trial, as well as eliminate the need to have available witnesses to provide "foundation" testimony for most items of documentary evidence. The listing of a potential objection does not constitute the making of that objection or require the court to rule on the objection; rather, it preserves the right of the party to make the objection when and as appropriate during trial. The court may, however, elect to treat the listing as a motion "in limine" and rule upon the objections in advance of trial to the extent appropriate.

The time specified in the rule for the final pretrial disclosures is relatively close to the trial date. The objective is to eliminate the time and expense in making these disclosures of evidence and objections in those cases that settle shortly before trial, while affording a reasonable time for final preparation for trial in those cases that do not settle. In many cases, it will be desirable for the court in a scheduling or pretrial order to set an earlier time for disclosures of evidence and provide more time for disclosing potential objections.

Paragraph (4). This paragraph prescribes the form of disclosures. A signed written statement is required, reminding the parties and counsel of the solemnity of the obligations imposed; and the signature on the initial or pretrial disclosure is a certification under subdivision (g)(1) that it is complete and correct as of the time when made. Consistent with Rule 5(d), these disclosures are to be filed with the court unless otherwise directed. It is anticipated that many courts will direct that expert reports required under paragraph (2)(B) not be filed until needed in connection with a motion or for trial.

Paragraph (5). This paragraph is revised to take note of the availability of revised Rule 45 for inspection from non-parties of documents and premises without the need for a deposition.

Subdivision (b). This subdivision is revised in several respects. First, former paragraph (1) is subdivided into two paragraphs for ease of reference and to avoid renumbering of paragraphs (3) and (4). Textual changes are then made in new paragraph (2) to enable the court to keep tighter rein on the extent of discovery. The information explosion of recent decades has greatly increased both the potential cost of wide-ranging discovery and the potential for discovery to be used as an instrument for delay or oppression. Amendments to Rules 30, 31, and 33 place presumptive limits on the number of depositions and interrogatories, subject to leave of court to pursue additional discovery. The revisions in Rule 26(b)(2) are intended to provide the court with broader discretion to impose additional restrictions on the scope and extent of discovery and to authorize courts that develop case tracking systems based on the complexity of cases to increase or decrease by local rule the presumptive number of depositions and interrogatories allowed in particular types or classifications of cases. The revision also dispels any doubt as to the power of the court to impose limitations on the length of depositions under Rule 30 or on the number of requests for admission under Rule 36.

Second, former paragraph (2), relating to insurance, has been relocated as part of the required initial disclosures under subdivision (a)(1)(D), and revised to provide for disclosure of the policy itself.

Third, paragraph (4)(A) is revised to provide that experts who are expected to be witnesses will be subject to deposition prior to trial, conforming the norm stated in the rule to the actual practice followed in most courts, in which depositions of experts have become standard. Concerns regarding the expense of such depositions should be mitigated by the fact that the expert's fees for the deposition will ordinarily be borne by the party taking the deposition. The requirement under subdivision (a)(2)(B) of a complete and detailed report of the expected testimony of certain forensic experts may, moreover, eliminate the need for some such depositions or at least reduce the length of the depositions. Accordingly, the deposition of an expert required by subdivision (a)(2)(B) to provide a written report may be taken only after the report has been served.

Paragraph (4)(C), bearing on compensation of experts, is revised to take account of the changes in paragraph (4)(A).

Paragraph (5) is a new provision. A party must notify other parties if it is withholding materials otherwise subject to disclosure under the rule or pursuant to a discovery request because it is asserting a claim of privilege or work product protection. To withhold materials without such notice is contrary to the rule, subjects the party to sanctions under Rule 37(b)(2), and may be viewed as a waiver of the privilege or protection.

The party must also provide sufficient information to enable other parties to evaluate the applicability of the claimed privilege or protection. Although the person from whom the discovery is sought decides whether to claim a privilege or protection, the court ultimately decides whether, if this claim is challenged, the privilege or protection applies. Providing information pertinent to the applicability of the privilege or protection should reduce the need for in camera examination of the documents.

The rule does not attempt to define for each case what information must be provided when a party asserts a claim of privilege or work product protection. Details concerning time, persons, general subject matter, etc., may be appropriate if only a few items are withheld, but may be unduly burdensome when voluminous documents are claimed to be privileged or protected, particularly if the items can be described by categories. A party can seek relief through a protective order under subdivision (c) if compliance with the requirement for providing this information would be an unreasonable burden. In rare circumstances some of the pertinent information affecting applicability of the claim, such as the identity of the client, may itself be privileged; the rule provides that such information need not be disclosed.

The obligation to provide pertinent information concerning withheld privileged materials applies only to items "otherwise discoverable." If a broad discovery request is made—for example, for all documents of a particular type during a twenty year period—and the responding party believes in good faith that production of documents for more than the past three years would be unduly burdensome, it should make its objection to the breadth of the request and, with respect to the documents generated in that three year period, produce the unprivileged documents and describe those withheld under the claim of privilege. If the court later rules that documents for a seven year period are properly discoverable, the documents for the additional four years should then be either produced (if not privileged) or described (if claimed to be privileged).

Subdivision (c). The revision requires that before filing a motion for a protective order the movant must confer—either in person or by telephone—with the other affected parties in a good faith effort to resolve the discovery dispute without the need for court intervention. If the movant is unable to get opposing parties even to discuss the matter, the efforts in attempting to arrange such a conference should be indicated in the certificate.

Subdivision (d). This subdivision is revised to provide that formal discovery—as distinguished from interviews of potential witnesses and other informal discovery—not commence until the parties have met and conferred as required by subdivision (f). Discovery can begin earlier if authorized under Rule 30(a)(2)(C) (deposition of person about to leave the country) or by local rule, order, or stipulation. This will be appropriate in some cases, such as those involving requests for a preliminary injunction or motions challenging personal jurisdiction. If a local rule exempts any types of cases in which discovery may be needed from the requirement of a meeting under Rule 26(f), it should specify when discovery may commence in those cases.

The meeting of counsel is to take place as soon as practicable and in any event at least 14 days before the date of the scheduling conference under Rule 16(b) or the date a scheduling order is due under Rule 16(b). The court can assure that discovery is not unduly delayed either by entering a special order or by setting the case for a scheduling conference.

Subdivision (e). This subdivision is revised to provide that the requirement for supplementation applies to all disclosures required by subdivision (a)(1)–(3). Like the former rule, the duty, while imposed on a "party," applies whether the corrective information is learned by the client or by the attorney. Supplementations need not be made as each new item of information is learned but should be made at appropriate intervals during the discovery period, and with special promptness as the trial date approaches. It may be useful for the scheduling order to specify the time or times when supplementations should be made.

The revision also clarifies that the obligation to supplement responses to formal discovery requests applies to interrogatories, requests for production, and requests for admissions, but not ordinarily to deposition testimony. However, with respect to experts from whom a written report is required under subdivision (a)(2)(B), changes in the opinions expressed by the expert whether in the report or at a subsequent deposition are subject to a duty of supplemental disclosure under subdivision (e)(1).

The obligation to supplement disclosures and discovery responses applies whenever a party learns that its prior disclosures or responses are in some material respect incomplete or incorrect. There is, however, no obligation to provide supplemental or corrective information that has been otherwise made known to the parties in writing or during the discovery process, as when a witness not previously disclosed is identified during the taking of a deposition or when an expert during a deposition corrects information contained in an earlier report.

Subdivision (f). This subdivision was added in 1980 to provide a party threatened with abusive discovery with a special means for obtaining judicial intervention other than through discrete motions under Rules 26(c) and 37(a). The amendment envisioned a two-step process: first, the parties would attempt to frame a mutually agreeable plan; second, the court would hold a "discovery conference" and then enter an order establishing a schedule and limitations for the conduct of discovery. It was contemplated that the procedure, an elective one triggered on request of a party, would be used in special cases rather than as a routine matter. As expected, the device has been used only sparingly in most courts, and judicial controls over the discovery process have ordinarily been imposed through scheduling orders under Rule 16(b) or through rulings on discovery motions.

The provisions relating to a conference with the court are removed from subdivision (f). This change does not signal any lessening of the importance of judicial supervision. Indeed, there is a greater need for early judicial involvement to consider the scope and timing of the disclosure requirements of Rule 26(a) and the presumptive limits on discovery imposed under these rules or by local rules. Rather, the change is made because the provisions addressing the use of conferences with the court to control discovery are more properly included in Rule 16, which is being revised to highlight the court's powers regarding the discovery process.

The desirability of some judicial control of discovery can hardly be doubted. Rule 16, as revised, requires that the court set a time for completion of discovery and authorizes various other orders affecting the scope, timing, and extent of discovery and disclosures. Before entering such orders, the court should consider the views of the parties, preferably by means of a conference, but at the least through written submissions. Moreover, it is desirable that the parties' proposals regarding discovery be developed through a process where they meet in person, informally explore the nature and basis of the issues, and discuss how discovery can be conducted most efficiently and economically.

As noted above, former subdivision (f) envisioned the development of proposed discovery plans as an optional procedure to be used in relatively few cases. The revised rule directs that in all cases not exempted by local rule or special order the litigants must meet in person and plan for discovery. Following this meeting, the parties submit to the court their proposals for a discovery plan and can begin formal discovery. Their report will assist the court in seeing that the timing and scope of disclosures under revised Rule 26(a) and the limitations on the extent of discovery under these rules and local rules are tailored to the circumstances of the particular case.

To assure that the court has the litigants' proposals before deciding on a scheduling order and that the commencement of discovery is not delayed unduly, the rule provides that the meeting of the parties take place as soon as practicable and in any event at least 14 days before a scheduling conference is held or before a scheduling order is due under Rule 16(b). (Rule 16(b) requires that a scheduling order be entered within 90 days after the first appearance of a defendant or, if earlier, within 120 days after the complaint has been served on any defendant.) The obligation to participate in the planning process is imposed on all parties that have appeared in the case, including defendants who, because of a pending Rule 12 motion, may not have yet filed an answer in the case. Each such party should attend the meeting, either through one of its attorneys or in person if unrepresented. If more parties are joined or appear after the initial meeting, an additional meeting may be desirable.

Subdivision (f) describes certain matters that should be accomplished at the meeting and included in the proposed discovery plan. This listing does not exclude consider- ation of other subjects, such as the time when any dispositive motions should be filed and when the case should be ready for trial.

The parties are directed under subdivision (a)(1) to make the disclosures required by that subdivision at or within 10 days after this meeting. In many cases the parties should use the meeting to exchange, discuss, and clarify their respective disclosures. In other cases, it may be more useful if the disclosures are delayed until after the parties have discussed at the meeting the claims and defenses in order to define the issues with respect to which the initial disclosures should be made. As discussed in the Notes to subdivision (a)(1), the parties may also need to consider whether a stipulation extending this 10-day period would be appropriate, as when a defendant would otherwise have less than 60 days after being served in which to make its initial disclosure. The parties should also discuss at the meeting what additional information, although not subject to the disclosure requirements, can be made available informally without the necessity for formal discovery requests.

The report is to be submitted to the court within 10 days after the meeting and should not be difficult to prepare. In most cases counsel should be able to agree that one of them will be responsible for its preparation and submission to the court. * * *

The litigants are expected to attempt in good faith to agree on the contents of the proposed discovery plan. If they cannot agree on all aspects of the plan, their report to the court should indicate the competing proposals of the parties on those items, as well as the matters on which they agree. Unfortunately, there may be cases in which, because of disagreements about time or place or for other reasons, the meeting is not attended by all parties or, indeed, no meeting takes place. In such situations, the report—or reports—should describe the circumstances and the court may need to consider sanctions under Rule 37(g).

* * *

Subdivision (g). Paragraph (1) is added to require signatures on disclosures, a requirement that parallels the provisions of paragraph (2) with respect to discovery requests, responses, and objections. The provisions of paragraph (3) have been modified to be consistent with Rules 37(a)(4) and 37(c)(1); in combination, these rules establish sanctions for violation of the rules regarding disclosures and discovery matters. Amended Rule 11 no longer applies to such violations.

RULE 27.　DEPOSITIONS TO PERPETUATE TESTIMONY.

(a) Before an Action is Filed.

(1) *Petition.*

A person who wants to perpetuate testimony about any matter cognizable in a United States court may file a verified petition in the district court for the district where any expected adverse party resides. The petition must ask for an order authorizing the petitioner to depose the named persons in order to perpetuate their testimony. The petition must be titled in the petitioner's name and must show:

> (A) that the petitioner expects to be a party to an action cognizable in a United States court but cannot presently bring it or cause it to be brought;

> (B) the subject matter of the expected action and the petitioner's interest;

> (C) the facts that the petitioner wants to establish by the proposed testimony and the reasons to perpetuate it;

> (D) the names or a description of the persons whom the petitioner expects to be adverse parties and their addresses, so far as known; and

> (E) the name, address, and expected substance of the testimony of each deponent.

(2) *Notice and Service.*

At least 21 days before the hearing date, the petitioner must serve each expected adverse party with a copy of the petition and a notice stating the time and place of the hearing. The notice may be served either inside or outside the district or state in the manner provided in Rule 4. If that service cannot be made with reasonable diligence on an expected adverse party, the court may order service by publication or otherwise. The court must appoint an attorney to represent persons not served in the manner provided in Rule 4 and to cross-examine the deponent if an unserved person is not otherwise represented. If any expected adverse party is a minor or is incompetent, Rule 17(c) applies.

(3) *Order and Examination.*

If satisfied that perpetuating the testimony may prevent a failure or delay of justice, the court must issue an order that designates or describes the persons whose depositions may be taken, specifies the subject matter of the examinations, and states whether the depositions will be taken orally or by written interrogato- ries. The depositions may then be taken under these rules, and the court may issue orders like those authorized by Rules 34 and 35. A reference in these rules to the court where an action is pending means, for purposes of this rule, the court where the petition for the deposition was filed.

(4) *Using the Deposition.*

A deposition to perpetuate testimony may be used under Rule 32(a) in any later-filed district-court action involving the same subject matter if the deposition either was taken under these rules or, although not so taken, would be admissible in evidence in the courts of the state where it was taken.

(b) Pending Appeal.

(1) *In General.*

The court where a judgment has been rendered may, if an appeal has been taken or may still be taken, permit a party to depose witnesses to perpetuate their testimony for use in the event of further proceedings in that court.

(2) *Motion.*

The party who wants to perpetuate testimony may move for leave to take the depositions, on the same notice and service as if the action were pending in the district court. The motion must show:

(A) the name, address, and expected substance of the testimony of each deponent; and

(B) the reasons for perpetuating the testimony.

(3) *Court Order.*

If the court finds that perpetuating the testimony may prevent a failure or delay of justice, the court may permit the depositions to be taken and may issue orders like those authorized by Rules 34 and 35. The depositions may be taken and used as any other deposition taken in a pending district-court action.

(c) Perpetuation by an Action.

This rule does not limit a court's power to entertain an action to perpetuate testimony.

[*Adopted Dec. 20, 1937, effective Sept. 16, 1938; amended Dec. 27, 1946, effective Mar. 19, 1948; Dec. 29, 1948, effective Oct. 20, 1949; Mar. 1, 1971, effective July 1, 1971;*

Mar. 2, 1987, effective Aug. 1, 1987; Apr. 25, 2005, eff. Dec. 1, 2005, amended April 30, 2007, effective Dec. 1, 2007; amended March 26, 2009, effective Dec. 1, 2009.]

RULE 28.   PERSONS BEFORE WHOM DEPOSITIONS MAY BE TAKEN.

(a) Within the United States.

(1) *In General.*

Within the United States or a territory or insular possession subject to United States jurisdiction, a deposition must be taken before:

> (A) an officer authorized to administer oaths either by federal law or by the law in the place of examination; or

> (B) a person appointed by the court where the action is pending to administer oaths and take testimony.

(2) *Definition of "Officer."*

The term "officer" in Rules 30, 31, and 32 includes a person appointed by the court under this rule or designated by the parties under Rule 29(a).

(b) In a Foreign Country.

(1) *In General.*

A deposition may be taken in a foreign country:

> (A) under an applicable treaty or convention;

> (B) under a letter of request, whether or not captioned a "letter rogatory";

> (C) on notice, before a person authorized to administer oaths either by federal law or by the law in the place of examination; or

> (D) before a person commissioned by the court to administer any necessary oath and take testimony.

(2) *Issuing a Letter of Request or a Commission.*

A letter of request, a commission, or both may be issued:

> (A) on appropriate terms after an application and notice of it; and

> (B) without a showing that taking the deposition in another manner is impracticable or inconvenient.

(3) *Form of a Request, Notice, or Commission.*

When a letter of request or any other device is used according to a treaty or convention, it must be captioned in the form prescribed by that treaty or convention. A letter of request may be addressed "To the Appropriate Authority in [name of country]." A deposition notice or a commission must designate by name or descriptive title the person before whom the deposition is to be taken.

(4) *Letter of Request—Admitting Evidence.*

Evidence obtained in response to a letter of request need not be excluded merely because it is not a verbatim transcript, because the testimony was not taken under oath, or because of any similar departure from the requirements for depositions taken within the United States.

(c) Disqualification.

A deposition must not be taken before a person who is any party's relative, employee, or attorney; who is related to or employed by any party's attorney; or who is financially interested in the action.

[*Adopted Dec. 20, 1937, effective Sept. 16, 1938; amended Dec. 27, 1946, effective Mar. 19, 1948; Jan. 21, 1963, effective July 1, 1963; Apr. 29, 1980, effective Aug. 1, 1980; Mar. 2, 1987, effective Aug. 1, 1987; Apr. 22, 1993, effective Dec. 1, 1993; amended April 30, 2007, effective Dec. 1, 2007.*]

RULE 29.   STIPULATIONS ABOUT DISCOVERY PROCEDURE.

Unless the court orders otherwise, the parties may stipulate that:

(a) a deposition may be taken before any person, at any time or place, on any notice, and in the manner specified—in which event it may be used in the same way as any other deposition; and

(b) other procedures governing or limiting discovery be modified—but a stipulation extending the time for any form of discovery must have court approval if it would interfere with the time set for completing discovery, for hearing a motion, or for trial.

[*Adopted Dec. 20, 1937, effective Sept. 16, 1938; amended Mar. 30, 1970, effective July 1, 1970; Apr. 22, 1993, effective Dec. 1, 1993; amended April 30, 2007, effective Dec. 1, 2007.*]

RULE 30.   DEPOSITIONS BY ORAL EXAMINATION.

(a) When a Deposition may be Taken.

(1) *Without Leave.*

A party may, by oral questions, depose any person, including a party, without leave of court except as provided in Rule 30(a)(2). The deponent's attendance may be compelled by subpoena under Rule 45.

(2) *With Leave.*

A party must obtain leave of court, and the court must grant leave to the extent consistent with Rule 26(b)(1) and (2):

    (A) if the parties have not stipulated to the deposition and:

        (i) the deposition would result in more than 10 depositions being taken under this rule or Rule 31 by the plaintiffs, or by the defendants, or by the third-party defendants;

(ii) the deponent has already been deposed in the case; or

(iii) the party seeks to take the deposition before the time specified in Rule 26(d), unless the party certifies in the notice, with supporting facts, that the deponent is expected to leave the United States and be unavailable for examination in this country after that time; or

(B) if the deponent is confined in prison.

(b) Notice of the Deposition; Other Formal Requirements.

(1) *Notice in General.*

A party who wants to depose a person by oral questions must give reasonable written notice to every other party. The notice must state the time and place of the deposition and, if known, the deponent's name and address. If the name is unknown, the notice must provide a general description sufficient to identify the person or the particular class or group to which the person belongs.

(2) *Producing Documents.*

If a subpoena duces tecum is to be served on the deponent, the materials designated for production, as set out in the subpoena, must be listed in the notice or in an attachment. The notice to a party deponent may be accompanied by a request under Rule 34 to produce documents and tangible things at the deposition.

(3) *Method of Recording.*

(A) *Method Stated in the Notice.*

The party who notices the deposition must state in the notice the method for recording the testimony. Unless the court orders otherwise, testimony may be recorded by audio, audiovisual, or stenographic means. The noticing party bears the recording costs. Any party may arrange to transcribe a deposition.

(B) *Additional Method.*

With prior notice to the deponent and other parties, any party may designate another method for recording the testimony in addition to that specified in the original notice. That party bears the expense of the additional record or transcript unless the court orders otherwise.

(4) *By Remote Means.*

The parties may stipulate — or the court may on motion order — that a deposition be taken by telephone or other remote means. For the purpose of this rule and Rules 28(a), 37(a)(2), and 37(b)(1), the deposition takes place where the deponent answers the questions.

(5) *Officer's Duties.*

(A) *Before the Deposition.*

Unless the parties stipulate otherwise, a deposition must be conducted before an officer appointed or designated under Rule 28. The officer must begin the deposition with an on-the-record statement that includes:

(i) the officer's name and business address;

(ii) the date, time, and place of the deposition;

(iii) the deponent's name;

(iv) the officer's administration of the oath or affirmation to the deponent; and

(v) the identity of all persons present.

(B) *Conducting the Deposition; Avoiding Distortion.*

If the deposition is recorded nonstenographically, the officer must repeat the items in Rule 30(b)(5)(A)(i)–(iii) at the beginning of each unit of the recording medium. The deponent's and attorneys' appearance or demeanor must not be distorted through recording techniques.

(C) *After the Deposition.*

At the end of a deposition, the officer must state on the record that the deposition is complete and must set out any stipulations made by the attorneys about custody of the transcript or recording and of the exhibits, or about any other pertinent matters.

(6) *Notice or Subpoena Directed to an Organization.*

In its notice or subpoena, a party may name as the deponent a public or private corporation, a partnership, an association, a governmental agency, or other entity and must describe with reasonable particularity the matters for examination. The named organization must designate one or more officers, directors, or managing agents, or designate other persons who consent to testify on its behalf; and it may set out the matters on which each person designated will testify. Before or promptly after the notice or subpoena is served, the serving party and the organization must confer in good faith about the matters for examination. A subpoena must advise a nonparty organization of its duty to confer with the serving party and to designate each person who will testify. The persons designated must testify about information known or reasonably available to the organization. This paragraph (6) does not preclude a deposition by any other procedure allowed by these rules.

(c) **Examination and Cross-Examination; Record of the Examination; Objections; Written Questions.**

(1) *Examination and Cross-Examination.*

The examination and cross-examination of a deponent proceed as they would at trial under the Federal Rules of Evidence, except Rules 103 and 615. After putting the deponent under oath or affirmation, the officer must record the testimony by the method designated under Rule 30(b)(3)(A). The testimony must be recorded by the officer personally or by a person acting in the presence and under the direction of the officer.

(2) *Objections.*

An objection at the time of the examination—whether to evidence, to a party's conduct, to the officer's qualifications, to the manner of taking the deposition, or to any other aspect of the deposition—must be noted on the record, but the examination still proceeds; the testimony is taken subject to any objection. An objection must be stated concisely in a nonargumentative and nonsuggestive manner. A person may instruct a deponent not to answer only when necessary to preserve a privilege, to enforce a limitation ordered by the court, or to present a motion under Rule 30(d)(3).

(3) *Participating Through Written Questions.*

Instead of participating in the oral examination, a party may serve written questions in a sealed envelope on the party noticing the deposition, who must deliver them to the officer. The officer must ask the deponent those questions and record the answers verbatim.

(d) Duration; Sanction; Motion to Terminate or Limit.

(1) *Duration.*

Unless otherwise stipulated or ordered by the court, a deposition is limited to 1 day of 7 hours. The court must allow additional time consistent with Rule 26(b)(1) and (2) if needed to fairly examine the deponent or if the deponent, another person, or any other circumstance impedes or delays the examination.

(2) *Sanction.*

The court may impose an appropriate sanction—including the reasonable expenses and attorney's fees incurred by any party—on a person who impedes, delays, or frustrates the fair examination of the deponent.

(3) *Motion to Terminate or Limit.*

(A) *Grounds.*

At any time during a deposition, the deponent or a party may move to terminate or limit it on the ground that it is being conducted in bad faith or in a manner that unreasonably annoys, embarrasses, or oppresses the deponent or party. The motion may be filed in the court where the action is pending or the deposition is being taken. If the objecting deponent or party so demands, the deposition must be suspended for the time necessary to obtain an order.

(B) *Order.*

The court may order that the deposition be terminated or may limit its scope and manner as provided in Rule 26(c). If terminated, the deposition may be resumed only by order of the court where the action is pending.

(C) *Award of Expenses.*

Rule 37(a)(5) applies to the award of expenses.

(e) Review by the Witness; Changes.

(1) *Review; Statement of Changes.*

On request by the deponent or a party before the deposition is completed, the deponent must be allowed 30 days after being notified by the officer that the transcript or recording is available in which:

(A) to review the transcript or recording; and

(B) if there are changes in form or substance, to sign a statement listing the changes and the reasons for making them.

(2) *Changes Indicated in the Officer's Certificate.*

The officer must note in the certificate prescribed by Rule 30(f)(1) whether a review was requested and, if so, must attach any changes the deponent makes during the 30-day period.

(f) Certification and Delivery; Exhibits; Copies of the Transcript or Recording; Filing.

(1) *Certification and Delivery.*

The officer must certify in writing that the witness was duly sworn and that the deposition accurately records the witness's testimony. The certificate must accompany the record of the deposition. Unless the court orders otherwise, the officer must seal the deposition in an envelope or package bearing the title of the action and marked "Deposition of [witness's name]" and must promptly send it to the attorney who arranged for the transcript or recording. The attorney must store it under conditions that will protect it against loss, destruction, tampering, or deterioration.

(2) *Documents and Tangible Things.*

(A) *Originals and Copies.*

Documents and tangible things produced for inspection during a deposition must, on a party's request, be marked for identification and attached to the deposition. Any party may inspect and copy them. But if the person who produced them wants to keep the originals, the person may:

(i) offer copies to be marked, attached to the deposition, and then used as originals — after giving all parties a fair opportunity to verify the copies by comparing them with the originals; or

(ii) give all parties a fair opportunity to inspect and copy the originals after they are marked — in which event the originals may be used as if attached to the deposition.

(B) *Order Regarding the Originals.*

Any party may move for an order that the originals be attached to the deposition pending final disposition of the case.

(3) *Copies of the Transcript or Recording.*

Unless otherwise stipulated or ordered by the court, the officer must retain the stenographic notes of a deposition taken stenographically or a copy of the recording of a deposition taken by another method. When paid reasonable charges, the officer must furnish a copy of the transcript or recording to any party or the deponent.

(4) *Notice of Filing.*

A party who files the deposition must promptly notify all other parties of the filing.

(g) Failure to Attend a Deposition or Serve a Subpoena; Expenses.

A party who, expecting a deposition to be taken, attends in person or by an attorney may recover reasonable expenses for attending, including attorney's fees, if the noticing party failed to:

(1) attend and proceed with the deposition; or

(2) serve a subpoena on a nonparty deponent, who consequently did not attend. [*Adopted Dec. 20, 1937, effective Sept. 16, 1938; amended Apr. 17, 2000, effective Dec. 1, 2000; amended April 30, 2007, effective Dec. 1, 2007; amended April 27, 2020, effective Dec. 1, 2020.*]

ADVISORY COMMITTEE'S NOTE TO 2000 AMENDMENT

Subdivision (d). Paragraph (1) has been amended to clarify the terms regarding behavior during depositions. The references to objections "to evidence" and limitations "on evidence" have been removed to avoid disputes about what is "evidence" and whether an objection is to, or a limitation is on, discovery instead. It is intended that the rule apply to any objection to a question or other issue arising during a deposition, and to any limitation imposed by the court in connection with a deposition, which might relate to duration or other matters.

The current rule places limitations on instructions that a witness not answer only when the instruction is made by a "party." Similar limitations should apply with regard to anyone who might purport to instruct a witness not to answer a question. Accordingly, the rule is amended to apply the limitation to instructions by any person. The amendment is not intended to confer new authority on nonparties to instruct witnesses to refuse to answer deposition questions. The amendment makes it clear that, whatever the legitimacy of giving such instructions, the nonparty is subject to the same limitations as parties.

Paragraph (2) imposes a presumptive durational limitation of one day of seven hours for any deposition. The Committee has been informed that overlong depositions can result in undue costs and delays in some circumstances. This limitation contemplates that there will be reasonable breaks during the day for lunch and other reasons, and that the only time to be counted is the time occupied by the actual deposition. For purposes of this durational limit, the deposition of each person designated under Rule 30(b)(6) should be considered a separate deposition. The presumptive duration may be extended, or otherwise altered, by agreement. Absent agreement, a court order is needed. The party seeking a court order to extend the examination, or otherwise alter the limitations, is expected to show good cause to justify such an order.

Parties considering extending the time for a deposition—and courts asked to order an extension—might consider a variety of factors. For example, if the witness needs an interpreter, that may prolong the examination. If the examination will cover events occurring over a long period of time, that may justify allowing additional time. In cases in which the witness will be questioned about numerous or lengthy documents, it is often desirable for the interrogating party to send copies of the documents to the witness sufficiently in advance of the deposition so that the witness can become familiar with them. Should the witness nevertheless not read the documents in advance, thereby prolonging the deposition, a court could consider that a reason for extending the time limit. If the examination reveals that documents have been requested but not produced, that may justify further examination once production has occurred. In multi-party cases, the need for each party to examine the witness may warrant additional time, although duplicative questioning should be avoided and parties with similar interests should strive to designate one lawyer to question about areas of common interest. Similarly, should the lawyer for the witness want to examine the witness, that may require additional time. Finally, with regard to expert witnesses, there may more often be a need for additional time — even after the submission of the report required by Rule 26(a)(2) — for full exploration of the theories upon which the witness relies.

It is expected that in most instances the parties and the witness will make reasonable accommodations to avoid the need for resort to the court. The limitation is phrased in terms of a single day on the assumption that ordinarily a single day would be preferable to a deposition extending over multiple days; if alternative arrangements would better suit the parties, they may agree to them. It is also assumed that there will be reasonable breaks during the day. Preoccupation with timing is to be avoided.

The rule directs the court to allow additional time where consistent with Rule 26(b)(2) if needed for a fair examination of the deponent. In addition, if the deponent or another person impedes or delays the examination, the court must authorize extra time. The amendment makes clear that additional time should also be allowed where the examination is impeded by an "other circumstance," which might include a power outage, a health emergency, or other event.

In keeping with the amendment to Rule 26(b)(2), the provision added in 1993 granting authority to adopt a local rule limiting the time permitted for depositions has been removed. The court may enter a case-specific order directing shorter depositions for all depositions in a case or with regard to a specific witness. The court may also order that a deposition be taken for limited periods on several days.

Paragraph (3) includes sanctions provisions formerly included in paragraph (2). It authorizes the court to impose an appropriate sanction on any person responsible for an impediment that frustrated the fair examination of the deponent. This could include the deponent, any party, or any other person involved in the deposition. If the impediment or delay results from an "other circumstance" under paragraph (2), ordinarily no sanction would be appropriate.

Former paragraph (3) has been renumbered (4) but is otherwise unchanged.

Subdivision (f)(1). This subdivision is amended because Rule 5(d) has been amended to direct that discovery materials, including depositions, ordinarily should not be filed. The rule already has provisions directing that the lawyer who arranged for the transcript or recording preserve the deposition. Rule 5(d) provides that, once the deposition is used in the proceeding, the attorney must file it with the court.

"Shall" is replaced by "must" or "may" under the program to conform amended rules to current style conventions when there is no ambiguity.

RULE 31.   DEPOSITIONS BY WRITTEN QUESTIONS.

(a) When a Deposition May Be Taken.

(1) *Without Leave.*

A party may, by written questions, depose any person, including a party, without leave of court except as provided in Rule 31(a)(2). The deponent's attendance may be compelled by subpoena under Rule 45.

(2) *With Leave.*

A party must obtain leave of court, and the court must grant leave to the extent consistent with Rule 26(b)(1) and (2):

  (A) if the parties have not stipulated to the deposition and:

   (i) the deposition would result in more than 10 depositions being taken under this rule or Rule 30 by the plaintiffs, or by the defendants, or by the third-party defendants;

   (ii) the deponent has already been deposed in the case; or

   (iii) the party seeks to take a deposition before the time specified in Rule 26(d); or

  (B) if the deponent is confined in prison.

(3) *Service; Required Notice.*

A party who wants to depose a person by written questions must serve them on every other party, with a notice stating, if known, the deponent's name and address. If the name is unknown, the notice must provide a general description sufficient to identify the person or the particular class or group to which the person belongs. The notice must also state the name or descriptive title and the address of the officer before whom the deposition will be taken.

(4) *Questions Directed to an Organization.*

A public or private corporation, a partnership, an association, or a governmental agency may be deposed by written questions in accordance with Rule 30(b)(6).

(5) *Questions from Other Parties.*

Any questions to the deponent from other parties must be served on all parties as follows: cross-questions, within 14 days after being served with the notice and direct questions; redirect questions, within 7 days after being served with cross- questions; and recross-questions, within 7 days after being served with redirect questions. The court may, for good cause, extend or shorten these times.

(b) Delivery to the Officer; Officer's Duties.

The party who noticed the deposition must deliver to the officer a copy of all the questions served and of the notice. The officer must promptly proceed in the manner provided in Rule 30(c), (e), and (f) to:

(1) take the deponent's testimony in response to the questions;

(2) prepare and certify the deposition; and

(3) send it to the party, attaching a copy of the questions and of the notice.

(c) Notice of Completion or Filing.

(1) *Completion.*

The party who noticed the deposition must notify all other parties when it is completed.

(2) *Filing.*

A party who files the deposition must promptly notify all other parties of the filing.

[*Adopted Dec. 20, 1937, effective Sept. 16, 1938; amended Mar. 30, 1970, effective July 1, 1970; Mar. 2, 1987, effective Aug. 1, 1987; Apr. 22, 1993, effective Dec. 1, 1993; amended April 30, 2007, effective Dec. 1, 2007; amended April 29, 2015, effective Dec. 1 2015.*]

RULE 32.   USING DEPOSITIONS IN COURT PROCEEDINGS.

(a) Using Depositions.

(1) *In General.*

At a hearing or trial, all or part of a deposition may be used against a party on these conditions:

(A) the party was present or represented at the taking of the deposition or had reasonable notice of it;

(B) it is used to the extent it would be admissible under the Federal Rules of Evidence if the deponent were present and testifying; and

(C) the use is allowed by Rule 32(a)(2) through (8).

(2) *Impeachment and Other Uses.*

Any party may use a deposition to contradict or impeach the testimony given by the deponent as a witness, or for any other purpose allowed by the Federal Rules of Evidence.

(3) *Deposition of Party, Agent, or Designee.*

An adverse party may use for any purpose the deposition of a party or anyone who, when deposed, was the party's officer, director, managing agent, or designee under Rule 30(b)(6) or 31(a)(4).

(4) *Unavailable Witness.*

A party may use for any purpose the deposition of a witness, whether or not a party, if the court finds:

    (A) that the witness is dead;

    (B) that the witness is more than 100 miles from the place of hearing or trial or is outside the United States, unless it appears that the witness's absence was procured by the party offering the deposition;

    (C) that the witness cannot attend or testify because of age, illness, infirmity, or imprisonment;

    (D) that the party offering the deposition could not procure the witness's attendance by subpoena; or

    (E) on motion and notice, that exceptional circumstances make it desirable—in the interest of justice and with due regard to the importance of live testimony in open court—to permit the deposition to be used.

(5) *Limitations on Use.*

    (A) *Deposition Taken on Short Notice.*

    A deposition must not be used against a party who, having received less than 14 days' notice of the deposition, promptly moved for a protective order under Rule 26(c)(1)(B) requesting that it not be taken or be taken at a different time or place—and this motion was still pending when the deposition was taken.

    (B) *Unavailable Deponent; Party Could Not Obtain an Attorney.*

    A deposition taken without leave of court under the unavailability provision of Rule 30(a)(2)(A)(iii) must not be used against a party who shows that, when served with the notice, it could not, despite diligent efforts, obtain an attorney to represent it at the deposition.

(6) *Using Part of a Deposition.*

If a party offers in evidence only part of a deposition, an adverse party may require the offeror to introduce other parts that in fairness should be considered with the part introduced, and any party may itself introduce any other parts.

(7) *Substituting a Party.*

Substituting a party under Rule 25 does not affect the right to use a deposition previously taken.

(8) *Deposition Taken in an Earlier Action.*

A deposition lawfully taken and, if required, filed in any federal- or state-court action may be used in a later action involving the same subject matter between the same parties, or their representatives or successors in interest, to the same extent as if taken in the later action. A deposition previously taken may also be used as allowed by the Federal Rules of Evidence.

(b) Objections to Admissibility.

Subject to Rules 28(b) and 32(d)(3), an objection may be made at a hearing or trial to the admission of any deposition testimony that would be inadmissible if the witness were present and testifying.

(c) Form of Presentation.

Unless the court orders otherwise, a party must provide a transcript of any deposition testimony the party offers, but may provide the court with the testimony in nontranscript form as well. On any party's request, deposition testimony offered in a jury trial for any purpose other than impeachment must be presented in nontranscript form, if available, unless the court for good cause orders otherwise.

(d) Waiver of Objections.

(1) *To the Notice.*

An objection to an error or irregularity in a deposition notice is waived unless promptly served in writing on the party giving the notice.

(2) *To the Officer's Qualification.*

An objection based on disqualification of the officer before whom a deposition is to be taken is waived if not made:

(A) before the deposition begins; or

(B) promptly after the basis for disqualification becomes known or, with reasonable diligence, could have been known.

(3) *To the Taking of the Deposition.*

(A) *Objection to Competence, Relevance, or Materiality.*

An objection to a deponent's competence — or to the competence, relevance, or materiality of testimony — is not waived by a failure to make the objection before or during the deposition, unless the ground for it might have been corrected at that time.

(B) *Objection to an Error or Irregularity.*

An objection to an error or irregularity at an oral examination is waived if:

(i) it relates to the manner of taking the deposition, the form of a question or answer, the oath or affirmation, a party's conduct, or other matters that might have been corrected at that time; and

(ii) it is not timely made during the deposition.

(C) *Objection to a Written Question.*

An objection to the form of a written question under Rule 31 is waived if not served in writing on the party submitting the question within the time for serving responsive questions or, if the question is a recross-question, within 7 days after being served with it.

(4) *To Completing and Returning the Deposition.*

An objection to how the officer transcribed the testimony—or prepared, signed, certified, sealed, endorsed, sent, or otherwise dealt with the deposition—is waived unless a motion to suppress is made promptly after the error or irregularity becomes known or, with reasonable diligence, could have been known.

[*Adopted Dec. 20, 1937, effective Sept. 16, 1938; amended April 30, 2007, effective Dec. 1, 2007, amended March 26, 2009, effective Dec. 1, 2009.*]

RULE 33. INTERROGATORIES TO PARTIES.

(a) In General.

(1) *Number.*

Unless otherwise stipulated or ordered by the court, a party may serve on any other party no more than 25 written interrogatories, including all discrete subparts. Leave to serve additional interrogatories may be granted to the extent consistent with Rule 26(b)(1) and (2).

(2) *Scope.*

An interrogatory may relate to any matter that may be inquired into under Rule 26(b). An interrogatory is not objectionable merely because it asks for an opinion or contention that relates to fact or the application of law to fact, but the court may order that the interrogatory need not be answered until designated discovery is complete, or until a pretrial conference or some other time.

(b) Answers and Objections.

(1) *Responding Party.*

The interrogatories must be answered:

(A) by the party to whom they are directed; or

(B) if that party is a public or private corporation, a partnership, an association, or a governmental agency, by any officer or agent, who must furnish the information available to the party.

(2) *Time to Respond.*

The responding party must serve its answers and any objections within 30 days after being served with the interrogatories. A shorter or longer time may be stipulated to under Rule 29 or be ordered by the court.

(3) *Answering Each Interrogatory.*

Each interrogatory must, to the extent it is not objected to, be answered separately and fully in writing under oath.

(4) *Objections.*

The grounds for objecting to an interrogatory must be stated with specificity. Any ground not stated in a timely objection is waived unless the court, for good cause, excuses the failure.

(5) *Signature.*

The person who makes the answers must sign them, and the attorney who objects must sign any objections.

(c) Use.

An answer to an interrogatory may be used to the extent allowed by the Federal Rules of Evidence.

(d) Option to Produce Business Records.

If the answer to an interrogatory may be determined by examining, auditing, compiling, abstracting, or summarizing a party's business records (including electroni- cally stored information), and if the burden of deriving or ascertaining the answer will be substantially the same for either party, the responding party may answer by:

> (1) specifying the records that must be reviewed, in sufficient detail to enable the interrogating party to locate and identify them as readily as the responding party could; and

> (2) giving the interrogating party a reasonable opportunity to examine and audit the records and to make copies, compilations, abstracts, or summaries.

[*Adopted Dec. 20, 1937, effective Sept. 16, 1938; amended April 12, 2006, effective* December 1, 2006; amended April 30, 2007, effective Dec. 1, 2007; amended April 29, 2015, effective Dec. 1, 2015.]

ADVISORY COMMITTEE'S NOTE TO 2006 AMENDMENT TO RULE 33

Rule 33(d) is amended to parallel Rule 34(a) by recognizing the importance of electronically stored information. The term "electronically stored information" has the same broad meaning in Rule 33(d) as in Rule 34(a). Much business information is stored only in electronic form; the Rule 33(d) option should be available with respect to such records as well.

Special difficulties may arise in using electronically stored information, either due to its form or because it is dependent on a particular computer system. Rule 33(d) allows a responding party to substitute access to documents or electronically stored information for an answer only if the burden of deriving the answer will be substantially the same for either party. Rule 33(d) states that a party electing to respond to an interrogatory by providing electronically stored information must ensure that the interrogating party can locate and identify it "as readily as can the party served," and that the responding party must give the interrogating party a "reasonable opportunity to examine, audit, or inspect" the information. Depending on the circumstances, satisfying these provisions with regard to electronically stored information may require the responding party to provide some combination of technical support, information on application software, or other assistance. The key question is whether such support enables the interrogating party to derive or ascertain the answer from the electronically stored information as readily as the responding party. A party that wishes to invoke Rule 33(d) by specifying electronically stored information may be required to provide direct access to its electronic information system, but only if that is necessary to afford the requesting party an adequate opportunity to derive or ascertain the answer to the interrogatory. In that situation, the responding party's need to protect sensitive interests of confidentiality or privacy may mean that it must derive or ascertain and provide the answer itself rather than invoke Rule 33(d).

RULE 34. PRODUCING DOCUMENTS, ELECTRONICALLY STORED INFORMATION, AND TANGIBLE THINGS, OR ENTERING ONTO LAND, FOR INSPECTION AND OTHER PURPOSES.

(a) In General.

A party may serve on any other party a request within the scope of Rule 26(b):

(1) to produce and permit the requesting party or its representative to inspect, copy, test, or sample the following items in the responding party's possession, custody, or control:

(A) any designated documents or electronically stored information—including writings, drawings, graphs, charts, photographs, sound recordings, images, and other data or data compilations—stored in any medium from which information can be obtained either directly or, if necessary, after translation by the responding party into a reasonably usable form; or

(B) any designated tangible things; or

(2) to permit entry onto designated land or other property possessed or controlled by the responding party, so that the requesting party may inspect, measure, survey, photograph, test, or sample the property or any designated object or operation on it.

(b) Procedure.

(1) *Contents of the Request.* The request:

(A) must describe with reasonable particularity each item or category of items to be inspected;

(B) must specify a reasonable time, place, and manner for the inspection and for performing the related acts; and

(C) may specify the form or forms in which electronically stored information is to be produced.

(2) *Responses and Objections.*

(A) Time to Respond. The party to whom the request is directed must respond in writing within 30 days after being served or—if the request was delivered under Rule 26(d)(2)—within 30 days after the parties' first Rule

26(f) conference. A shorter or longer time may be stipulated to under Rule 29 or be ordered by the court.

(B) Responding to Each Item. For each item or category, the response must either state that inspection and related activities will be permitted as requested or state with specificity the grounds for objecting to the request, including the reasons. The responding party may state that it will produce copies of documents or of electronically stored information instead of permitting inspection. The production must then be completed no later than the time for inspection specified in the request or another reasonable time specified in the response.

(C) Objections. An objection must state whether any responsive materials are being withheld on the basis of that objection. An objection to part of a request must specify the part and permit inspection of the rest.

(D) Responding to a Request for Production of Electronically Stored Information. The response may state an objection to a requested form for producing electronically stored information. If the responding party objects to a requested form — or if no form was specified in the request — the party must state the form or forms it intends to use.

(E) Producing the Documents or Electronically Stored Information. Unless otherwise stipulated or ordered by the court, these procedures apply to producing documents or electronically stored information:

(i) A party must produce documents as they are kept in the usual course of business or must organize and label them to correspond to the categories in the request;

(ii) If a request does not specify a form for producing electronically stored information, a party must produce it in a form or forms in which it is ordinarily maintained or in a reasonably usable form or forms; and

(iii) A party need not produce the same electronically stored information in more than one form.

(c) Nonparties.

As provided in Rule 45, a nonparty may be compelled to produce documents and tangible things or to permit an inspection.

[*Adopted Dec. 20, 1937, effective Sept. 16, 1938; amended April 12, 2006, effective Dec. 1, 2006; amended April 30, 2007, effective Dec. 1, 2007; amended April 29, 2015, effective Dec. 1, 2015.*]

NOTES OF ADVISORY COMMITTEE ON 2015 AMENDMENT TO RULE 34

Several amendments are made in Rule 34, aimed at reducing the potential to impose unreasonable burdens by objections to requests to produce. * * *

Rule 34(b)(2)(B) is amended to require that objections to Rule 34 requests be stated with specificity. This provision adopts the language of Rule 33(b)(4), eliminating any doubt that less specific objections might be suitable under Rule 34. The specificity of the objection ties to the new provision in Rule 34(b)(2)(C) directing that an objection must state whether any responsive materials are being withheld on the basis of that objection. An objection may state that a request is overbroad, but if the objection recognizes that some part of the request is appropriate the objection should state the scope that is not overbroad. Examples would be a statement that the responding party will limit the search to documents or electronically stored information created within a given period of time prior to the events in suit, or to specified sources. When there is such an objection, the statement of what has been withheld can properly identify as matters "withheld" anything beyond the scope of the search specified in the objection.

Rule 34(b)(2)(B) is further amended to reflect the common practice of producing copies of documents or electronically stored information rather than simply permitting inspection. The response to the request must state that copies will be produced. The production must be completed either by the time for inspection specified in the request or by another reasonable time specifically identified in the response. When it is necessary to make the production in stages the response should specify the beginning and end dates of the production.

Rule 34(b)(2)(C) is amended to provide that an objection to a Rule 34 request must state whether anything is being withheld on the basis of the objection. This amendment should end the confusion that frequently arises when a producing party states several objections and still produces information, leaving the requesting party uncertain whether any relevant and responsive information has been withheld on the basis of the objections. The producing party does not need to provide a detailed description or log of all documents withheld, but does need to alert other parties to the fact that documents have been withheld and thereby facilitate an informed discussion of the objection. An objection that states the limits that have controlled the search for responsive and relevant materials qualifies as a statement that the materials have been "withheld."

ADVISORY COMMITTEE'S NOTE TO 2006 AMENDMENT TO RULE 34

Subdivision (a). As originally adopted, Rule 34 focused on discovery of "documents" and "things." In 1970, Rule 34(a) was amended to include discovery of data compilations, anticipating that the use of computerized information would increase. Since then, the growth in electronically stored information and in the variety of systems for creating and storing such information has been dramatic. Lawyers and judges interpreted the term "documents" to include electronically stored information because it was obviously improper to allow a party to evade discovery obligations on the basis that the label had not kept pace with changes in information technology. But it has become increasingly difficult to say that all forms of electronically stored information, many dynamic in nature, fit within the traditional concept of a "document." Electronically stored information may exist in dynamic databases and other forms far different from fixed expression on paper. Rule 34(a) is amended to confirm that discovery of electronically stored information stands on equal footing with discovery of paper documents. The change clarifies that Rule 34 applies to information that is fixed in a tangible form and to information that is stored in a medium from which it can be retrieved and examined. At the same time, a Rule 34 request for production of "documents" should be understood to encompass, and the response should include, electronically stored information unless discovery in the action has clearly distinguished between electronically stored information and "documents."

Discoverable information often exists in both paper and electronic form, and the same or similar information might exist in both. The items listed in Rule 34(a) show different ways in which information may be recorded or stored. Images, for example, might be hard-copy documents or electronically stored information. The wide variety of computer systems currently in use, and the rapidity of technological change, counsel against a limiting or precise definition of electronically stored information. Rule 34(a)(1) is expansive and includes any type of information that is stored electronically. A common example often sought in discovery is electronic communications, such as e-mail. The rule covers—either as documents or as electronically stored information—information "stored in any medium," to encompass future developments in computer technology. Rule 34(a)(1) is intended to be broad enough to cover all current types of computer-based information, and flexible enough to encompass future changes and developments.

References elsewhere in the rules to "electronically stored information" should be understood to invoke this expansive approach. A companion change is made to Rule 33(d), making it explicit that parties choosing to respond to an interrogatory by permitting access to responsive records may do so by providing access to electronically stored information. More generally, the term used in Rule 34(a)(1) appears in a number of other amendments, such as those to Rules 26(a)(1), 26(b)(2), 26(b)(5)(B), 26(f), 34(b), 37(f), and 45. In each of these rules, electronically stored information has the same broad meaning it has under Rule 34(a)(1). References to "documents" appear in discovery rules that are not amended, including Rules 30(f), 36(a), and 37(c)(2). These references should be interpreted to include electronically stored information as circumstances warrant.

The term "electronically stored information" is broad, but whether material that falls within this term should be produced, and in what form, are separate questions that must be addressed under Rules 26(b), 26(c), and 34(b).

The Rule 34(a) requirement that, if necessary, a party producing electronically stored information translate it into reasonably usable form does not address the issue of translating from one human language to another. *See In re Puerto Rico Elect. Power Auth.*, 687 F.2d 501, 504–510 (1st Cir. 1989).

Rule 34(a)(1) is also amended to make clear that parties may request an opportunity to test or sample materials sought under the rule in addition to inspecting and copying them. That opportunity may be important for both electronically stored information and hard-copy materials. The current rule is not clear that such testing or sampling is authorized; the amendment expressly permits it. As with any other form of discovery, issues of burden and intrusiveness raised by requests to test or sample can be addressed under Rules 26(b)(2) and 26(c). Inspection or testing of certain types of electronically stored information or of a responding party's electronic information system may raise issues of confidentiality or privacy. The addition of testing and sampling to Rule 34(a) with regard to documents and electronically stored information is not meant to create a routine right of direct access to a party's electronic information system, although such access might be justified in some circumstances. Courts should guard against undue intrusiveness resulting from inspecting or testing such systems.

Rule 34(a)(1) is further amended to make clear that tangible things must—like documents and land sought to be examined—be designated in the request.

Subdivision (b). Rule 34(b) provides that a party must produce documents as they are kept in the usual course of business or must organize and label them to correspond with the categories in the discovery request. The production of electronically stored information should be subject to comparable requirements to protect against deliberate or inadvertent production in ways that raise unnecessary obstacles for the requesting party. Rule 34(b) is amended to ensure similar protection for electronically stored information.

The amendment to Rule 34(b) permits the requesting party to designate the form or forms in which it wants electronically stored information produced. The form of production is more important to the exchange of electronically stored information than of hard-copy materials, although a party might specify hard copy as the requested form. Specification of the desired form or forms may facilitate the orderly, efficient, and cost-effective discovery of electronically stored information. The rule recognizes that different forms of production may be appropriate for different types of electronically stored information. Using current technology, for example, a party might be called upon to produce word processing documents, e-mail messages, electronic spreadsheets, different image or sound files, and material from databases. Requiring that such diverse types of electronically stored information all be produced in the same form could prove impossible, and even if possible could increase the cost and burdens of producing and using the information. The rule therefore provides that the requesting party may ask for different forms of production for different types of electronically stored information.

The rule does not require that the requesting party choose a form or forms of production. The requesting party may not have a preference. In some cases, the requesting party may not know what form the producing party uses to maintain its electronically stored information, although Rule 26(f)(3) is amended to call for discussion of the form of production in the parties' prediscovery conference.

The responding party also is involved in determining the form of production. In the written response to the production request that Rule 34 requires, the responding party must state the form it intends to use for producing electronically stored information if the requesting party does not specify a form or if the responding party objects to a form that the requesting party specifies. Stating the intended form before the production occurs may permit the parties to identify and seek to resolve disputes before the expense and work of the production occurs. A party that responds to a discovery request by simply producing electronically stored information in a form of its choice, without identifying that form in advance of the production in the response required by Rule 34(b), runs a risk that the requesting party can show that the produced form is not reasonably usable and that it is entitled to production of some or all of the information in an additional form. Additional time might be required to permit a responding party to assess the appropriate form or forms of production.

If the requesting party is not satisfied with the form stated by the responding party, or if the responding party has objected to the form specified by the requesting party, the parties must meet and confer under Rule 37(a)(2)(B) in an effort to resolve the matter before the requesting party can file a motion to compel. If they cannot agree and the court resolves the dispute, the court is not limited to the forms initially chosen by the requesting party, stated by the responding party, or specified in this rule for situations in which there is no court order or party agreement.

If the form of production is not specified by party agreement or court order, the responding party must produce electronically stored information either in a form or forms in which it is ordinarily maintained or in a form or forms that are reasonably usable. Rule 34(a) requires that, if necessary, a responding party "translate" information it produces into a "reasonably usable" form. Under some circumstances, the responding party may need to provide some reasonable amount of technical support, information on application software, or other reasonable assistance to enable the requesting party to use the information. The rule does not require a party to produce electronically stored information in the form it which it is ordinarily maintained, as long as it is produced in a reasonably usable form. But the option to produce in a reasonably usable form does not mean that a responding party is free to convert electronically stored information from the form in which it is ordinarily maintained to a different form that makes it more difficult or burdensome for the requesting party to use the information efficiently in the litigation. If the responding party ordinarily maintains the information it is producing in a way that makes it searchable by electronic means, the information should not be produced in a form that removes or significantly degrades this feature.

Some electronically stored information may be ordinarily maintained in a form that is not reasonably usable by any party. One example is "legacy" data that can be used only by superseded systems. The questions whether a producing party should be required to convert such information to a more usable form, or should be required to produce it at all, should be addressed under Rule 26(b)(2)(B).

Whether or not the requesting party specified the form of production, Rule 34(b) provides that the same electronically stored information ordinarily need be produced in only one form.

RULE 35.   PHYSICAL AND MENTAL EXAMINATIONS.

(a) Order for an Examination.

(1) *In General.*

The court where the action is pending may order a party whose mental or physical condition—including blood group—is in controversy to submit to a physical or mental examination by a suitably licensed or certified examiner. The court has the same authority to order a party to produce for examination a person who is in its custody or under its legal control.

(2) *Motion and Notice; Contents of the Order.*

The order:

   (A) may be made only on motion for good cause and on notice to all parties and the person to be examined; and

   (B) must specify the time, place, manner, conditions, and scope of the examination, as well as the person or persons who will perform it.

(b) Examiner's Report.

(1) *Request by the Party or Person Examined.*

The party who moved for the examination must, on request, deliver to the requester a copy of the examiner's report, together with like reports of all earlier examinations of the same condition. The request may be made by the party against whom the examination order was issued or by the person examined.

(2) *Contents.*

The examiner's report must be in writing and must set out in detail the examiner's findings, including diagnoses, conclusions, and the results of any tests.

(3) *Request by the Moving Party.*

After delivering the reports, the party who moved for the examination may request—and is entitled to receive—from the party against whom the examination order was issued like reports of all earlier or later examinations of the same condition. But those reports need not be delivered by the party with custody or control of the person examined if the party shows that it could not obtain them.

(4) *Waiver of Privilege.*

By requesting and obtaining the examiner's report, or by deposing the examiner, the party examined waives any privilege it may have—in that action or any other action involving the same controversy—concerning testimony about all examinations of the same condition.

(5) *Failure to Deliver a Report.*

The court on motion may order—on just terms—that a party deliver the report of an examination. If the report is not provided, the court may exclude the examiner's testimony at trial.

(6) *Scope.*

This subdivision (b) applies also to an examination made by the parties' agreement, unless the agreement states otherwise. This subdivision does not preclude obtaining an examiner's report or deposing an examiner under other rules.

[*Adopted Dec. 20, 1937, effective Sept. 16, 1938; amended Mar. 30, 1970, effective July 1, 1970; Mar. 2, 1987, effective Aug. 1, 1987; Nov. 18, 1988; Apr. 30, 1991, effective Dec. 1, 1991; amended April 30. 2007, effective Dec. 1, 2007.*]

Rule 36. Requests for Admission.

(a) Scope and Procedure.

(1) *Scope.*

A party may serve on any other party a written request to admit, for purposes of the pending action only, the truth of any matters within the scope of Rule 26(b)(1) relating to:

  (A) facts, the application of law to fact, or opinions about either; and

  (B) the genuineness of any described documents.

(2) *Form; Copy of a Document.*

Each matter must be separately stated. A request to admit the genuineness of a document must be accompanied by a copy of the document unless it is, or has been, otherwise furnished or made available for inspection and copying.

(3) *Time to Respond; Effect of Not Responding.*

A matter is admitted unless, within 30 days after being served, the party to whom the request is directed serves on the requesting party a written answer or objection addressed to the matter and signed by the party or its attorney. A shorter or longer time for responding may be stipulated to under Rule 29 or be ordered by the court.

(4) *Answer.*

If a matter is not admitted, the answer must specifically deny it or state in detail why the answering party cannot truthfully admit or deny it. A denial must fairly respond to the substance of the matter; and when good faith requires that a party qualify an answer or deny only a part of a matter, the answer must specify the part admitted and qualify or deny the rest. The answering party may assert lack of knowledge or information as a reason for failing to admit or deny only if the party states that it has made reasonable inquiry and that the information it knows or can readily obtain is insufficient to enable it to admit or deny.

(5) *Objections.*

The grounds for objecting to a request must be stated. A party must not object solely on the ground that the request presents a genuine issue for trial.

(6) *Motion Regarding the Sufficiency of an Answer or Objection.*

The requesting party may move to determine the sufficiency of an answer or objection. Unless the court finds an objection justified, it must order that an answer be served. On finding that an answer does not comply with this rule, the court may order either that the matter is admitted or that an amended answer be served. The court may defer its final decision until a pretrial conference or a specified time before trial. Rule 37(a)(5) applies to an award of expenses.

(b) Effect of an Admission; Withdrawing or Amending It.

A matter admitted under this rule is conclusively established unless the court, on motion, permits the admission to be withdrawn or amended. Subject to Rule 16(e), the court may permit withdrawal or amendment if it would promote the presentation of the merits of the action and if the court is not persuaded that it would prejudice the requesting party in maintaining or defending the action on the merits. An admission under this rule is not an admission for any other purpose and cannot be used against the party in any other proceeding.

[*Adopted Dec. 20, 1937, effective Sept. 16, 1938; amended Dec. 27, 1946, effective Mar. 19, 1948; Mar. 30, 1970, effective July 1, 1970; Mar. 2, 1987, effective Aug. 1, 1987; Apr. 22, 1993, effective Dec. 1, 1993; amended April 30, 2007, effective Dec. 1, 2007.*]

ADVISORY COMMITTEE'S NOTE OF 1970 TO SUBDIVISION (A)

Subdivision (a). As revised, the subdivision provides that a request may be made to admit any matters within the scope of Rule 26(b) that relate to statements or opinions of fact or of the application of law to fact. It thereby eliminates the requirement that the matters be "of fact." This change resolves conflicts in the court decisions as to whether a request to admit matters of "opinion" and matters involving "mixed law and fact" is proper under the rule. . . .

Not only is it difficult as a practical matter to separate "fact" from "opinion," see 4 *Moore's Federal Practice* ¶ 36.04 (2d ed. 1966); *cf.* 2A Barron & Holtzoff, *Federal Practice and Procedure* 317 (Wright ed. 1961), but an admission on a matter of opinion may facilitate proof or narrow the issues or both. An admission of a matter involving the application of law to fact may, in a given case, even more clearly narrow the issues. For example, an admission that an employee acted in the scope of his employment may remove a major issue from the trial. In *McSparran v. Hanigan, supra,* plaintiff admitted that "the premises on which said accident occurred, were occupied or under the control" of one of the defendants, 225 F. Supp. at 636. This admission, involving law as well as fact, removed one of the issues from the lawsuit and thereby reduced the proof required at trial. The amended provision does not authorize requests for admissions of law unrelated to the facts of the case.

Requests for admission involving the application of law to fact may create disputes between the parties which are best resolved in the presence of the judge after much or all of the other discovery has been completed. Power is therefore expressly conferred upon the court to defer decision until a pretrial conference is held or until a designated time prior to trial. On the other hand, the court should not automatically defer decision; in many instances, the importance of the admission lies in enabling the requesting party to avoid the burdensome accumulation of proof prior to the pretrial conference.

Courts have also divided on whether an answering party may properly object to requests for admission as to matters which that party regards as "in dispute." . . . The proper response in such cases is an answer. The very purpose of the request is to ascertain whether the answering party is prepared to admit or regards the matter as presenting a genuine issue for trial. In his answer, the party may deny, or he may give as his reason for inability to admit or deny the existence of a genuine issue. The party runs no risk of sanctions if the matter is genuinely in issue, since Rule 37(c) provides a sanction of costs only when there are no good reasons for a failure to admit.

On the other hand, requests to admit may be so voluminous and so framed that the answering party finds the task of identifying what is in dispute and what is not unduly burdensome. If so, the responding party may obtain a protective order and under Rule 26(c). Some of the decisions sustaining objections on "disputability" grounds could have been justified by the burdensome character of the requests. See, e.g., *Syracuse Broadcasting Corp. v. Newhouse, supra.*

Another sharp split of authority exists on the question whether a party may base his answer on lack of information or knowledge without seeking out additional information. . . .

The rule as revised adopts the majority view, as in keeping with a basic principle of the discovery rules that a reasonable burden may be imposed on the parties when its discharge will facilitate preparation for trial and ease the trial process. It has been argued against this view that one side should not have the burden of "proving" the other side's case. The revised rule requires only that the answering party make reasonable inquiry and secure such knowledge and information as are readily obtainable by him. In most instances, the investigation will be necessary either to his own case or to preparation for rebuttal. Even when it is not, the information may be close enough at hand to be "readily obtainable." Rule 36 requires only that the party state that he has taken these steps. The sanction for failure of a party to inform himself before he answers lies in the award of costs after trial, as provided in Rule 37(c). . . .

RULE 37.   FAILURE TO MAKE DISCLOSURES OR TO COOPERATE IN DISCOVERY; SANCTIONS.

(a) Motion for an Order Compelling Disclosure or Discovery.

(1) *In General.*

On notice to other parties and all affected persons, a party may move for an order compelling disclosure or discovery. The motion must include a certification that the movant has in good faith conferred or attempted to confer with the person or party failing to make disclosure or discovery in an effort to obtain it without court action.

(2) *Appropriate Court.*

A motion for an order to a party must be made in the court where the action is pending. A motion for an order to a nonparty must be made in the court where the discovery is or will be taken.

(3) *Specific Motions.*

(A) *To Compel Disclosure.*

If a party fails to make a disclosure required by Rule 26(a), any other party may move to compel disclosure and for appropriate sanctions.

(B) *To Compel a Discovery Response.*

A party seeking discovery may move for an order compelling an answer, designation, production, or inspection. This motion may be made if:

(i) a deponent fails to answer a question asked under Rule 30 or 31;

(ii) a corporation or other entity fails to make a designation under Rule 30(b)(6) or 31(a)(4);

(iii) a party fails to answer an interrogatory submitted under Rule 33; or

(iv) a party fails to produce documents or fails to respond that inspection will be permitted—or fails to permit inspection—as requested under Rule 34.

(C) *Related to a Deposition.*

When taking an oral deposition, the party asking a question may complete or adjourn the examination before moving for an order.

(4) *Evasive or Incomplete Disclosure, Answer, or Response.*

For purposes of this subdivision (a), an evasive or incomplete disclosure, answer, or response must be treated as a failure to disclose, answer, or respond.

(5) *Payment of Expenses; Protective Orders.*

(A) *If the Motion Is Granted (or Disclosure or Discovery Is Provided After Filing).*

If the motion is granted—or if the disclosure or requested discovery is provided after the motion was filed—the court must, after giving an opportunity to be heard, require the party or deponent whose conduct necessitated the motion, the party or attorney advising that conduct, or both to pay the movant's reasonable expenses incurred in making the motion, including attorney's fees. But the court must not order this payment if:

> (i) the movant filed the motion before attempting in good faith to obtain the disclosure or discovery without court action;

> (ii) the opposing party's nondisclosure, response, or objection was substantially justified; or

> (iii) other circumstances make an award of expenses unjust.

(B) *If the Motion Is Denied.*

If the motion is denied, the court may issue any protective order authorized under Rule 26(c) and must, after giving an opportunity to be heard, require the movant, the attorney filing the motion, or both to pay the party or deponent who opposed the motion its reasonable expenses incurred in opposing the motion, including attorney's fees. But the court must not order this payment if the motion was substantially justified or other circumstances make an award of expenses unjust.

(C) *If the Motion Is Granted in Part and Denied in Part.*

If the motion is granted in part and denied in part, the court may issue any protective order authorized under Rule 26(c) and may, after giving an opportunity to be heard, apportion the reasonable expenses for the motion.

(b) Failure to Comply with a Court Order.

(1) *Sanctions in the District Where the Deposition Is Taken.*

If the court where the discovery is taken orders a deponent to be sworn or to answer a question and the deponent fails to obey, the failure may be treated as contempt of court. If a deposition-related motion is transferred to the court where the action is pending, and that court orders a deponent to be sworn or to answer a question and the deponent fails to obey, the failure may be treated as contempt of either the court where the discovery is taken or the court where the action is pending.

(2) *Sanctions in the District Where the Action Is Pending.*

(A) *For Not Obeying a Discovery Order.*

If a party or a party's officer, director, or managing agent — or a witness designated under Rule 30(b)(6) or 31(a)(4) — fails to obey an order to provide or permit discovery, including an order under Rule 26(f), 35, or 37(a), the court where the action is pending may issue further just orders. They may include the following:

> (i) directing that the matters embraced in the order or other designated facts be taken as established for purposes of the action, as the prevailing party claims;

> (ii) prohibiting the disobedient party from supporting or opposing designated claims or defenses, or from introducing designated matters in evidence;

(iii) striking pleadings in whole or in part;

(iv) staying further proceedings until the order is obeyed;

(v) dismissing the action or proceeding in whole or in part;

(vi) rendering a default judgment against the disobedient party; or

(vii) treating as contempt of court the failure to obey any order except an order to submit to a physical or mental examination.

(B) *For Not Producing a Person for Examination.*

If a party fails to comply with an order under Rule 35(a) requiring it to produce another person for examination, the court may issue any of the orders listed in Rule 37(b)(2)(A)(i)–(vi), unless the disobedient party shows that it cannot produce the other person.

(C) *Payment of Expenses.*

Instead of or in addition to the orders above, the court must order the disobedient party, the attorney advising that party, or both to pay the reasonable expenses, including attorney's fees, caused by the failure, unless the failure was substantially justified or other circumstances make an award of expenses unjust.

(c) Failure to Disclose, to Supplement an Earlier Response, or to Admit.

(1) *Failure to Disclose or Supplement.*

If a party fails to provide information or identify a witness as required by Rule 26(a) or (e), the party is not allowed to use that information or witness to supply evidence on a motion, at a hearing, or at a trial, unless the failure was substantially justified or is harmless. In addition to or instead of this sanction, the court, on motion and after giving an opportunity to be heard:

(A) may order payment of the reasonable expenses, including attorney's fees, caused by the failure;

(B) may inform the jury of the party's failure; and

(C) may impose other appropriate sanctions, including any of the orders listed in Rule 37(b)(2)(A)(i)–(vi).

(2) *Failure to Admit.*

If a party fails to admit what is requested under Rule 36 and if the requesting party later proves a document to be genuine or the matter true, the requesting party may move that the party who failed to admit pay the reasonable expenses, including attorney's fees, incurred in making that proof. The court must so order unless:

(A) the request was held objectionable under Rule 36(a);

(B) the admission sought was of no substantial importance;

(C) the party failing to admit had a reasonable ground to believe that it might prevail on the matter; or

(D) there was other good reason for the failure to admit.

(d) Party's Failure to Attend Its Own Deposition, Serve Answers to Interrogatories, or Respond to a Request for Inspection.

(1) *In General.*

(A) *Motion; Grounds for Sanctions.*

The court where the action is pending may, on motion, order sanctions if:

(i) a party or a party's officer, director, or managing agent — or a person designated under Rule 30(b)(6) or 31(a)(4) — fails, after being served with proper notice, to appear for that person's deposition; or

(ii) a party, after being properly served with interrogatories under Rule 33 or a request for inspection under Rule 34, fails to serve its answers, objections, or written response.

(B) *Certification.*

A motion for sanctions for failing to answer or respond must include a certification that the movant has in good faith conferred or attempted to confer with the party failing to act in an effort to obtain the answer or response without court action.

(2) *Unacceptable Excuse for Failing to Act.*

A failure described in Rule 37(d)(1)(A) is not excused on the ground that the discovery sought was objectionable, unless the party failing to act has a pending motion for a protective order under Rule 26(c).

(3) *Types of Sanctions.*

Sanctions may include any of the orders listed in Rule 37(b)(2)(A)(i)–(vi). Instead of or in addition to these sanctions, the court must require the party failing to act, the attorney advising that party, or both to pay the reasonable expenses, including attorney's fees, caused by the failure, unless the failure was substantially justified or other circumstances make an award of expenses unjust.

(e) Failure to Preserve Electronically Stored Information.

If electronically stored information that should have been preserved in the anticipation or conduct of litigation is lost because a party failed to take reasonable steps to preserve it, and it cannot be restored or replaced through additional discovery, the court:

(1) upon finding prejudice to another party from loss of the information, may order measures no greater than necessary to cure the prejudice; or

(2) only upon finding that the party acted with the intent to deprive another party of the information's use in the litigation may:

(A) presume that the lost information was unfavorable to the party;

(B) instruct the jury that it may or must presume the information was unfavorable to the party; or

(C) dismiss the action or enter a default judgment.

(f) Failure to Participate in Framing a Discovery Plan.

If a party or its attorney fails to participate in good faith in developing and submitting a proposed discovery plan as required by Rule 26(f), the court may, after giving an opportunity to be heard, require that party or attorney to pay to any other party the reasonable expenses, including attorney's fees, caused by the failure.

[*Adopted Dec. 20, 1937, effective Sept. 16, 1938; as amended Dec. 1, 2013; amended April 29, 2015, effective Dec. 1, 2015.*]

NOTES OF ADVISORY COMMITTEE ON 2015 AMENDMENTS TO RULE 37

*   *   *

Subdivision (e). Present Rule 37(e), adopted in 2006, provides: "Absent exceptional circumstances, a court may not impose sanctions under these rules on a party for failing to provide electronically stored information lost as a result of the routine, good-faith operation of an electronic information system." This limited rule has not adequately addressed the serious problems resulting from the continued exponential growth in the volume of such information. Federal circuits have established significantly different standards for imposing sanctions or curative measures on parties who fail to preserve electronically stored information. These developments have caused litigants to expend excessive effort and money on preservation in order to avoid the risk of severe sanctions if a court finds they did not do enough.

New Rule 37(e) replaces the 2006 rule. It authorizes and specifies measures a court may employ if information that should have been preserved is lost, and specifies the findings necessary to justify these measures. It therefore forecloses reliance on inherent authority or state law to determine when certain measures should be used. The rule does not affect the validity of an independent tort claim for spoliation if state law applies in a case and authorizes the claim.

The new rule applies only to electronically stored information, also the focus of the 2006 rule. It applies only when such information is lost. Because electronically stored information often exists in multiple locations, loss from one source may often be harmless when substitute information can be found elsewhere.

The new rule applies only if the lost information should have been preserved in the anticipation or conduct of litigation and the party failed to take reasonable steps to preserve it. Many court decisions hold that potential litigants have a duty to preserve relevant information when litigation is reasonably foreseeable. Rule 37(e) is based on this common-law duty; it does not attempt to create a new duty to preserve. The rule does not apply when information is lost before a duty to preserve arises.

In applying the rule, a court may need to decide whether and when a duty to preserve arose. Courts should consider the extent to which a party was on notice that litigation was likely and that the information would be relevant. A variety of events may alert a party to the prospect of litigation. Often these events provide only limited information about that prospective litigation, however, so that the scope of information that should be preserved may remain uncertain. It is important not to be blinded to this reality by hindsight arising from familiarity with an action as it is actually filed.

Although the rule focuses on the common-law obligation to preserve in the anticipation or conduct of litigation, courts may sometimes consider whether there was an independent requirement that the lost information be preserved. Such require- ments arise from many sources—statutes, administrative regulations, an order in another case, or a party's own information-retention protocols. The court should be sensitive, however, to the fact that such independent preservation require- ments may be addressed to a wide variety of concerns unrelated to the current litiga- tion. The fact that a party had an independent obligation to preserve information does not necessarily mean that it had such a duty with respect to the litigation, and the fact that the party failed to observe some other preservation obligation does not itself prove that its efforts to preserve were not reasonable with respect to a particu- lar case.

The duty to preserve may in some instances be triggered or clarified by a court order in the case. Preservation orders may become more common, in part because Rules 16(b)(3)(B)(iii) and 26(f)(3)(C) are amended to encourage discovery plans and orders that address preservation. Once litigation has commenced, if the parties cannot reach agreement about preservation issues, promptly seeking judicial guid- ance about the extent of reasonable preservation may be important.

The rule applies only if the information was lost because the party failed to take reasonable steps to preserve the information. Due to the ever-increasing volume of electronically stored information and the multitude of devices that generate such information, perfection in preserving all relevant electronically stored information is often impossible. As under the current rule, the routine, good-faith operation of an electronic information system would be a relevant factor for the court to con- sider in evaluating whether a party failed to take reasonable steps to preserve lost information, although the prospect of litigation may call for reasonable steps to pre- serve information by intervening in that routine operation. This rule recognizes that "reasonable steps" to preserve suffice; it does not call for perfection. The court should be sensitive to the party's sophistication with regard to litigation in evaluat- ing preservation efforts; some litigants, particularly individual litigants, may be less familiar with preservation obligations than others who have considerable experi- ence in litigation.

Because the rule calls only for reasonable steps to preserve, it is inapplicable when the loss of information occurs despite the party's reasonable steps to preserve. For example, the information may not be in the party's control. Or information the party has preserved may be destroyed by events outside the party's control—the computer room may be flooded, a "cloud" service may fail, a malign software attack may dis- rupt a storage system, and so on. Courts may, however, need to assess the extent to which a party knew of and protected against such risks.

Another factor in evaluating the reasonableness of preservation efforts is propor-tionality. The court should be sensitive to party resources; aggressive preservation efforts can be extremely costly, and parties (including governmental parties) may have limited staff and resources to devote to those efforts. A party may act reasonably by choosing a less costly form of information preservation, if it is substantially as effective as more costly forms. It is important that counsel become familiar with their clients' information systems and digital data—including social media—to address these issues. A party urging that preservation requests are disproportionate may need to provide specifics about these matters in order to enable meaningful dis-cussion of the appropriate preservation regime.

When a party fails to take reasonable steps to preserve electronically stored infor-mation that should have been preserved in the anticipation or conduct of litigation, and the information is lost as a result, Rule 37(e) directs that the initial focus should be on whether the lost information can be restored or replaced through additional discovery. Nothing in the rule limits the court's powers under Rules 16 and 26 to authorize additional discovery. Orders under Rule 26(b)(2)(B) regarding discov- ery from sources that would ordinarily be considered inaccessible or under Rule 26(c)(1)(B) on allocation of expenses may be pertinent to solving such problems. If the information is restored or replaced, no further measures should be taken. At the same time, it is important to emphasize that efforts to restore or replace lost infor-mation through discovery should be proportional to the apparent importance of the lost information to claims or defenses in the litigation. For example, substantial mea-sures should not be employed to restore or replace information that is marginally relevant or duplicative. * * *

TITLE VI.   TRIALS

RULE 38.   RIGHT TO A JURY TRIAL; DEMAND.

(a) Right Preserved.

The right of trial by jury as declared by the Seventh Amendment to the Constitution—or as provided by a federal statute—is preserved to the parties inviolate.

(b) Demand.

On any issue triable of right by a jury, a party may demand a jury trial by:

(1) serving the other parties with a written demand—which may be included in a pleading—no later than 14 days after the last pleading directed to the issue is served; and

(2) filing the demand in accordance with Rule 5(d).

(c) Specifying Issues.

In its demand, a party may specify the issues that it wishes to have tried by a jury; otherwise, it is considered to have demanded a jury trial on all the issues so triable. If the party has demanded a jury trial on only some issues, any other party may—within 14 days after being served with the demand or within a shorter time ordered by the court—serve a demand for a jury trial on any other or all factual issues triable by jury.

(d) Waiver; Withdrawal.

A party waives a jury trial unless its demand is properly served and filed. A proper demand may be withdrawn only if the parties consent.

(e) Admiralty and Maritime Claims.

These rules do not create a right to a jury trial on issues in a claim that is an admiralty or maritime claim under Rule 9(h).

[*Adopted Dec. 20, 1937, effective Sept. 16, 1938; amended Feb. 28, 1966, effective July 1, 1966; Mar. 2, 1987, effective Aug. 1, 1987; Apr. 22, 1993, effective Dec. 1, 1993; amended April 30, 2007, effective Dec. 1, 2007; amended March 26, 2009, effective Dec. 1, 2009.*]

RULE 39. TRIAL BY JURY OR BY THE COURT.

(a) When a Demand Is Made.

When a jury trial has been demanded under Rule 38, the action must be designated on the docket as a jury action. The trial on all issues so demanded must be by jury unless:

> (1) the parties or their attorneys file a stipulation to a nonjury trial or so stipulate on the record; or

> (2) the court, on motion or on its own, finds that on some or all of those issues there is no federal right to a jury trial.

(b) When No Demand Is Made.

Issues on which a jury trial is not properly demanded are to be tried by the court. But the court may, on motion, order a jury trial on any issue for which a jury might have been demanded.

(c) Advisory Jury; Jury Trial by Consent.

In an action not triable of right by a jury, the court, on motion or on its own:

> (1) may try any issue with an advisory jury; or

> (2) may, with the parties' consent, try any issue by a jury whose verdict has the same effect as if a jury trial had been a matter of right, unless the action is against the United States and a federal statute provides for a nonjury trial.

[*Adopted Dec. 20, 1937, effective Sept. 16, 1938; amended July 30, 2007, effective Dec. 1, 2007.*]

RULE 40. SCHEDULING CASES FOR TRIAL.

Each court must provide by rule for scheduling trials. The court must give priority to actions entitled to priority by a federal statute.

[*Adopted Dec. 20, 1937, effective Sept. 16, 1938; amended April 30, 2007, effective Dec. 1, 2007.*]

RULE 41.　DISMISSAL OF ACTIONS.

(a) Voluntary Dismissal.

(1) *By the Plaintiff.*

(A) *Without a Court Order.*

Subject to Rules 23(e), 23.1(c), 23.2, and 66 and any applicable federal statute, the plaintiff may dismiss an action without a court order by filing:

(i) a notice of dismissal before the opposing party serves either an answer or a motion for summary judgment; or

(ii) a stipulation of dismissal signed by all parties who have appeared.

(B) *Effect.*

Unless the notice or stipulation states otherwise, the dismissal is without prejudice. But if the plaintiff previously dismissed any federal- or state-court action based on or including the same claim, a notice of dismissal operates as an adjudication on the merits.

(2) *By Court Order; Effect.*

Except as provided in Rule 41(a)(1), an action may be dismissed at the plaintiff's request only by court order, on terms that the court considers proper. If a defendant has pleaded a counterclaim before being served with the plaintiff's motion to dismiss, the action may be dismissed over the defendant's objection only if the counterclaim can remain pending for independent adjudication. Unless the order states otherwise, a dismissal under this paragraph (2) is without prejudice.

(b) Involuntary Dismissal; Effect.

If the plaintiff fails to prosecute or to comply with these rules or a court order, a defendant may move to dismiss the action or any claim against it. Unless the dismissal order states otherwise, a dismissal under this subdivision (b) and any dismissal not under this rule—except one for lack of jurisdiction, improper venue, or failure to join a party under Rule 19—operates as an adjudication on the merits.

(c) Dismissing a Counterclaim, Crossclaim, or Third-Party Claim.

This rule applies to a dismissal of any counterclaim, crossclaim, or third-party claim. A claimant's voluntary dismissal under Rule 41(a)(1)(A)(i) must be made:

(1) before a responsive pleading is served; or

(2) if there is no responsive pleading, before evidence is introduced at a hearing or trial.

(d) Costs of a Previously Dismissed Action.

If a plaintiff who previously dismissed an action in any court files an action based on or including the same claim against the same defendant, the court:

(1) may order the plaintiff to pay all or part of the costs of that previous action; and

(2) may stay the proceedings until the plaintiff has complied.

[*Adopted Dec. 20, 1937, effective Sept. 16, 1938; amended Dec. 27, 1946, effective Mar. 19, 1948; Jan. 21, 1963, effective July 1, 1963; Feb. 28, 1966, effective July 1, 1966; Dec. 4, 1967, effective July 1, 1968; Mar. 2, 1987, effective Aug. 1, 1987; Apr. 30, 1991, effective Dec. 1, 1991; amended April 30, 2007, effective Dec. 1, 2007.*]

RULE 42.   CONSOLIDATION; SEPARATE TRIALS.

(a) Consolidation.

If actions before the court involve a common question of law or fact, the court may:

(1) join for hearing or trial any or all matters at issue in the actions;

(2) consolidate the actions; or

(3) issue any other orders to avoid unnecessary cost or delay.

(b) Separate Trials.

For convenience, to avoid prejudice, or to expedite and economize, the court may order a separate trial of one or more separate issues, claims, crossclaims, counterclaims, or third-party claims. When ordering a separate trial, the court must preserve any federal right to a jury trial.

[*Adopted Dec. 20, 1937, effective Sept. 16, 1938; amended Feb. 28, 1966, effective July 1, 1966; amended April 30, 2007, effective Dec. 1, 2007.*]

RULE 43.   TAKING TESTIMONY.

(a) In Open Court.

At trial, the witnesses' testimony must be taken in open court unless a federal statute, the Federal Rules of Evidence, these rules, or other rules adopted by the Supreme Court provide otherwise. For good cause in compelling circumstances and with appropriate safeguards, the court may permit testimony in open court by contemporaneous transmission from a different location.

(b) Affirmation Instead of an Oath.

When these rules require an oath, a solemn affirmation suffices.

(c) Evidence on a Motion.

When a motion relies on facts outside the record, the court may hear the matter on affidavits or may hear it wholly or partly on oral testimony or on depositions.

(d) Interpreter.

The court may appoint an interpreter of its choosing; fix reasonable compensation to be paid from funds provided by law or by one or more parties; and tax the compensation as costs.

[*Adopted Dec. 20, 1937, effective Sept. 16, 1938; amended Feb. 28, 1966, effective July 1, 1966; Nov. 20, 1972, and Dec. 18, 1972, effective July 1, 1975; Mar. 2, 1987, effective Aug. 1, 1987; Apr. 23, 1996, effective Dec. 1, 1996; amended April 30, 2007, effective Dec. 1, 2007.*]

RULE 44. PROVING AN OFFICIAL RECORD.

(a) Means of Proving.

(1) *Domestic Record.*

Each of the following evidences an official record—or an entry in it—that is otherwise admissible and is kept within the United States, any state, district, or commonwealth, or any territory subject to the administrative or judicial jurisdiction of the United States:

> (A) an official publication of the record; or

> (B) a copy attested by the officer with legal custody of the record—or by the officer's deputy—and accompanied by a certificate that the officer has custody. The certificate must be made under seal:

>> (i) by a judge of a court of record in the district or political subdivision where the record is kept; or

>> (ii) by any public officer with a seal of office and with official duties in the district or political subdivision where the record is kept.

(2) *Foreign Record.*

(A) *In General.*

Each of the following evidences a foreign official record—or an entry in it—that is otherwise admissible:

>> (i) an official publication of the record; or

>> (ii) the record—or a copy—that is attested by an authorized person and is accompanied either by a final certification of genuineness or by a certification under a treaty or convention to which the United States and the country where the record is located are parties.

(B) *Final Certification of Genuineness.*

A final certification must certify the genuineness of the signature and official position of the attester or of any foreign official whose certificate of genuineness relates to the attestation or is in a chain of certificates of genuineness relating to the attestation. A final certification may be made by a secretary of a United States embassy or legation; by a consul general, vice consul, or consular agent of the United States; or by a diplomatic or consular official of the foreign country assigned or accredited to the United States.

(C) *Other Means of Proof.*

If all parties have had a reasonable opportunity to investigate a foreign record's authenticity and accuracy, the court may, for good cause, either:

(i) admit an attested copy without final certification; or

(ii) permit the record to be evidenced by an attested summary with or without a final certification.

(b) Lack of a Record.

A written statement that a diligent search of designated records revealed no record or entry of a specified tenor is admissible as evidence that the records contain no such record or entry. For domestic records, the statement must be authenticated under Rule 44(a)(1). For foreign records, the statement must comply with (a)(2)(C)(ii).

(c) Other Proof.

A party may prove an official record—or an entry or lack of an entry in it—by any other method authorized by law.

[*Adopted Dec. 20, 1937, effective Sept. 16, 1938; amended Feb. 28, 1966, effective July 1, 1966; Mar. 2, 1987, effective Aug. 1, 1987; Apr. 30, 1991, effective Dec. 1, 1991; amended April 30, 2007, effective Dec. 1, 2007.*]

RULE 44.1. DETERMINING FOREIGN LAW.

A party who intends to raise an issue about a foreign country's law must give notice by a pleading or other writing. In determining foreign law, the court may consider any relevant material or source, including testimony, whether or not submitted by a party or admissible under the Federal Rules of Evidence. The court's determination must be treated as a ruling on a question of law.

[*Adopted Feb. 28, 1966, effective July 1, 1966; amended Nov. 20, 1972, effective July 1, 1975; Mar. 2, 1987, effective Aug. 1, 1987; amended April 30, 2007, effective Dec. 1, 2007.*]

RULE 45. SUBPOENA.

(a) In General.

(1) *Form and Contents.*

(A) *Requirements—In General.*

Every subpoena must:

(i) state the court from which it issued;

(ii) state the title of the action and its civil-action number;

(iii) command each person to whom it is directed to do the following at a specified time and place: attend and testify; produce designated documents, electronically stored information, or tangible things in that person's possession, custody, or control; or permit the inspection of premises; and

(iv) set out the text of Rule 45(d) and (e).

(B) *Command to Attend a Deposition—Notice of the Recording Method.*

A subpoena commanding attendance at a deposition must state the method for recording the testimony.

(C) *Combining or Separating a Command to Produce or to Permit Inspection; Specifying the Form for Electronically Stored Information.*

A command to produce documents, electronically stored information, or tangible things or to permit the inspection of premises may be included in a subpoena commanding attendance at a deposition, hearing, or trial, or may be set out in a separate subpoena. A subpoena may specify the form or forms in which electronically stored information is to be produced.

(D) *Command to Produce; Included Obligations.*

A command in a subpoena to produce documents, electronically stored information, or tangible things requires the responding party to permit inspection, copying, testing, or sampling of the materials.

(2) *Issuing Court.*

A subpoena must issue from the court where the action is pending.

(3) *Issued by Whom.*

The clerk must issue a subpoena, signed but otherwise in blank, to a party who requests it. That party must complete it before service. An attorney also may issue and sign a subpoena if the attorney is authorized to practice in the issuing court.

(4) *Notice to Other Parties Before Service.*

If the subpoena commands the production of documents, electronically stored information, or tangible things or the inspection of premises before trial, then before it is served on the person to whom it is directed, a notice and a copy of the subpoena must be served on each party.

(b) Service.

(1) *By Whom and How; Tendering Fees.*

Any person who is at least 18 years old and not a party may serve a subpoena. Serving a subpoena requires delivering a copy to the named person and, if the subpoena requires that person's attendance, tendering the fees for 1 day's attendance and the mileage allowed by law. Fees and mileage need not be tendered when the subpoena issues on behalf of the United States or any of its officers or agencies.

(2) *Service in the United States.*

A subpoena may be served at any place within the United States.

(3) *Service in a Foreign Country.*

28 U.S.C. § 1783 governs issuing and serving a subpoena directed to a United States national or resident who is in a foreign country.

(4) *Proof of Service.*

Proving service, when necessary, requires filing with the issuing court a statement showing the date and manner of service and the names of the persons served. The statement must be certified by the server.

(c) Place of Compliance.

(1) *For a Trial, Hearing, or Deposition.*

A subpoena may command a person to attend a trial, hearing, or deposition only as follows:

(A) within 100 miles of where the person resides, is employed, or regularly transacts business in person; or

(B) within the state where the person resides, is employed, or regularly transacts business in person, if the person

(i) is a party or a party's officer; or

(ii) is commanded to attend a trial and would not incur substantial expense.

(2) *For Other Discovery.*

A subpoena may command:

(A) production of documents, electronically stored information, or tangible things at a place within 100 miles of where the person resides, is employed, or regularly transacts business in person; and

(B) inspection of premises at the premises to be inspected.

(d) Protecting a Person Subject to a Subpoena; Enforcement.

(1) *Avoiding Undue Burden or Expense; Sanctions.*

A party or attorney responsible for issuing and serving a subpoena must take reasonable steps to avoid imposing undue burden or expense on a person subject to the subpoena. The court for the district where compliance is required must enforce this duty and impose an appropriate sanction—which may include lost earnings and reasonable attorney's fees—on a party or attorney who fails to comply.

(2) *Command to Produce Materials or Permit Inspection.*

(A) *Appearance Not Required.*

A person commanded to produce documents, electronically stored information, or tangible things, or to permit the inspection of premises, need not appear in person at the place of production or inspection unless also commanded to appear for a deposition, hearing, or trial.

(B) *Objections.*

A person commanded to produce documents or tangible things or to permit inspection may serve on the party or attorney designated in the subpoena a written objection to inspecting, copying, testing, or sampling any or all of the materials or to inspecting the premises—or to producing electronically stored information in the form or forms requested. The objection must be served before the earlier of the time specified for compliance or 14 days after the subpoena is served. If an objection is made, the following rules apply:

> (i) At any time, on notice to the commanded person, the serving party may move the court for the district where compliance is required for an order compelling production or inspection.

> (ii) These acts may be required only as directed in the order, and the order must protect a person who is neither a party nor a party's officer from significant expense resulting from compliance.

(3) *Quashing or Modifying a Subpoena.*

(A) *When Required.*

On timely motion, the court for the district where compliance is required must quash or modify a subpoena that:

> (i) fails to allow a reasonable time to comply;

> (ii) requires a person to comply beyond the geographical limits specified in Rule 45(c);

> (iii) requires disclosure of privileged or other protected matter, if no exception or waiver applies; or

> (iv) subjects a person to undue burden.

(B) *When Permitted.*

To protect a person subject to or affected by a subpoena, the court for the district where compliance is required may, on motion, quash or modify the subpoena if it requires:

> (i) disclosing a trade secret or other confidential research, development, or commercial information; or

> (ii) disclosing an unretained expert's opinion or information that does not describe specific occurrences in dispute and results from the expert's study that was not requested by a party.

(C) *Specifying Conditions as an Alternative.*

In the circumstances described in Rule 45(d)(3)(B), the court may, instead of quashing or modifying a subpoena, order appearance or production under specified conditions if the serving party:

> (i) shows a substantial need for the testimony or material that cannot be otherwise met without undue hardship; and

> (ii) ensures that the subpoenaed person will be reasonably compensated.

(e) Duties in Responding to a Subpoena.

(1) *Producing Documents or Electronically Stored Information.*

These procedures apply to producing documents or electronically stored information:

(A) *Documents.*

A person responding to a subpoena to produce documents must produce them as they are kept in the ordinary course of business or must organize and label them to correspond to the categories in the demand.

(B) *Form for Producing Electronically Stored Information Not Specified.*

If a subpoena does not specify a form for producing electronically stored information, the person responding must produce it in a form or forms in which it is ordinarily maintained or in a reasonably usable form or forms.

(C) *Electronically Stored Information Produced in Only One Form.*

The person responding need not produce the same electronically stored information in more than one form.

(D) *Inaccessible Electronically Stored Information.*

The person responding need not provide discovery of electronically stored information from sources that the person identifies as not reasonably accessible because of undue burden or cost. On motion to compel discovery or for a protective order, the person responding must show that the information is not reasonably accessible because of undue burden or cost. If that showing is made, the court may nonetheless order discovery from such sources if the requesting party shows good cause, considering the limitations of Rule 26(b)(2)(C). The court may specify conditions for the discovery.

(2) *Claiming Privilege or Protection.*

(A) *Information Withheld.*

A person withholding subpoenaed information under a claim that it is privileged or subject to protection as trial-preparation material must:

> (i) expressly make the claim; and

> (ii) describe the nature of the withheld documents, communications, or tangible things in a manner that, without revealing information itself privileged or protected, will enable the parties to assess the claim.

(B) *Information Produced.*

If information produced in response to a subpoena is subject to a claim of privilege or of protection as trial-preparation material, the person making the claim may notify any party that received the information of the claim and the basis for it. After being notified, a party must promptly return, sequester, or destroy the specified information and any copies it has; must not use or disclose the information until the claim is resolved; must take reasonable steps to retrieve the information if the party disclosed it before being notified; and may promptly present the information under seal to the court for the district where compliance is required for a determination of the claim. The person who produced the information must preserve the information until the claim is resolved.

(f) **Transferring a Subpoena-Related Motion.**

When the court where compliance is required did not issue the subpoena, it may transfer a motion under this rule to the issuing court if the person subject to the subpoena consents or if the court finds exceptional circumstances. Then, if the attorney for a person subject to a subpoena is authorized to practice in the court where the motion was made, the attorney may file papers and appear on the motion as an officer of the issuing court. To enforce its order, the issuing court may transfer the order to the court where the motion was made.

(g) **Contempt.**

The court for the district where compliance is required—and also, after a motion is transferred, the issuing court—may hold in contempt a person who, having been served, fails without adequate excuse to obey the subpoena or an order related to it.

[*Adopted Dec. 20, 1937, effective Sept. 16, 1938; as amended Apr. 16, 2013, effective Dec. 1, 2013.*]

ADVISORY COMMITTEE'S NOTE TO 2006 AMENDMENT TO RULE 45

Rule 45 is amended to conform the provisions for subpoenas to changes in other discovery rules, largely related to discovery of electronically stored information. Rule 34 is amended to provide in greater detail for the production of electronically stored information. Rule 45(a)(1)(C) is amended to recognize that electronically stored information, as defined in Rule 34(a), can also be sought by subpoena. Like Rule 34(b), Rule 45(a)(l) is amended to provide that the subpoena can designate a form or forms for production of electronic data. Rule 45(c)(2) is amended, like Rule 34(b), to authorize the person served with a subpoena to object to the requested form or forms. In addition, as under Rule 34(b), Rule 45(d)(1)(B) is amended to provide that if the subpoena does not specify the form or forms for electronically stored information, the person served with the subpoena must produce electronically stored information in a form or forms in which it is usually maintained or in a form or forms that are reasonably usable. Rule 45(d)(1)(C) is added to provide that the person producing electronically stored information should not have to produce the same information in more than one form unless so ordered by the court for good cause.

As with discovery of electronically stored information from parties, complying with a subpoena for such information may impose burdens on the responding person. Rule 45(c) provides protection against undue impositions on nonparties. For example, Rule 45(c)(l) directs that a party serving a subpoena "shall take reasonable steps to avoid imposing undue burden or expense on a person subject to the subpoena," and Rule 45(c)(2)(B) permits the person served with the subpoena to object to it and directs that an order requiring compliance "shall protect a person who is neither a party nor a party's officer from significant expense resulting from" compliance. Rule 45(d)(l)(D) is added to provide that the responding person need not provide discovery of electronically stored information from sources the party identifies as not reasonably accessible, unless the court orders such discovery for good cause, considering the limitations of Rule 26(b)(2)(C), on terms that protect a nonparty against significant expense. A parallel provision is added to Rule 26(b)(2).

Rule 45(a)(1)(B) is also amended, as is Rule 34(a), to provide that a subpoena is available to permit testing and sampling as well as inspection and copying. As in Rule 34, this change recognizes that on occasion the opportunity to perform testing or sampling may be important, both for documents and for electronically stored information. Because testing or sampling may present particular issues of burden or intrusion for the person served with the subpoena, however, the protective provisions of Rule 45(c) should be enforced with vigilance when such demands are made. Inspection or testing of certain types of electronically stored information or of a person's electronic information system may raise issues of confidentiality or privacy. The addition of sampling and testing to Rule 45(a) with regard to documents and electronically stored information is not meant to create a routine right of direct access to a person's electronic information system, although such access might be justified in some circumstances. Courts should guard against undue intrusiveness resulting from inspecting or testing such systems.

Rule 45(d)(2) is amended, as is Rule 26(b)(5), to add a procedure for assertion of privilege or of protection as trial-preparation materials after production. The receiving party may submit the information to the court for resolution of the privilege claim, as under Rule 26(b)(5)(B).

Other minor amendments are made to conform the rule to the changes described above.

ADVISORY COMMITTEE'S NOTES TO 1991 AMENDMENT OF RULE 45

Purposes of Revision. The purposes of this revision are (1) to clarify and enlarge the protections afforded persons who are required to assist the court by giving information or evidence; (2) to facilitate access outside the deposition procedure provided by Rule 30 to documents and other information in the possession of persons who are not parties; (3) to facilitate service of subpoenas for depositions or productions of evidence at places distant from the district in which an action is proceeding; (4) to enable the court to compel a witness found within the state in which the court sits to attend trial; (5) to clarify the organization of the text of the rule.

Subdivision (a). This subdivision is amended in seven significant respects.

First, Paragraph (a)(3) modifies the requirement that a subpoena be issued by the clerk of court. Provision is made for the issuance of subpoenas by attorneys as officers of the court. This revision perhaps culminates an evolution. Subpoenas were long issued by specific order of the court. As this became a burden to the court, general orders were made authorizing clerks to issue subpoenas on request. Since 1948, they have been issued in blank by the clerk of any federal court to any lawyer, the clerk serving as stationer to the bar. In allowing counsel to issue the subpoena, the rule is merely a recognition of present reality.

Although the subpoena is in a sense the command of the attorney who completes the form, defiance of a subpoena is nevertheless an act in defiance of a court order and exposes the defiant witness to contempt sanctions. * * *

Necessarily accompanying the evolution of this power of the lawyer as officer of the court is the development of increased responsibility and liability for the misuse of this power. The latter development is reflected in the provisions of subdivision (c) of this rule, and also in the requirement imposed by paragraph (3) of this subdivision that the attorney issuing a subpoena must sign it.

Second, Paragraph (a)(3) authorizes attorneys in distant districts to serve as officers authorized to issue commands in the name of the court. Any attorney permitted to represent a client in a federal court, even one admitted pro haec vice, has the same authority as a clerk to issue a subpoena from any federal court for the district in which the subpoena is served and enforced. In authorizing attorneys to issue subpoenas from distant courts, the amended rule effectively authorizes service of a subpoena anywhere in the United States by an attorney representing any party. This change is intended to ease the administrative burdens of inter-district law practice. The former rule resulted in delay and expense caused by the need to secure forms from clerks' offices some distance from the place at which the action proceeds. This change does not enlarge the burden on the witness.

Pursuant to Paragraph (a)(2), a subpoena for a deposition must still issue from the court in which the deposition or production would be compelled. Accordingly, a motion to quash such a subpoena if it overbears the limits of the subpoena power must, as under the previous rule, be presented to the court for the district in which the deposition would occur. Likewise, the court in whose name the subpoena is issued is responsible for its enforcement.

Third, in order to relieve attorneys of the need to secure an appropriate seal to affix to a subpoena issued as an officer of a distant court, the requirement that a subpoena be under seal is abolished by the provisions of Paragraph (a)(1).

Fourth, Paragraph (a)(1) authorizes the issuance of a subpoena to compel a non-party to produce evidence independent of any deposition. This revision spares the necessity of a deposition of the custodian of evidentiary material required to be produced. A party seeking additional production from a person subject to such a subpoena may serve an additional subpoena requiring additional production at the same time and place.

Fifth, Paragraph (a)(2) makes clear that the person subject to the subpoena is required to produce materials in that person's control whether or not the materials are located within the district or within the territory within which the subpoena can be served. The non-party witness is subject to the same scope of discovery under this rule as that person would be as a party to whom a request is addressed pursuant to Rule 34.

Sixth, Paragraph (a)(1) requires that the subpoena include a statement of the rights and duties of witnesses by setting forth in full the text of the new subdivisions (c) and (d).

Seventh, the revised rule authorizes the issuance of a subpoena to compel the inspection of premises in the possession of a non-party. Rule 34 has authorized such inspections of premises in the possession of a party as discovery compelled under Rule 37, but prior practice required an independent proceeding to secure such relief ancillary to the federal proceeding when the premises were not in the possession of a party. Practice in some states has long authorized such use of a subpoena for this purpose without apparent adverse consequence.

*   *   *

Subdivision (c). This provision is new and states the rights of witnesses. It is not intended to diminish rights conferred by Rules 26–37 or any other authority.

Paragraph (c)(1) gives specific application to the principle stated in Rule 26(g) and specifies liability for earnings lost by a non-party witness as a result of a misuse of the subpoena. No change in existing law is thereby effected. Abuse of a subpoena is an actionable tort, *Board of Ed. v. Farmingdale Classroom Teach. Ass'n,* 38 N.Y.2d 397, 380 N.Y.S.2d 635, 343 N.E.2d 278 (1975), and the duty of the attorney to the non-party is also embodied in Model Rule of Professional Conduct 4.4. The liability of the attorney is correlative to the expanded power of the attorney to issue subpoenas. The liability may include the cost of fees to collect attorneys' fees owed as a result of a breach of this duty.

Paragraph (c)(2) retains language from the former subdivision (b) and paragraph (d)(1). The 10-day period for response to a subpoena is extended to 14 days to avoid the complex calculations associated with short time periods under Rule 6 and to allow a bit more time for such objections to be made.

A non-party required to produce documents or materials is protected against significant expense resulting from involuntary assistance to the court. This provision applies, for example, to a non-party required to provide a list of class members. The court is not required to fix the costs in advance of production, although this will often be the most satisfactory accommodation to protect the party seeking discovery from excessive costs. In some instances, it may be preferable to leave uncertain costs to be determined after the materials have been produced, provided that the risk of uncertainty is fully disclosed to the discovering party. See, *e.g., United States v. Columbia Broadcasting System, Inc.* 666 F.2d 364 (9th Cir. 1982).

Paragraph (c)(3) explicitly authorizes the quashing of a subpoena as a means of protecting a witness from misuse of the subpoena power. It replaces and enlarges on the former subdivision (b) of this rule and tracks the provisions of Rule 26(c). While largely repetitious, this rule is addressed to the witness who may read it on the subpoena, where it is required to be printed by the revised paragraph (a)(1) of this rule.

Subparagraph (c)(3)(A) identifies those circumstances in which a subpoena must be quashed or modified. It restates the former provisions with respect to the limits of mandatory travel that are set forth in the former paragraphs (d)(2) and (e)(1), with one important change. Under the revised rule, a federal court can compel a witness to come from any place in the state to attend trial, whether or not the local state law so provides. This extension is subject to the qualification provided in the next paragraph, which authorizes the court to condition enforcement of a subpoena compelling a non-party witness to bear substantial expense to attend trial. The traveling non-party witness may be entitled to reasonable compensation for the time and effort entailed.

Clause (c)(3)(A)(iv) requires the court to protect all persons from undue burden imposed by the use of the subpoena power. Illustratively, it might be unduly burdensome to compel an adversary to attend trial as a witness if the adversary is known to have no personal knowledge of matters in dispute, especially so if the adversary would be required to incur substantial travel burdens.

Subparagraph (c)(3)(B) identifies circumstances in which a subpoena should be quashed unless the party serving the subpoena shows a substantial need and the court can devise an appropriate accommodation to protect the interests of the witness. An additional circumstance in which such action is required is a request for costly production of documents; that situation is expressly governed by subparagraph (b)(2)(B).

Clause (c)(3)(B)(i) authorizes the court to quash, modify, or condition a subpoena to protect the person subject to or affected by the subpoena from unnecessary or unduly harmful disclosures of confidential information. It corresponds to Rule 26(c)(7).

Clause (c)(3)(B)(ii) provides appropriate protection for the intellectual property of the non-party witness; it does not apply to the expert retained by a party, whose information is subject to the provisions of Rule 26(b)(4). A growing problem has been the use of subpoenas to compel the giving of evidence and information by unretained experts. Experts are not exempt from the duty to give evidence, even if they cannot be compelled to prepare themselves to give effective testimony, *e.g.*, *Carter-Wallace, Inc. v. Otte*, 474 F.2d 529 (2d Cir. 1972), but compulsion to give evidence may threaten the intellectual property of experts denied the opportunity to bargain for the value of their services. See generally Maurer, *Compelling the Expert Witness: Fairness and Utility Under the Federal Rules of Civil Procedure*, 19 GA.L.REV. 71 (1984); Note, *Discovery and Testimony of Unretained Experts*, 1987 DUKE L.J. 140. Arguably the compulsion to testify can be regarded as a "taking" of intellectual property. The rule establishes the right of such persons to withhold their expertise, at least unless the party seeking it makes the kind of showing required for a conditional denial of a motion to quash as provided in the final sentence of subparagraph (c)(3)

(B); that requirement is the same as that necessary to secure work product under Rule 26(b)(3) and gives assurance of reasonable compensation. The Rule thus approves the accommodation of competing interests exemplified in *United States v. Columbia Broadcasting System, Inc.*, 666 F.2d 364 (9th Cir. 1982). See also *Wright v. Jeep Corporation*, 547 F.Supp. 871 (E.D. Mich. 1982).

As stated in *Kaufman v. Edelstein*, 539 F.2d 811, 822 (2d Cir. 1976), the district court's discretion in these matters should be informed by "the degree to which the expert is being called because of his knowledge of facts relevant to the case rather than in order to give opinion testimony; the difference between testifying to a previously formed or expressed opinion and forming a new one; the possibility that, for other reasons, the witness is a unique expert; the extent to which the calling party is able to show the unlikelihood that any comparable witness will willingly testify; and the degree to which the witness is able to show that he has been oppressed by having continually to testify. . . ."

Clause (c)(3)(B)(iii) protects non-party witnesses who may be burdened to perform the duty to travel in order to provide testimony at trial. The provision requires the court to condition a subpoena requiring travel of more than 100 miles on reasonable compensation.

Subdivision (d). This provision is new. Paragraph (d)(1) extends to non-parties the duty imposed on parties by the last paragraph of Rule 34(b), which was added in 1980.

Paragraph (d)(2) is new. . . . Its purpose is to provide a party whose discovery is constrained by a claim of privilege or work product protection with information sufficient to evaluate such a claim and to resist if it seems unjustified. The person claiming a privilege or protection cannot decide the limits of that party's own entitlement.

A party receiving a discovery request who asserts a privilege or protection but fails to disclose that claim is at risk of waiving the privilege or protection. A person claiming a privilege or protection who fails to provide adequate information about the privilege or protection claim to the party seeking the information is subject to an order to show cause why the person should not be held in contempt under subdivision (e). Motions for such orders and responses to motions are subject to the sanctions provisions of Rules 7 and 11.

A person served a subpoena that is too broad may be faced with a burdensome task to provide full information regarding all that person's claims to privilege or work product protection. Such a person is entitled to protection that may be secured through an objection made pursuant to subparagraph (c)(2).

Subdivision (e). This provision retains most of the language of the former subdivision (f).

"Adequate cause" for a failure to obey a subpoena remains undefined. In at least some circumstances, a non-party might be guilty of contempt for refusing to obey a subpoena even though the subpoena manifestly overreaches the appropriate limits of the subpoena power. *E.g., Walker v. City of Birmingham*, 388 U.S. 307 (1967). But, because the command of the subpoena is not in fact one uttered by a judicial officer, contempt should be very sparingly applied when the non-party witness has been overborne by a party or attorney. The language added to subdivision (f) is intended to assure that result where a non-party has been commanded, on the signature of an attorney, to travel greater distances than can be compelled pursuant to this rule.

RULE 46.   OBJECTING TO A RULING OR ORDER.

A formal exception to a ruling or order is unnecessary. When the ruling or order is requested or made, a party need only state the action that it wants the court to take or objects to, along with the grounds for the request or objection. Failing to object does not prejudice a party who had no opportunity to do so when the ruling or order was made.

[*Adopted Dec. 20, 1937, effective Sept. 16, 1938; amended Mar. 2, 1987, effective Aug. 1, 1987; amended April 30, 2007, effective Dec. 1, 2007.*]

RULE 47.   SELECTING JURORS.

(a) Examining Jurors.

The court may permit the parties or their attorneys to examine prospective jurors or may itself do so. If the court examines the jurors, it must permit the parties or their attorneys to make any further inquiry it considers proper, or must itself ask any of their additional questions it considers proper.

(b) Peremptory Challenges.

The court must allow the number of peremptory challenges provided by 28 U.S.C. § 1870.

(c) Excusing a Juror.

During trial or deliberation, the court may excuse a juror for good cause. [*Adopted Dec. 20, 1937, effective Sept. 16, 1938; amended Feb. 28, 1966, effective July 1, 1966; Apr. 30, 1991, effective Dec. 1, 1991; amended April 30, 2007, effective Dec. 1, 2007.*]

RULE 48.   NUMBER OF JURORS; VERDICT.

(a) Number of Jurors.

A jury must begin with at least 6 and no more than 12 members, and each juror must participate in the verdict unless excused under Rule 47(c).

(b) Verdict.

Unless the parties stipulate otherwise, the verdict must be unanimous and must be returned by a jury of at least 6 members.

(c) Polling.

After a verdict is returned but before the jury is discharged, the court must on a party's request, or may on its own, poll the jurors individually. If the poll reveals a lack of unanimity or lack of assent by the number of jurors that the parties stipulated to, the court may direct the jury to deliberate further or may order a new trial.

[*Adopted Dec. 20, 1937, effective Sept. 16, 1938; amended Apr. 30, 1991, effective Dec. 1, 1991; amended April 30, 2007, effective Dec. 1, 2007; amended March 26, 2009, effective Dec. 1, 2009.*]

RULE 49.   SPECIAL VERDICT; GENERAL VERDICT AND QUESTIONS.

(a) Special Verdict.

(1) *In General.*

The court may require a jury to return only a special verdict in the form of a special written finding on each issue of fact. The court may do so by:

> (A) submitting written questions susceptible of a categorical or other brief answer;

> (B) submitting written forms of the special findings that might properly be made under the pleadings and evidence; or

> (C) using any other method that the court considers appropriate.

(2) *Instructions.*

The court must give the instructions and explanations necessary to enable the jury to make its findings on each submitted issue.

(3) *Issues Not Submitted.*

A party waives the right to a jury trial on any issue of fact raised by the pleadings or evidence but not submitted to the jury unless, before the jury retires, the party demands its submission to the jury. If the party does not demand submission, the court may make a finding on the issue. If the court makes no finding, it is considered to have made a finding consistent with its judgment on the special verdict.

(b) General Verdict with Answers to Written Questions.

(1) *In General.*

The court may submit to the jury forms for a general verdict, together with written questions on one or more issues of fact that the jury must decide. The court must give the instructions and explanations necessary to enable the jury to render a general verdict and answer the questions in writing, and must direct the jury to do both.

(2) *Verdict and Answers Consistent.*

When the general verdict and the answers are consistent, the court must approve, for entry under Rule 58, an appropriate judgment on the verdict and answers.

(3) *Answers Inconsistent with the Verdict.*

When the answers are consistent with each other but one or more is inconsistent with the general verdict, the court may:

>   (A) approve, for entry under Rule 58, an appropriate judgment according to the answers, notwithstanding the general verdict;

>   (B) direct the jury to further consider its answers and verdict; or

>   (C) order a new trial.

(4) *Answers Inconsistent with Each Other and the Verdict.*

When the answers are inconsistent with each other and one or more is also inconsistent with the general verdict, judgment must not be entered; instead, the court must direct the jury to further consider its answers and verdict, or must order a new trial.

[*Adopted Dec. 20, 1937, effective Sept. 16, 1938; amended Jan. 21, 1963, effective July 1, 1963; Mar. 2, 1987, effective Aug. 1, 1987; amended April 30, 2007, effective Dec. 1, 2007.*]

RULE 50. JUDGMENT AS A MATTER OF LAW IN A JURY TRIAL; RELATED MOTION FOR A NEW TRIAL; CONDITIONAL RULING.

(a) Judgment as a Matter of Law.

(1) *In General.*

If a party has been fully heard on an issue during a jury trial and the court finds that a reasonable jury would not have a legally sufficient evidentiary basis to find for the party on that issue, the court may:

>   (A) resolve the issue against the party; and

>   (B) grant a motion for judgment as a matter of law against the party on a claim or defense that, under the controlling law, can be maintained or defeated only with a favorable finding on that issue.

(2) *Motion.*

A motion for judgment as a matter of law may be made at any time before the case is submitted to the jury. The motion must specify the judgment sought and the law and facts that entitle the movant to the judgment.

(b) Renewing the Motion After Trial; Alternative Motion for a New Trial.

If the court does not grant a motion for judgment as a matter of law made under Rule 50(a), the court is considered to have submitted the action to the jury subject to the court's later deciding the legal questions raised by the motion. No later than 28 days after the entry of judgment—or if the motion addresses a jury issue not decided by a verdict, no later than 28 days after the jury was discharged—the movant may file a renewed motion for judgment as a matter of law and may include an alternative or joint request a new trial under Rule 59. In ruling on the renewed motion, the court may:

(1) allow the judgment on the verdict, if the jury returned a verdict;

(2) order a new trial; or

(3) direct the entry of judgment as a matter of law.

(c) Granting the Renewed Motion; Conditional Ruling on a motion for a New Trial.

(1) *In General.*

If the court grants a renewed motion for judgment as a matter of law, it must also conditionally rule on any motion for a new trial by determining whether a new trial should be granted if the judgment is later vacated or reversed. The court must state the grounds for conditionally granting or denying the motion for a new trial.

(2) *Effect of a Conditional Ruling.*

Conditionally granting the motion for a new trial does not affect the judgment's finality; if the judgment is reversed, the new trial must proceed unless the appellate court orders otherwise. If the motion for a new trial is conditionally denied, the appellee may assert error in that denial; if the judgment is reversed, the case must proceed as the appellate court orders.

(d) Time for a Losing Party's New-Trial Motion.

Any motion for a new trial under Rule 59 by a party against whom judgment as a matter of law is rendered must be filed no later than 28 days after the entry of the judgment.

(e) Denying the Motion for Judgment as a Matter of Law; Reversal on Appeal.

If the court denies the motion for judgment as a matter of law, the prevailing party may, as appellee, assert grounds entitling it to a new trial should the appellate court conclude that the trial court erred in denying the motion. If the appellate court reverses the judgment, it may order a new trial, direct the trial court to determine whether a new trial should be granted, or direct the entry of judgment.

[*Adopted Dec. 20, 1937, effective Sept. 16, 1938; amended Jan. 21, 1963, effective July 1, 1963; Mar. 2, 1987, effective Aug. 1, 1987; Apr. 30, 1991, effective Dec. 1, 1991; Apr. 22, 1993, effective Dec. 1, 1993; Apr. 27, 1995, effective Dec. 1, 1995; April 12, 2006, effective Dec. 1, 2006; amended April 30, 2007, effective Dec. 1, 2007; amended March 26, 2009, effective Dec. 1, 2009.*]

ADVISORY COMMITTEE'S NOTE TO 2006 AMENDMENT TO RULE 50

The language of Rule 50(a) has been amended as part of the general restyling of the Civil Rules to make them more easily understood and to make style and terminology consistent throughout the rules. These changes are intended to be stylistic only.

Rule 50(b) is amended to permit renewal of any Rule 50(a) motion for judgment as a matter of law, deleting the requirement that a motion be made at the close of all the evidence. Because the Rule 50(b) motion is only a renewal of the preverdict motion, it can be granted only on grounds advanced in the preverdict motion. The earlier motion informs the opposing party of the challenge to the sufficiency of the evidence and affords a clear opportunity to provide additional evidence that may be available. The earlier motion also alerts the court to the opportunity to simplify the trial by resolving some issues, or even all issues, without submission to the jury. This fulfillment of the functional needs that underlie present Rule 50(b) also satisfies the Seventh Amendment. Automatic reservation of the legal questions raised by the motion conforms to the decision in *Baltimore & Carolina Line v. Redman*, 295 U.S. 654 (1935).

This change responds to many decisions that have begun to move away from requiring a motion for judgment as a matter of law at the literal close of all the evidence. Although the requirement has been clearly established for several decades, lawyers continue to overlook it. The courts are slowly working away from the formal requirement. The amendment establishes the functional approach that courts have been unable to reach under the present rule and makes practice more consistent and predictable.

Many judges expressly invite motions at the close of all the evidence. The amendment is not intended to discourage this useful practice.

* * *

ADVISORY COMMITTEE'S NOTE TO 1991
AMENDMENT OF RULE 50

Subdivision (a). The revision of this subdivision aims to facilitate the exercise by the court of its responsibility to assure the fidelity of its judgment to the controlling law, a responsibility imposed by the Due Process Clause of the Fifth Amendment. *Cf. Galloway v. United States*, 319 U.S. 372 (1943).

The revision abandons the familiar terminology of *direction of verdict* for several reasons. The term is misleading as a description of the relationship between judge and jury. It is also freighted with anachronisms some of which are the subject of the text of former subdivision (a) of this rule that is deleted in this revision. Thus, it should not be necessary to state in the text of this rule that a motion made pursuant to it is not a waiver of the right to jury trial, and only the antiquities of directed verdict practice suggest that it might have been. The term "judgment as a matter of law" is an almost equally familiar term and appears in the text of Rule 56; its use in Rule 50 calls attention to the relationship between the two rules. Finally, the change enables the rule to refer to pre-verdict and post-verdict motions with a terminology that does not conceal the common identity of two motions made at different times in the proceeding.

If a motion is denominated a motion for directed verdict or for judgment notwithstanding the verdict, the party's error is merely formal. Such a motion should be treated as a motion for judgment as a matter of law in accordance with this rule.

Paragraph (a)(1) articulates the standard for the granting of a motion for judgment as a matter of law. It effects no change in the existing standard. That existing standard was not expressed in the former rule, but was articulated in long-standing case law. *See generally* Cooper, *Directions for Directed Verdicts: A compass for Federal Courts,* 55 Minn.L.Rev. 903 (1971). The expressed standard makes clear that action taken under the rule is a performance of the court's duty to assure enforcement of the controlling law and is not an intrusion on any responsibility for factual determinations conferred on the jury by the Seventh Amendment or any other provision of federal law. Because this standard is also used as a reference point for entry of summary judgment under 56(a), it serves to link the two related provisions.

The revision authorizes the court to perform its duty to enter judgment as a matter of law at any time during the trial, as soon as it is apparent that either party is unable to carry a burden of proof that is essential to that party's case. Thus, the second sentence of paragraph (a)(1) authorizes the court to consider a motion for judgment as a matter of law as soon as a party has completed a presentation on a fact essential to that party's case. Such early action is appropriate when economy and expedition will be served. In no event, however, should the court enter judgment against a party who has not been apprised of the materiality of the dispositive fact and been afforded an opportunity to present any available evidence bearing on that fact. In order further to facilitate the exercise of the authority provided by this rule, Rule 16 is also revised to encourage the court to schedule an order of trial that proceeds first with a presentation on an issue that is likely to be dispositive, if such an issue is identified in the course of pretrial. Such scheduling can be appropriate where the court is uncertain whether favorable action should be taken under Rule 56. Thus, the revision affords the court the alternative of denying a motion for summary judgment while scheduling a separate trial of the issues under Rule 42(b) or scheduling the trial to begin with a presentation on that essential fact which the opposing party seems unlikely to be able to maintain.

Paragraph (a)(2) retains the requirement that a motion for judgment be made prior to the close of the trial, subject to renewal after a jury verdict has been rendered. The purpose of this requirement is to assure the responding party an opportunity to cure any deficiency in that party's proof that may have been overlooked until called to the party's attention by a late motion for judgment.... At one time, this requirement was held to be of constitutional stature, being compelled by the Seventh Amendment. Cf. *Slocum v. New York Insurance Co.,* 228 U.S. 364 (1913). But cf. *Baltimore & Carolina Line v. Redman,* 295 U.S. 654 (1935).

The second sentence of paragraph (a)(2) does impose a requirement that the moving party articulate the basis on which a judgment as a matter of law might be rendered. The articulation is necessary to achieve the purpose of the requirement that the motion be made before the case is submitted to the jury, so that the responding party may seek to correct any overlooked deficiencies in the proof. The revision thus alters the result in cases in which courts have used various techniques to avoid the requirement that a motion for a directed verdict be made as a predicate to a motion for judgment notwithstanding the verdict. E.g., *Benson v. Allphin*, 786 F.2d 268 (7th Cir.1986) ("this circuit has allowed something less than a formal motion for directed verdict to preserve a party's right to move for judgment notwithstanding the verdict"). *See generally* 9 Wright & Miller, Federal Practice and Procedure § 2537 (1971 and Supp.). The information required with the motion may be supplied by explicit reference to materials and argument previously supplied by the court.

This subdivision deals only with the entry of judgment and not with the resolution of particular factual issues as a matter of law. The court may, as before, properly refuse to instruct a jury to decide an issue if a reasonable jury could on the evidence presented decide that issue in only one way.

Subdivision (b). This provision retains the concept of the former rule that the post- verdict motion is a renewal of an earlier motion made at the close of the evidence. One purpose of this concept was to avoid any question arising under the Seventh Amendment. *Montgomery Ward & Co. v. Duncan,* 311 U.S. 243 (1940). It remains useful as a means of defining the appropriate issue posed by the post-verdict motion. A post-trial motion for judgment can be granted only on grounds advanced in the pre- verdict motion. *E.g., Kutner Buick, Inc. v. American Motors Corp.,* 868 F.2d 614 (3d Cir.1989).

Often it appears to the court or to the moving party that a motion for judgment as a matter of law made at the close of the evidence should be reserved for a post-verdict decision. This is so because a jury verdict for the moving party moots the issue and because a pre-verdict ruling gambles that a reversal may result in a new trial that might have been avoided. For these reasons, the court may often wisely decline to rule on a motion for judgment as a matter of law made at the close of the evidence, and it is not inappropriate for the moving party to suggest such a postponement of the ruling until after the verdict has been rendered.

In ruling on such a motion, the court should disregard any jury determination for which there is no legally sufficient evidentiary basis enabling a reasonable jury to make it. The court may then decide such issues as a matter of law and enter judgment if all other material issues have been decided by the jury on the basis of legally sufficient evidence, or by the court as a matter of law.

The revised rule is intended for use in this manner with Rule 49. Thus, the court may combine facts established as a matter of law either before trial under Rule 56 or at trial on the basis of the evidence presented with other facts determined by the jury under instructions provided under Rule 49 to support a proper judgment under this rule.

This provision also retains the former requirement that a post-trial motion under the rule must be made within 10 days after entry of a contrary judgment. The renewed motion must be served and filed as provided by Rule 5. A purpose of this requirement is to meet the requirements of F.R.App.P. 4(a)(4).

RULE 51. INSTRUCTIONS TO THE JURY; OBJECTIONS; PRESERVING A CLAIM OF ERROR.

(a) Requests.

(1) *Before or at the Close of the Evidence.*

At the close of the evidence or at any earlier reasonable time that the court orders, a party may file and furnish to every other party written requests for the jury instructions it wants the court to give.

(2) *After the Close of the Evidence.*

After the close of the evidence, a party may:

(A) file requests for instructions on issues that could not reasonably have been anticipated by an earlier time that the court set for requests; and

(B) with the court's permission, file untimely requests for instructions on any issue.

(b) Instructions.

The court:

(1) must inform the parties of its proposed instructions and proposed action on the requests before instructing the jury and before final jury arguments;

(2) must give the parties an opportunity to object on the record and out of the jury's hearing before the instructions and arguments are delivered; and

(3) may instruct the jury at any time before the jury is discharged.

(c) Objections.

(1) *How to Make.*

A party who objects to an instruction or the failure to give an instruction must do so on the record, stating distinctly the matter objected to and the grounds for the objection.

(2) *When to Make.*

An objection is timely if:

(A) a party objects at the opportunity provided under Rule 51(b)(2); or

(B) a party was not informed of an instruction or action on a request before that opportunity to object, and the party objects promptly after learning that the instruction or request will be, or has been, given or refused.

(d) Assigning Error; Plain Error.

(1) *Assigning Error.*

A party may assign as error:

> (A) an error in an instruction actually given, if that party properly objected; or

> (B) a failure to give an instruction, if that party properly requested it and — unless the court rejected the request in a definitive ruling on the record — also properly objected.

(2) *Plain Error.*

A court may consider a plain error in the instructions that has not been preserved as required by Rule 51(d)(1) if the error affects substantial rights.

[*Adopted Dec. 20, 1937, effective Sept. 16, 1938; amended Mar. 2, 1987, effective Aug. 1, 1987; Mar. 27, 2003, effective Dec. 1, 2003; amended April 30, 2007, effective Dec. 1, 2007.*]

ADVISORY COMMITTEE'S NOTE TO 2003
AMENDMENT OF RULE 51 COMMITTEE NOTE

Rule 51 is revised to capture many of the interpretations that have emerged in practice. The revisions in text will make uniform the conclusions reached by a majority of decisions on each point. Additions also are made to cover some practices that cannot now be anchored in the text of Rule 51.

Scope. Rule 51 governs instructions to the trial jury on the law that governs the verdict. A variety of other instructions cannot practically be brought within Rule 51. Among these instructions are preliminary instructions to a venire, and cautionary or limiting instructions delivered in immediate response to events at trial.

Requests. Subdivision (a) governs requests. Apart from the plain error doctrine recognized in subdivision (d)(2), a court is not obliged to instruct the jury on issues raised by the evidence unless a party requests an instruction. The revised rule recognizes the court's authority to direct that requests be submitted before trial.

The close-of-the-evidence deadline may come before trial is completed on all potential issues. Trial may be formally bifurcated or may be sequenced in some less formal manner. The close of the evidence is measured by the occurrence of two events: completion of all intended evidence on an identified phase of the trial and impending submission to the jury with instructions.

The risk in directing a pretrial request deadline is that trial evidence may raise new issues or reshape issues the parties thought they had understood. Courts need not insist on pretrial requests in all cases. Even if the request time is set before trial or early in the trial, subdivision (a)(2)(A) permits requests after the close of the evidence to address issues that could not reasonably have been anticipated at the earlier time for requests set by the court.

Subdivision (a)(2)(B) expressly recognizes the court's discretion to act on an untimely request. The most important consideration in exercising the discretion confirmed by subdivision (a)(2)(B) is the importance of the issue to the case — the closer the issue lies to the "plain error" that would be recognized under subdivision (d)(2), the better the reason to give an instruction. The cogency of the reason for failing to make a timely request also should be considered. To be considered under subdivision (a)(2)(B) a request should be made before final instructions and before final jury arguments. What is a "final" instruction and argument depends on the sequence of submitting the case to the jury. If separate portions of the case are submitted to the jury in sequence, the final arguments and final instructions are those made on submitting to the jury the portion of the case addressed by the arguments and instructions.

Instructions. Subdivision (b)(1) requires the court to inform the parties, before instructing the jury and before final jury arguments related to the instruction, of the proposed instructions as well as the proposed action on instruction requests. The time limit is addressed to final jury arguments to reflect the practice that allows interim arguments during trial in complex cases; it may not be feasible to develop final instructions before such interim arguments. It is enough that counsel know of the intended instructions before making final arguments addressed to the issue. If the trial is sequenced or bifurcated, the final arguments addressed to an issue may occur before the close of the entire trial.

Subdivision (b)(2) complements subdivision (b)(1) by carrying forward the opportunity to object established by present Rule 51. It makes explicit the opportunity to object on the record, ensuring a clear memorial of the objection.

Subdivision (b)(3) reflects common practice by authorizing instructions at any time after trial begins and before the jury is discharged.

Objections. Subdivision (c) states the right to object to an instruction or the failure to give an instruction. It carries forward the formula of present Rule 51 requiring that the objection state distinctly the matter objected to and the grounds of the objection, and makes explicit the requirement that the objection be made on the record. The provisions on the time to object make clear that it is timely to object promptly after learning of an instruction or action on a request when the court has not provided advance information as required by subdivision (b)(1). The need to repeat a request by way of objection is continued by new subdivision (d)(1)(B) except where the court made a definitive ruling on the record.

Preserving a claim of error and plain error. Many cases hold that a proper request for a jury instruction is not alone enough to preserve the right to appeal failure to give the instruction. The request must be renewed by objection. This doctrine is appropriate when the court may not have sufficiently focused on the request, or may believe that the request has been granted in substance although in different words. But this doctrine may also prove a trap for the unwary who fail to add an objection after the court has made it clear that the request has been considered and rejected on the merits. Subdivision (d)(1)(B) establishes authority to review the failure to grant a timely request, despite a failure to add an objection, when the court has made a definitive ruling on the record rejecting the request.

Many circuits have recognized that an error not preserved under Rule 51 may be reviewed in exceptional circumstances. The language adopted to capture these decisions in subdivision (d)(2) is borrowed from Criminal Rule 52. Although the language is the same, the context of civil litigation often differs from the context of criminal prosecution; actual application of the plain-error standard takes account of the differences. The Supreme Court has summarized application of Criminal Rule 52 as involving four elements: (1) there must be an error; (2) the error must be plain; (3) the error must affect substantial rights; and (4) the error must seriously affect the fairness, integrity, or public reputation of judicial proceedings. *Johnson v. U.S.*, 520 U.S. 461, 466–467, 469–470 (1997). (The Johnson case quoted the fourth element from its decision in a civil action, *U.S. v. Atkinson*, 297 U.S. 157, 160 (1936): "In exceptional circumstances, especially in criminal cases, appellate courts, in the public interest, may, of their own motion, notice errors to which no exception has been taken, if the errors are obvious, or if they otherwise substantially affect the fairness, integrity, or public reputation of judicial proceedings.")

The court's duty to give correct jury instructions in a civil action is shaped by at least four factors.

The factor most directly implied by a "plain" error rule is the obviousness of the mistake. The importance of the error is a second major factor. The costs of correcting an error reflect a third factor that is affected by a variety of circumstances. In a case that seems close to the fundamental error line, account also may be taken of the impact a verdict may have on nonparties.

ADVISORY COMMITTEE'S NOTE TO 1987 AMENDMENT OF RULE 51

Although Rule 51 in its present form specifies that the court shall instruct the jury only after the arguments of the parties are completed, in some districts (typically those in states where the practice is otherwise) it is common for the parties to stipulate to instruction before the arguments. The purpose of the amendment is to give the court discretion to instruct the jury either before or after argument. Thus the rule as revised will permit resort to the long-standing federal practice or to an alternative procedure, which has been praised because it gives counsel the opportunity to explain the instructions, argue their application to the facts and thereby give the jury the maximum assistance in determining the issues and arriving at a good verdict on the law and the evidence. As an ancillary benefit, this approach aids counsel by supplying a natural outline so that arguments may be directed to the essential fact issues which the jury must decide. *See generally* Raymond, *Merits and Demerits of the Missouri System of Instructing Juries,* 5 St. Louis U.L.J. 317 (1959). Moreover, if the court instructs before an argument, counsel then know the precise words the court has chosen and need not speculate as to the words the court will later use in its instructions. Finally, by instructing ahead of argument the court has the attention of the jurors when they are fresh and can give their full attention to the court's instructions. It is more difficult to hold the attention of jurors after lengthy arguments.

Rule 52. Findings and Conclusions by the Court; Judgment on Partial Findings.

(a) Findings and Conclusions.

(1) *In General.*

In an action tried on the facts without a jury or with an advisory jury, the court must find the facts specially and state its conclusions of law separately. The findings and conclusions may be stated on the record after the close of the evidence or may appear in an opinion or a memorandum of decision filed by the court. Judgment must be entered under Rule 58.

(2) *For an Interlocutory Injunction.*

In granting or refusing an interlocutory injunction, the court must similarly state the findings and conclusions that support its action.

(3) *For a Motion.*

The court is not required to state findings or conclusions when ruling on a motion under Rule 12 or 56 or, unless these rules provide otherwise, on any other motion.

(4) *Effect of a Master's Findings.*

A master's findings, to the extent adopted by the court, must be considered the court's findings.

(5) *Questioning the Evidentiary Support.*

A party may later question the sufficiency of the evidence supporting the findings, whether or not the party requested findings, objected to them, moved to amend them, or moved for partial findings.

(6) *Setting Aside the Findings.*

Findings of fact, whether based on oral or other evidence, must not be set aside unless clearly erroneous, and the reviewing court must give due regard to the trial court's opportunity to judge the witnesses' credibility.

(b) Amended or Additional Findings.

On a party's motion filed no later than 28 days after the entry of judgment, the court may amend its findings—or make additional findings—and may amend the judgment accordingly. The motion may accompany a motion for a new trial under Rule 59.

(c) Judgment on Partial Findings.

If a party has been fully heard on an issue during a nonjury trial and the court finds against the party on that issue, the court may enter judgment against the party on a claim or defense that, under the controlling law, can be maintained or defeated only with a favorable finding on that issue. The court may, however, decline to render any judgment until the close of the evidence. A judgment on partial findings must be supported by findings of fact and conclusions of law as required by Rule 52(a).

[*Adopted Dec. 20, 1937, effective Sept. 16, 1938; amended Dec. 27, 1946, effective Mar. 19, 1948; Jan. 21, 1963, effective July 1, 1963; Apr. 28, 1983, effective Aug. 1, 1983; Apr. 29, 1985, effective Aug. 1, 1985; Apr. 30, 1991, effective Dec. 1, 1991; Apr. 22, 1993, effective Dec. 1, 1993; Apr. 27, 1995, effective Dec. 1, 1995; amended April 30, 2007, effective Dec. 1, 2007; amended March 26, 2009, effective Dec. 1, 2009.*]

RULE 53. MASTERS.

(a) Appointment.

(1) *Scope.*

Unless a statute provides otherwise, a court may appoint a master only to:

(A) perform duties consented to by the parties;

(B) hold trial proceedings and make or recommend findings of fact on issues to be decided without a jury if appointment is warranted by:

(i) some exceptional condition; or

(ii) the need to perform an accounting or resolve a difficult computation of damages; or

(C) address pretrial and posttrial matters that cannot be effectively and timely addressed by an available district judge or magistrate judge of the district.

(2) *Disqualification.*

A master must not have a relationship to the parties, attorneys, action, or court that would require disqualification of a judge under 28 U.S.C. § 455, unless the parties, with the court's approval, consent to the appointment after the master discloses any potential grounds for disqualification.

(3) *Possible Expense or Delay.*

In appointing a master, the court must consider the fairness of imposing the likely expenses on the parties and must protect against unreasonable expense or delay.

(b) Order Appointing a Master.

(1) *Notice.*

Before appointing a master, the court must give the parties notice and an opportunity to be heard. Any party may suggest candidates for appointment.

(2) *Contents.*

The appointing order must direct the master to proceed with all reasonable diligence and must state:

(A) the master's duties, including any investigation or enforcement duties, and any limits on the master's authority under Rule 53(c);

(B) the circumstances, if any, in which the master may communicate ex parte with the court or a party;

(C) the nature of the materials to be preserved and filed as the record of the master's activities;

(D) the time limits, method of filing the record, other procedures, and standards for reviewing the master's orders, findings, and recommendations; and

(E) the basis, terms, and procedure for fixing the master's compensation under Rule 53(g).

(3) *Issuing.*

The court may issue the order only after:

(A) the master files an affidavit disclosing whether there is any ground for disqualification under 28 U.S.C. §455; and

(B) if a ground is disclosed, the parties, with the court's approval, waive the disqualification.

(4) *Amending.*

The order may be amended at any time after notice to the parties and an opportunity to be heard.

(c) **Master's Authority.**

(1) *In General.*

In General. Unless the appointing order directs otherwise, a master may:

(A) regulate all proceedings;

(B) take all appropriate measures to perform the assigned duties fairly and efficiently; and

(C) if conducting an evidentiary hearing, exercise the appointing court's power to compel, take, and record evidence.

(2) *Sanctions.*

The master may by order impose on a party any noncontempt sanction provided by Rule 37 or 45, and may recommend a contempt sanction against a party and sanctions against a nonparty.

(d) **Master's Orders.**

A master who issues an order must file it and promptly serve a copy on each party. The clerk must enter the order on the docket.

(e) **Master's Reports.**

A master must report to the court as required by the appointing order. The master must file the report and promptly serve a copy on each party, unless the court orders otherwise.

(f) **Action on the Master's Order, Report, or Recommendations.**

(1) *Opportunity for a Hearing; Action in General.*

In acting on a master's order, report, or recommendations, the court must give the parties notice and an opportunity to be heard; may receive evidence; and may adopt or affirm, modify, wholly or partly reject or reverse, or resubmit to the master with instructions.

(2) *Time to Object or Move to Adopt or Modify.*

A party may file objections to—or a motion to adopt or modify—the master's order, report, or recommendations no later than 21 days after a copy is served, unless the court sets a different time.

(3) *Reviewing Factual Findings.*

The court must decide de novo all objections to findings of fact made or recommended by a master, unless the parties, with the court's approval, stipulate that:

    (A) the findings will be reviewed for clear error; or

    (B) the findings of a master appointed under Rule 53(a)(1)(A) or (C) will be final.

(4) *Reviewing Legal Conclusions.*

The court must decide de novo all objections to conclusions of law made or recommended by a master.

(5) *Reviewing Procedural Matters.*

Unless the appointing order establishes a different standard of review, the court may set aside a master's ruling on a procedural matter only for an abuse of discretion.

(g) **Compensation.**

(1) *Fixing Compensation.*

Before or after judgment, the court must fix the master's compensation on the basis and terms stated in the appointing order, but the court may set a new basis and terms after giving notice and an opportunity to be heard.

(2) *Payment.*

The compensation must be paid either:

    (A) by a party or parties; or

    (B) from a fund or subject matter of the action within the court's control.

(3) *Allocating Payment.*

The court must allocate payment among the parties after considering the nature and amount of the controversy, the parties' means, and the extent to which any party is more responsible than other parties for the reference to a master. An interim allocation may be amended to reflect a decision on the merits.

(h) **Appointing a Magistrate Judge.**

A magistrate judge is subject to this rule only when the order referring a matter to the magistrate judge states that the reference is made under this rule.

[Adopted Dec. 20, 1937, effective Sept. 16, 1938; amended Feb. 28, 1966, effective July 1, 1966; Apr. 28, 1983, effective Aug. 1, 1983; Mar. 2, 1987, effective Aug. 1, 1987; Apr. 30, 1991, effective Dec. 1, 1991; Apr. 22, 1993, effective Dec. 1, 1993; Mar. 27, 2003, effective Dec. 1, 2003; amended April 30, 2007, effective Dec. 1, 2007; amended March 26, 2009, effective Dec. 1, 2009.]

TITLE VII.   JUDGMENT

RULE 54.   JUDGMENT; COSTS.

(a) Definition; Form.

"Judgment" as used in these rules includes a decree and any order from which an appeal lies. A judgment should not include recitals of pleadings, a master's report, or a record of prior proceedings.

(b) Judgment on Multiple Claims or Involving Multiple Parties.

When an action presents more than one claim for relief—whether as a claim, counterclaim, crossclaim, or third-party claim—or when multiple parties are involved, the court may direct entry of a final judgment as to one or more, but fewer than all, claims or parties only if the court expressly determines that there is no just reason for delay. Otherwise, any order or other decision, however designated, that adjudicates fewer than all the claims or the rights and liabilities of fewer than all the parties does not end the action as to any of the claims or parties and may be revised at any time before the entry of a judgment adjudicating all the claims and all the parties' rights and liabilities.

(c) Demand for Judgment; Relief to Be Granted.

A default judgment must not differ in kind from, or exceed in amount, what is demanded in the pleadings. Every other final judgment should grant the relief to which each party is entitled, even if the party has not demanded that relief in its pleadings.

(d) Costs; Attorney's Fees.

(1) *Costs Other Than Attorney's Fees.*

Unless a federal statute, these rules, or a court order provides otherwise, costs—other than attorney's fees—should be allowed to the prevailing party. But costs against the United States, its officers, and its agencies may be imposed only to the extent allowed by law. The clerk may tax costs on 14 days' notice. On motion served within the next 7 days, the court may review the clerk's action.

(2) *Attorney's Fees.*

(A) *Claim to Be by Motion.*

A claim for attorney's fees and related nontaxable expenses must be made by motion unless the substantive law requires those fees to be proved at trial as an element of damages.

(B) *Timing and Contents of the Motion.*

Unless a statute or a court order provides otherwise, the motion must:

(i) be filed no later than 14 days after the entry of judgment;

(ii) specify the judgment and the statute, rule, or other grounds entitling the movant to the award;

(iii) state the amount sought or provide a fair estimate of it; and

(iv) disclose, if the court so orders, the terms of any agreement about fees for the services for which the claim is made.

(C) *Proceedings.*

Subject to Rule 23(h), the court must, on a party's request, give an opportunity for adversary submissions on the motion in accordance with Rule 43(c) or 78. The court may decide issues of liability for fees before receiving submissions on the value of services. The court must find the facts and state its conclusions of law as provided in Rule 52(a).

(D) *Special Procedures by Local Rule; Reference to a Master or a Magistrate Judge.*

By local rule, the court may establish special procedures to resolve fee-related issues without extensive evidentiary hearings. Also, the court may refer issues concerning the value of services to a special master under Rule 53 without regard to the limitations of Rule 53(a)(1), and may refer a motion for attorney's fees to a magistrate judge under Rule 72(b) as if it were a dispositive pretrial matter.

(E) *Exceptions.*

Subparagraphs (A)–(D) do not apply to claims for fees and expenses as sanctions for violating these rules or as sanctions under 28 U.S.C. § 1927.

[*Adopted Dec. 20, 1937, effective Sept. 16, 1938; amended Dec. 27, 1946, effective Mar. 19, 1948; Apr. 17, 1961, effective July 19, 1961; Mar. 2, 1987, effective Aug. 1, 1987; Apr. 22, 1993, effective Dec. 1, 1993; Apr. 29, 2002, effective Dec. 1, 2002; Mar. 27, 2003, effective Dec. 1, 2003; amended April 30, 2007, effective Dec. 1, 2007; amended March 26, 2009, effective Dec. 1, 2009.*]

RULE 55.   DEFAULT; DEFAULT JUDGMENT.

(a) Entering a Default.

When a party against whom a judgment for affirmative relief is sought has failed to plead or otherwise defend, and that failure is shown by affidavit or otherwise, the clerk must enter the party's default.

(b) Entering a Default Judgment.

(1) *By the Clerk.*

If the plaintiff's claim is for a sum certain or a sum that can be made certain by computation, the clerk—on the plaintiff's request, with an affidavit showing the amount due—must enter judgment for that amount and costs against a defendant who has been defaulted for not appearing and who is neither a minor nor an incompetent person.

(2) *By the Court.*

In all other cases, the party must apply to the court for a default judgment. A default judgment may be entered against a minor or incompetent person only if represented by a general guardian, conservator, or other like fiduciary who has appeared. If the party against whom a default judgment is sought has appeared personally or by a representative, that party or its representative must be served with written notice of the application at least 7 days before the hearing. The court may conduct hearings or make referrals—preserving any federal statutory right to a jury trial—when, to enter or effectuate judgment, it needs to:

(A) conduct an accounting;

(B) determine the amount of damages;

(C) establish the truth of any allegation by evidence; or

(D) investigate any other matter.

(c) Setting Aside a Default or a Default Judgment.

The court may set aside an entry of default for good cause, and it may set aside a final default judgment under Rule 60(b).

(d) Judgment Against the United States.

A default judgment may be entered against the United States, its officers, or its agencies only if the claimant establishes a claim or right to relief by evidence that satisfies the court.

[*Adopted Dec. 20, 1937, effective Sept. 16, 1938; amended Mar. 2, 1987, effective Aug. 1, 1987; amended April 30, 2007, effective Dec. 1, 2007; amended March 26, 2009, effective Dec. 1, 2009; amended April 29, 2015, effective Dec. 1, 2015.*]

NOTES OF ADVISORY COMMITTEE ON 2015 AMENDMENTS TO RULE 55

Rule 55(c) is amended to make plain the interplay between Rules 54(b), 55(c), and 60(b). A default judgment that does not dispose of all of the claims among all parties is not a final judgment unless the court directs entry of final judgment under Rule 54(b). Until final judgment is entered, Rule 54(b) allows revision of the default judgment at any time. The demanding standards set by Rule 60(b) apply only in seeking relief from a final judgment.

RULE 56. SUMMARY JUDGMENT.

(a) Motion for Summary Judgment or Partial Summary Judgment.

A party may move for summary judgment, identifying each claim or defense—or the part of each claim or defense—on which summary judgment is sought. The court shall grant summary judgment if the movant shows that there is no genuine dispute as to any material fact and the movant is entitled to judgment as a matter of law. The court should state on the record the reasons for granting or denying the motion.

(b) Time to File a Motion.

Unless a different time is set by local rule or the court orders otherwise, a party may file a motion for summary judgment at any time until 30 days after the close of all discovery.

(c) Procedures.

(1) *Supporting Factual Positions.* A party asserting that a fact cannot be or is genuinely disputed must support the assertion by:

(A) citing to particular parts of materials in the record, including depositions, documents, electronically stored information, affidavits or declarations, stipulations (including those made for purposes of the motion only), admissions, interrogatory answers, or other materials; or

(B) showing that the materials cited do not establish the absence or presence of a genuine dispute, or that an adverse party cannot produce admissible evidence to support the fact.

(2) *Objection That a Fact Is Not Supported by Admissible Evidence.*

A party may object that the material cited to support or dispute a fact cannot be presented in a form that would be admissible in evidence.

(3) *Materials Not Cited.*

The court need consider only the cited materials, but it may consider other materials in the record.

(4) *Affidavits or Declarations.*

An affidavit or declaration used to support or oppose a motion must be made on personal knowledge, set out facts that would be admissible in evidence, and show that the affiant or declarant is competent to testify on the matters stated.

(d) When Facts Are Unavailable to the Nonmovant.

If a nonmovant shows by affidavit or declaration that, for specified reasons, it cannot present facts essential to justify its opposition, the court may:

(1) defer considering the motion or deny it;

(2) allow time to obtain affidavits or declarations or to take discovery; or

(3) issue any other appropriate order.

(e) Failing to Properly Support or Address a Fact.

If a party fails to properly support an assertion of fact or fails to properly address another party's assertion of fact as required by Rule 56(c), the court may:

(1) give an opportunity to properly support or address the fact;

(2) consider the fact undisputed for purposes of the motion;

(3) grant summary judgment if the motion and supporting materials—including the facts considered undisputed—show that the movant is entitled to it; or

(4) issue any other appropriate order.

(f) Judgment Independent of the Motion.

After giving notice and a reasonable time to respond, the court may:

(1) grant summary judgment for a nonmovant;

(2) grant the motion on grounds not raised by a party; or

(3) consider summary judgment on its own after identifying for the parties material facts that may not be genuinely in dispute.

(g) Failing to Grant All the Requested Relief.

If the court does not grant all the relief requested by the motion, it may enter an order stating any material fact—including an item of damages or other relief—that is not genuinely in dispute and treating the fact as established in the case.

(h) Affidavit or Declaration Submitted in Bad Faith.

If satisfied that an affidavit or declaration under this rule is submitted in bad faith or solely for delay, the court—after notice and a reasonable time to respond—may order the submitting party to pay the other party the reasonable expenses, including attorney's fees, it incurred as a result. An offending party or attorney may also be held in contempt or subjected to other appropriate sanctions.

[*Adopted Dec. 20, 1937, effective Sept. 16, 1938; amended Dec. 27, 1946, effective Mar. 19, 1948; Jan. 21, 1963, effective July 1, 1963; Mar 2, 1987, effective Aug. 1, 1987; amended April 30, 2007, effective Dec. 1, 2007; amended March 26, 2009, effective Dec. 1, 2009; amended April 28, 2010, effective Dec. 1, 2010.*]

ADVISORY COMMITTEE NOTE (2010)

Rule 56 is revised to improve the procedures for presenting and deciding summary-judgment motions and to make the procedures more consistent with those already used in many courts. The standard for granting summary judgment remains unchanged. The language of subdivision (a) continues to require that there be no genuine dispute as to any material fact and that the movant be entitled to judgment as a matter of law. The amendments will not affect continuing development of the decisional law construing and applying these phrases.

Subdivision (a). Subdivision (a) carries forward the summary-judgment standard expressed in former subdivision (c), changing only one word—genuine "issue" becomes genuine "dispute." "Dispute" better reflects the focus of a summary- judgment determination. As explained below, "shall" also is restored to the place it held from 1938 to 2007.

The first sentence is added to make clear at the beginning that summary judgment may be requested not only as to an entire case but also as to a claim, defense, or part of a claim or defense. The subdivision caption adopts the common phrase "partial summary judgment" to describe disposition of less than the whole action, whether or not the order grants all the relief requested by the motion.

"Shall" is restored to express the direction to grant summary judgment. The word "shall" in Rule 56 acquired significance over many decades of use. Rule 56 was amended in 2007 to replace "shall" with "should" as part of the Style Project, acting under a convention that prohibited any use of "shall." Comments on proposals to amend Rule 56, as published in 2008, have shown that neither of the choices available under the Style Project conventions—"must" or "should"—is suitable in light of the case law on whether a district court has discretion to deny summary judgment when there appears to be no genuine dispute as to any material fact. Compare *Anderson v. Liberty Lobby, Inc.*, 477 U.S. 242, 255 (1986) ("Neither do we suggest that the trial courts should act other than with caution in granting summary judgment or that the trial court may not deny summary judgment in a case in which there is reason to believe that the better course would be to proceed to a full trial. *Kennedy v. Silas Mason Co.*, 334 U.S. 249 * * * (1948))," with *Celotex Corp. v. Catrett*, 477 U.S. 317, 322 (1986) ("In our view, the plain language of Rule 56(c) mandates the entry of summary judgment, after adequate time for discovery and upon motion, against a party who fails to make a showing sufficient to establish the existence of an element essential to that party's case, and on which that party will bear the burden of proof at trial."). Eliminating "shall" created an unacceptable risk of changing the summary-judgment standard. Restoring "shall" avoids the unintended consequences of any other word.

Subdivision (a) also adds a new direction that the court should state on the record the reasons for granting or denying the motion. Most courts recognize this practice. Among other advantages, a statement of reasons can facilitate an appeal or subsequent trial-court proceedings. It is particularly important to state the reasons for granting summary judgment. The form and detail of the statement of reasons are left to the court's discretion.

The statement on denying summary judgment need not address every available reason. But identification of central issues may help the parties to focus further proceedings. * * *

Subdivision (c). Subdivision (c) is new. It establishes a common procedure for several aspects of summary-judgment motions synthesized from similar elements developed in the cases or found in many local rules.

Subdivision (c)(1) addresses the ways to support an assertion that a fact can or cannot be genuinely disputed. * * * Subdivision (c)(1)(A) describes the familiar record materials commonly relied upon and requires that the movant cite the particular parts of the materials that support its fact positions. * * *

Subdivision (c)(1)(B) recognizes that a party need not always point to specific record materials. One party, without citing any other materials, may respond or reply that materials cited to dispute or support a fact do not establish the absence or presence of a genuine dispute. And a party who does not have the trial burden of production may rely on a showing that a party who does have the trial burden cannot produce admissible evidence to carry its burden as to the fact.

Subdivision (c)(2) provides that a party may object that material cited to support or dispute a fact cannot be presented in a form that would be admissible in evidence. The objection functions much as an objection at trial, adjusted for the pretrial setting. The burden is on the proponent to show that the material is admissible as presented or to explain the admissible form that is anticipated. There is no need to make a separate motion to strike. If the case goes to trial, failure to challenge admissibility at the summary-judgment stage does not forfeit the right to challenge admissibility at trial.

Subdivision (c)(3) reflects judicial opinions and local rules provisions stating that the court may decide a motion for summary judgment without undertaking an independent search of the record. Nonetheless, the rule also recognizes that a court may consider record materials not called to its attention by the parties. * * *

A formal affidavit is no longer required. 28 U.S.C. § 1746 allows a written unsworn declaration, certificate, verification, or statement subscribed in proper form as true under penalty of perjury to substitute for an affidavit. * * *

Subdivision (e). Subdivision (e) addresses questions that arise when a party fails to support an assertion of fact or fails to properly address another party's assertion of fact as required by Rule 56(c). As explained below, summary judgment cannot be granted by default even if there is a complete failure to respond to the motion, much less when an attempted response fails to comply with Rule 56(c) requirements. Nor should it be denied by default even if the movant completely fails to reply to a nonmovant's response. Before deciding on other possible action, subdivision (e)(1) recognizes that the court may afford an opportunity to properly support or address the fact. In many circumstances this opportunity will be the court's preferred first step.

Subdivision (e)(2) authorizes the court to consider a fact as undisputed for purposes of the motion when response or reply requirements are not satisfied. This approach reflects the "deemed admitted" provisions in many local rules. The fact is considered undisputed only for purposes of the motion; if summary judgment is denied, a party who failed to make a proper Rule 56 response or reply remains free to contest the fact in further proceedings. And the court may choose not to consider the fact as undisputed, particularly if the court knows of record materials that show grounds for genuine dispute.

Subdivision (e)(3) recognizes that the court may grant summary judgment only if the motion and supporting materials — including the facts considered undisputed under subdivision (e)(2)—show that the movant is entitled to it. Considering some facts undisputed does not of itself allow summary judgment. If there is a proper response or reply as to some facts, the court cannot grant summary judgment without determining whether those facts can be genuinely disputed. Once the court has determined the set of facts—both those it has chosen to consider undisputed for want of a proper response or reply and any that cannot be genuinely disputed despite a procedurally proper response or reply—it must determine the legal consequences of these facts and permissible inferences from them. * * *

Subdivision (f). Subdivision (f) brings into Rule 56 text a number of related procedures that have grown up in practice. After giving notice and a reasonable time to respond the court may grant summary judgment for the nonmoving party; grant a motion on legal or factual grounds not raised by the parties; or consider summary judgment on its own. In many cases it may prove useful first to invite a motion; the invited motion will automatically trigger the regular procedure of subdivision (c).

RULE 57. DECLARATORY JUDGMENT.

These rules govern the procedure for obtaining a declaratory judgment under 28 U.S.C. § 2201. Rules 38 and 39 govern a demand for a jury trial. The existence of another adequate remedy does not preclude a declaratory judgment that is otherwise appropriate. The court may order a speedy hearing of a declaratory-judgment action.

[*Adopted Dec. 20, 1937, effective Sept. 16, 1938; amended Dec. 29, 1948, effective Oct. 20, 1949; amended April 30, 2007, effective Dec. 1, 2007.*]

RULE 58. ENTERING JUDGMENT.

(a) Separate Document.

Every judgment and amended judgment must be set out in a separate document, but a separate document is not required for an order disposing of a motion:

> (1) for judgment under Rule 50(b);

> (2) to amend or make additional findings under Rule 52(b);

> (3) for attorney's fees under Rule 54;

> (4) for a new trial, or to alter or amend the judgment, under Rule 59; or

> (5) for relief under Rule 60.

(b) Entering Judgment.

(1) *Without the Court's Direction.*

Subject to Rule 54(b) and unless the court orders otherwise, the clerk must, without awaiting the court's direction, promptly prepare, sign, and enter the judgment when:

> (A) the jury returns a general verdict;

(B) the court awards only costs or a sum certain; or

(C) the court denies all relief.

(2) *Court's Approval Required.*

Subject to Rule 54(b), the court must promptly approve the form of the judgment, which the clerk must promptly enter, when:

(A) the jury returns a special verdict or a general verdict with answers to written questions; or

(B) the court grants other relief not described in this subdivision (b).

(c) Time of Entry.

For purposes of these rules, judgment is entered at the following times:

(1) if a separate document is not required, when the judgment is entered in the civil docket under Rule 79(a); or

(2) if a separate document is required, when the judgment is entered in the civil docket under Rule 79(a) and the earlier of these events occurs:

(A) it is set out in a separate document; or

(B) 150 days have run from the entry in the civil docket.

(d) Request for Entry.

A party may request that judgment be set out in a separate document as required by Rule 58(a).

(e) Cost or Fee Awards.

Ordinarily, the entry of judgment may not be delayed, nor the time for appeal extended, in order to tax costs or award fees. But if a timely motion for attorney's fees is made under Rule 54(d)(2), the court may act before a notice of appeal has been filed and become effective to order that the motion have the same effect under Federal Rule of Appellate Procedure 4(a)(4) as a timely motion under Rule 59.

[*Adopted Dec. 20, 1937, effective Sept. 16, 1938; amended Dec. 27, 1946, effective Mar. 19, 1948; Jan. 21, 1963, effective July 1, 1963; Apr. 22, 1993, effective Dec. 1, 1993; Apr. 29, 2002, effective Dec. 1, 2002; amended April 30, 2007, effective Dec. 1, 2007.*]

RULE 59.   NEW TRIALS; ALTERING OR AMENDING A JUDGMENT.

(a) In General.

(1) *Grounds for New Trial.*

The court may, on motion, grant a new trial on all or some of the issues—and to any party—as follows:

(A) after a jury trial, for any reason for which a new trial has heretofore been granted in an action at law in federal court; or

(B) after a nonjury trial, for any reason for which a rehearing has heretofore been granted in a suit in equity in federal court.

(2) *Further Action After a Nonjury Trial.*

After a nonjury trial, the court may, on motion for a new trial, open the judgment if one has been entered, take additional testimony, amend findings of fact and conclusions of law or make new ones, and direct the entry of a new judgment.

(b) Time to File a Motion for a New Trial.

A motion for a new trial must be filed no later than 28 days after the entry of judgment.

(c) Time to Serve Affidavits.

When a motion for a new trial is based on affidavits, they must be filed with the motion. The opposing party has 14 days after being served to file opposing affidavits. The court may permit reply affidavits.

(d) New Trial on the Court's Initiative or for Reasons Not in the Motion.

No later than 28 days after the entry of judgment, the court, on its own, may order a new trial for any reason that would justify granting one on a party's motion. After giving the parties notice and an opportunity to be heard, the court may grant a timely motion for a new trial for a reason not stated in the motion. In either event, the court must specify the reasons in its order.

(e) Motion to Alter or Amend a Judgment.

A motion to alter or amend a judgment must be filed no later than 28 days after the entry of the judgment.

[*Adopted Dec. 20, 1937, effective Sept. 16, 1938; amended Dec. 27, 1946, effective Mar. 19, 1948; Feb. 28, 1966, effective July 1, 1966; Apr. 27, 1995, effective Dec. 1, 1995; amended April 30, 2007, effective Dec. 1, 2007; amended March 26, 2009, effective Dec. 1, 2009.*]

RULE 60.   RELIEF FROM A JUDGMENT OR ORDER.

(a) Corrections Based on Clerical Mistakes; Oversights and Omissions.

The court may correct a clerical mistake or a mistake arising from oversight or omission whenever one is found in a judgment, order, or other part of the record. The court may do so on motion or on its own, with or without notice. But after an appeal has been docketed in the appellate court and while it is pending, such a mistake may be corrected only with the appellate court's leave.

(b) Grounds for Relief from a Final Judgment, Order, or Proceeding.

On motion and just terms, the court may relieve a party or its legal representative from a final judgment, order, or proceeding for the following reasons:

(1) mistake, inadvertence, surprise, or excusable neglect;

(2) newly discovered evidence that, with reasonable diligence, could not have been discovered in time to move for a new trial under Rule 59(b);

(3) fraud (whether previously called intrinsic or extrinsic), misrepresentation, or misconduct by an opposing party;

(4) the judgment is void;

(5) the judgment has been satisfied, released or discharged; it is based on an earlier judgment that has been reversed or vacated; or applying it prospectively is no longer equitable; or

(6) any other reason that justifies relief.

(c) **Timing and Effect of the Motion.**

(1) *Timing.*

A motion under Rule 60(b) must be made within a reasonable time—and for reasons (1), (2), and (3) no more than a year after the entry of the judgment or order or the date of the proceeding.

(2) *Effect on Finality.*

The motion does not affect the judgment's finality or suspend its operation.

(d) **Other Powers to Grant Relief.**

This rule does not limit a court's power to:

(1) entertain an independent action to relieve a party from a judgment, order, or proceeding;

(2) grant relief under 28 U.S.C. § 1655 to a defendant who was not personally notified of the action; or

(3) set aside a judgment for fraud on the court.

(e) **Bills and Writs Abolished.**

The following are abolished: bills of review, bills in the nature of bills of review, and writs of coram nobis, coram vobis, and audita querela.

[*Adopted Dec. 20, 1937, effective Sept. 16, 1938; amended Dec. 27, 1946, effective Mar. 19, 1948; Dec. 29, 1948, effective Oct. 20, 1949; Mar. 2, 1987, effective Aug. 1, 1987; amended April 30, 2007, effective Dec. 1, 2007*].

Rule 61.   Harmless Error.

Unless justice requires otherwise, no error in admitting or excluding evidence—or any other error by the court or a party—is ground for granting a new trial, for setting aside a verdict, or for vacating, modifying, or otherwise disturbing a judgment or order. At every stage of the proceeding, the court must disregard all errors and defects that do not affect any party's substantial rights.

[*Adopted Dec. 20, 1937, effective Sept. 16, 1938; amended April 30, 2007, effective Dec. 1, 2007.*]

RULE 62. STAY OF PROCEEDINGS TO ENFORCE A JUDGMENT.

(a) Automatic Stay.

Except as provided in Rule 62(c) and (d), execution on a judgment and proceedings to enforce it are stayed for 30 days after its entry, unless the court orders otherwise.

(b) Stay by Bond or Other Security.

At any time after judgment is entered, a party may obtain a stay by providing a bond or other security. The stay takes effect when the court approves the bond or other security and remains in effect for the time specified in the bond or other security.

(c) Stay of an Injunction, Receivership, or Patent Accounting Order.

Unless the court orders otherwise, the following are not stayed after being entered, even if an appeal is taken:

(1) an interlocutory or final judgment in an action for an injunction or receivership; or

(2) a judgment or order that directs an accounting in an action for patent infringement.

(d) Injunction Pending an Appeal.

While an appeal is pending from an interlocutory order or final judgment that grants, continues, modifies, refuses, dissolves, or refuses to dissolve or modify an injunction, the court may suspend, modify, restore, or grant an injunction on terms for bond or other terms that secure the opposing party's rights. If the judgment appealed from is rendered by a statutory three-judge district court, the order must be made either:

(1) by that court sitting in open session; or

(2) by the assent of all its judges, as evidenced by their signatures.

(e) Stay Without Bond on an Appeal by the United States, Its Officers, or Its Agencies.

The court must not require a bond, obligation, or other security from the appellant when granting a stay on an appeal by the United States, its officers, or its agencies or on an appeal directed by a department of the federal government.

(f) Stay in Favor of a Judgment Debtor Under State Law.

If a judgment is a lien on the judgment debtor's property under the law of the state where the court is located, the judgment debtor is entitled to the same stay of execution the state court would give.

(g) Appellate Court's Power Not Limited.

This rule does not limit the power of the appellate court or one of its judges or justices:

(1) to stay proceedings—or suspend, modify, restore, or grant an injunction—while an appeal is pending; or

(2) to issue an order to preserve the status quo or the effectiveness of the judgment to be entered.

(h) Stay with Multiple Claims or Parties.

A court may stay the enforcement of a final judgment entered under Rule 54(b) until it enters a later judgment or judgments, and may prescribe terms necessary to secure the benefit of the stayed judgment for the party in whose favor it was entered.

[*Adopted Dec. 20, 1937, effective Sept. 16, 1938; as amended April 26, 2018, effective Dec. 1, 2018.*]

RULE 62.1. INDICATIVE RULING ON A MOTION FOR RELIEF THAT IS BARRED BY A PENDING APPEAL.

(a) Relief Pending Appeal.

If a timely motion is made for relief that the court lacks authority to grant because of an appeal that has been docketed and is pending, the court may:

(1) defer considering the motion;

(2) deny the motion; or

(3) state either that it would grant the motion if the court of appeals remands for that purpose or that the motion raises a substantial issue.

(b) Notice to the Court of Appeals.

The movant must promptly notify the circuit clerk under Federal Rule of Appellate Procedure 12.1 if the district court states that it would grant the motion or that the motion raises a substantial issue.

(c) Remand.

The district court may decide the motion if the court of appeals remands for that purpose.

[*Adopted Dec. 1, 2009.*]

RULE 63. JUDGE'S INABILITY TO PROCEED.

If a judge conducting a hearing or trial is unable to proceed, any other judge may proceed upon certifying familiarity with the record and determining that the case may be completed without prejudice to the parties. In a hearing or a nonjury trial, the successor judge must, at a party's request, recall any witness whose testimony is material and disputed and who is available to testify again without undue burden. The successor judge may also recall any other witness.

[*Adopted Dec. 20, 1937, effective Sept. 16, 1938; amended Mar. 2, 1987, effective Aug. 1, 1987; Apr. 30, 1991, effective Dec. 1, 1991; amended April 30, 2007, effective Dec. 1, 2007.*]

TITLE VIII. PROVISIONAL AND FINAL REMEDIES

RULE 64. SEIZING A PERSON OR PROPERTY.

(a) Remedies Under State Law—In General.

At the commencement of and throughout an action, every remedy is available that, under the law of the state where the court is located, provides for seizing a person or property to secure satisfaction of the potential judgment. But a federal statute governs to the extent it applies.

(b) Specific Kinds of Remedies.

The remedies available under this rule include the following—however designated and regardless of whether state procedure requires an independent action:

- arrest;
- attachment;
- garnishment;
- replevin;
- sequestration; and
- other corresponding or equivalent remedies.

[*Adopted Dec. 20, 1937, effective Sept. 16, 1938; amended April 30, 2007, effective Dec. 1, 2007.*]

RULE 65. INJUNCTIONS AND RESTRAINING ORDERS.

(a) Preliminary Injunction.

(1) *Notice.*

The court may issue a preliminary injunction only on notice to the adverse party.

(2) *Consolidating the Hearing with the Trial on the Merits.*

Before or after beginning the hearing on a motion for a preliminary injunction, the court may advance the trial on the merits and consolidate it with the hearing. Even when consolidation is not ordered, evidence that is received on the motion and that would be admissible at trial becomes part of the trial record and need not be repeated at trial. But the court must preserve any party's right to a jury trial.

(b) Temporary Restraining Order.

(1) *Issuing Without Notice.*

The court may issue a temporary restraining order without written or oral notice to the adverse party or its attorney only if:

> (A) specific facts in an affidavit or a verified complaint clearly show that immediate and irreparable injury, loss, or damage will result to the movant before the adverse party can be heard in opposition; and

> (B) the movant's attorney certifies in writing any efforts made to give notice and the reasons why it should not be required.

(2) *Contents; Expiration.*

Every temporary restraining order issued without notice must state the date and hour it was issued; describe the injury and state why it is irreparable; state why the order was issued without notice; and be promptly filed in the clerk's office and entered in the record. The order expires at the time after entry—not to exceed 14 days—that the court sets, unless before that time the court, for good cause, extends it for a like period or the adverse party consents to a longer extension. The reasons for an extension must be entered in the record.

(3) *Expediting the Preliminary-Injunction Hearing.*

If the order is issued without notice, the motion for a preliminary injunction must be set for hearing at the earliest possible time, taking precedence over all other matters except hearings on older matters of the same character. At the hearing, the party who obtained the order must proceed with the motion; if the party does not, the court must dissolve the order.

(4) *Motion to Dissolve.*

On 2 days' notice to the party who obtained the order without notice—or on shorter notice set by the court—the adverse party may appear and move to dissolve or modify the order. The court must then hear and decide the motion as promptly as justice requires.

(c) Security.

The court may issue a preliminary injunction or a temporary restraining order only if the movant gives security in an amount that the court considers proper to pay the costs and damages sustained by any party found to have been wrongfully enjoined or restrained. The United States, its officers, and its agencies are not required to give security.

(d) Contents and Scope of Every Injunction and Restraining Order.

(1) *Contents.*

Every order granting an injunction and every restraining order must:

> (A) state the reasons why it issued;

(B) state its terms specifically; and

(C) describe in reasonable detail—and not by referring to the complaint or other document—the act or acts restrained or required.

(2) *Persons Bound.*

The order binds only the following who receive actual notice of it by personal service or otherwise:

(A) the parties;

(B) the parties' officers, agents, servants, employees, and attorneys; and

(C) other persons who are in active concert or participation with anyone described in Rule 65(d)(2)(A) or (B).

(e) Other Laws Not Modified.

These rules do not modify the following:

(1) any federal statute relating to temporary restraining orders or preliminary injunctions in actions affecting employer and employee;

(2) 28 U.S.C. § 2361, which relates to preliminary injunctions in actions of interpleader or in the nature of interpleader; or

(3) 28 U.S.C. § 2284, which relates to actions that must be heard and decided by a three-judge district court.

(f) Copyright Impoundment.

This rule applies to copyright-impoundment proceedings.

[*Adopted Dec. 20, 1937, effective Sept. 16, 1938; amended Dec. 27, 1946, effective Mar. 19, 1948; Dec. 29, 1948, effective Oct. 20, 1949; Feb. 28, 1966, effective July 1, 1966; Mar. 2, 1987, effective Aug. 1, 1987; Apr. 23, 2001, effective Dec. 1, 2001; amended April 30, 2007, effective Dec. 1, 2007; amended March 26, 2009, effective Dec. 1, 2009.*]

RULE 65.1.   PROCEEDINGS AGAINST A SURETY.

Whenever these rules (including the Supplemental Rules for Admiralty or Maritime Claims and Asset Forfeiture Actions) require or allow a party to give security, and security is given with one or more security providers, each provider submits to the court's jurisdiction and irrevocably appoints the court clerk as its agent for receiving service of any papers that affect its liability on the security. The security provider's liability may be enforced on motion without an independent action. The motion and any notice that the court orders may be served on the court clerk, who must promptly send a copy of each to every security provider whose address is known.

[*Adopted Feb. 28, 1966, effective July 1, 1966; as amended April 26, 2018, effective Dec. 1, 2018.*]

RULE 66.   RECEIVERS.

These rules govern an action in which the appointment of a receiver is sought or a receiver sues or is sued. But the practice in administering an estate by a receiver or a similar court-appointed officer must accord with the historical practice in federal courts or with a local rule. An action in which a receiver has been appointed may be dismissed only by court order.

[*Adopted Dec. 20, 1937, effective Sept. 16, 1938; amended Dec. 27, 1946, effective Mar. 19, 1948; Dec. 29, 1948, effective Oct. 20, 1949; amended April 30, 2007, effective Dec. 1, 2007.*]

RULE 67.   DEPOSIT INTO COURT.

(a) Depositing Property.

If any part of the relief sought is a money judgment or the disposition of a sum of money or some other deliverable thing, a party — on notice to every other party and by leave of court — may deposit with the court all or part of the money or thing, whether or not that party claims any of it. The depositing party must deliver to the clerk a copy of the order permitting deposit.

(b) Investing and Withdrawing Funds.

Money paid into court under this rule must be deposited and withdrawn in accordance with 28 U.S.C. §§ 2041 and 2042 and any like statute. The money must be deposited in an interest-bearing account or invested in a court-approved, interest-bearing instrument.

[*Adopted Dec. 20, 1937, effective Sept. 16, 1938; amended Dec. 29, 1948, effective Oct. 20, 1949; Apr. 28, 1983, effective Aug. 1, 1983; amended April 30, 2007, effective Dec. 1, 2007.*]

RULE 68.   OFFER OF JUDGMENT.

(a) Making an Offer; Judgment on an Accepted Offer.

More than 14 days before the trial begins, a party defending against a claim may serve on an opposing party an offer to allow judgment on specified terms, with the costs then accrued. If, within 14 days after being served, the opposing party serves written notice accepting the offer, either party may then file the offer and notice ofacceptance, plus proof of service. The clerk must then enter judgment.

(b) Unaccepted Offer.

An unaccepted offer is considered withdrawn, but it does not preclude a later offer. Evidence of an unaccepted offer is not admissible except in a proceeding to determine costs.

(c) Offer After Liability Is Determined.

When one party's liability to another has been determined but the extent of liability remains to be determined by further proceedings, the party held liable may make an offer of judgment. It must be served within a reasonable time—but at least 14 days—before a hearing to determine the extent of liability.

(d) Paying Costs After an Unaccepted Offer.

If the judgment that the offeree finally obtains is not more favorable than the unaccepted offer, the offeree must pay the costs incurred after the offer was made.

[*Adopted Dec. 20, 1937, effective Sept. 16, 1938; amended Dec. 27, 1946, effective Mar. 19, 1948; Feb. 28, 1966, effective July 1, 1966; Mar. 2, 1987, effective Aug. 1, 1987; amended April 30, 2007, effective December 1, 2007; amended March 26, 2009, effective Dec. 1, 2009.*]

RULE 69. EXECUTION.

(a) In General.

(1) *Money Judgment; Applicable Procedure.*

A money judgment is enforced by a writ of execution, unless the court directs otherwise. The procedure on execution—and in proceedings supplementary to and in aid of judgment or execution—must accord with the procedure of the state where the court is located, but a federal statute governs to the extent it applies.

(2) *Obtaining Discovery.*

In aid of the judgment or execution, the judgment creditor or a successor in interest whose interest appears of record may obtain discovery from any person—including the judgment debtor—as provided in these rules or by the procedure of the state where the court is located.

(b) Against Certain Public Officers.

When a judgment has been entered against a revenue officer in the circumstances stated in 28 U.S.C. § 2006, or against an officer of Congress in the circumstances stated in 2 U.S.C. § 118, the judgment must be satisfied as those statutes provide.

[*Adopted Dec. 20, 1937, effective Sept. 16, 1938; amended Dec. 29, 1948, effective Oct. 20, 1949; Mar. 30, 1970, effective July 1, 1970; Mar. 2, 1987, effective Aug. 1, 1987; amended April 30, 2007, effective Dec. 1, 2007.*]

RULE 70.   ENFORCING A JUDGMENT FOR A SPECIFIC ACT.

(a) Party's Failure to Act; Ordering Another to Act.

If a judgment requires a party to convey land, to deliver a deed or other document, or to perform any other specific act and the party fails to comply within the time specified, the court may order the act to be done—at the disobedient party's expense—by another person appointed by the court. When done, the act has the same effect as if done by the party.

(b) Vesting Title.

If the real or personal property is within the district, the court—instead of ordering a conveyance—may enter a judgment divesting any party's title and vesting it in others. That judgment has the effect of a legally executed conveyance.

(c) Obtaining a Writ of Attachment or Sequestration.

On application by a party entitled to performance of an act, the clerk must issue a writ of attachment or sequestration against the disobedient party's property to compel obedience.

(d) Obtaining a Writ of Execution or Assistance.

On application by a party who obtains a judgment or order for possession, the clerk must issue a writ of execution or assistance.

(e) Holding in Contempt.

The court may also hold the disobedient party in contempt.

[*Adopted Dec. 20, 1937, effective Sept. 16, 1938; amended April 30, 2007, effective Dec. 1, 2007.*]

RULE 71.   ENFORCING RELIEF FOR OR AGAINST A NONPARTY.

When an order grants relief for a nonparty or may be enforced against a nonparty, the procedure for enforcing the order is the same as for a party.

[*Adopted Dec. 20, 1937, effective Sept. 16, 1938; amended Mar. 2, 1987, effective Aug. 1, 1987; amended April 30, 2007, effective Dec. 1, 2007.*]

TITLE IX.   SPECIAL PROCEEDINGS

RULE 71.1.   CONDEMNING REAL OR PERSONAL PROPERTY.

(a) Applicability of Other Rules.

These rules govern proceedings to condemn real and personal property by eminent domain, except as this rule provides otherwise.

(b) Joinder of Properties.

The plaintiff may join separate pieces of property in a single action, no matter whether they are owned by the same persons or sought for the same use.

(c) Complaint.

(1) *Caption.*

The complaint must contain a caption as provided in Rule 10(a). The plaintiff must, however, name as defendants both the property C designated generally by kind, quantity, and location—and at least one owner of some part of or interest in the property.

(2) *Contents.*

The complaint must contain a short and plain statement of the following:

(A) the authority for the taking;

(B) the uses for which the property is to be taken;

(C) a description sufficient to identify the property;

(D) the interests to be acquired; and

(E) for each piece of property, a designation of each defendant who has been joined as an owner or owner of an interest in it.

(3) *Parties.*

When the action commences, the plaintiff need join as defendants only those persons who have or claim an interest in the property and whose names are then known. But before any hearing on compensation, the plaintiff must add as defendants all those persons who have or claim an interest and whose names have become known or can be found by a reasonably diligent search of the records, considering both the property's character and value and the interests to be acquired. All others may be made defendants under the designation "Unknown Owners."

(4) *Procedure.*

Notice must be served on all defendants as provided in Rule 71.1(d), whether they were named as defendants when the action commenced or were added later. A defendant may answer as provided in Rule 71.1(e). The court, meanwhile, may order any distribution of a deposit that the facts warrant.

(5) *Filing; Additional Copies.*

In addition to filing the complaint, the plaintiff must give the clerk at least one copy for the defendants' use and additional copies at the request of the clerk or a defendant.

(d) Process.

(1) *Delivering Notice to the Clerk.*

On filing a complaint, the plaintiff must promptly deliver to the clerk joint or several notices directed to the named defendants. When adding defendants, the plaintiff must deliver to the clerk additional notices directed to the new defendants.

(2) *Contents of the Notice.*

(A) *Main Contents.*

Each notice must name the court, the title of the action, and the defendant to whom it is directed. It must describe the property sufficiently to identify it, but need not describe any property other than that to be taken from the named defendant. The notice must also state:

> (i) that the action is to condemn property;

> (ii) the interest to be taken;

> (iii) the authority for the taking;

> (iv) the uses for which the property is to be taken;

> (v) that the defendant may serve an answer on the plaintiff's attorney within 21 days after being served with the notice;

> (vi) that the failure to so serve an answer constitutes consent to the taking and to the court's authority to proceed with the action and fix the compensation; and

> (vii) that a defendant who does not serve an answer may file a notice of appearance.

(B) *Conclusion.*

The notice must conclude with the name, telephone number, and e-mail address of the plaintiff's attorney and an address within the district in which the action is brought where the attorney may be served.

(3) *Serving the Notice.*

(A) *Personal Service.*

When a defendant whose address is known resides within the United States or a territory subject to the administrative or judicial jurisdiction of the United States, personal service of the notice (without a copy of the complaint) must be made in accordance with Rule 4.

(B) *Service by Publication.*

> (i) A defendant may be served by publication only when the plaintiff's attorney files a certificate stating that the attorney believes the defendant cannot be personally served, because after diligent inquiry within the state where the complaint is filed, the defendant's place of residence is still unknown or, if known, that it is beyond the territorial limits of personal service. Service is then made by publishing the notice—once a week for at least three successive weeks—in a newspaper published in the county where the property is located or, if there is no such newspaper, in a newspaper with general circulation where the property is located. Before the last publication, a copy of the notice must also be mailed to every defendant who cannot be personally served but whose place of residence is then known. Unknown owners may be served by publication in the same manner by a notice addressed to "Unknown Owners."

(ii) Service by publication is complete on the date of the last publication. The plaintiff's attorney must prove publication and mailing by a certificate, attach a printed copy of the published notice, and mark on the copy the newspaper's name and the dates of publication.

(4) *Effect of Delivery and Service.*

Delivering the notice to the clerk and serving it have the same effect as serving a summons under Rule 4.

(5) *Proof of Service; Amending the Proof or Notice.*

Rule 4(l) governs proof of service. The court may permit the proof or the notice to be amended.

(e) Appearance or Answer.

(1) *Notice of Appearance.*

A defendant that has no objection or defense to the taking of its property may serve a notice of appearance designating the property in which it claims an interest. The defendant must then be given notice of all later proceedings affecting the defendant.

(2) *Answer.*

A defendant that has an objection or defense to the taking must serve an answer within 21 days after being served with the notice. The answer must:

(A) identify the property in which the defendant claims an interest;

(B) state the nature and extent of the interest; and

(C) state all the defendant's objections and defenses to the taking.

(3) *Waiver of Other Objections and Defenses; Evidence on Compensation.*

A defendant waives all objections and defenses not stated in its answer. No other pleading or motion asserting an additional objection or defense is allowed. But at the trial on compensation, a defendant—whether or not it has previously appeared or answered—may present evidence on the amount of compensation to be paid and may share in the award.

(f) Amending Pleadings.

Without leave of court, the plaintiff may—as often as it wants—amend the complaint at any time before the trial on compensation. But no amendment may be made if it would result in a dismissal inconsistent with Rule 71.1(i)(1) or (2). The plaintiff need not serve a copy of an amendment, but must serve notice of the filing, as provided in Rule 5(b), on every affected party who has appeared and, as provided in Rule 71.1(d), on every affected party who has not appeared. In addition, the plaintiff must give the clerk at least one copy of each amendment for the defendants' use, and additional copies at the request of the clerk or a defendant. A defendant may appear or answer in the time and manner and with the same effect as provided in Rule 71.1(e).

(g) Substituting Parties.

If a defendant dies, becomes incompetent, or transfers an interest after being joined, the court may, on motion and notice of hearing, order that the proper party be substituted. Service of the motion and notice on a nonparty must be made as provided in Rule 71.1(d)(3).

(h) Trial of the Issues.

(1) *Issues Other Than Compensation; Compensation.*

In an action involving eminent domain under federal law, the court tries all issues, including compensation, except when compensation must be determined:

(A) by any tribunal specially constituted by a federal statute to determine compensation; or

(B) if there is no such tribunal, by a jury when a party demands one within the time to answer or within any additional time the court sets, unless the court appoints a commission.

(2) *Appointing a Commission; Commission's Powers and Report.*

(A) *Reasons for Appointing.*

If a party has demanded a jury, the court may instead appoint a three-person commission to determine compensation because of the character, location, or quantity of the property to be condemned or for other just reasons.

(B) *Alternate Commissioners.*

The court may appoint up to two additional persons to serve as alternate commissioners to hear the case and replace commissioners who, before a decision is filed, the court finds unable or disqualified to perform their duties. Once the commission renders its final decision, the court must discharge any alternate who has not replaced a commissioner.

(C) *Examining the Prospective Commissioners.*

Before making its appointments, the court must advise the parties of the identity and qualifications of each prospective commissioner and alternate, and may permit the parties to examine them. The parties may not suggest appointees, but for good cause may object to a prospective commissioner or alternate.

(D) *Commission's Powers and Report.*

A commission has the powers of a master under Rule 53(c). Its action and report are determined by a majority. Rule 53(d), (e), and (f) apply to its action and report.

(i) Dismissal of the Action or a Defendant.

(1) *Dismissing the Action.*

(A) *By the Plaintiff.*

If no compensation hearing on a piece of property has begun, and if the plaintiff has not acquired title or a lesser interest or taken possession, the plaintiff may, without a court order, dismiss the action as to that property by filing a notice of dismissal briefly describing the property.

(B) *By Stipulation.*

Before a judgment is entered vesting the plaintiff with title or a lesser interest in or possession of property, the plaintiff and affected defendants may, without a court order, dismiss the action in whole or in part by filing a stipulation of dismissal. And if the parties so stipulate, the court may vacate a judgment already entered.

(C) *By Court Order.*

At any time before compensation has been determined and paid, the court may, after a motion and hearing, dismiss the action as to a piece of property. But if the plaintiff has already taken title, a lesser interest, or possession as to any part of it, the court must award compensation for the title, lesser interest, or possession taken.

(2) *Dismissing a Defendant.*

The court may at any time dismiss a defendant who was unnecessarily or improperly joined.

(3) *Effect.*

A dismissal is without prejudice unless otherwise stated in the notice, stipulation, or court order.

(j) **Deposit and Its Distribution.**

(1) *Deposit.*

The plaintiff must deposit with the court any money required by law as a condition to the exercise of eminent domain and may make a deposit when allowed by statute.

(2) *Distribution; Adjusting Distribution.*

After a deposit, the court and attorneys must expedite the proceedings so as to distribute the deposit and to determine and pay compensation. If the compensation finally awarded to a defendant exceeds the amount distributed to that defendant, the court must enter judgment against the plaintiff for the deficiency. If the compensation awarded to a defendant is less than the amount distributed to that defendant, the court must enter judgment against that defendant for the overpayment.

(k) **Condemnation Under a State's Power of Eminent Domain.**

This rule governs an action involving eminent domain under state law. But if state law provides for trying an issue by jury—or for trying the issue of compensation by jury or commission or both—that law governs.

(l) **Costs.**

Costs are not subject to Rule 54(d).

[*Adopted Apr. 30, 1951, effective Aug. 1, 1951; amended Jan. 21, 1963, effective July 1, 1963; Apr. 29, 1985, effective Aug. 1, 1985; Mar. 2, 1987, effective Aug. 1, 1987; Apr. 25, 1988, effective Aug. 1, 1988; Nov. 18, 1988; Apr. 22, 1993, effective Dec. 1, 1993; Mar. 27, 2003, effective Dec. 1, 2003; amended April 30, 2007, effective Dec. 1, 2007; amended March 26, 2009, effective Dec. 1, 2009.*]

RULE 72.   MAGISTRATE JUDGES: PRETRIAL ORDER.

(a) Nondispositive Matters.

When a pretrial matter not dispositive of a party's claim or defense is referred to a magistrate judge to hear and decide, the magistrate judge must promptly conduct the required proceedings and, when appropriate, issue a written order stating the decision. A party may serve and file objections to the order within 14 days after being served with a copy. A party may not assign as error a defect in the order not timely objected to. The district judge in the case must consider timely objections and modify or set aside any part of the order that is clearly erroneous or is contrary to law.

(b) Dispositive Motions and Prisoner Petitions.

(1) *Findings and Recommendations.*

A magistrate judge must promptly conduct the required proceedings when assigned, without the parties' consent, to hear a pretrial matter dispositive of a claim or defense or a prisoner petition challenging the conditions of confinement. A record must be made of all evidentiary proceedings and may, at the magistrate judge's discretion, be made of any other proceedings. The magistrate judge must enter a recommended disposition, including, if appropriate, proposed findings of fact. The clerk must promptly mail a copy to each party.

(2) *Objections.*

Within 14 days after being served with a copy of the recommended disposition, a party may serve and file specific written objections to the proposed findings and recommendations. A party may respond to another party's objections within 14 days after being served with a copy. Unless the district judge orders otherwise, the objecting party must promptly arrange for transcribing the record, or whatever portions of it the parties agree to or the magistrate judge considers sufficient.

(3) *Resolving Objections.*

The district judge must determine de novo any part of the magistrate judge's disposition that has been properly objected to. The district judge may accept, reject, or modify the recommended disposition; receive further evidence; or return the matter to the magistrate judge with instructions.

[*Adopted Apr. 28, 1983, effective Aug. 1, 1983; amended Apr. 30, 1991, effective Dec. 1, 1991; Apr. 22, 1993, effective Dec. 1, 1993; amended April 30, 2007, effective Dec. 1, 2007; amended March 26, 2009, effective Dec. 1, 2009.*]

RULE 73.   MAGISTRATE JUDGES: TRIAL BY CONSENT; APPEAL.

(a) Trial by Consent.

When authorized under 28 U.S.C. § 636(c), a magistrate judge may, if all parties consent, conduct a civil action or proceeding, including a jury or nonjury trial. A record must be made in accordance with 28 U.S.C. § 636(c)(5).

(b) Consent Procedure.

(1) *In General.*

When a magistrate judge has been designated to conduct civil actions or proceedings, the clerk must give the parties written notice of their opportunity to consent under 28 U.S.C. § 636(c). To signify their consent, the parties must jointly or separately file a statement consenting to the referral. A district judge or magistrate judge may be informed of a party's response to the clerk's notice only if all parties have consented to the referral.

(2) *Reminding the Parties About Consenting.*

A district judge, magistrate judge, or other court official may remind the parties of the magistrate judge's availability, but must also advise them that they are free to withhold consent without adverse substantive consequences.

(3) *Vacating a Referral.*

On its own for good cause — or when a party shows extraordinary circumstances — the district judge may vacate a referral to a magistrate judge under this rule.

(c) Appealing a Judgment.

In accordance with 28 U.S.C. § 636(c)(3), an appeal from a judgment entered at a magistrate judge's direction may be taken to the court of appeals as would any other appeal from a district-court judgment.

[*Adopted Apr. 28, 1983, effective Aug. 1, 1983; amended Mar. 2, 1987, effective Aug. 1, 1987; Apr. 22, 1993, effective Dec. 1, 1993; amended Apr. 11, 1997, effective Dec. 1, 1997; amended April 30, 2007, effective Dec. 1, 2007.*]

RULE 74.   METHOD OF APPEAL FROM MAGISTRATE JUDGE TO DISTRICT JUDGE UNDER TITLE 28, U.S.C. § 636(c)(4) AND RULE 73(D).

(Abrogated-December 1, 1997.)

RULE 75.   PROCEEDINGS ON APPEAL FROM MAGISTRATE JUDGE TO DISTRICT JUDGE UNDER RULE 73(D).

(Abrogated-December 1, 1997.)

Rule 76. Judgment of the District Judge on the Appeal Under Rule 73(d) and Costs.

(Abrogated-December 1, 1997.)

TITLE X.   DISTRICT COURTS AND CLERKS: CONDUCTING BUSINESS; ISSUING ORDERS

Rule 77.   Conducting Business; Clerk's Authority; Notice of an Order or Judgment.

(a) When Court Is Open.

Every district court is considered always open for filing any paper, issuing and returning process, making a motion, or entering an order.

(b) Place for Trial and Other Proceedings.

Every trial on the merits must be conducted in open court and, so far as convenient, in a regular courtroom. Any other act or proceeding may be done or conducted by a judge in chambers, without the attendance of the clerk or other court official, and anywhere inside or outside the district. But no hearing—other than one exparte—may be conducted outside the district unless all the affected parties consent.

(c) Clerk's Office Hours; Clerk's Orders.

(1) *Hours.*

The clerk's office—with a clerk or deputy on duty—must be open during business hours every day except Saturdays, Sundays, and legal holidays. But a court may, by local rule or order, require that the office be open for specified hours on Saturday or a particular legal holiday other than one listed in Rule 6(a)(6)(A).

(2) *Orders.*

Subject to the court's power to suspend, alter, or rescind the clerk's action for good cause, the clerk may:

(A) issue process;

(B) enter a default;

(C) enter a default judgment under Rule 55(b)(1); and

(D) act on any other matter that does not require the court's action.

(d) Serving Notice of an Order or Judgment.

(1) *Service.*

Immediately after entering an order or judgment, the clerk must serve notice of the entry, as provided in Rule 5(b), on each party who is not in default for failing to appear. The clerk must record the service on the docket. A party also may serve notice of the entry as provided in Rule 5(b).

(2) *Time to Appeal Not Affected by Lack of Notice.*

Lack of notice of the entry does not affect the time for appeal or relieve—or authorize the court to relieve—a party for failing to appeal within the time allowed, except as allowed by Federal Rule of Appellate Procedure (4)(a).

[*Adopted Dec. 20, 1937, effective Sept. 16, 1938; amended Dec. 27, 1946, effective Mar. 19, 1948; Jan. 21, 1963, effective July 1, 1963; Dec. 4, 1967, effective July 1, 1968; Mar. 1, 1971, effective July 1, 1971; Mar. 2, 1987, effective Aug. 1, 1987; Apr. 30, 1991, effective Dec. 1, 1991; Apr. 23, 2001, effective Dec. 1, 2001; amended April 30, 2007, effective Dec. 1, 2007; amended April 25, 2014, effective Dec. 1, 2014.*]

ADVISORY COMMITTEE'S NOTE TO 2001 AMENDMENT

Rule 77(d) is amended to reflect changes in Rule 5(b). A few courts have experimented with serving Rule 77(d) notices by electronic means on parties who consent to this procedure. The success of these experiments warrants express authorization. Because service is made in the manner provided in Rule 5(b), party consent is required for service by electronic or other means described in Rule 5(b)(2)(D). The same provision is made for a party who wishes to ensure actual communication of the Rule 77(d) notice by also serving notice.

ADVISORY COMMITTEES NOTE TO 1991 AMENDMENT OF SUBDIVISION (D)

This revision is a companion to the concurrent amendment to Rule 4 of the Federal Rules of Appellate Procedure. The purpose of the revisions is to permit district courts to ease strict sanctions now imposed on appellants whose notices of appeal are filed late because of their failure to receive notice of entry of a judgment.

Failure to receive notice may have increased in frequency with the growth in the caseload in the clerks' offices. The present strict rule imposes a duty on counsel to maintain contact with the court while a case is under submission. Such contact is more difficult to maintain if counsel is outside the district, as is increasingly common, and can be a burden to the court as well as counsel.

The effect of the revisions is to place a burden on prevailing parties who desire certainty that the time for appeal is running. Such parties can take the initiative to assure that their adversaries receive effective notice. An appropriate procedure for such notice is provided in Rule 5.

The revised rule lightens the responsibility but not the workload of the clerk's offices, for the duty of that office to give notice of entry of judgment must be maintained.

RULE 78. HEARING MOTIONS; SUBMISSION ON BRIEFS.

(a) Providing a Regular Schedule for Oral Hearings.

A court may establish regular times and places for oral hearings on motions.

(b) Providing for Submission on Briefs.

By rule or order, the court may provide for submitting and determining motions on briefs, without oral hearings.

[*Adopted Dec. 20, 1937, effective Sept. 16, 1938; amended Mar. 2, 1987, effective Aug. 1, 1987; amended April 30, 2007, effective Dec. 1, 2007.*]

RULE 79.   RECORDS KEPT BY THE CLERK.

(a) Civil Docket.

(1) *In General.*

The clerk must keep a record known as the "civil docket" in the form and manner prescribed by the Director of the Administrative Office of the United States Courts with the approval of the Judicial Conference of the United States. The clerk must enter each civil action in the docket. Actions must be assigned consecutive file numbers, which must be noted in the docket where the first entry of the action is made.

(2) *Items to be Entered.*

The following items must be marked with the file number and entered chronologically in the docket:

(A) papers filed with the clerk;

(B) process issued, and proofs of service or other returns showing execution; and

(C) appearances, orders, verdicts, and judgments.

(3) *Contents of Entries; Jury Trial Demanded.*

Each entry must briefly show the nature of the paper filed or writ issued, the substance of each proof of service or other return, and the substance and date of entry of each order and judgment. When a jury trial has been properly demanded or ordered, the clerk must enter the word "jury" in the docket.

(b) Civil Judgments and Orders.

The clerk must keep a copy of every final judgment and appealable order; of every order affecting title to or a lien on real or personal property; and of any other order that the court directs to be kept. The clerk must keep these in the form and manner prescribed by the Director of the Administrative Office of the United States Courts with the approval of the Judicial Conference of the United States.

(c) Indexes; Calendars.

Under the court's direction, the clerk must:

(1) keep indexes of the docket and of the judgments and orders described in Rule 79(b); and

(2) prepare calendars of all actions ready for trial, distinguishing jury trials from nonjury trials.

(d) Other Records.

The clerk must keep any other records required by the Director of the Administrative Office of the United States Courts with the approval of the Judicial Conference of the United States.

[*Adopted Dec. 20, 1937, effective Sept. 16, 1938; amended Dec. 27, 1946, effective Mar. 19, 1948; Dec. 29, 1948, effective Oct. 20, 1949; Jan. 21, 1963, effective July 1, 1963; amended April 30, 2007, effective Dec. 1, 2007.*]

RULE 80. STENOGRAPHIC TRANSCRIPT AS EVIDENCE.

If stenographically reported testimony at a hearing or trial is admissible in evidence at a later trial, the testimony may be proved by a transcript certified by the person who reported it.

[*Adopted Dec. 20, 1937, effective Sept. 16, 1938; amended Dec. 27, 1946, effective Mar. 19, 1948; amended April 30, 2007, effective Dec. 1, 2007.*]

TITLE XI. GENERAL PROVISIONS

RULE 81. APPLICABILITY OF THE RULES IN GENERAL; REMOVED ACTIONS.

(a) Applicability to Particular Proceedings.

(1) *Prize Proceedings.*

These rules do not apply to prize proceedings in admiralty governed by 10 U.S.C. §§ 7651–7681.

(2) *Bankruptcy.*

These rules apply to bankruptcy proceedings to the extent provided by the Federal Rules of Bankruptcy Procedure.

(3) *Citizenship.*

These rules apply to proceedings for admission to citizenship to the extent that the practice in those proceedings is not specified in federal statutes and has previously conformed to the practice in civil actions. The provisions of 8 U.S.C. § 1451 for service by publication and for answer apply in proceedings to cancel citizenship certificates.

(4) *Special Writs.*

These rules apply to proceedings for habeas corpus and for quo warranto to the extent that the practice in those proceedings:

(A) is not specified in a federal statute, the Rules Governing Section 2254 Cases, or the Rules Governing Section 2255 Cases; and

(B) has previously conformed to the practice in civil actions.

(5) *Proceedings Involving a Subpoena.*

These rules apply to proceedings to compel testimony or the production of documents through a subpoena issued by a United States officer or agency under a federal statute, except as otherwise provided by statute, by local rule, or by court order in the proceedings.

(6) *Other Proceedings.*

These rules, to the extent applicable, govern proceedings under the following laws, except as these laws provide other procedures:

>(A) 7 U.S.C. §§ 292, 499g(c), for reviewing an order of the Secretary of Agriculture;

>(B) 9 U.S.C., relating to arbitration;

>(C) 15 U.S.C. § 522, for reviewing an order of the Secretary of the Interior;

>(D) 15 U.S.C. § 715d(c), for reviewing an order denying a certificate of clearance;

>(E) 29 U.S.C. §§ 159, 160, for enforcing an order of the National Labor Relations Board;

>(F) 33 U.S.C. §§ 918, 921, for enforcing or reviewing a compensation order under the Longshore and Harbor Workers' Compensation Act; and

>(G) 45 U.S.C. § 159, for reviewing an arbitration award in a railway-labor dispute.

(b) Scire Facias and Mandamus.

The writs of scire facias and mandamus are abolished. Relief previously available through them may be obtained by appropriate action or motion under these rules.

(c) Removed Actions.

(1) *Applicability.*

These rules apply to a civil action after it is removed from a state court.

(2) *Further Pleading.*

After removal, repleading is unnecessary unless the court orders it. A defendant who did not answer before removal must answer or present other defenses or objections under these rules within the longest of these periods:

>(A) 21 days after receiving—through service or otherwise—a copy of the initial pleading stating the claim for relief;

>(B) 21 days after being served with the summons for an initial pleading on file at the time of service; or

>(C) 7 days after the notice of removal is filed.

(3) *Demand for a Jury Trial.*

(A) *As Affected by State Law.*

A party who, before removal, expressly demanded a jury trial in accordance with state law need not renew the demand after removal. If the state law did not require an express demand for a jury trial, a party need not make one after removal unless the court orders the parties to do so within a specified time. The court must so order at a party's request and may so order on its own. A party who fails to make a demand when so ordered waives a jury trial.

(B) *Under Rule 38.*

If all necessary pleadings have been served at the time of removal, a party entitled to a jury trial under Rule 38 must be given one if the party serves a demand within 14 days after:

     (i) it files a notice of removal; or

     (ii) it is served with a notice of removal filed by another party.

(d) Law Applicable.

(1) *"State Law" Defined.*

When these rules refer to state law, the term "law" includes the state's statutes and the state's judicial decisions.

(2) *"State" Defined.*

The term "state" includes, where appropriate, the District of Columbia and any United States commonwealth or territory.

(3) *"Federal Statute" Defined in the District of Columbia.*

In the United States District Court for the District of Columbia, the term "federal statute" includes any Act of Congress that applies locally to the District.

[*Adopted Dec. 20, 1937, effective Sept. 16, 1938; amended Dec. 28, 1939, effective Apr. 3, 1941; Dec. 27, 1946, effective Mar. 19, 1948; Dec. 29, 1948, effective Oct. 20, 1949; Apr. 30 1951, effective Aug. 1, 1951; Jan. 21, 1963, effective July 1, 1963; Feb. 28, 1966, effective July 1, 1966; Dec. 4, 1967, effective July 1, 1968; Mar. 1, 1971, effective July 1, 1971; Mar. 2, 1987, effective Aug. 1, 1987; Apr. 23, 2001, effective Dec. 1, 2001; Apr. 29, 2002, effective Dec. 1, 2002; amended April 30, 2007, effective Dec. 1, 2007; amended March 26, 2009, effective Dec. 1, 2009.*]

RULE 82. JURISDICTION AND VENUE UNAFFECTED.

These rules do not to extend or limit the jurisdiction of the district courts or the venue of actions in those courts. An admiralty or maritime claim under Rule 9(h) is governed by 28 U.S.C. § 1390.

[*Adopted Dec. 20, 1937, effective Sept. 16, 1938; as amended April 28, 2016, effective Dec. 1, 2016.*]

RULE 83. RULES BY DISTRICT COURTS; JUDGE'S DIRECTIVES.

(a) Local Rules.

(1) *In General.*

After giving public notice and an opportunity for comment, a district court, acting by a majority of its district judges, may adopt and amend rules governing its practice. A local rule must be consistent with—but not duplicate—federal statutes and rules adopted under 28 U.S.C. §§ 2072 and 2075, and must conform to any uniform numbering system prescribed by the Judicial Conference of the United States. A local rule takes effect on the date specified by the district court and remains in effect unless amended by the court or abrogated by the judicial council of the circuit. Copies of rules and amendments must, on their adoption, be furnished to the judicial council and the Administrative Office of the United States Courts and be made available to the public.

(2) *Requirement of Form.*

A local rule imposing a requirement of form must not be enforced in a way that causes a party to lose any right because of a nonwillful failure to comply.

(b) Procedure When There Is No Controlling Law.

A judge may regulate practice in any manner consistent with federal law, rules adopted under 28 U.S.C. §§ 2072 and 2075, and the district's local rules. No sanction or other disadvantage may be imposed for noncompliance with any requirement not in federal law, federal rules, or the local rules unless the alleged violator has been furnished in the particular case with actual notice of the requirement.

[*Adopted Dec. 20, 1937, effective Sept. 16, 1938; amended Apr. 29, 1985, effective Aug. 1, 1985; Apr. 27, 1995, effective Dec. 1, 1995; amended April 30, 2007, effective Dec. 1, 2007.*]

ADVISORY COMMITTEE'S NOTE TO 1985—AMENDMENT OF RULE 83

Rule 83, which has not been amended since the Federal Rules were promulgated in 1938, permits each district to adopt local rules not inconsistent with the Federal Rules by a majority of the judges. The only other requirement is that copies be furnished to the Supreme Court.

The widespread adoption of local rules and the modest procedural prerequisites for their promulgation have led many commentators to question the soundness of the process as well as the validity of some rules. *See* 12 C. Wright & A. Miller, *Federal Practice and Procedure: Civil* § 3152, at 217 (1973); Caballero, *Is There an Over- Exercise of Local Rule-Making Powers by the United States District Courts?* 24 Fed. Bar News 325 (1977). Although the desirability of local rules for promoting uniform practice within a district is widely accepted, several commentators also have suggested reforms to increase the quality, simplicity, and uniformity of the local rules. *See* Note, *Rule 83 and the Local Federal Rules,* 67 Colum. L. Rev. 1251 (1967), and Comment, *The Local Rules of Civil Procedure in the Federal District Courts-A Survey,* 1966 Duke L.J. 1011.

The amended Rule attempts, without impairing the procedural validity of existing local rules, to enhance the local rulemaking process by requiring appropriate public notice of proposed rules and an opportunity to comment on them. Although some district courts apparently consult the local bar before promulgating rules, many do not, which has led to criticism of a process that has district judges consulting only with each other. *See* 12 C. Wright & A. Miller, *supra*, § 3152, at 217; Blair, *The New Local Rules for Federal Practice in Iowa*, 23 Drake L. Rev. 517 (1974). The new language subjects local rulemaking to scrutiny similar to that accompanying the Federal Rules, administrative rulemaking, and legislation. It attempts to assure that the expert advice of practitioners and scholars is made available to the district court before local rules are promulgated. *See* Weinstein, *Reform of Court Rule-Making Procedures* 84–87, 127–37, 151 (1977).

The amended Rule does not detail the procedure for giving notice and an opportunity to be heard since conditions vary from district to district. Thus, there is no explicit requirement for a public hearing, although a district may consider that procedure appropriate in all or some rulemaking situations. See generally, Weinstein, *supra*, at 117–37, 151. The new Rule does not foreclose any other form of consultation. For example, it can be accomplished through the mechanism of an "Advisory Committee" similar to that employed by the Supreme Court in connection with the Federal Rules themselves.

The amended Rule provides that a local rule will take effect upon the date specified by the district court and will remain in effect unless amended by the district court or abrogated by the judicial council. The effectiveness of a local rule should not be deferred until approved by the judicial council because that might unduly delay promulgation of a local rule that should become effective immediately, especially since some councils do not meet frequently. Similarly, it was thought that to delay a local rule's effectiveness for a fixed period of time would be arbitrary and that to require the judicial council to abrogate a local rule within a specified time would be inconsistent with its power under 28 U.S.C. § 332 (1976) to nullify a local rule at any time. The expectation is that the judicial council will examine all local rules, including those currently in effect, with an eye toward determining whether they are valid and consistent with the Federal Rules, promote inter-district uniformity and efficiency, and do not undermine the basic objectives of the Federal Rules.

The amended Rule requires copies of local rules to be sent upon their promulgation to the judicial council and the Administrative Office of the United States Courts rather than to the Supreme Court. The Supreme Court was the appropriate filing place in 1938, when Rule 83 originally was promulgated, but the establishment of the Administrative Office makes it a more logical place to develop a centralized file of local rules. This procedure is consistent with both the Criminal and the Appellate Rules. See Fed. R. Crim. P. 57(a); Fed. R. App. P. 47. The Administrative Office also will be able to provide improved utilization of the file because of its recent development of a Local Rules Index.

The practice pursued by some judges of issuing standing orders has been controversial, particularly among members of the practicing bar. The last sentence in Rule 83 has been amended to make certain that standing orders are not inconsistent with the Federal Rules or any local district court rules. Beyond that, it is hoped that each district will adopt procedures, perhaps by local rule, for promulgating and reviewing single-judge standing orders.

Rule 84.   [Abrogated.]

[This Rule (adopted in 1938; amended Dec. 27, 1946, eff. March 19, 1948; April 30, 2007, eff. Dec. 1, 2007) was abrogated April 29, 2015, eff. Dec. 1, 2015. It related to the forms Appendix.]

NOTES OF THE ADVISORY COMMITTEE
ON THE ABROGATION OF RULE 84

Rule 84 was adopted when the Civil Rules were established in 1938 "to indicate, subject to the provisions of these rules, the simplicity and brevity of statement which the rules contemplate." The purpose of providing illustrations for the rules, although useful when the rules were adopted, has been fulfilled. Accordingly, recognizing that there are many excellent alternative sources for forms, including the website of the Administrative Office of the United States Courts, the websites of many district courts, and local law libraries that contain many commercially published forms, Rule 84 and the Appendix of Forms are no longer necessary and have been abrogated. The abrogation of Rule 84 does not alter existing pleading standards or otherwise change the requirements of Civil Rule 8.

Rule 85.   Title.

These rules may be cited as the Federal Rules of Civil Procedure.

[*Adopted Dec. 20, 1937, effective Sept. 16, 1938; amended April 30, 2007, effective Dec. 1, 2007.*]

Rule 86.   Effective Dates.

(a) In General.

These rules and any amendments take effect at the time specified by the Supreme Court, subject to 28 U.S.C. § 2074. They govern:

(1) proceedings in an action commenced after their effective date; and

(2) proceedings after that date in an action then pending unless:

(A) the Supreme Court specifies otherwise; or

(B) the court determines that applying them in a particular action would be infeasible or work an injustice.

(b) December 1, 2007 Amendments.

If any provision in Rules 1–5.1, 6–73, or 77–86 conflicts with another law, priority in time for the purpose of 28 U.S.C. § 2072(b) is not affected by the amendments taking effect on December 1, 2007.

[*Adopted Dec. 20, 1937, effective Sept. 16, 1938; amended Dec. 27, 1946, effective Mar. 19, 1948; Dec. 29, 1948, effective Oct. 20, 1949; Apr. 17, 1961, effective July 19, 1961; Jan. 21 and Mar. 18, 1963, effective July 1, 1963; amended April 30, 2007, effective Dec. 1, 2007.*]

II. APPENDIX OF FORMS [Abrogated.]

[Abrogated (Apr. 29, 2015, effective Dec. 1, 2015).]

FORMS

III.   SELECTED FEDERAL RULES AND FORMS OF APPELLATE PROCEDURE FOR THE UNITED STATES COURTS OF APPEALS

FEDERAL RULES OF APPELLATE PROCEDURE

RULE 1. SCOPE OF RULES; TITLE.

(a) Scope of Rules.

(1) These rules govern procedure in the United States courts of appeals.

(2) When these rules provide for filing a motion or other document in the district court, the procedure must comply with the practice of the district court.

(b) Definition.

In these rules, "state" includes the District of Columbia and any United States commonwealth or territory.

(c) Title.

These rules are to be known as the Federal Rules of Appellate Procedure. [*Adopted Dec. 4, 1967, effective July 1, 1968; amended Apr. 30, 1979, effective Aug. 1, 1979; Apr. 25, 1989, effective Dec. 1, 1989; Apr. 29, 1994, effective Dec. 1, 1994; Apr. 24, 1998, effective Dec. 1, 1998; Apr. 29, 2002, effective Dec. 1, 2002; Apr. 28, 2010, effective Dec. 1, 2010.*]

RULE 3.   APPEAL AS OF RIGHT — HOW TAKEN.

(a) Filing the Notice of Appeal.

(1) An appeal permitted by law as of right from a district court to a court of appeals may be taken only by filing a notice of appeal with the district clerk within the time allowed by Rule 4. At the time of filing, the appellant must furnish the clerk with enough copies of the notice to enable the clerk to comply with Rule 3(d).

(2) An appellant's failure to take any step other than the timely filing of a notice of appeal does not affect the validity of the appeal, but is ground only for the court of appeals to act as it considers appropriate, including dismissing the appeal.

(3) An appeal from a judgment by a magistrate judge in a civil case is taken in the same way as an appeal from any other district court judgment.

(4) An appeal by permission under 28 U.S.C. § 1292(b) or an appeal in a bankruptcy case may be taken only in the manner prescribed by Rules 5 and 6, respectively.

(b) Joint or Consolidated Appeals.

(1) When two or more parties are entitled to appeal from a district-court judgment or order, and their interests make joinder practicable, they may file a joint notice of appeal. They may then proceed on appeal as a single appellant.

(2) When the parties have filed separate timely notices of appeal, the appeals may be joined or consolidated by the court of appeals.

(c) **Contents of the Notice of Appeal.**

(1) The notice of appeal must:

(A) specify the party or parties taking the appeal by naming each one in the caption or body of the notice, but an attorney representing more than one party may describe those parties with such terms as "all plaintiffs," "the defendants," "the plaintiffs A, B, et al.," or "all defendants except X";

(B) designate the judgment, order, or part thereof being appealed; and

(C) name the court to which the appeal is taken.

(2) A pro se notice of appeal is considered filed on behalf of the signer and the signer's spouse and minor children (if they are parties), unless the notice clearly indicates otherwise.

(3) In a class action, whether or not the class has been certified, the notice of appeal is sufficient if it names one person qualified to bring the appeal as representative of the class.

(4) An appeal must not be dismissed for informality of form or title of the notice of appeal, or for failure to name a party whose intent to appeal is otherwise clear from the notice.

(5) Form 1 in the Appendix of Forms is a suggested form of a notice of appeal.

(d) **Serving the Notice of Appeal.**

(1) The district clerk must serve notice of the filing of a notice of appeal by sending a copy to each party's counsel of record-excluding the appellant's-or, if a party is proceeding pro se, to the party's last known address. When a defendant in a criminal case appeals, the clerk must also serve a copy of the notice of appeal on the defendant. The clerk must promptly send a copy of the notice of appeal and of the docket entries-and any later docket entries-to the clerk of the court of appeals named in the notice. The district clerk must note, on each copy, the date when the notice of appeal was filed.

(2) If an inmate confined in an institution files a notice of appeal in the manner provided by Rule 4(c), the district clerk must also note the date when the clerk docketed the notice.

(3) The district clerk's failure to serve notice does not affect the validity of the appeal. The clerk must note on the docket the names of the parties to whom the clerk sends copies, with the date of sending. Service is sufficient despite the death of a party or the party's counsel.

(e) Payment of Fees.

Upon filing a notice of appeal, the appellant must pay the district clerk all required fees. The district clerk receives the appellate docket fee on behalf of the court of appeals.

[*Adopted Dec. 4, 1967, effective July 1, 1968; as amended April 25, 2019, eff. Dec. 1, 2019.*]

Rule 4.   Appeal as of Right — When Taken.

(a) Appeal in a Civil Case.

(1) *Time for Filing a Notice of Appeal.*

(A) In a civil case, except as provided in Rules 4(a)(1)(B), 4(a)(4), and 4(c), the notice of appeal required by Rule 3 must be filed with the district clerk within 30 days after entry of the judgment or order appealed from.

(B) The notice of appeal may be filed by any party within 60 days after entry of the judgment or order appealed from if one of the parties is:

(i) the United States;

(ii) a United States agency;

(iii) a United States officer or employee sued in an official capacity; or

(iv) a current or former United States officer or employee sued in an individual capacity for an act or omission occurring in connection with duties performed on the United States' behalf—including all instances in which the United States represents that person when the judgment or order is entered or files the appeal for that person.

(C) An appeal from an order granting or denying an application for a writ of error *coram nobis* is an appeal in a civil case for purposes of Rule 4(a).

(2) *Filing Before Entry of Judgment.*

A notice of appeal filed after the court announces a decision or order—but before the entry of the judgment or order—is treated as filed on the date of and after the entry.

(3) *Multiple Appeals.*

If one party timely files a notice of appeal, any other party may file a notice of appeal within 14 days after the date when the first notice was filed, or within the time otherwise prescribed by this Rule 4(a), whichever period ends later.

(4) *Effect of a Motion on a Notice of Appeal.*

(A) If a party files in the district court any of the following motions under the Federal Rules of Civil Procedure—and does so within the time allowed by those rules—the time to file an appeal runs for all parties from the entry of the order disposing of the last such remaining motion:

> (i) for judgment under Rule 50(b);

> (ii) to amend or make additional factual findings under Rule 52(b), whether or not granting the motion would alter the judgment;

> (iii) for attorney's fees under Rule 54 if the district court extends the time to appeal under Rule 58;

> (iv) to alter or amend the judgment under Rule 59;

> (v) for a new trial under Rule 59; or

> (vi) for relief under Rule 60 if the motion is filed no later than 28 days after the judgment is entered.

(B) (i) If a party files a notice of appeal after the court announces or enters a judgment—but before it disposes of any motion listed in Rule 4(a)(4)(A)—the notice becomes effective to appeal a judgment or order, in whole or in part, when the order disposing of the last such remaining motion is entered.

> (ii) A party intending to challenge an order disposing of any motion listed in Rule 4(a)(4)(A), or a judgment altered or amended upon such a motion, must file a notice of appeal, or an amended notice of appeal—in compliance with Rule 3(c)—within the time prescribed by this Rule measured from the entry of the order disposing of the last such remaining motion.

> (iii) No additional fee is required to file an amended notice.

(5) *Motion for Extension of Time.*

(A) The district court may extend the time to file a notice of appeal if:

> (i) a party so moves no later than 30 days after the time prescribed by this Rule 4(a) expires; and

> (ii) regardless of whether its motion is filed before or during the 30 days after the time prescribed by this Rule 4(a) expires, that party shows excusable neglect or good cause.

(B) A motion filed before the expiration of the time prescribed in Rule 4(a) (1) or (3) may be ex parte unless the court requires otherwise. If the motion is filed after the expiration of the prescribed time, notice must be given to the other parties in accordance with local rules.

(C) No extension under this Rule 4(a)(5) may exceed 30 days after the prescribed time or 14 days after the date when the order granting the motion is entered, whichever is later.

(6) *Reopening the Time to File an Appeal.*

The district court may reopen the time to file an appeal for a period of 14 days after the date when its order to reopen is entered, but only if all the following conditions are satisfied:

> (A) the court finds that the moving party did not receive notice under Federal Rule of Civil Procedure 77(d) of the entry of the judgment or order sought to be appealed within 21 days after entry;

> (B) the motion is filed within 180 days after the judgment or order is entered or within 14 days after the moving party receives notice under Federal Rule of Civil Procedure 77(d) of the entry, whichever is earlier; and

> (C) the court finds that no party would be prejudiced.

(7) *Entry Defined.*

> (A) A judgment or order is entered for purposes of this Rule 4(a):

>> (i) if Federal Rule of Civil Procedure 58(a) does not require a separate document, when the judgment or order is entered in the civil docket under Federal Rule of Civil Procedure 79(a); or

>> (ii) if Federal Rule of Civil Procedure 58(a) requires a separate document, when the judgment or order is entered in the civil docket under Federal Rule of Civil Procedure 79(a) and when the earlier of these events occurs:

>>> • the judgment or order is set forth on a separate document, or

>>> • 150 days have run from entry of the judgment or order in the civil docket under Federal Rule of Civil Procedure 79(a).

> (B) A failure to set forth a judgment or order on a separate document when required by Federal Rule of Civil Procedure 58(a) does not affect the validity of an appeal from that judgment or order.

(b) Appeal in a Criminal Case.

[omitted]

(c) Appeal by an Inmate Confined in an Institution.

[omitted]

(d) Mistaken Filing in the Court of Appeals.

If a notice of appeal in either a civil or a criminal case is mistakenly filed in the court of appeals, the clerk of that court must note on the notice the date when it was received and send it to the district clerk. The notice is then considered filed in the district court on the date so noted.

[*Adopted Dec. 4, 1967, eff. July 1, 1968; as amended Apr. 27, 2017, effective Dec. 1, 2017.*]

RULE 5.   APPEAL BY PERMISSION.

(a) Petition for Permission to Appeal.

(1) To request permission to appeal when an appeal is within the court of appeals' discretion, a party must file a petition with the circuit clerk and serve it on all other parties to the district-court action.

(2) The petition must be filed within the time specified by the statute or rule authorizing the appeal or, if no such time is specified, within the time provided by Rule 4(a) for filing a notice of appeal.

(3) If a party cannot petition for appeal unless the district court first enters an order granting permission to do so or stating that the necessary conditions are met, the district court may amend its order, either on its own or in response to a party's motion, to include the required permission or statement. In that event, the time to petition runs from entry of the amended order.

(b) Contents of the Petition; Answer or Cross-Petition; Oral Argument.

(1) The petition must include the following:

(A) the facts necessary to understand the question presented;

(B) the question itself;

(C) the relief sought;

(D) he reasons why the appeal should be allowed and is authorized by a statute or rule; and

(E) an attached copy of:

(i) the order, decree, or judgment complained of and any related opinion or memorandum, and

(ii) any order stating the district court's permission to appeal or finding that the necessary conditions are met.

(2) A party may file an answer in opposition or a cross-petition within 10 days after the petition is served.

(3) The petition and answer will be submitted without oral argument unless the court of appeals orders otherwise.

(c) Form of Papers; Number of Copies; Length Limits.

All papers must conform to Rule 32(c)(2). An original and 3 copies must be filed unless the court requires a different number by local rule or by order in a particular case. Except by the court's permission, and excluding the accompanying documents required by Rule 5(b)(1)(E):

(1) a paper produced using a computer must not exceed 5,200 words; and

(2) a handwritten or typewritten paper must not exceed 20 pages.

(d) **Grant of Permission; Fees; Cost Bond; Filing the Record.**

(1) Within 14 days after the entry of the order granting permission to appeal, the appellant must:

(A) pay the district clerk all required fees; and

(B) file a cost bond if required under Rule 7.

(2) A notice of appeal need not be filed. The date when the order granting permission to appeal is entered serves as the date of the notice of appeal for calculating time under these rules.

(3) The district clerk must notify the circuit clerk once the petitioner has paid the fees. Upon receiving this notice, the circuit clerk must enter the appeal on the docket. The record must be forwarded and filed in accordance with Rules 11 and 12(c).

[*Adopted Dec. 4, 1967, effective July 1, 1968; as amended April 25, 2019, effective Dec. 1, 2019.*]

RULE 8.   STAY OR INJUNCTION PENDING APPEAL.

(a) **Motion For Stay.**

(1) *Initial Motion in the District Court.*

A party must ordinarily move first in the district court for the following relief:

(A) a stay of the judgment or order of a district court pending appeal;

(B) approval of a bond or other security provided to obtain a stay of judgment; or

(C) an order suspending, modifying, restoring, or granting an injunction while an appeal is pending.

(2) *Motion in the Court of Appeals; Conditions on Relief.*

A motion for the relief mentioned in Rule 8(a)(1) may be made to the court of appeals or to one of its judges.

(A) The motion must:

(i) show that moving first in the district court would be impracticable; or

(ii) state that, a motion having been made, the district court denied the motion or failed to afford the relief requested and state any reasons given by the district court for its action.

(B) The motion must also include:

(i) the reasons for granting the relief requested and the facts relied on;

(ii) originals or copies of affidavits or other sworn statements supporting facts subject to dispute; and

(iii) relevant parts of the record.

(C) The moving party must give reasonable notice of the motion to all parties.

(D) A motion under this Rule 8(a)(2) must be filed with the circuit clerk and normally will be considered by a panel of the court. But in an exceptional case in which time requirements make that procedure impracticable, the motion may be made to and considered by a single judge.

(E) The court may condition relief on a party's filing a bond or other security in the district court.

(b) Proceeding Against a Security Provider.

If a party gives security with one or more security providers, each provider submits to the jurisdiction of the district court and irrevocably appoints the district clerk as its agent on whom any papers affecting its liability on the security may be served. On motion, a security provider's liability may be enforced in the district court without the necessity of an independent action. The motion and any notice that the district court prescribes may be served on the district clerk, who must promptly send a copy to each security provider whose address is known.

(c) Stay in a Criminal Case.

Rule 38 of the Federal Rules of Criminal Procedure governs a stay in a criminal case.

[*Adopted Dec. 4, 1967, effective July 1, 1968; as amended April 26, 2018, effective Dec. 1, 2018.*]

RULE 10.   THE RECORD ON APPEAL.

(a) Composition of the Record on Appeal.

The following items constitute the record on appeal:

(1) the original papers and exhibits filed in the district court;

(2) the transcript of proceedings, if any; and

(3) a certified copy of the docket entries prepared by the district clerk.

(b) The Transcript of Proceedings.

(1) *Appellant's Duty to Order.*

Within 14 days after filing the notice of appeal or entry of an order disposing of the last timely remaining motion of a type specified in Rule 4(a)(4)(A), whichever is later, the appellant must do either of the following:

(A) order from the reporter a transcript of such parts of the proceedings not already on file as the appellant considers necessary, subject to a local rule of the court of appeals and with the following qualifications:

(i) the order must be in writing;

(ii) if the cost of the transcript is to be paid by the United States under the Criminal Justice Act, the order must so state; and

(iii) the appellant must, within the same period, file a copy of the order with the district clerk; or

(B) file a certificate stating that no transcript will be ordered.

(2) *Unsupported Finding or Conclusion.*

If the appellant intends to urge on appeal that a finding or conclusion is unsupported by the evidence or is contrary to the evidence, the appellant must include in the record a transcript of all evidence relevant to that finding or conclusion.

(3) *Partial Transcript.*

Unless the entire transcript is ordered:

(A) the appellant must—within the 14 days provided in Rule 10(b)(1)— file a statement of the issues that the appellant intends to present on the appeal and must serve on the appellee a copy of both the order or certificate and the statement;

(B) if the appellee considers it necessary to have a transcript of other parts of the proceedings, the appellee must, within 14 days after the service of the order or certificate and the statement of the issues, file and serve on the appellant a designation of additional parts to be ordered; and

(C) unless within 14 days after service of that designation the appellant has ordered all such parts, and has so notified the appellee, the appellee may within the following 14 days either order the parts or move in the district court for an order requiring the appellant to do so.

(4) *Payment.*

At the time of ordering, a party must make satisfactory arrangements with the reporter for paying the cost of the transcript.

(c) Statement of the Evidence When the Proceedings Were Not Recorded or When a Transcript Is Unavailable.

If the transcript of a hearing or trial is unavailable, the appellant may prepare a statement of the evidence or proceedings from the best available means, including the appellant's recollection. The statement must be served on the appellee, who may serve objections or proposed amendments within 14 days after being served. The statement and any objections or proposed amendments must then be submitted to the district court for settlement and approval. As settled and approved, the statement must be included by the district clerk in the record on appeal.

(d) Agreed Statement as the Record on Appeal.

In place of the record on appeal as defined in Rule 10(a), the parties may prepare, sign, and submit to the district court a statement of the case showing how the issues presented by the appeal arose and were decided in the district court. The statement must set forth only those facts averred and proved or sought to be proved that are essential to the court's resolution of the issues. If the statement is truthful, it— together with any additions that the district court may consider necessary to a full presentation of the issues on appeal—must be approved by the district court and must then be certified to the court of appeals as the record on appeal. The district clerk must then send it to the circuit clerk within the time provided by Rule 11. A copy of the agreed statement may be filed in place of the appendix required by Rule 30.

(e) **Correction or Modification of the Record.**

(1) If any difference arises about whether the record truly discloses what occurred in the district court, the difference must be submitted to and settled by that court and the record conformed accordingly.

(2) If anything material to either party is omitted from or misstated in the record by error or accident, the omission or misstatement may be corrected and a supplemental record may be certified and forwarded:

(A) on stipulation of the parties;

(B) by the district court before or after the record has been forwarded; or

(C) by the court of appeals.

(3) All other questions as to the form and content of the record must be presented to the court of appeals.

[*Adopted Dec. 4, 1967, effective July 1, 1968; amended Apr. 30, 1979, effective Aug. 1, 1979; Mar. 10, 1986, effective July 1, 1986; Apr. 30, 1991, effective Dec. 1, 1991; Apr. 22, 1993, effective Dec. 1, 1993; Apr. 27, 1995, effective Dec. 1, 1995; Apr. 24, 1998, effective Dec. 1, 1998; amended March 26, 2009, eff. Dec. 1, 2009.*]

RULE 12.1. REMAND AFTER AN INDICATIVE RULING BY THE DISTRICT COURT ON A MOTION FOR RELIEF THAT IS BARRED BY A PENDING APPEAL.

(a) **Notice to the Court of Appeals.**

If a timely motion is made in the district court for relief that it lacks authority to grant because of an appeal that has been docketed and is pending, the movant must promptly notify the circuit clerk if the district court states either that it would grant the motion or that the motion raises a substantial issue.

(b) **Remand After an Indicative Ruling.**

If the district court states that it would grant the motion or that the motion raises a substantial issue, the court of appeals may remand for further proceedings but retains jurisdiction unless it expressly dismisses the appeal. If the court of appeals remands but retains jurisdiction, the parties must promptly notify the circuit clerk when the district court has decided the motion on remand.

[*Adopted Dec. 1, 2009.*]

RULE 25.   FILING AND SERVICE.

(a) Filing.

(1) *Filing with the Clerk.*

A paper required or permitted to be filed in a court of appeals must be filed with the clerk.

(2) *Filing: Method and Timeliness.*

(A) *Nonelectronic Filing.*

(i) *In General.*

For a paper not filed electronically, filing may be accomplished by mail addressed to the clerk, but filing is not timely unless the clerk receives the papers within the time fixed for filing.

(ii) *A Brief or Appendix.* A brief or appendix not filed electronically is timely filed, however, if on or before the last day for filing, it is:

- mailed to the clerk by first-class mail, or other class of mail that is at least as expeditious, postage prepaid; or

- dispatched to a third-party commercial carrier for delivery to the clerk within 3 days.

(iii) *Inmate Filing.* If an institution has a system designed for legal mail, an inmate confined there must use that system to receive the benefit of this Rule 25(a)(2)(A)(iii) A paper not filed electronically by an inmate is timely if it is deposited in the institution's internal mail system on or before the last day for filing and:

it is accompanied by:

- a declaration in compliance with 28 U.S.C. § 1746—or a notarized statement—setting out the date of deposit and stating that first-class postage is being prepaid; or

- evidence (such as a postmark or date stamp) showing that the paper was so deposited and that postage was prepaid; or

- the court of appeals exercises its discretion to permit the later filing of a declaration or notarized statement that satisfies Rule 25(a)(2)(A)(iii).

(B) *Electronic Filing and Signing.*

(i) *By a Represented Person—Generally Required; Exceptions.* A person represented by an attorney must file electronically, unless nonelectronic filing is allowed by the court for good cause or is allowed or required by a local rule.

(ii) *By an Unrepresented Person—When Allowed or Required.* A person not represented by an attorney:

- may file electronically only if allowed by court order or by local rule; and

- may be required to file electronically only by court order, or by a local rule that includes reasonable exceptions.

(iii) *Signing.* A filing made through a person's electronic-filing account and authorized by that person, together with that person's name on a signature block, constitutes the person's signature.

(iv) *Same as a Written Paper.* A paper filed electronically is a written paper for purposes of these rules.

(3) *Filing a Motion with a Judge.*

If a motion requests relief that may be granted by a single judge, the judge may permit the motion to be filed with the judge; the judge must note the filing date on the motion and give it to the clerk.

(4) *Clerk's Refusal of Documents.*

The clerk must not refuse to accept for filing any paper presented for that purpose solely because it is not presented in proper form as required by these rules or by any local rule or practice.

(5) *Privacy Protection.*

An appeal in a case whose privacy protection was governed by Federal Rule of Bankruptcy Procedure 9037, Federal Rule of Civil Procedure 5.2, or Federal Rule of Criminal Procedure 49.1 is governed by the same rule on appeal. In all other proceedings, privacy protection is governed by Federal Rule of Civil Procedure 5.2, except that Federal Rule of Criminal Procedure 49.1 governs when an extraordinary writ is sought in a criminal case.

(b) Service of All Papers Required.

Unless a rule requires service by the clerk, a party must, at or before the time of filing a paper, serve a copy on the other parties to the appeal or review. Service on a party represented by counsel must be made on the party's counsel.

(c) Manner of Service.

(1) Nonelectronic service may be any of the following:

(A) personal, including delivery to a responsible person at the office of counsel;

(B) by mail; or

(C) by third-party commercial carrier for delivery within 3 days

(2) Electronic service of a paper may be made

(A) by sending it to a registered user by filing it with the court's electronic-filing system or (B) by sending it by other electronic means that the person to be served consented in writing.

(3) When reasonable considering such factors as the immediacy of the relief sought, distance, and cost, service on a party must be by a manner at least as expeditious as the manner used to file the paper with the court.

(4) Service by mail or by commercial carrier is complete on mailing or delivery to the carrier. Service by electronic means is complete on filing or sending, unless the party making service is notified that the paper was not received by the party served.

(d) **Proof of Service.**

(1) A paper presented for filing must contain either of the following if it was served other than through the court's electronic-filing system:

(A) an acknowledgment of service by the person served; or

(B) proof of service consisting of a statement by the person who made service certifying:

(i) the date and manner of service;

(ii) the names of the persons served; and

(iii) their mail or electronic addresses, facsimile numbers, or the addresses of the places of delivery, as appropriate for the manner of service.

(2) When a brief or appendix is filed by mailing or dispatch in accordance with Rule 25(a)(2)(A)(ii), the proof of service must also state the date and manner by which the document was mailed or dispatched to the clerk.

(3) Proof of service may appear on or be affixed to the papers filed.

(e) **Number of Copies.**

When these rules require the filing or furnishing of a number of copies, a court may require a different number by local rule or by order in a particular case.

[*Amended July 1, 1986; Dec. 1, 1991; as amended, April 25, 2019, effective Dec. 1, 2019.*]

Rule 28. Briefs.

(a) **Appellant's Brief.**

The appellant's brief must contain, under appropriate headings and in the order indicated:

(1) a corporate disclosure statement if required by Rule 26.1;

(2) a table of contents, with page references;

(3) a table of authorities—cases (alphabetically arranged), statutes, and other authorities—with references to the pages of the brief where they are cited;

(4) a jurisdictional statement, including:

(A) the basis for the district court's or agency's subject-matter jurisdiction, with citations to applicable statutory provisions and stating relevant facts establishing jurisdiction;

(B) the basis for the court of appeals' jurisdiction, with citations to applicable statutory provisions and stating relevant facts establishing jurisdiction;

(C) the filing dates establishing the timeliness of the appeal or petition for review; and

(D) an assertion that the appeal is from a final order or judgment that disposes of all parties' claims, or information establishing the court of appeals' jurisdiction on some other basis;

(5) a statement of the issues presented for review;

(6) a concise statement of the case setting out the facts relevant to the issues submitted for review, describing the relevant procedural history, and identifying the rulings presented for review, with appropriate references to the record (see Rule 28(e));

(7) a summary of the argument, which must contain a succinct, clear, and accurate statement of the arguments made in the body of the brief, and which must not merely repeat the argument headings;

(8) the argument, which must contain:

(A) appellant's contentions and the reasons for them, with citations to the authorities and parts of the record on which the appellant relies; and

(B) for each issue, a concise statement of the applicable standard of review (which may appear in the discussion of the issue or under a separate heading placed before the discussion of the issues);

(9) a short conclusion stating the precise relief sought; and

(10) the certificate of compliance, if required by Rule 32(g)(1).

(b) Appellee's Brief.

The appellee's brief must conform to the requirements of Rule 28(a)(1)-(9) and (10), except that none of the following need appear unless the appellee is dissatisfied with the appellant's statement:

(1) the jurisdictional statement;

(2) the statement of the issues;

(3) the statement of the case;

(4) the statement of the standard of review.

(c) Reply Brief.

The appellant may file a brief in reply to the appellee's brief. Unless the court permits, no further briefs may be filed. A reply brief must contain a table of contents, with page references, and a table of authorities-cases (alphabetically arranged), statutes, and other authorities-with references to the pages of the reply brief where they are cited.

(d) References to Parties.

In briefs and at oral argument, counsel should minimize use of the terms "appellant" and "appellee." To make briefs clear, counsel should use the parties' actual names or the designations used in the lower court or agency proceeding, or such descriptive terms as the "employee," "the injured person," "the taxpayer," "the ship," "the stevedore."

(e) References to the Record.

References to the parts of the record contained in the appendix filed with the appellant's brief must be to the pages of the appendix. If the appendix is prepared after the briefs are filed, a party referring to the record must follow one of the methods detailed in Rule 30(c). If the original record is used under Rule 30(f) and is not consecutively paginated, or if the brief refers to an unreproduced part of the record, any reference must be to the page of the original document. For example:

- Answer p. 7;

- Motion for Judgment p. 2;

- Transcript p. 231.

Only clear abbreviations may be used. A party referring to evidence whose admissibility is in controversy must cite the pages of the appendix or of the transcript at which the evidence was identified, offered, and received or rejected.

(f) Reproduction of Statutes, Rules, Regulations, Etc.

If the court's determination of the issues presented requires the study of statutes, rules, regulations, etc., the relevant parts must be set out in the brief or in an addendum at the end, or may be supplied to the court in pamphlet form.

(g) [Reserved]

(h) [Reserved]

(i) Briefs in a Case Involving Multiple Appellants or Appellees.

In a case involving more than one appellant or appellee, including consolidated cases, any number of appellants or appellees may join in a brief, and any party may adopt by reference a part of another's brief. Parties may also join in reply briefs.

(j) Citation of Supplemental Authorities.

If pertinent and significant authorities come to a party's attention after the party's brief has been filed-or after oral argument but before decision-a party may promptly advise the circuit clerk by letter, with a copy to all other parties, setting forth the citations. The letter must state the reasons for the supplemental citations, referring either to the page of the brief or to a point argued orally. The body of the letter must not exceed 350 words. Any response must be made promptly and must be similarly limited.

[*Adopted Dec. 4, 1967, effective July 1, 1968; as amended April 28, 2016, effective, Dec. 1, 2016.*]

Rule 28.1. Cross-Appeals.

(a) Applicability.

This rule applies to a case in which a cross-appeal is filed. Rules 28(a)-(c), 31(a)(1), 32(a)(2), and 32(a)(7)(A)-(B) do not apply to such a case, except as otherwise provided in this rule.

(b) Designation of Appellant.

The party who files a notice of appeal first is the appellant for the purposes of this rule and Rules 30 and 34. If notices are filed on the same day, the plaintiff in the proceeding below is the appellant. These designations may be modified by the parties' agreement or by court order.

(c) Briefs.

In a case involving a cross-appeal:

(1) *Appellant's Principal Brief.*

The appellant must file a principal brief in the appeal. That brief must comply with Rule 28(a).

(2) *Appellee's Principal and Response Brief.*

The appellee must file a principal brief in the cross-appeal and must, in the same brief, respond to the principal brief in the appeal. That appellee's brief must comply with Rule 28(a), except that the brief need not include a statement of the case unless the appellee is dissatisfied with the appellant's statement.

(3) *Appellant's Response and Reply Brief.*

The appellant must file a brief that responds to the principal brief in the cross-appeal and may, in the same brief, reply to the response in the appeal. That brief must comply with Rule 28(a)(2)-(8) and (10), except that none of the following need appear unless the appellant is dissatisfied with the appellee's statement in the cross-appeal:

      (A) the jurisdictional statement;

      (B) the statement of the issues;

      (C) the statement of the case;

      (D) the statement of the standard of review.

(4) *Appellee's Reply Brief.*

The appellee may file a brief in reply to the response in the cross-appeal. That brief must comply with Rule 28(a)(2)-(3) and (10) and must be limited to the issues presented by the cross-appeal.

(5) *No Further Briefs.*

Unless the court permits, no further briefs may be filed in a case involving a cross-appeal.

(d) Cover.

Except for filings by unrepresented parties, the cover of the appellant's principal brief must be blue; the appellee's principal and response brief, red; the appellant's response and reply brief, yellow; the appellee's reply brief, gray; an intervenor's or amicus curiae's brief, green; and any supplemental brief, tan. The front cover of a brief must contain the information required by Rule 32(a)(2).

(e) Length.

(1) *Page Limitation.*

Unless it complies with Rule 28.1(e)(2), the appellant's principal brief must not exceed 30 pages; the appellee's principal and response brief, 35 pages; the appellant's response and reply brief, 30 pages; and the appellee's reply brief, 15 pages.

(2) *Type-Volume Limitation.*

    (A) The appellant's principal brief or the appellant's response and reply brief is acceptable if it:

        (i) contains no more than 13,000 words; or

        (ii) uses a monospaced face and contains no more than 1,300 lines of text.

    (B) The appellee's principal and response brief is acceptable if it:

        (i) contains no more than 15,300 words; or

        (ii) uses a monospaced face and contains no more than 1,500 lines of text.

    (C) The appellee's reply brief is acceptable if it contains no more than half of the type volume specified in Rule 28.1(e)(2)(A).

(3) *Certificate of Compliance.*

A brief submitted under Rule 28.1(e)(2) must comply with Rule 32(a)(7)(C).

(f) Time to Serve and File a Brief.

Briefs must be served and filed as follows:

    (1) the appellant's principal brief, within 40 days after the record is filed;

    (2) the appellee's principal and response brief, within 30 days after the appellant's principal brief is served;

    (3) the appellant's response and reply brief, within 30 days after the appellee's principal and response brief is served; and

    (4) the appellee's reply brief, within 14 days after the appellant's response and reply brief is served, but at least 7 days before argument unless the court, for good cause, allows a later filing.

[*Adopted Dec. 1, 2009; as amended April 28, 2016, effective Dec. 1, 2016.*]

RULE 30.   APPENDIX TO THE BRIEFS.

(a) Appellant's Responsibility.

(1) *Contents of the Appendix.*

The appellant must prepare and file an appendix to the briefs containing:

(A) the relevant docket entries in the proceeding below;

(B) the relevant portions of the pleadings, charge, findings, or opinion;

(C) the judgment, order, or decision in question; and

(D) other parts of the record to which the parties wish to direct the court's attention.

(2) *Excluded Material.*

Memoranda of law in the district court should not be included in the appendix unless they have independent relevance. Parts of the record may be relied on by the court or the parties even though not included in the appendix.

(3) *Time to File; Number of Copies.*

Unless filing is deferred under Rule 30(c), the appellant must file 10 copies of the appendix with the brief and must serve one copy on counsel for each party separately represented. An unrepresented party proceeding in forma pauperis must file 4 legible copies with the clerk, and one copy must be served on counsel for each separately represented party. The court may by local rule or by order in a particular case require the filing or service of a different number.

(b) All Parties' Responsibilities.

(1) *Determining the Contents of the Appendix.*

The parties are encouraged to agree on the contents of the appendix. In the absence of an agreement, the appellant must, within 14 days after the record is filed, serve on the appellee a designation of the parts of the record the appellant intends to include in the appendix and a statement of the issues the appellant intends to present for review. The appellee may, within 14 days after receiving the designation, serve on the appellant a designation of additional parts to which it wishes to direct the court's attention. The appellant must include the designated parts in the appendix. The parties must not engage in unnecessary designation of parts of the record, because the entire record is available to the court. This paragraph applies also to a cross-appellant and a cross-appellee.

(2) *Costs of Appendix.*

Unless the parties agree otherwise, the appellant must pay the cost of the appendix. If the appellant considers parts of the record designated by the appellee to be unnecessary, the appellant may advise the appellee, who must then advance the cost of including those parts. The cost of the appendix is a taxable cost. But if any party causes unnecessary parts of the record to be included in the appendix, the court may impose the cost of those parts on that party. Each circuit must, by local rule, provide for sanctions against attorneys who unreasonably and vexatiously increase litigation costs by including unnecessary material in the appendix.

(c) **Deferred Appendix.**

(1) *Deferral Until After Briefs Are Filed.*

The court may provide by rule for classes of cases or by order in a particular case that preparation of the appendix may be deferred until after the briefs have been filed and that the appendix may be filed 21 days after the appellee's brief is served. Even though the filing of the appendix may be deferred, Rule 30(b) applies; except that a party must designate the parts of the record it wants included in the appendix when it serves its brief, and need not include a statement of the issues presented.

(2) *References to the Record.*

(A) If the deferred appendix is used, the parties may cite in their briefs the pertinent pages of the record. When the appendix is prepared, the record pages cited in the briefs must be indicated by inserting record page numbers, in brackets, at places in the appendix where those pages of the record appear.

(B) A party who wants to refer directly to pages of the appendix may serve and file copies of the brief within the time required by Rule 31(a), containing appropriate references to pertinent pages of the record. In that event, within 14 days after the appendix is filed, the party must serve and file copies of the brief, containing references to the pages of the appendix in place of or in addition to the references to the pertinent pages of the record. Except for the correction of typographical errors, no other changes may be made to the brief.

(d) **Format of the Appendix.**

The appendix must begin with a table of contents identifying the page at which each part begins. The relevant docket entries must follow the table of contents. Other parts of the record must follow chronologically. When pages from the transcript of proceedings are placed in the appendix, the transcript page numbers must be shown in brackets immediately before the included pages. Omissions in the text of papers or of the transcript must be indicated by asterisks. Immaterial formal matters (captions, subscriptions, acknowledgments, etc.) should be omitted.

(e) **Reproduction of Exhibits.**

Exhibits designated for inclusion in the appendix may be reproduced in a separate volume, or volumes, suitably indexed. Four copies must be filed with the appendix, and one copy must be served on counsel for each separately represented party. If a transcript of a proceeding before an administrative agency, board, commission, or officer was used in a district-court action and has been designated for inclusion in the appendix, the transcript must be placed in the appendix as an exhibit.

(f) **Appeal on the Original Record Without an Appendix.**

The court may, either by rule for all cases or classes of cases or by order in a particular case, dispense with the appendix and permit an appeal to proceed on the original record with any copies of the record, or relevant parts, that the court may order the parties to file.

[*Adopted Dec. 4, 1967, effective July 1, 1968; amended Mar. 30, 1970, effective July 1, 1970; Mar. 10, 1986, effective July 1, 1986; Apr. 30, 1991, effective Dec. 1, 1991; Apr. 29, 1994, effective Dec. 1, 1994; Apr. 24, 1998, effective Dec. 1, 1998; amended March 26, 2009, eff. Dec. 1, 2009.*]

RULE 31.   SERVING AND FILING BRIEFS.

(a) Time to Serve and File a Brief.

(1) The appellant must serve and file a brief within 40 days after the record is filed. The appellee must serve and file a brief within 30 days after the appellant's brief is served. The appellant may serve and file a reply brief within 21 days after service of the appellee's brief but a reply brief must be filed at least 7 days before argument, unless the court, for good cause, allows a later filing.

(2) A court of appeals that routinely considers cases on the merits promptly after the briefs are filed may shorten the time to serve and file briefs, either by local rule or by order in a particular case.

(b) Number of Copies.

Twenty-five copies of each brief must be filed with the clerk and 2 copies must be served on each unrepresented party and on counsel for each separately represented party. An unrepresented party proceeding in forma pauperis must file 4 legible copies with the clerk, and one copy must be served on each unrepresented party and on counsel for each separately represented party. The court may by local rule or by order in a particular case require the filing or service of a different number.

(c) Consequence of Failure to File.

If an appellant fails to file a brief within the time provided by this rule, or within an extended time, an appellee may move to dismiss the appeal. An appellee who fails to file a brief will not be heard at oral argument unless the court grants permission.

[*Adopted Dec. 4, 1967, effective July 1, 1968; as amended April 26, 2018, eff. Dec. 1, 2018.*]

RULE 32.   FORM OF BRIEFS, APPENDICES, AND OTHER PAPERS.

(a) Form of a Brief.

(1) *Reproduction.*

(A) A brief may be reproduced by any process that yields a clear black image on light paper. The paper must be opaque and unglazed. Only one side of the paper may be used.

(B) Text must be reproduced with a clarity that equals or exceeds the output of a laser printer.

(C) Photographs, illustrations, and tables may be reproduced by any method that results in a good copy of the original; a glossy finish is acceptable if the original is glossy.

(2) *Cover.*

Except for filings by unrepresented parties, the cover of the appellant's brief must be blue; the appellee's, red; an intervenor's or amicus curiae's, green; any reply brief, gray; and any supplemental brief, tan. The front cover of a brief must contain:

(A) the number of the case centered at the top;

(B) the name of the court;

(C) the title of the case (see Rule 12(a));

(D) the nature of the proceeding (e.g., Appeal, Petition for Review) and the name of the court, agency, or board below;

(E) the title of the brief, identifying the party or parties for whom the brief is filed; and

(F) the name, office address, and telephone number of counsel representing the party for whom the brief is filed.

(3) *Binding.*

The brief must be bound in any manner that is secure, does not obscure the text, and permits the brief to lie reasonably flat when open.

(4) *Paper Size, Line Spacing, and Margins.*

The brief must be on 8 1/2 by 11 inch paper. The text must be double-spaced, but quotations more than 2 lines long may be indented and single-spaced. Headings and footnotes may be single-spaced. Margins must be at least one inch on all four sides. Page numbers may be placed in the margins, but no text may appear there.

(5) *Typeface.*

Either a proportionally spaced or a monospaced face may be used.

(A) A proportionally spaced face must include serifs, but sans-serif type may be used in headings and captions. A proportionally spaced face must be 14-point or larger.

(B) A monospaced face may not contain more than 10 1/2 characters per inch.

(6) *Type Styles.*

A brief must be set in a plain, roman style, although italics or boldface may be used for emphasis. Case names must be italicized or underlined.

(7) *Length.*

(A) Page limitation.

A principal brief may not exceed 30 pages, or a reply brief 15 pages, unless it complies with Rule 32(a)(7)(B).

(B) Type-volume limitation.

(i) A principal brief is acceptable if it:

- contains no more than 13,000 words; or

- uses a monospaced face and contains no more than 1,300 lines of text.

(ii) A reply brief is acceptable if it contains no more than half of the type volume specified in Rule 32(a)(7)(B)(i).

(iii) Headings, footnotes, and quotations count toward the word and line limitations. The corporate disclosure statement, table of contents, table of citations, statement with respect to oral argument, any addendum containing statutes, rules or regulations, and any certificates of counsel do not count toward the limitation.

(C) Certificate of compliance.

(i) A brief submitted under Rules 28.1(e)(2) or 32(a)(7)(B) must include a certificate by the attorney, or an unrepresented party, that the brief complies with the type-volume limitation. The person preparing the certificate may rely on the word or line count of the word-processing system used to prepare the brief. The certificate must state either:

- the number of words in the brief; or

- the number of lines of monospaced type in the brief.

(ii) Form 6 in the Appendix of Forms is a suggested form of a certificate of compliance. Use of Form 6 must be regarded as sufficient to meet the requirements of Rules 28.1(e)(3) and 32(a)(7)(C)(i).

(b) Form of an Appendix.

An appendix must comply with Rule 32(a)(1), (2), (3), and (4), with the following exceptions:

(1) The cover of a separately bound appendix must be white.

(2) An appendix may include a legible photocopy of any document found in the record or of a printed judicial or agency decision.

(3) When necessary to facilitate inclusion of odd-sized documents such as technical drawings, an appendix may be a size other than 8 1 / 2 by 11 inches, and need not lie reasonably flat when opened.

(c) Form of Other Papers.

(1) *Motion.*

The form of a motion is governed by Rule 27(d).

(2) *Other Papers.*

Any other paper, including a petition for panel rehearing and a petition for hearing or rehearing en banc, and any response to such a petition, must be reproduced in the manner prescribed by Rule 32(a), with the following exceptions:

> (A) A cover is not necessary if the caption and signature page of the paper together contain the information required by Rule 32(a)(2). If a cover is used, it must be white.

> (B) Rule 32(a)(7) does not apply.

(d) Signature.

Every brief, motion, or other paper filed with the court must be signed by the party filing the paper or, if the party is represented, by one of the party's attorneys.

(e) Local Variation.

Every court of appeals must accept documents that comply with the form requirements of this rule and the length limits set by these rules. By local rule or order in a particular case, a court of appeals may accept documents that do not meet all the form requirements of this rule or the length limits set by these rules.

(f) Items Excluded from Length. In computing any length limit, headings, footnotes, and quotations count toward the limit but the following items do not:

- cover page;
- disclosure statement;
- table of contents;
- table of citations;
- statement regarding oral argument;
- addendum containing statutes, rules, or regulations;
- certificate of counsel;
- signature block;
- proof of service; and
- any item specifically excluded by these rules or by local rule.

(g) Certificate of Compliance.

(1) Briefs and Papers That Require a Certificate. A brief submitted under Rules 28.1(e)(2), 29(b)(4), or 32(a)(7)(B)—and a paper submitted under Rules 5(c)(1), 21(d)(1), 27(d)(2)(A), 27(d)(2)(C), 35(b)(2)(A), or 40(b)(1)—must include a certificate by the attorney, or an unrepresented party, that the document complies with the type-volume limitation. The person preparing the certificate may rely on the word or line count of the word-processing system used to prepare the document. The certificate must state the number of words—or the number of lines of monospaced type—in the document.

(2) Acceptable Form. Form 6 in the Appendix of Forms meets the requirements for a certificate of compliance.

[Adopted Dec. 4, 1967, effective July 1, 1968; as amended Apr. 25, 2019, eff. Dec.1, 2019.]

RULE 32.1. CITING JUDICIAL DISPOSITIONS.

(a) Citation Permitted.

A court may not prohibit or restrict the citation of federal judicial opinions, orders, judgments, or other written dispositions that have been:

> (i) designated as "unpublished," "not for publication," "non-precedential," "not precedent," or the like; and

> (ii) issued on or after January 1, 2007.

(b) Copies Required.

If a party cites a federal judicial opinion, order, judgment, or other written disposition that is not available in a publicly accessible electronic database, the party must file and serve a copy of that opinion, order, judgment, or disposition with the brief or other paper in which it is cited.

[Adopted April 12, 2006, effective December 1, 2006.]

ADVISORY COMMITTEE'S NOTE TO 2006 ADOPTION OF RULE 32.1

Rule 32.1 is a new rule addressing the citation of judicial opinions, orders, judgments, or other written dispositions that have been designated by a federal court as "unpublished," "not for publication," "non-precedential," "not precedent," or the like. This Committee Note will refer to these dispositions collectively as "unpublished" opinions.

Rule 32.1 is extremely limited. It does not require any court to issue an unpublished opinion or forbid any court from doing so. It does not dictate the circumstances under which a court may choose to designate an opinion as "unpublished" or specify the procedure that a court must follow in making that determination. It says nothing about what effect a court must give to one of its unpublished opinions or to the unpublished opinions of another court. Rule 32.1 addresses only the *citation* of federal judicial dispositions that have been *designated* as "unpublished" or "non-precedential"—whether or not those dispositions have been published in some way or are precedential in some sense.

Subdivision (a). Every court of appeals has allowed unpublished opinions to be cited in some circumstances, such as to support a contention of issue preclusion or claim preclusion. But the circuits have differed dramatically with respect to the restrictions that they have placed on the citation of unpublished opinions for their persuasive value. Some circuits have freely permitted such citation, others have discouraged it but permitted it in limited circumstances, and still others have forbidden it altogether.

Rule 32.1(a) is intended to replace these inconsistent standards with one uniform rule. Under Rule 32.1(a), a court of appeals may not prohibit a party from citing an unpublished opinion of a federal court for its persuasive value or for any other reason. In addition, under Rule 32.1(a), a court may not place any restriction on the citation of such opinions. For example, a court may not instruct parties that the citation of unpublished opinions is discouraged, nor may a court forbid parties to cite unpublished opinions when a published opinion addresses the same issue.

Rule 32.1(a) applies only to unpublished opinions issued on or after January 1, 2007. The citation of unpublished opinions issued before January 1, 2007, will continue to be governed by the local rules of the circuits.

Subdivision (b). Under Rule 32.1(b), a party who cites an opinion of a federal court must provide a copy of that opinion to the court of appeals and to the other parties, unless that opinion is available in a publicly accessible electronic database — such as a commercial database maintained by a legal research service or a database maintained by a court. A party who is required under Rule 32.1(b) to provide a copy of an opinion must file and serve the copy with the brief or other paper in which the opinion is cited. Rule 32.1(b) applies to all unpublished opinions, regardless of when they were issued.

RULE 34. ORAL ARGUMENT.

(a) In General.

(1) *Party's Statement.*

Any party may file, or a court may require by local rule, a statement explaining why oral argument should, or need not, be permitted.

(2) *Standards.*

Oral argument must be allowed in every case unless a panel of three judges who have examined the briefs and record unanimously agrees that oral argument is unnecessary for any of the following reasons:

> (A) the appeal is frivolous;

> (B) the dispositive issue or issues have been authoritatively decided; or

> (C) the facts and legal arguments are adequately presented in the briefs and record, and the decisional process would not be significantly aided by oral argument.

(b) Notice of Argument; Postponement.

The clerk must advise all parties whether oral argument will be scheduled, and, if so, the date, time, and place for it, and the time allowed for each side. A motion to postpone the argument or to allow longer argument must be filed reasonably in advance of the hearing date.

(c) Order and Contents of Argument.

The appellant opens and concludes the argument. Counsel must not read at length from briefs, records, or authorities.

(d) Cross-Appeals and Separate Appeals.

If there is a cross-appeal, Rule 28.1(b) determines which party is the appellant and which is the appellee for purposes of oral argument. Unless the court directs otherwise, a cross-appeal or separate appeal must be argued when the initial appeal is argued. Separate parties should avoid duplicative argument.

(e) Nonappearance of a Party.

If the appellee fails to appear for argument, the court must hear appellant's argument. If the appellant fails to appear for argument, the court may hear the appellee's argument. If neither party appears, the case will be decided on the briefs, unless the court orders otherwise.

(f) Submission on Briefs.

The parties may agree to submit a case for decision on the briefs, but the court may direct that the case be argued.

(g) Use of Physical Exhibits at Argument; Removal.

Counsel intending to use physical exhibits other than documents at the argument must arrange to place them in the courtroom on the day of the argument before the court convenes. After the argument, counsel must remove the exhibits from the courtroom, unless the court directs otherwise. The clerk may destroy or dispose of the exhibits if counsel does not reclaim them within a reasonable time after the clerk gives notice to remove them.

[*Adopted Dec. 4, 1967, effective July 1, 1968; amended Apr. 1, 1979, effective Aug. 1, 1979; Mar. 10, 1986, effective July 1, 1986; Apr. 30, 1991, effective Dec. 1, 1991; Apr. 22, 1993, effective Dec. 1, 1993; Apr. 24, 1998, effective Dec. 1, 1998; Apr. 25, 2005, eff. Dec. 1, 2005.*]

RULE 35. EN BANC DETERMINATION.

(a) When Hearing or Rehearing En Banc May Be Ordered.

A majority of the circuit judges who are in regular active service and who are not disqualified may order that an appeal or other proceeding be heard or reheard by the court of appeals en banc. An en banc hearing or rehearing is not favored and ordinarily will not be ordered unless:

(1) en banc consideration is necessary to secure or maintain uniformity of the court's decisions; or

(2) the proceeding involves a question of exceptional importance.

(b) Petition for Hearing or Rehearing En Banc.

A party may petition for a hearing or rehearing en banc.

(1) The petition must begin with a statement that either:

(A) the panel decision conflicts with a decision of the United States Supreme Court or of the court to which the petition is addressed (with citation to the conflicting case or cases) and consideration by the full court is therefore necessary to secure and maintain uniformity of the court's decisions; or

(B) the proceeding involves one or more questions of exceptional importance, each of which must be concisely stated; for example, a petition may assert that a proceeding presents a question of exceptional importance if it involves an issue on which the panel decision conflicts with the authoritative decisions of other United States Courts of Appeals that have addressed the issue.

(2) Except by the court's permission:

(A) a petition for an en banc hearing or rehearing produced using a computer must not exceed 3,900 words; and

(B) a handwritten or typewritten petition for an en banc hearing or rehearing must not exceed 15 pages.

(3) For purposes of the limits in Rule 35(b)(2), if a party files both a petition for panel rehearing and a petition for rehearing en banc, they are considered a single document even if they are filed separately, unless separate filing is required by local rule.

(c) **Time to Petition for Hearing or Rehearing En Banc.**

A petition that an appeal be heard initially en banc must be filed by the date when the appellee's brief is due. A petition for a rehearing en banc must be filed within the time prescribed by Rule 40 for filing a petition for rehearing.

(d) **Number of Copies.**

The number of copies to be filed must be prescribed by local rule and may be altered by order in a particular case.

(e) **Response.**

No response may be filed to a petition for an en banc consideration unless the court orders a response. The length limits in Rule 35(b)(2) apply to a response.

(f) **Call for a Vote.**

A vote need not be taken to determine whether the case will be heard or reheard en banc unless a judge calls for a vote.

[*Adopted Dec. 4, 1967, effective July 1, 1968; as amended Apr. 27, 2020, eff. Dec. 1, 2020.*]

RULE 36.   ENTRY OF JUDGMENT; NOTICE.

(a) **Entry.**

A judgment is entered when it is noted on the docket. The clerk must prepare, sign, and enter the judgment:

(1) after receiving the court's opinion-but if settlement of the judgment's form is required, after final settlement; or

(2) if a judgment is rendered without an opinion, as the court instructs.

(b) Notice.

On the date when judgment is entered, the clerk must serve on all parties a copy of the opinion—or the judgment, if no opinion was written—and a notice of the date when the judgment was entered.

[*Adopted Dec. 4, 1967, effective July 1, 1968; amended Apr. 24, 1998, effective Dec. 1, 1998; Apr. 29, 2002, effective Dec. 1, 2002.*]

RULE 37.   INTEREST ON JUDGMENT.

(a) When the Court Affirms.

Unless the law provides otherwise, if a money judgment in a civil case is affirmed, whatever interest is allowed by law is payable from the date when the district court's judgment was entered.

(b) When the Court Reverses.

If the court modifies or reverses a judgment with a direction that a money judgment be entered in the district court, the mandate must contain instructions about the allowance of interest.

[*Adopted Dec. 4, 1967, effective July 1, 1968; amended Apr. 24, 1998, effective Dec. 1, 1998.*]

RULE 38.   FRIVOLOUS APPEAL — DAMAGES AND COSTS.

If a court of appeals determines that an appeal is frivolous, it may, after a separately filed motion or notice from the court and reasonable opportunity to respond, award just damages and single or double costs to the appellee.

[*Adopted Dec. 4, 1967, effective July 1, 1968; amended Apr. 29, 1994, effective Dec. 1, 1994; Apr. 24, 1998, effective Dec. 1, 1998.*]

RULE 39.   COSTS.

(a) Against Whom Assessed.

The following rules apply unless the law provides or the court orders otherwise:

(1) if an appeal is dismissed, costs are taxed against the appellant, unless the parties agree otherwise;

(2) if a judgment is affirmed, costs are taxed against the appellant;

(3) if a judgment is reversed, costs are taxed against the appellee;

(4) if a judgment is affirmed in part, reversed in part, modified, or vacated, costs are taxed only as the court orders.

(b) Costs For and Against the United States.

Costs for or against the United States, its agency, or officer will be assessed under Rule 39(a) only if authorized by law.

(c) Costs of Copies.

Each court of appeals must, by local rule, fix the maximum rate for taxing the cost of producing necessary copies of a brief or appendix, or copies of records authorized by Rule 30(f). The rate must not exceed that generally charged for such work in the area where the clerk's office is located and should encourage economical methods of copying.

(d) Bill of Costs: Objections; Insertion in Mandate.

(1) A party who wants costs taxed must—within 14 days after entry of judgment—file with the circuit clerk and serve an itemized and verified bill of costs.

(2) Objections must be filed within 14 days after service of the bill of costs, unless the court extends the time.

(3) The clerk must prepare and certify an itemized statement of costs for insertion in the mandate, but issuance of the mandate must not be delayed for taxing costs. If the mandate issues before costs are finally determined, the district clerk must-upon the circuit clerk's request-add the statement of costs, or any amendment of it, to the mandate.

(e) Costs on Appeal Taxable in the District Court.

The following costs on appeal are taxable in the district court for the benefit of the party entitled to costs under this rule:

(1) the preparation and transmission of the record;

(2) the reporter's transcript, if needed to determine the appeal;

(3) premiums paid for a bond or other security to preserve rights pending appeal; and

(4) the fee for filing the notice of appeal.

[*Adopted Dec. 4, 1967, effective July 1, 1968; as amended April 25, 2019, eff. Dec. 1, 2019.*]

RULE 40.   PETITION FOR PANEL REHEARING.

(a) Time to File; Contents; Response; Action by the Court if Granted.

(1) *Time.*

Unless the time is shortened or extended by order or local rule, a petition for panel rehearing may be filed within 14 days after entry of judgment. But in a civil case, unless an order shortens or extends the time, the petition may be filed by any party within 45 days after entry of judgment if one of the parties is:

(A) the United States;

(B) a United States agency;

(C) a United States officer or employee sued in an official capacity; or

(D) a current or former United States officer or employee sued in an individual capacity for an act or omission occurring in connection with duties performed on the United States' behalf—including all instances in which the United States represents that person when the court of appeals' judgment is entered or files the petition for that person.

(2) *Contents.*

The petition must state with particularity each point of law or fact that the petitioner believes the court has overlooked or misapprehended and must argue in support of the petition. Oral argument is not permitted.

(3) *Response.*

Unless the court requests, no response to a petition for panel rehearing is permitted. Ordinarily, rehearing will not be granted in the absence of such a request. If a response is requested, the requirements of Rule 40(b) apply to the response.

(4) *Action by the Court.*

If a petition for panel rehearing is granted, the court may do any of the following:

(A) make a final disposition of the case without reargument;

(B) restore the case to the calendar for reargument or resubmission; or

(C) issue any other appropriate order.

(b) Form of Petition; Length.

The petition must comply in form with Rule 32. Copies must be served and filed as Rule 31 prescribes. Except by the court's permission:

(1) a petition for panel rehearing produced using a computer must not exceed 3,900 words; and

(2) a handwritten or typewritten petition for panel rehearing must not exceed 15 pages.

[*Adopted Dec. 4, 1967, eff. July 1, 1968; as amended Apr. 27, 2020, eff. Dec. 1, 2020.*]

RULE 41. MANDATE: CONTENTS; ISSUANCE AND EFFECTIVE DATE; STAY.

(a) Contents.

Unless the court directs that a formal mandate issue, the mandate consists of a certified copy of the judgment, a copy of the court's opinion, if any, and any direction about costs.

(b) When Issued.

The court's mandate must issue 7 days after the time to file a petition for rehearing expires, or 7 days after entry of an order denying a timely petition for panel rehearing, petition for rehearing en banc, or motion for stay of mandate, whichever is later. The court may shorten or extend the time by order.

(c) Effective Date.

The mandate is effective when issued.

(d) Staying the Mandate Pending a Petition for Certiorari.

(1) *Motion to Stay.*

A party may move to stay the mandate pending the filing of a petition for a writ of certiorari in the Supreme Court. The motion must be served on all parties and must show that the petition would present a substantial question and that there is good cause for a stay.

(2) *Duration of Stay; Extensions.*

The stay must not exceed 90 days, unless:

(A) the period is extended for good cause; or

(B) the party who obtained the stay notifies the circuit clerk in writing within the period of the stay:

> (i) that the time for filing a petition has been extended, in which case the stay continues for the extended period; or

> (ii) that the petition has been filed, in which case the stay continues until the Supreme Court's final disposition.

(3) *Security.*

The court may require a bond or other security as a condition to granting or continuing a stay of the mandate.

(4) *Issuance of Mandate.*

The court of appeals must issue the mandate immediately on receiving a copy of a Supreme Court order denying the petition, unless extraordinary circumstances exist.

[*Adopted Dec. 4, 1967, effective July 1, 1968; as amended Apr. 26, 2018, eff. Dec. 1, 2018.*]

RULE 47. LOCAL RULES BY COURTS OF APPEALS.

(a) Local Rules.

(1) Each court of appeals acting by a majority of its judges in regular active service may, after giving appropriate public notice and opportunity for comment, make and amend rules governing its practice. A generally applicable direction to

parties or lawyers regarding practice before a court must be in a local rule rather than an internal operating procedure or standing order. A local rule must be consistent with — but not duplicative of — Acts of Congress and rules adopted under 28 U.S.C. §2072 and must conform to any uniform numbering system prescribed by the Judicial Conference of the United States. Each circuit clerk must send the Administrative Office of the United States Courts a copy of each local rule and internal operating procedure when it is promulgated or amended.

(2) A local rule imposing a requirement of form must not be enforced in a manner that causes a party to lose rights because of a nonwillful failure to comply with the requirement.

(b) Procedure When There Is No Controlling Law.

A court of appeals may regulate practice in a particular case in any manner consistent with federal law, these rules, and local rules of the circuit. No sanction or other disadvantage may be imposed for noncompliance with any requirement not in federal law, federal rules, or the local circuit rules unless the alleged violator has been furnished in the particular case with actual notice of the requirement.

[*Adopted Dec. 4, 1967, effective July 1, 1968; amended Apr. 27, 1995, effective Dec. 1, 1995; Apr. 24, 1998, effective Dec. 1, 1998.*]

FORM 1. NOTICE OF APPEAL TO A COURT OF APPEALS FROM A JUDGMENT OR ORDER OF A DISTRICT COURT

United States District Court for the

_____ District of _____

File Number _____

A.B.,
 	
                Plaintiff
 	
        v.
 	
C.D.,   Defendant
	Notice of Appeal

   Notice is hereby given that ___(here name all parties taking the appeal)__, (plaintiffs) (defendants) in the above named case, hereby appeal to the United States Court of Appeals for the _____ Circuit (from the final judgment) (from an order (describing it)) entered in this action on the _____ day of _____, 20___.

(s) _____

Attorney for _____

Address: _____

[*As amended April 28, 2016, eff. Dec. 1, 2016.*]

FORM 6. CERTIFICATE OF COMPLIANCE WITH TYPE-VOLUME LIMIT

Certificate of Compliance With Type-Volume Limit,

Typeface Requirements, and Type-Style Requirements

1. This document complies with [the type-volume limit of Fed. R. App. P. [*insert Rule citation; e.g., 32(a)(7)(B)*]] [the word limit of Fed. R. App. P. [*insert Rule citation; e.g., 5(c)(1)*]]] because, excluding the parts of the document exempted by Fed. R. App. P. 32(f) [and [*insert applicable Rule citation, if any*]]:

☐ this document contains [*state the number of*] words, **or**

☐ this brief uses a monospaced typeface and contains [*state the number of*] lines of text.

2. This document complies with the typeface requirements of Fed. R. App. P. 32(a)(5) and the type-style requirements of Fed. R. App. P. 32(a)(6) because:

☐ this document has been prepared in a proportionally spaced typeface using [*state name and version of word-processing program*] in [*state font size and name of type style*], **or**

☐ this document has been prepared in a monospaced typeface using [*state name and version of word-processing program*] with [*state number of characters per inch and name of type style*].

(s) _____

Attorney for _____

Dated: _____

[*As amended Apr. 28, 2016, effective Dec. 1, 2016.*]

IV.   SELECTED RULE OF THE SUPREME COURT OF THE UNITED STATES

PART III.   JURISDICTION ON WRIT OF CERTIORARI

Rule 10. Considerations Governing Review on Certiorari.

Review on a writ of certiorari is not a matter of right, but of judicial discretion. A petition for a writ of certiorari will be granted only for compelling reasons. The following, although neither controlling nor fully measuring the Court's discretion, indicate the character of the reasons the Court considers:

(a) a United States court of appeals has entered a decision in conflict with the decision of another United States court of appeals on the same important matter; has decided an important federal question in a way that conflicts with a decision by a state court of last resort; or has so far departed from the accepted and usual course of judicial proceedings, or sanctioned such a departure by a lower court, as to call for an exercise of this Court's supervisory power;

(b) a state court of last resort has decided an important federal question in a way that conflicts with the decision of another state court of last resort or of a United States court of appeals;

(c) a state court or a United States court of appeals has decided an important question of federal law that has not been, but should be, settled by this Court, or has decided an important federal question in a way that conflicts with relevant decisions of this Court.

A petition for a writ of certiorari is rarely granted when the asserted error consists of erroneous factual findings or the misapplication of a properly stated rule of law.

[*Adopted 1997.*]

SUP. CT. R.

V. SELECTED FEDERAL RULES OF EVIDENCE

ARTICLE I. GENERAL PROVISIONS

RULE 103. RULINGS ON EVIDENCE.

(a) Preserving a Claim of Error.

A party may claim error in a ruling to admit or exclude evidence only if the error affects a substantial right of the party and:

> (1) if the ruling admits evidence, a party, on the record:

>> (A) timely objects or moves to strike; and

>> (B) states the specific ground, unless it was apparent from the context; or

> (2) if the ruling excludes evidence, a party informs the court of its substance by an offer of proof, unless the substance was apparent from the context.

(b) Not Needing to Renew an Objection or Offer of Proof.

Once the court rules definitively on the record—either before or at trial—a party need not renew an objection or offer of proof to preserve a claim of error for appeal.

(c) Court's Statement About the Ruling; Directing an Offer of Proof.

The court may make any statement about the character or form of the evidence, the objection made, and the ruling. The court may direct that an offer of proof be made in question-and-answer form.

(d) Preventing the Jury from Hearing Inadmissible Evidence.

To the extent practicable, the court must conduct a jury trial so that inadmissible evidence is not suggested to the jury by any means.

(e) Taking Notice of Plain Error.

A court may take notice of a plain error affecting a substantial right, even if the claim of error was not properly preserved.

[*As amended Apr. 17, 2000, eff. Dec. 1, 2000; Apr. 26, 2011, eff. Dec. 1, 2011.*]

ARTICLE IV. RELEVANCE AND ITS LIMITS

RULE 401. TEST FOR RELEVANT EVIDENCE

Evidence is relevant if:

(a) it has any tendency to make a fact more or less probable than it would be without the evidence; and

(b) the fact is of consequence in determining the action. [*(As amended Apr. 26, 2011, eff. Dec. 1, 2011.)*]

RULE 402.   GENERALLY ADMISSIBILITY OF RELEVANT EVIDENCE

Relevant evidence is admissible unless any of the following provides otherwise:

- the United States Constitution;
- a federal statute;
- these rules; or
- other rules prescribed by the Supreme Court. Irrelevant evidence is not admissible.

[*As amended Apr. 26, 2011, eff. Dec. 1, 2011.*]

RULE 403.   EXCLUDING RELEVANT EVIDENCE FOR PREJUDICE, CONFUSION, WASTE OF TIME, OR OTHER REASONS

The court may exclude relevant evidence if its probative value is substantially outweighed by a danger of one or more of the following: unfair prejudice, confusing the issues, misleading the jury, undue delay, wasting time, or needlessly presenting cumulative evidence.

[*As amended Apr. 26, 2011, eff. Dec. 1, 2011.*]

ARTICLE V.   PRIVILEGES

RULE 501.   PRIVILEGE IN GENERAL.

The common law—as interpreted by United States courts in the light of reason and experience—governs a claim of privilege unless any of the following provides otherwise:

- the United States Constitution;
- a federal statute; or
- rules prescribed by the Supreme Court.

But in a civil case, state law governs privilege regarding a claim or defense for which state law supplies the rule of decision.

[*As amended Apr. 26, 2011, eff. Dec. 1, 2011.*]

RULE 502.   ATTORNEY-CLIENT PRIVILEGE AND WORK PRODUCT; LIMITATIONS ON WAIVER.

The following provisions apply, in the circumstances set out, to disclosure of a communication or information covered by the attorney-client privilege or work- product protection.

(a) Disclosure made in a Federal proceeding or to a Federal office or agency; scope of a waiver.

When the disclosure is made in a Federal proceeding or to a Federal office or agency and waives the attorney-client privilege or work-product protection, the waiver extends to an undisclosed communication or information in a Federal or State proceeding only if:

(1) the waiver is intentional;

(2) the disclosed and undisclosed communications or information concern the same subject matter; and

(3) they ought in fairness to be considered together.

(b) Inadvertent disclosure.

When made in a Federal proceeding or to a Federal office or agency, the disclosure does not operate as a waiver in a Federal or State proceeding if:

(1) the disclosure is inadvertent;

(2) the holder of the privilege or protection took reasonable steps to prevent disclosure; and

(3) the holder promptly took reasonable steps to rectify the error, including (if applicable) following Federal Rule of Civil Procedure 26(b)(5)(B).

(c) Disclosure made in a State proceeding.

When the disclosure is made in a State proceeding and is not the subject of a State-court order concerning waiver, the disclosure does not operate as a waiver in a Federal proceeding if the disclosure:

(1) would not be a waiver under this rule if it had been made in a Federal proceeding; or

(2) is not a waiver under the law of the State where the disclosure occurred.

(d) Controlling effect of a court order.

A Federal court may order that the privilege or protection is not waived by disclosure connected with the litigation pending before the court — in which event the disclosure is also not a waiver in any other Federal or State proceeding.

(e) Controlling effect of a party agreement.

An agreement on the effect of disclosure in a Federal proceeding is binding only on the parties to the agreement, unless it is incorporated into a court order.

(f) Controlling effect of this rule.

Notwithstanding Rules 101 and 1101, this rule applies to State proceedings and to Federal court-annexed and Federal court-mandated arbitration proceedings, in the circumstances set out in the rule. And notwithstanding Rule 501, this rule applies even if State law provides the rule of decision.

(g) Definitions.

In this rule:

(1) "attorney-client privilege" means the protection that applicable law provides for confidential attorney-client communications; and

(2) "work-product protection" means the protection that applicable law provides for tangible material (or its intangible equivalent) prepared in anticipation of litigation or for trial.

[*As amended Pub. L. 110–322, § 1(a), Sept. 19, 2008, 122 Stat. 3537; amended Apr. 26, 2011, eff. Dec. 1, 2011.*]

ARTICLE VI.   WITNESSES

RULE 601.   COMPETENCY TO TESTIFY IN GENERAL

Every person is competent to be a witness unless these rules provide otherwise. But in a civil case, state law governs the witness's competency regarding a claim or defense for which state law supplies the rule of decision.

[*As amended April 26, 2011, eff. Dec. 1, 2011.*]

RULE 602.   NEED FOR PERSONAL KNOWLEDGE.

A witness may testify to a matter only if evidence is introduced sufficient to support a finding that the witness has personal knowledge of the matter. Evidence to prove personal knowledge may consist of the witness's own testimony. This rule does not apply to a witness's expert testimony under Rule 703.

[*As amended Mar. 2, 1987, eff. Oct. 1, 1987; Apr. 25, 1988, eff. Nov. 1, 1988; Apr. 26, 2001, eff. Dec. 1, 2011.*]

RULE 606.   JUROR'S COMPETENCE AS A WITNESS

(a) *At the trial.* A juror may not testify as a witness before the other jurors at the trial. If a juror is called to testify, the court must give a party an opportunity to object outside the jury's presence.

(b) *During an Inquiry into the Validity of a Verdict or Indictment.*

(1) *Prohibited Testimony or Other Evidence.* During an inquiry into the validity of a verdict or indictment, a juror may not testify about any statement made or incident that occurred during the jury's deliberations; the effect of anything on that juror's or another juror's vote; or any juror's mental processes concerning the verdict or indictment. The court may not receive a juror's affidavit or evidence of a juror's statement on these matters.

(2) *Exceptions.* A juror may testify about whether:

(A) extraneous prejudicial information was improperly brought to the jury's attention;

(B) an outside influence was improperly brought to bear on any juror; or

(C) a mistake was made in entering the verdict on the verdict form.

[As amended Pub. L. 94–149, § 1(10), Dec. 12, 1975, 89 Stat. 805; Mar. 2, 1987, eff. Oct. 1, 1987; Apr. 12, 2006, eff. Dec. 1, 2006; Apr. 26, 2011, eff. Dec. 1, 2011.]

ARTICLE VII.   OPINIONS AND EXPERT TESTIMONY

RULE 701.   OPINION TESTIMONY BY LAY WITNESSES.

If a witness is not testifying as an expert, testimony in the form of an opinion is limited to one that is:

(a) rationally based on the witness's perception;

(b) helpful to clearly understanding the witness's testimony or to determining a fact in issue; and

(c) not based on scientific, technical, or other specialized knowledge within the scope of Rule 702.

[As amended Mar. 2, 1987, eff. Oct. 1, 1087; Apr. 17, 2000, eff. Dec. 1, 2000; Apr. 26, 2011, eff. Dec. 1, 2011.]

RULE 702.   TESTIMONY BY EXPERT WITNESSES.

A witness who is qualified as an expert by knowledge, skill, experience, training, or education may testify in the form of an opinion or otherwise if:

(a) the expert's scientific, technical, or other specialized knowledge will help the trier of fact to understand the evidence or to determine a fact in issue;

(b) the testimony is based on sufficient facts or data;

(c) the testimony is the product of reliable principles and methods; and

(d) the expert has reliably applied the principles and methods to the facts of the case.

[As amended Apr. 17, 2000, eff. Dec. 1, 2000; Apr. 26, 2011, eff. Dec. 1, 2011.]

ARTICLE VIII.   HEARSAY

RULE 801.   DEFINITIONS THAT APPLY TO THIS ARTICLE; EXCLUSIONS FROM HEARSAY.

The following definitions apply under this article:

(a) Statement.

"Statement" means a person's oral assertion, written assertion, or nonverbal conduct, if the person intended it as an assertion.

(b) Declarant.

"Declarant" means the person who made the statement.

(c) Hearsay.

"Hearsay" means a statement that:

(1) the declarant does not make while testifying at the current trial or hearing; and

(2) a party offers in evidence to prove the truth of the matter asserted in the statement.

(d) Statements that are not hearsay.

A statement that meets the following conditions is not hearsay:

(1) *A Declarant-Witness's Prior Statement.*

The declarant testifies and is subject to cross-examination about a prior statement, and the statement:

(A) is inconsistent with the declarant's testimony and was given under penalty of perjury at a trial, hearing, or other proceeding or in a deposition;

(B) is consistent with the declarant's testimony and is offered:

(i) to rebut an express or implied charge that the declarant recently fabricated it or acted from a recent improper influence or motive in so testifying; or

(ii) to rehabilitate the declarant's credibility as a witness when attacked on another ground; or

(C) identifies a person as someone the declarant perceived earlier.

(2) *An Opposing Party's Statement.*

The statement is offered against an opposing party and:

(A) was made by the party in an individual or representative capacity;

(B) is one the party manifested that it adopted or believed to be true;

(C) was made by a person whom the party authorized to make a statement on the subject;

(D) was made by the party's agent or employee on a matter within the scope of that relationship and while it existed; or

(E) was made by the party's coconspirator during and in furtherance of the conspiracy.

The statement must be considered but does not by itself establish the declarant's authority under (C); the existence or scope of the relationship under (D); or the existence of the conspiracy or participation in it under (E).

[*As amended Pub. L. 94–113, § 1, Oct. 16, 1975, 89 Stat. 575, eff. Oct. 31, 1975; Mar. 2, 1987, eff. Oct. 1, 1987; Apr. 11, 1997, eff. Dec. 1, 1997; Apr. 26, 2011, eff. Dec. 1, 2011; amended April 25, 2014, eff. Dec. 1, 2014.*]

RULE 802.   THE RULE AGAINST HEARSAY.

Hearsay is not admissible unless any of the following provides otherwise:

- a federal statute;

- these rules; or

- other rules prescribed by the Supreme Court. [*As amended Apr. 26, 2011, eff. Dec. 1, 2011.*]

RULE 803.   EXCEPTIONS TO THE RULE AGAINST HEARSAY — REGARDLESS OF WHETHER THE DECLARANT IS AVAILABLE AS A WITNESS

The following are not excluded by the rule against hearsay, regardless of whether the declarant is available as a witness:

(1) *Present sense impression.*

A statement describing or explaining an event or condition, made while or immediately after the declarant perceived it.

(2) *Excited utterance.*

A statement relating to a startling event or condition, made while the declarant was under the stress of excitement that it caused.

(3) *Then existing mental, emotional, or physical condition.*

A statement of the declarant's then-existing state of mind (such as motive, intent, or plan) or emotional, sensory, or physical condition (such as mental feeling, pain, or bodily health), but not including a statement of memory or belief to prove the fact remembered or believed unless it relates to the validity or terms of the declarant's will.

(4) *Statements made for purposes of medical diagnosis or treatment.*

A statement that:

(A) is made for—and is reasonably pertinent to—medical diagnosis or treatment; and

(B) describes medical history; past or present symptoms or sensations; their inception; or their general cause.

(5) *Recorded recollection.*

A record that:

(A) is on a matter the witness once knew about but now cannot recall well enough to testify fully and accurately;

(B) was made or adopted by the witness when the matter was fresh in the witness's memory; and

(C) accurately reflects the witness's knowledge.

If admitted, the record may be read into evidence but may be received as an exhibit only if offered by an adverse party.

(6) *Records of a regularly conducted activity.*

A record of an act, event, condition, opinion, or diagnosis if:

(A) the record was made at or near the time by—or from information transmitted by—someone with knowledge;

(B) the record was kept in the course of a regularly conducted activity of a business, organization, occupation, or calling, whether or not for profit;

(C) making the record was a regular practice of that activity;

(D) all these conditions are shown by the testimony of the custodian or another qualified witness, or by a certification that complies with Rule 902(11) or (12) or with a statute permitting certification; and

(E) the opponent does not show that the source of information or the method or circumstances of preparation indicate a lack of trustworthiness.

(7) *Absence of a record of a regularly conducted activity.*

Evidence that a matter is not included in a record described in paragraph (6) if:

(A) the evidence is admitted to prove that the matter did not occur or exist;

(B) a record was regularly kept for a matter of that kind; and

(C) the opponent does not show that the possible source of the information or other circumstances indicate a lack of trustworthiness.

(8) *Public records.*

A record or statement of a public office if:

(A) it sets out:

(i) the offices activities;

(ii) a matter observed while under a legal duty to report, but not including, in a criminal case, a matter observed by law-enforcement personnel; or

(iii) in a civil case or against the government in a criminal case, factual findings from a legally authorized investigation; and

(B) the opponent does not show that the source of information or other circumstances indicate a lack of trustworthiness.

(9) *Public records of vital statistics.*

A record of a birth, death, or marriage, if reported to a public office in accordance with a legal duty.

(10) *Absence of a Public Record.*

Testimony—or a certification under Rule 902—that a diligent search failed to disclose a public record or statement if:

(A) the testimony or certification is admitted to prove that

(i) the record or statement does not exist; or

(ii) a matter did not occur or exist, if a public office regularly kept a record or statement for a matter of that kind; and

(B) in a criminal case, a prosecutor who intends to offer a certification provides written notice of that intent at least 14 days before trial, and the defendant does not object in writing within 7 days of receiving the notice— unless the court sets a different time for the notice or the objection.

(11) *Records of religious organizations concerning personal or family history.*

A statement of birth, legitimacy, ancestry, marriage, divorce, death, relationship by blood or marriage, or similar facts of personal or family history, contained in a regularly kept record of a religious organization.

(12) *Certificates of marriage, baptism, and similar ceremonies.*

A statement of fact contained in a certificate:

(A) made by a person who is authorized by a religious organization or by law to perform the act certified;

(B) attesting that the person performed a marriage or similar ceremony or administered a sacrament; and

(C) purporting to have been issued at the time of the act or within a reasonable time after it.

(13) *Family records.*

A statement of fact about personal or family history contained in a family record, such as a Bible, genealogy, chart, engraving on a ring, inscription on a portrait, or engraving on an urn or burial marker.

(14) *Records of documents that affect an interest in property.*

The record of a document that purports to establish or affect an interest in property if:

(A) the record is admitted to prove the content of the original recorded document, along with its signing and its delivery by each person who purports to have signed it;

(B) the record is kept in a public office; and

(C) a statute authorizes recording documents of that kind in that office.

(15) *Statements in documents that affect an interest in property.*

A statement contained in a document that purports to establish or affect an interest in property if the matter stated was relevant to the document's purpose— unless later dealings with the property are inconsistent with the truth of the statement or the purport of the document.

(16) *Statements in ancient documents.*

A statement in a document that was prepared before January 1, 1998 and whose authenticity is established.

(17) *Market reports and similar commercial publications.*

Market quotations, lists, directories, or other compilations that are generally relied on by the public or by persons in particular occupations.

(18) *Statements in learned treatises, periodicals, and pamphlets.*

A statement contained in a treatise, periodical, or pamphlet if:

(A) the statement is called to the attention of an expert witness on cross-examination or relied on by the expert on direct examination; and

(B) the publication is established as a reliable authority by the expert's admission or testimony, by another expert's testimony, or by judicial notice.

If admitted, the statement may be read into evidence but not received as an exhibit.

(19) *Reputation concerning personal or family history.*

A reputation among a person's family by blood, adoption, or marriage — or among a person's associates or in the community — concerning the person's birth, adoption, legitimacy, ancestry, marriage, divorce, death, relationship by blood, adoption, or marriage, or similar facts of personal or family history.

(20) *Reputation concerning boundaries or general history.*

A reputation in a community — arising before the controversy — concerning boundaries of land in the community or customs that affect the land, or concerning general historical events important to that community, state, or nation.

(21) *Reputation concerning character.*

A reputation among a person's associates or in the community concerning the person's character.

(22) *Judgment of a previous conviction.*

Evidence of a final judgment of conviction if:

(A) the judgment was entered after a trial or guilty plea, but not a nolo contendere plea;

(B) the conviction was for a crime punishable by death or by imprisonment for more than a year;

(C) the evidence is admitted to prove any fact essential to the judgment; and

(D) when offered by the prosecutor in a criminal case for a purpose other than impeachment, the judgment was against the defendant.

The pendency of an appeal may be shown but does not affect admissibility.

(23) *Judgments involving personal, family, or general history, or a boundary.*

A judgment that is admitted to prove a matter of personal, family, or general history, or boundaries, if the matter:

(A) was essential to the judgment; and

(B) could be proved by evidence of reputation.

(24) [Other exceptions.] [Transferred to Rule 807.]

[*As amended Pub. L. 94–149, § 1(11), Dec. 12, 1975, 89 Stat. 805; Mar. 2, 1987, eff. Oct. 1, 1987; amended April 27, 2017, eff. Dec. 1, 2017.*]

RULE 804. EXCEPTIONS TO THE RULE AGAINST HEARSAY — WHEN THE DECLARANT IS UNAVAILABLE AS A WITNESS.

(a) Criteria for being unavailable.

A declarant is considered to be unavailable as a witness if the declarant:

(1) is exempted from testifying about the subject matter of the declarant's statement because the court rules that a privilege applies;

(2) refuses to testify about the subject matter despite a court order to do so;

(3) testifies to not remembering the subject matter;

(4) cannot be present or testify at the trial or hearing because of death or a then-existing infirmity, physical illness, or mental illness; or

(5) is absent from the trial or hearing and the statement's proponent has not been able, by process or other reasonable means, to procure:

(A) the declarant's attendance, in the case of a hearsay exception under Rule 804(b)(1) or (6); or

(B) the declarant's attendance or testimony, in the case of a hearsay exception under Rule 804(b)(2), (3), or (4).

But this subdivision (a) does not apply if the statement's proponent procured or wrongfully caused the declarant's unavailability as a witness in order to prevent the declarant from attending or testifying.

(b) The exceptions.

The following are not excluded by the rule against hearsay if the declarant is unavailable as a witness:

(1) *Former testimony.* Testimony that:

(A) was given as a witness at a trial, hearing, or lawful deposition, whether given during the current proceeding or a different one; and

(B) is now offered against a party who had—or, in a civil case, whose predecessor in interest had—an opportunity and similar motive to develop it by direct, cross-, or redirect examination.

(2) *Statement Under the Belief of Imminent Death.* In a prosecution for homicide or in a civil case, a statement that the declarant, while believing the declarant's death to be imminent, made about its cause or circumstances.

(3) *Statement Against Interest.* A statement that:

(A) a reasonable person in the declarant's position would have made only if the person believed it to be true because, when made, it was so contrary to the declarant's proprietary or pecuniary interest or had so great a tendency to invalidate the declarant's claim against someone else or to expose the declarant to civil or criminal liability; and

(B) is supported by corroborating circumstances that clearly indicate its trustworthiness, if it is offered in a criminal case as one that tends to expose the declarant to criminal liability.

(4) *Statement of personal or family history.* A statement about:

(A) the declarant's own birth, adoption, legitimacy, ancestry, marriage, divorce, relationship by blood, adoption, or marriage, or similar facts of personal or family history, even though the declarant had no way of acquiring personal knowledge about that fact; or

(B) another person concerning any of these facts, as well as death, if the declarant was related to the person by blood, adoption, or marriage or was so intimately associated with the person's family that the declarant's information is likely to be accurate.

(5) *Other exceptions.* [Transferred to Rule 807.]

(6) *Statement offered against a party that wrongfully caused the declarant's unavailability.* A statement offered against a party that wrong- fully caused— or acquiesced in wrongfully causing—the declarant's unavailability as a witness, and did so intending that result.

[*As amended Dec. 12, 1975; Mar. 2, 1987, eff. Oct. 1, 1987; Nov. 18, 1988; Apr. 11, 1997, eff. Dec. 1, 1997; Apr. 28, 2010, eff. Dec. 1, 2010; Apr. 26, 2011, eff. Dec. 1, 2011.*]

RULE 807.   RESIDUAL EXCEPTION.

(a) In general.

Under the following conditions, a hearsay statement is not excluded by the rule against hearsay even if the statement is not admissible under a hearsay exception in Rule 803 or 804:

(1) the statement is supported by sufficient guarantees of trustworthiness—after considering the totality of circumstances under which it was made and evidence, if any, corroborating the statement; and

(2) it is more probative on the point for which it is offered than any other evidence that the proponent can obtain through reasonable efforts.

(b) Notice.

The statement is admissible only if the proponent gives an adverse party reasonable notice of the intent to offer the statement—including its substance and the declarant's name—so that the party has a fair opportunity to meet it. The notice must be provided in writing before the trial or hearing—or in any form during the trial or hearing if the court, for good cause, excuses a lack of earlier notice.

[*Added Apr. 11, 1997, eff. Dec. 1, 1997; Apr. 26, 2011, eff. Dec. 1, 2011; amended April 25, 2019, eff. Dec. 1, 2019.*]

VI.   SELECTED PROVISIONS FROM THE CONSTITUTION OF THE UNITED STATES

We the People of the United States, in Order to form a more perfect Union, establish Justice, insure domestic Tranquility, provide for the common defence, promote the general Welfare, and secure the Blessings of Liberty to ourselves and our Posterity, do ordain and establish this Constitution for the United States of America.

ARTICLE I

Section 1. All legislative Powers herein granted shall be vested in a Congress of the United States, which shall consist of a Senate and House of Representatives.

*   *   *

Section 8. The Congress shall have Power To Lay and collect Taxes, Duties, Imposts and Excises, to pay the Debts and provide for the common Defence and general Welfare of the United States; but all Duties, Imposts and Excises shall be uniform throughout the United States;

To borrow Money on the credit of the United States;

To regulate Commerce with foreign Nations, and among the several States, and with the Indian Tribes;

To establish an uniform Rule of Naturalization, and uniform Laws on the subject of Bankruptcies throughout the United States;

To coin Money, regulate the Value thereof, and of foreign Coin, and fix the Standard of Weights and Measures;

To provide for the Punishment of counterfeiting the Securities and current Coin of the United States;

To establish Post Offices and Post Roads;

To promote the Progress of Science and useful Arts, by securing for limited Times to Authors and Inventors the exclusive Right to their respective Writings and Discoveries;

To constitute Tribunals inferior to the supreme Court;

To define and punish Piracies and Felonies committed on the high Seas, and Offenses against the Law of Nations;

To declare War, grant Letters of Marque and Reprisal, and make Rules concerning Captures on Land and Water;

To raise and support Armies, but no Appropriation of Money to that Use shall be for a longer Term than two Years;

To provide and maintain a Navy;

CONSTITUTION

To make Rules for the Government and Regulation of the land and naval Forces; To provide for calling forth the Militia to execute the Laws of the Union, suppress

Insurrections and repel Invasions;

To provide for organizing, arming, and disciplining, the Militia, and for governing such Part of them as may be employed in the Service of the United States, reserving to the States respectively, the Appointment of the Officers, and the Authority of training the Militia according to the discipline prescribed by Congress;

To exercise exclusive Legislation in all Cases whatsoever, over such District (not exceeding ten Miles square) as may, by Cession of Particular States, and the Acceptance of Congress, become the Seat of the Government of the United States, and to exercise like Authority over all Places purchased by the Consent of the Legislature of the State in which the Same shall be, for the Erection of Forts, Magazines, Arsenals, dock-Yards, and other needful Buildings:—And

To make all Laws which shall be necessary and proper for carrying into Execution the foregoing Powers, and all other Powers vested by this Constitution in the Government of the United States, or in any Department or Officer thereof.

*　*　*

ARTICLE II

Section 1. The executive Power shall be vested in a President of the United States of America.

ARTICLE III

Section 1. The judicial Power of the United States, shall be vested in one supreme Court, and in such inferior Courts as the Congress may from time to time ordain and establish. The Judges, both of the supreme and inferior Courts, shall hold their Offices during good Behaviour, and shall, at stated Times, receive for their Services, a Compensation, which shall not be diminished during their Continuance in Office.

Section 2. The judicial Power shall extend to all Cases, in Law and Equity, arising under this Constitution, the Laws of the United States, and Treaties made, or which shall be made, under their Authority;—to all Cases affecting Ambassadors, other public Ministers and Consuls;—to all Cases of admiralty and maritime Jurisdiction;—to Controversies to which the United States shall be a Party;—to Controversies between two or more States;—between a State and Citizens of another State;—between Citizens of different States; between Citizens of the same State claiming Lands under Grants of different States, and between a State, or the Citizens thereof, and foreign States, Citizens or Subjects.

In all Cases affecting Ambassadors, other public Ministers and Consuls, and those in which a State shall be Party, the supreme Court shall have original Jurisdiction. In all the other Cases before mentioned, the supreme Court shall have appellate Jurisdiction, both as to Law and Fact, with such Exceptions, and under such Regulations as the Congress shall make.

The Trial of all Crimes, except in Cases of Impeachment, shall be by Jury; and such Trial shall be held in the State where the said Crimes shall have been committed; but when not committed within any State, the Trial shall be at such Place or Places as the Congress may by Law have directed.

* * *

ARTICLE IV

Section 1. Full Faith and Credit shall be given in each State to the public Acts, Records, and judicial Proceedings of every other State. And the Congress may by general Laws prescribe the Manner in which such Acts, Records and Proceedings shall be proved, and the Effect thereof.

Section 2. The Citizens of each State shall be entitled to all Privileges and Immunities of Citizens in the several States.

* * *

Section 4. The United States shall guarantee to every State in this Union a Republican Form of Government, and shall protect each of them against Invasion; and on Application of the Legislature, or of the Executive (when the Legislature cannot be convened) against domestic Violence.

ARTICLE VI

* * *

This Constitution, and the Laws of the United States which shall be made in Pursuance thereof; and all Treaties made, or which shall be made, under the Authority of the United States, shall be the supreme Law of the Land; and the Judges in every State shall be bound thereby, any Thing in the Constitution or Laws of any State to the Contrary notwithstanding.

* * *

AMENDMENT I

Congress shall make no law respecting an establishment of religion, or prohibiting the free exercise thereof; or abridging the freedom of speech, or of the press; or the right of the people peaceably to assemble, and to petition the Government for a redress of grievances.

AMENDMENT IV

The right of the people to be secure in their persons, houses, papers, and effects, against unreasonable searches and seizures, shall not be violated, and no Warrants shall issue, but upon probable cause, supported by Oath or affirmation, and particularly describing the place to be searched, and the persons or things to be seized.

AMENDMENT V

No person shall be held to answer for a capital, or otherwise infamous crime, unless on a presentment or indictment of a Grand Jury, except in cases arising in the land or naval forces, or in the Militia, when in actual service in time of War or public danger; nor shall any person be subject for the same offence to be twice put in jeopardy of life or limb; nor shall be compelled in any criminal case to be a witness against himself, nor be deprived of life, liberty, or property, without due process of law; nor shall private property be taken for public use, without just compensation.

AMENDMENT VI

In all criminal prosecutions, the accused shall enjoy the right to a speedy and public trial, by an impartial jury of the State and district wherein the crime shall have been committed, which district shall have been previously ascertained by law, and to be informed of the nature and cause of the accusation; to be confronted with the witnesses against him; to have compulsory process for obtaining witnesses in his favor, and to have the Assistance of Counsel for his defence.

AMENDMENT VII

In Suits at common law, where the value in controversy shall exceed twenty dollars, the right of trial by jury shall be preserved, and no fact tried by a jury, shall be otherwise reexamined in any Court of the United States, than according to the rules of the common law.

AMENDMENT VIII

Excessive bail shall not be required, nor excessive fines imposed, nor cruel and unusual punishments inflicted.

AMENDMENT IX

The enumeration in the Constitution, of certain rights, shall not be construed to deny or disparage others retained by the people.

AMENDMENT X

The powers not delegated to the United States by the Constitution, nor prohibited by it to the States, are reserved to the States respectively, or to the people.

AMENDMENT XI

The Judicial power of the United States shall not be construed to extend to any suit in law or equity, commenced or prosecuted against one of the United States by Citizens of another State, or by Citizens or Subjects of any Foreign State.

AMENDMENT XIV

Section 1. All persons born or naturalized in the United States and subject to the jurisdiction thereof, are citizens of the United States and of the State wherein they reside. No State shall make or enforce any law which shall abridge the privileges or immunities of citizens of the United States; nor shall any State deprive any person of life, liberty, or property, without due process of law; nor deny to any person within its jurisdiction the equal protection of the laws.

*   *   *

Section 5. The Congress shall have the power to enforce, by appropriate legislation, the provisions of this article.

Appendix 2

United States Code

STATUTES

PART V — PROCEDURE

PART VI — PARTICULAR PROCEEDINGS

SELECTED PROVISIONS
FROM TITLE 42 OF THE UNITED STATES CODE

PART I   ORGANIZATION OF COURTS

CHAPTER 1.   SUPREME COURT

§ 1.   NUMBER OF JUSTICES; QUORUM.

The Supreme Court of the United States shall consist of a Chief Justice of the United States and eight associate justices, any six of whom shall constitute a quorum.

(Added June 25, 1948, ch. 646, 62 Stat. 869)

§ 2.   TERMS OF COURT.

The Supreme Court shall hold at the seat of government a term of court commencing on the first Monday in October of each year and may hold such adjourned or special terms as may be necessary.

(Added June 25, 1948, ch. 646, 62 Stat. 869)

CHAPTER 3.   COURTS OF APPEALS

§ 41.   NUMBER AND COMPOSITION OF CIRCUITS.

The thirteen judicial circuits of the United States are constituted as follows:

CIRCUITS	*COMPOSITION*
District of Columbia	District of Columbia.
First	Maine, Massachusetts, New Hampshire, Puerto Rico, Rhode Island.
Second	Connecticut, New York, Vermont.
Third	Delaware, New Jersey, Pennsylvania, Virgin Islands.

Fourth	Maryland, North Carolina, South Carolina, Virginia, West Virginia.
Fifth	District of the Canal Zone, Louisiana, Mississippi, Texas.
Sixth.........................	Kentucky, Michigan, Ohio, Tennessee.
Seventh	Illinois, Indiana, Wisconsin.
Eighth	Arkansas, Iowa, Minnesota, Missouri, Nebraska, North Dakota, South Dakota.
Ninth	Alaska, Arizona, California, Idaho, Montana, Nevada, Oregon, Washington, Guam, Hawaii.
Tenth	Colorado, Kansas, New Mexico, Oklahoma, Utah, Wyoming.
Eleventh......................	Alabama, Florida, Georgia.
Federal	All Federal judicial districts.

(As amended Oct. 31, 1951, ch. 655, § 34, 65 Stat. 723; 1980, Pub. L. 96-452; Apr. 2, 1982, Pub. L. 97-164, § 101, 96 Stat. 25.)

§ 43.   CREATION AND COMPOSITION OF COURTS.

(a) There shall be in each circuit a court of appeals, which shall be a court of record, known as the United States Court of Appeals for the circuit.

(b) Each court of appeals shall consist of the circuit judges of the circuit in regular active service. The circuit justice and justices or judges designated or assigned shall also be competent to sit as judges of the court.

(As amended Nov. 13, 1963, Pub. L. 88-176, § 1(a), 77 Stat. 331.)

§ 44.   APPOINTMENT, TENURE, RESIDENCE AND SALARY OF CIRCUIT JUDGES.

(a) The President shall appoint, by and with the advice and consent of the Senate, circuit judges for the several circuits as follows:

CIRCUITS	NUMBER OF JUDGES
District of Columbia	11
First	6
Second	13
Third	14
Fourth	15
Fifth	17

(b) Circuit judges shall hold office during good behavior.

(c) Except in the District of Columbia, each circuit judge shall be a resident of the circuit for which appointed at the time of his appointment and thereafter while in active service. While in active service, each circuit judge of the Federal judicial circuit appointed after the effective date of the Federal Courts Improvement Act of 1982, and the chief judge of the Federal judicial circuit, whenever appointed, shall reside within fifty miles of the District of Columbia. In each circuit (other than the Federal judicial circuit) there shall be at least one circuit judge in regular active service appointed from the residents of each state in that circuit.

(d) Each circuit judge shall receive a salary at an annual rate determined under section 225 of the Federal Salary Act of 1967 (2 U.S.C. 351–361), as adjusted by section 461 of this title.

(Latest amendment Jan. 7, 2008, Pub.L. 110-177, Title V, § 509(a), 121 Stat. 2543.)

§ 46. ASSIGNMENT OF JUDGES; PANELS; HEARINGS; QUORUM.

(a) Circuit judges shall sit on the court and its panels in such order and at such times as the court directs.

(b) In each circuit the court may authorize the hearing and determination of cases and controversies by separate panels, each consisting of three judges, at least a majority of whom shall be judges of that court, unless such judges cannot sit because recused or disqualified, or unless the chief judge of that court certifies that there is an emergency including, but not limited to, the unavailability of a judge of the court because of illness. Such panels shall sit at the times and places and hear the cases and controversies assigned as the court directs. The United States Court of Appeals for the Federal Circuit shall determine by rule a procedure for the rotation of judges from panel to panel to ensure that all of the judges sit on a representative cross section of the cases heard and, notwithstanding the first sentence of this subsection, may determine by rule the number of judges, not less than three, who constitute a panel.

(c) Cases and controversies shall be heard and determined by a court or panel of not more than three judges (except that the United States Court of Appeals for the Federal Circuit may sit in panels of more than three judges if its rules so provide), unless a hearing or rehearing before the court in banc is ordered by a majority of the circuit judges of the circuit who are in regular active service. A court in banc shall consist of all circuit judges in regular active service, or such number of judges as may be prescribed in accordance with section 6 of Public Law 95-486 (92 Stat. 1633), except that any senior circuit judge of the circuit shall be eligible (1) to participate, at his election and upon designation and assignment pursuant to section 294(c) of this title and the rules of the circuit, as a member of an in banc court reviewing a decision of a panel of which such judge was a member, or (2) to continue to participate in the decision of a case or controversy that was heard or reheard by the court in banc at a time when such judge was in regular active service.

(d) A majority of the number of judges authorized to constitute a court or panel thereof, as provided in paragraph (c), shall constitute a quorum.

(As amended Nov. 13, 1963, Pub. L. 88-176, § 1(b), 77 Stat. 331; Oct. 20, 1978, Pub. L. 95-486, 92 Stat. 1633; Apr. 2, 1982, Pub. L. 97-164, §§ 103, 205, 96 Stat. 25, 53; Aug. 6, 1996, Pub. L. 104-175, § 1, 110 Stat. 1556.)

§ 47.　Disqualification of Trial Judge to Hear Appeal.

No judge shall hear or determine an appeal from the decision of a case or issue tried by him.

(Added June 25, 1948, ch. 646, 62 Stat. 872)

§ 48.　Terms of Court.

(a) The courts of appeals shall hold regular sessions at the places listed below, and at such other places within the respective circuit as each court may designate by rule.

Circuits	Places
District of Columbia	Washington.
First	Boston.
Second	New York.
Third	Philadelphia.
Fourth	Richmond, Asheville.
Fifth	New Orleans, Fort Worth, Jackson.
Sixth	Cincinnati.
Seventh	Chicago.
Eighth	St. Louis, Kansas City, Omaha, St. Paul.
Ninth	San Francisco, Los Angeles, Portland, Seattle.
Tenth	Denver, Wichita, Oklahoma City.

| Eleventh............................. | Atlanta, Jacksonville, Montgomery. |
| Federal.............................. | District of Columbia, and in any other place listed above as the court by rule directs. |

(b) Each court of appeals may hold special sessions at any place within its circuit as the nature of the business may require, and upon such notice as the court orders. The court may transact any business at a special session which it might transact at a regular session.

(c) Any court of appeals may pretermit any regular session of court at any place for insufficient business or other good cause.

(d) The times and places of the sessions of the Court of Appeals for the Federal Circuit shall be prescribed with a view to securing reasonable opportunity to citizens to appear before the court with as little inconvenience and expense to citizens as is practicable.

(e) Each court of appeals may hold special sessions at any place within the United States outside the circuit as the nature of the business may require and upon such notice as the court orders, upon a finding by either the chief judge of the court of appeals (or, if the chief judge is unavailable, the most senior available active judge of the court of appeals) or the judicial council of the circuit that, because of emergency conditions, no location within the circuit is reasonably available where such special sessions could be held. The court may transact any business at a special session outside the circuit which it might transact at a regular session.

(f) If a court of appeals issues an order exercising its authority under subsection (e), the court—

(1) through the Administrative Office of the United States Courts, shall—

(A) send notice of such order, including the reasons for the issuance of such order, to the Committee on the Judiciary of the Senate and the Committee on the Judiciary of the House of Representatives; and

(B) not later than 180 days after the expiration of such court order submit a brief report to the Committee on the Judiciary of the Senate and the Committee on the Judiciary of the House of Representatives describing the impact of such order, including—

(i) the reasons for the issuance of such order;

(ii) the duration of such order;

(iii) the impact of such order on litigants; and

(iv) the costs to the judiciary resulting from such order; and

(2) shall provide reasonable notice to the United States Marshals Service before the commencement of any special session held pursuant to such order.

(As amended Oct. 31, 1951, ch. 655, § 36, 65 Stat. 723; Oct. 14, 1980, Pub. L. 96-452; Apr. 2, 1982, Pub. L. 97-164, § 104, 96 Stat. 26; Oct. 29, 1992, Pub. L. 102-572, § 501, 106 Stat. 4512; Sept. 9, 2005, Pub. L. 109-63, § 2(a), 119 Stat. 1993.)

CHAPTER 5.   DISTRICT COURTS

§ 84. CALIFORNIA.

California is divided into four judicial districts to be known as the Northern, Eastern, Central, and Southern Districts of California.

Northern District

(a) The Northern District comprises the counties of Alameda, Contra Costa, Del Norte, Humboldt, Lake, Marin, Mendocino, Monterey, Napa, San Benito, Santa Clara, Santa Cruz, San Francisco, San Mateo, and Sonoma.

Court for the Northern District shall be held at Eureka, Oakland, San Francisco, and San Jose.

Eastern District

(b) The Eastern District comprises the counties of Alpine, Amador, Butte, Calaveras, Colusa, El Dorado, Fresno, Glenn, Inyo, Kern, Kings, Lassen, Madera, Mariposa, Merced, Modoc, Mono, Nevada, Placer, Plumas, Sacramento, San Joaquin, Shasta, Sierra, Siskiyou, Solano, Stanislaus, Sutter, Tehama, Trinity, Tulare, Tuolumne, Yolo, and Yuba.

Court for the Eastern District shall be held at Fresno, Redding, and Sacramento.

Central District

(c) The Central District comprises 3 divisions.

(1) The Eastern Division comprises the counties of Riverside and San Bernardino.

Court for the Eastern Division shall be held at a suitable site in the city of Riverside, the city of San Bernardino, or not more than 5 miles from the boundary of either such city.

(2) The Western Division comprises the counties of Los Angeles, San Luis Obispo, Santa Barbara, and Ventura.

Court for the Western Division shall be held at Los Angeles.

(3) The Southern Division comprises Orange County.

Court for the Southern Division shall be held at Santa Ana.

Southern District

Court for the Southern District shall be held at San Diego.

(d) The Southern District comprises the counties of Imperial and San Diego. (June 25, 1948, ch. 646, 62 Stat. 875; March 18, 1966, Pub. L. 89-372, § 3(a), 80 Stat. 75; Oct. 15, 1980, Pub. L. 96-462, § 2, 94 Stat. 1053; Aug. 26, 1992, Pub. L. 102-357, § 2, 106 Stat. 958.)

§ 132.   CREATION AND COMPOSITION OF DISTRICT COURTS.

(a) There shall be in each judicial district a district court which shall be a court of record known as the United States District Court for the district.

(b) Each district court shall consist of the district judge or judges for the district in regular active service. Justices or judges designated or assigned shall be competent to sit as judges of the court.

(c) Except as otherwise provided by law, or rule or order of court, the judicial power of a district court with respect to any action, suit or proceeding may be exercised by a single judge, who may preside alone and hold a regular or special session of court at the same time other sessions are held by other judges.

(As amended Nov. 13, 1963, Pub. L. 88-176, § 2, 77 Stat. 331.)

§ 133.   APPOINTMENT AND NUMBER OF DISTRICT JUDGES.

(a) The President shall appoint, by and with the advice and consent of the Senate, district judges for the several judicial districts, as follows:

DISTRICTS	JUDGES
Alabama:	
Northern	7
Middle	3
Southern	3
Alaska	3
Arizona	12
Arkansas:	
Eastern	5
Western	3
California:	
Northern	14
Eastern	6
Central	27
Southern	8
Colorado	7
Connecticut	8

Delaware 4

District of Columbia 15

Florida:

    Northern 4

    Middle 15

    Southern 17

Georgia:

    Northern 11

    Middle 4

    Southern 3

Hawaii 3

Idaho 2

Illinois:

    Northern 22

    Central......................... 4

    Southern 4

Indiana:

    Northern 5

    Southern 5

Iowa:

    Northern 2

    Southern 3

Kansas 5

Kentucky:

    Eastern......................... 5

    Western 4

    Eastern and Western............. 1

Louisiana:

    Eastern......................... 12

    Middle 3

    Western 7

Maine............................. 3

Maryland.......................... 10

Massachusetts 13

Michigan:

    Eastern 15

    Western 4

Minnesota 7

Mississippi:

    Northern 3

    Southern 6

Missouri:

    Eastern 6

    Western 5

    Eastern and Western 2

Montana 3

Nebraska 3

Nevada 7

New Hampshire 3

New Jersey 17

New Mexico 6

New York:

    Northern 5

    Southern 28

    Eastern 15

    Western 4

North Carolina:

    Eastern 4

    Middle 4

    Western 3

North Dakota 2

Ohio:

    Northern 11

    Southern 8

Oklahoma:

    Northern 3

    Eastern 1

    Western 6

    Northern, Eastern, and Western 1

(b) (1)In any case in which a judge of the United States (other than a senior judge) assumes the duties of a full-time office of Federal judicial administration, the President shall appoint, by and with the advice and consent of the Senate, an additional judge for the court on which such judge serves. If the judge who assumes the duties of such full-time office leaves that office and resumes the duties as an active judge of the court, then the President shall not appoint a judge to fill the first vacancy which occurs thereafter in that court.

(2) For purposes of paragraph (1), the term "office of Federal judicial administration" means a position as Director of the Federal Judicial Center, Director of the Administrative Office of the United States Courts, or counselor to the Chief Justice.

(Latest amendment Oct. 13, 2008, P.L. 110-402, § 1(b)(1), 122 Stat. 4254.)

§ 134. TENURE AND RESIDENCE OF DISTRICT JUDGES.

(a) The district judges shall hold office during good behavior.

(b) Each district judge, except in the District of Columbia, the Southern District of New York, and the Eastern District of New York, shall reside in the district or one of the districts for which he is appointed. Each district judge of the Southern District of New York and the Eastern District of New York may reside within 20 miles of the district to which he or she is appointed.

(c) If the public interest and the nature of the business of a district court require that a district judge should maintain his abode at or near a particular place for holding court in the district or within a particular part of the district the judicial council of the circuit may so declare and may make an appropriate order. If the district judges of such a district are unable to agree as to which of them shall maintain his abode at or near the place or within the area specified in such an order the judicial council of the circuit may decide which of them shall do so.

(Latest amendment Oct. 19, 1996, Pub. L. 104-317, § 607, 110 Stat. 3860.)

§ 144. BIAS OR PREJUDICE OF JUDGE.

Whenever a party to any proceeding in a district court makes and files a timely and sufficient affidavit that the judge before whom the matter is pending has a personal bias or prejudice either against him or in favor of any adverse party, such judge shall proceed no further therein, but another judge shall be assigned to hear such proceeding.

The affidavit shall state the facts and the reasons for the belief that bias or prejudice exists, and shall be filed not less than ten days before the beginning of the term at which the proceeding is to be heard, or good cause shall be shown for failure to file it within such time. A party may file only one such affidavit in any case. It shall be accompanied by a certificate of counsel of record stating that it is made in good faith.

(Added June 25, 1948, Ch. 646, 62 Stat. 898; amended May 24, 1949, ch. 139, § 65, 63 Stat. 99.)

CHAPTER 15.   CONFERENCES AND COUNCILS OF JUDGES

§ 331.   Judicial Conference of the United States.

The Chief Justice of the United States shall summon annually the chief judge of each judicial circuit, the chief judge of the Court of International Trade, and a district judge from each judicial circuit to a conference at such time and place in the United States as he may designate. He shall preside at such conference which shall be known as the Judicial Conference of the United States. Special sessions of the Conference may be called by the Chief Justice at such times and places as he may designate.

* * *

The Conference shall make a comprehensive survey of the condition of business in the courts of the United States and prepare plans for assignment of judges to or from circuits or districts where necessary. It shall also submit suggestions and recommendations to the various courts to promote uniformity of management procedures and the expeditious conduct of court business. The Conference is authorized to exercise the authority provided in chapter 16 of this title as the Conference, or through a standing committee. If the Conference elects to establish a standing committee, it shall be appointed by the Chief Justice and all petitions for review shall be reviewed by that committee. The Conference or the standing committee may hold hearings, take sworn testimony, issue subpoenas and subpoenas duces tecum, and make necessary and appropriate orders in the exercise of its authority. Subpoenas and subpoenas duces tecum shall be issued by the clerk of the Supreme Court or by the clerk of any court of appeals, at the direction of the Chief Justice or his designee and under the seal of the court, and shall be served in the manner provided in rule 45(c) of the Federal Rules of Civil Procedure for subpoenas and subpoenas duces tecum issued on behalf of the United States or an officer or any agency thereof. The Conference may also prescribe and modify rules for the exercise of the authority provided in chapter 16 of this title. All judicial officers and employees of the United States shall promptly carry into effect all orders of the Judicial Conference or the standing committee established pursuant to this section.

The Conference shall also carry on a continuous study of the operation and effect of the general rules of practice and procedure now or hereafter in use as prescribed by the Supreme Court for the other courts of the United States pursuant to law. Such changes in and additions to those rules as the Conference may deem desirable to promote simplicity in procedure, fairness in administration, the just determination of litigation, and the elimination of unjustifiable expense and delay shall be recommended by the Conference from time to time to the Supreme Court for its consideration and adoption, modification or rejection, in accordance with law.

The Judicial Conference shall review rules prescribed under section 2071 of this title by the courts, other than the Supreme Court and the district courts, for consistency with Federal law. The Judicial Conference may modify or abrogate any such rule so reviewed found inconsistent in the course of such a review.

The Attorney General shall, upon request of the Chief Justice, report to such Conference on matters relating to the business of the several courts of the United States, with particular reference to cases to which the United States is a party.

The Chief Justice shall submit to Congress an annual report of the proceedings of the Judicial Conference and its recommendations for legislation.

The Judicial Conference shall consult with the Director of United States Marshals Service on a continuing basis regarding the security requirements for the judicial branch of the United States Government, to ensure that the views of the Judicial Conference regarding the security requirements for the judicial branch of the Federal Government are taken into account when determining staffing levels, setting priorities for programs regarding judicial security, and allocating judicial security resources. In this paragraph, the term "judicial security" includes the security of buildings housing the judiciary, the personal security of judicial officers, the assessment of threats made to judicial officers, and the protection of all other judicial personnel. The United States Marshals Service retains final authority regarding security requirements for the judicial branch of the Federal Government.

(Latest amendment Nov. 2, 2002, Pub. L. 107-273, § 11043(b), 116 Stat. 1855.)

CHAPTER 21.   GENERAL PROVISIONS APPLICABLE TO COURTS AND JUDGES

§ 451.   DEFINITIONS.

As used in this title:

The term "court of the United States" includes the Supreme Court of the United States, courts of appeals, district courts constituted by chapter 5 of this title, including the Court of International Trade and any court created by Act of Congress the judges of which are entitled to hold office during good behavior.

The terms "district court" and "district court of the United States" means the courts constituted by chapter 5 of this title.

The term "judge of the United States" includes judges of the courts of appeals, district courts, Court of International Trade and any court created by Act of Congress, the judges of which are entitled to hold office during good behavior.

The term "justice of the United States" includes the Chief Justice of the United States and the associate justices of the Supreme Court.

The term "district" and "judicial district" mean the districts enumerated in Chapter 5 of this title.

The term "department" means one of the executive departments enumerated in section 1 of Title 5, unless the context shows that such term was intended to describe the executive, legislative, or judicial branches of the government.

The term "agency" includes any department, independent establishment, commission, administration, authority, board or bureau of the United States or any corporation in which the United States has a proprietary interest, unless the context shows that such term was intended to be used in a more limited sense.

(Latest amendment July 10, 1984, Pub. L. 98-353, § 113, 98 Stat. 343.)

§ 452. Courts Always Open; Power Unrestricted by Expiration of Sessions.

All courts of the United States shall be deemed always open for the purpose of filing proper papers, issuing and returning process, and making motions and orders.

The continued existence or expiration of a session of court in no way affects the power of the court to do any act or take any proceeding.

(As amended Oct. 16, 1963, Pub. L. 88-139, § 2, 77 Stat. 248.)

§ 453. Oaths of Justices and Judges.

Each justice or judge of the United States shall take the following oath or affirmation before performing the duties of his office: "I, _____, do solemnly swear (or affirm) that I will administer justice without respect to persons, and do equal right to the poor and to the rich, and that I will faithfully and impartially discharge and perform all the duties incumbent upon me as _____ under the Constitution and laws of the United States. So help me God." (As amended Dec. 1, 1990, Pub. L. 101-650, § 404, 104 Stat. 5089.)

§ 454. Practice of Law by Justices and Judges.

Any justice or judge appointed under the authority of the United States who engages in the practice of law is guilty of a high misdemeanor.

(Added June 25, 1948, ch. 646, 62 Stat. 908)

§ 455. Disqualification of Justice, Judge, or Magistrate.

(a) Any justice, judge, or magistrate of the United States shall disqualify himself in any proceeding in which his impartiality might reasonably be questioned.

(b) He shall also disqualify himself in the following circumstances:

(1) Where he has a personal bias or prejudice concerning a party, or personal knowledge of disputed evidentiary facts concerning the proceeding; Where in private practice he served as lawyer in the matter in controversy, or a lawyer with whom he previously practiced law served during such association as a lawyer concerning the matter, or the judge or such lawyer has been a material witness concerning it;

(2) Where he has served in governmental employment and in such capacity participated as counsel, adviser or material witness concerning the proceeding or expressed an opinion concerning the merits of the particular case in controversy;

(3) He knows that he, individually or as a fiduciary, or his spouse or minor child residing in his household, has a financial interest in the subject matter in controversy or in a party to the proceeding, or any other interest that could be substantially affected by the outcome of the proceeding;

(4) He or his spouse, or a person within the third degree of relationship to either of them, or the spouse of such a person:

(i) Is a party to the proceeding, or an officer, director, or trustee of a party;

(ii) Is acting as a lawyer in the proceeding;

(iii) Is known by the judge to have an interest that could be substantially affected by the outcome of the proceeding;

(iv) Is to the judge's knowledge likely to be a material witness in the proceeding.

(c) A judge should inform himself about his personal and fiduciary financial interests, and make a reasonable effort to inform himself about the personal financial interests of his spouse and minor children residing in his household.

(d) For the purposes of this section the following words or phrases shall have the meaning indicated:

(1) "proceeding" includes pretrial, trial, appellate review, or other stages of litigation;

(2) the degree of relationship is calculated according to the civil law system;

(3) "fiduciary" includes such relationships as executor, administrator, trustee, and guardian;

(4) "financial interest" means ownership of a legal or equitable interest, however small, or a relationship as director, adviser, or other active participant in the affairs of a party, except that:

(i) Ownership in a mutual or common investment fund that holds securities is not a "financial interest" in such securities unless the judge participates in the management of the fund;

(ii) An office in an educational, religious, charitable, fraternal, or civic organization is not a "financial interest" in securities held by the organization;

(iii) The proprietary interest of a policyholder in a mutual insurance company, of a depositor in a mutual savings association, or a similar proprietary interest, is a "financial interest" in the organization only if the outcome of the proceeding could substantially affect the value of the interest;

(iv) Ownership of government securities is a "financial interest" in the issuer only if the outcome of the proceeding could substantially affect the value of the securities.

(e) No justice, judge, or magistrate shall accept from the parties to the proceeding a waiver of any ground for disqualification enumerated in subsection (b). Where the ground for disqualification arises only under subsection (a), waiver may be accepted provided it is preceded by a full disclosure on the record of the basis for disqualification.

(f) Notwithstanding the preceding provisions of this section, if any justice, judge, magistrate, or bankruptcy judge to whom a matter has been assigned would be disqualified, after substantial judicial time has been devoted to the matter, because of the appearance or discovery, after the matter was assigned to him or her, that he or she individually or as a fiduciary, or his or her spouse or minor child residing in his or her household, has a financial interest in a party (other than an interest that could be substantially affected by the outcome), disqualification is not required if the justice, judge, magistrate, bankruptcy judge, spouse or minor child, as the case may be, divests himself or herself of the interest that provides the grounds for the disqualification.

(Added June 25, 1948, ch. 646, 62 Stat. 908; amended Dec. 5, 1974, Pub. L. 93-512, § 1, 88 Stat. 1609; Nov. 6, 1978, Pub. L. 95-598, title II, § 214(a), (b), 92 Stat. 2661; Nov. 19, 1988, Pub. L. 100-702, title X, § 1007, 102 Stat. 4667.)

PART III COURT OFFICERS AND EMPLOYEES

CHAPTER 43. UNITED STATES MAGISTRATES

§ 636. JURISDICTION, POWERS, AND TEMPORARY ASSIGNMENT.

(a) Each United States magistrate serving under this chapter shall have within the district in which sessions are held by the court that appointed the magistrate judge, at other places where that court may function, and elsewhere as authorized by law—

(1) all powers and duties conferred or imposed upon United States commissioners by law or by the Rules of Criminal Procedure for the United States District Courts;

(2) the power to administer oaths and affirmations, issue orders pursuant to section 3142 of title 18 concerning release or detention of persons pending trial, and take acknowledgments, affidavits, and depositions;

(3) the power to conduct trials under section 3401, title 18, United States Code, in conformity with and subject to the limitations of that section;

(4) the power to enter a sentence for a petty offense; and

(5) the power to enter a sentence for a class A misdemeanor in a case in which the parties have consented.

(b) (1) Notwithstanding any provision of law to the contrary—

(A) a judge may designate a magistrate to hear and determine any pretrial matter pending before the court, except a motion for injunctive relief, for judgment on the pleadings, for summary judgment, to dismiss or quash an indictment or information made by the defendant, to suppress evidence in a criminal case, to dismiss or to permit maintenance of a class action, to dismiss for failure to state a claim upon which relief can be granted, and to involuntarily dismiss an action. A judge of the court may reconsider any pretrial matter under this subparagraph (A) where it has been shown that the magistrate's [magistrate judge's] order is clearly erroneous or contrary to law.

(B) a judge may also designate a magistrate to conduct hearings, including evidentiary hearings, and to submit to a judge of the court proposed findings of fact and recommendations for the disposition, by a judge of the court, of any motion excepted in subparagraph (A), of applications for posttrial relief made by individuals convicted of criminal offenses and of prisoner petitions challenging conditions of confinement.

(C) the magistrate shall file his proposed findings and recommendations under subparagraph (B) with the court and a copy shall forthwith be mailed to all parties.

Within fourteen days after being served with a copy, any party may serve and file written objections to such proposed findings and recommendations as provided by rules of court. A judge of the court shall make a de novo determination of those portions of the report or specified proposed findings or recommendations to which objection is made. A judge of the court may accept, reject, or modify, in whole or in part, the findings or recommendations made by the magistrate. The judge may also receive further evidence or recommit the matter to the magistrate with instructions.

(2) A judge may designate a magistrate to serve as a special master pursuant to the applicable provisions of this title and the Federal Rules of Civil Procedure for the United States district courts. A judge may designate a magistrate to serve as a special master in any civil case, upon consent of the parties, without regard to the provisions of rule 53(b) of the Federal Rules of Civil Procedure for the United States district courts.

(3) A magistrate may be assigned such additional duties as are not inconsistent with the Constitution and laws of the United States.

(4) Each district court shall establish rules pursuant to which the magistrates [magistrate judge's] shall discharge their duties.

(c) Notwithstanding any provision of law to the contrary—

(1) Upon the consent of the parties, a full-time United States magistrate or a part-time United States magistrate who serves as a full-time judicial officer may conduct any or all proceedings in a jury or nonjury civil matter and order the entry of judgment in the case, when specially designated to exercise such jurisdiction by the district court or courts he serves. Upon the consent of the parties, pursuant to their specific written request, any other part-time magistrate may exercise such jurisdiction, if such magistrate meets the bar membership requirements set forth in section 631(b)(1) and the chief judge of the district court certifies that a full-time magistrate is not reasonably available in accordance with guidelines established by the judicial council of the circuit. When there is more than one judge of a district court, designation under this paragraph shall be by the concurrence of a majority of all the judges of such district court, and when there is no such concurrence, then by the chief judge.

(2) If a magistrate is designated to exercise civil jurisdiction under paragraph (1) of this subsection, the clerk of court shall, at the time the action is filed, notify the parties of the availability of a magistrate to exercise such jurisdiction. The decision of the parties shall be communicated to the clerk of court. Thereafter, either the district court judge or the magistrate may again advise the parties of the availability of the magistrate, but in so doing, shall also advise the parties that they are free to withhold consent without adverse substantive consequences. Rules of court for the reference of civil matters to magistrates shall include procedures to protect the voluntariness of the parties' consent.

(3) Upon entry of judgment in any case referred under paragraph (1) of this subsection, an aggrieved party may appeal directly to the appropriate United States court of appeals from the judgment of the magistrate in the same manner as an appeal from any other judgment of a district court. The consent of the parties allows a magistrate designated to exercise civil jurisdiction under paragraph (1) of this subsection to direct the entry of a judgment of the district court in accordance with the Federal Rules of Civil Procedure. Nothing in this paragraph shall be construed as a limitation of any party's right to seek review by the Supreme Court of the United States.

(4) The court may, for good cause shown on its own motion, or under extraordinary circumstances shown by any party, vacate a reference of a civil matter to a magistrate under this subsection.

(5) The magistrate shall, subject to guidelines of the Judicial Conference, determine whether the record taken pursuant to this section shall be taken by electronic sound recording, by a court reporter, or by other means.

(d) The practice and procedure for the trial of cases before officers serving under this chapter shall conform to rules promulgated by the Supreme Court pursuant to section 2072 of this title.

(e) Contempt authority—

(1) In general. United States magistrate judge serving under this chapter shall have within the territorial jurisdiction prescribed by the appointment of such magistrate judge the power to exercise contempt authority as set forth in this subsection.

(2) Summary criminal contempt authority. A magistrate judge shall have the power to punish summarily by fine or imprisonment, or both, such contempt of the authority of such magistrate judge constituting misbehavior of any person in the magistrate judge's presence so as to obstruct the administration of justice. The order of contempt shall be issued under the Federal Rules of Criminal Procedure.

(3) Additional criminal contempt authority in civil consent and misdemeanor cases. In any case in which a United States magistrate judge presides with the consent of the parties under subsection (c) of this section, and in any misdemeanor case proceeding before a magistrate judge under section 3401 of title 18, the magistrate judge shall have the power to punish, by fine or imprisonment, or both, criminal contempt constituting disobedience or resistance to the magistrate judge's lawful writ, process, order, rule, decree, or command. Disposition of such contempt shall be conducted upon notice and hearing under the Federal Rules of Criminal Procedure.

(4) Civil contempt authority in civil consent and misdemeanor cases. In any case in which a United States magistrate judge presides with the consent of the parties under subsection (c) of this section, and in any misdemeanor case proceeding before a magistrate judge under section 3401 of title 18, the magistrate judge may exercise the civil contempt authority of the district court. This paragraph shall not be construed to limit the authority of a magistrate judge to order sanctions under any other statute, the Federal Rules of Civil Procedure, or the Federal Rules of Criminal Procedure.

(5) Criminal contempt penalties. The sentence imposed by a magistrate judge for any criminal contempt provided for in paragraphs (2) and (3) shall not exceed the penalties for a Class C misdemeanor as set forth in sections 3581(b)(8) and 3571(b)(6) of title 18.

(6) Certification of other contempts to the district court. Upon the commission of any such act—

(A) in any case in which a United States magistrate judge presides with the consent of the parties under subsection (c) of this section, or in any misdemeanor case proceeding before a magistrate judge under section 3401 of title 18, that may, in the opinion of the magistrate judge, constitute a serious criminal contempt punishable by penalties exceeding those set forth in paragraph (5) of this subsection, or

(B) in any other case or proceeding under subsection (a) or (b) of this section, or any other statute, where—

(i) the act committed in the magistrate judge's presence may, in the opinion of the magistrate judge, constitute a serious criminal contempt punishable by penalties exceeding those set forth in paragraph (5) of this subsection,

(ii) the act that constitutes a criminal contempt occurs outside the presence of the magistrate judge, or

(iii) the act constitutes a civil contempt, the magistrate judge shall forthwith certify the facts to a district judge and may serve or cause to be served, upon any person whose behavior is brought into question under this paragraph, an order requiring such person to appear before a district judge upon a day certain to show cause why that person should not be adjudged in contempt by reason of the facts so certified. The district judge shall thereupon hear the evidence as to the act or conduct complained of and, if it is such as to warrant punishment, punish such person in the same manner and to the same extent as for a contempt committed before a district judge.

(7) Appeals of magistrate judge contempt orders. The appeal of an order of contempt under this subsection shall be made to the court of appeals in cases proceeding under subsection (c) of this section. The appeal of any other order of contempt issued under this section shall be made to the district court.

(f) In an emergency and upon the concurrence of the chief judges of the districts involved, a United States magistrate may be temporarily assigned to perform any of the duties specified in subsection (a), (b), or (c) of this section in a judicial district other than the judicial district for which he has been appointed. No magistrate shall perform any of such duties in a district to which he has been temporarily assigned until an order has been issued by the chief judge of such district specifying (1) the emergency by reason of which he has been transferred, (2) the duration of his assignment, and (3) the duties which he is authorized to perform. A magistrate so assigned shall not be entitled to additional compensation but shall be reimbursed for actual and necessary expenses incurred in the performance of his duties in accordance with section 635.

(g) A United States magistrate may perform the verification function required by section 4107 of title 18, United States Code. A magistrate may be assigned by a judge of any United States district court to perform the verification required by section 4108 and the appointment of counsel authorized by section 4109 of title 18, United States Code, and may perform such functions beyond the territorial limits of the United States. A magistrate assigned such functions shall have no authority to perform any other function within the territory of a foreign country.

(h) A United States magistrate who has retired may, upon the consent of the chief judge of the district involved, be recalled to serve as a magistrate in any judicial district by the judicial council of the circuit within which such district is located. Upon recall, a magistrate may receive a salary for such service in accordance with regulations promulgated by the Judicial Conference, subject to the restrictions on the payment of an annuity set forth in section 377 of this title or in subchapter III of chapter 83, and chapter 84, of title 5 which are applicable to such magistrate. The requirements set forth in subsections (a), (b)(3), and (d) of section 631, and paragraph (1) of subsection (b) of such section to the extent such paragraph requires membership of the bar of the location in which an individual is to serve as a magistrate, shall not apply to the recall of a retired magistrate under this subsection or section 375 of this title. Any other requirement set forth in section 631(b) shall apply to the recall of a retired magistrate under this subsection or section 375 of this title unless such retired magistrate met such requirement upon appointment or reappointment as a magistrate under section 631.

(Added June 25, 1948, ch. 646, 62 Stat. 917; latest amendment Sept. 9, 2005, Pub. L. 109-63, § 2(d), 119 Stat. 1995.)

PART IV JURISDICTION AND VENUE

CHAPTER 81. SUPREME COURT

§ 1251. ORIGINAL JURISDICTION.

(a) The Supreme Court shall have original and exclusive jurisdiction of all controversies between two or more States.

(b) The Supreme Court shall have original but not exclusive jurisdiction of:

(1) All actions or proceedings to which ambassadors, other public ministers, consuls, or vice consuls of foreign states are parties;

(2) All controversies between the United States and a State;

(3) All actions or proceedings by a State against the citizens of another State or against aliens.

(Added June 25, 1948, ch. 646, 62 Stat. 927; amended Sept. 30, 1978, Pub. L. 95-393, § 8(b), 92 Stat. 810.)

§ 1253. DIRECT APPEALS FROM DECISIONS OF THREE-JUDGE COURTS.

Except as otherwise provided by law, any party may appeal to the Supreme Court from an order granting or denying, after notice and hearing, an interlocutory or permanent injunction in any civil action, suit or proceeding required by an Act of Congress to be heard and determined by a district court of three judges.

(Added June 25, 1948, ch. 646, 62 Stat. 928.)

§ 1254. Courts of Appeals; Certiorari; Certified Questions.

Cases in the courts of appeals may be reviewed by the Supreme Court by the following methods:

(1) By writ of certiorari granted upon the petition of any party to any civil or criminal case, before or after rendition of judgment or decree;

(2) By certification at any time by a court of appeals of any question of law in any civil or criminal case as to which instructions are desired, and upon such certification the Supreme Court may give binding instructions or require the entire record to be sent up for decision of the entire matter in controversy.

(Added June 25, 1948, ch. 646, 62 Stat. 928; amended June 27, 1988, Pub. L. 100-352, § 2(a), (b), 102 Stat. 662.)

§ 1257. State Courts; Certiorari.

(a) Final judgments or decrees rendered by the highest court of a State in which a decision could be had, may be reviewed by the Supreme Court by writ of certiorari where the validity of a treaty or statute of the United States is drawn in question or where the validity of a statute of any state is drawn in question on the ground of its being repugnant to the Constitution, treaties, or laws of the United States, or where any title, right, privilege, or immunity is specially set up or claimed under the Constitution or the treaties or statutes of, or any commission held or authority exercised under, the United States.

(b) For the purposes of this section, the term "highest court of a State" includes the District of Columbia Court of Appeals.

(Added June 25, 1948, ch. 646, 62 Stat. 929; amended July 29, 1970, Pub. L. 91-358, title I, § 172(a)(1), 84 Stat. 590; June 27, 1988, Pub. L. 100-352, § 3, 102 Stat. 662.)

CHAPTER 83.   COURTS OF APPEALS

§ 1291. Final Decisions of District Courts.

The courts of appeals (other than the United States Court of Appeals for the Federal Circuit) shall have jurisdiction of appeals from all final decisions of the district courts of the United States, the United States District Court for the District of the Canal Zone, the District Court of Guam, and the District Court of the Virgin Islands, except where a direct review may be had in the Supreme Court. The jurisdiction of the United States Court of Appeals for the Federal Circuit shall be limited to the jurisdiction described in sections 1292(c) and (d) and 1295 of this title.

(Added June 25, 1948, ch. 646, 62 Stat. 929; amended Oct. 31, 1951, ch. 655, § 48, 65 Stat. 726; July 7, 1958, Pub. L. 85-508, § 12(e); 72 Stat. 348; April 2, 1982, Pub. L. 97-164, § 124, 96 Stat. 36.)

§ 1292. INTERLOCUTORY DECISIONS.

(a) Except as provided in subsections (c) and (d) of this section, the courts of appeals shall have jurisdiction of appeals from:

(1) Interlocutory orders of the district courts of the United States, the United States District Court for the District of the Canal Zone, the District Court of Guam, and the District Court of the Virgin Islands, or of the judges thereof, granting, continuing, modifying, refusing or dissolving injunctions, or refusing to dissolve or modify injunctions, except where a direct review may be had in the Supreme Court;

(2) Interlocutory orders appointing receivers, or refusing orders to wind up receiverships or to take steps to accomplish the purposes thereof, such as directing sales or other disposals of property;

(3) Interlocutory decrees of such district courts or the judges thereof determining the rights and liabilities of the parties to admiralty cases in which appeals from final decrees are allowed.

(b) When a district judge, in making in a civil action an order not otherwise appealable under this section, shall be of the opinion that such order involves a controlling question of law as to which there is substantial ground for difference of opinion and that an immediate appeal from the order may materially advance the ultimate termination of the litigation, he shall so state in writing in such order. The Court of Appeals which would have jurisdiction of an appeal of such action may thereupon, in its discretion, permit an appeal to be taken from such order, if application is made to it within ten days after the entry of the order: *Provided, however,* That application for an appeal hereunder shall not stay proceedings in the district court unless the district judge or the Court of Appeals or a judge thereof shall so order.

(c) The United States Court of Appeals for the Federal Circuit shall have exclusive jurisdiction—

(1) of an appeal from an interlocutory order or decree described in subsection (a) or (b) of this section in any case over which the court would have jurisdiction of an appeal under section 1295 of this title; and

(2) of an appeal from a judgment in a civil action for patent infringement which would otherwise be appealable to the United States Court of Appeals for the Federal Circuit and is final except for an accounting.

(d) (1)When the chief judge of the Court of International Trade issues an order under the provisions of section 256(b) of this title, or when any judge of the Court of International Trade, in issuing any other interlocutory order, includes in the order a statement that a controlling question of law is involved with respect to which there is a substantial ground for difference of opinion and that an immediate appeal from that order may materially advance the ultimate termination of the litigation, the United States Court of Appeals for the Federal Circuit may, in its discretion, permit an appeal to be taken from such order, if application is made to that Court within ten days after the entry of such order.

(2) When the chief judge of the United States Court of Federal Claims issues an order under section 798(b) of this title, or when any judge of the United States Court of Federal Claims, in issuing an interlocutory order, includes in the order a statement that a controlling question of law is involved with respect to which there is a substantial ground for difference of opinion and that an immediate appeal from that order may materially advance the ultimate termination of the litigation, the United States Court of Appeals for the Federal Circuit may, in its discretion, permit an appeal to be taken from such order, if application is made to that Court within ten days after the entry of such order.

(3) Neither the application for nor the granting of an appeal under this subsection shall stay proceedings in the Court of International Trade or in the Court of Federal Claims, as the case may be, unless a stay is ordered by a judge of the Court of International Trade or of the Court of Federal Claims or by the United States Court of Appeals for the Federal Circuit or a judge of that court.

(4) (A)The United States Court of Appeals for the Federal Circuit shall have exclusive jurisdiction of an appeal from an interlocutory order of a district court of the United States, the District Court of Guam, the District Court of the Virgin Islands, or the District Court for the Northern Mariana Islands, granting or denying, in whole or in part, a motion to transfer an action to the United States Court of Federal Claims under section 1631 of this title.

(B) When a motion to transfer an action to the Court of Federal Claims is filed in a district court, no further proceedings shall be taken in the district court until 60 days after the court has ruled upon the motion. If an appeal is taken from the district court's grant or denial of the motion, proceedings shall be further stayed until the appeal has been decided by the Court of Appeals for the Federal Circuit. The stay of proceedings in the district court shall not bar the granting of preliminary or injunctive relief, where appropriate and where expedition is reasonably necessary. However, during the period in which proceedings are stayed as provided in this subparagraph, no transfer to the Court of Federal Claims pursuant to the motion shall be carried out.

(e) The Supreme Court may prescribe rules, in accordance with section 2072 of this title, to provide for an appeal of an interlocutory decision to the courts of appeals that is not otherwise provided for under subsection (a), (b), (c), or (d).

(Added June 25, 1948, ch. 646, 62 Stat. 929; amended Oct. 31, 1951, ch 655, § 49, 65 Stat. 726; July 7, 1958, Pub. L. 85-508, § 12(e), 72 Stat. 348; Sept. 2, 1958, Pub. L. 85-919, 72 Stat. 1770; April 2, 1982, Pub L. No. 97-164, § 125, 96 Stat. 36; Nov. 8, 1985, Pub. L. 98-620, § 412, 98 Stat. 3362; Nov. 19, 1988, Pub. L. 100-702, § 501; as amended Oct. 29, 1992, Pub. L. 102-572, §§ 101, 902(b), 906(c), 106 Stat. 4506, 4516, 4518.)

§ 1294. Circuits in Which Decisions Reviewable.

Except as provided in sections 1292(c), 1292(d), and 1295 of this title, appeals from reviewable decisions of the district and territorial courts shall be taken to the courts of appeals as follows:

(1) From a district court of the United States to the court of appeals for the circuit embracing the district;

(2) From the United States District Court for the District of the Canal Zone, to the Court of Appeals for the Fifth Circuit;

(3) From the District Court of the Virgin Islands, to the Court of Appeals for the Third Circuit;

(4) From the District Court of Guam, to the Court of Appeals for the Ninth Circuit.

(As amended Oct. 31, 1951, ch. 655, § 50(a), 65 Stat. 727; July 7, 1958, Pub. L. 85-508 § 12(g), 72 Stat. 348; Mar. 18, 1959, Pub. L. 86-3, § 14(c), 73 Stat. 10; Aug 30, 1961, Pub. L. 87-189, § 5, 75 Stat. 417; Nov. 6, 1978, Pub. L. 95-598, § 237, 92 Stat. 2667; April 2, 1982, Pub. L. 97-164, § 126, 96 Stat. 37; July 10, 1984, Pub. L. 98-353, § 113, 98 Stat. 343.)

§ 1295. Jurisdiction of the United States Court of Appeals for the Federal Circuit.

(a) The United States Court of Appeals for the Federal Circuit shall have exclusive jurisdiction—

(1) of an appeal from a final decision of a district court of the United States, the United States District Court for the District of the Canal Zone, the District Court of Guam, the District Court of the Virgin Islands, or the District Court for the Northern Mariana Islands, if the jurisdiction of that court was based, in whole or in part, on section 1338 of this title, except that a case involving a claim arising under any Act of Congress relating to copyrights, exclusive rights in mask works, or trademarks and no other claims under section 1338(a) shall be governed by sections 1291, 1292, and 1294 of this title;

(2) of an appeal from a final decision of a district court of the United States, the United States District Court for the District of the Canal Zone, the District Court of Guam, the District Court of the Virgin Islands, or the District Court for the Northern Mariana Islands, if the jurisdiction of that court was based, in whole or in part, on section 1346 of this title, except that jurisdiction of an appeal in a case brought in a district court under section 1346(a)(1), 1346(b), 1346(e), or 1346(f) of this title or under section 1346(a)(2) when the claim is founded upon an Act of Congress or a regulation of an executive department providing for internal revenue shall be governed by sections 1291, 1292, and 1294 of this title;

(3) of an appeal from a final decision of the United States Court of Federal Claims;

(4) of an appeal from a decision of—

(A) the Patent Trial and Appeal Board of the United States Patent and Trademark Office with respect to a patent application, derivation proceeding, reexamination, post-grant review, or inter partes review under title 35, at the instance of a party who exercised that party's right to participate in the applicable proceeding before or appeal to the Board, except that an applicant or a party to a derivation proceeding may also have remedy by civil action pursuant to section 145 or 146 of title 35; an appeal under this subparagraph of a decision of the Board with respect to an application or derivation proceeding shall waive the right of such applicant or party to proceed under section 145 or 146 of title 35;

(B) the Under Secretary of Commerce for Intellectual Property and Director of the United States Patent and Trademark Office or the Trademark Trial and Appeal Board with respect to applications for registration of marks and other proceedings as provided in section 21 of the Trademark Act of 1946 (15 U.S.C. 1071); or

(C) a district court to which a case was directed pursuant to section 145, 146, or 154(b) of title 35;

(5) of an appeal from a final decision of the United States Court of International Trade;

(6) to review the final determinations of the United States International Trade Commission relating to unfair practices in import trade, made under section 337 of the Tariff Act of 1930 (19 U.S.C. 1337);

(7) to review, by appeal on questions of law only, findings of the Secretary of Commerce under U.S. note 6 to subchapter X of chapter 98 of the Harmonized Tariff Schedule of the United States (relating to importation of instruments or apparatus);

(8) of an appeal under section 71 of the Plant Variety Protection Act (7 U.S.C. 2461);

(9) of an appeal from a final order or final decision of the Merit Systems Protection Board, pursuant to sections 7703(b)(1) and 7703(d) of title 5;

(10) of an appeal from a final decision of an agency board of contract appeals pursuant to section 7107(a)(1) of title 41;

(11) of an appeal under section 211 of the Economic Stabilization Act of 1970;

(12) of an appeal under section 5 of the Emergency Petroleum Allocation Act of 1973;

(13) of an appeal under section 506(c) of the Natural Gas Policy Act of 1978; and

(14) of an appeal under section 523 of the Energy Policy and Conservation Act.

(b) The head of any executive department or agency may, with the approval of the Attorney General, refer to the Court of Appeals for the Federal Circuit for judicial review any final decision rendered by a board of contract appeals pursuant to the terms of any contract with the United States awarded by that department or agency which the head of such department or agency has concluded is not entitled to finality pursuant to the review standards specified in section 7107(a)(1) of title 41. The head of each executive department or agency shall make any referral under this section within one hundred and twenty days after the receipt of a copy of the final appeal decision.

(c) The Court of Appeals for the Federal Circuit shall review the matter referred in accordance with the standards specified in section 7107(a)(1) of title 41. The court shall proceed with judicial review on the administrative record made before the board of contract appeals on matters so referred as in other cases pending in such court, shall determine the issue of finality of the appeal decision, and shall, if appropriate, render judgment thereon, or remand the matter to any administrative or executive body or official with such direction as it may deem proper and just.

(Added April 2, 1982, Pub. L. 97-164, § 127(a), 96 Stat. 39; latest amendment Sept. 16, 2012. Act Sept. 16, 2011, P.L. 112-29, § 7(c)(2), 125 Stat. 314.)

CHAPTER 85.   DISTRICT COURTS; JURISDICTION

§ 1330.   Actions Against Foreign States.

(a) The district courts shall have original jurisdiction without regard to amount in controversy of any nonjury civil action against a foreign state as defined in section 1603(a) of this title as to any claim for relief in personam with respect to which the foreign state is not entitled to immunity either under sections 1605–1607 of this title or under any applicable international agreement.

(b) Personal jurisdiction over a foreign state shall exist as to every claim for relief over which the district courts have jurisdiction under subsection (a) where service has been made under section 1608 of this title.

(c) For purposes of subsection (b), an appearance by a foreign state does not confer personal jurisdiction with respect to any claim for relief not arising out of any transaction or occurrence enumerated in sections 1605–1607 of this title.

(Added Oct. 21, 1976, Pub. L. 94-583, § 2(a), 90 Stat. 2891.)

§ 1331.   Federal Question.

The district courts shall have original jurisdiction of all civil actions arising under the Constitution, laws, or treaties of the United States.

(Added June 25, 1948, ch. 646, 62 Stat. 930; amended July 25, 1958, Pub. L. 85-554, § 1, 72 Stat. 415; Oct. 21, 1976, Pub. L. 94-574, § 2, 90 Stat. 2721; Dec. 1, 1980, Pub. L. 96-486, § 2(a), 94 Stat. 2369.)

§ 1332.   Diversity of Citizenship; Amount in Controversy; Costs.

(a) The district courts shall have original jurisdiction of all civil actions where the matter in controversy exceeds the sum or value of $ 75,000, exclusive of interest and costs, and is between —

(1) citizens of different States;

(2) citizens of a State and citizens or subjects of a foreign state, except that the district courts shall not have original jurisdiction under this subsection of an action between citizens of a State and citizens or subjects of a foreign state who are lawfully admitted for permanent residence in the United States and are domiciled in the same State;

(3) citizens of different States and in which citizens or subjects of a foreign state are additional parties; and

(4) a foreign state, defined in section 1603(a) of this title, as plaintiff and citizens of a State or of different States.

(b) Except when express provision therefor is otherwise made in a statute of the United States, where the plaintiff who files the case originally in the Federal courts is finally adjudged to be entitled to recover less than the sum or value of $75,000, computed without regard to any setoff or counterclaim to which the defendant may be adjudged to be entitled, and exclusive of interest and costs, the district court may deny costs to the plaintiff and, in addition, may impose costs on the plaintiff.

(c) For the purposes of this section and section 1441 of this title —

(1) a corporation shall be deemed to be a citizen of every State and foreign state by which it has been incorporated and of the State or foreign state where it has its principal place of business, except that in any direct action against the insurer of a policy or contract of liability insurance, whether incorporated or unincorporated, to which action the insured is not joined as a party-defendant, such insurer shall be deemed a citizen of —

(a) every State and foreign state of which the insured is a citizen;

(b) every State and foreign state by which the insurer has been incorporated; and

(c) the State or foreign state where the insurer has its principal place of business; and

(2) the legal representative of the estate of a decedent shall be deemed to be a citizen only of the same State as the decedent, and the legal representative of an infant or incompetent shall be deemed to be a citizen only of the same State as the infant or incompetent.

(d) (1)In this subsection —

(A) the term "class" means all of the class members in a class action;

(B) the term "class action" means any civil action filed under rule 23 of the Federal Rules of Civil Procedure or similar State statute or rule of judicial procedure authorizing an action to be brought by 1 or more representative persons as a class action;

(C) the term "class certification order" means an order issued by a court approving the treatment of some or all aspects of a civil action as a class action; and

(D) the term "class members" means the persons (named or unnamed) who fall within the definition of the proposed or certified class in a class action.

(2) The district courts shall have original jurisdiction of any civil action in which the matter in controversy exceeds the sum or value of $5,000,000, exclusive of interest and costs, and is a class action in which—

(A) any member of a class of plaintiffs is a citizen of a State different from any defendant;

(B) any member of a class of plaintiffs is a foreign state or a citizen or subject of a foreign state and any defendant is a citizen of a State; or

(C) any member of a class of plaintiffs is a citizen of a State and any defendant is a foreign state or a citizen or subject of a foreign state.

(3) A district court may, in the interests of justice and looking at the totality of the circumstances, decline to exercise jurisdiction under paragraph (2) over a class action in which greater than one-third but less than two-thirds of the members of all proposed plaintiff classes in the aggregate and the primary defendants are citizens of the State in which the action was originally filed based on consideration of—

(A) whether the claims asserted involve matters of national or interstate interest;

(B) whether the claims asserted will be governed by laws of the State in which the action was originally filed or by the laws of other States;

(C) whether the class action has been pleaded in a manner that seeks to avoid Federal jurisdiction;

(D) whether the action was brought in a forum with a distinct nexus with the class members, the alleged harm, or the defendants;

(E) whether the number of citizens of the State in which the action was originally filed in all proposed plaintiff classes in the aggregate is substantially larger than the number of citizens from any other State, and the citizenship of the other members of the proposed class is dispersed among a substantial number of States; and

(F) whether, during the 3-year period preceding the filing of that class action, 1 or more other class actions asserting the same or similar claims on behalf of the same or other persons have been filed.

(4) A district court shall decline to exercise jurisdiction under paragraph (2)—

(A) (i) over a class action in which—

(I) greater than two-thirds of the members of all proposed plaintiff classes in the aggregate are citizens of the State in which the action was originally filed;

(II) at least 1 defendant is a defendant—

(aa) from whom significant relief is sought by members of the plaintiff class;

(bb) whose alleged conduct forms a significant basis for the claims asserted by the proposed plaintiff class; and

(cc) who is a citizen of the State in which the action was originally filed; and

(III) principal injuries resulting from the alleged conduct or any related conduct of each defendant were incurred in the State in which the action was originally filed; and

(ii) during the 3-year period preceding the filing of that class action, no other class action has been filed asserting the same or similar factual allegations against any of the defendants on behalf of the same or other persons; or

(B) two-thirds or more of the members of all proposed plaintiff classes in the aggregate, and the primary defendants, are citizens of the State in which the action was originally filed.

(5) Paragraphs (2) through (4) shall not apply to any class action in which—

(A) the primary defendants are States, State officials, or other governmental entities against whom the district court may be foreclosed from ordering relief; or

(B) the number of members of all proposed plaintiff classes in the aggregate is less than 100.

(6) In any class action, the claims of the individual class members shall be aggregated to determine whether the matter in controversy exceeds the sum or value of $5,000,000, exclusive of interest and costs.

(7) Citizenship of the members of the proposed plaintiff classes shall be determined for purposes of paragraphs (2) through (6) as of the date of filing of the complaint or amended complaint, or, if the case stated by the initial pleading is not subject to Federal jurisdiction, as of the date of service by plaintiffs of an

amended pleading, motion, or other paper, indicating the existence of Federal jurisdiction.

(8) This subsection shall apply to any class action before or after the entry of a class certification order by the court with respect to that action.

(9) Paragraph (2) shall not apply to any class action that solely involves a claim —

(A) concerning a covered security as defined under 16(f)(3) of the Securities Act of 1933 (15 U.S.C. 78p(f)(3)) and section 28(f)(5)(E) of the Securities Exchange Act of 1934 (15 U.S.C. 78bb(f)(5)(E));

(B) that relates to the internal affairs or governance of a corporation or other form of business enterprise and that arises under or by virtue of the laws of the State in which such corporation or business enterprise is incorporated or organized; or

(C) that relates to the rights, duties (including fiduciary duties), and obligations relating to or created by or pursuant to any security (as defined under section 2(a)(1) of the Securities Act of 1933 (15 U.S.C. 77b(a)(1)) and the regulations issued thereunder).

(10) For purposes of this subsection and section 1453, an unincorporated association shall be deemed to be a citizen of the State where it has its principal place of business and the State under whose laws it is organized.

(11) (A)For purposes of this subsection and section 1453, a mass action shall be deemed to be a class action removable under paragraphs (2) through (10) if it otherwise meets the provisions of those paragraphs.

(B) (i)As used in subparagraph (A), the term "mass action" means any civil action (except a civil action within the scope of section 1711(2)) in which monetary relief claims of 100 or more persons are proposed to be tried jointly on the ground that the plaintiffs' claims involve common questions of law or fact, except that jurisdiction shall exist only over those plaintiffs whose claims in a mass action satisfy the jurisdictional amount requirements under subsection (a).

(ii) As used in subparagraph (A), the term "mass action" shall not include any civil action in which —

(I) all of the claims in the action arise from an event or occurrence in the State in which the action was filed, and that allegedly resulted in injuries in that State or in States contiguous to that State;

(II) the claims are joined upon motion of a defendant;

(III) all of the claims in the action are asserted on behalf of the general public (and not on behalf of individual claimants or members of a purported class) pursuant to a State statute specifically authorizing such action; or

(IV) the claims have been consolidated or coordinated solely for pre-trial proceedings.

(C) (i)Any action(s) removed to Federal court pursuant to this subsection shall not thereafter be transferred to any other court pursuant to section 1407, or the rules promulgated thereunder, unless a majority of the plaintiffs in the action request transfer pursuant to section 1407.

(ii) This subparagraph will not apply—

(I) to cases certified pursuant to rule 23 of the Federal Rules of Civil Procedure; or

(II) if plaintiffs propose that the action proceed as a class action pursuant to rule 23 of the Federal Rules of Civil Procedure.

(D) The limitations periods on any claims asserted in a mass action that is removed to Federal court pursuant to this subsection shall be deemed tolled during the period that the action is pending in Federal court.

(e) The word "States", as used in this section, includes the Territories, the District of Columbia, and the Commonwealth of Puerto Rico.

(Added June 25, 1948, ch. 646, 62 Stat. 930; amended July 26, 1956, ch. 740, 70 Stat. 658; July 25, 1958, Pub. L. 85-554, § 2, 72 Stat. 415; Aug. 14, 1964, Pub. L. 88-439 § 1, 78 Stat. 445; October 21, 1976, Pub. L. 94-583, § 3, 90 Stat. 2891; Nov. 19, 1988, Pub. L. 100-702, §§ 201(a), 202(a), 203(a), 102 Stat. 4646; Oct. 19, 1996, Pub. L. 104-317, § 205, 110 Stat. 3850; Feb. 18, 2005, Pub. L. 109-2, § 4(a), 119 Stat. 9; Dec. 8, 2011, P.L. 112–63, Title I, §§ 101, 102, 125 Stat. 758.)

§ 1333. ADMIRALTY, MARITIME AND PRIZE CASES.

The district courts shall have original jurisdiction, exclusive of the courts of the States, of:

(1) Any civil case of admiralty or maritime jurisdiction, saving to suitors in all cases all other remedies to which they are otherwise entitled.

(2) Any prize brought into the United States and all proceedings for the condemnation of property taken as prize.

(As amended May 24, 1949, ch. 139, § 79, 63 Stat. 101.)

§ 1334. BANKRUPTCY CASES AND PROCEEDINGS.

(a) Except as provided in subsection (b) of this section, the district courts shall have original and exclusive jurisdiction of all cases under title 11.

(b) Except as provided in subsection (e)(2), and notwithstanding any Act of Congress that confers exclusive jurisdiction on a court or courts other than the district courts, the district courts shall have original but not exclusive jurisdiction of all civil proceedings arising under title 11, or arising in or related to cases under title 11.

(c) (1)Except with respect to a case under chapter 15 of title 11, nothing in this section prevents a district court in the interest of justice, or in the interest of comity with State courts or respect for State law, from abstaining from hearing a particular proceeding arising under title 11 or arising in or related to a case under title 11.

(2) Upon timely motion of a party in a proceeding based upon a State law claim or State law cause of action, related to a case under title 11 but not arising under title 11 or arising in a case under title 11, with respect to which an action could not have been commenced in a court of the United States absent jurisdiction under this section, the district court shall abstain from hearing such proceeding if an action is commenced, and can be timely adjudicated, in a State forum of appropriate jurisdiction.

(d) Any decision to abstain or not to abstain made under subsection (c) (other than a decision not to abstain in a proceeding described in subsection (c)(2)) is not reviewable by appeal or otherwise by the court of appeals under section 158(d), 1291, or 1292 of this title or by the Supreme Court of the United States under section 1254 of this title. Subsection (c) and this subsection shall not be construed to limit the applicability of the stay provided for by section 362 of title 11, United States Code, as such section applies to an action affecting the property of the estate in bankruptcy.

(e) The district court in which a case under title 11 is commenced or is pending shall have exclusive jurisdiction—

(1) of all the property, wherever located, of the debtor as of the commencement of such case, and of property of the estate; and

(2) over all claims or causes of action that involve construction of section 327 of title 11, United States Code, or rules relating to disclosure requirements under section 327.

(As amended Nov. 6, 1978, Pub. L. 95-598, § 238, 92 Stat. 2668; July 10, 1984, Pub. L. 98-353, § 101(a), 98 Stat. 333; Dec. 1, 1990, Pub. L. 101-650, § 309, 104 Stat. 5089; Oct. 22, 1994, Pub. L. 103-394, § 104, 108 Stat. 4109; Apr. 20, 2005, Pub. L. 109-8, § 324(a), § 802(c)(2), § 1219, 119 Stat. 98, 145, 195.)

§ 1335. INTERPLEADER.

(a) The district courts shall have original jurisdiction of any civil action of interpleader or in the nature of interpleader filed by any person, firm, or corporation, association, or society having in his or its custody or possession money or property of the value of $500 or more, or having issued a note, bond, certificate, policy of insurance, or other instrument of value or amount of $500 or more, or providing for the delivery or payment or the loan of money or property of such amount or value, or being under any obligation written or unwritten to the amount of $500 or more, if—

(1) Two or more adverse claimants, of diverse citizenship as defined in subsection (a) or (d) of section 1332 of this title, are claiming or may claim to be entitled to such money or property, or to any one or more of the benefits arising by virtue of any note, bond, certificate, policy or other instrument, or arising by virtue of any such obligation; and if—

(2) the plaintiff has deposited such money or property or has paid the amount of or the loan or other value of such instrument or the amount due under such obligation into the registry of the court, there to abide the judgment of the court, or has given bond payable to the clerk of the court in such amount and with such surety as the court or judge may deem proper, conditioned upon the compliance by the plaintiff with the future order or judgment of the court with respect to the subject matter of the controversy.

(b) Such an action may be entertained although the titles or claims of the conflicting claimants do not have a common origin, or are not identical, but are adverse to and independent of one another.

(Added June 25, 1948, ch. 646, 62 Stat. 931; amended Feb. 18, 2005, Pub. L. 109-2, § 4(b)(1), 119 Stat. 12.)

§ 1337. Commerce and Antitrust Regulations; Amount in Controversy, Costs.

(a) The district courts shall have original jurisdiction of any civil action or proceeding arising under any Act of Congress regulating commerce or protecting trade and commerce against restraints and monopolies: *Provided, however,* That the district courts shall have original jurisdiction of an action brought under section 11706 or 14706 of title 49, only if the matter in controversy for each receipt or bill of lading exceeds $10,000, exclusive of interest and costs.

(b) Except when express provision therefor is otherwise made in a statute of the United States, where a plaintiff who files the case under section 11706 or 14706 of title 49, originally in the Federal courts is finally adjudged to be entitled to recover less than the sum or value of $10,000, computed without regard to any setoff or counterclaim to which the defendant may be adjudged to be entitled, and exclusive of any interest and costs, the district court may deny costs to the plaintiff and, in addition, may impose costs on the plaintiff.

(c) The district courts shall not have jurisdiction under this section of any matter within the exclusive jurisdiction of the Court of International Trade under chapter 95 of this title.

(As amended Oct. 10, 1980, Pub. L. 96-417, § 505, 94 Stat. 1743; Jan. 12, 1983, Pub. L. 97-449, § 5, 96 Stat. 2413; Dec. 29, 1995, Pub. L. 104-88, § 305(a)(3), 109 Stat. 944.)

§ 1338.　Patents, Plant Variety Protection, Copyrights, Mask Works, Designs, Trademarks, and Unfair Competition.

(a) The district courts shall have original jurisdiction of any civil action arising under any Act of Congress relating to patents, plant variety protection, copyrights and trademarks. No State court shall have jurisdiction over any claim for relief arising under any Act of Congress relating to patents, plant variety protection, or copyrights. For purposes of this subsection, the term "State" includes any State of the United States, the District of Columbia, the Commonwealth of Puerto Rico, the United States Virgin Islands, American Samoa, Guam, and the Northern Mariana Islands.

(b) The district courts shall have original jurisdiction of any civil action asserting a claim of unfair competition when joined with a substantial and related claim under the copyright, patent, plant variety protection or trademark laws.

(c) Subsections (a) and (b) apply to exclusive rights in mask works under chapter 9 of title 17, and to exclusive rights in designs under chapter 13 of title 17, to the same extent as such subsections apply to copyrights.

(Added June 25, 1948, ch. 646, 62 Stat. 931; latest amendment Sept. 16, 2011, P.L. 112–29, § 19(a), 125 Stat. 331.)

§ 1343.　Civil Rights and Elective Franchise.

(a) The district courts shall have original jurisdiction of any civil action authorized by law to be commenced by any person:

(1) To recover damages for injury to his person or property, or because of the deprivation of any right or privilege of a citizen of the United States, by any act done in furtherance of any conspiracy mentioned in section 1985 of Title 42;

(2) To recover damages from any person who fails to prevent or to aid in preventing any wrongs mentioned in section 1985 of Title 42 which he had knowledge were about to occur and power to prevent;

(3) To redress the deprivation, under color of any State law, statute, ordinance, regulation, custom or usage, of any right, privilege or immunity secured by the Constitution of the United States or by any Act of Congress providing for equal rights of citizens or of all persons within the jurisdiction of the United States;

(4) To recover damages or to secure equitable or other relief under any Act of Congress providing for the protection of civil rights, including the right to vote.

(b) For purposes of this section—

(1) the District of Columbia shall be considered to be a State; and

(2) any Act of Congress applicable exclusively to the District of Columbia shall be considered to be a statute of the District of Columbia.

(As amended Sept. 3, 1954, ch. 1263, § 42, 68 Stat. 1241; Sept. 9, 1957, Pub. L. 85-315, Part III § 121, 71 Stat. 637; Dec. 29, 1979, Pub. L. 96-170, § 2, 93 Stat. 1284.)

§ 1345. UNITED STATES AS PLAINTIFF.

Except as otherwise provided by Act of Congress, the district courts shall have original jurisdiction of all civil actions, suits or proceedings commenced by the United States, or by any agency or officer thereof expressly authorized to sue by Act of Congress.

(Added June 25, 1948, ch. 646, 62 Stat. 933.)

§ 1346. UNITED STATES AS DEFENDANT.

(a) The district courts shall have original jurisdiction, concurrent with the United States Court of Federal Claims, of:

(1) Any civil action against the United States for the recovery of any internal-revenue tax alleged to have been erroneously or illegally assessed or collected, or any penalty claimed to have been collected without authority or any sum alleged to have been excessive or in any manner wrongfully collected under the internal revenue laws;

(2) Any other civil action or claim against the United States, not exceeding $10,000 in amount, founded either upon the Constitution, or any Act of Congress, or any regulation of an executive department, or upon any express or implied contract with the United States, or for liquidated or unliquidated damages in cases not sounding in tort, except that the district courts shall not have jurisdiction of any civil action or claim against the United States founded upon any express or implied contract with the United States or for liquidated or unliquidated damages in cases not sounding in tort which are subject to sections 7104(b)(1) and 7107(a)(1) of title 41. For the purpose of this paragraph, an express or implied contract with the Army and Air Force Exchange Service, Navy Exchanges, Marine Corps Exchanges, Coast Guard Exchanges, or Exchange Councils of the National Aeronautics and Space Administration shall be considered an express or implied contract with the United States.

(b)(1) Subject to the provisions of chapter 171 of this title, the district courts, together with the United States District Court for the District of the Canal Zone and the District Court of the Virgin Islands, shall have exclusive jurisdiction of civil actions on claims against the United States, for money damages, accruing on and after January 1, 1945, for injury or loss of property, or personal injury or death caused by the negligent or wrongful act or omission of any employee of the Government while acting within the scope of his office or employment, under circumstances where the United States, if a private person, would be liable to the claimant in accordance with the law of the place where the act or omission occurred.

(2) No person convicted of a felony who is incarcerated while awaiting sentencing or while serving a sentence may bring a civil action against the United States or an agency, officer, or employee of the Government, for mental or emotional injury suffered while in custody without a prior showing of physical injury or the commission of a sexual act (as defined in section 2246 of title 18).

(c) The jurisdiction conferred by this section includes jurisdiction of any set-off, counterclaim, or other claim or demand whatever on the part of the United States against any plaintiff commencing an action under this section.

(d) The district courts shall not have jurisdiction under this section of any civil action or claim for a pension.

(e) The district courts shall have original jurisdiction of any civil action against the United States provided in section 6226, 6228(a), 7426, or 7428 (in the case of the United States district court for the District of Columbia) or section 7429 of the Internal Revenue Code of 1986.

(f) The district courts shall have exclusive original jurisdiction of civil actions under section 2409a to quiet title to an estate or interest in real property in which an interest is claimed by the United States.

(g) Subject to the provisions of chapter 179, the district courts of the United States shall have exclusive jurisdiction over any civil action commenced under section 453(2) of title 3, by a covered employee under chapter 5 of such title.

(Added June 25, 1948, ch. 646, 62 Stat. 933; latest amendment Mar. 7, 2013, P.L. 113–4, Title XI, § 1101(b), 127 Stat. 134.)

§ 1350.   ALIEN'S ACTION FOR TORT.

The district court shall have original jurisdiction of any civil action by an alien for a tort only, committed in violation of the law of nations or a treaty of the United States.

(Added June 25, 1948, ch. 646, § 1, 62 Stat. 935.)

STATUTORY NOTE

TORTURE VICTIM PROTECTION ACT OF 1991.

Act March 12, 1992, P.L. 102-256, 106 Stat. 73, provides:

"Section 1. Short title.

"This Act may be cited as the 'Torture Victim Protection Act of 1991'. "**Sec. 2. Establishment of civil action.**

"(a) **Liability.** —

An individual who, under actual or apparent authority, or color of law, of any foreign nation—

"(1) subjects an individual to torture shall, in a civil action, be liable for damages to that individual; or

"(2) subjects an individual to extrajudicial killing shall, in a civil action, be liable for damages to the individual's legal representative, or to any person who may be a claimant in an action for wrongful death.

"(b) **Exhaustion of remedies.** —

A court shall decline to hear a claim under this section if the claimant has not exhausted adequate and available remedies in the place in which the conduct giving rise to the claim occurred.

"(c) Statute of limitations. —

No action shall be maintained under this section unless it is commenced within 10 years after the cause of action arose.

"Sec. 3. Definitions.

"(a) Extrajudicial killing. —

For the purposes of this Act, the term 'extrajudicial killing' means a deliberated killing not authorized by a previous judgment pronounced by a regularly constituted court affording all the judicial guarantees which are recognized as indispensable by civilized peoples. Such term, however, does not include any such killing that, under international law, is lawfully carried out under the authority of a foreign nation.

"(b) Torture. —

For the purposes of this Act —

"(1) the term 'torture' means any act, directed against an individual in the offender's custody or physical control, by which severe pain or suffering (other than pain or suffering arising only from or inherent in, or incidental to, lawful sanctions), whether physical or mental, is intentionally inflicted on that individual for such purposes as obtaining from that individual or a third person information or a confession, punishing that individual for an act that individual or a third person has committed or is suspected of having committed, intimidating or coercing that individual or a third person, or for any reason based on discrimination of any kind; and

"(2) mental pain or suffering refers to prolonged mental harm caused by or resulting from —

"(A) the intentional infliction or threatened infliction of severe physical pain or suffering;

"(B) the administration or application, or threatened administration or application, of mind altering substances or other procedures calculated to disrupt profoundly the senses or the personality;

"(C) the threat of imminent death; or

"(D) the threat that another individual will imminently be subjected to death, severe physical pain or suffering, or the administration or application of mind altering substances or other procedures calculated to disrupt profoundly the senses or personality."

§ 1359.   Parties Collusively Joined or Made.

A district court shall not have jurisdiction of a civil action in which any party, by assignment or otherwise, has been improperly or collusively made or joined to invoke the jurisdiction of such court.

(Added June 25, 1948, ch. 646, § 1, 62 Stat. 935.)

§ 1361.   Action to Compel an Officer of the United States to Perform His Duty.

The district courts shall have original jurisdiction of any action in the nature of mandamus to compel an officer or employee of the United States or any agency thereof to perform a duty owed to the plaintiff.

(Added Oct. 5, 1962, Pub. L. 87-748, § 1(a), 76 Stat. 744.)

§ 1367.   Supplemental Jurisdiction.

(a) Except as provided in subsections (b) and (c) or as expressly provided otherwise by Federal statute, in any civil action of which the district courts have original jurisdiction, the district courts shall have supplemental jurisdiction over all other claims that are so related to claims in the action within such original jurisdiction that they form part of the same case or controversy under Article III of the United States Constitution. Such supplemental jurisdiction shall include claims that involve the joinder or intervention of additional parties.

(b) In any civil action of which the district courts have original jurisdiction founded solely on section 1332 of this title, the district courts shall not have supplemental jurisdiction under subsection (a) over claims by plaintiffs against persons made parties under Rule 14, 19, 20, or 24 of the Federal Rules of Civil Procedure, or over claims by persons proposed to be joined as plaintiffs under Rule 19 of such rules, or seeking to intervene as plaintiffs under Rule 24 of such rules, when exercising supplemental jurisdiction over such claims would be inconsistent with the jurisdictional requirements of section 1332.

(c) The district courts may decline to exercise supplemental jurisdiction over a claim under subsection (a) if —

(1) the claim raises a novel or complex issue of State law,

(2) the claim substantially predominates over the claim or claims over which the district court has original jurisdiction,

(3) the district court has dismissed all claims over which it has original jurisdiction, or

(4) in exceptional circumstances, there are other compelling reasons for declining jurisdiction.

(d) The period of limitations for any claim asserted under subsection (a), and for any other claim in the same action that is voluntarily dismissed at the same time as or after the dismissal of the claim under subsection (a), shall be tolled while the claim is pending and for a period of 30 days after it is dismissed unless State law provides for a longer tolling period.

(e) As used in this section, the term "State" includes the District of Columbia, the Commonwealth of Puerto Rico, and any territory or possession of the United States.

(Added Dec. 1, 1990, Pub. L. 101-650, § 310(a), 104 Stat. 5113.)

§ 1369.   Multiparty, Multiforum Jurisdiction.

(a) In general. The district courts shall have original jurisdiction of any civil action involving minimal diversity between adverse parties that arises from a single accident, where at least 75 natural persons have died in the accident at a discrete location, if—

> (1) a defendant resides in a State and a substantial part of the accident took place in another State or other location, regardless of whether that defendant is also a resident of the State where a substantial part of the accident took place;

> (2) any two defendants reside in different States, regardless of whether such defendants are also residents of the same State or States; or

> (3) substantial parts of the accident took place in different States.

(b) Limitation of jurisdiction of district courts. The district court shall abstain from hearing any civil action described in subsection (a) in which—

> (1) the substantial majority of all plaintiffs are citizens of a single State of which the primary defendants are also citizens; and

> (2) the claims asserted will be governed primarily by the laws of that State.

(c) Special rules and definitions. For purposes of this section—

> (1) minimal diversity exists between adverse parties if any party is a citizen of a State and any adverse party is a citizen of another State, a citizen or subject of a foreign state, or a foreign state as defined in section 1603(a) of this title;

> (2) a corporation is deemed to be a citizen of any State, and a citizen or subject of any foreign state, in which it is incorporated or has its principal place of business, and is deemed to be a resident of any State in which it is incorporated or licensed to do business or is doing business;

> (3) the term "injury" means—

>> (A) physical harm to a natural person; and

>> (B) physical damage to or destruction of tangible property, but only if physical harm described in subparagraph (A) exists;

> (4) the term "accident" means a sudden accident, or a natural event culminating in an accident, that results in death incurred at a discrete location by at least 75 natural persons; and

(5) the term "State" includes the District of Columbia, the Commonwealth of Puerto Rico, and any territory or possession of the United States.

(d) Intervening parties. In any action in a district court which is or could have been brought, in whole or in part, under this section, any person with a claim arising from the accident described in subsection (a) shall be permitted to intervene as a party plaintiff in the action, even if that person could not have brought an action in a district court as an original matter.

(e) Notification of judicial panel on multidistrict litigation. A district court in which an action under this section is pending shall promptly notify the judicial panel on multidistrict litigation of the pendency of the action.

(Added Nov. 2, 2002, Pub. L. 107-273, § 11020(b)(1)(A), 116 Stat. 1826.)

CHAPTER 87.   DISTRICT COURTS; VENUE

§ 1390.   SCOPE.

(a) *Venue defined.* As used in this chapter, the term "venue" refers to the geographic specification of the proper court or courts for the litigation of a civil action that is within the subject-matter jurisdiction of the district courts in general, and does not refer to any grant or restriction of subject-matter jurisdiction providing for a civil action to be adjudicated only by the district court for a particular district or districts.

(b) *Exclusion of certain cases.* Except as otherwise provided by law, this chapter shall not govern the venue of a civil action in which the district court exercises the jurisdiction conferred by section 1333, except that such civil actions may be transferred between district courts as provided in this chapter.

(c) *Clarification regarding cases removed from State courts.* This chapter shall not determine the district court to which a civil action pending in a State court may be removed, but shall govern the transfer of an action so removed as between districts and divisions of the United States district courts.

(Added Dec. 7, 2011, P.L. 112–63, Title II, § 201(a), 125 Stat. 762.)

§ 1391.   VENUE GENERALLY.

(a) *Applicability of section.* Except as otherwise provided by law—

(1) this section shall govern the venue of all civil actions brought in district courts of the United States; and

(2) the proper venue for a civil action shall be determined without regard to whether the action is local or transitory in nature.

(b) *Venue in general.* A civil action may be brought in—

(1) a judicial district in which any defendant resides, if all defendants are residents of the State in which the district is located;

(2) a judicial district in which a substantial part of the events or omissions giving rise to the claim occurred, or a substantial part of property that is the subject of the action is situated; or

(3) if there is no district in which an action may otherwise be brought as provided in this section, any judicial district in which any defendant is subject to the court's personal jurisdiction with respect to such action.

(c) *Residency.* For all venue purposes—

(1) a natural person, including an alien lawfully admitted for permanent residence in the United States, shall be deemed to reside in the judicial district in which that person is domiciled;

(2) an entity with the capacity to sue and be sued in its common name under applicable law, whether or not incorporated, shall be deemed to reside, if a defendant, in any judicial district in which such defendant is subject to the court's personal jurisdiction with respect to the civil action in question and, if a plaintiff, only in the judicial district in which it maintains its principal place of business; and

(3) a defendant not resident in the United States may be sued in any judicial district, and the joinder of such a defendant shall be disregarded in determining where the action may be brought with respect to other defendants.

(d) *Residency of corporations in States with multiple districts.* For purposes of venue under this chapter, in a State which has more than one judicial district and in which a defendant that is a corporation is subject to personal jurisdiction at the time an action is commenced, such corporation shall be deemed to reside in any district in that State within which its contacts would be sufficient to subject it to personal jurisdiction if that district were a separate State, and, if there is no such district, the corporation shall be deemed to reside in the district within which it has the most significant contacts.

(e) *Actions where defendant is officer or employee of the United States.*

(1) *In general.* A civil action in which a defendant is an officer or employee of the United States or any agency thereof acting in his official capacity or under color of legal authority, or an agency of the United States, or the United States, may, except as otherwise provided by law, be brought in any judicial district in which (A) a defendant in the action resides, (B) a substantial part of the events or omissions giving rise to the claim occurred, or a substantial part of property that is the subject of the action is situated, or (C) the plaintiff resides if no real property is involved in the action. Additional persons may be joined as parties to any such action in accordance with the Federal Rules of Civil Procedure and with such other venue requirements as would be applicable if the United States or one of its officers, employees, or agencies were not a party.

(2) *Service.* The summons and complaint in such an action shall be served as provided by the Federal Rules of Civil Procedure except that the delivery of the summons and complaint to the officer or agency as required by the rules may be made by certified mail beyond the territorial limits of the district in which the action is brought.

(f) *Civil actions against a foreign state.* A civil action against a foreign state as defined in section 1603(a) of this title may be brought—

(1) in any judicial district in which a substantial part of the events or omissions giving rise to the claim occurred, or a substantial part of property that is the subject of the action is situated;

(2) in any judicial district in which the vessel or cargo of a foreign state is situated, if the claim is asserted under section 1605(b) of this title;

(3) in any judicial district in which the agency or instrumentality is licensed to do business or is doing business, if the action is brought against an agency or instrumentality of a foreign state as defined in section 1603(b) of this title; or

(4) in the United States District Court for the District of Columbia if the action is brought against a foreign state or political subdivision thereof.

(g) *Multiparty, multiforum litigation.* A civil action in which jurisdiction of the district court is based upon section 1369 of this title may be brought in any district in which any defendant resides or in which a substantial part of the accident giving rise to the action took place.

(Added June 25, 1948, ch. 646, 62 Stat. 935; latest amendment Dec. 7, 2011, P.L. 112–63, Title II, § 202, 125 Stat. 763.)

§ 1397. INTERPLEADER.

Any civil action of interpleader or in the nature of interpleader under section 1335 of this title may be brought in the judicial district in which one or more of the claimants reside.

(Added June 25, 1948, ch. 646, 62 Stat. 936.)

§ 1400. PATENTS AND COPYRIGHTS, MASK WORKS, AND DESIGNS.

(a) Civil actions, suits, proceedings arising under any Act of Congress relating to copyrights or exclusive rights in mask works or designs may be instituted in the district in which the defendant or his agent resides or may be found.

(b) Any civil action for patent infringement may be brought in the judicial district where the defendant resides, or where the defendant has committed acts of infringement and has a regular and established place of business.

(Added June 25, 1948, ch. 646, 62 Stat. 936; amended Nov. 19, 1988, Pub. L. 100-702, § 1020(a)(5), 102 Stat. 4671; Oct. 28, 1998, Pub. L. 105-304, § 503(c), 112 Stat. 2917; Aug. 5, 1999, Pub. L. 106-44, § 2(a), 113 Stat. 223.)

§ 1401.   Stockholder's Derivative Action.

Any civil action by a stockholder on behalf of his corporation may be prosecuted in any judicial district where the corporation might have sued the same defendants.

(Added June 25, 1948, ch. 646, 62 Stat. 936.)

§ 1402.   United States as Defendant.

(a) Any civil action in a district court against the United States under subsection (a) of section 1346 of this title may be prosecuted only:

(1) Except as provided in paragraph (2), in the judicial district where the plaintiff resides;

(2) In the case of a civil action by a corporation under paragraph (1) of subsection (a) of section 1346, in the judicial district in which is located the principal place of business or principal office or agency of the corporation; or if it has no principal place of business or principal office or agency in any judicial district (A) in the judicial district in which is located the office to which was made the return of the tax in respect of which the claim is made, or (B) if no return was made, in the judicial district in which lies the District of Columbia. Notwithstanding the foregoing provisions of this paragraph a district court, for the convenience of the parties and witnesses, in the interest of justice, may transfer any such action to any other district or division.

(b) Any civil action on a tort claim against the United States under subsection (b) of section 1346 of this title may be prosecuted only in the judicial district where the plaintiff resides or wherein the act or omission complained of occurred.

(c) Any civil action against the United States under subsection (e) of section 1346 of this title may be prosecuted only in the judicial district where the property is situated at the time of levy, or if no levy is made, in the judicial district in which the event occurred which gave rise to the cause of action.

(d) Any civil action under section 2409a to quiet title to an estate or interest in real property in which an interest is claimed by the United States shall be brought in the district court of the district where the property is located or, if located in different districts, in any of such districts.

(Added June 25, 1948, ch. 646, 62 Stat. 937; amended Sept. 2, 1958, Pub. L. 85-920, 72 Stat. 1770; Nov. 2, 1966, Pub. L. 89-719, § 202(b), 80 Stat. 1149; Oct. 25, 1972, Pub. L. 92-562, 86 Stat. 1176; April 2, 1982, Pub. L. 97-164, § 131, 96 Stat. 39.)

§ 1404. CHANGE OF VENUE.

(a) For the convenience of parties and witnesses, in the interest of justice, a district court may transfer any civil action to any other district or division where it might have been brought or to any district or division to which all parties have consented.

(b) Upon motion, consent or stipulation of all parties, any action, suit or proceeding of a civil nature or any motion or hearing thereof, may be transferred, in the discretion of the court, from the division in which pending to any other division in the same district. Transfer of proceedings in rem brought by or on behalf of the United States may be transferred under this section without the consent of the United States where all other parties request transfer.

(c) A district court may order any civil action to be tried at any place within the division in which it is pending.

(d) Transfers from a district court of the United States to the District Court of Guam, the District Court for the Northern Mariana Islands, or the District Court of the Virgin Islands shall not be permitted under this section. As otherwise used in this section, the term "district court" includes the District Court of Guam, the District Court for the Northern Mariana Islands, and the District Court of the Virgin Islands, and the term "district" includes the territorial jurisdiction of each such court.

(Added June 25, 1948, ch. 646, 62 Stat. 937; amended October 18, 1962, Pub. L. 87-845, § 9, 76A Stat. 699; Oct. 19, 1996, Pub. L. 104-317, § 610, 110 Stat. 3860; Dec. 7, 2011, P.L. 112–63, Title I, § 103(a), 125 Stat. 759.)

§ 1406. CURE OR WAIVER OF DEFECTS.

(a) The district court of a district in which is filed a case laying venue in the wrong division or district shall dismiss, or if it be in the interest of justice, transfer such case to any district or division in which it could have been brought.

(b) Nothing in this chapter shall impair the jurisdiction of a district court of any matter involving a party who does not interpose timely and sufficient objection to the venue.

(c) As used in this section, the term "district court" includes the District Court of Guam, the District Court for the Northern Mariana Islands, and the District Court of the Virgin Islands, and the term "district" includes the territorial jurisdiction of each such court.

(Added June 25, 1948, ch. 646, 62 Stat. 937; amended May 24, 1949, ch. 139, § 81, 63 Stat. 101; Sept. 13, 1960, Pub. L. 86-770, § 1, 74 Stat. 912; Oct. 18, 1962, Pub. L. 87-845, § 10, 76A Stat. 699; April 2, 1982, Pub. L. 97-164, § 132, 96 Stat. 39; Oct. 19, 1996, Pub. L. 104-317, § 610, 110 Stat. 3860.)

§ 1407. Multidistrict Litigation.

(a) When civil actions involving one or more common questions of fact are pending in different districts, such actions may be transferred to any district for coordinated or consolidated pretrial proceedings. Such transfers shall be made by the judicial panel on multidistrict litigation authorized by this section upon its determination that transfers for such proceedings will be for the convenience of parties and witnesses and will promote the just and efficient conduct of such actions. Each action so transferred shall be remanded by the panel at or before the conclusion of such pretrial proceedings to the district from which it was transferred unless it shall have been previously terminated: *Provided, however,* That the panel may separate any claim, cross-claim, counter-claim, or third-party claim and remand any of such claims before the remainder of the action is remanded.

(b) Such coordinated or consolidated pretrial proceedings shall be conducted by a judge or judges to whom such actions are assigned by the judicial panel on multidistrict litigation. For this purpose, upon request of the panel, a circuit judge or a district judge may be designated and assigned temporarily for service in the transferee district by the Chief Justice of the United States or the chief judge of the circuit, as may be required, in accordance with the provisions of chapter 13 of this title. With the consent of the transferee district court, such actions may be assigned by the panel to a judge or judges of such district. The judge or judges to whom such actions are assigned, the members of the judicial panel on multidistrict litigation, and other circuit and district judges designated when needed by the panel may exercise the powers of a district judge in any district for the purpose of conducting pretrial depositions in such coordinated or consolidated pretrial proceedings.

(c) Proceedings for the transfer of an action under this section may be initiated by—

> (i) the judicial panel on multidistrict litigation upon its own initiative, or

> (ii) motion filed with the panel by a party in any action in which transfer for coordinated or consolidated pretrial proceedings under this section may be appropriate. A copy of such motion shall be filed in the district court in which the moving party's action is pending.

The panel shall give notice to the parties in all actions in which transfers for coordinated or consolidated pretrial proceedings are contemplated, and such notice shall specify the time and place of any hearing to determine whether such transfer shall be made. Orders of the panel to set a hearing and other orders of the panel issued prior to the order either directing or denying transfer shall be filed in the office of the clerk of the district court in which a transfer hearing is to be or has been held. The panel's order of transfer shall be based upon a record of such hearing at which material evidence may be offered by any party to an action pending in any district that would be affected by the proceedings under this section, and shall be supported by findings of fact and conclusions of law based upon such record. Orders of transfer and such other orders as the panel may make thereafter shall be filed in the office of the clerk of the district court of the transferee district and shall be effective when thus filed. The clerk of the transferee district court shall forthwith transmit a certified copy of the panel's order to transfer to the clerk of the district court from which the action is being transferred. An order denying transfer shall be filed in each district wherein there is a case pending in which the motion for transfer has been made.

(d) The judicial panel on multidistrict litigation shall consist of seven circuit and district judges designated from time to time by the Chief Justice of the United States, no two of whom shall be from the same circuit. The concurrence of four members shall be necessary to any action by the panel.

(e) No proceedings for review of any order of the panel may be permitted except by extraordinary writ pursuant to the provisions of title 28, section 1651, United States Code. Petitions for an extraordinary writ to review an order of the panel to set a transfer hearing and other orders of the panel issued prior to the order either directing or denying transfer shall be filed only in the court of appeals having jurisdiction over the district in which a hearing is to be or has been held. Petitions for an extraordinary writ to review an order to transfer or orders subsequent to transfer shall be filed only in the court of appeals having jurisdiction over the transferee district. There shall be no appeal or review of an order of the panel denying a motion to transfer for consolidated or coordinated proceedings.

(f) The panel may prescribe rules for the conduct of its business not inconsistent with Acts of Congress and the Federal Rules of Civil Procedure.

(g) Nothing in this section shall apply to any action in which the United States is a complainant arising under the antitrust laws. "Antitrust laws" as used herein include those acts referred to in the Act of October 15, 1914, as amended (38 Stat. 730; 15 U.S.C. 12), and also include the Act of June 19, 1936 (49 Stat. 1526; 15 U.S.C. 13, 13a, and 13b) and the Act of September 26, 1914, as added March 21, 1938 (52 Stat. 116, 117; 15 U.S.C. 56); but shall not include section 4A of the Act of October 15, 1914, as added July 7, 1955 (69 Stat. 282; 15 U.S.C. 15a).

(h) Notwithstanding the provisions of section 1404 or subsection (f) of this section, the judicial panel on multidistrict litigation may consolidate and transfer with or without the consent of the parties, for both pretrial purposes and for trial, any action brought under section 4C of the Clayton Act.

(Added April 29, 1968, Pub. L. 90-296, § 1, 82 Stat. 109; amended September 30, 1976, Pub. L. 94-435, § 303, 90 Stat. 1396.)

CHAPTER 89.   DISTRICT COURTS; REMOVAL OF CASES FROM STATE COURTS

§ 1441.   REMOVAL OF CIVIL ACTIONS.

(a) *Generally.* Except as otherwise expressly provided by Act of Congress, any civil action brought in a State court of which the district courts of the United States have original jurisdiction, may be removed by the defendant or the defendants, to the district court of the United States for the district and division embracing the place where such action is pending.

(b) *Removal based on diversity of citizenship.*

(1) In determining whether a civil action is removable on the basis of the jurisdiction under section 1332(a) of this title, the citizenship of defendants sued under fictitious names shall be disregarded.

(2) A civil action otherwise removable solely on the basis of the jurisdiction under section 1332(a) of this title may not be removed if any of the parties in interest properly joined and served as defendants is a citizen of the State in which such action is brought.

(c) *Joinder of Federal law claims and State law claims.*

(1) If a civil action includes —

(A) a claim arising under the Constitution, laws, or treaties of the United States (within the meaning of section 1331 of this title), and

(B) a claim not within the original or supplemental jurisdiction of the district court or a claim that has been made nonremovable by statute, the entire action may be removed if the action would be removable without the inclusion of the claim described in subparagraph (B).

(2) Upon removal of an action described in paragraph (1), the district court shall sever from the action all claims described in paragraph (1)(B) and shall remand the severed claims to the State court from which the action was removed. Only defendants against whom a claim described in paragraph (1)(A) has been asserted are required to join in or consent to the removal under paragraph (1).

(d) *Actions against foreign states.* Any civil action brought in a State court against a foreign state as defined in section 1603(a) of this title may be removed by the foreign state to the district court of the United States for the district and division embracing the place where such action is pending. Upon removal the action shall be tried by the court without jury. Where removal is based upon this subsection, the time limitations of section 1446(b) of this chapter may be enlarged at any time for cause shown.

(e) *Multiparty, multiforum jurisdiction.*

(1) Notwithstanding the provisions of subsection (b) of this section, a defendant in a civil action in a State court may remove the action to the district court of the United States for the district and division embracing the place where the action is pending if—

(A) the action could have been brought in a United States district court under section 1369 of this title; or

(B) the defendant is a party to an action which is or could have been brought, in whole or in part, under section 1369 in a United States district court and arises from the same accident as the action in State court, even if the action to be removed could not have been brought in a district court as an original matter.

The removal of an action under this subsection shall be made in accordance with section 1446 of this title, except that a notice of removal may also be filed before trial of the action in State court within 30 days after the date on which the defendant first becomes a party to an action under section 1369 in a United States district court that arises from the same accident as the action in State court, or at a later time with leave of the district court.

(2) Whenever an action is removed under this subsection and the district court to which it is removed or transferred under section 1407(j) has made a liability determination requiring further proceedings as to damages, the district court shall remand the action to the State court from which it had been removed for the determination of damages, unless the court finds that, for the convenience of parties and witnesses and in the interest of justice, the action should be retained for the determination of damages.

(3) Any remand under paragraph (2) shall not be effective until 60 days after the district court has issued an order determining liability and has certified its intention to remand the removed action for the determination of damages. An appeal with respect to the liability determination of the district court may be taken during that 60-day period to the court of appeals with appellate jurisdiction over the district court. In the event a party files such an appeal, the remand shall not be effective until the appeal has been finally disposed of. Once the remand has become effective, the liability determination shall not be subject to further review by appeal or otherwise.

(4) Any decision under this subsection concerning remand for the determination of damages shall not be reviewable by appeal or otherwise.

(5) An action removed under this subsection shall be deemed to be an action under section 1369 and an action in which jurisdiction is based on section 1369 of this title for purposes of this section and sections 1407, 1697, and 1785 of this title.

(6) Nothing in this subsection shall restrict the authority of the district court to transfer or dismiss an action on the ground of inconvenient forum.

(f) *Derivative removal jurisdiction.* The court to which a civil action is removed under this section is not precluded from hearing and determining any claim in such civil action because the State court from which such civil action is removed did not have jurisdiction over that claim.

(Added June 25, 1948, ch. 646, 62 Stat. 937; amended Oct. 21, 1976, Pub. L. 94-583, § 6, 90 Stat. 2898; June 19, 1986, Pub. L. 99-336, § 3(a), 100 Stat. 637; Nov. 19, 1988, Pub. L. 100-702, § 1016(a), 102 Stat. 4669; Dec. 1, 1990, Pub. L. 101-650, § 312, 104 Stat. 5114; Dec. 9, 1991, Pub. L. 102-198, § 4, 105 Stat. 1623; Nov. 2, 2002, Pub. L. 107-273, § 11020(b)(3), 116 Stat. 1827; Dec. 7, 2011, P.L. 112–63, Title I, § 103(a), 125 Stat. 759.)

§ 1442.   FEDERAL OFFICERS OR AGENCIES SUED OR PROSECUTED.

(a) A civil action or criminal prosecution that is commenced in a State court and that is against or directed to any of the following may be removed by them to the district court of the United States for the district and division embracing the place wherein it is pending:

(1) The United States or any agency thereof or any officer (or any person acting under that officer) of the United States or of any agency thereof, in an official or individual capacity, for or relating to any act under color of such office or on account of any right, title or authority claimed under any Act of Congress for the apprehension or punishment of criminals or the collection of the revenue.

(2) A property holder whose title is derived from any such officer, where such action or prosecution affects the validity of any law of the United States.

(3) Any officer of the courts of the United States, for or relating to any Act under color of office or in the performance of his duties;

(4) Any officer of either House of Congress, for or relating to any act in the discharge of his official duty under an order of such House.

(b) A personal action commenced in any State court by an alien against any citizen of a State who is, or at the time the alleged action accrued was, a civil officer of the United States and is a nonresident of such State, wherein jurisdiction is obtained by the State court by personal service of process, may be removed by the defendant to the district court of the United States for the district and division in which the defendant was served with process.

(c) Solely for purposes of determining the propriety of removal under subsection (a), a law enforcement officer, who is the defendant in a criminal prosecution, shall be deemed to have been acting under the color of his office if the officer —

(1) protected an individual in the presence of the officer from a crime of violence;

(2) provided immediate assistance to an individual who suffered, or who was threatened with, bodily harm; or

(3) prevented the escape of any individual who the officer reasonably believed to have committed, or was about to commit, in the presence of the officer, a crime of violence that resulted in, or was likely to result in, death or serious bodily injury.

(d) In this section, the following definitions apply:

(1) The terms "civil action" and "criminal prosecution" include any proceeding (whether or not ancilary to another proceeding) to the extent that in such proceeding a judicial order, including a subpoena for testimony or documents, is sought or issued. If removal is sought for a proceeding described in the previous sentence, and there is no other basis for removal, only that proceeding may be removed to the district court.

(2) The term "crime of violence" has the meaning given that term in section 16 of title 18.

(3) The term "law enforcement officer" means any employee described in subparagraph (A), (B), or (C) of section 8401(17) of title 5 and any special agent in the Diplomatic Security Service of the Department of State.

(4) The term "serious bodily injury" has the meaning given that term in section 1365 of title 18.

(5) The term "State" includes the District of Columbia, United States territories and insular possessions, and Indian country (as defined in section 1151 of title 18).

(6) The term "State court" includes the Superior Court of the District of Columbia, a court of a United States territory or insular possession, and a tribal court.

(Added June 25, 1948, ch. 646, 62 Stat. 938; amended Oct. 19, 1996, Pub. L. 104-317, § 206(a), 110 Stat. 3850; Nov. 9, 2011, P.L. 112–51, § 2(a), (b), 125 Stat. 545; Jan. 2, 2013, Pub. L. 112-239, Title X, § 1087, 126 Stat. 1969.)

§ 1443.   Civil Rights Cases.

Any of the following civil actions or criminal prosecutions, commenced in a State court may be removed by the defendant to the district court of the United States for the district and division embracing the place wherein it is pending:

(1) Against any person who is denied or cannot enforce in the courts of such State a right under any law providing for the equal civil rights of citizens of the United States, or of all persons within the jurisdiction thereof;

(2) For any act under color of authority derived from any law providing for equal rights, or for refusing to do any act on the ground that it would be inconsistent with such law.

(Added June 25, 1948, ch. 646, 62 Stat. 938.)

§ 1445. Nonremovable Actions.

(a) A civil action in any State court against a railroad or its receivers or trustees, arising under sections 1–4 and 5–10 of the Act of April 22, 1908 (45 U.S.C. 51–54, 55–60), may not be removed to any district court of the United States.

(b) A civil action in any State court against a carrier or its receivers or trustees to recover damages for delay, loss, or injury of shipments, arising under section 11706 or 14706 of title 49, may not be removed to any district court of the United States unless the matter in controversy exceeds $10,000, exclusive of interest and costs.

(c) A civil action in any State court arising under the workmen's compensation laws of such State may not be removed to any district court of the United States.

(d) A civil action in any State court arising under section 40302 of the Violence Against Women Act of 1994 may not be removed to any district court of the United States.

(Added June 25, 1948, ch. 646, 62 Stat. 939; amended July 25, 1958, Pub. L. 85-554, § 5, 72 Stat. 415; Oct. 17, 1978, Pub. L. 95-473, § 2(a)(3)(A), 92 Stat. 1465; Oct. 20, 1978, Pub. L. 95-486, § 9(b), 92 Stat. 1634; subsection (d) added Sept. 13, 1994, Pub. L. 103-322, § 40302(e)(5), 108 Stat. 1942; Dec. 29, 1995, Pub. L. 104-88, § 305(b), 109 Stat. 944; Oct. 11, 1996, Pub. L. 104-287, § 3, 110 Stat. 3388.)

§ 1446. Procedure for Removal of Civil Actions.

(a) *Generally.* A defendant or defendants desiring to remove any civil action from a State court shall file in the district court of the United States for the district and division within which such action is pending a notice of removal signed pursuant to Rule 11 of the Federal Rules of Civil Procedure and containing a short and plain statement of the grounds for removal, together with a copy of all process, pleadings, and orders served upon such defendant or defendants in such action.

(b) *Requirements; generally.*

(1) The notice of removal of a civil action or proceeding shall be filed within 30 days after the receipt by the defendant, through service or otherwise, of a copy of the initial pleading setting forth the claim for relief upon which such action or proceeding is based, or within 30 days after the service of summons upon the defendant if such initial pleading has then been filed in court and is not required to be served on the defendant, whichever period is shorter.

(2) (A) When a civil action is removed solely under section 1441(a), all defendants who have been properly joined and served must join in or consent to the removal of the action.

(B) Each defendant shall have 30 days after receipt by or service on that defendant of the initial pleading or summons described in paragraph (1) to file the notice of removal.

(C) If defendants are served at different times, and a later-served defendant files a notice of removal, any earlier-served defendant may consent to the removal even though that earlier-served defendant did not previously initiate or consent to removal.

(3) Except as provided in subsection (c), if the case stated by the initial pleading is not removable, a notice of removal may be filed within 30 days after receipt by the defendant, through service or otherwise, of a copy of an amended pleading, motion, order or other paper from which it may first be ascertained that the case is one which is or has become removable.

(c) *Requirements; removal based on diversity of citizenship.*

(1) A case may not be removed under subsection (b)(3) on the basis of jurisdiction conferred by section 1332 more than 1 year after commencement of the action, unless the district court finds that the plaintiff has acted in bad faith in order to prevent a defendant from removing the action.

(2) If removal of a civil action is sought on the basis of the jurisdiction conferred by section 1332(a), the sum demanded in good faith in the initial pleading shall be deemed to be the amount in controversy, except that—

(A) the notice of removal may assert the amount in controversy if the initial pleading seeks—(i) nonmonetary relief; or (ii) a money judgment, but the State practice either does not permit demand for a specific sum or permits recovery of damages in excess of the amount demanded; and

(B) removal of the action is proper on the basis of an amount in controversy asserted under subparagraph (A) if the district court finds, by the preponderance of the evidence, that the amount in controversy exceeds the amount specified in section 1332(a).

(3) (A)If the case stated by the initial pleading is not removable solely because the amount in controversy does not exceed the amount specified in section 1332(a), information relating to the amount in controversy in the record of the State proceeding, or in responses to discovery, shall be treated as an "other paper" under subsection (b)(3).

(B) If the notice of removal is filed more than 1 year after commencement of the action and the district court finds that the plaintiff deliberately failed to disclose the actual amount in controversy to prevent removal, that finding shall be deemed bad faith under paragraph (1).

(d) *Notice to adverse parties and State court.* Promptly after the filing of such notice of removal of a civil action the defendant or defendants shall give written notice thereof to all adverse parties and shall file a copy of the notice with the clerk of such State court, which shall effect removal and the State court shall proceed no further unless and until the case is remanded.

(e) *Counterclaim in 337 proceeding.* With respect to any counterclaim removed to a district court pursuant to section 337(c) of the Tariff Act of 1930, the district court shall resolve such counterclaim in the same manner as an original complaint under the Federal Rules of Civil Procedure, except that the payment of a filing fee shall not be required in such cases and the counterclaim shall relate back to the date of the original complaint in the proceeding before the International Trade Commission under section 337 of that Act.

(f) [Redesignated.]

(g) Where the civil action or criminal prosecution that is removable under section 1442(a) is a proceeding in which a judicial order for testimony or documents is sought or issued or sought to be enforced, the 30-day requirement of subsection (b) of this section and paragraph (1) of section 1455(b) is satisfied if the person or entity desiring to remove the proceeding files the notice of removal not later than 30 days after receiving, through service, notice of any such proceeding.

(Added June 25, 1948, ch. 646, 62 Stat. 939; amended May 24, 1949, ch. 139, § 83, 63 Stat. 101; Sept. 29, 1965, Pub. L. 89-215, 79 Stat. 887; July 30, 1977, Pub. L. 95-78, § 3, 91 Stat. 321; Nov. 19, 1988, Pub. L. 100-702, § 1016; Dec. 9, 1991, Pub. L. 102-198, § 10(a), 105 Stat. 1626; Dec. 8, 1994, Pub. L. 103-465, § 321(b)(2), 108 Stat. 4946; Oct. 19, 1996, Pub. L. 104-317, § 603, 110 Stat. 3857; Dec. 7, 2011, P.L. 112–63, Title I, §§ 103(b), 104, 125 Stat. 760, 762.)

§ 1447. PROCEDURE AFTER REMOVAL GENERALLY.

(a) In any case removed from a State court, the district court may issue all necessary orders and process to bring before it all proper parties whether served by process issued by the State court or otherwise.

(b) It may require the removing party to file with its clerk copies of all records and proceedings in such State court or may cause the same to be brought before it by writ of certiorari issued to such State court.

(c) A motion to remand the case on the basis of any defect other than lack of subject matter jurisdiction must be made within 30 days after the filing of the notice of removal under section 1446(a). If at any time before final judgment it appears that the district court lacks subject matter jurisdiction, the case shall be remanded. An order remanding the case may require payment of just costs and any actual expenses, including attorney fees, incurred as a result of the removal. A certified copy of the order of remand shall be mailed by the clerk to the clerk of the State court. The State court may thereupon proceed with such case.

(d) An order remanding a case to the State court from which it was removed is not reviewable on appeal or otherwise, except that an order remanding a case to the State court from which it was removed pursuant to section 1442 or 1443 of this title shall be reviewable by appeal or otherwise.

(e) If after removal the plaintiff seeks to join additional defendants whose joinder would destroy subject matter jurisdiction, the court may deny joinder, or permit joinder and remand the action to the State court.

(Added June 25, 1948, ch. 646, 62 Stat. 939; amended May 24, 1949, ch. 139, § 84, 63 Stat. 102; July 2, 1964, Pub. L. 88-352, Title IX, § 901, 78 Stat. 266; Nov. 19, 1988, Pub. L. 100-702, § 1016(c), 102 Stat. 4670; Dec. 9, 1991, Pub. L. 102-198, § 10(b), 105 Stat. 1626; Oct. 1, 1996, Pub. L. 104-219, § 1, 110 Stat. 3022.)

§ 1448.   PROCESS AFTER REMOVAL.

In all cases removed from any State court to any district court of the United States in which any one or more of the defendants has not been served with process or in which the service has not been perfected prior to removal, or in which process served proves to be defective, such process or service may be completed or new process issued in the same manner as in cases originally filed in such district court.

This section shall not deprive any defendant upon whom process is served after removal of his right to move to remand the case.

§ 1450.   ATTACHMENT OR SEQUESTRATION; SECURITIES.

Whenever any action is removed from a State court to a district court of the United States, any attachment or sequestration of the goods or estate of the defendant in such action in the State court shall hold the goods or estate to answer the final judgment or decree in the same manner as they would have been held to answer final judgment or decree had it been rendered by the State court.

All bonds, undertakings, or security given by either party in such action prior to its removal shall remain valid and effectual notwithstanding such removal.

All injunctions, orders, and other proceedings had in such action prior to its removal shall remain in full force and effect until dissolved or modified by the district court.

(Added June 25, 1948, ch. 646, 62 Stat. 940)

§ 1451.   DEFINITIONS.

For purposes of this chapter —

    (1) The term "State court" includes the Superior Court of the District of Columbia.

    (2) The term "State" includes the District of Columbia. (Added July 29, 1970, Pub. L. 91-358, § 172, 84 Stat. 591.)

§ 1453.   REMOVAL OF CLASS ACTIONS.

(a) *Definitions.* In this section, the terms "class," "class action," "class certification order," and "class member" shall have the meanings given such terms under section 1332(d)(1).

(b) *In general.* A class action may be removed to a district court of the United States in accordance with section 1446 (except that the 1-year limitation under section 1446(c)(1) shall not apply), without regard to whether any defendant is a citizen of the State in which the action is brought, except that such action may be removed by any defendant without the consent of all defendants.

(c) *Review of remand orders.*

(1) *In general.* Section 1447 shall apply to any removal of a case under this section, except that notwithstanding section 1447(d), a court of appeals may accept an appeal from an order of a district court granting or denying a motion to remand a class action to the State court from which it was removed if application is made to the court of appeals not more than 10 days after entry of the order.

(2) *Time period for judgment.* If the court of appeals accepts an appeal under paragraph (1), the court shall complete all action on such appeal, including rendering judgment, not later than 60 days after the date on which such appeal was filed, unless an extension is granted under paragraph (3).

(3) *Extension of time period.* The court of appeals may grant an extension of the 60-day period described in paragraph (2) if—

(A) all parties to the proceeding agree to such extension, for any period of time; or

(B) such extension is for good cause shown and in the interests of justice, for a period not to exceed 10 days.

(4) *Denial of appeal.* If a final judgment on the appeal under paragraph (1) is not issued before the end of the period described in paragraph (2), including any extension under paragraph (3), the appeal shall be denied.

(d) *Exception.* This section shall not apply to any class action that solely involves—

(1) a claim concerning a covered security as defined under section 16(f)(3) of the Securities Act of 1933 (15 U.S.C. 78p(f)(3)) and section 28(f)(5)(E) of the Securities Exchange Act of 1934 (15 U.S.C. 78bb(f)(5)(E));

(2) a claim that relates to the internal affairs or governance of a corporation or other form of business enterprise and arises under or by virtue of the laws of the State in which such corporation or business enterprise is incorporated or organized; or

(3) a claim that relates to the rights, duties (including fiduciary duties), and obligations relating to or created by or pursuant to any security (as defined under section 2(a)(1) of the Securities Act of 1933 (15 U.S.C. 77b(a)(1)) and the regulations issued thereunder).

(Added Feb. 18, 2005, Pub. L. 109-2, § 5(a), 119 Stat. 12; amended Dec. 7, 2011, P.L. 112–63, Title I, § 103(d)(2), 125 Stat. 762.)

§ 1454.   Patent, Plant Variety Protection, and Copyright Cases

(a) *In general.* A civil action in which any party asserts a claim for relief arising under any Act of Congress relating to patents, plant variety protection, or copyrights may be removed to the district court of the United States for the district and division embracing the place where the action is pending.

(b) *Special rules.* The removal of an action under this section shall be made in accordance with section 1446, except that if the removal is based solely on this section—

(1) the action may be removed by any party; and

(2) the time limitations contained in section 1446(b) may be extended at any time for cause shown.

(c) *Clarification of jurisdiction in certain cases.* The court to which a civil action is removed under this section is not precluded from hearing and determining any claim in the civil action because the State court from which the civil action is removed did not have jurisdiction over that claim.

(d) *Remand.* If a civil action is removed solely under this section, the district court

(1) shall remand all claims that are neither a basis for removal under subsection (a) nor within the original or supplemental jurisdiction of the district court under any Act of Congress; and

(2) may, under the circumstances specified in section 1367(c), remand any claims within the supplemental jurisdiction of the district court under section 1367.

(Added Sept. 16, 2011, P.L. 112-29, § 19(c)(1), 125 Stat. 332)

CHAPTER 97.   JURISDICTIONAL IMMUNITIES OF FOREIGN STATES

§ 1602.   Findings and Declaration of Purpose.

The Congress finds that the determination by United States courts of the claims of foreign states to immunity from the jurisdiction of such courts would serve the interests of justice and would protect the rights of both foreign states and litigants in United States courts. Under international law, states are not immune from the jurisdiction of foreign courts insofar as their commercial activities are concerned, and their commercial property may be levied upon for the satisfaction of judgments rendered against them in connection with their commercial activities. Claims of foreign states to immunity should henceforth be decided by courts of the United States and of the States in conformity with the principles set forth in this chapter.

(Added Oct. 21, 1976, P.L. 94-583, § 4(a), 90 Stat. 2892.)

§ 1603.   Definitions.

For purposes of this chapter—

(a) A "foreign state," except as used in section 1608 of this title, includes a political subdivision of a foreign state or an agency or instrumentality of a foreign state as defined in subsection (b).

(b) An "agency or instrumentality of a foreign state" means any entity—

(1) which is a separate legal person, corporate or otherwise, and

(2) which is an organ of a foreign state or political subdivision thereof, or a majority of whose shares or other ownership interest is owned by a foreign state or political subdivision thereof, and

(3) which is neither a citizen of a State of the United States as defined in section 1332(c) and (e) of this title, nor created under the laws of any third country.

(c) The "United States" includes all territory and waters, continental or insular, subject to the jurisdiction of the United States.

(d) A "commercial activity" means either a regular course of commercial conduct or a particular commercial transaction or act. The commercial character of an activity shall be determined by reference to the nature of the course of conduct or particular transaction or act, rather than by reference to its purpose.

(e) A "commercial activity carried on in the United States by a foreign state" means commercial activity carried on by such state and having substantial contact with the United States.

(Added Oct. 21, 1976, Pub. L. 94-583, § 4(a), 90 Stat. 2892; amended Feb. 18, 2005, Pub. L. 109-2, § 4(b)(2), 119 Stat. 12.)

§ 1604.   Immunity of a Foreign State From Jurisdiction.

Subject to existing international agreements to which the United States is a party at the time of enactment of this Act a foreign state shall be immune from the jurisdiction of the courts of the United States and of the States except as provided in sections 1605 to 1607 of this chapter.

(Added Oct. 21, 1976, Pub. L. 94-583, § 4(a), 90 Stat. 2892.)

§ 1605.   General Exceptions to the Jurisdictional Immunity of a Foreign State.

(a) A foreign state shall not be immune from the jurisdiction of courts of the United States or of the States in any case—

(1) in which the foreign state has waived its immunity either explicitly or by implication, notwithstanding any withdrawal of the waiver which the foreign state may purport to effect except in accordance with the terms of the waiver;

(2) in which the action is based upon a commercial activity carried on in the United States by the foreign state; or upon an act performed in the United States in connection with a commercial activity of the foreign state elsewhere; or upon an act outside the territory of the United States in connection with a commercial activity of the foreign state elsewhere and that act causes a direct effect in the United States;

(3) in which rights in property taken in violation of international law are in issue and that property or any property exchanged for such property is present in the United States in connection with a commercial activity carried on in the United States by the foreign state; or that property or any property exchanged for such property is owned or operated by an agency or instrumentality of the foreign state and that agency or instrumentality is engaged in a commercial activity in the United States;

(4) in which rights in property in the United States acquired by succession or gift or rights in immovable property situated in the United States are in issue;

(5) not otherwise encompassed in paragraph (2) above, in which money damages are sought against a foreign state for personal injury or death, or damage to or loss of property, occurring in the United States and caused by the tortious act or omission of that foreign state or of any official or employee of that foreign state while acting within the scope of his office or employment; except this paragraph shall not apply to—

(A) any claim based upon the exercise or performance or the failure to exercise or perform a discretionary function regardless of whether the discretion be abused, or

(B) any claim arising out of malicious prosecution, abuse of process, libel, slander, misrepresentation, deceit, or interference with contract rights;

(6) in which the action is brought, either to enforce an agreement made by the foreign state with or for the benefit of a private party to submit to arbitration all or any differences which have arisen or which may arise between the parties with respect to a defined legal relationship, whether contractual or not, concerning a subject matter capable of settlement by arbitration under the laws of the United States, or to confirm an award made pursuant to such an agreement to arbitrate, if (A) the arbitration takes place or is intended to take place in the United States, (B) the agreement or award is or may be governed by a treaty or other international agreement in force for the United States calling for the recognition and enforce- ment of arbitral awards, (C) the underlying claim, save for the agreement to arbitrate, could have been brought in a United States court under this section or section 1607, or (D) paragraph (1) of this subsection is otherwise applicable[.]

(7) [deleted.]

(b) A foreign state shall not be immune from the jurisdiction of the courts of the United States in any case in which a suit in admiralty is brought to enforce a maritime lien against a vessel or cargo of the foreign state, which maritime lien is based upon a commercial activity of the foreign state: *Provided*, That—

(1) notice of the suit is given by delivery of a copy of the summons and of the complaint to the person, or his agent, having possession of the vessel or cargo against which the maritime lien is asserted; and if the vessel or cargo is arrested pursuant to process obtained on behalf of the party bringing the suit, the service of process of arrest shall be deemed to constitute valid delivery of such notice, but the party bringing the suit shall be liable for any damages sustained by the foreign state as a result of the arrest if the party bringing the suit had actual or constructive knowledge that the vessel or cargo of a foreign state was involved; and

(2) notice to the foreign state of the commencement of suit as provided in section 1608 of this title is initiated within ten days either of the delivery of notice as provided in paragraph (1) of this subsection or, in the case of a party who was unaware that the vessel or cargo of a foreign state was involved, of the date such party determined the existence of the foreign state's interest.

(c) Whenever notice is delivered under subsection (b)(1), the suit to enforce a maritime lien shall thereafter proceed and shall be heard and determined according to the principles of law and rules of practice of suits in rem whenever it appears that, had the vessel been privately owned and possessed, a suit in rem might have been maintained. A decree against the foreign state may include costs of the suit and, if the decree is for a money judgment, interest as ordered by the court, except that the court may not award judgment against the foreign state in an amount greater than the value of the vessel or cargo upon which the maritime lien arose. Such value shall be determined as of the time notice is served under subsection (b)(1). Decrees shall be subject to appeal and revision as provided in other cases of admiralty and maritime jurisdiction. Nothing shall preclude the plaintiff in any proper case from seeking relief in personam in the same action brought to enforce a maritime lien as provided in this section.

(d) A foreign state shall not be immune from the jurisdiction of the courts of the United States in any action brought to foreclose a preferred mortgage, as defined in the Ship Mortgage Act, 1920 (46 U.S.C. 911 and following [46 USCS Appx. §§ 911 et seq.]). Such action shall be brought, heard, and determined in accordance with the provisions of that Act and in accordance with the principles of law and rules of practice of suits in rem, whenever it appears that had the vessel been privately owned and possessed a suit in rem might have been maintained.

(e) [Repealed.]

(f) [Repealed.]

(g) Limitation on discovery.

    (1) In general.

        (A) Subject to paragraph (2), if an action is filed that would otherwise be barred by section 1604, but for Section 1605A or Section 1605B, the court, upon request of the Attorney General, shall stay any request, demand, or order for discovery on the United States that the Attorney General certifies would significantly interfere with a criminal investigation or prosecution, or a national security operation, related to the incident that gave rise to the cause of action, until such time as the Attorney General advises the court that such request, demand, or order will no longer so interfere.

        (B) A stay under this paragraph shall be in effect during the 12-month period beginning on the date on which the court issues the order to stay discovery. The court shall renew the order to stay discovery for additional 12-month periods upon motion by the United States if the Attorney General certifies that discovery would significantly interfere with a criminal investigation or prosecution, or a national security operation, related to the incident that gave rise to the cause of action.

    (2) Sunset.

        (A) Subject to subparagraph (B), no stay shall be granted or continued in effect under paragraph (1) after the date that is 10 years after the date on which the incident that gave rise to the cause of action occurred.

        (B) After the period referred to in subparagraph (A), the court, upon request of the Attorney General, may stay any request, demand, or order for discovery on the United States that the court finds a substantial likelihood would—

            (i) create a serious threat of death or serious bodily injury to any person;

            (ii) adversely affect the ability of the United States to work in cooperation with foreign and international law enforcement agencies in investigating violations of United States law; or

            (iii) obstruct the criminal case related to the incident that gave rise to the cause of action or undermine the potential for a conviction in such case.

    (3) Evaluation of evidence. The court's evaluation of any request for a stay under this subsection filed by the Attorney General shall be conducted ex parte and in camera.

    (4) Bar on motions to dismiss. A stay of discovery under this subsection shall constitute a bar to the granting of a motion to dismiss under rules 12(b)(6) and 56 of the Federal Rules of Civil Procedure.

(5) Construction. Nothing in this subsection shall prevent the United States from seeking protective orders or asserting privileges ordinarily available to the United States.

(h) Jurisdiction immunity for certain art exhibition activities. [omitted]

(Added Oct. 21, 1976, P.L. 94-583, § 4(a), 90 Stat. 2892; latest amendments Sept. 28, 2016, P.L. 114-222, § 3(b)(2), 130 Stat. 853; Dec. 16, 2016, P.L. 114-319, § 2(a), 130 Stat. 1618.)

STATUTORY NOTE

Liability of agents of state sponsors of terrorism to U.S. nationals.

Act Sept. 30, 1996, P.L. 104-208, Div A, Title I, § 101(c) [Title V, § 589], 110 Stat. 3009-172, provides:

"(a) An official, employee, or agent of a foreign state designated as a state sponsor of terrorism designated under section 6(j) of the Export Administration Act of 1979 [50 USCS Appx § 2405(j)] while acting within the scope of his or her office, employment, or agency shall be liable to a United States national or the national's legal representative for personal injury or death caused by acts of that official, employee, or agent for which the courts of the United States may maintain jurisdiction under section 1605(a)(7) of title 28, United States Code, for money damages which may include economic damages, solatium, pain, and suffering, and punitive damages if the acts were among those described in section 1605(a)(7)."

"(b) Provisions related to statute of limitations and limitations on discovery that would apply to an action brought under 28 U.S.C. 1605(f) and (g) shall also apply to actions brought under this section. No action shall be maintained under this action if an official, employee, or agent of the United States, while acting within the scope of his or her office, employment, or agency would not be liable for such acts if carried out within the United States."

§ 1605A. Terrorism Exception to the Jurisdictional Immunity of a Foreign State.

(a) In general.

(1) No immunity. A foreign state shall not be immune from the jurisdiction of courts of the United States or of the States in any case not otherwise covered by this chapter in which money damages are sought against a foreign state for personal injury or death that was caused by an act of torture, extrajudicial killing, aircraft sabotage, hostage taking, or the provision of material support or resources for such an act if such act or provision of material support or resources is engaged in by an official, employee, or agent of such foreign state while acting within the scope of his or her office, employment, or agency.

(2) Claim heard. The court shall hear a claim under this section if—

(A) (i) (I)the foreign state was designated as a state sponsor of terrorism at the time the act described in paragraph (1) occurred, or was so designated as a result of such act, and, subject to subclause (II), either remains so designated when the claim is filed under this section or was so designated within the 6-month period before the claim is filed under this section; or

(II)in the case of an action that is refiled under this section by reason of section 1083(c)(2)(A) of the National Defense Authorization Act for Fiscal Year 2008 or is filed under this section by reason of section 1083(c)(3) of that Act, the foreign state was designated as a state sponsor of terrorism when the original action or the related action under section 1605(a)(7) (as in effect before the enactment of this section [enacted Jan. 28, 2008]) or section 589 of the Foreign Operations, Export Financing, and Related Programs Appropriations Act, 1997 (as contained in section 101(c) of division A of Public Law 104-208) was filed;

(ii) the claimant or the victim was, at the time the act described in paragraph (1) occurred—

(I) a national of the United States;

(II) a member of the armed forces; or

(III) otherwise an employee of the Government of the United States, or of an individual performing a contract awarded by the United States Government, acting within the scope of the employee's employment; and

(iii) in a case in which the act occurred in the foreign state against which the claim has been brought, the claimant has afforded the foreign state a reasonable opportunity to arbitrate the claim in accordance with the accepted international rules of arbitration; or

(B) the act described in paragraph (1) is related to Case Number 1:00CV03110 (EGS) in the United States District Court for the District of Columbia.

(b) Limitations. An action may be brought or maintained under this section if the action is commenced, or a related action was commenced under section 1605(a)(7) (before the date of the enactment of this section) or section 589 of the Foreign Operations, Export Financing, and Related Programs Appropriations Act, 1997 (as contained in section 101(c) of division A of Public Law 104-208) not later than the latter of—

(1) 10 years after April 24, 1996; or

(2) 10 years after the date on which the cause of action arose.

(c) Private right of action. A foreign state that is or was a state sponsor of terrorism as described in subsection (a)(2)(A)(i), and any official, employee, or agent of that foreign state while acting within the scope of his or her office, employment, or agency, shall be liable to—

(1) a national of the United States,

(2) a member of the armed forces,

(3) an employee of the Government of the United States, or of an individual performing a contract awarded by the United States Government, acting within the scope of the employee's employment, or

(4) the legal representative of a person described in paragraph (1), (2), or (3), for personal injury or death caused by acts described in subsection (a)(1) of that foreign state, or of an official, employee, or agent of that foreign state, for which the courts of the United States may maintain jurisdiction under this section for money damages. In any such action, damages may include economic damages, solatium, pain and suffering, and punitive damages. In any such action, a foreign state shall be vicariously liable for the acts of its officials, employees, or agents.

(d) Additional damages. After an action has been brought under subsection (c), actions may also be brought for reasonably foreseeable property loss, whether insured or uninsured, third party liability, and loss claims under life and property insurance policies, by reason of the same acts on which the action under subsection (c) is based.

(e) Special masters.

(1) In general. The courts of the United States may appoint special masters to hear damage claims brought under this section.

(2) Transfer of funds. The Attorney General shall transfer, from funds available for the program under section 1404C of the Victims of Crime Act of 1984 (42 U.S.C. 10603c), to the Administrator of the United States district court in which any case is pending which has been brought or maintained under this section such funds as may be required to cover the costs of special masters appointed under paragraph (1). Any amount paid in compensation to any such special master shall constitute an item of court costs.

(f) Appeal. In an action brought under this section, appeals from orders not conclusively ending the litigation may only be taken pursuant to section 1292(b) of this title.

(g) Property disposition.

(1) In general. In every action filed in a United States district court in which jurisdiction is alleged under this section, the filing of a notice of pending action pursuant to this section, to which is attached a copy of the complaint filed in the action, shall have the effect of establishing a lien of lis pendens upon any real property or tangible personal property that is—

(A) subject to attachment in aid of execution, or execution, under section 1610;

(B) located within that judicial district; and

(C) titled in the name of any defendant, or titled in the name of any entity controlled by any defendant if such notice contains a statement listing such controlled entity.

(2) Notice. A notice of pending action pursuant to this section shall be filed by the clerk of the district court in the same manner as any pending action and shall be indexed by listing as defendants all named defendants and all entities listed as controlled by any defendant.

(3) Enforceability. Liens established by reason of this subsection shall be enforceable as provided in chapter 111 of this title.

(h) Definitions. For purposes of this section—

(1) the term "aircraft sabotage" has the meaning given that term in Article 1 of the Convention for the Suppression of Unlawful Acts Against the Safety of Civil Aviation;

(2) the term "hostage taking" has the meaning given that term in Article 1 of the International Convention Against the Taking of Hostages;

(3) the term "material support or resources" has the meaning given that term in section 2339A of title 18;

(4) the term "armed forces" has the meaning given that term in section 101 of title 10;

(5) the term "national of the United States" has the meaning given that term in section 101(a)(22) of the Immigration and Nationality Act (8 U.S.C. 1101(a)(22));

(6) the term "state sponsor of terrorism" means a country the government of which the Secretary of State has determined, for purposes of section 6(j) of the Export Administration Act of 1979 (50 U.S.C. App. 2405(j)), section 620A of the Foreign Assistance Act of 1961 (22 U.S.C. 2371), section 40 of the Arms Export Control Act (22 U.S.C. 2780), or any other provision of law, is a government that has repeatedly provided support for acts of international terrorism; and

(7) the terms "torture" and "extrajudicial killing" have the meaning given those terms in section 3 of the Torture Victim Protection Act of 1991 (28 U.S.C. 1350 note).

(Added Jan. 28, 2008, P.L. 110-181, Div A, Title X, Subtitle F, § 1083(a)(1), 122 Stat. 338.)

§ 1605B. RESPONSIBILITY OF FOREIGN STATES FOR INTERNATIONAL TERRORISM AGAINST THE UNITED STATES.

(a) Definition. In this section, the term "international terrorism"—

(1) has the meaning given the term in section 2331 of title 18, United States Code; and

(2) does not include any act of war (as defined in that section).

(b) Responsibility of foreign states. A foreign state shall not be immune from the jurisdiction of the courts of the United States in any case in which money damages are sought against a foreign state for physical injury to person or property or death occurring in the United States and caused by—

(1) an act of international terrorism in the United States; and

(2) a tortious act or acts of the foreign state, or of any official, employee, or agent of that foreign state while acting within the scope of his or her office, employment, or agency, regardless where the tortious act or acts of the foreign state occurred.

(c) Claims by nationals of the United States. Notwithstanding section 2337(2) of title 18, a national of the United States may bring a claim against a foreign state in accordance with section 2333 of that title if the foreign state would not be immune under subsection (b).

(d) Rule of construction. A foreign state shall not be subject to the jurisdiction of the courts of the United States under subsection (b) on the basis of an omission or a tortious act or acts that constitute mere negligence.

(Added Sept. 28, 2016, P.L. 114-222, § 3(a), 130 Stat. 853.)

§ 1606.   EXTENT OF LIABILITY.

As to any claim for relief with respect to which a foreign state is not entitled to immunity under section 1605 or 1607 of this chapter [28 USCS § 1605 or 1607], the foreign state shall be liable in the same manner and to the same extent as a private individual under like circumstances; but a foreign state except for an agency or instrumentality thereof shall not be liable for punitive damages; if, however, in any case wherein death was caused, the law of the place where the action or omission occurred provides, or has been construed to provide, for damages only punitive in nature, the foreign state shall be liable for actual or compensatory damages measured by the pecuniary injuries resulting from such death which were incurred by the persons for whose benefit the action was brought.

(Added Oct. 21, 1976, P.L. 94-583, § 4(a), 90 Stat. 2894; as amended Oct. 21, 1998, Pub. L. 105-277, Div. A, § 101(h), 112 Stat. 2681-491; Oct. 28, 2000, Pub.L. 106-386, Div. C. § 2002(f)(2), 114 Stat. 1543.)

§ 1607.   COUNTERCLAIMS.

In any action brought by a foreign state, or in which a foreign state intervenes, in a court of the United States or of a State, the foreign state shall not be accorded immunity with respect to any counterclaim—

(a) for which a foreign state would not be entitled to immunity under section 1605 or 1605A of this chapter had such claim been brought in a separate action against the foreign state; or

(b) arising out of the transaction or occurrence that is the subject matter of the claim of the foreign state; or

(c) to the extent that the counterclaim does not seek relief exceeding in amount or differing in kind from that sought by the foreign state.

(Added Oct. 21, 1976, P.L. 94-583, § 4(a), 90 Stat. 2894; amended Jan. 28, 2008, P.L. 110-181, Div A, Title X, Subtitle F, § 1083(b)(2), 122 Stat. 341.)

§ 1610. EXCEPTIONS TO THE IMMUNITY FROM ATTACHMENT OR EXECUTION.

(a) The property in the United States of a foreign state, as defined in section 1603(a) of this chapter, used for a commercial activity in the United States, shall not be immune from attachment in aid of execution, or from execution, upon a judgment entered by a court of the United States or of a State after the effective date of this Act, if—

(1) the foreign state has waived its immunity from attachment in aid of execution or from execution either explicitly or by implication, notwithstanding any withdrawal of the waiver the foreign state may purport to effect except in accordance with the terms of the waiver, or

(2) the property is or was used for the commercial activity upon which the claim is based, or

(3) the execution relates to a judgment establishing rights in property which has been taken in violation of international law or which has been exchanged for property taken in violation of international law, or

(4) the execution relates to a judgment establishing rights in property—

(A) which is acquired by succession or gift, or

(B) which is immovable and situated in the United States: *Provided*, That such property is not used for purposes of maintaining a diplomatic or consular mission or the residence of the Chief of such mission, or

(5) the property consists of any contractual obligation or any proceeds from such a contractual obligation to indemnify or hold harmless the foreign state or its employees under a policy of automobile or other liability or casualty insurance covering the claim which merged into the judgment, or

(6) the judgment is based on an order confirming an arbitral award rendered against the foreign state, provided that attachment in aid of execution, or execution, would not be inconsistent with any provision in the arbitral agreement, or

(7) the judgment relates to a claim for which the foreign state is not immune under section 1605A, regardless of whether the property is or was involved with the act upon which the claim is based.

(b) In addition to subsection (a), any property in the United States of an agency or instrumentality of a foreign state engaged in commercial activity in the United States shall not be immune from attachment in aid of execution, or from execution, upon a judgment entered by a court of the United States or of a State after the effective date of this Act if—

(1) the agency or instrumentality has waived its immunity from attachment in aid of execution or from execution either explicitly or implicitly, notwithstanding any withdrawal of the waiver the agency or instrumentality may purport to effect except in accordance with the terms of the waiver, or

(2) the judgment relates to a claim for which the agency or instrumentality is not immune by virtue of section 1605(a)(2), (3), or (5) or 1605(b) of this chapter, regardless of whether the property is or was involved in the act upon which the claim is based.

(3) the judgment relates to a claim for which the agency or instrumentality is not immune by virtue of section 1605A of this chapter or section 1605(a)(7) of this chapter (as such section was in effect on January 27, 2008), regardless of whether the property is or was involved in the act upon which the claim is based.

(c) No attachment or execution referred to in subsections (a) and (b) of this section shall be permitted until the court has ordered such attachment and execution after having determined that a reasonable period of time has elapsed following the entry of judgment and the giving of any notice required under section 1608(e) of this chapter.

(d) The property of a foreign state, as defined in section 1603(a) of this chapter, used for a commercial activity in the United States, shall not be immune from attachment prior to the entry of judgment in any action brought in a court of the United States or of a State, or prior to the elapse of the period of time provided in subsection (c) of this section, if—

(1) the foreign state has explicitly waived its immunity from attachment prior to judgment, notwithstanding any withdrawal of the waiver the foreign state may purport to effect except in accordance with the terms of the waiver, and

(2) the purpose of the attachment is to secure satisfaction of a judgment that has been or may ultimately be entered against the foreign state, and not to obtain jurisdiction.

(e) The vessels of a foreign state shall not be immune from arrest in rem, interlocutory sale, and execution in actions brought to foreclose a preferred mortgage as provided in section 1605(d).

(f) (1) (A)Notwithstanding any other provision of law, including but not limited to section 208(f) of the Foreign Missions Act (22 U.S.C. 4308(f)), and except as provided in subparagraph (B), any property with respect to which financial transactions are prohibited or regulated pursuant to section 5(b) of the Trading with the Enemy Act (50 U.S.C. App. 5(b)), section 620(a) of the Foreign Assistance Act of 1961 (22 U.S.C. 2370(a)), sections 202 and 203 of the International Emergency Economic Powers Act (50 U.S.C. 1701-1702), or any other proclamation, order, regulation, or license issued pursuant thereto, shall be subject to execution or attachment in aid of execution of any judgment relating to a claim for which a foreign state (including any agency or instrumentality or such state) claiming such property is not immune under section 1605(a)(7) (as in effect before the enactment of section 1605A [enacted Jan. 28, 2008]) or section 1605A.

> (B)Subparagraph (A) shall not apply if, at the time the property is expropriated or seized by the foreign state, the property has been held in title by a natural person or, if held in trust, has been held for the benefit of a natural person or persons.

(2) (A)At the request of any party in whose favor a judgment has been issued with respect to a claim for which the foreign state is not immune under section 1605(a)(7) (as in effect before the enactment of section 1605A [enacted Jan. 28, 2008]) or section 1605A, the Secretary of the Treasury and the Secretary of State should make every effort to fully, promptly, and effectively assist any judgment creditor or any court that has issued any such judgment in identifying, locating, and executing against the property of that foreign state or any agency or instrumentality of such state.

> (B) In providing such assistance, the Secretaries—

>> (i) may provide such information to the court under seal; and

>> (ii) should make every effort to provide the information in a manner sufficient to allow the court to direct the United States Marshall's office to promptly and effectively execute against that property.

(3) Waiver. The President may waive any provision of paragraph (1) in the interest of national security.

(g) Property in certain actions.

(1) In general. Subject to paragraph (3), the property of a foreign state against which a judgment is entered under section 1605A, and the property of an agency or instrumentality of such a state, including property that is a separate juridical entity or is an interest held directly or indirectly in a separate juridical entity, is subject to attachment in aid of execution, and execution, upon that judgment as provided in this section, regardless of—

> (A) the level of economic control over the property by the government of the foreign state;

> (B) whether the profits of the property go to that government;

(C) the degree to which officials of that government manage the property or otherwise control its daily affairs;

(D) whether that government is the sole beneficiary in interest of the property; or

(E) whether establishing the property as a separate entity would entitle the foreign state to benefits in United States courts while avoiding its obligations.

(2) United States sovereign immunity inapplicable. Any property of a foreign state, or agency or instrumentality of a foreign state, to which paragraph (1) applies shall not be immune from attachment in aid of execution, or execution, upon a judgment entered under section 1605A because the property is regulated by the United States Government by reason of action taken against that foreign state under the Trading With the Enemy Act or the International Emergency Economic Powers Act.

(3) Third-party joint property holders. Nothing in this subsection shall be construed to supersede the authority of a court to prevent appropriately the impairment of an interest held by a person who is not liable in the action giving rise to a judgment in property subject to attachment in aid of execution, or execution, upon such judgment.

(Added Oct. 21, 1976, P.L. 94-583, § 4(a), 90 Stat. 2896; latest amendment Aug. 10, 2012, Pub. L. 112-158, Title V, § 502(e)(1), 126 Stat. 1260.)

CHAPTER 99.   GENERAL PROVISIONS

§ 1631.   Transfer to Cure Want of Jurisdiction.

Whenever a civil action is filed in a court as defined in section 610 of this title or an appeal, including a petition for review of administrative action, is noticed for or filed with such a court and that court finds that there is a want of jurisdiction, the court shall, if it is in the interest of justice, transfer such action or appeal to any other such court (or, for cases within the jurisdiction of the United States Tax Court, to that court) in which the action or appeal could have been brought at the time it was filed or noticed, and the action or appeal shall proceed as if it had been filed in or noticed for the court to which it is transferred on the date upon which it was actually filed in or noticed for the court from which it is transferred.

(Added Apr. 2, 1982, Pub. L. 97-164, § 301(a), 96 Stat. 55, amended Dec. 19, 2018, Pub. l. 155-332, § 2, 132 Stat. 4487.)

PART V   PROCEDURE

CHAPTER 111.   GENERAL PROVISIONS

§ 1651.   WRITS.

(a) The Supreme Court and all courts established by Act of Congress may issue all writs necessary or appropriate in aid of their respective jurisdictions and agreeable to the usages and principles of law.

(b) An alternative writ or rule nisi may be issued by a justice or judge of a court which has jurisdiction.

(Added June 25, 1948, ch. 646, 62 Stat. 944; amended May 24, 1949, ch. 139, § 90, 63 Stat. 102.)

§ 1652.   STATE LAWS AS RULES OF DECISION.

The laws of the several states, except where the Constitution or treaties of the United States or Acts of Congress otherwise require or provide, shall be regarded as rules of decision in civil actions in the courts of the United States, in cases where they apply.

(Added June 25, 1948, ch. 646, 62 Stat. 944.)

§ 1653.   AMENDMENT OF PLEADINGS TO SHOW JURISDICTION.

Defective allegations of jurisdiction may be amended, upon terms, in the trial or appellate courts.

(Added June 25, 1948, ch. 646, 62 Stat. 944.)

§ 1654.   APPEARANCE PERSONALLY OR BY COUNSEL.

In all courts of the United States the parties may plead and conduct their own cases personally or by counsel as, by the rules of such courts, respectively, are permitted to manage and conduct causes therein.

(As amended May 24, 1949, ch. 139, § 91, 63 Stat. 103.)

§ 1655.   LIEN ENFORCEMENT; ABSENT DEFENDANTS.

In an action in a district court to enforce any lien upon or claim to, or to remove any incumbrance or lien or cloud upon the title to, real or personal property within the district, where any defendant cannot be served within the State, or does not voluntarily appear, the court may order the absent defendant to appear or plead by a day certain.

Such order shall be served on the absent defendant personally if practicable, wherever found, and also upon the person or persons in possession or charge of such property, if any. Where personal service is not practicable, the order shall be published as the court may direct, not less than once a week for six consecutive weeks.

If an absent defendant does not appear or plead within the time allowed, the court may proceed as if the absent defendant had been served with process within the State, but any adjudication shall, as regards the absent defendant without appearance, affect only the property which is the subject of the action. When a part of the property is within another district, but within the same state, such action may be brought in either district.

Any defendant not so personally notified may, at any time within one year after final judgment, enter his appearance, and thereupon the court shall set aside the judgment and permit such defendant to plead on payment of such costs as the court deems just.

(Added June 25, 1948, ch. 646, 62 Stat. 944.)

§ 1657.　PRIORITY OF CIVIL ACTIONS.

(a) Notwithstanding any other provision of law, each court of the United States shall determine the order in which civil actions are heard and determined, except that the court shall expedite the consideration of any action brought under chapter 153 or section 1826 of this title, any action for temporary or preliminary injunctive relief, or any other action if good cause therefor is shown. For purposes of this subsection, "good cause" is shown if a right under the Constitution of the United States or a Federal Statute (including rights under section 552 of title 5) would be maintained in a factual context that indicates that a request for expedited consideration has merit.

(b) The Judicial Conference of the United States may modify the rules adopted by the courts to determine the order in which civil actions are heard and determined, in order to establish consistency among the judicial circuits.

(Added Nov. 8, 1984, P.L. 98-620, Title IV, Subtitle A, § 401(a), 98 Stat. 3356.)

§ 1658.　TIME LIMITATIONS ON THE COMMENCEMENT OF CIVIL ACTIONS ARISING UNDER ACTS OF CONGRESS.

(a) Except as otherwise provided by law, a civil action arising under an Act of Congress enacted after the date of the enactment of this section may not be commenced later than 4 years after the cause of action accrues.

(b) Notwithstanding subsection (a), a private right of action that involves a claim of fraud, deceit, manipulation, or contrivance in contravention of a regulatory requirement concerning the securities laws, as defined in section 3(a)(47) of the Securities Exchange Act of 1934 (15 U.S.C. 78c(a)(47)), may be brought not later than the earlier of—

(1) 2 years after the discovery of the facts constituting the violation; or

(2) 5 years after such violation.

(Added Dec. 1, 1990, Pub. L. 101-650, § 313, 104 Stat. 5089; July 30, 2002, Pub. L. 107-204, § 804(a), 116 Stat. 801.)

CHAPTER 113. PROCESS

§ 1691. Seal and Teste of Process.

All writs and process issuing from a court of the United States shall be under the seal of the court and signed by the clerk thereof.

(Added June 25, 1948, ch. 646, 62 Stat. 944.)

§ 1693. Place of Arrest in Civil Action.

Except as otherwise provided by Act of Congress, no person shall be arrested in one district for trial in another in any civil action in a district court.

(Added June 25, 1948, ch. 646, 62 Stat. 944.)

§ 1694. Patent infringement action.

In a patent infringement action commenced in a district where the defendant is not a resident but has a regular and established place of business, service of process, summons or subpoena upon such defendant may be made upon his agent or agents conducting such business.

(June 25, 1948, ch 646, 62 Stat. 945.)

§ 1695. Stockholder's Derivative Action.

Process in a stockholder's action in behalf of his corporation may be served upon such corporation in any district where it is organized or licensed to do business or is doing business.

(Added June 25, 1948, ch. 646, 62 Stat. 944.)

§ 1696. Service in Foreign and International Litigation.

(a) The district court of the district in which a person resides or is found may order service upon him of any document issued in connection with a proceeding in a foreign or international tribunal. The order may be made pursuant to a letter rogatory issued, or request made, by a foreign or international tribunal or upon application of any interested person and shall direct the manner of service. Service pursuant to this subsection does not, of itself, require the recognition or enforcement in the United States of a judgment, decree, or order rendered by a foreign or international tribunal.

(b) This section does not preclude service of such a document without an order of court.

(Added Oct. 3, 1964, Pub. L. 88-619, § 4(a), 78 Stat. 995.)

§ 1697.   Service in Multiparty, Multiforum Actions.

When the jurisdiction of the district court is based in whole or in part upon section 1369 of this title, process, other than subpoenas, may be served at any place within the United States, or anywhere outside the United States if otherwise permitted by law.

(Added Nov. 2, 2002, Pub. L. 107-273, § 11020(b)(4)(A)(i), 116 Stat. 1828.)

CHAPTER 114.   CLASS ACTIONS

§ 1711.   Definitions.

In this chapter:

(1) Class. The term "class" means all of the class members in a class action.

(2) Class action. The term "class action" means any civil action filed in a district court of the United States under rule 23 of the Federal Rules of Civil Procedure or any civil action that is removed to a district court of the United States that was originally filed under a State statute or rule of judicial procedure authorizing an action to be brought by 1 or more representatives as a class action.

(3) Class counsel. The term "class counsel" means the persons who serve as the attorneys for the class members in a proposed or certified class action.

(4) Class members. The term "class members" means the persons (named or unnamed) who fall within the definition of the proposed or certified class in a class action.

(5) Plaintiff class action. The term "plaintiff class action" means a class action in which class members are plaintiffs.

(6) Proposed settlement. The term "proposed settlement" means an agreement regarding a class action that is subject to court approval and that, if approved, would be binding on some or all class members.

(Added Feb. 18, 2005, Pub. L. 109-2, § 3(a), 119 Stat. 5.)

§ 1712.   Coupon Settlements.

(a) Contingent fees in coupon settlements.

If a proposed settlement in a class action provides for a recovery of coupons to a class member, the portion of any attorney's fee award to class counsel that is attributable to the award of the coupons shall be based on the value to class members of the coupons that are redeemed.

(b) Other attorney's fee awards in coupon settlements.

(1) In general. If a proposed settlement in a class action provides for a recovery of coupons to class members, and a portion of the recovery of the coupons is

not used to determine the attorney's fee to be paid to class counsel, any attorney's fee award shall be based upon the amount of time class counsel reasonably expended working on the action.

(2) Court approval. Any attorney's fee under this subsection shall be subject to approval by the court and shall include an appropriate attorney's fee, if any, for obtaining equitable relief, including an injunction, if applicable. Nothing in this subsection shall be construed to prohibit application of a lodestar with a multiplier method of determining attorney's fees.

(c) Attorney's fee awards calculated on a mixed basis in coupon settlements. If a proposed settlement in a class action provides for an award of coupons to class members and also provides for equitable relief, including injunctive relief—

(1) that portion of the attorney's fee to be paid to class counsel that is based upon a portion of the recovery of the coupons shall be calculated in accordance with subsection (a); and

(2) that portion of the attorney's fee to be paid to class counsel that is not based upon a portion of the recovery of the coupons shall be calculated in accordance with subsection (b).

(d) Settlement valuation expertise. In a class action involving the awarding of coupons, the court may, in its discretion upon the motion of a party, receive expert testimony from a witness qualified to provide information on the actual value to the class members of the coupons that are redeemed.

(e) Judicial scrutiny of coupon settlements. In a proposed settlement under which class members would be awarded coupons, the court may approve the proposed settlement only after a hearing to determine whether, and making a written finding that, the settlement is fair, reasonable, and adequate for class members. The court, in its discretion, may also require that a proposed settlement agreement provide for the distribution of a portion of the value of unclaimed coupons to 1 or more charitable or governmental organizations, as agreed to by the parties. The distribution and redemption of any proceeds under this subsection shall not be used to calculate attorneys' fees under this section.

(Added Feb. 18, 2005, Pub. L. 109-2, § 3(a), 119 Stat. 6.)

§ 1713. PROTECTION AGAINST LOSS BY CLASS MEMBERS.

The court may approve a proposed settlement under which any class member is obligated to pay sums to class counsel that would result in a net loss to the class member only if the court makes a written finding that nonmonetary benefits to the class member substantially outweigh the monetary loss.

(Added Feb. 18, 2005, Pub. L. 109-2, § 3(a), 119 Stat. 7.)

§ 1714. Protection Against Discrimination Based on Geographic Location.

The court may not approve a proposed settlement that provides for the payment of greater sums to some class members than to others solely on the basis that the class members to whom the greater sums are to be paid are located in closer geographic proximity to the court.

(Added Feb. 18, 2005, Pub. L. 109-2, § 3(a), 119 Stat. 7.)

§ 1715. Notifications to Appropriate Federal and State Officials.

(a) Definitions.

(1) Appropriate Federal official. In this section, the term "appropriate Federal official" means —

(A) the Attorney General of the United States; or

(B) in any case in which the defendant is a Federal depository institution, a State depository institution, a depository institution holding company, a foreign bank, or a nondepository institution subsidiary of the foregoing (as such terms are defined in section 3 of the Federal Deposit Insurance Act (12 U.S.C. 1813)), the person who has the primary Federal regulatory or supervisory responsibility with respect to the defendant, if some or all of the matters alleged in the class action are subject to regulation or supervision by that person.

(2) Appropriate State official. In this section, the term "appropriate State official" means the person in the State who has the primary regulatory or supervisory responsibility with respect to the defendant, or who licenses or otherwise authorizes the defendant to conduct business in the State, if some or all of the matters alleged in the class action are subject to regulation by that person. If there is no primary regulator, supervisor, or licensing authority, or the matters alleged in the class action are not subject to regulation or supervision by that person, then the appropriate State official shall be the State attorney general.

(b) In general. Not later than 10 days after a proposed settlement of a class action is filed in court, each defendant that is participating in the proposed settlement shall serve upon the appropriate State official of each State in which a class member resides and the appropriate Federal official, a notice of the proposed settlement consisting of—

(1) a copy of the complaint and any materials filed with the complaint and any amended complaints (except such materials shall not be required to be served if such materials are made electronically available through the Internet and such service includes notice of how to electronically access such material);

(2) notice of any scheduled judicial hearing in the class action;

(3) any proposed or final notification to class members of —

    (A) (i)the members' rights to request exclusion from the class action; or

        (ii) if no right to request exclusion exists, a statement that no such right exists; and

    (B) a proposed settlement of a class action;

(4) any proposed or final class action settlement;

(5) any settlement or other agreement contemporaneously made between class counsel and counsel for the defendants;

(6) any final judgment or notice of dismissal;

(7) (A)if feasible, the names of class members who reside in each State and the estimated proportionate share of the claims of such members to the entire settlement to that State's appropriate State official; or

    (B) if the provision of information under subparagraph (A) is not feasible, a reasonable estimate of the number of class members residing in each State and the estimated proportionate share of the claims of such members to the entire settlement; and

(8) any written judicial opinion relating to the materials described under subparagraphs (3) through (6).

(c) Depository institutions notification.

(1) Federal and other depository institutions. In any case in which the defendant is a Federal depository institution, a depository institution holding company, a foreign bank, or a non-depository institution subsidiary of the foregoing, the notice requirements of this section are satisfied by serving the notice required under subsection (b) upon the person who has the primary Federal regulatory or supervisory responsibility with respect to the defendant, if some or all of the matters alleged in the class action are subject to regulation or supervision by that person.

(2) State depository institutions. In any case in which the defendant is a State depository institution (as that term is defined in section 3 of the Federal Deposit Insurance Act (12 U.S.C. 1813)), the notice requirements of this section are satisfied by serving the notice required under subsection (b) upon the State bank supervisor (as that term is defined in section 3 of the Federal Deposit Insurance Act (12 U.S.C. 1813)) of the State in which the defendant is incorporated or chartered, if some or all of the matters alleged in the class action are subject to regulation or supervision by that person, and upon the appropriate Federal official.

(d) Final approval. An order giving final approval of a proposed settlement may not be issued earlier than 90 days after the later of the dates on which the appropriate

Federal official and the appropriate State official are served with the notice required under subsection (b).

(e) Noncompliance if notice not provided.

(1) In general. A class member may refuse to comply with and may choose not to be bound by a settlement agreement or consent decree in a class action if the class member demonstrates that the notice required under subsection (b) has not been provided.

(2) Limitation. A class member may not refuse to comply with or to be bound by a settlement agreement or consent decree under paragraph (1) if the notice required under subsection (b) was directed to the appropriate Federal official and to either the State attorney general or the person that has primary regulatory, supervisory, or licensing authority over the defendant.

(3) Application of rights. The rights created by this subsection shall apply only to class members or any person acting on a class member's behalf, and shall not be construed to limit any other rights affecting a class member's participation in the settlement.

(f) Rule of construction. Nothing in this section shall be construed to expand the authority of, or impose any obligations, duties, or responsibilities upon, Federal or State officials.

(Added Feb. 18, 2005, Pub. L. 109-2, § 3(a), 119 Stat. 7.)

CHAPTER 115.   EVIDENCE; DOCUMENTARY

§ 1738.   STATE AND TERRITORIAL STATUTES AND JUDICIAL PROCEEDINGS; FULL FAITH AND CREDIT.

The Acts of the legislature of any State, Territory, or Possession of the United States, or copies thereof, shall be authenticated by affixing the seal of such State, Territory or Possession thereto.

The records and judicial proceedings of any court of any such State, Territory or Possession, or copies thereof, shall be proved or admitted in other courts within the United States and its Territories and Possessions by the attestation of the clerk and seal of the court annexed, if a seal exists, together with a certificate of a judge of the court that the said attestation is in proper form.

Such Acts, records and judicial proceedings or copies thereof, so authenticated, shall have the same full faith and credit in every court within the United States and its Territories and Possessions as they have by law or usage in the courts of such State, Territory or Possession from which they are taken.

(Added June 25, 1948, ch. 646, 62 Stat. 947.)

§ 1738A. Full Faith and Credit Given to Child Custody Determinations.

(a) The appropriate authorities of every State shall enforce according to its terms, and shall not modify except as provided in subsections (f), (g), and (h) of this section, any custody determination or visitation determination made consistently with the provisions of this section by a court of another State.

(b) As used in this section, the term —

(1) "child" means a person under the age of eighteen;

(2) "contestant" means a person, including a parent or grandparent, who claims a right to custody or visitation of a child;

(3) "custody determination" means a judgment, decree, or other order of a court providing for the custody of a child, and includes permanent and temporary orders, and initial orders and modifications;

(4) "home State" means the State in which, immediately preceding the time involved, the child lived with his parents, a parent, or a person acting as parent, for at least six consecutive months, and in the case of a child less than six months old, the State in which the child lived from birth with any of such persons. Periods of temporary absence of any of such persons are counted as part of the six-month or other period;

(5) "modification" and "modify" refer to a custody or visitation determination which modifies, replaces, supersedes, or otherwise is made subsequent to, a prior custody or visitation determination concerning the same child, whether made by the same court or not;

(6) "person acting as a parent" means a person, other than a parent, who has physical custody of a child and who has either been awarded custody by a court or claims a right to custody;

(7) "physical custody" means actual possession and control of a child;

(8) "State" means a State of the United States, the District of Columbia, the Commonwealth of Puerto Rico, or a territory or possession of the United States; and

(9) "visitation determination" means a judgment, decree, or other order of a court providing for the visitation of a child and includes permanent and temporary orders and initial orders and modifications.

(c) A child custody or visitation determination made by a court of a State is consistent with the provisions of this section only if —

(1) such court has jurisdiction under the law of such State; and

(2) one of the following conditions is met:

(A) such State (i) is the home State of the child on the date of the commencement of the proceeding, or (ii) had been the child's home State within six months before the date of the commencement of the proceeding and the child is absent from such State because of his removal or retention by a contestant or for other reasons, and a contestant continues to live in such State;

(B) (i) it appears that no other State would have jurisdiction under subparagraph (A), and (ii) it is in the best interest of the child that a court of such State assume jurisdiction because (I) the child and his parents, or the child and at least one contestant, have a significant connection with such State other than mere physical presence in such State, and (II) there is available in such State substantial evidence concerning the child's present or future care, protection, training, and personal relationships;

(C) the child is physically present in such State and (i) the child has been abandoned, or (ii) it is necessary in an emergency to protect the child because the child, a sibling, or parent of the child has been subjected to or threatened with mistreatment or abuse;

(D) it appears that no other State would have jurisdiction under subparagraph (A), (B), (C), or (E), or another State has declined to exercise jurisdiction on the ground that the State whose jurisdiction is in issue is the more appropriate forum to determine the custody or visitation of the child, and (ii) it is in the best interest of the child that such court assume jurisdiction; or

(E) the court has continuing jurisdiction pursuant to subsection (d) of this section.

(d) The jurisdiction of a court of a State which has made a child custody or visitation determination consistently with the provisions of this section continues as long as the requirement of subsection (c)(1) of this section continues to be met and such State remains the residence of the child or of any contestant.

(e) Before a child custody or visitation determination is made, reasonable notice and opportunity to be heard shall be given to the contestants, any parent whose parental rights have not been previously terminated and any person who has physical custody of a child.

(f) A court of a State may modify a determination of the custody of the same child made by a court of another State, if—

(1) it has jurisdiction to make such a child custody determination; and

(2) the court of the other State no longer has jurisdiction, or it has declined to exercise such jurisdiction to modify such determination.

(g) A court of a State shall not exercise jurisdiction in any proceeding for a custody or visitation determination commenced during the pendency of a proceeding in a court of another State where such court of that other State is exercising jurisdiction consistently with the provisions of this section to make a custody or visitation determination.

(h) A court of a State may not modify a visitation determination made by a court of another State unless the court of the other State no longer has jurisdiction to modify such determination or has declined to exercise jurisdiction to modify such determination.

(Added Dec. 28, 1980, Pub. L. 96-611, § 8, 94 Stat. 3569; amended Nov. 12, 1998, Pub. L. 105-374, § 1, 112 Stat. 3383; Oct. 28, 2000, Pub. L. 106-386, § 1303(d), 114 Stat. 1512.)

§ 1738B.   Full Faith and Credit for Child Support Orders.

(a) General Rule. The appropriate authorities of each State—

(1) shall enforce according to its terms a child support order made consistently with this section by a court of another State; and

(2) shall not seek or make a modification of such an order except in accordance with subsections (e), (f), and (i).

(b) Definitions.—

In this section: "child" means:

(A) a person under 18 years of age; and

(B) a person 18 or more years of age with respect to whom a child support order has been issued pursuant to the laws of a State.

"child's State" means the State in which a child resides.

"child's home State" means the State in which a child lived with a parent or a person acting as parent for at least 6 consecutive months immediately preceding the time of filing of a petition or comparable pleading for support and, if a child is less than 6 months old, the State in which the child lived from birth with any of them. A period of temporary absence of any of them is counted as part of the 6-month period.

"child support" means a payment of money, continuing support, or arrearages or the provision of a benefit (including payment of health insurance, child care, and educational expenses) for the support of a child.

"child support order"—

(A) means a judgment, decree, or order of a court requiring the payment of child support in periodic amounts or in a lump sum; and

(B) includes—

(i) a permanent or temporary order; and

(ii) an initial order or a modification of an order. "contestant" means—

(A) a person (including a parent) who—

(i) claims a right to receive child support;

(ii) is a party to a proceeding that may result in the issuance of a child support order; or

(iii) is under a child support order; and

(B) a State or political subdivision of a State to which the right to obtain child support has been assigned.

"court" means a court or administrative agency of a State that is authorized by State law to establish the amount of child support payable by a contestant or make a modification of a child support order.

"modification" means a change in a child support order that affects the amount, scope, or duration of the order and modifies, replaces, supersedes, or otherwise is made subsequent to the child support order.

"State" means a State of the United States, the District of Columbia, the Commonwealth of Puerto Rico, the territories and possessions of the United States, and Indian country (as defined in section 1151 of title 18).

(c) Requirements of Child Support Orders. A child support order made by a court of a State is made consistently with this section if—

(1) a court that makes the order, pursuant to the laws of the State in which the court is located and subsections (e), (f), and (g)—

(A) has subject matter jurisdiction to hear the matter and enter such an order; and

(B) has personal jurisdiction over the contestants; and

(2) reasonable notice and opportunity to be heard is given to the contestants.

(d) Continuing Jurisdiction. A court of a State that has made a child support order consistently with this section has continuing, exclusive jurisdiction over the order if the State is the child's State or the residence of any individual contestant unless the court of another State, acting in accordance with subsections (e) and (f), has made a modification of the order.

(e) Authority To Modify Orders. A court of a State may modify a child support order issued by a court of another State if—

(1) the court has jurisdiction to make such a child support order pursuant to subsection (i); and

(2) (A) the court of the other State no longer has continuing, exclusive jurisdiction of the child support order because that State no longer is the child's State or the residence of any individual contestant; or

(B) each individual contestant has filed written consent with the State of continuing, exclusive jurisdiction for a court of another State to modify the order and assume continuing, exclusive jurisdiction over the order.

(f) Recognition of Child Support Orders. If 1 or more child support orders have been issued with regard to an obligor and a child, a court shall apply the following rules in determining which order to recognize for purposes of continuing, exclusive jurisdiction and enforcement:

(1) If only 1 court has issued a child support order, the order of that court must be recognized.

(2) If 2 or more courts have issued child support orders for the same obligor and child, and only 1 of the courts would have continuing, exclusive jurisdiction under this section, the order of that court must be recognized.

(3) If 2 or more courts have issued child support orders for the same obligor and child, and more than 1 of the courts would have continuing, exclusive jurisdiction under this section, an order issued by a court in the current home State of the child must be recognized, but if an order has not been issued in the current home State of the child, the order most recently issued must be recognized.

(4) If 2 or more courts have issued child support orders for the same obligor and child, and none of the courts would have continuing, exclusive jurisdiction under this section, a court having jurisdiction over the parties shall issue a child support order, which must be recognized.

(5) The court that has issued an order recognized under this subsection is the court having continuing, exclusive jurisdiction under subsection (d).

(g) Enforcement of Modified Orders. A court of a State that no longer has continuing, exclusive jurisdiction of a child support order may enforce the order with respect to nonmodifiable obligations and unsatisfied obligations that accrued before the date on which a modification of the order is made under subsections (e) and (f).

(h) Choice of Law.—

(1) In general. In a proceeding to establish, modify, or enforce a child support order, the forum State's law shall apply except as provided in paragraphs (2) and (3).

(2) Law of state of issuance of order. In interpreting a child support order including the duration of current payments and other obligations of support, a court shall apply the law of the State of the court that issued the order.

(3) Period of limitation. In an action to enforce arrears under a child support order, a court shall apply the statute of limitation of the forum State or the State of the court that issued the order, whichever statute provides the longer period of limitation.

(i) Registration for Modification. If there is no individual contestant or child residing in the issuing State, the party or support enforcement agency seeking to modify, or to modify and enforce, a child support order issued in another State shall register that order in a State with jurisdiction over the nonmovant for the purpose of modification.

(Added Oct. 22, 1994, Pub. L. 103-383, § 3(a), 108 Stat. 4064; Aug. 22, 1996, Pub. L. 104-193, § 322, 110 Stat. 2221, 2222; Aug. 22, 1996, Pub. L. 105-33, § 5554, 111 Stat. 636.)

§ 1738C. Certain Acts, Records, and Proceedings and the Effect Thereof.

No State, territory, or possession of the United States, or Indian tribe, shall be required to give effect to any public act, record, or judicial proceeding of any other State, territory, possession, or tribe respecting a relationship between persons of the same sex that is treated as a marriage under the laws of such other State, territory, possession, or tribe, or a right or claim arising from such relationship.

(Added Sept. 21, 1996, P.L. 104-199, § 2(a), 110 Stat. 2419.)

§ 1739. State and Territorial Nonjudicial Records; Full Faith and Credit.

All nonjudicial records or books kept in any public office of any State, Territory, or Possession of the United States, or copies thereof, shall be proved or admitted in any court or office in any other State, Territory, or Possession by the attestation of the custodian of such records or books, and the seal of his office annexed, if there be a seal, together with a certificate of a judge of a court of record of the county, parish, or district in which such office may be kept, or of the Governor, or secretary of state, the chancellor or keeper of the great seal, of the State, Territory, or Possession that the said attestation is in due form and by the proper officers.

If the certificate is given by a judge, it shall be further authenticated by the clerk or prothonotary of the court, who shall certify, under his hand and the seal of his office, that such judge is duly commissioned and qualified; or, if given by such Governor, secretary, chancellor, or keeper of the great seal, it shall be under the great seal of the State, Territory, or Possession in which it is made.

Such records or books, or copies thereof, so authenticated, shall have the same full faith and credit in every court and office within the United States and its Territories and Possessions as they have by law or usage in the courts or offices of the State, Territory, or Possession from which they are taken.

(Added June 25, 1948, ch. 646, 62 Stat. 947.)

§ 1746. Unsworn Declarations Under Penalty of Perjury.

Wherever, under any law of the United States or under any rule, regulation, order, or requirement made pursuant to law, any matter is required or permitted to be supported, evidenced, established, or proved by the sworn declaration, verification, certificate, statement, oath, or affidavit, in writing of the person making the same (other than a deposition, or an oath of office, or an oath required to be taken before a specified official other than a notary public), such matter may, with like force and effect, be supported, evidenced, established, or proved by the unsworn declaration, certificate, verification, or statement, in writing of such person which is subscribed by him, as true under penalty of perjury, and dated, in substantially the following form:

> (1) If executed without the United States: "I declare (or certify, verify, or state) under penalty of perjury under the laws of the United States of America that the foregoing is true and correct.

Executed on (date).

(Signature)".

> (2) If executed within the United States, its territories, possessions, or commonwealths: "I declare (or certify, verify, or state) under penalty of perjury that the foregoing is true and correct.

Executed on (date).

(Signature)".

(Added Oct. 18, 1976, P.L. 94-550, § 1(a), 90 Stat. 2534.)

CHAPTER 117.   EVIDENCE; DEPOSITIONS

§ 1782.   Assistance to Foreign and International Tribunals and to Litigants Before Such Tribunals.

(a) The district court of the district in which a person resides or is found may order him to give his testimony or statement or to produce a document or other thing for use in a proceeding in a foreign or international tribunal, including criminal investigations conducted before formal accusation. The order may be made pursuant to a letter rogatory issued, or request made, by a foreign or international tribunal or upon the application of any interested person and may direct that the testimony or statement be given, or the document or other thing be produced, before a person appointed by the court. By virtue of his appointment, the person appointed has power to administer any necessary oath and take the testimony or statement. The order may prescribe the practice and procedure, which may be in whole or part the practice and procedure of the foreign country or the international tribunal, for taking the testimony or statement or producing the document or other thing. To the extent that the order does not prescribe otherwise, the testimony or statement shall be taken, and the document or other thing produced, in accordance with the Federal Rules of Civil Procedure.

A person may not be compelled to give his testimony or statement or to produce a document or other thing in violation of any legally applicable privilege.

(b) This chapter does not preclude a person within the United States from voluntarily giving his testimony or statement, or producing a document or other thing, for use in a proceeding in a foreign or international tribunal before any person and in any manner acceptable to him.

(As amended Act. 3, 1964, Pub. L. 88-619, § 9(a), 78 Stat. 997; Feb. 10, 1996, Pub. L. 104-106, § 1342(b), 110 Stat. 486.)

CHAPTER 121.   JURIES; TRIAL BY JURY

§ 1861.   DECLARATION OF POLICY.

It is the policy of the United States that all litigants in Federal courts entitled to trial by jury shall have the right to grand and petit juries selected at random from a fair cross section of the community in the district or division wherein the court convenes. It is further the policy of the United States that all citizens shall have the opportunity to be considered for service on grand and petit juries in the district courts of the United States, and shall have an obligation to serve as jurors when summoned for that purpose.

(Added June 25, 1948, ch. 646, 62 Stat. 952; amended March 27, 1968, Pub. L. 90-274, § 101, 82 Stat. 54.)

§ 1862.   DISCRIMINATION PROHIBITED.

No citizen shall be excluded from service as a grand or petit juror in the district court of the United States or in the Court of International Trade on account of race, color, religion, sex, national origin, or economic status.

(Added June 25, 1948, ch. 646, 62 Stat. 952; amended March 27, 1968, Pub. L. 90-274, § 101, 82 Stat. 54; Oct. 10, 1980, Pub. L. 96-417, § 302(c), 94 Stat. 1739.)

§ 1863.   PLAN FOR RANDOM JURY SELECTION.

(a) Each United States district court shall devise and place into operation a written plan for random selection of grand and petit jurors that shall be designed to achieve the objectives of sections 1861 and 1862 of this title, and that shall otherwise comply with the provisions of this title. The plan shall be placed into operation after approval by a reviewing panel consisting of the members of the judicial council of the circuit and either the chief judge of the district whose plan is being reviewed or such other active district judge of that district as the chief judge of the district may designate. The panel shall examine the plan to ascertain that it complies with the provisions of this title. If the reviewing panel finds that the plan does not comply, the panel shall state the particular in which the plan fails to comply and direct the district court to present within a reasonable time an alternative plan remedying the defect or defects. Separate plans may be adopted for each division or combination of divisions within a judicial district. The district court may modify a plan at any time and it shall modify the plan when so directed by the reviewing panel. The district court shall promptly notify the panel, the Administrative Office of the United States Courts, and the Attorney General of the United States, of the initial adoption and future modifications of the plan by filing copies therewith. Modifications of the plan made at the instance of the district court shall become effective after approval by the panel. Each district court shall submit a report on the jury selection process within its jurisdiction to the Administrative Office of the United States in such form and at such times as the Judicial Conference of the United States may specify. The Judicial Conference of the United States may, from time to time, adopt rules and regulations governing the provisions and the operation of the plans formulated under this title.

(b) Among other things, such plan shall—

(1) either establish a jury commission, or authorize the clerk of the court, to manage the jury selection process. If the plan establishes a jury commission, the district court shall appoint one citizen to serve with the clerk of the court as the jury commission: *Provided, however,* That the plan for the District of Columbia may establish a jury commission consisting of three citizens. The citizen jury commissioner shall not belong to the same political party as the clerk serving with him. The clerk or the jury commission, as the case may be, shall act under the supervision and control of the chief judge of the district court or such other judge of the district court as the plan may provide. Each jury commissioner shall, during his tenure in office, reside in the judicial district or division for which he is appointed. Each citizen jury commissioner shall receive compensation to be fixed by the district court plan at a rate not to exceed $50 per day for each day necessarily employed in the performance of his duties, plus reimbursement for travel, subsistence, and other necessary expenses incurred by him in the performance of such duties. The Judicial Conference of the United States may establish standards for allowance of travel, subsistence, and other necessary expenses incurred by jury commissioners.

(2) specify whether the names of prospective jurors shall be selected from the voter registration lists or the lists of actual voters of the political subdivisions within the district or division. The plan shall prescribe some other source or sources of names in addition to voter lists where necessary to foster the policy and protect the rights secured by sections 1861 and 1862 of this title. The plan for the District of Columbia may require the names of prospective jurors to be selected from the city directory rather than from voter lists. The plans for the districts of Puerto Rico and the Canal Zone may prescribe some other source or sources of names of prospective jurors in lieu of voter lists, the use of which shall be consistent with the policies declared and rights secured by sections 1861 and 1862 of this title. The plan for the district of Massachusetts may require the names of prospective jurors to be selected from the resident list provided for in chapter 234A, Massachusetts General Laws, or comparable authority, rather than from voter lists.

(3) specify detailed procedures to be followed by the jury commission or clerk in selecting names from the sources specified in paragraph (2) of this subsection. These procedures shall be designed to ensure the random selection of a fair cross section of the persons residing in the community in the district or

division wherein the court convenes. They shall ensure that names of persons, residing in each of the counties, parishes, or similar political subdivisions within the judicial district or division are placed in a master jury wheel; and shall ensure that each county, parish, or similar political subdivision within the district or division is substantially proportionally represented in the master jury wheel for that judicial district, division, or combination of divisions. For the purposes of determining proportional representation in the master jury wheel, either the number of actual voters at the last general election in each county, parish, or similar political subdivision, or the number of registered voters if registration of voters is uniformly required throughout the district or division, may be used.

(4) provide for a master jury wheel (or a device similar in purpose and function) into which the names of those randomly selected shall be placed. The plan shall fix a minimum number of names to be placed initially in the master jury wheel, which shall be at least one-half of 1 per centum of the total number of persons on the lists used as a source of names for the district or division; but if this number of names is believed to be cumbersome and unnecessary, the plan may fix a smaller number of names to be placed in the master wheel, but in no event less than one thousand. The chief judge of the district court, or such other district court judge as the plan may provide, may order additional names to be placed in the master jury wheel from time to time as necessary. The plan shall provide for periodic emptying and refilling of the master jury wheel at specified times, the interval for which shall not exceed four years.

(5) (A)except as provided in subparagraph (B), specify those groups of persons or occupational classes whose members shall, on individual request therefor, be excused from jury service. Such groups or classes shall be excused only if the district court finds, and the plan states, that jury service by such class or group would entail undue hardship or extreme inconvenience to the members thereof, and excuse of members thereof would not be inconsistent with sections 1861 and 1862 of this title.

(B) specify that volunteer safety personnel, upon individual request, shall be excused from jury service. For purposes of this subparagraph, the term "volunteer safety personnel" means individuals serving a public agency (as defined in section 1203(6) of title I of the Omnibus Crime Control and Safe Streets Act of 1968) in an official capacity, without compensation, as firefighters or members of a rescue squad or ambulance crew.

(6) specify that the following persons are barred from jury service on the ground that they are exempt: (A) members in active service in the Armed Forces of the United States; (B) members of the fire or police departments of any State, the District of Columbia, any territory or possession of the United States, or any subdivision of a State, the District of Columbia, or such territory or possession; (C) public officers in the executive, legislative, or judicial branches of the Government of the United States, or of any State, the District

of Columbia, any territory or possession of the United States, or any subdivision of a State, the District of Columbia, or such territory or possession, who are actively engaged in the performance of official duties.

(7) fix the time when the names drawn from the qualified jury wheel shall be disclosed to parties and to the public. If the plan permits these names to be made public, it may nevertheless permit the chief judge of the district court, or such other district court judge as the plan may provide, to keep these names confidential in any case where the interests of justice so require.

(8) specify the procedures to be followed by the clerk or jury commission in assigning persons whose names have been drawn from the qualified jury wheel to grand and petit jury panels.

(c) The initial plan shall be devised by each district court and transmitted to the reviewing panel specified in subsection (a) of this section within one hundred and twenty days of the date of enactment of the Jury Selection and Service Act of 1968. The panel shall approve or direct the modification of each plan so submitted within sixty days thereafter. Each plan or modification made at the direction of the panel shall become effective after approval at such time thereafter as the panel directs, in no event to exceed ninety days from the date of approval. Modifications made at the instance of the district court under subsection (a) of this section shall be effective at such time thereafter as the panel directs, in no event to exceed ninety days from the date of modification.

(d) State, local, and Federal officials having custody, possession, or control of voter registration lists, lists of actual voters, or other appropriate records shall make such lists and records available to the jury commission or clerks for inspection, reproduction, and copying at all reasonable times as the commission or clerk may deem necessary and proper for the performance of duties under this title. The district courts shall have jurisdiction upon application by the Attorney General of the United States to compel compliance with this subsection by appropriate process.

(Added June 25, 1948, ch. 646, 62 Stat. 952; latest amended Oct. 29, 1992, Pub. L. 102-572, § 401, 106 Stat. 4511.)

§ 1864. Drawing of Names From the Master Jury Wheel; Completion of Juror Qualification Form.

(a) From time to time as directed by the district court, the clerk or a district judge shall draw at random from the master jury wheel the names of as many persons as may be required for jury service. The clerk or jury commission shall post a general notice for public review in the clerk's office and on the court's website explaining the process by which names and are periodically and randomly drawn. The clerk or jury commission may, upon order of the court, prepare an alphabetical list of the names drawn from the master jury wheel. Any list so prepared shall not be disclosed to any person except pursuant to the district court plan or pursuant to section 1867 or 1868 of this title. The clerk or jury commission shall mail to every person whose name is drawn from the master wheel a juror qualification form accompanied by instructions to fill out and return the form, duly signed and sworn, to the clerk or jury commission by mail within ten days. If the person is unable to fill out the form, another shall do it for him, and shall indicate that he has done so and the reason therefor. In any case in which it appears that there is an omission, ambiguity, or error in a form, the clerk or jury commission shall return the form with instructions to the person to make such additions or corrections as may be necessary and to return the form to the clerk or jury commission within ten days. Any person who fails to return a completed juror qualification form as instructed may be summoned by the clerk or jury commission forthwith to appear before the clerk or jury commission to fill out a juror qualification form. A person summoned to appear because of failure to return a juror qualification form as instructed who personally appears and executes a juror qualification form before the clerk or jury commission may, at the discretion of the district court, except where his prior failure to execute and mail such forms was willful, be entitled to receive for such appearance the same fees and travel allowances paid to jurors under section 1871 of this title. At the time of his appearance for jury service, any person may be required to fill out another juror qualification form in the presence of the jury commission or the clerk or the court, at which time, in such cases as it appears warranted, the person may be questioned, but only with regard to his responses to questions contained on the form. Any information thus acquired by the clerk or jury commission may be noted on the juror qualification form and transmitted to the chief judge or such district court judge as the plan may provide.

(b) Any person summoned pursuant to subsection (a) of this section who fails to appear as directed shall be ordered by the district court forthwith to appear and show cause for his failure to comply with the summons. Any person who fails to appear pursuant to such order or who fails to show good cause for noncompliance with the summons may be fined not more than $1000, imprisoned not more than three days, ordered to perform community services, or any combination thereof. Any person who willfully misrepresents a material fact on a juror qualification form for the purpose of avoiding or securing service as a juror may be fined not more than $1000, imprisoned not more than three days, ordered to perform community services, or any combination thereof.

(Added June 25, 1948, ch. 646, 62 Stat. 952; last amended Oct. 13, 2008, P.L. 110-406, §§ 5(a), 17(a), 122 Stat. 4292, 4295.)

§ 1865.   QUALIFICATIONS FOR JURY SERVICE.

(a) The chief judge of the district court, or such other district court judge as the plan may provide, on his initiative or upon recommendation of the clerk or jury commission, or the clerk under supervision of the court if the court's jury selection plan so authorizes, shall determine solely on the basis of information provided on the juror qualification form and other competent evidence whether a person is unqualified for, or exempt, or to be excused from jury service. The clerk shall enter such determination in the space provided on the juror qualification form and in any alphabetical list of names drawn from the master jury wheel. If a person did not appear in response to a summons, such fact shall be noted on said list.

(b) In making such determination the chief judge of the district court, or such other district court judge as the plan may provide, or the clerk if the court's jury selection plan so provides, shall deem any person qualified to serve on grand and petit juries in the district court unless he—

(1) is not a citizen of the United States eighteen years old who has resided for a period of one year within the judicial district;

(2) is unable to read, write, and understand the English language with a degree of proficiency sufficient to fill out satisfactorily the juror qualification form;

(3) is unable to speak the English language;

(4) is incapable, by reason of mental or physical infirmity, to render satisfactory jury service; or

(5) has a charge pending against him for the commission of, or has been convicted in a State or Federal court of record of, a crime punishable by imprisonment for more than one year and his civil rights have not been restored.

(Added June 25, 1948, ch. 646, 62 Stat. 952; last amended Nov. 13, 2000, P.L. 106-518, § 305. 114 Stat. 2418.)

§ 1866. SELECTION AND SUMMONING OF JURY PANELS.

(a) The jury commission, or in the absence thereof the clerk, shall maintain a qualified jury wheel and shall place in such wheel names of all persons drawn from the master jury wheel who are determined to be qualified as jurors and not exempt or excused pursuant to the district court plan. From time to time, the jury commission or the clerk shall draw at random from the qualified jury wheel such number of names of persons as may be required for assignment to grand and petit jury panels. The clerk or jury commission shall post a general notice for public review in the clerk's office and on the court's website explaining the process by which names are periodically and randomly drawn. The jury commission or the clerk shall prepare a separate list of names of persons assigned to each grand and petit jury panel.

(b) When the court orders a grand or petit jury to be drawn, the clerk or jury commission or their duly designated deputies shall issue summonses for the required number of jurors.

Each person drawn for jury service may be served personally, or by registered, certified, or first-class mail addressed to such person at his usual residence or business address.

If such service is made personally the summons shall be delivered by the clerk or the jury commission or their duly designated deputies to the marshal who shall make such service.

If such service is made by mail, the summons may be served by the marshal or by the clerk, the jury commission or their duly designated deputies, who shall make affidavit of service and shall attach thereto any receipt from the addressee for a registered or certified summons.

(c) Except as provided in section 1865 of this title or in any jury selection plan provision adopted pursuant to paragraph (5) or (6) of section 1863(b) of this title, no person or class of persons shall be disqualified, excluded, excused, or exempt from service as jurors: *Provided*, That any person summoned for jury service may be (1) excused by the court, or by the clerk under supervision of the court if the court's jury selection plan so authorizes, upon a showing of undue hardship or extreme inconvenience, for such period as the court deems necessary, at the conclusion of which such person either shall be summoned again for jury service under subsections (b) and (c) of this section or, if the court's jury selection plan so provides, the name of such person shall be reinserted into the qualified jury wheel for selection pursuant to subsection (a) of this section, or (2) excluded by the court on the ground that such person may be unable to render impartial jury service or that his service as a juror would be likely to disrupt the proceedings, or (3) excluded upon peremptory challenge as provided by law, or (4) excluded pursuant to the procedure specified by law upon a challenge by any party for good cause shown, or (5) excluded upon determination by the court that his service as a juror would be likely to threaten the secrecy of the proceedings, or otherwise adversely affect the integrity of jury deliberations. No person shall be excluded under clause (5) of this subsection unless the judge, in open court, determines that such is warranted and that exclusion of the person will not be inconsistent with sections 1861 and 1862 of this title. The number of persons excluded under clause (5) of this subsection shall not exceed one per centum of the number of persons who return executed jury qualification forms during the period, specified in the plan, between two consecutive fillings of the master jury wheel. The names of persons excluded under clause (5) of this subsection, together with detailed explanations for the exclusions, shall be forwarded immediately to the judicial council of the circuit, which shall have the power to make any appropriate order, prospective or retroactive, to redress any misapplication of clause (5) of this subsection, but otherwise exclusions effectuated under such clause shall not be subject to challenge under the provisions of this title. Any person excluded from a particular jury under clause (2), (3), or (4) of this subsection shall be eligible to sit on another jury if the basis for his initial exclusion would not be relevant to his ability to serve on such other jury.

(d) Whenever a person is disqualified, excused, exempt, or excluded from jury service, the jury commission or clerk shall note in the space provided on his juror qualification form or on the juror's card drawn from the qualified jury wheel the specific reason therefor.

(e) In any two-year period, no person shall be required to (1) serve or attend court for prospective service as a petit juror for a total of more than thirty days, except when necessary to complete service in a particular case, or (2) serve on more than one grand jury, or (3) serve as both a grand and petit juror.

(f) When there is an unanticipated shortage of available petit jurors drawn from the qualified jury wheel, the court may require the marshal to summon a sufficient number of petit jurors selected at random from the voter registration lists, lists of actual voters, or other lists specified in the plan, in a manner ordered by the court consistent with sections 1861 and 1862 of this title.

(g) Any person summoned for jury service who fails to appear as directed may be ordered by the district court to appear forthwith and show cause for failure to comply with the summons. Any person who fails to show good cause for noncompliance with a summons may be fined not more than $1000, imprisoned not more than three days, ordered to perform community service, or any combination thereof.

(Added June 25, 1948, ch. 646, 62 Stat. 952; latest amendment Oct. 13, 2008, P.L. 110-406, §§ 4, 5(b), 17(b), 122 Stat. 4292, 4295.)

§ 1867. CHALLENGING COMPLIANCE WITH SELECTION PROCEDURES.

(a), (b) [Not Reproduced.]

(c) In civil cases, before the voir dire examination begins, or within seven days after the party discovered or could have discovered, by the exercise of diligence, the grounds therefor, whichever is earlier, any party may move to stay the proceedings on the ground of substantial failure to comply with the provisions of this title in selecting the petit jury.

(d) Upon motion filed under subsection (a), (b), or (c) of this section, containing a sworn statement of facts which, if true, would constitute a substantial failure to comply with the provisions of this title, the moving party shall be entitled to present in support of such motion the testimony of the jury commission or clerk, if available, any relevant records and papers not public or otherwise available used by the jury commissioner or clerk, and any other relevant evidence. If the court determines that there has been a substantial failure to comply with the provisions of this title in selecting the grand jury, the court shall stay the proceedings pending the selection of a grand jury in conformity with this title or dismiss the indictment, whichever is appropriate. If the court determines that there has been a substantial failure to comply with the provisions of this title in selecting the petit jury, the court shall stay the proceedings pending the selection of a petit jury in conformity with this title.

(e) The procedures prescribed by this section shall be the exclusive means by which a person accused of a Federal crime, the Attorney General of the United States or a party in a civil case may challenge any jury on the ground that such jury was not selected in conformity with the provisions of this title. Nothing in this section shall preclude any person or the United States from pursuing any other remedy, civil or criminal, which may be available for the vindication or enforcement of any law prohibiting discrimination on account of race, color, religion, sex, national origin or economic status in the selection of persons for service on grand or petit juries.

(f) The contents of records or papers used by the jury commission or clerk in connection with the jury selection process shall not be disclosed, except pursuant to the district court plan or as may be necessary in the preparation or presentation of a motion under subsection (a), (b), or (c) of this section, until after the master jury wheel has been emptied and refilled pursuant to section 1863(b)(4) of this title and all persons selected to serve as jurors before the master wheel was emptied have completed such service. The parties in a case shall be allowed to inspect, reproduce, and copy such records or papers at all reasonable times during the preparation and pendency of such a motion. Any person who discloses the contents of any record or paper in violation of this subsection may be fined not more than $1,000 or imprisoned not more than one year, or both.

(Added June 25, 1948, ch. 646, 62 Stat. 953; amended Sept. 2, 1957, Pub. L. 85-259, 71 Stat. 583; March 27, 1968, Pub. L. 90-274, § 101, 82 Stat. 59.)

§ 1869. DEFINITIONS.

For purposes of this chapter—

(a) "clerk" and "clerk of the court" shall mean the clerk of the district court of the United States, any authorized deputy clerk, and any other person authorized by the court to assist the clerk in the performance of functions under this chapter;

(b) "chief judge" shall mean the chief judge of any district court of the United States;

(c) "voter registration lists" shall mean the official records maintained by State or local election officials of persons registered to vote in either the most recent State or the most recent Federal general election, or, in the case of a State or political subdivision thereof that does not require registration as a prerequisite to voting, other official lists of persons qualified to vote in such election. The term shall also include the list of eligible voters maintained by any Federal examiner pursuant to the Voting Rights Act of 1965 where the names on such list have not been included on the official registration lists or other official lists maintained by the appropriate State or local officials. With respect to the districts of Guam and the Virgin Islands, "voter registration lists" shall mean the official records maintained by territorial election officials of persons registered to vote in the most recent territorial general election;

(d) "lists of actual voters" shall mean the official lists of persons actually voting in either the most recent State or the most recent Federal general election;

(e) "division" shall mean: (1) one or more statutory divisions of a judicial district; or (2) in statutory divisions that contain more than one place of holding court, or in judicial districts where there are no statutory divisions, such counties, parishes, or similar political subdivisions surrounding the places where court is held as the district court plan shall determine: *Provided*, That each county, parish, or similar political subdivision shall be included in some such division;

(f) "district court of the United States," "district court," and "court" shall mean any district court established by chapter 5 of this title, and any court which is created by Act of Congress in a territory and is invested with any jurisdiction of a district court established by chapter 5 of this title;

(g) "jury wheel" shall include any device or system similar in purpose or function, such as a properly programmed electronic data processing system or device;

(h) "juror qualification form" shall mean a form prescribed by the Administrative Office of the United States Courts and approved by the Judicial Conference of the United States, which shall elicit the name, address, age, race, occupation, education, length of residence within the judicial district, distance from residence to place of holding court, prior jury service, and citizenship of a potential juror, and whether he should be excused or exempted from jury service, has any physical or mental infirmity impairing his capacity to serve as juror, is able to read, write, speak, and understand the English language, has pending against him any charge for the commission of a State or Federal criminal offense punishable by imprisonment for more than one year, or has been convicted in any State or Federal court of record of a crime punishable by imprisonment for more than one year and has not had his civil rights restored. The form shall request, but not require, any other information not inconsistent with the provisions of this title and required by the district court plan in the interests of the sound administration of justice. The form shall also elicit the sworn statement that his responses are true to the best of his knowledge. Notarization shall not be required. The form shall contain words clearly informing the person that the furnishing of any information with respect to his religion, national origin, or economic status is not a prerequisite to his qualification for jury service, that such information need not be furnished if the person finds it objectionable to do so, and that information concerning race is required solely to enforce nondiscrimination in jury selection and has no bearing on an individual's qualification for jury service.

(i) "public officer" shall mean a person who is either elected to public office or who is directly appointed by a person elected to public office;

(j) "undue hardship or extreme inconvenience", as a basis for excuse from immediate jury service under section 1866(c)(1) of this chapter, shall mean great distance, either in miles or travel-time, from the place of holding court, grave illness in the family or any other emergency which outweighs in immediacy and urgency the obligation to serve as a juror when summoned, or any other factor which the court determines to constitute an undue hardship or to create an extreme inconvenience to the juror; and in addition, in situations where it is anticipated that a trial or grand jury proceeding may require more than thirty days of service, the court may consider, as a further basis for temporary excuse, severe economic hardship to an employer which would result from the absence of a key employee during the period of such service; and

(k) "jury summons" shall mean a summons issued by a clerk of court, jury commission, or their duly designated deputies, containing either a preprinted or stamped seal of court, and containing the name of the issuing clerk imprinted in preprinted, type, or facsimile manner on the summons or the envelopes transmitting the summons.

(Added June 25, 1948, ch. 646, 62 Stat. 953; latest amendment Oct. 13, 2008, P.L. 110-406, § 5(c), 122 Stat. 4292.)

§ 1870.   CHALLENGES.

In civil cases, each party shall be entitled to three peremptory challenges. Several defendants or several plaintiffs may be considered as a single party for the purposes of making challenges, or the court may allow additional peremptory challenges and permit them to be exercised separately or jointly.

All challenges for cause or favor, whether to the array or panel or to individual jurors, shall be determined by the court.

(Added June 25, 1948, ch. 646, 62 Stat. 953; amended Sept. 16, 1959, Pub. L. 86-282, 73 Stat. 565.)

§ 1872.   ISSUES OF FACT IN SUPREME COURT.

In all original actions at law in the Supreme Court against citizens of the United States, issues of fact shall be tried by a jury.

(Added June 25, 1948, ch. 646, 62 Stat. 953)

§ 1873.   ADMIRALTY AND MARITIME CASES.

In any case of admiralty and maritime jurisdiction relating to any matter of contract or tort arising upon or concerning any vessel of twenty tons or upward, enrolled and licensed for the coasting trade, and employed in the business of commerce and navigation between places in different states upon the lakes and navigable waters connecting said lakes, the trial of all issues of fact shall be by jury if either party demands it.

(Added June 25, 1948, ch. 646, 62 Stat. 953)

CHAPTER 123.   FEES AND COSTS

§ 1912.   DAMAGES AND COSTS ON AFFIRMANCE.

Where a judgment is affirmed by the Supreme Court or a court of appeals, the court in its discretion may adjudge to the prevailing party just damages for his delay, and single or double costs.

(Added June 25, 1948, ch. 646, 62 Stat. 953)

§ 1914. District Court; Filing and Miscellaneous Fees; Rules of Court.

(a) The clerk of each district court shall require the parties instituting any civil action, suit or proceeding in such court, whether by original process, removal or otherwise, to pay a filing fee of $350 except that on application for a writ of habeas corpus the filing fee shall be $5.

(b) The clerk shall collect from the parties such additional fees only as are prescribed by the Judicial Conference of the United States.

(c) Each district court by rule or standing order may require advance payment of fees.

(As amended Feb. 8, 2006, Pub. L. 109-171, § 10001(a), 120 Stat. 183.)

§ 1915. Proceedings In Forma Pauperis.

(a) (1)Subject to subsection (b), any court of the United States may authorize the commencement, prosecution, or defense of any suit, action or proceeding, civil or criminal, or appeal therein, without prepayment of fees or security therefor, by a person who submits an affidavit that includes a statement of all assets such prisoner possesses that the person is unable to pay such fees or give security therefor. Such affidavit shall state the nature of the action, defense or appeal and affiant's belief that the person is entitled to redress.

(2) A prisoner seeking to bring a civil action or appeal a judgment in a civil action or proceeding without prepayment of fees or security therefor, in addition to filing the affidavit filed under paragraph (1), shall submit a certified copy of the trust fund account statement (or institutional equivalent) for the prisoner for the 6-month period immediately preceding the filing of the complaint or notice of appeal, obtained from the appropriate official of each prison at which the prisoner is or was confined.

(3) An appeal may not be taken in forma pauperis if the trial court certifies in writing that it is not taken in good faith.

(b) (1)Notwithstanding subsection (a), if a prisoner brings a civil action or files an appeal in forma pauperis, the prisoner shall be required to pay the full amount of a filing fee. The court shall assess and, when funds exist, collect, as a partial payment of any court fees required by law, an initial partial filing fee of 20 percent of the greater of—

(A) the average monthly deposits to the prisoner's account; or

(B) the average monthly balance in the prisoner's account for the 6-month period immediately preceding the filing of the complaint or notice of appeal.

(2) After payment of the initial partial filing fee, the prisoner shall be required to make monthly payments of 20 percent of the preceding month's

income credited to the prisoner's account. The agency having custody of the prisoner shall forward payments from the prisoner's account to the clerk of the court each time the amount in the account exceeds $10 until the filing fees are paid.

(3) In no event shall the filing fee collected exceed the amount of fees permitted by statute for the commencement of a civil action or an appeal of a civil action or criminal judgment.

(4) In no event shall a prisoner be prohibited from bringing a civil action or appealing a civil or criminal judgment for the reason that the prisoner has no assets and no means by which to pay the initial partial filing fee.

(c) Upon the filing of an affidavit in accordance with subsections (a) and (b) and the prepayment of any partial filing fee as may be required under subsection (b), the court may direct payment by the United States of the expenses of (1) printing the record on appeal in any civil or criminal case, if such printing is required by the appellate court; (2) preparing a transcript of proceedings before a United States magistrate in any civil or criminal case, if such transcript is required by the district court, in the case of proceedings conducted under section 636(b) of this title or under section 3401(b) of title 18, United States Code; and (3) printing the record on appeal if such printing is required by the appellate court, in the case of proceedings conducted pursuant to section 636(c) of this title. Such expenses shall be paid when authorized by the Director of the Administrative Office of the United States Courts.

(d) The officers of the court shall issue and serve all process, and perform all duties in such cases. Witnesses shall attend as in other cases, and the same remedies shall be available as are provided for by law in other cases.

(e) (1) The court may request an attorney to represent any person unable to afford counsel.

(2) Notwithstanding any filing fee, or any portion thereof, that may have been paid, the court shall dismiss the case at any time if the court determines that—

(A) the allegation of poverty is untrue; or

(B) the action or appeal—

(i) is frivolous or malicious;

(ii) fails to state a claim on which relief may be granted; or

(iii) seeks monetary relief against a defendant who is immune from such relief.

(f) (1) Judgment may be rendered for costs at the conclusion of the suit or action as in other proceedings, but the United States shall not be liable for any of the costs thus incurred. If the United States has paid the cost of a stenographic transcript or printed record for the prevailing party, the same shall be taxed in favor of the United States.

(2) (A)If the judgment against a prisoner includes the payment of costs under this subsection, the prisoner shall be required to pay the full amount of the costs ordered.

(B) The prisoner shall be required to make payments for costs under this subsection in the same manner as is provided for filing fees under subsection (a)(2).

(C) In no event shall the costs collected exceed the amount of the costs ordered by the court.

(g) In no event shall a prisoner bring a civil action or appeal a judgment in a civil action or proceeding under this section if the prisoner has, on 3 or more prior occasions, while incarcerated or detained in any facility, brought an action or appeal in a court of the United States that was dismissed on the grounds that it is frivolous, malicious, or fails to state a claim upon which relief may be granted, unless the prisoner is under imminent danger of serious physical injury.

(h) As used in this section, the term "prisoner" means any person incarcerated or detained in any facility who is accused of, convicted of, sentenced for, or adjudicated delinquent for, violations of criminal law or the terms and conditions of parole, probation, pretrial release, or diversionary program.

(Added June 25, 1948, ch. 646, 62 Stat. 954; latest amendment Apr. 26, 1996, Pub. L. 104-134, § 804(a), (c), (d), (e), 110 Stat. 1321.)

§ 1915A. SCREENING.

(a) Screening.—

The court shall review, before docketing, if feasible or, in any event, as soon as practicable after docketing, a complaint in a civil action in which a prisoner seeks redress from a governmental entity or officer or employee of a governmental entity.

(b) Grounds for Dismissal.—

On review, the court shall identify cognizable claims or dismiss the complaint, or any portion of the complaint, if the complaint—

(1) is frivolous, malicious, or fails to state a claim upon which relief may be granted; or

(2) seeks monetary relief from a defendant who is immune from such relief.

(c) Definition.—

As used in this section, the term "prisoner" means any person incarcerated or detained in any facility who is accused of, convicted of, sentenced for, or adjudicated delinquent for, violations of criminal law or the terms and conditions of parole, probation, pretrial release, or diversionary program.

(As added Apr. 26, 1996, Pub. L. 104-134, § 805(a), 110 Stat. 1321.)

§ 1919.   Dismissal for Lack of Jurisdiction.

Whenever any action or suit is dismissed in any district court, the Court of International Trade, or the Court of Federal Claims for want of jurisdiction, such court may order the payment of just costs.

(As amended Oct. 10, 1980, Pub. L. 96-417, § 510, 94 Stat. 1743; October 29, 1992, Pub. L. 102-572, § 908(a), (b)(1), 106 Stat. 4519.)

§ 1920.   Taxation of Costs.

A judge or clerk of any court of the United States may tax as costs the following:

(1) Fees of the clerk and marshal;

(2) Fees for printed or electronically recorded transcripts necessarily obtained for use in the case;

(3) Fees and disbursements for printing and witnesses;

(4) Fees for exemplification and the costs of making copies of any materials where the copies are necessarily obtained for use in the case;

(5) Docket fees under section 1923 of this title;

(6) Compensation of court appointed experts, compensation of interpreters, and salaries, fees, expenses, and costs of special interpretation services under section 1828 of this title.

A bill of costs shall be filed in the case and, upon allowance, included in the judgment or decree.

(Added June 25, 1948, ch. 646, 62 Stat. 955; amended Oct. 28, 1978, Pub. L. 95-539, § 7, 92 Stat. 2044.)

§ 1924.   Verification of Bill of Costs.

Before any bill of costs is taxed, the party claiming any item of cost or disbursement shall attach thereto an affidavit, made by himself or by his duly authorized attorney or agent having knowledge of the facts, that such item is correct and has been necessarily incurred in the case and that the services for which fees have been charged were actually and necessarily performed.

§ 1927.   Counsel's Liability for Excessive Costs.

Any attorney or other person admitted to conduct cases in any court of the United States or any Territory thereof who so multiplies the proceedings in any case unreasonably and vexatiously may be required by the court to satisfy personally the excess costs, expenses, and attorneys' fees reasonably incurred because of such conduct.

(As amended September 12, 1980, Pub. L. 96-349, § 3, 94 Stat. 1156.)

CHAPTER 125.   PENDING ACTIONS AND JUDGMENTS

§ 1961.   INTEREST.

(a) Interest shall be allowed on any money judgment in a civil case recovered in a district court. Execution therefor may be levied by the marshal, in any case where, by the law of the State in which such court is held, execution may be levied for interest on judgments recovered in the courts of the State. Such interest shall be calculated from the date of the entry of the judgment, at a rate equal to the weekly average 1-year constant maturity Treasury yield, as published by the Board of Governors of the Federal Reserve System, for the calendar week preceding the date of the judgment. The Director of the Administrative Office of the United States Courts shall distribute notice of that rate and any changes in it to all Federal judges.

(b) Interest shall be computed daily to the date of payment except as provided in section 2516(b) of this title and section 1304(b) of title 31, and shall be compounded annually.

(c) (1)This section shall not apply in any judgment of any court with respect to any internal revenue tax case. Interest shall be allowed in such cases at the underpayment rate or overpayment rate (whichever is appropriate) established under section 6621 of the Internal Revenue Code of 1986.

(2) Except as otherwise provided in paragraph (1) of this subsection, interest shall be allowed on all final judgments against the United States in the United States Court of Appeals for the Federal circuit, at the rate provided in subsection (a) and as provided in subsection (b).

(3) Interest shall be allowed, computed, and paid on judgments of the United States Court of Federal Claims only as provided in paragraph (1) of this subsection or in any other provision of law.

(4) This section shall not be construed to affect the interest on any judgment of any court not specified in this section.

(As amended Apr. 2, 1982, Pub. L. 97-164, § 302, 96 Stat. 55; September 13, 1982, Pub. L. 97-258, § 2(m)(1), 96 Stat. 1060; Jan. 12, 1983, Pub. L. 97-452, § 2, 96 Stat. 2467; Oct. 22, 1986, Pub. L. 99-514, 100 Stat. 2745; Oct. 29, 1992, Pub. L. 102-572, § 902(b) (1), 106 Stat. 4516; Dec. 21, 2000, Pub. L. 106-554, § 1(a)(7) [307(d)(1)], 114 Stat. 3763A-636.)

§ 1963.   REGISTRATION OF JUDGMENTS FOR ENFORCEMENT IN OTHER DISTRICTS.

A judgment in an action for the recovery of money or property entered in any court of appeals, district court, bankruptcy court, or in the Court of International Trade may be registered by filing a certified copy of the judgment in any other district or, with respect to the Court of International Trade, in any judicial district, when the judgment has become final by appeal or expiration of the time for appeal or when ordered by the court that entered the judgment for good cause shown. Such a judgment entered in favor of the United States may be so registered any time after judgment is entered. A judgment so registered shall have the same effect as a judgment of the district court of the district where registered and may be enforced in like manner.

A certified copy of the satisfaction of any judgment in whole or in part may be registered in like manner in any district in which the judgment is a lien.

The procedure prescribed under this section is in addition to other procedures provided by law for the enforcement of judgments.

(As amended Aug. 23, 1954, c837, Stat. 772; July 7, 1958, Pub. L. 85-508, § 12(o), 72 Stat. 349; Nov. 19, 1988, Pub. L. 100-702, § 1002; Nov. 29, 1990, Pub. L. 101-647, § 3628, 104 Stat. 4965; Oct. 19, 1996, Pub. L. 104-317, § 203, 110 Stat. 3849.)

CHAPTER 131.   RULES OF COURTS

§ 2071.   Rule-Making Power Generally.

(a) The Supreme Court and all courts established by Act of Congress may from time to time prescribe rules for the conduct of their business. Such rules shall be consistent with Acts of Congress and rules of practice and procedure prescribed under section 2072 of this title.

(b) Any rule prescribed by a court, other than the Supreme Court, under subsection (a) shall be prescribed only after giving appropriate public notice and an opportunity for comment. Such rule shall take effect upon the date specified by the prescribing court and shall have such effect on pending proceedings as the prescribing court may order.

(c) (1)A rule of a district court prescribed under subsection (a) shall remain in effect unless modified or abrogated by the judicial council of the relevant circuit.

(2) Any other rule prescribed by a court other than the Supreme Court under subsection (a) shall remain in effect unless modified or abrogated by the Judicial Conference.

(d) Copies of rules prescribed under subsection (a) by a district court shall be furnished to the judicial council, and copies of all rules prescribed by a court other than the Supreme Court under subsection (a) shall be furnished to the Director of the Administrative Office of the United States Courts and made available to the public.

(e) If the prescribing court determines that there is an immediate need for a rule, such court may proceed under this section without public notice and opportunity for comment, but such court shall promptly thereafter afford such notice and opportunity for comment.

(f) No rule may be prescribed by a district court other than under this section. (As amended May 24, 1949, ch. 139, § 102, 63 Stat. 104; Nov. 19, 1988, Pub. L. 100-702, § 403.)

§ 2072. Rules of Procedure and Evidence; Power to Prescribe.

(a) The Supreme Court shall have the power to prescribe general rules of practice and procedure and rules of evidence for cases in the United States district courts (including proceedings before magistrates thereof) and courts of appeals.

(b) Such rules shall not abridge, enlarge or modify any substantive right. All laws in conflict with such rules shall be of no further force or effect after such rules have taken effect.

(c) Such rules may define when a ruling of a district court is final for the purposes of appeal under section 1291 of this title.

(As amended May 24, 1949, ch. 139, § 103, 63 Stat. 104; July 18, 1949, ch. 343, § 2, 63 Stat. 446; May 10, 1950, ch. 174, § 2, 64 Stat. 158; July 7, 1958, Pub. L. 85-508, § 12(m), 72 Stat. 348; Nov. 6, 1966, Pub 89-773, § 1, 80 Stat. 1323; Nov. 19, 1988, Pub. L. 100-702, § 401; Dec. 1, 1990, Pub. L. 101-650, § 315, 104 Stat. 5115.)

§ 2073. Rules of Procedure and Evidence; Method of Prescribing.

(a) (1) The Judicial Conference shall prescribe and publish the procedures for the consideration of proposed rules under this section.

(2) The Judicial Conference may authorize the appointment of committees to assist the Conference by recommending rules to be prescribed under sections 2072 and 2075 of this title. Each such committee shall consist of members of the bench and the professional bar, and trial and appellate judges.

(b) The Judicial Conference shall authorize the appointment of a standing committee on rules of practice, procedure, and evidence under subsection (a) of this section. Such standing committee shall review each recommendation of any other committees so appointed and recommend to the Judicial Conference rules of practice, procedure, and evidence and such changes in rules proposed by a committee appointed under subsection (a)(2) of this section as may be necessary to maintain consistency and otherwise promote the interest of justice.

(c) (1) Each meeting for the transaction of business under this chapter by any committee appointed under this section shall be open to the public, except when the committee so meeting, in open session and with a majority present, determines that it is in the public interest that all or part of the remainder of the meeting on that day shall be closed to the public, and states the reason for so closing the meeting. Minutes of each meeting for the transaction of business under this chapter shall be maintained by the committee and made available to the public, except that any portion of such minutes, relating to a closed meeting and made available to the public, may contain such deletions as may be necessary to avoid frustrating the purposes of closing the meeting.

(2) Any meeting for the transaction of business under this chapter, by a committee appointed under this section, shall be preceded by sufficient notice to enable all interested persons to attend.

(d) In making a recommendation under this section or under section 2072 or 2075, the body making that recommendation shall provide a proposed rule, an explanatory note on the rule, and a written report explaining the body's action, including any minority or other separate views.

(e) Failure to comply with this section does not invalidate a rule prescribed under section 2072 or 2075 of this title.

(Added Nov. 19, 1988, Pub. L. 100-702, § 401; amended Oct. 22, 1994, Pub. L. 103-394, § 104(e), 108 Stat. 4110.)

§ 2074. Rules of Procedure and Evidence; Submission to Congress; Effective Date.

(a) The Supreme Court shall transmit to the Congress not later than May 1 of the year in which a rule prescribed under section 2072 is to become effective a copy of the proposed rule. Such rule shall take effect no earlier than December 1 of the year in which such rule is so transmitted unless otherwise provided by law. The Supreme Court may fix the extent such rule shall apply to proceedings then pending, except that the Supreme Court shall not require the application of such rule to further proceed- ings then pending to the extent that, in the opinion of the court in which such proceedings are pending, the application of such rule in such proceedings would not be feasible or would work injustice, in which event the former rule applies.

(b) Any such rule creating, abolishing, or modifying an evidentiary privilege shall have no force or effect unless approved by Act of Congress.

(Added Nov. 19, 1988, Pub. L. 100-702, § 401.)

§ 2077. Publication of Rules; Advisory Committees.

(a) The rules for the conduct of the business of each court of appeals, including the operating procedures of such court, shall be published. Each court of appeals shall print or cause to be printed necessary copies of the rules. The Judicial Conference shall prescribe the fees for sales of copies under section 1913 of this title, but the Judicial Conference may provide for free distribution of copies to members of the bar of each court and to other interested persons.

(b) Each court, except the Supreme Court, that is authorized to prescribe rules of the conduct of such court's business under section 2071 of this title shall appoint an advisory committee for the study of the rules of practice and internal operating procedures of such court and, in the case of an advisory committee appointed by a court of appeals, of the rules of the judicial council of the circuit. The advisory committee shall make recommendations to the court concerning such rules and procedures. Members of the committee shall serve without compensation, but the Director may pay travel and transportation expenses in accordance with section 5703 of title 5.

(Added Apr. 2, 1982, Pub. L. 97-164, § 208, 96 Stat. 54; as amended Nov. 19, 1988, Pub. L. 100-702, § 401; Dec. 1, 1990, Pub. L. 101-650, § 406, 104 Stat. 5089.)

CHAPTER 133.   REVIEW—MISCELLANEOUS PROVISIONS

§ 2101.   Supreme Court; Time for Appeal or Certiorari; Docketing; Stay.

(a) A direct appeal to the Supreme Court from any decision under section 1253 of this title, holding unconstitutional in whole or in part, any Act of Congress, shall be taken within thirty days after the entry of the interlocutory or final order, judgment or decree. The record shall be made up and the case docketed within sixty days from the time such appeal is taken under rules prescribed by the Supreme Court.

(b) Any other direct appeal to the Supreme Court which is authorized by law, from a decision of a district court in any civil action, suit or proceeding, shall be taken within thirty days from the judgment, order or decree, appealed from, if interlocutory, and within sixty days if final.

(c) Any other appeal or any writ of certiorari intended to bring any judgment or decree in a civil action, suit or proceeding before the Supreme Court for review shall be taken or applied for within ninety days after the entry of such judgment or decree. A justice of the Supreme Court, for good cause shown, may extend the time for applying for a writ of certiorari for a period not exceeding sixty days.

(d) The time for appeal or application for a writ of certiorari to review the judgment of a State court in a criminal case shall be as prescribed by rules of the Supreme Court.

(e) An application to the Supreme Court for a writ of certiorari to review a case before judgment has been rendered in the court of appeals may be made at any time before judgment.

(f) In any case in which the final judgment or decree of any court is subject to review by the Supreme Court on writ of certiorari, the execution and enforcement of such judgment or decree may be stayed for a reasonable time to enable the party aggrieved to obtain a writ of certiorari from the Supreme Court. The stay may be granted by a judge of the court rendering the judgment or decree or by a justice of the Supreme Court, and may be conditioned on the giving of security, approved by such judge or justice, that if the aggrieved party fails to make application for such writ within the period allotted therefor, or fails to obtain an order granting his application, or fails to make his plea good in the Supreme Court, he shall answer for all damages and costs which the other party may sustain by reason of the stay.

(g) The time for application for a writ of certiorari to review a decision of the United States Court of Appeals for the Armed Forces shall be as prescribed by rules of the Supreme Court.

(As amended May 24, 1949, ch. 139 § 106, 63 Stat. 104; Dec. 6, 1983, Pub. L. 98-209, § 10(b), 97 Stat. 1405; June 27, 1988, Pub. L. 100-352, § 5(b), 102 Stat. 663; Oct. 5, 1994, Pub. L. 103-337, § 924(d)(1)(C).)

§ 2104. Reviews of State Court Decisions.

A review by the Supreme Court of a judgment or decree of a State court shall be conducted in the same manner and under the same regulations, and shall have the same effect, as if the judgment or decree reviewed had been rendered in a court of the United States.

(As amended June 27, 1988, Pub. L. 100-352, § 5(d)(1), 102 Stat. 663.)

§ 2105. Scope of Review; Abatement.

There shall be no reversal in the Supreme Court or a court of appeals for error in ruling upon matters in abatement which do not involve jurisdiction.

(Added June 25, 1948, ch.646, 62 Stat. 963.)

§ 2106. Determination.

The Supreme Court or any other court of appellate jurisdiction may affirm, modify, vacate, set aside or reverse any judgment, decree, or order of a court lawfully brought before it for review, and may remand the cause and direct the entry of such appropriate judgment, decree, or order, or require such further proceedings to be had as may be just under the circumstances.

(Added June 25, 1948, ch. 646, 62 Stat. 963.)

§ 2107. Time for Appeal to Court of Appeals

(a) Except as otherwise provided in this section, no appeal shall bring any judgment, order or decree in an action, suit or proceeding of a civil nature before a court of appeals for review unless notice of appeal is filed, within thirty days after the entry of such judgment, order or decree.

(b) In any such action, suit, or proceeding, the time as to all parties shall be 60 days from such entry if one of the parties is—

(1) the United States;

(2) a United States agency;

(3) a United States officer or employee sued in an official capacity; or

(4) a current or former United States officer or employee sued in an individual capacity for an act or omission occurring in connection with duties performed on behalf of the United States, including all instances in which the United States represents that officer or employee when the judgment, order, or decree is entered or files the appeal for that officer or employee.

(c) The district court may, upon motion filed not later than 30 days after the expiration of the time otherwise set for bringing appeal, extend the time for appeal upon a showing of excusable neglect or good cause. In addition, if the district court finds—

(1) that a party entitled to notice of the entry of a judgment or order did not receive such notice from the clerk or any party within 21 days of its entry, and

(2) that no party would be prejudiced,

the district court may, upon motion filed within 180 days after entry of the judgment or order or within 14 days after receipt of such notice, whichever is earlier, reopen the time for appeal for a period of 14 days from the date of entry of the order reopening the time for appeal.

(d) This section shall not apply to bankruptcy matters or other proceedings under Title 11.

(June 25, 1948, ch 646, 62 Stat. 963; latest amendment Nov. 29, 2011, P.L. 112-62, § 3, 125 Stat. 757.)

§ 2111. HARMLESS ERROR.

On the hearing of any appeal or writ of certiorari in any case, the court shall give judgment after an examination of the record without regard to errors or defects which do not affect the substantial rights of the parties.

(Added May 24, 1949, c. 139, § 110, 63 Stat. 105.)

§ 2113. DEFINITION.

For purposes of this chapter, the terms "State court", "State courts", and "highest court of a State" include the District of Columbia Court of Appeals.

(Added July 29, 1970, Pub. L. 91-358, title I, § 172(a)(2)(A), 84 Stat. 590.)

PART VI   PARTICULAR PROCEEDINGS

CHAPTER 151.   DECLARATORY JUDGMENTS

§ 2201. CREATION OF REMEDY.

(a) In a case of actual controversy within its jurisdiction, except with respect to Federal taxes other than actions brought under section 7428 of the Internal Revenue Code of 1986, a proceeding under section 505 or 1146 of title 11, or in any civil action involving an antidumping or countervailing duty proceeding regarding a class or kind of merchandise of a free trade area country (as defined in section 516A(f)(9) of the Tariff Act of 1930), as determined by the administering authority, any court of the United States, upon the filing of an appropriate pleading, may declare the rights and other legal relations of any interested party seeking such declaration, whether or not further relief is or could be sought. Any such declaration shall have the force and effect of a final judgment or decree and shall be reviewable as such.

(b) For limitations on actions brought with respect to drug patents see section 505 or 512 of the Federal Food, Drug, and Cosmetic Act, or section 351 of the Public Health Service Act.

(Added June 25, 1948, ch. 646, 62 Stat. 964; latest amendment July 1, 2020, P. L. 116-113.)

§ 2202. FURTHER RELIEF.

Further necessary or proper relief based on a declaratory judgment or decree may be granted, after reasonable notice and hearing, against any adverse party whose rights have been determined by such judgment.

(Added June 25, 1948, ch. 646, 62 Stat. 968.)

CHAPTER 155.   INJUNCTIONS; THREE-JUDGE COURTS

§ 2283. STAY OF STATE COURT PROCEEDINGS.

A court of the United States may not grant an injunction to stay proceedings in a State court except as expressly authorized by Act of Congress, or where necessary in aid of its jurisdiction, or to protect or effectuate its judgments.

(Added June 25, 1948, ch. 646, 62 Stat. 968.)

§ 2284. THREE-JUDGE COURT; WHEN REQUIRED; COMPOSITION; PROCEDURE.

(a) A district court of three judges shall be convened when otherwise required by Act of Congress, or when an action is filed challenging the constitutionality of the apportionment of congressional districts or the apportionment of any statewide legislative body.

(b) In any action required to be heard and determined by a district court of three judges under subsection (a) of this section, the composition and procedure of the court shall be as follows:

(1) Upon the filing of a request for three judges, the judge to whom the request is presented shall, unless he determines that three judges are not required, immediately notify the chief judge of the circuit, who shall designate two other judges, at least one of whom shall be a circuit judge. The judges so designated, and the judge to whom the request was presented, shall serve as members of the court to hear and determine the action or proceeding.

(2) If the action is against a State, or officer or agency thereof, at least five days' notice of hearing of the action shall be given by registered or certified mail to the Governor and attorney general of the State.

(3) A single judge may conduct all proceedings except the trial, and enter all orders permitted by the rules of civil procedure except as provided in this subsection. He may grant a temporary restraining order on a specific finding,

based on evidence submitted, that specified irreparable damage will result if the order is not granted, which order, unless previously revoked by the district judge, shall remain in force only until the hearing and determination by the district court of three judges of an application for a preliminary injunction. A single judge shall not appoint a master, or order a reference, or hear and determine any application for a preliminary or permanent injunction or motion to vacate such an injunction, or enter judgment on the merits. Any action of a single judge may be reviewed by the full court at any time before final judgment.

(Added June 25, 1948, ch. 646, 62 Stat. 968; amended June 11, 1960, Pub. L. 86-507, § 1(19), 74 Stat. 201; Aug. 12, 1976, Pub. L. 94-381, § 3, 90 Stat. 1119; November 8, 1984, Pub. L. 98-620, § 402(29)(E), 98 Stat. 3359.)

CHAPTER 159. INTERPLEADER

§ 2361. PROCESS AND PROCEDURE.

In any civil action of interpleader or in the nature of interpleader under section 1335 of this title, a district court may issue its process for all claimants and enter its order restraining them from instituting or prosecuting any proceeding in any State or United States court affecting the property, instrument or obligation involved in the interpleader action until further order of the court. Such process and order shall be returnable at such time as the court or judge thereof directs, and shall be addressed to and served by the United States marshals for the respective districts where the claimants reside or may be found.

Such district court shall hear and determine the case, and may discharge the plaintiff from further liability, make the injunction permanent, and make all appropriate orders to enforce its judgment. [*See also* §§ 1335 and 1397.]

(As amended May 24, 1949, ch. 139, § 117, 63 Stat 105.)

CHAPTER 161. UNITED STATES AS PARTY GENERALLY

§ 2401. TIME FOR COMMENCING ACTION AGAINST UNITED STATES.

(a) Except as provided by chapter 71 of title 41, every civil action commenced against the United States shall be barred unless the complaint is filed within six years after the right of action first accrues. The action of any person under legal disability or beyond the seas at the time the claim accrues may be commenced within three years after the disability ceases.

(b) [A] tort claim against the United States shall be forever barred unless it is presented in writing to the appropriate Federal agency within two years after such claim accrues or unless action is begun within six months after the date of mailing, by certified or registered mail, of notice of final denial of the claim by the agency to which it was presented.

(June 25, 1948, ch 646, 62 Stat. 971; April 25, 1949, ch 92, § 1, 63 Stat. 62; Sept. 8, 1959, P.L. 86-238, § 1(3), 73 Stat. 472; July 18, 1966, P.L. 89-506, § 7, 80 Stat. 307; Nov. 1, 1978, P.L. 95-563, § 14(b), 92 Stat. 2389; Jan. 4, 2011, P.L. 111-350, § 5(g)(8), 124 Stat. 3848.)

§ 2402.   Jury Trial in Actions Against United States.

Subject to chapter 179 of this title, any action against the United States under section 1346 shall be tried by the court without a jury, except that any action against the United States under section 1346(a)(1) shall, at the request of either party to such action, be tried by the court with a jury.

(June 25, 1948, ch 646, 62 Stat. 971; July 30, 1954, ch. 648, § 2(a), 68 Stat. 589; Oct. 26, 1996, P.L. 104-331, § 3(b)(3), 110 Stat. 4069.)

§ 2403.   Intervention by United States or a State; Constitutional Question.

(a) In any action, suit or proceeding in a court of the United States to which the United States or any agency, officer or employee thereof is not a party, wherein the constitutionality of any Act of Congress affecting the public interest is drawn in question, the court shall certify such fact to the Attorney General, and shall permit the United States to intervene for presentation of evidence, if evidence is otherwise admissible in the case, and for argument on the question of constitutionality. The United States shall, subject to the applicable provisions of law, have all the rights of a party and be subject to all liabilities of a party as to court costs to the extent necessary for a proper presentation of the facts and law relating to the question of constitutionality.

(b) In any action, suit, or proceeding in a court of the United States to which a State or any agency, officer, or employee thereof is not a party, wherein the constitutionality of any statute of that State affecting the public interest is drawn in question, the court shall certify such fact to the attorney general of the State, and shall permit the State to intervene for presentation of evidence, if evidence is otherwise admissible in the case, and for argument on the question of constitutionality. The State shall, subject to the applicable provisions of law, have all the rights of a party and be subject to all liabilities of a party as to court costs to the extent necessary for a proper presentation of the facts and law relating to the question of constitutionality.

(As amended by Act of Aug. 12, 1976, Pub. L. 94-381, § 5, 90 Stat. 1120.)

§ 2412.   Costs and Fees.

(a) (1)Except as otherwise specifically provided by statute, a judgment for costs, as enumerated in section 1920 of this title, but not including the fees and expenses of attorneys, may be awarded to the prevailing party in any civil action brought by or against the United States or any agency or any official of the United States acting in his or her official capacity in any court having jurisdiction of such action. A judgment for costs when taxed against the United States shall, in an amount established by statute, court rule, or order, be limited to reimbursing in whole or in part the prevailing party for the costs incurred by such party in the litigation.

(2) A judgment for costs, when awarded in favor of the United States in an action brought by the United States, may include an amount equal to the filing fee prescribed under section 1914(a) of this title. The preceding sentence shall not be construed as requiring the United States to pay any filing fee.

(b) Unless expressly prohibited by statute, a court may award reasonable fees and expenses of attorneys, in addition to the costs which may be awarded pursuant to subsection (a), to the prevailing party in any civil action brought by or against the United States or any agency or any official of the United States acting in his or her official capacity in any court having jurisdiction of such action. The United States shall be liable for such fees and expenses to the same extent that any other party would be liable under the common law or under the terms of any statute which specifically provides for such an award.

(c) (1) Any judgment against the United States or any agency and any official of the United States acting in his or her official capacity for costs pursuant to subsection (a) shall be paid as provided in sections 2414 and 2517 of this title and shall be in addition to any relief provided in the judgment.

(2) Any judgment against the United States or any agency and any official of the United States acting in his or her official capacity for fees and expenses of attorneys pursuant to subsection (b) shall be paid as provided in sections 2414 and 2517 of this title, except that if the basis for the award is a finding that the United States acted in bad faith, then the award shall be paid by any agency found to have acted in bad faith and shall be in addition to any relief provided in the judgment.

(d) (1) (A)Except as otherwise specifically provided by statute, a court shall award to a prevailing party other than the United States fees and other expenses, in addition to any costs awarded pursuant to subsection (a), incurred by that party in any civil action (other than cases sounding in tort), including proceedings for judicial review of agency action, brought by or against the United States in any court having jurisdiction of that action, unless the court finds that the position of the United States was substantially justified or that special circumstances make an award unjust.

(B)A party seeking an award of fees and other expenses shall, within thirty days of final judgment in the action, submit to the court an application for fees and other expenses which shows that the party is a prevailing party and is eligible to receive an award under this subsection, and the amount sought, including an itemized statement from any attorney or expert witness representing or appearing in behalf of the party stating the actual time expended and the rate at which fees and other expenses were computed. The party shall also allege that the position of the United States was not substantially justified. Whether or not the position of the United States was substantially justified shall be determined on the basis of the record (including the record with respect to the action or failure to act by the agency upon which the civil action is based) which is made in the civil action for which fees and other expenses are sought.

(C) The court, in its discretion, may reduce the amount to be awarded pursuant to this subsection, or deny an award, to the extent that the prevailing party during the course of the proceedings engaged in conduct which unduly and unreasonably protracted the final resolution of the matter in controversy.

(D) If, in a civil action brought by the United States or a proceeding for judicial review of an adversary adjudication described in section 504(a)(4) of title 5, the demand by the United States is substantially in excess of the judgment finally obtained by the United States and is unreasonable when compared with such judgment, under the facts and circumstances of the case, the court shall award to the party the fees and other expenses related to defending against the excessive demand, unless the party has committed a willful violation of law or otherwise acted in bad faith, or special circumstances make an award unjust. Fees and expenses awarded under this subparagraph shall be paid only as a consequence of appropriations provided in advance.

(2) For the purposes of this subsection—

(A) "fees and other expenses" includes the reasonable expenses of expert witnesses, the reasonable cost of any study, analysis, engineering report, test, or project which is found by the court to be necessary for the preparation of the party's case, and reasonable attorney fees (The amount of fees awarded under this subsection shall be based upon prevailing market rates for the kind and quality of the services furnished, except that (i) no expert witness shall be compensated at a rate in excess of the highest rate of compensation for expert witnesses paid by the United States; and (ii) attorney fees shall not be awarded in excess of $125 per hour unless the court determines that an increase in the cost of living or a special factor, such as the limited availability of qualified attorneys for the proceedings involved, justifies a higher fee.);

(B) "party" means (i) an individual whose net worth did not exceed $2,000,000 at the time the civil action was filed, or (ii) any owner of an unincorporated business, or any partnership, corporation, association, unit of local government, or organization, the net worth of which did not exceed $7,000,000 at the time the civil action was filed, and which had not more than 500 employees at the time the civil action was filed; except that an organization described in section 501(c)(3) of the Internal Revenue Code of 1986 (26 U.S.C. 501(c)(3)) exempt from taxation under section 501(a) of such Code, or a cooperative association as defined in section 15(a) of the Agricultural Marketing Act (12 U.S.C. 1141j(a)), may be a party regardless of the net worth of such organization or cooperative association or for purposes of subsection (d)(1)(D), a small entity as defined in section 601 of title 5;

(C) "United States" includes any agency and any official of the United States acting in his or her official capacity;

(D) "position of the United States" means, in addition to the position taken by the United States in the civil action, the action or failure to act by the agency upon which the civil action is based; except that fees and expenses may not be awarded to a party for any portion of the litigation in which the party has unreasonably protracted the proceedings;

(E) "civil action brought by or against the United States" includes an appeal by a party, other than the United States, from a decision of a contracting officer rendered pursuant to a disputes clause in a contract with the Government or pursuant to chapter 71 of title 41;

(F) "court" includes the United States Court of Federal Claims and the United States Court of Appeals for Veterans Claims;

(G) "final judgment" means a judgment that is final and not appealable, and includes an order of settlement;

(H) "prevailing party", in the case of eminent domain proceedings, means a party who obtains a final judgment (other than by settlement), exclusive of interest, the amount of which is at least as close to the highest valuation of the property involved that is attested to at trial on behalf of the property owner as it is to the highest valuation of the property involved that is attested to at trial on behalf of the Government; and

(I) "demand" means the express demand of the United States which led to the adversary adjudication, but shall not include a recitation of the maximum statutory penalty (i) in the complaint, or (ii) elsewhere when accompanied by an express demand for a lesser amount.

(3) In awarding fees and other expenses under this subsection to a prevailing party in any action for judicial review of an adversary adjudication, as defined in subsection (b)(1)(C) of section 504 of title 5, or an adversary adjudication subject to chapter 71 of title 41, the court shall include in that award fees and other expenses to the same extent authorized in subsection (a) of such section, unless the court finds that during such adversary adjudication the position of the United States was substantially justified, or that special circumstances make an award unjust.

(4) Fees and other expenses awarded under this subsection to a party shall be paid by any agency over which the party prevails from any funds made available to the agency by appropriation or otherwise.

(5) (A) Not later than March 31 of the first fiscal year beginning after the date of enactment of the John D. Dingell, Jr. Conservation, Management, and Recreation Act [enacted March 12, 2019], and every fiscal year thereafter, the

Chairman of the Administrative Conference of the United States shall submit to Congress and make publicly available online a report on the amount of fees and other expenses awarded during the preceding fiscal year pursuant to this subsection.

(B) Each report under subparagraph (A) shall describe the number, nature, and amount of the awards, the claims involved in the controversy, and any other relevant information that may aid Congress in evaluating the scope and impact of such awards.

(C) (i) Each report under subparagraph (A) shall account for all payments of fees and other expenses awarded under this subsection that are made pursuant to a settlement agreement, regardless of whether the settlement agreement is sealed or otherwise subject to a nondisclosure provision.

(ii) The disclosure of fees and other expenses required under clause (i) shall not affect any other information that is subject to a nondisclosure provision in a settlement agreement.

(D) The Chairman of the Administrative Conference of the United States shall include and clearly identify in each annual report under subparagraph (A), for each case in which an award of fees and other expenses is included in the report—

(i) any amounts paid under section 1304 of title 31 for a judgment in the case;

(ii) the amount of the award of fees and other expenses; and

(iii) the statute under which the plaintiff filed suit.

(6) As soon as practicable, and in any event not later than the date on which the first report under paragraph (5)(A) is required to be submitted, the Chairman of the Administrative Conference of the United States shall create and maintain online a searchable database containing, with respect to each award of fees and other expenses under this subsection made on or after the date of enactment of the John D. Dingell, Jr. Conservation, Management, and Recreation Act [enacted March 12, 2019], the following information:

(A) The case name and number, hyperlinked to the case, if available.

(B) The name of the agency involved in the case.

(C) The name of each party to whom the award was made as such party is identified in the order or other court document making the award.

(D) A description of the claims in the case.

(E) The amount of the award.

(F) The basis for the finding that the position of the agency concerned was not substantially justified.

(7) The online searchable database described in paragraph (6) may not reveal any information the disclosure of which is prohibited by law or a court order.

(8) The head of each agency (including the Attorney General of the United States) shall provide to the Chairman of the Administrative Conference of the United States in a timely manner all information requested by the Chairman to comply with the requirements of paragraphs (5), (6), and (7).

(e) The provisions of this section shall not apply to any costs, fees, and other expenses in connection with any proceeding to which section 7430 of the Internal Revenue Code of 1986 applies (determined without regard to subsections (b) and (f) of such section). Nothing in the preceding sentence shall prevent the awarding under subsection (a) of this section, of costs enumerated in section 1920 of this title (as in effect on October 1, 1981).

(f) If the United States appeals an award of costs or fees and other expenses made against the United States under this section and the award is affirmed in whole or in part, interest shall be paid on the amount of the award as affirmed. Such interest shall be computed at the rate determined under section 1961(a) of this title, and shall run from the date of the award through the day before the date of the mandate of affirmance.

(As amended July 18, 1966, Pub. L. 89-507, § 1, 80 Stat. 308; latest amendment May 12, 2019, P.L. 116-9, § 4201, 133 Stat. 763, 764.)

§ 2672. ADMINISTRATIVE ADJUSTMENT OF CLAIMS.

The head of each Federal agency or his designee, in accordance with regulations prescribed by the Attorney General, may consider, ascertain, adjust, determine, compromise, and settle any claim for money damages against the United States for injury or loss of property or personal injury or death caused by the negligent or wrongful act or omission of any employee of the agency while acting within the scope of his office or employment, under circumstances where the United States, if a private person, would be liable to the claimant in accordance with the law of the place where the act or omission occurred: *Provided*, That any award, compromise, or settlement in excess of $25,000 shall be effected only with the prior written approval of the Attorney General or his designee. Notwithstanding the proviso contained in the preceding sentence, any award, compromise, or settlement may be effected without the prior written approval of the Attorney General or his or her designee, to the extent that the Attorney General delegates to the head of the agency the authority to make such award, compromise, or settlement. Such delegations may not exceed the authority delegated by the Attorney General to the United States attorneys to settle claims for money damages against the United States. Each Federal agency may use arbitration, or other alternative means of dispute resolution under the provisions of subchapter IV of chapter 5 of title 5, to settle any tort claim against the United States, to the extent of the agency's authority to award, compromise, or settle such claim without the prior written approval of the Attorney General or his or her designee.

Subject to the provisions of this title relating to civil actions on tort claims against the United States, any such award, compromise, settlement, or determination shall be final and conclusive on all officers of the Government, except when procured by means of fraud.

Any award, compromise, or settlement in an amount of $2,500 or less made pursuant to this section shall be paid by the head of the Federal agency concerned out of appropriations available to that agency. Payment of any award, compromise, or settlement in an amount in excess of $2,500 made pursuant to this section or made by the Attorney General in any amount pursuant to section 2677 of this title shall be paid in a manner similar to judgments and compromises in like causes and appropriations or funds available for the payment of such judgments and compromises are hereby made available for the payment of awards, compromises, or settlements under this chapter.

The acceptance by the claimant of any such award, compromise, or settlement shall be final and conclusive on the claimant, and shall constitute a complete release of any claim against the United States and against the employee of the government whose act or omission gave rise to the claim, by reason of the same subject matter.

(June 25, 1948, ch 646, 62 Stat. 983; latest amendment Nov. 15, 1990, P.L. 101-552, § 8(a), 104 Stat. 2746.)

§ 2674. LIABILITY OF UNITED STATES.

The United States shall be liable, respecting the provisions of this title relating to tort claims, in the same manner and to the same extent as a private individual under like circumstances, but shall not be liable for interest prior to judgment or for punitive damages.

If, however, in any case wherein death was caused, the law of the place where the act or omission complained of occurred provides, or has been construed to provide, for damages only punitive in nature, the United States shall be liable for actual or compensatory damages, measured by the pecuniary injuries resulting from such death to the persons respectively, for whose benefit the action was brought, in lieu thereof.

With respect to any claim under this chapter, the United States shall be entitled to assert any defense based upon judicial or legislative immunity which otherwise would have been available to the employee of the United States whose act or omission gave rise to the claim, as well as any other defenses to which the United States is entitled.

With respect to any claim to which this section applies, the Tennessee Valley Authority shall be entitled to assert any defense which otherwise would have been available to the employee based upon judicial or legislative immunity, which otherwise would have been available to the employee of the Tennessee Valley Authority whose act or omission gave rise to the claim as well as any other defenses to which the Tennessee Valley Authority is entitled under this chapter.

(June 25, 1948, ch 646, 62 Stat. 983; Nov. 18, 1988, P.L. 100-694, §§ 4, 9(c), 102 Stat. 4564, 4567.)

§ 2675.   DISPOSITION BY FEDERAL AGENCY AS PREREQUISITE; EVIDENCE.

(a) An action shall not be instituted upon a claim against the United States for money damages for injury or loss of property or personal injury or death caused by the negligent or wrongful act or omission of any employee of the Government while acting within the scope of his office or employment, unless the claimant shall have first presented the claim to the appropriate Federal agency and his claim shall have been finally denied by the agency in writing and sent by certified or registered mail. The failure of an agency to make final disposition of a claim within six months after it is filed shall, at the option of the claimant any time thereafter, be deemed a final denial of the claim for purposes of this section. The provisions of this subsection shall not apply to such claims as may be asserted under the Federal Rules of Civil Procedure by third party complaint, cross-claim, or counterclaim.

(b) Action under this section shall not be instituted for any sum in excess of the amount of the claim presented to the federal agency, except where the increased amount is based upon newly discovered evidence not reasonably discoverable at the time of presenting the claim to the federal agency, or upon allegation and proof of intervening facts, relating to the amount of the claim.

(c) Disposition of any claim by the Attorney General or other head of a federal agency shall not be competent evidence of liability or amount of damages.

(June 25, 1948, ch 646, 62 Stat. 983; May 24, 1949, ch 139, § 126, 63 Stat. 107; July 18, 1966, P.L. 89-506, § 2, 80 Stat. 306.)

§ 2676.   JUDGMENT AS BAR.

The judgment in an action under section 1346(b) of this title shall constitute a complete bar to any action by the claimant, by reason of the same subject matter, against the employee of the government whose act or omission gave rise to the claim.

(June 25, 1948, ch 646, 62 Stat. 984.)

§ 2677.   COMPROMISE.

The Attorney General or his designee may arbitrate, compromise, or settle any claim cognizable under section 1346(b) of this title, after the commencement of an action thereon.

(June 25, 1948, ch 646, 62 Stat. 984; July 18, 1966, P.L. 89-506, § 3, 80 Stat. 307.)

§ 2678.   ATTORNEY FEES; PENALTY.

No attorney shall charge, demand, receive, or collect for services rendered, fees in excess of 25 per centum of any judgment rendered pursuant to section 1346(b) of this title or any settlement made pursuant to section 2677 of this title, or in excess of 20 per centum of any award, compromise, or settlement made pursuant to section 2672 of this title.

Any attorney who charges, demands, receives, or collects for services rendered in connection with such claim any amount in excess of that allowed under this section, if recovery be had, shall be fined not more than $2,000 or imprisoned not more than one year, or both.

(June 25, 1948, ch 646, 62 Stat. 984; July 18, 1966, P.L. 89-506, § 4, 80 Stat. 307.)

§ 2679. Exclusiveness of Remedy.

(a) The authority of any federal agency to sue and be sued in its own name shall not be construed to authorize suits against such federal agency on claims which are cognizable under section 1346(b) of this title, and the remedies provided by this title in such cases shall be exclusive.

(b) (1)The remedy against the United States provided by sections 1346(b) and 2672 of this title for injury or loss of property, or personal injury or death arising or resulting from the negligent or wrongful act or omission of any employee of the Government while acting within the scope of his office or employment is exclusive of any other civil action or proceeding for money damages by reason of the same subject matter against the employee whose act or omission gave rise to the claim or against the estate of such employee. Any other civil action or proceeding for money damages arising out of or relating to the same subject matter against the employee or the employee's estate is precluded without regard to when the act or omission occurred.

(2) Paragraph (1) does not extend or apply to a civil action against an employee of the Government —

(A) which is brought for a violation of the Constitution of the United States, or

(B) which is brought for a violation of a statute of the United States under which such action against an individual is otherwise authorized.

(c) The Attorney General shall defend any civil action or proceeding brought in any court against any employee of the Government or his estate for any such damage or injury. The employee against whom such civil action or proceeding is brought shall deliver within such time after date of service or knowledge of service as determined by the Attorney General, all process served upon him or an attested true copy thereof to his immediate superior or to whomever was designated by the head of his department to receive such papers and such person shall promptly furnish copies of the pleadings and process therein to the United States attorney for the district embracing the place wherein the proceeding is brought, to the Attorney General, and to the head of his employing Federal agency.

(d) (1) Upon certification by the Attorney General that the defendant employee was acting within the scope of his office or employment at the time of the incident out of which the claim arose, any civil action or proceeding commenced upon such claim in a United States district court shall be deemed an action against the United States under the provisions of this title and all references thereto, and the United States shall be substituted as the party defendant.

(2) Upon certification by the Attorney General that the defendant employee was acting within the scope of his office or employment at the time of the incident out of which the claim arose, any civil action or proceeding commenced upon such claim in a State court shall be removed without bond at any time before trial by the Attorney General to the district court of the United States for the district and division embracing the place in which the action or proceeding is pending. Such action or proceeding shall be deemed to be an action or proceeding brought against the United States under the provisions of this title and all references thereto, and the United States shall be substituted as the party defendant. This certification of the Attorney General shall conclusively establish scope of office or employment for purposes of removal.

(3) In the event that the Attorney General has refused to certify scope of office or employment under this section, the employee may at any time before trial petition the court to find and certify that the employee was acting within the scope of his office or employment. Upon such certification by the court, such action or proceeding shall be deemed to be an action or proceeding brought against the United States under the provisions of this title and all references thereto, and the United States shall be substituted as the party defendant. A copy of the petition shall be served upon the United States in accordance with the provisions of Rule 4(d)(4) of the Federal Rules of Civil Procedure. In the event the petition is filed in a civil action or proceeding pending in a State court, the action or proceeding may be removed without bond by the Attorney General to the district court of the United States for the district and division embracing the place in which it is pending. If, in considering the petition, the district court determines that the employee was not acting within the scope of his office or employment, the action or proceeding shall be remanded to the State court.

(4) Upon certification, any action or proceeding subject to paragraph (1), (2), or (3) shall proceed in the same manner as any action against the United States filed pursuant to section 1346(b) of this title and shall be subject to the limitations and exceptions applicable to those actions.

(5) Whenever an action or proceeding in which the United States is substituted as the party defendant under this subsection is dismissed for failure first to present a claim pursuant to section 2675(a) of this title, such a claim shall be deemed to be timely presented under section 2401(b) of this title if—

  (A) the claim would have been timely had it been filed on the date the underlying civil action was commenced, and

  (B) the claim is presented to the appropriate Federal agency within 60 days after dismissal of the civil action.

  (e) The Attorney General may compromise or settle any claim asserted in such civil action or proceeding in the manner provided in section 2677, and with the same effect.

(June 25, 1948, ch 646, 62 Stat. 984; Sept. 21, 1961, P.L. 87-258, § 1, 75 Stat. 539; July 18, 1966, P.L. 89-506, § 5(a), 80 Stat. 307; Nov. 18, 1988, P.L. 100-694, §§ 5, 6, 102 Stat. 4564.)

§ 2680. Exceptions.

The provisions of this chapter and section 1346(b) of this title shall not apply to—

(a) Any claim based upon an act or omission of an employee of the Government, exercising due care, in the execution of a statute or regulation, whether or not such statute or regulation be valid, or based upon the exercise or performance or the failure to exercise or perform a discretionary function or duty on the part of a federal agency or an employee of the Government, whether or not the discretion involved be abused.

(b) Any claim arising out of the loss, miscarriage, or negligent transmission of letters or postal matter.

(c) Any claim arising in respect of the assessment or collection of any tax or customs duty, or the detention of any goods, merchandise, or other property by any officer of customs or excise or any other law enforcement officer, except that the provisions of this chapter and section 1346(b) of this title apply to any claim based on injury or loss of goods, merchandise, or other property, while in the possession of any officer of customs or excise or any other law enforcement officer, if—

(1) the property was seized for the purpose of forfeiture under any provision of Federal law providing for the forfeiture of property other than as a sentence imposed upon conviction of a criminal offense;

(2) the interest of the claimant was not forfeited;

(3) the interest of the claimant was not remitted or mitigated (if the property was subject to forfeiture); and

(4) the claimant was not convicted of a crime for which the interest of the claimant in the property was subject to forfeiture under a Federal criminal forfeiture law.

(d) Any claim for which a remedy is provided by chapter 309 or 311 of title 46 relating to claims or suits in admiralty against the United States.

(e) Any claim arising out of an act or omission of any employee of the Government in administering the provisions of sections 1-31 of Title 50, Appendix.

(f) Any claim for damages caused by the imposition or establishment of a quarantine by the United States.

(g) [Repealed.]

(h) Any claim arising out of assault, battery, false imprisonment, false arrest, malicious prosecution, abuse of process, libel, slander, misrepresentation, deceit, or interference with contract rights: *Provided*, That, with regard to acts or omissions of investigative or law enforcement officers of the United States Government, the provisions of this chapter and section 1346(b) of this title shall apply to any claim arising, on or after the date of the enactment of this proviso, out of assault, battery, false imprisonment, false arrest, abuse of process, or malicious prosecution. For the purpose of this subsection, "investigative or law enforcement officer" means any officer of the United States who is empowered by law to execute searches, to seize evidence, or to make arrests for violations of Federal law.

(i) Any claim for damages caused by the fiscal operations of the Treasury or by the regulation of the monetary system.

(j) Any claim arising out of the combatant activities of the military or naval forces, or the Coast Guard, during time of war.

(k) Any claim arising in a foreign country.

(l) Any claim arising from the activities of the Tennessee Valley Authority.

(m) Any claim arising from the activities of the Panama Canal Company.

(n) Any claim arising from the activities of a Federal land bank, a Federal intermediate credit bank, or a bank for co-operatives.

(As amended Oct. 6, 2006, P.L. 109-304, § 17(f)(4), 120 Stat. 1708.)

§ 4101. DEFINITIONS.

In this chapter:

(1) Defamation. The term "defamation" means any action or other proceeding for defamation, libel, slander, or similar claim alleging that forms of speech are false, have caused damage to reputation or emotional distress, have presented any person in a false light, or have resulted in criticism, dishonor, or condemnation of any person.

(2) Domestic court. The term "domestic court" means a Federal court or a court of any State.

(3) Foreign court. The term "foreign court" means a court, administrative body, or other tribunal of a foreign country.

(4) Foreign judgment. The term "foreign judgment" means a final judgment rendered by a foreign court.

(5) State. The term "State" means each of the several States, the District of Columbia, and any commonwealth, territory, or possession of the United States.

(6) United states person. The term "United States person" means—

(A) a United States citizen;

(B) an alien lawfully admitted for permanent residence to the United States;

(C) an alien lawfully residing in the United States at the time that the speech that is the subject of the foreign defamation action was researched, prepared, or disseminated; or

(D) a business entity incorporated in, or with its primary location or place of operation in, the United States.

(Added Aug. 10, 2010, P.L. 111-223, § 3(a), 124 Stat. 2381)

§ 4102.   RECOGNITION OF FOREIGN DEFAMATION JUDGMENTS.

(a) First Amendment considerations.

(1) In general. Notwithstanding any other provision of Federal or State law, a domestic court shall not recognize or enforce a foreign judgment for defamation unless the domestic court determines that—

(A) the defamation law applied in the foreign court's adjudication provided at least as much protection for freedom of speech and press in that case as would be provided by the first amendment to the Constitution of the United States and by the constitution and law of the State in which the domestic court is located; or

(B) even if the defamation law applied in the foreign court's adjudication did not provide as much protection for freedom of speech and press as the first amendment to the Constitution of the United States and the constitution and law of the State, the party opposing recognition or enforcement of that foreign judgment would have been found liable for defamation by a domestic court applying the first amendment to the Constitution of the United States and the constitution and law of the State in which the domestic court is located.

(2) Burden of establishing application of defamation laws. The party seeking recognition or enforcement of the foreign judgment shall bear the burden of making the showings required under subparagraph (A) or (B).

(b) Jurisdictional considerations.

(1) In general. Notwithstanding any other provision of Federal or State law, a domestic court shall not recognize or enforce a foreign judgment for defamation unless the domestic court determines that the exercise of personal jurisdiction by the foreign court comported with the due process requirements that are imposed on domestic courts by the Constitution of the United States.

(2) Burden of establishing exercise of jurisdiction. The party seeking recognition or enforcement of the foreign judgment shall bear the burden of making the showing that the foreign court's exercise of personal jurisdiction comported with the due process requirements that are imposed on domestic courts by the Constitution of the United States.

(c) Judgment against provider of interactive computer service.

(1) In general. Notwithstanding any other provision of Federal or State law, a domestic court shall not recognize or enforce a foreign judgment for defamation against the provider of an interactive computer service, as defined in section 230 of the Communications Act of 1934 (47 U.S.C. 230) unless the domestic court determines that the judgment would be consistent with section 230 if the information that is the subject of such judgment had been provided in the United States.

(2) Burden of establishing consistency of judgment. The party seeking recognition or enforcement of the foreign judgment shall bear the burden of establishing that the judgment is consistent with section 230.

(d) Appearances not a bar. An appearance by a party in a foreign court rendering a foreign judgment to which this section applies shall not deprive such party of the right to oppose the recognition or enforcement of the judgment under this section, or represent a waiver of any jurisdictional claims.

(e) Rule of construction. Nothing in this section shall be construed to—

(1) affect the enforceability of any foreign judgment other than a foreign judgment for defamation; or

(2) limit the applicability of section 230 of the Communications Act of 1934 (47 U.S.C. 230) to causes of action for defamation.

(Added Aug. 10, 2010, P.L. 111-223, § 3(a), 124 Stat. 2381.)

§ 4103. REMOVAL.

In addition to removal allowed under section 1441, any action brought in a State domestic court to enforce a foreign judgment for defamation in which—

(1) any plaintiff is a citizen of a State different from any defendant;

(2) any plaintiff is a foreign state or a citizen or subject of a foreign state and any defendant is a citizen of a State; or

(3) any plaintiff is a citizen of a State and any defendant is a foreign state or citizen or subject of a foreign state, may be removed by any defendant to the district court of the United States for the district and division embracing the place where such action is pending without regard to the amount in controversy between the parties.

(Added Aug. 10, 2010, P.L. 111-223, § 3(a), 124 Stat. 2383.)

§ 4104. DECLARATORY JUDGMENTS.

(a) Cause of action.

(1) In general. Any United States person against whom a foreign judgment is entered on the basis of the content of any writing, utterance, or other speech by that person that has been published, may bring an action in district court,

under section 2201(a), for a declaration that the foreign judgment is repugnant to the Constitution or laws of the United States. For the purposes of this paragraph, a judgment is repugnant to the Constitution or laws of the United States if it would not be enforceable under section 4102 (a), (b), or (c).

(2) Burden of establishing unenforceability of judgment. The party bringing an action under paragraph (1) shall bear the burden of establishing that the foreign judgment would not be enforceable under section 4102 (a), (b), or (c).

(b) Nationwide service of process.

Where an action under this section is brought in a district court of the United States, process may be served in the judicial district where the case is brought or any other judicial district of the United States where the defendant may be found, resides, has an agent, or transacts business.

(Added Aug. 10, 2010, P.L. 111-223, § 3(a), 124 Stat. 2383.)

§ 4105. Attorneys' Fees.

In any action brought in a domestic court to enforce a foreign judgment for defamation, including any such action removed from State court to Federal court, the domestic court shall, absent exceptional circumstances, allow the party opposing recognition or enforcement of the judgment a reasonable attorney's fee if such party prevails in the action on a ground specified in section 4102(a), (b), or (c).

(Added Aug. 10, 2010, P.L. 111-223, § 3(a), 124 Stat. 2383.)

TITLE 42   UNITED STATES CODE

§ 1983. Civil Action for Deprivation of Rights.

Every person who, under color of any statute, ordinance, regulation, custom, or usage, of any State or Territory or the District of Columbia, subjects, or causes to be subjected, any citizen of the United States or other person within the jurisdiction thereof to the deprivation of any rights, privileges, or immunities secured by the Constitution and laws, shall be liable to the party injured in an action at law, suit in equity, or other proper proceeding for redress, except that in any action brought against a judicial officer for an act or omission taken in such officer's judicial capacity, injunctive relief shall not be granted unless a declaratory decree was violated or declaratory relief was unavailable. For the purposes of this section, any Act of Congress applicable exclusively to the District of Columbia shall be considered to be a statute of the District of Columbia.

(Amended Oct. 19, 1996, Pub. L. 104-317, § 309(c), 110 Stat. 3853.)

§ 1988. Proceedings in Vindication of Civil Rights; Attorney's Fees.

(a) [Not Reproduced.]

(b) Attorney's Fees

In any action or proceeding to enforce a provision of sections 1981, 1981a, 1982, 1983, 1985, and 1986 of this title, title IX of Public Law 92-318, the Religious Freedom Restoration Act of 1993, the Religious Land Use and Institutionalized Persons Act of 2000, or title VI of the Civil Rights Act of 1964, or section 40302 of the Violence Against Women Act of 1994, the court, in its discretion, may allow the prevailing party, other than the United States, a reasonable attorney's fee as part of the costs, except that in any action brought against a judicial officer for an act or omission taken in such officer's judicial capacity such officer shall not be held liable for any costs, including attorney's fees, unless such action was clearly in excess of such officer's jurisdiction.

(c) Expert Fees

In awarding an attorney's fee under subsection (b) in any action or proceeding to enforce a provision of section 1981 or 1981a of this title, the court, in its discretion, may include expert fees as part of the attorney's fees.

(As amended Oct. 19, 1996, Pub. L. 104-317, § 309(b), 110 Stat. 3853; Sept. 22, 2000, Pub. L. 106-274, § 4(d)(1), 113 Stat. 804.)

Table of Cases

[References are to page numbers.]

Index

[References are to section numbers.]